The World Since 1919

The World Since 1919

Walter Consuelo Langsam
President, University of Cincinnati

Otis C. Mitchell
University of Cincinnati

Eighth Edition

THE MACMILLAN COMPANY, NEW YORK
COLLIER-MACMILLAN LIMITED, LONDON

THE MACMILLAN COMPANY
866 THIRD AVENUE, NEW YORK, NEW YORK 10022
COLLIER-MACMILLAN CANADA, LTD., TORONTO, ONTARIO

Library of Congress catalog card number: 70–123532
First Printing

TO JULIE
whose help makes every
task a pleasure
W. C. L.

TO MY FATHER'S MEMORY
O. C. M.

Foreword to the Eighth Edition

The seventh and eighth editions of this work are separated by seventeen years, that is, by one third of the entire period covered. This fact necessitated the most thorough revision of the several noted here. The first twenty chapters have been extensively revised and shortened. Chapters 3 and 4 of the previous edition were combined, so that the number of chapters dealing with events to the end of World War II has been reduced to nineteen. The chapters dealing with the post-World War II period are new. New also are the footnotes, added from place to place throughout the book, in which are noted the development of widely differing historical opinions on certain controversial questions. Many things that seemed important from the perspective of 1954 now seem of greater or lesser significance, and adjustments have been made accordingly. The bibliography of this new work is approximately the same size as that of its predecessor, but it has been revised to achieve a balance between the important old books and some of the worthwhile new ones that have appeared since the seventh edition was published.

The world of the twentieth century is becoming ever more homogeneous, as technology shapes societies into similar molds. It has therefore become increasingly important for histories of the twentieth century to paint an integrated and balanced picture of both Western and non-Western governments and societies. As non-Western currents surge with greater force into the stream of contemporary events, it has seemed appropriate to avoid the very heavy emphasis on Western activities that is typical of many past writings on the current century. Hence, the eighth edition of *The World Since 1919* has become more completely than ever a "world" history, as the authors have attempted to respond to tendencies observed in scholarship and, more broadly, in the global society about them.

January 1971   W.C.L. and O.C.M.

Foreword to the Seventh Edition

This seventh edition is, in effect, a new work. The original chapters on the First World War were eliminated, and the story was made to begin with the Paris Peace Conference. This was done partly because a survey showed such omission to be the classroom trend and partly in order to leave more room for a description of events since 1948 (when the sixth edition was published) without unduly enlarging the book. The remaining chapters all were rewritten or at least revised. In some cases the emphases were shifted as history made certain backgrounds more, or less, important. Organizational changes were made for the sake of better comprehension and in line with the more recent approaches to the study of world affairs.

June 1954   W.C.L.

Foreword to the Sixth Edition

The chief difference between this edition and its immediate predecessor is the addition of five years' crowded history, covering the period 1943–1948. At the same time some minor changes have been made throughout the text. The particular form of organization adopted for the new part of the book has seemed to be the most teachable one for a confused, turbulent, and exciting period. Let it be repeated from an earlier foreword that the whole story is so organized as to make it feasible to begin the course in 1918 with Chapter IV or 1919 with Chapter V. Thus the reading matter may be shortened by from eighty to one hundred pages.

July 1948   W.C.L.

Foreword to the Fifth Edition

Every chapter in this edition has been rewritten, so that not one page has remained without some change, large or small. The changes generally were made for one or more of three reasons: either because new material had come to light, or because recent events dictated a shift in emphasis, or to conserve space. All material formerly printed in supplements has been rewritten and woven into the body of the text. The volume fortunately reverses an earlier trend by being somewhat shorter than its predecessor. But the lengthy bibliography has been retained and brought up to date. Throughout I have tried—how successfully remains for the reader to judge—to keep the narrative balanced, though it was written in a time, not merely of national, but of world crisis.

June 1943   W.C.L.

Foreword to the Fourth Edition

The chief innovation of this edition is the inclusion of a Part IV, entitled "The Road to Another War." This part covers the major European and Asiatic developments since 1935 and carries the story of international relations down to the outbreak of the new European war in September 1939. The organization of this part parallels that in the main body of the text and, wherever necessary, cross-references have been provided to tie up all portions of the book. The bibliography has been enlarged, brought up to date, and subdivided for the longer chapters. The index is unusually full. The whole story is related in such a way that the teacher or reader who feels that the account is somewhat lengthy may, by beginning with either Chapter IV or Chapter V, start his study with the year 1918 rather than go back to 1914.

January 1940   W. C. L.

Foreword to the Third Edition

The organization adopted in this edition is, in general, the same as that of the original issue. Every chapter, however, has been entirely rewritten and one new chapter—on Latin America—has been added. The map equipment has, it is hoped, been greatly improved. The spellings of place names vary somewhat from the forms used in the earlier editions because it has seemed advisable, for the sake of uniformity, to employ in every case the orthography of the *Sixth Report of the United States Geographic Board 1890–1932*, 1933. Names of governing bodies are capitalized only when given in exact or full and literally translated form. For the convenience of the reader, the dates of treaties and of the births and deaths of important individuals have been included in the index. The bibliography has been brought up to date, annotated, and extended so as to include references to each subject from differing viewpoints.

December 1935   W. C. L.

Foreword to the Second Edition

[This edition contained no special foreword, since it merely included a supplementary chapter summarizing recent developments. It was published in October 1933.]

                                                                 W. C. L.

Foreword to the First Edition

Today more than at any previous time it is essential for the preservation of civilization that citizens everywhere be familiar with the outstanding issues that confront the nations. The period since 1914 has been crowded with events of world importance, with complex questions of war guilt, reparation, war debts, disarmament, reconstruction, national minorities, territorial readjustments, economic upheaval, and dictatorships. The mind is easily confused by the magnitude of some of the problems and by the technical aspects of others. Yet, only in the widespread knowledge of the origins and history of these factors can there be any real hope of future international harmony.

It is the aim of this volume to contribute to a clarification of the issues and to provide a readable, organized, and compact exposition of the world developments which, at the time of writing, appeared to be the most promising–or the most portentous.

February 1933   W.C.L.

Table of Contents

I The Aftermath of War

II National Developments, 1919–1939

III   The Second World War and After

Maps and Charts

The Aftermath of War

I

The Peace of Paris, 1919-1920 | 1

COST OF THE FIRST WORLD WAR

The First World War, which lasted 1565 days, was the bloodiest and costliest war that had yet been fought. During the conflict about 65,000,000 men participated in the economically unproductive activity of organized destruction. Approximately one out of five of these men was killed in action or died later of wounds received in battle. One in three was wounded, and some 7,000,000 of these were permanently disabled. Many of the wounded died within a few years after the end of hostilities as a consequence of war-inflicted disabilities.

More than twice as many men were killed in battle during the First World War as in all the major wars from 1790 to 1913 added together. Two-thirds of the men mobilized and two-thirds of those killed were on the Allied side. This conflict was total, in that the estimated number of civilian deaths was even greater than that of soldiers. In consequence, the various national birth rates declined.

Equally staggering were the monetary costs of the combat and the destruction of property on land and sea. When the costs of conducting the war are added to the economic value of property destroyed, they amount to a sum equal to five and a half times as many dollars as the number of seconds that have elapsed since the birth of Christ. Considering the lives spent on the field of battle, the noncombatants taken by privation and disease, and the nearly incalculable wealth lost, it seemed to civilized men everywhere that they now rightfully could expect an era of peace and good will. Thus, the men who met to consider the terms of peace after World War I were charged with a grave responsibility. It was their moral burden to assure that the loss in lives and goods should not have been in vain.

THE PEACE CONFERENCE LEADERS

Long before the armistice celebrations of November 1918 subsided, Paris, having been chosen as the site for the conclusion of
peace, made ready for this new festival. The French capital prepared
to receive some of the most distinguished statesmen, jurists, and
scholars from the Allied world. The defeated Central Powers, however, were not to be represented at the conference. They would be
called in later to sign the already completed treaty.

In December 1918, President Woodrow Wilson embarked for
Europe, having determined to attend the conference in person. His
arrival in Europe was eagerly anticipated, not so much by the statesmen as by the people. His recent addresses, based on his earlier list
of "Fourteen Points"[1] and couched in the form of categorical demands, aimed at the somewhat unrealistic but apparently popular
goal of revising the normal European pattern of peace making.[2]
Consequently, a general feeling prevailed that he was the one person
who could "rise above the tumult of passion" that surged through
the world. Everywhere the President's reception was commensurate
with the glamour attached to his name. In Great Britain, in France,
and even in Germany, where many regarded him as a savior,
Wilson's name aroused emotion and his presence moved men to
tears. The reception was such that Wilson came to think of himself
in control of matters in Paris.

But the glamor was deceptive. Wilson was not supported by a
majority of his own countrymen. His party had been defeated in
the American congressional elections and the new Senate was hostile
to the Administration. Yet Wilson did not take with him to Paris
any representatives of the opposition. As far as Republican Senators
were concerned, the peace would be "Democratic" and many, as a
matter of party loyalty, would automatically vote against it.

Wilson's tactical mistakes were, in some measure, the result of his
personality. He was a rational idealist, convinced of his moral and
intellectual superiority. His knowledge of European problems and
affairs was limited; yet, he was so convinced of the moral correctness
of his positions that he rarely consulted the technical experts he had

[1] See Footnote 3 for a listing of the "Fourteen Points."
[2] The visionary and utopian aspects of Wilson's political thought have been
pointed out by English historian A. J. P. Taylor. He indicates his belief
that the two foremost political Utopians of the early twentieth century
were Wilson and V. I. Lenin. See: A. J. P. Taylor, *From Sarajevo to
Potsdam* (New York: Harcourt, Brace & World, 1965), p. 45. Another
historian, Arno J. Mayer, has developed this argument, holding that the
First World War was transformed by the ideological confrontation of
Wilson and Lenin from a traditional conflict into a crusade of ideals,
thus forming a "watershed" from which flow the major opposing currents
of twentieth century international politics. See: Arno J. Mayer, *Wilson
vs. Lenin, Political Origins of the New Diplomacy* (Cleveland: World
Publishing Co., 1964), pp. 368–393.

taken to Europe to advise him. In consequence, embodying the idealistic state of mind, he often was at the practical mercy of his more realistic colleagues.

In contrast to Wilsonian idealism was the realism of Georges Clemenceau, who led the French deputation. Georges Clemenceau, nicknamed "Tiger" and *Père la Victoire,* came to the conference a disillusioned old man, who seemed to have seen all the evils of life. Until he came to power, he had been known for his violent opposition to censorship and governmental controls. Yet, when he became Premier and Minister of War, he devised an efficient "gagging machine" of his own. Clemenceau probably was the most artful diplomat at the conference. The extent of his realism was indicated by his prudence in paying lip service to Wilson's ideals while pursuing the goals of exalting and securing France as he weakened Germany.

David Lloyd George, energetic, relentless, and alert, represented the British. The clever Welsh attorney was rarely at a loss to find the most appealing argument to touch the "vanity, weakness, or self-interest" of his immediate listener. Head of the Liberal Party and Prime Minister, he rode to electoral victory in 1918 with the aid of slogans such as "Make Germany Pay" and "Hang the Kaiser." He was backed in Lord Northcliffe's London *Daily Mail* by the cry: "They will cheat you yet—those Huns." His attitude at the conference thus to some extent was determined by the promises made during his election and the nature of his support.

Premier Vittorio Orlando headed the Italian delegation. He was a learned and eloquent diplomat. However, the Sicilian ex-professor of law had no command of English and thus could exert relatively little direct influence on the general proceedings. Besides, he irritated Wilson by insisting that certain secret treaties, which had been the price of Italy's participation in the war, be fulfilled.

Thirty-two states were represented at Paris. In addition to the "Big Four" just mentioned, numerous other powers sent a host of delegates streaming to Paris. From Greece came Eleutherios Venizelos, the "Ulysses of the Conference." The Poles eventually sent the famed pianist, Ignace Jan Paderewski, who soon discovered that he was no match for the international politicians gathered at Paris. The representatives of Japan, led by Kimmochi Saionji and Nobuaki Makino, generally voted with the United States and Great Britain as they tried to build Western good will while furthering their Far Eastern interests.

All the world brought its cares to Paris, hoping to benefit from the institution of a new order. The Armenians sought to better their lot by recounting the massacres they had suffered before and during the recent conflict. The new states of Central Europe sought hearings to improve their positions. The Zionist Jews, the Portuguese, the Siamese, Estonians, Livonians, Lebanese, Georgians, and even the far-off Koreans sent delegates filled with high hopes. Many, however, were to go away from the conference empty-handed and with their aspirations replaced by general disillusionment.

ORGANIZATION AND PROBLEMS OF THE CONFERENCE

The leading belligerent governments, long before the armistice, had appointed experts to collect data on all subjects that might come up at the expected peace conference. Although some of the labor was wasted, a large portion of it was invaluable, and frequently "ideas appeared at the conference which could be traced back to laborious pens working at a time when the Germans seemed almost invincible."

In the United States, a group of experts had studied the linguistic, economic, and ethnographic factors in Central and Eastern European history. The activities of this group provided the background for the Fourteen Points and furnished President Wilson with a tentative scheme for territorial settlements. Similar preparations were made in other countries, and such national groups as the Poles and Czechs developed efficient propaganda committees that did considerable work of a similar nature. As a result, every delegation that came to Paris brought with it a clutter of statistics and memoranda.

The Peace Conference formally opened in plenary session on January 18, 1919. Large and small nations of the world were represented. Accompanying each delegation was a large staff including representatives of varied interests. There were at least fifty or sixty nationals who came from even the smaller countries. So large a group could not do business efficiently. It thus became the general rule for the conference to hold only rare plenary sessions. To make business possible, more than fifty commissions of various sorts were established and coordination among them was effected by the Council of Ten.

The Supreme Council, or Council of Ten, was made up of the two chief delegates from the United States, Great Britain, France, Italy, and Japan. For all practical purposes, this was the working body of the conference. Its principal members demanded and received membership on all commissions. As Clemenceau pointed out, the great powers were supported by twelve million soldiers and the lesser states could not hope to assert themselves effectively against them.

It soon developed that even a body of ten was too large for efficiency and secrecy, and in March 1919 it was announced that the brunt of the work was being taken over by the Council of Four, consisting of the chiefs from the United States, Great Britain, France, and Italy. The "Big Four" continued working until April, when Orlando left Paris in a huff because Wilson appealed to the Italian people over his head. Thereafter, the "Big Three" continued to meet in strictest secrecy. Clemenceau's knowledge of English made it possible even to dispense with the services of an interpreter.

The routine work of the conference was accomplished by the commissions and committees. Because the final treaty was basically a summation of the work of many separate committees, its terms probably were more severe than they otherwise would have been. Each separate comittee went ahead with its work, oblivious of what the other committees were doing. In the end, this produced a whole greater than the sum of its parts. But by that time the conference seemed to have lasted too long and the delegates were impatient to go home.

The number of knotty problems facing the conference was legion. The Paris assemblage had to draw up terms to satisfy at least the more important Allies. They had to attempt the feeding of the starving millions in Central and Eastern Europe. There had to be drawn up a covenant for a league of nations. And all this had to be done in a Europe which, in those dark days immediately following the war, resembled a seething cauldron. Many nations still were involved in combat. The great powers themselves were at odds over policies and viewpoints. In retrospect it seems miraculous that any treaty was devised in the pandemonium that was Europe in 1919.

Wilson's advocacy of "open covenants of peace, openly arrived at" made the question of conference publicity of first importance. Yet, most of the crucial meetings were held behind closed doors and precisely what went on during the Big Three meetings could only be guessed, since few minutes were kept. Normally newspapermen were admitted only to the general sessions of the conference. Reports from France to the United States and from the United States to France were censored to prevent "bad" news from leaking in either direction. The secrecy often was justifiable, as the proceedings of the conference were surrounded by an increasing fear of further warfare.

Perhaps the greatest difficulty confronting the delegates was that of reconciling the "Secret Treaties," agreed upon in wartime, with the idealistic principles, laid down by Wilson in his Fourteen Points and accepted by Germany—in modified form—as the basis for the peace discussions.[3] Throughout 1918, Wilson had repeated his Four-

---

[3] The Fourteen Points summarized Wilson's program for "peace without victory." They were demands for: (1) "open covenants of peace" and the abolition of secret diplomacy; (2) freedom of the seas; (3) "removal of all economic barriers and the establishment of an equality of trade conditions;" (4) the reduction of armaments "to the lowest point consistent with domestic safety;" (5) an "open-minded" and "impartial adjustment of all colonial claims;" (6) "the evacuation of all Russian territory" and the settlement of difficulties arising out of the Russian situation in a spirit of "intelligent and unselfish sympathy;" (7) the evacuation and restoration of Belgium; (8) German release of invaded French territory and the retrocession to France of Alsace-Lorraine; (9) "a readjustment" of Italian frontiers along "clearly recognizable lines of nationality;" (10) the "freest opportunity of autonomous development" for the peoples of Austria-

teen Points in an attempt to convince the world that they were the aims for which the Allies waged war. The Germans, too, had received declarations of the Wilsonian scheme to revolutionize the European order—through leaflets scattered in the trenches from the air, as the "points" became an instrument of psychological warfare aimed at weakening the Kaiser's Government.

The authorities in Great Britain, France, and Italy, however, had never officially accepted all the points. In fact, between 1915 and 1917, the leading Allied states had concluded several secret agreements that were in conflict with Wilson's statement of war aims. They had virtually apportioned the Ottoman Empire among themselves. Italy had been promised territory held by Austria-Hungary, Albania, and Turkey as well as some land in Africa. The Allies did not see fit to protest the Wilsonian doctrine during the war. Yet, the existence of the secret agreements made a protracted quarrel between Wilson and the Allied statesmen inevitable at the peace conference.

Although Wilson seemed to have been aware of the Secret Treaties, he appears to have thought that he could persuade the Allies to his way of thinking. Soon enough, however, the treaties became a major obstacle to Wilson's plans for the settlement.

There were many such obstacles, especially when Wilson's idealism came into sharp conflict with materialism at the conference —and in most cases materialism triumphed. Sometimes Wilson was firm. During an impasse over the Saar question, he threatened to withdraw from the conference unless he had his way. Again, he displayed firmness in refusing to give Fiume to Italy, and Orlando went home, ill-humored and piqued. These instances, however, were not common enough to ensure the survival of the Fourteen Points intact.

Last among the general obstacles to progress at the conference was the temporary return of both Wilson and Lloyd George to their homelands. President Wilson returned to consider the bills that Congress had passed during his absence and to explain to the Senate the tentative draft of the League of Nations' Covenant. Lloyd George's absence was necessitated by the pressing problem of widespread unemployment in Great Britain. During this interim, too, Clemenceau was shot by a dim-witted anarchist. Although confined to his apartment for some days, the old French statesman was able to return to his duties by the time Wilson returned to Paris on March 14, 1919. The Big Four now could begin to consider the peace treaties.[4]

Hungary; (11) the evacuation and restoration of Romania, Serbia, and Montenegro; (12) autonomous development of the non-Turkish possessions of the Sultan and internationalization of the Dardanelles; (13) the creation of an independent Poland with an outlet to the sea; and (14) the establishment of a League of Nations.

[4] Because of delays, the armistice with Germany, which had been renewed in December 1918 and January 1919, was again extended in February 1919.

DRAFTING AND SIGNING THE VERSAILLES TREATY

The greatest difficulty in the actual drawing up of the treaty terms was experienced in connection with the following points: (1) the wording of a league of nations' covenant; (2) the question of French security and the fate of the left bank of the Rhine; (3) the Italian and Polish claims; (4) the disposition of the erstwhile German colonies and the former possessions of the Turkish Empire; and (5) the reparation for damages that soon was to be exacted from Germany.

A serious difference of opinion arose over the advisability of incorporating the projected covenant in the general peace agreement. Wilson insisted on having it included in the treaty, lest the nations, in their preoccupation with other matters, shelve the covenant indefinitely. He had his way,[5] and the second plenary session, in January 1919, appointed him chairman of a committee to draft the covenant. In February, Wilson presented a completed report to another plenary session of the conference. It met with considerable criticism and was changed significantly before the covenant finally was adopted on April 28. Against the wishes of France, a new article was added, giving recognition for the first time in a diplomatic document to the Monroe Doctrine.

Simultaneously with the problem of wording a covenant arose the question of providing France with the security for which she longed. Reminiscences of what had happened along the Rhine frontier during the past century, and the fear of possible German revenge, made the French, in panic, seek security against future invasion. The only means of achieving this security, or so it appeared to the French, was to cripple Germany—politically, militarily, economically, and commercially—thus ensuring that she never again could threaten France.

In accordance with this view, Marshal Ferdinand Foch, former Commander in Chief of the Allied Armies in France, and his followers demanded that Germany's western frontier be fixed at the Rhine and that the 10,000 square miles of territory between the Rhine and the Netherlands, Belgium, and France to the west, be transformed into a buffer state under French protection. This arrangement, however, was not viewed favorably by the British and United States delegations, both of which firmly opposed the establishment of another Alsace-Lorraine.

After prolonged bargaining Clemenceau agreed to a compromise. The area in question was divided into three sections, to be occupied by Allied troops for respective periods of five, ten, and fifteen years. All the time limits, however, were made contingent upon Germany's prompt fulfillment of the other parts of the treaty; otherwise the occupation might continue indefinitely. In addition, Germany was

[5] Wilson probably was correct in his reasoning, but the fact that the covenant formed an integral part of the peace treaties later proved to be a weakening factor in the life of the League.

not to build fortifications or assemble armed forces in a demilitarized zone extending thirty-one miles east of the Rhine. The German army's traditional *Wacht am Rhein* was to be terminated.

To reassure the French further, Woodrow Wilson and Lloyd George promised to sign special treaties which would guarantee that the United States and Great Britain would come to the aid of France in case of "invasion" by Germany. Upon Clemenceau's insistence the term *invasion* was changed to the more general *aggression*. At the signing of the Versailles Treaty, two supplementary guarantee treaties, one Franco-British and the other Franco-United States, were signed to ensure Allied protection of France's eastern boundary against the possible German aggression that Clemenceau feared.

The problem of the Saar Basin, one of the world's greatest coal-producing regions, also assumed a position of importance in the deliberations of Wilson, Lloyd George, and Clemenceau. The estimated coal reserves of the Saar were greater than those in all France. Since the Germans had destroyed many coal mines in northern France, it was believed by the Allies that compensation in kind should be paid to the French. Clemenceau, although the French had no real historical or ethnological claim to the region, demanded the cession of the Basin. In consequence, the coal mines of the Saar were transferred to France for a period of fifteen years in "full and absolute possession." During the fifteen-year period, the Saar was to be administered by the League of Nations. At the end of the fifteen years a plebiscite of the inhabitants would decide the future status of the territory. If the plebiscite brought the Saar back to Germany, the Germans were to repurchase control of the mines from the French at a price to be determined by a board of experts appointed by the League.

The single item that took up more of the conference leaders' time than any other arose from the conflict of Italian demands with those of newly formed Yugoslavia. Italy wanted territory extending from the Brenner Pass in the Tirol to the port of Valona in Albania, the Dodecanese Islands, land in Asia and Africa, the port of Fiume, and an extra part of the Dalmatian coast. The fact that the demanded territories contained German-speaking Austrians, South Slavs, and Greeks did not deter the Italians.

Italy desired Fiume particularly. There were commercial reasons for this. However, by far the most important consideration for the Italians was the fact that, with the removal of Austria-Hungary by the war as a rival for control of the Adriatic, Italy did not propose to allow the newly created Yugoslavia to replace the Austro-Hungarian state as a major maritime rival in the area.

The Italian delegation advanced several claims to the territories they desired. Some were based on the sacrifices made and hardships suffered by Italy during the war. Beyond these, stategic and geographic reasons were advanced to establish Italy's claim to Fiume, it being demonstrated that the port was directly *connected* with Italy by sea, but *separated* from Yugoslavia by mountains. To this the Yugoslav delegates replied that the principle of national self-determination would be violated if an area in which the Italians were a small minority were incorporated into Italy.

After the Council of Four had listened to all arguments, a Dalmatian line was drawn, giving Italy somewhat less than she desired. The Italian delegates rejected what they regarded as a Wilsonian compromise and angrily quitted Paris. They returned some days later, but the Fiume-Adriatic controversy was not settled and raged on after the conference ended.

The Polish Question was solved in a fashion that left behind a residue of ill-will to trouble Polish-German relations. A corridor, including the city of Danzig with its German population of 300,000, was carved out of Posen and West Prussia. The territorial settlement severed East Prussia from Germany. In this "corridor" Germans and Poles had intermingled, but the intermixing had been under German control. Now the situation was reversed and the Poles governed Germans, who counted among their number many militant nationalists.

The establishment of the "Polish Corridor" fitted in well with French schemes to weaken Germany. France wanted a powerful Poland to the east of Germany, occupying the same place in the French alliance system that Russia had taken before World War I.

The disposal and distribution of the overseas territories of Germany and the crumbling Ottoman Empire posed a problem that was solved by the development of a scheme which later came to be known as the "mandate system." The original plan was to dispose of the territories taken from Russia, Austria-Hungary, and Turkey by assigning them to the League of Nations. The League then was to "delegate its authority" to some other state, which would serve as a mandatory power, acting as steward for the League in the protection of people who as yet were unready to stand alone in the complexity of the modern world.

This pattern of mandates eventually was applied, on Wilson's initiative, to approximately 1,250,000 square miles of land formerly held as German colonies and as non-Turkish parts of the Ottoman Empire. Despite the high principles involved in the idea of protecting "backward" peoples, the actual distribution followed closely the terms of the secret agreements made during the war. All League members were promised equal commercial and trading opportunities in the mandates.

One of the last items to be settled was one of the first to be mentioned. Under the reparation clauses of the final treaty, it was stated that Germany was principally responsible for starting the war and hence must pay for damage done. This concept of "war guilt" and consequent reparative obligation was incorporated in clauses requiring Germany to accept "the responsibility ... for causing all the loss and damage to which the Allied and Associated Governments and their nationals have been subjected as a consequence of the war imposed upon them by the aggression of Germany and her Allies."[6] The Allies recognized that Germany's immediate resources were not adequate to cover large reparations. It therefore was decided that the defeated nation should pay its debt to the victors over a thirty-year period and that a Reparation Commission would be appointed to determine the annual amounts and the method of their transfer. Meanwhile, Germany was to pay the equivalent of 20,000,000,000 marks in gold by May 21, 1921. In addition, the Germans were required to deliver timber and coal to France and ships to Britain, to compensate those states for corresponding losses.

The treaty now was completed and the Germans were told to come and learn the terms devised by the conference. A delegation of six, led by Ulrich von Brockdorff-Rantzau, former envoy to Denmark and now Foreign Minister of the new German Republic, arrived at Versailles. The German delegates were guarded by Allied officers, kept in their hotel behind barbed wire, and forbidden to communicate with the Allied deputies.

On May 7, 1919, the fourth anniversary of the sinking of the liner *Lusitania,* the peace terms were formally presented by Clemenceau in the small Trianon Palace near Versailles. Clemenceau ignored the birth of the German Republic as he addressed the representatives of Germany as "delegates of the German Empire." He said, "the time has come when we must settle our accounts. You have asked for peace. We are ready to give you peace."

Brockdorff-Rantzau admitted that his countrymen "were under no illusion as to the extent of their defeat and the degree of their helplessness." He denied, however, that Germany was solely responsible for the war and announced that Germans still had right and justice on their side. This attitude was widely interpreted as

---

[6] Historians have revised and re-revised the concept of war guilt since the signing of the Treaty of Versailles. It first was widely assumed that Germany was indeed guilty of beginning the war. Then, in the late 1920's, historical writing was altered by the appearance of the "revisionist" view. Exponents of revisionism sought to refute the "war guilt" thesis that had been used to justify the punitive terms of the Versailles Treaty.

German scholars, of course, had attempted to disprove the guilt thesis from the time of the treaty's signing. Then, in the 1920's, an American sociologist-historian, Harry Elmer Barnes, in his *Genesis of the World War,* sought to shift the blame for starting the war to other European powers. The revisionist view then was given more scholarly treatment by Sidney B. Fay in his *Origins of the World War.* This appeared in 1928 and held that "Germany did not plot" and "did not want" a European war.

Later the pendulum of historical opinion swung back once again toward the idea of German guilt. In the early 1960's, working with newly unearthed documents, German historian Fritz Fischer emphasized the imperialistic ambitions of leading Germans before 1914 and linked such aspirations to German war aims. In the 1960's, also, Bernadotte E. Schmidt reaffirmed his earlier (1934) interpretation upholding German culpability.

additional proof of Germany's inability to understand any language other than force.

The announcement of the terms in Germany resulted in a fierce outburst. Radicals, moderates, and reactionaries alike denounced Allied "treachery" and "deceit." Popular sentiment was well expressed by Chancellor Philipp Scheidemann when he said: "What hand would not wither that sought to lay itself and us in those chains?"[7] Matthias Erzberger, who had headed the German Armistice Commission that had signed the November 11, 1918, agreement suspending hostilities, pleaded, "Do not ask to be our own executioners." Germany denied that it alone was responsible for the war, and emphasized the impossibility of fulfilling all terms set down by the Allies.

Despite the objections from Germany, only few modifications were made. The main alteration concerned the withholding of Upper Silesia from Poland until a plebiscite could be held to indicate the wishes of those who lived in the area. The Germans were given five days, and then two more, in which to accept the revised treaty. Failure to do so, they were told, would mean invasion.

Although many Germans appeared ready to renew the struggle rather than sign the document, Field Marshal Paul von Hindenburg announced that further resistance in the west was impossible. The Scheidemann Government, including Foreign Minister Brockdorff-Rantzau, resigned and Gustav Bauer, a Social Democrat like his predecessor, became Chancellor. The German assembly at Weimar voted a conditional acceptance, objecting to articles saddling Germany with the guilt of beginning the conflict, demanding the surrender of certain "war criminals," and accusing her of violating the code of war. The Allies refused to satisfy the objections and repeated the demand for unconditional acceptance. The Weimar Government was forced to accept the treaty as an inescapable disaster, and immediately was saddled in Germany by ultranationalists with the onus of having betrayed the Fatherland.

At three o'clock in the afternoon of June 28, 1919, the fifth anniversary of the assassination of Austrian Archduke Francis Ferdinand, the Germans were admitted to the Hall of Mirrors at Versailles, where almost fifty years before the king of Prussia had been declared German Emperor in a celebration of Germanic triumph. The new German Foreign Minister, Hermann Müller, "pale and nervous," moved forward to sign the treaty. The Allied delegates followed in alphabetical order. *Amérique du Nord* headed the list, and thus Wilson's signature came first.[8]

---

[7] Special criticism was aimed at the section of the treaty which demanded that hungry Germany hand over to France and Belgium 140,000 cows and 120,000 sheep within three months after the signing of the document.
[8] Ratifications between the Allies and Germany were exchanged in Paris on January 10, 1920. Four other treaties were drawn up by the peace conference, with Austria, Hungary, Bulgaria, and Turkey. Collectively the five treaties were known as the Peace of Paris.

THE TREATY OF VERSAILLES

The Treaty of Versailles comprised 440 articles and almost a score of annexes.[9] Alsace and Lorraine were returned to France. Belgium, Denmark, and the new Czechoslovakia were enlarged. To Poland was ceded the Polish Corridor, a territory 260 miles long and ranging up to 80 miles in width.

In industrial Upper Silesia a plebiscite was ordered held under the supervision of an Allied commission. The ballot returns showed more than 700,000 votes for Germany and 480,000 for Poland; of the communes, 754 voted for adherence to Germany, whereas 699 preferred incorporation into Poland. The Poles thereupon claimed all the areas with Polish majorities, whereas Germany maintained that the entire region was an indivisible economic unit and rightfully belonged to her. Strife ensued and the matter was referred to the League of Nations Council. The latter partitioned Silesia, leaving Germany more than half of the people and land area, but giving Poland more of the economic resources. Danzig, with a population almost wholly German, was made a free city under League control, but Poland was accorded special diplomatic and economic rights in the city. The Memel district, at the northeastern tip of Germany and controlling the mouth of the Niemen River, was ceded to the Allies.[10]

Germany renounced all her rights and titles to oversea possessions, these being later apportioned among the Allies as mandates of the League of Nations. The Allied and Associated Powers reserved "the right to retain and liquidate all property, rights, and interest" belonging to private German nationals or companies within the territories belonging to Allied governments or newly ceded to them. Compensation to these deprived owners was to be made by the German Government.[11]

Germany recognized the severance of Luxembourg from the German customs union. Germany was forbidden to "maintain or construct any fortifications either on the left bank of the Rhine or on the right bank" or within "fifty kilometers to the east of the Rhine." Armed forces could not be assembled, nor maneuvers held, in this area, and existing fortifications were to be dismantled.

"As compensation for the destruction" of the French coal mines and as a beginning payment towards the total reparation due from

---

[9] The text of the most important articles of the treaties with Germany and Austria may be found in Langsam, W. C. *Documents and Readings in the History of Europe Since 1918*, rev. and enl. ed., 1951, pp. 12–38.
[10] In 1923 a Lithuanian force seized Memel (1110 square miles) from the French garrison which had been holding it. The League Council in 1924 sponsored a convention signed by Lithuania, France, Great Britain, Italy, and Japan providing for the transfer of Memel to Lithuania as an autonomous territory.
[11] Some of this property, notably in the United States, later was returned to the German owners.

Germany, Berlin ceded to France the coal mines in the Saar Basin. The government of the Saar was to be entrusted for fifteen years to the League of Nations. Then there was to be a plebiscite. The fortifications and harbors of the islands of Dune and Helgoland were to be destroyed. Germany promised to respect Austrian independence.

To limit Germany's military potential, the German General Staff was abolished. The army was limited to 100,000 men, including a maximum of 4000 officers. The manufacture, import, and export of armaments was limited and such materials could be stored only "at points to be notified to the Governments" of the Allies. Compulsory military service was abolished and only voluntary enlistments were permitted. As a result of these provisions, many rootless military men were cast into a civilian society which they despised.

The naval provisions permitted Germany to retain only six battleships, six light cruisers, twelve destroyers, and twelve torpedo boats. No submarines were allowed her and no new warships might be built except to replace those worn out. Naval personnel was limited to 15,000 men. No one in the merchant marine was to receive naval training. All war vessels in excess of the stated quota were either to be dismantled and converted into merchant ships or turned over to the Allies.[12] Germany was forbidden to have any military or naval air forces and all aeronautical war material had to be surrendered.

Allied control commissions were to supervise the execution of the disarmament clauses. The commissions, whose expenses Germany had to bear, were given extensive powers of investigation. By 1927, however, they all had been abolished. Although the armament restrictions were designed to last as long as the treaty itself, many of the clauses soon were modified in practice, with Allied consent. The treaty indicated, moreover, that the restrictions upon Germany's fighting establishments were not merely calculated to render it impossible for her "to resume military aggression," but were the first steps toward a general reduction of armaments throughout the world. It was declared to be one of the first duties of the League to promote widespread disarmament.

"William II of Hohenzollern, formerly German Emperor," was publicly arraigned in the treaty "for a supreme offense against international morality and the sanctity of treaties." A special Allied tribunal was to be appointed to try him. However, the Netherlands refused to extradite William. Germany also was required to surrender for trial before Allied courts any designated "persons accused of having committed acts in violation of the laws and customs of

---

[12] In June 1919 the crews of the surrendered German warships, which had been ordered to Scapa Flow in the Orkneys, opened the sea cocks and sank fifty-three vessels. Germany thereupon was ordered to build additional merchantmen for the Allies.

war." Eventually the Allies permitted the trials to be held in Leipzig, where the court procedure was perfunctory. Only a few of the less important "war criminals" were tried, and they received light sentences.

The legal justification for demanding reparation from Germany was put into the so-called guilt clause of the treaty, Article 231:

> The Allied and Associated Governments affirm and Germany accepts the responsibility of Germany and her allies for causing all the loss and damage to which the Allied and Associated Governments and their nationals have been subjected as a consequence of the war imposed upon them by the aggression of Germany and her Allies.

Courtesy, Foreign Policy Association, *Headline Series.*

In Article 232, it was recognized that the resources of Germany were not adequate "to make complete reparation for all such loss and damage," and Germany was required only "to make compensation for all damage done to the civilian population of the Allied and Associated Powers and to their property . . . ." In addition, Germany was to reimburse Belgium with interest at 5 per cent for all the money the latter had borrowed from the Allied governments during the war years.

A reparation commission was to be appointed by the Allies to determine the total amount of reparation and to "draw up a schedule of payments" distributed over thirty years beginning May 1, 1921. Meanwhile, Germany was to pay the equivalent of nearly $5,000,000,000. Out of this advance sum the cost of the army of occupation was to be met, and the balance applied to reparation. Since full reparation could not be paid in cash, it was stipulated that Germany might pay part in the form of specified commodities.

Courtesy, Foreign Policy Association, *Headline Series.*

The right of the Allies was recognized to replace at German expense all merchant-marine ships and fishing boats lost or damaged during the war. Germany therefore was made to surrender one-half of her ships and one-fourth of her steam trawlers and fishing boats.

The economic resources of Germany were to be devoted "directly to the physical restoration of the invaded areas." The Allies, consequently, were permitted to file with the Reparation Commission lists showing various articles seized by Germany or destroyed in consequence of military operations, as well as lists of building materials that the Allies wished to have produced and manufactured in Germany and delivered to them to permit restoration of the invaded areas. Germany agreed also to make large annual coal deliveries for ten years to France, Italy, and Luxembourg.

The Reparation Commission was empowered to recommend action in case of any German failure to pay reparation. In addition, Germany was forced to agree not to regard as an act of war any punitive action taken by the Allies because of such a German default.

The remainder of the treaty was concerned with a variety of items. Among them was the assurance by Germany that Allied manufactures would be accorded a most-favored-nation treatment in the markets of the Fatherland. In addition, certain German waterways were internationalized so that free access to the sea might be provided for the landlocked states of Central Europe.

To ensure the proper execution of the treaty, the German territory to the west of the Rhine was to be occupied by Allied troops for a period of fifteen years. There was established a plan for a progressive evacuation of this area, but the occupation could be extended indefinitely or an evacuated part reoccupied, if Germany misbehaved. Actually, the last of the troops were withdrawn from this zone in 1930. The United States and British troops in the occupied territory got along fairly well with the inhabitants, but a situation, ominous for future events, developed from the hatred aroused by the French.

The Versailles Treaty, in summary, reduced the European area of Germany by one eighth and its population by 6,500,000. All colonies and most investments abroad were stripped away. The German merchant marine was reduced from more than 5,000,000 tons to fewer than 500,000. The navy was virtually wiped out and the army that remained was only slightly larger than Belgium's. Germany lost vast mineral resources, including major portions of her coal reserves, iron ore, lead, and zinc. The loss of colonies made it more expensive to obtain oil and rubber. The treaty so broke down the prewar industrial complex that for a long time Germany was incapable of producing a healthy economy functioning anywhere near its former level of efficiency. Finally, the defeated nation signed a blank reparation check.

THE LESSER TREATIES

The Council of Four at Paris did not confine its treaty-making activities to the German situation. Before Wilson and Lloyd George left Paris late in June 1919, the Big Four sketched a preliminary draft treaty with Austria, decided on the boundaries of Hungary, and considered the cases of Bulgaria and Turkey. But the final form of the treaties with Germany's allies was largely the work of a special Council of Five. This body consisted of Chairman Clemenceau and one representative each from the United States, Great Britain, France, and Italy.

The Austrian delegates arrived at St. Germain-en-Laye in May 1919, and were restrained, as had been the Germans at Versailles. There was some delay while the deliberations at Versailles were being finished, and the Austrian delegation was forced to wait nearly three weeks before it was presented with a treaty. There were immediate protests and the document was altered somewhat. But the Allies would not give in on the major issue: Austria was not to be considered as a truly new nation, as its delegation indicated it should be, and consequently deserving of better treatment. New Austria was burdened with the sins of old Austria and had to pay for them "as a consequence of the war imposed upon" the Allies "by the aggression of Austria-Hungary."

The Treaty of St. Germain was so completely modeled on Versailles that whole clauses were taken from the first treaty and reincorporated into the second without changing a word. Austria ceded to Italy the South Tirol up to the Brenner Pass, Trieste, Istria, the Trentino, and some islands off Dalmatia. To Czechoslovakia went Bohemia, Moravia, part of lower Austria, and nearly all Austrian Silesia, these areas containing about 3,000,000 *Sudetendeutsche*. Poland received Austrian Galicia. Romania was awarded Bukovina, whereas Bosnia, Herzegovina, and the Dalmatian coast and islands went to Yugoslavia. Union (*Anschluss*) with Germany was prohibited without the consent of the League of Nations. Austria's army was limited to 30,000 volunteers. In addition, there were other penalties and reparation modeled after those in the Versailles Treaty.

What was left to Austria was only a shadow image of the former empire. The former Austrian half of the Dual Monarchy was reduced in area and population by three-fourths.

The Treaty of Neuilly with Bulgaria also was delayed. The Bulgarian delegates came to Paris in July 1919, but were forced to wait almost two months before they learned their terms. Though the Bulgarians developed a position much like that held earlier by Austria, and indicated that their country was a new state—a democracy, deserving a mild peace—the Allies curtly refused to accept these views and reminded Bulgaria that she was a defeated power. Bulgaria had no choice other than to sign, and did so at Neuilly-sur-Seine on November 27, 1919.

Again Versailles served as a model. Four small regions in western Bulgaria were given to Yugoslavia for strategic reasons. Otherwise, Bulgaria retained much the same frontiers it had had in 1914 except for the loss of Western Thrace to Greece. Bulgaria's army was reduced to 20,000, and other armed officials numbering 13,000 were allowed. The net result was to make Bulgaria one of the weakest of the Balkan powers.

Because of unsettled affairs in Hungary, where the collapse of the Habsburgs resulted in a struggle for control among Monarchists, Republicans, Socialists, and Communists, the treaty with Hungary was not signed until June 4, 1920, in the Trianon Palace at Versailles. The treaty was signed under protest for, territorially, it was the harshest of the postwar settlements. Romania alone was enlarged by the cession of an area severed from Hungary which was larger than the total rump state remaining. Three million Magyars came under other than Hungarian control. The army was cut to 35,000 men and the navy reduced to a few patrol boats. Hungary, too, was made liable for reparation through a guilt clause.

In 1920 Lloyd George told the House of Commons that the arrangements contemplated by the forthcoming treaty with the sultan would at last release "all non-Turkish populations from Turkish sway." In reality the treaty contemplated a reversal of the situation by subjecting the Turks to the sway of Europeans. The Treaty of Sèvres with Turkey freed the Arab states from Turkish control, but the more important Arab states simply exchanged one foreign ruler for another when they became Class A mandates under the direction of France and Britain. The Allies, moreover, went beyond this diminution of traditional Turkish influence and began to divide up the Turkish homeland in Asia Minor itself—by honoring the secret agreements reached during the war.

Because the treaty was signed by representatives of a Turkish Government momentarily overawed by Allied ships at Constantinople, Turkish nationalist sentiment rebelled against ratification. An energetic group of nationalists led by Mustapha Kemal quickly rose in arms against it. The story of their success is told in another chapter.

THE PROTECTION OF MINORITIES

The boundary adjustments of the treaties created an acute problem of national minorities. The flame of national spirit was fanned by the war and the peace conference, and national jealousies were aroused. Vengeful reprisals were to be expected. To prevent trouble, safeguards for the minorities had to be established. It appeared essential to guarantee at least a modicum of racial, religious, social, linguistic, and economic equality for the numerous national minorities.

In the cases of the defeated powers, such guarantees were included in the peace treaties. Newly established, enlarged, or liberated states such as Poland, Yugoslavia, Czechoslovakia, Greece, and Romania were required to sign special agreements embodying similar guarantees. Most of the countries concerned objected to the treaties as an infringement of national sovereignty and as an encouragement to the establishment of separatist movements within their borders. But once again the views of the great powers were more important than those of the small, and protective obligations had to be assumed. In each instance the supervision of minorities became the responsibility of the League of Nations.

The treaties followed a somewhat uniform pattern in that they included guarantees of life and liberty to all subjects regardless of race, nationality, religion, or creed. They also generally protected the use of minority languages, even, in certain circumstances, in business and the schools.

CRITIQUE OF THE PEACE OF PARIS

The treaties arising from the "war to end wars" were replete with unstable compromises. Wilson's Fourteen Points had not fared well. Only five were put into effect as stated. The others either were carried out in a manner to benefit the Allies or were disregarded. The settlements contained the seeds of future conflict. Yet, in appraising the work of the treaty-makers of 1919 and 1920, the enormous material and psychological difficulties that troubled the conference must be remembered. Some of their mistakes were obvious at the time they were made, but many stood out more clearly only after the passing of years. There was a spirit of vengeance surrounding the deliberations in Paris, growing out of four years of blood and mire. Man had not had a broad enough experience in peacemaking. As someone has well said, war appears to be as old as mankind, but peace is a relatively modern invention.

Among the criticisms which can be made of the Peace of Paris are the following: (1) It probably was unwise to enunciate broad principles that would not be carried out in practice; thus, in the matter of self-determination of peoples, since the victorious powers were willing to grant such rights in only limited fashion, their earlier promises incited minorities to thoughts of revenge against those responsible for the unfulfilled pledges. (2) The victors should not have made promises, such as that to disarm, which they could not realistically expect to keep. (3) The economic clauses of the settlement, bearing little relation to economic facts, brought on situations, such as a prolonged depression in British shipbuilding, because the British appropriated most of the German merchant fleet as reparation and thus for a long time needed no new ships.

(4) It soon became apparent that western "democracy" could not arbitrarily be imposed upon people who had few democratic traditions—as in Germany, where it was difficult to convert an autocratic monarchy into a smoothly functioning republic simply because the

Allies wished it so. (5) The peace settlement left both Germany and Russia as large, revengeful, and potentially powerful nations surrounded by a cordon of small, weak states; the "Balkanization of Central Europe" made it relatively easy later on for Nazi Germany and the Soviet Union to absorb some of their smaller neighbors. And (6) the history of events after the Peace of Paris made it clear that victorious powers needed later to cooperate in upholding whatever peace settlement they had agreed upon at the peace conference itself. The validity of this point soon became apparent, as Britain and France began to follow divergent paths. The British wanted to see the Germans recover for purposes of trade, whereas the French were anxious to keep Germany weak. And so, after 1920, a succession of German treaty modifications was winked at by one or another of the Allies, as each sought to serve its own purposes.

As finally drafted and later applied, the Peace of Paris was neither severe enough to hold down the Germans forever, nor generous enough to help the vanquished adjust to the new situation. Consequently, the world eventually was reduced to crying, in the manner of Jeremiah, "Peace, peace, when there is no peace."

THE NEW WORLD: FUTURE IMPERFECT

During the war, a young German soldier had looked to the future and written: "This war [has] stamped its whole character on the period which it began. A surging age is being born, breaking forth here in wars, there in revolutions, here in social transformations. . . ." How accurate he was, he could not have known, but the changes wrought by the war and the peace that followed were manifold. A few are summarized here:

(1)   Four imperial governments were swept away, in Germany, Austria-Hungary, Russia, and Turkey.

(2)   A wave of republicanism swept over Europe. In 1914 there were only five republican governments on the continent. By 1932 there were sixteen.

(3)   Owing partly to the inability of many new republican governments to solve the complex postwar problems, there arose a distrust of democracy, which later nourished dictatorship.

(4)   Three great politico-economic experiments were inaugurated: Bolshevism, Fascism, and Nazism.

(5)   There was a decided change in the relative importance of nations in Europe. Before the war six great powers determined international situations in Europe. Now Germany, Russia, and Austria-Hungary were at least temporarily eclipsed, while the emergence of a number of smaller states increased the number of actors on the international stage.

(6)   The great emphasis on nationality during the war, coupled with the concept of self-determination so widely considered at the

Paris Conference, complicated political and economic relations among nations. Thus, the flames of old hatreds were fanned and a dangerous hysteria developed.

(7)   These same spirits of nationality and self-determination that caused so much unrest in Europe spread to the oversea possessions of the Allied powers in the Near East, Asia, and Africa.

(8)   Despite the optimistic hopes of many, the peace treaties did not establish a new code of international behavior. New wounds were created in the process of healing old ones. As new alliances were formed, Europe was divided anew into hostile camps, and soon the world's military and naval budgets again were weighing heavily on national economies.

(9)   Although instruments for international cooperation and the peaceful settlement of international disputes were now provided by the League of Nations and the World Court, these were not always given effective support.

(10)   In many countries democratic reforms were introduced, particularly in the direction of suffrage extension.

(11)   Labor assumed a new importance in the world order. There was a general realization that the man on the fighting line would have been helpless without the support of the man at the factory. There was also, in the economic distress which followed the war, a tendency for labor movements to cluster in their hardship and, newly organized, to move toward political influence.

(12)   There was a general, if temporary, religious revival. Many of the men who had been surrounded by death in the war sought refuge in religion and, in some instances, even mysticism or spiritualism.

(13)   There arose a general feeling that in the proper education of the young lay the best guarantee against a repetition of the catastrophe. Consequently, as money became available and the economic distress of the lean years following the war abated, increased attention was paid to the educative process.

(14)   Young people, especially in China, Germany, Italy, and the Soviet Union—made serious and political-minded by periods of crisis in which they had lived and were living—trained themselves in eager anticipation of the wholesale regeneration of their homelands.

(15)   The lesson of cooperation among nations taught by the war was at least partially learned. World conferences became frequent, if not always successful, occurrences.

(16)   The United States emerged from the war as the world's greatest creditor and its new importance was the cause of much ill will and jealousy.

(17)   Through their participation in the war, their membership in the League of Nations, and their increasing importance as markets, the Latin American states came to have a new and more prominent standing in world affairs.

(18)   The war served as a stimulus, not only to the development of more efficient machines of destruction, but to advances in such fields as medicine, shipbuilding, and aviation.

(19)   Temporary impetus was given to a movement for general disarmament, but progress in this direction was halting.

(20)   A complete and worldwide economic rehabilitation was necessitated, for the war had dislocated the economic machinery of all participants and the Peace of Paris had tended to forego proper consideration of the economic aspects of the settlement to concentrate almost exclusively on political and territorial questions.

These major alterations in the world order left the future indeed uncertain. Those who feared the changes wrought by the war saw their fears realized when the world depression in 1929 bankrupted nations and caused international unrest. By 1939, the renewing of the worldwide conflagration gave proof that the preceding score of years in reality had been only a protracted armistice.

The League of Nations | 2

ORIGIN, MEMBERSHIP, AND ORGANIZATION

The pertinence of the observation regarding the absence of anything new under the sun is strikingly illustrated in the history of plans for an association of the nations. Most of the costly wars in history have produced new plans to preserve peace and settle international disputes by arbitration rather than armed conflict. The First World War similarly aroused agitation for the establishment of an instrument that would replace warfare as a means of settling international difficulties. By the end of the war, it was generally understood that the forthcoming peace conference would give earnest consideration to an international organization for the prevention of international hostilities.

As a result, the Covenant of the League of Nations was made an integral part of each peace treaty, and the organization which it created was given supervision over the fulfillment of many treaty clauses. This fact, however, proved to be a disadvantage in the defeated countries, for many became prejudiced against the League simply *because* it was so closely tied to the Paris settlement. Moreover, the League's assigned task of "implementing the peace" was made more difficult by the refusal of the United States to become a member.

No better explanation of the purpose of the League can be given than by quoting the preamble to the Covenant:

> The High Contracting Parties,
> In order to promote international cooperation and to achieve international peace and security
> by the acceptance of obligations not to resort to war,

by the prescription of open, just and honourable relations between nations,

by the firm establishment of the understandings of international law as the actual rule of conduct among Governments,

and by the maintenance of justice and a scrupulous respect for all treaty obligations in the dealings of organized peoples with one another,

Agree to this Covenant of the League of Nations.

The League that began meeting on November 15, 1920, was an outgrowth of the settlement of the war which had supposedly made the world safe for democracy. Thus, it was decided that any state might join or resign with relative ease. Any member nation might withdraw from the League after two years' notice. As a result, in the difficult years after 1933, many states withdrew. The League had sixty members in 1934, but only forty-six at the outbreak of the Second World War.

The League functioned through an Assembly, a Council, and a Secretariat. The Assembly consisted of representatives of all members, each state having one vote. The Assembly might consider "any matter affecting the peace of the world." The body was to be a forum in which any member nation might offer a general view or air a grievance. In addition, it had specific duties, among them the admission of new members, and, with the Council, the election of the judges of the World Court.

The Council corresponded to the executive branch in a national government. Originally, the Covenant provided for five permanent and four nonpermanent Council seats, permanency to be awarded to the United States, Great Britain, France, Italy, and Japan. Because of the refusal of the United States to join the League, there were, until 1922, only eight members in the Council. Then it was decided to increase the nonpermanent members, thus giving the smaller states a majority. When Germany and the Soviet Union joined the League, they were given permanent seats.

After 1929, the Council normally held three meetings a year, but there were frequent special meetings. Except in matters of procedure, decisions of the Council had to be unanimous. Like the Assembly, the Council might consider any question affecting world peace or threatening the harmony of international relations. Since this body was smaller than the Assembly and could be gathered more quickly, it was called upon to handle most of the emergency situations.

The specific duties assigned to the Council by the Covenant included working for the reduction of armaments, evaluating the mandate system, and preventing international aggression. It was to inquire into any disputes which might be submitted to it and could refer such disputes to the Assembly. Finally, the Council had the responsibility of summoning the member states to the defense of "the Covenants of the League," should the need arise.

The third agency of the League was the Secretariat, or "civil service," established at Geneva. It consisted of a secretary-general and a staff selected by him with the approval of the Council. The first secretary-general was Sir James Eric Drummond, who soon proved himself an officer of remarkable ability. Further secretaries-general were to be appointed by the Council with the approval of the Assembly. In 1933, Drummond relinquished his post and was succeeded by two more secretaries before the final Assembly of the League in 1946.

The secretary-general eventually came to be assisted by a staff of almost 700 employees, who, theoretically at least, did not represent the interests of their respective countries. The Secretariat was divided into eleven sections, which were concerned with general League business and the publication of all League-produced documents in their original language, as well as in French and English.

To lighten the work of these three main bodies, the League created several additional organs known as "technical organizations" and "advisory committees." These entities worked with diverse situations ranging from problems in world communications to attempts to limit the world's opium traffic. Most of these agencies later were taken over by the United Nations when it was established at the close of the Second World War.

THE PERMANENT COURT AND THE ILO

Two other major agencies technically formed part of the machinery of the League: The Permanent Court of International Justice, or World Court, and the International Labor Organization. According to Article 14 of the League Covenant:

The Council shall formulate and submit to the Members of the League for adoption plans for the establishment of a Permanent Court of International Justice. The Court shall be competent to hear and determine any dispute of an international character which the parties thereto submit to it. The Court may also give an advisory opinion upon any dispute or question referred to it by the Council or by the Assembly.

In execution of this mandate the Council at its second session appointed a committee of jurists to draw up a statute for such a court. The Statute was prepared, and adopted unanimously by the Assembly.

The court was to come into existence as soon as a majority of the League members ratified a Council-prepared protocol of acceptance. By September 1921, ratification was secured and the first group of judges elected. The Hague was picked as the seat of the court.

The World Court, eventually composed of fifteen judges who met throughout the year, had jurisdiction of two kinds, voluntary and compulsory. When two or more states were in dispute and referred their argument to the court for settlement, the tribunal's voluntary jurisdiction was invoked. A certain number of states, however, signed a so-called Optional Clause, which bound them to accept the compulsory arbitration of the tribunal when there was involved a charge of breach of international law or obligation. At one time or another, fifty states were bound by compulsory agreements.

The procedure of the court was like that of any regular tribunal. Only states might bring suit before the court. If a state failed to answer a proper trial summons, it might be judged in default. The court also was empowered to give advisory opinions to the Council and Assembly of the League. These opinions were not binding, but, in practice, generally were accepted as valid.

The Permanent Court did not entirely replace the old Hague Tribunal, first established in 1899, which provided a panel of 132 jurists who could be called upon to arbitrate international disputes. The World Court did not arbitrate quarrels; it interpreted international law and decided on treaty violations. By the time the court's membership was dispersed after the 1940 Nazi invasion of the Netherlands, thirty-one decisions and twenty-seven advisory opinions had been handed down. After the Second World War, the Permanent Court was transformed into the International Court of Justice of the United Nations.

The International Labor Organization was an autonomous organ of the League. It was brought into being through the Versailles Treaty to serve the interests of labor. Since the League was pledged to better labor conditions internationally, it agreed to support the ILO and make membership in it automatic with League membership. Germany, however, was a member of the ILO before her entry into the League; Brazil remained an ILO member after quitting the League; and the United States joined the ILO without ever becoming a League member.

The ILO was similar in structure to the League itself. There was a General Conference, which could focus world attention on certain evils and point the way to improved labor conditions. It accomplished its mission through the recommendation of broad principles to guide national legislation in behalf of the working man. There also existed a Governing Body, whose main function was to elect and control the director of the International Labor Office.

This office had its headquarters in Geneva. There it collected information on all phases of industrial life and labor, prepared the agenda for the annual General Conference meetings, and maintained contact with volunteer labor societies throughout the world.

During the Second World War, the ILO transferred its working center to Montreal. In 1948 it moved back to Geneva, having meanwhile become one of the "specialized agencies" affiliated with the United Nations. In the post-1945 period, the ILO remained active, making what it considered fair progress toward the establishment of a "uniform movement for social reform throughout the world."

THE PACIFIC SETTLEMENT OF DISPUTES

Any "war or threat of war" was declared to be a matter of concern to the whole League, and any member had the right to bring any dangerous international circumstances before the organization. As an inducement to states to seek Council consideration of major disputes, the members promised not to go to war against any state that accepted the arbitration and the resulting decision of the Council. In no case was a state to resort to war until three months after the Council's decision had been made.

The Covenant provided penalties for the infraction of its pledges. Whenever a nation resorted to armed hostilities in violation of its agreements, it was automatically "deemed to have committed an act of war against" the entire League. The culprit was to be subjected to immediate economic sanctions. This economic weapon might be applied to the private affairs of the guilty state's nationals as well as to its government. If the economic measures taken proved ineffective, the Council might *recommend,* but could not *order,* the contribution of armed forces from League members "to protect the covenants of the League."

In twenty years the League was called upon to examine about forty political disputes, most of them legacies of the First World War. Some of the earlier quarrels settled by the League, such as the 1923 disagreement between Italy and Greece over the murder of several Italians on Greek soil, were serious threats to world peace. More were of lesser importance, and some the League was unable to settle. Article 19 of the Covenant, advising a "reconsideration" of treaties that had become "unapplicable," was never implemented —despite the fact that it had been formulated to make possible a peaceable revision of the Peace of Paris.

The League generally was able to assert its political mission more strongly where small nations were involved. The larger nations were likely to regard League investigations as infringing their sovereign rights. They also were better able to bring pressure to bear in their favor. From 1931, the great powers demonstrated repeatedly that they were not prepared to uphold the ideal of collective resistance to aggression. The Covenant was violated with increasing frequency, and the League members simply refused to meet the challenge of the violations.[1]

ADMINISTRATION OF TERRITORY: THE SAAR

The Versailles Treaty gave the League responsibility for the government of the Saar Basin and the free city of Danzig. A govern-

[1] Some of the disputes that were referred to the League for settlement will be considered in connection with the histories of the countries concerned.

ing commission for the Saar was appointed by the Council and began operations in February 1920. (For the League and Danzig, see Chapter 9).

In its first proclamation to the Saar's inhabitants, the commission stressed its determination to work in "the letter and the spirit" of the Versailles Treaty. The people were warned that no attempt to spread disquiet, whether through open violence or passive resistance, would be tolerated.

In addition to the repressive powers granted the commission, the Saar situation was complicated by the privileges conceded to France in the district by the peace treaty. The French had the right to substitute French for German money in connection with the working of the mines that had been turned over to them. They had the option of establishing schools for mine employees' children, in which the instruction would be in French. Further, the entire basin was incorporated within the French customs regime. There were protective guarantees, however, as those living within the area could lodge complaints against the administration with the League Council.

Many Saarlanders soon were greatly annoyed by the French exercise of power in the basin. The people were allowed to elect deputies —who then were not consulted. German children were induced to attend French schools. When the natives complained, the members of the commission minimized the objections before passing them on to the League Council. Before long, despite a treaty stipulation that the area be policed by a local gendarmerie, a French army was stationed there.

In 1923, when the German miners in the Saar went on strike out of sympathy for their fellow workmen in the Ruhr district, which had been occupied by French troops, the commission responded by forbidding picketing, making it a penal offense to speak against the League, and muzzling the local press. This time the protests were so serious that the commission could not prevent their leaking out. The British Government requested the League to investigate.

In the resultant investigation of 1923, it was disclosed that the French-dominated membership of the commission felt duty bound to further the interests of France. The League Council expressed no criticism of this fact and whitewashed the situation. The only suggestion made was that the French army be replaced by a local gendarmerie. Yet, the prestige of the commission was undermined by the disclosure of the situation. It could no longer be asserted that it was an impartial group of international officials. Gradually its pro-French membership was revised and the change reduced the antagonism not only of the natives, but of Germans in the Reich who had sympathized with their vexed countrymen. By 1927 the French troops had been recalled and the "Saar garrison" thus eliminated.

According to the peace treaty the permanent status of the Saar was to be decided in 1935 by a plebiscite. As the year approached, it was decided that the voting would transpire on January 13, 1935.

Both France and Germany agreed not to exert official pressure to influence the voting and promised to prevent reprisals against persons because of their attitude during the plebiscite. Nazi Germany also promised, if the Saar were returned to the Fatherland, not to hinder any individuals who might wish to leave the basin, and not to apply any "Aryan legislation" for at least a year. Nonetheless, as the date for the balloting neared, friction developed in the Saar. Trouble arose out of the excesses of Nazi sympathizers and the fears of anti-Nazis. Accordingly, a League army of 3000 British, Italian, Swedish, and Netherlands soldiers was assembled in the Saar to help maintain order before and during the plebiscite.

As the day of balloting approached, many Saarlanders who had lived in the valley when the peace treaty was signed, but who had since emigrated to other lands as far removed as North America, returned to cast their votes. The Nazis were confident of overwhelming victory, whereas their opponents hoped that the Catholic, liberal, and left-wing votes might carry the decision for the status quo. There was little belief anywhere that a majority would favor incorporation into France.

In a tense atmosphere, but without serious outbreaks, the plebiscite was held according to schedule. More than 525,000 votes (98 per cent of those registered) were cast, and of these about 90 per cent were in favor of returning the Saar to Germany. Therefore, the basin was awarded to Germany, and on March 1, 1935, the formal transfer took place. Thus ended one of the most difficult tasks imposed on the League of Nations by the Peace of Paris.

THE MANDATES

Under Article 22 of the Covenant, the disposal and distribution of the foreign and overseas territories of Germany and the Ottoman Empire were accomplished. The territories were forfeited by the war's losers, but could not be annexed outright by the victors without violating the Wilsonian doctrines. Yet, since the areas were inhabited by peoples considered to be too backward "to stand by themselves" in the modern world, it was decided to give them the guidance of more modern nations. Thus, the Mandate System was developed and a commission was devised to sit at Geneva and receive the reports of nations to whom backward peoples were granted in trust.

There were three classes of mandates, graded A, B, and C, in rough accord with the political development of the societies included. Class A states were primarily the communities formerly attached to the Turkish Empire and were expected reasonably soon to become independent. The Class B mandates included the former German possessions in Central Africa. Independence for the inhabitants of these areas was remote. In Class C were placed

German South West Africa and the Pacific islands that once had belonged to Germany. These territories passed wholly "under the laws of the Mandatory as integral portions of its territory," subject to certain safeguards in the interests of the indigenous population.

The distribution of mandates was made at Allied conferences, essentially at Paris in 1919, and at San Remo in 1920. In general, the mandate system did help replace the pre-1914 idea of colonial exploitation by that of a general "guardianship" of "backward" areas. In 1932, Iraq became the first Class A state to stand among the nations as an equal; in that year she was admitted to the League as a sovereign state.

THE MINORITIES

Although the peace settlement after World War I at least attempted a realistic drawing of the European map along ethnographic lines, minorities still were included within many of the new frontiers. About 30,000,000 members of national groups, chiefly from the defeated states, were compelled to live under "alien" rule. These peoples were protected by special minorities treaties signed at, or soon after, the Paris Peace Conference. The responsibilities of the League with respect to the minorities were heavy. The Council of the League was given the task of shielding the minorities against mistreatment, and yet the Council had to be careful not to infringe the sovereignty or hurt the national pride of the majorities. It was not astonishing that this phase of the League's activities should have been subjected to frequent hostile criticism.

In an attempt to remedy some of the evils apparent in the system, the Council, in 1929, revised its procedure of dealing with minority disputes. A Minorities Committee was established and assigned the duty of deciding whether or not questions regarding minority rights should be laid before the Council. It eventually became the practice of the Council not to impose its decisions in minority disputes, but to indicate the path of conciliation and compromise.

Yet the problem of minorities remained, and in some parts of Europe it became a festering sore in the body politic. The handling of minority problems, indeed, continued to be guided more by emotion than by reason. The Fourteenth Assembly in 1933, moreover, expressed the view that the states not bound by minorities treaties ought to show "at least as high a standard of justice" in the treatment of their minorities as was required of other states by the treaties. On the other hand, at the next Assembly in 1934, Poland declared that, until a new general system of protecting minorities should be developed, she would refuse to cooperate. In addition, nationalists sometimes attacked the minorities treaties as tending to perpetuate undesirable internal differences.

THE WORTH OF THE LEAGUE

The Covenant imposed upon the League of Nations a multitude of tasks in addition to those mentioned. Financial assistance to needy states, attempts at armament reduction, and a variety of efforts to improve the human condition were all part of the League's activities.

Perhaps the greatest general contribution of the League was its influence in spreading the idea of international cooperation. More than any other agency, the League helped to make people aware of the existence of world conditions and problems, thus counteracting isolationist attitudes. It appeared to be a decided advantage merely to have a periodic assemblage of representatives from all over the world at one conference table, so that the delegates might come to know their respective worths and outlooks. In the end, the League failed to preserve peace because it was nothing less or more than its members were willing to make it.

Finally, "in its purposes and principles, its institutions and its methods, the United Nations bears at every point the mark of the experience of the League. In judgments upon the records of the League and all that it did, this truth must be always borne in mind. Whatever the fortunes of the United Nations may be, the fact that, at the close of the Second World War, its establishment was desired and approved by the whole community of civilized peoples, must stand to future generations as a vindication of the men who planned the League, of the thousands who worked for it, of the many millions who placed in it their hopes of a peaceful and prosperous world."[2]

[2] F. P. Walter, *A History of the League of Nations*, 2 v., 1952, II, p. 812. Reprinted by permission of the Oxford University Press.

The Postwar Search for International Equilibrium

3

THE INTERNATIONAL ECONOMIC SITUATION

In the Peace of Paris, the Allies demanded that the Central Powers, because of their presumed responsibility for the war, make complete financial restitution for the property damage and pension obligations done to and incurred by the Allied powers. War responsibility and reparation thus were expressly linked together.

To evaluate the amount of the damages and formulate a method of payment were tasks assigned by the peace treaty to a Reparation Commission. The Commissioners had until May 1921 to hear and approve or disapprove Allied claims for damages and to set a total reparation figure. Meanwhile, Germany was to pay on account about $5,000,000,000.

Early in 1921 Germany announced that she had completed payment of the advance in coal and other items, but the Reparation Commission found the Germans still 60 per cent short of the goal. Germany was declared in default, and the Allied zone of occupation was extended across the east bank of the Rhine to include several large industrial centers.

Seven weeks later the Reparation Commission announced that the total German indemnity should be about $32,000,000,000, some three times as high as the figure recommended by Allied economic experts at the peace conference. Following threats of an Allied occupation of the Ruhr, the schedule was accepted by Germany.

In order to make the annual payment of hundreds of millions of dollars, Germany needed a favorable trade balance. Instead, for some time after the war, she had an unfavorable balance. Despite this difficulty, Germany, in the opinion of some, might have been able to fulfill her obligations had she really been anxious to do so.

It became evident in Germany that the will to pay was lacking, deriving in part from the feeling of helplessness among Germans, who saw a massive outflow of money which did not even cover the interest charges on the total debt. As payments were met the mark declined in value and more paper money was printed. A moratorium therefore was asked until the end of 1924.

The French, however, were determined to apply pressure, for they were convinced that Germany could pay, if only she would. Under the Versailles Treaty the Allies might undertake reprisals whenever Germany voluntarily defaulted on her obligations. Consequently, the French looked for defaults and soon found them in the delivery of telegraph poles, coal, and cattle. The Reparation Commission was notified and Germany was declared in default. In January 1923, French, Belgian, and Italian troops occupied the Ruhr district as far east as Dortmund; the British regarded the action as illegal and refused to participate in it.

The Ruhr was the heart of German industry, producing 80 per cent of the country's coal, iron, and steel. By the occupation, therefore, the French in effect crushed the German economic body while demanding a continuation of reparation payments. The embittered Germans could not fight, but they inaugurated a passive resistance that caused communication services to come to a standstill and the mines and factories to be deserted.

The Berlin Government now stopped all reparation payments, forbade the Ruhr inhabitants to have any dealings with the intruders, and subsidized the striking miners and workmen with food, clothing, and freshly printed paper money. In an effort to keep economic life going, the French army attempted to work the mines and run the trains—with little success. In anger the invaders declared a state of siege and blood was shed. The mark, meanwhile, continued to decline and economic conditions throughout Germany worsened seriously. Finally, Berlin had to give in and the immediate cessation of passive resistance in the Ruhr was announced.

It seemed that the French had won, but the victory was illusory. Since the French policies had caused the total suspension of German reparation payments, the French currency was damaged along with the mark. There was an alarming drop in the value of the franc. It thus became necessary to appoint an international committee to re-study the whole problem of reparation. A body of experts was appointed and began work in January 1924. Under the chairmanship of the United States financier, General Charles G. Dawes, it submitted a comprehensive plan to the Reparation Commission in April.

The committeemen who drew up the "Dawes Plan" approached their tasks as "business men anxious to obtain effective results." Their deliberations produced numerous recommendations, among them the following: (1) the Ruhr should be evacuated; (2) there should be established a central bank to act as a depository for reparation payments and empowered to issue a new monetary unit, the *Reichs-*

mark, bearing a stable relation to gold; and (3) the Germans should pay reparation at an eventual fixed rate, which might, however, be raised or lowered in relation to the degree of prosperity in Germany.

The plan was endorsed by the European powers, eventually even by France, and became effective on September 1, 1924. Evacuation of the Ruhr began at once.

Initially, the Dawes Plan seemed to work well. German business picked up and reparation payments were made promptly. Nevertheless, the Plan had weaknesses. The Dawes Committee had not fixed a total reparation bill. Technically the total of $32,000,000,000 set in 1921 still was in force. The Germans could not be expected to make huge annual payments indefinitely with no knowledge of how long the assessments would continue. Moreover, the Plan provided for an elaborate system of economic control that was distasteful to both sides.

In 1928, the air was rife with talk about the desirability of a more satisfactory system of reparation payments. Again a committee of experts was appointed to work out a final settlement of the problem. The new body, known as "the Young Committee" after its United States chairman, Owen D. Young, held its first meeting in Paris in February 1929.

The Young Plan was signed on January 20, 1930, after several stormy conference sessions at The Hague. The new plan placed on Germany alone the responsibility for collecting the reparation payments and transferring them to the recipients. It also fixed a new total sum to be paid by Germany, namely, 37,000,000,000 marks (approximately $8,000,000,000), with interest at 5½ per cent. This time a termination date of 58½ years was set. On French urging, a "sanctions clause" was incorporated into the agreements, giving the creditor powers "free liberty of action" against Germany, should the World Court decide that she was in willful default. In addition, there was established a new institution, the Bank for International Settlements. The BIS was to act as a bank for the national banks in order to facilitate the movement of funds among nations and thus "contribute to the stability of international finance."

The Young Plan was fairly well received, except in Germany, where the financial interests and the nationalists strongly opposed it. The presumed continuation of payments until 1988 rankled many. It appeared to involve an unjust transfer of the idea of war guilt and the Versailles restrictions to generations yet unborn. Outside Germany the nations were relieved, believing that a "complete and final settlement" had at last been reached. Yet, within less than two years, the Young annuities had to be suspended, because of the onset of a worldwide Great Depression.

THE AUSTRO-GERMAN CUSTOMS UNION PLAN
AND THE HOOVER MORATORIUM

Following an unprecedented stock market crash in the United States in 1929, European stock exchanges also began to sag. By 1930 the situation was critical, as the structure of western political economy seemed to be breaking under the strain of postwar adjustments. Relief proposals were legion, but the only really important one in 1930 was a scheme for the creation of an economic federation of Europe, placed before the League of Nations by the French. Many objected that the idea of an economic Pan-Europa was visionary and that the situation was too critical for a plan whose development was bound to involve long-drawn-out negotiations. Instead, it was indicated, particularly by Austria, that a beginning could be made toward economic federation by the prompt conclusion of regional agreements.

The concept of an *Anschluss* or union between Austria and Germany had been traditionally popular in those countries. Now (1931) the idea was given economic expression in an Austro-German agreement to establish a customs union. This proposal was well received in Great Britain as a promising bilateral or regional trade pact. But elsewhere there were immediate storms of protest. Italy, and especially France, were profoundly agitated. French pressure forced Austria and Germany to suspend negotiations and the matter was placed before the World Court. The latter, by a vote of eight to seven, supported the French objection that Anschluss would jeopardize Austria's independence. Austria was left to struggle alone with a worsening economic situation.

Soon the major banking concern in Vienna, the *Kredit Anstalt*, which had interests in the financial systems of the whole Danubian area, became insolvent. Caught in a deepening crisis, Austria ignored politically weighted French offers of help and asked England for aid. The aid was forthcoming in the form of loans, but the temporary saving of one bank could not save the weakening economic structure of all Central Europe. By the end of May 1931, Germany, too, was forced to ask for help. Several large German businesses declared bankruptcy and rumors of a default on reparation spread. German President Paul von Hindenburg issued emergency edicts and then telegraphed an appeal to President Herbert Hoover of the United States calling for help in the Reich's financial crisis.

President Hoover, in the interest of the "economic recovery of the world," proposed a world moratorium, postponing for one year "all payments on intergovernmental debts." The scheme was agreeable to every country except France, which objected that the Hoover proposal bore no relation to the Young Plan. After a number of telegrams were exchanged between Washington and Paris, the Hoover Moratorium was agreed upon (July 1931). Meanwhile more German banks closed.

The worsening international economic situation forced a July meeting of premiers, foreign ministers, and finance ministers. This assemblage, however, produced little more than an assertion that nothing should be done to aggravate the international financial situation. Other conferences and conversations followed, resulting merely in the slowing down of international financial transactions to avoid panic withdrawals from banks. Panic withdrawals, nonetheless, became the order of the day. By the end of July, the Bank of England was losing gold at the rate of £2,500,000 per day. By September 1931 the pound, the basic unit of the world's money market, had dropped in value by 30 per cent.

Now even the French began to feel the financial pinch. The *Banque Nationale de Credit* was saved only through government aid. By December it was admitted that the French also suffered from rapidly rising unemployment.

At the end of 1931, too, an Advisory Committee provided for by the Young Plan reported that Germany probably could not pay reparation in 1932. Debtor countries simply could not continue to pay out huge sums annually to creditor countries that were "putting obstacles in the way of the free movement of goods." The Young Plan evidently was defunct, and a conference met at Lausanne in June 1932 to certify the fact. At this conference, a convention was signed in July that in effect abolished reparation.

The end of German reparation also brought up the question of the Inter-Allied war debts. During the war the various Allied powers had borrowed several billion dollars from Great Britain. After the United States entered the conflict it also loaned large amounts. At the end of the war the British announced their willingness to cancel the war debts owed them by the other Allies if the United States adopted a similar stand. But President Wilson had rejected this proposal and succeeding administrations, Democratic and Republican alike, chose the course of collection.

As long as Germany met her reparation installments, the Allies fulfilled their obligations to the United States. All payments, however, were suspended by the Hoover Moratorium. After the expiration of the moratorium, and with the appearance of the Great Depression, an increasing number of nations failed to pay their debt installments to the United States. American public opinion was divided on the subject of collection, but Congress stood firm against cancellation. To many Americans it seemed that Europeans always appeared able to find funds for war, but were short of cash to meet their contractual obligations.

In the hope that another international conference might solve the world's financial problems, a World Economic Conference was called in London in 1933. The conference met for some six weeks and adopted a few temporary expedients and pious resolutions. The general view was that the conference had failed.

Soon after the World Economic Conference adjourned there began a general debt default. In April 1934, the United States Congress passed the Johnson Act, closing American security markets to any foreign government which had defaulted on its debts. By June 1934, almost all the debtor states had defaulted. Throughout the remaining years before the beginning of World War II, nations placed more and more obstacles in the path of international trade. Nazi Germany, readily followed by the sister nations, led the way in erecting political barriers to the international movement of goods.

Thus, an international economic equilibrium could not be established. On the contrary, during the 1930's extreme economic nationalism so retarded international trade that many people came to look on the use of force as the only way to reinstitute a normal state of world financial and economic relations.

THE GENERAL SEARCH FOR SECURITY

Economic stability was not the only form of international order that proved difficult to establish. In the political relations established among nations there developed widespread uncertainty and eventual crisis as well. Long before the last echoes of war had died, France embarked upon a search for security against another German invasion. Twice within memory the pounding of German military boots had been heard on French soil, and Frenchmen were fearful of still another incursion. As long as Germany remained economically and militarily strong and as long as her population increased at a faster rate than that of France, it seemed necessary to Frenchmen to seek ironclad guarantees of protection and help. The leader in this hunt for security was Raymond Poincaré who, born in Lorraine, had nourished from early youth a hatred of Germany. The foreign policies of other French premiers, however, were all motivated by the same fear. Differ as they might on domestic policies, the statesmen of France invariably sought one goal in international affairs: security.

The first practical step in search of security was the signing, in June 1919, of identical treaties between France and Great Britain, and France and the United States. The Guarantee Treaties provided that Great Britain and the United States, respectively, should "come immediately to [France's] assistance in the event of any unprovoked movement of aggression against her being made by Germany." Whatever comfort France might have got from these agreements, it was short lived. The United States Senate would have nothing to do with President Wilson's treaty and thereupon the one with Great Britain, already ratified, automatically became void; its acceptance had been made "contingent upon the United States Government undertaking the same obligation."

France, looking upon the development as little short of betrayal, turned to the smaller states that also had cause to fear any change in the political status quo. First (1920) came a military alliance with Belgium. The secret terms of this agreement provided that each signatory should come to the support of the other in case of attack by Germany.

Next, France sought a substitute to take the place occupied in the prewar alliance scheme by Russia. The logical candidate was Poland, for the latter stood in as much fear of Germany as did France. The natural attachment between the two republics was increased when France, in 1920, lent Poland men, money, and munitions with which to fight the Bolsheviks, whom the French feared only less than they did the Germans. Therefore, a Franco-Polish mutual defense treaty was signed in 1921.

France, the pivot of two alliances, also determined once more to approach Great Britain. Late in 1921, accordingly, Paris advanced plans for a political alliance. The British, however, would promise immediate assistance only in case of a direct German invasion of France. But France was more apprehensive lest Germany attack Poland, for in that event the Third Republic was bound to aid her ally; it was against such a contingency that Paris sought assurance of British military support. Meanwhile, other differences had arisen between France and Great Britain. At the Washington Conference for the Limitation of Armaments in 1921–1922 (see Chapter 13), an Anglo-American proposal to abolish submarines was laid aside, largely because of opposition by France. The breach between the two former allies was widened still more by their opposing views on the reparation question. In the summer of 1922, therefore, alliance negotiations lapsed.

Worried by the complications arising from the Ruhr occupation, France set out to find additional friends. In 1924 a Franco-Czechoslovak pact was concluded. Two years later (1926), France concluded a security agreement with Romania. In 1927 France signed a similar treaty with Yugoslavia.

Meanwhile, the eastern allies of France had formed a partnership among themselves. In 1920 and 1921 a Little Entente was organized by Czechoslovakia, Yugoslavia, and Romania to keep intact the Treaty of Trianon and prevent a restoration of the Habsburgs. In 1921, moreover, Romania signed a treaty of alliance with Poland. During 1922 cordial relations were established between the remaining members of the Little Entente and Poland. Finally, to make possible economic as well as diplomatic cooperation, the foreign ministers of the entente states decided to hold periodic conferences to which Poland might be invited. The new French hegemony, thus created in the name of security, was founded upon an armed camp of the type that had proved so futile and so dangerous in 1914. It was one of the moving factors behind the conclusion of two other treaty systems centering, respectively, in the Soviet Union and Fascist Italy.

It happened that in April 1922 the representatives of thirty-four nations, including Germany and Russia, met at Genoa to devise means for improving the European economic situation. Discussions on loans and credits were well advanced when news reached the gathering that Walter Rathenau and George Chicherin, chiefs, respectively, of the German and Russian foreign offices, had signed a treaty at the Italian watering place of Rapallo.

It was understandable that these two powers should have been drawn together. Neither had as yet been restored to membership in good standing among the nations of Europe. Both were fearful of an unfriendly Allied- or French-controlled coalition and both were anxious to establish new trade contacts. To Germans, the pact seemed to clear the way toward an alliance with Russia and to make possible a defiance of the Allies and their treaty demands. To the Russian leaders it meant the restoration of diplomatic relations with a great power, the opportunity to secure credits, and lessened fear of the Franco-Polish alliance. By the terms of the treaty, the Soviet Government was accorded recognition by Germany, and all prewar debts and claims were mutually canceled. The news of the treaty angered the Allied delegates, and the Genoa Conference broke up without settling any major issue.

Soon after the conclusion of the Rapallo Treaty, the Bolsheviks began to fear the formation of a European bloc against Russia. Hence Moscow determined to negotiate nonaggression pacts with neighboring countries. The first such achievement was the signing in 1925 of a treaty of friendship and neutrality with Turkey, since the Turkish Republic shared the Soviet Union's distrust of the western states.

Four months later (April 1926) a similar covenant was signed in Berlin with Germany. The Reich was indignant over bickerings attending the vote on its admission to the League in that year and consequently looked with favor on closer relations with Moscow. Before the end of 1926 the Bolsheviks had concluded similar agreements with Afghanistan and Lithuania, and in 1927 a nonaggression treaty was negotiated with Iran.

It was not to be expected that Italy would remain isolated while the other continental states were engaged in so lively a search for security. The postwar period saw the development of a struggle between Italy and France for control of the western Mediterranean. The result was an armament race, and military preparations were made on both sides of the Franco-Italian border. Hostilities were further heightened by the fact that France had land in Europe and North Africa which, according to some Italians, should have been theirs. Finally, Italy placed chief blame upon France for Italian inability in 1919 to get more colonies.

Steps to protect Italy against French diplomatic maneuvers were undertaken shortly after Benito Mussolini's advent to power. Treaties of friendship and neutrality were signed in 1924 with Czechoslovakia and Yugoslavia. In 1926 similar agreements were reached with Romania and Spain. A political treaty of 1926 with Albania was strengthened in the following year by a defensive alliance. An Italo-Hungarian treaty was negotiated in 1927.

Thus, in 1927, nine years after the armistice, Europe was again divided into armed camps. In place of the two big prewar alliances (Triple Alliance and Triple Entente), each with a host of satellites, there now were three major groups. The outlook was hardly one to inspire confidence in the hearts of Europeans. France, in particular, was virtually bound by her various treaties to defend the frontiers of five protegés, not one of which was a first class power and each of which had numerous enemies.

THE ERA OF PACTS, 1923-1933

The members of the League recognized "that the maintenance of peace" required the reduction of national armaments to the lowest point consistent with national safety. The task of formulating specific plans for the reduction of armaments was entrusted to the Council. Even before the League started functioning, a beginning was made in compulsory disarmament by the arms clauses of the peace treaties with the defeated powers. Moreover, in a note to Germany in June 1919, the Allies plainly stated that German disarmament was to be regarded as one of the "first steps" toward a general reduction of armaments throughout the world.

Early in 1921, the Council appointed a commission to draw up proposals for the reduction of armaments. When the commission over several years was unable to produce a document the member states would accept, a resolution was introduced (1924) at the Fifth Assembly of the League, reopening the entire question of security and disarmament. As a result of this move the Assembly unanimously approved a Protocol for the Pacific Settlement of International Disputes.

The Geneva Protocol, as it came to be known, stigmatized aggressive war as an international crime. To prevent such conflicts, it stipulated that the nations adhering to its terms must agree to a variety of commitments aimed especially at defining the aggressor and thus reducing the likelihood of war. No part of the protocol was to go into effect until the efforts of a new conference to reduce armaments should have resulted in at least partial disarmament.

Although some of the smaller states displayed eagerness to ratify the Geneva Protocol, the great powers found objections to it and the document never went into force. This rejection of the first important attempt to define the aggressor in future conflicts was at least followed by the acceptance of another scheme which aimed at identifying any future aggressor in one of the worst of Europe's many sore spots: the Rhineland.

In hope of allaying the mutual suspicions with which the French and Germans regarded each other's every action, Berlin had several times (1922–1923) suggested to Paris the negotiation of frontier guarantees, antiwar pledges, and arbitration projects. Each time France had been cold to the proposals. Undismayed by these setbacks and by the fate of the Geneva Protocol, Germany, through Foreign Minister Gustav Stresemann, in 1925 once more broached the subject to France. This time Aristide Briand in France and Austen Chamberlain in Great Britain lent willing ears to the plan, but before definite negotiations could be inaugurated the French insisted that Italy, Belgium, Czechoslovakia, and Poland be invited to attend the parleys.

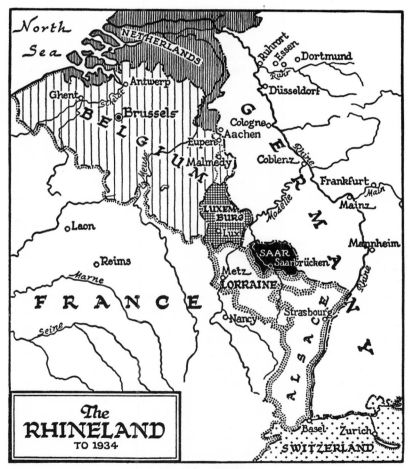

After Landman, J., *Outline History of the World Since 1914*, 1934.
Courtesy, Barnes and Noble, Inc.

In October 1925, delegates from the seven states met at Locarno in Switzerland. For the first time since the war all powers met on equal footing and the proceedings were carried on informally. So different were the attitudes of the delegates on this occasion from the usual diplomatic poses that the phrase "spirit of Locarno" was coined to describe the changed atmosphere. In this spirit seven treaties were initialed.

In the major pact the powers "collectively and severally" guaranteed "the maintenance of the territorial status quo resulting from the frontiers between Germany and Belgium and Germany and France" as fixed by the Versailles Treaty, and the demilitarization of the Rhineland as stipulated in the same treaty. Germany, France, and Belgium agreed that, except in "legitimate defense," they would not "attack or invade each other." The same states undertook to settle by peaceful means "all questions of every kind which may arise between them." The treaty was to go into effect immediately upon Germany's entry into the League.

The Locarno achievements were widely hailed as precursors of a new era in world history. But neither the pacts nor the spirit of Locarno were actual guarantees of peace. True, the Rhine frontier apparently was safeguarded. Germany supposedly gave up all claims to Alsace-Lorraine and France all hopes of a Rhineland protectorate. Yet the problem of Germany's eastern frontiers remained unsolved and there was no guarantee that it would be settled peaceably. The spirit of friendliness, moreover, was only sporadically evident in international affairs after 1925. Nonetheless, in 1927 it did lead French Foreign Minister Briand to dispatch a note to Washington suggesting a Franco-American engagement "mutually outlawing war."

After several months of correspondence, Secretary of State Frank B. Kellogg proposed that France and the United States join in an effort to induce a number of the powers to sign a general antiwar pact. It was not difficult to interest the members of the League in such a scheme, for by signing the Covenant they automatically had promised to have recourse to war only as a means of last resort. Eventually, in August 1928, delegates from fifteen nations subscribed to an antiwar agreement in Paris. The document came to be known as the Kellogg-Briand Pact or Pact of Paris.

The signers declared "in the names of their respective peoples" that they renounced war as an instrument of national policy. They agreed "that the settlement or solution of all disputes or conflicts of whatever nature or whatever origin they may be, which may arise among them, shall never be sought except by pacific means." Within four years sixty-two acceptances were recorded.

The efficacy of this "outlawry of war" was lessened by qualifications placed upon the text by a number of signatories. Fundamentally, only wars of aggression were outlawed, and even in such cases there was no provision for enforcement. The pact was founded on the hope that public opinion might be strong enough, even in time of emergency, to restrain any particular nation from violating what were simply moral obligations. But such incidents as the Sino-Japanese controversy, beginning in 1931, seemed to indicate that a warless future could be guaranteed only if the Pact of Paris were provided with "teeth," so that its violation would be regarded as something more serious than the perpetration of an immoral act. As it happened, one of the chief effects of the Paris Pact was the appearance of the so-called undeclared war.

The suspicion and antagonism that characterized European relations during the early depression years, and especially after Adolf Hitler became chancellor of Germany, led to the formulation of additional peace agreements, the most important of which was the Pact of Rome. The Pact of Rome was a ten-year agreement signed at Rome (1933) among Great Britain, France, Germany, and Italy, obligating them to consult automatically on all important international questions. The Soviet Union reacted to the Pact of Rome by promptly signing the so-called London Agreements with a number of small neighbors for mutual defense purposes.

DISARMAMENT AND REARMAMENT

The delegates who were gathered at Geneva in 1925 for the Sixth Assembly of the League faced a grave responsibility. Five Assemblies already had met, and yet the problem of disarmament was hardly nearer solution than in 1920. Hence the time had come to take some definite action that would be acceptable to the governments of the world. In this spirit the Assembly requested the Council to plan a conference for the reduction of armaments.

The Council thereupon appointed a Preparatory Commission for the Disarmament Conference, to meet at Geneva in 1926. The British and French Governments prepared draft conventions to serve as starting points for the talks of the Preparatory Commission. The drafts conflicted on nearly every vital issue. Moreover, the technical aspects of the disarmament problem regularly were pushed into the background by fear, jealousy, pride, and economics. In general, the United States, Germany, and Great Britain were on one side in the voting, and France and her allies on the other.

The commission, unable to reach final agreement, drew up (1927) a draft convention which embodied all the points that had secured general assent. This convention did not come up for a second reading until 1929. In the meantime many things had happened in the spheres of security and disarmament.

To understand the story of the further disarmament proceedings, it is necessary to refer back to the early postwar years. Inasmuch as the peace conference had ignored the question of freedom of the seas, influential groups in the United States agitated soon after the war for the building of a navy that would be able to enforce United States rights in any future war. For a time it appeared as if the pre-war Anglo-German naval rivalry would be replaced by an equally dangerous Anglo-American competition. By virtue of an Anglo-Japanese alliance, moreover, Japan might well be found on the side of Great Britain. The United States then invited a group of powers to attend a conference in Washington in the winter of 1921–1922 to consider naval limitation as well as the entire question of Pacific and Far Eastern relations.

Seven treaties were signed by the conference. One of these, effective from 1923, limited the total tonnage of aircraft carriers and restricted the number of capital ships to be allowed each signatory.[1] A ten year "naval holiday" was declared during which no new capital ships were to be built, and no capital ship could be replaced until it was twenty years old.

Five years after the signing of this treaty, President Calvin Coolidge invited the signatories to a conference to consider the limitation of cruisers, destroyers, and submarines. Only Great Britain and Japan accepted the invitation. France and Italy declared that such a conference would merely increase the difficulties of the Preparatory Commission. Hence it was a three-power conference that opened in 1927 at Geneva. After two months the conference broke up, with nothing accomplished except a renewal of the suspicion between the United States and Great Britain, which had temporarily subsided after the signing of the Washington treaties.

During 1929, there occurred a *rapprochement* between the United States and Great Britain. The ratification of the Kellogg Pact restored a measure of good feeling, and both President Hoover and Prime Minister James Ramsey MacDonald expressed renewed hopes for a further reduction of naval armaments. The outcome of resulting conversations was the calling in January 1930 of a London Naval Conference of the five great naval powers.

Almost exactly three months after the opening of the conference, the five powers signed a London Naval Treaty. Japan, England, and the United States were given equal submarine tonnage, no new capital ships were to be laid down until 1936, and the aircraft-carrier figures remained the same as in the Washington Treaty. Involved in a contest for control of the western Mediterranean, Italy and France refused to sign vital portions of the pact.

Perhaps the most discussed section of the treaty was the so-called safeguarding or escalator clause. This permitted any signatory to increase its tonnage in any category if, in its opinion, its national security was endangered by new construction on the part of any nonsignatory.

While the London Naval Conference was in progress, the Pre-

---

[1] A capital ship was defined as one with a greater displacement than 10,000 tons and guns of larger than eight-inch caliber.

paratory Commission had adjourned in hope that the naval deadlock might be broken. The failure of France and Italy to sign the whole London Treaty, however, emphasized the need for reaching results. Discussions were resumed and late in 1930 a final draft convention for a general disarmament conference was adopted. After almost five years of effort, disagreements persisted over virtually every important article. The League Council now selected Geneva as the site of the world's first disarmament conference, to open in February 1932. When the Geneva Disarmament Conference convened, there were present representatives from some sixty states.

The draft convention that was placed before the conference was a general document which indicated the methods of limitation that might be adopted, but which left to the conference the application of these methods and the decisions as to ratios and figures. It was a "skeleton lacking flesh and blood" and it offered blanks and dashes in place of figures.

Perhaps even more ominous for the success of the conference was the clash of French demands for security and German demands for equality. The French representatives steadfastly refused to vote for any reduction of armaments unless adequate security for France was assured, preferably by the placing of a powerful military, naval, and air force under the control of the League of Nations. This means of achieving security, though endorsed by the allies of France, satisfied none of the larger states. Deadlock therefore ensued.

The conference, unable to agree on any vital matter, adjourned in July 1932. One of the dangerous results of its failure was the reaction in Italy, the Soviet Union, and Germany. In the former two countries the authorities became more disdainful than ever of the impotence of the League. In Germany a fear of widespread military preparations and alliance formations, a resentment over the intransigence of France, and a desire for the restoration of the fatherland to equality with the other great powers, played directly into the hands of the restless nationalists. Through Defense Minister General Kurt von Schleicher these nationalists now officially demanded that the world either disarm to the level set for Germany in the Versailles Treaty or recognize the equality of the Germans by letting them arm to the degree of their neighbors.

Alarmed at the prospect that Germany might unilaterally abrogate the disarmament provisions of the Versailles Treaty, the powers declared in December 1932 that the Conference on Disarmament should grant to Germany and the other disarmed powers equality of rights. In February 1933 the conference resumed the work it had begun just one year previously. In the meantime (January 30, 1933) Adolf Hitler, leader of the National Socialist Party, had become German Chancellor.

The new German Government displayed no mood for temporizing, and once more Franco-German differences threatened to disrupt the proceedings. Whereas Germany was determined to rearm without further delay, France and her allies, alarmed by the nationalistic utterances of the Hitlerites, were unwilling to permit such rearming for some time to come. Meanwhile, the armament expenditures of every large state continued to mount. Into this atmosphere there burst the news, on October 14, 1933, that Germany was withdrawing from the disarmament conference. Simultaneously Germany served notice of her intended withdrawal from the League. A few months later, in 1934, the delegates to the disarmament conference dispersed, never to meet again. Thereafter most of the powers voted increasingly high appropriations for military measures.

FROM REVISIONIST BLOC TO AXIS

Toward the end of the first postwar decade it became apparent that the security system established shortly after the war was destined to undergo changes. As Germany regained strength and as the other defeated powers acquired more stability, there was a growing demand for broad revision of the peace settlement. Italy, moreover, because of her grievances against France and her general ambitions, gradually drew closer to her former enemies and began openly to side with them on matters pertaining to the peace treaties. By 1928, the Fascist kingdom began to emerge as the leader of a "revisionist bloc" whose most insistent member, Hungary, clamored for the return of the many Magyars assigned to the neighboring states by the Treaty of Trianon.

Between 1928 and 1930 Italy concluded treaties of friendship and neutrality with Turkey, Greece, and Austria. Italian friendship with Bulgaria was sealed in 1930 by the marriage of Princess Giovanna of Italy to King Boris. In 1933, Italy and the Soviet Union signed a pact of nonaggression.

In 1933 the rise to power of Adolf Hitler, who patterned some of his policies after those of Mussolini, seemed to foreshadow an Italo-German entente. The prospect for a time worried France, but Italy showed little sympathy for Germany's desire to absorb Austria. For strategic and economic reasons Mussolini preferred to see Austria independent and closely tied to Italy.

The new German nationalism, as voiced by the Hitlerites, and the continued activity of the revisionist bloc, also affected the interrelations of the Little Entente, France, and the Soviet Union. Already, in 1929, Czechoslovakia, Yugoslavia, and Romania had renewed the whole set of treaties that comprised the entente. Furthermore, to protect themselves, the members of the Little Entente in 1933 signed the London Agreements with the Soviet Union and then also drew closer to Poland. This step was especially important inasmuch as all these smaller countries seemed to have wearied of being regarded as French satellites. Poland in January 1934 signed a ten-year nonaggression pact with Nazi Germany. Soon thereafter Poland also renewed a nonaggression treaty that earlier had been signed with the Soviet Union.

The Third Republic, too, figured in a changed diplomatic lineup. As early as 1931, France, for years the leading foe of the Soviet Union, had begun to shift her position. She long had wanted access to the Russian oil resources. The Soviet Union placed huge orders abroad and France saw no reason why these should nearly all fall to Germany, Great Britain, and Italy. In Germany the nationalists were becoming strong enough to frighten both the French and the Bolsheviks: they threatened to repudiate the Versailles Treaty, vehemently denounced communism, and sometimes referred to Russia as a suitable field for eastward expansion. Hence Soviet-German relations cooled, and France in 1932 signed a neutrality treaty with the Soviet Union. Then, in 1935, France and the Soviet Union signed a nonaggression pact.[2]

Late in 1934 representatives of the United States, Great Britain, and Japan discussed the question of renewing the naval-limitation treaties. Japan demanded parity with the United States and Great Britain. When this was refused, Tokyo gave the required two years' notice of the termination of the naval agreements. By 1935 the matter was further complicated by Germany's determination to build a sizeable fleet.

This time the German naval ambitions appeared to worry France more than Great Britain. London, indeed, signed an agreement with Berlin in 1935 whereby the Nazis, regardless of Versailles restrictions, might acquire a naval tonnage equal to 35 per cent of that of the British Commonwealth.

Then came the autumn of 1935 and with it, following partial Franco-Italian reconciliation through a Pact of Rome, the Italian invasion of Ethiopia and the imposition of limited League sanctions against the Fascist aggressor. More and more did Rome now veer away from the states that at last—four years after a Japanese invasion of Manchuria—had come to act in the name of "collective security." More and more, therefore, did Rome now move towards the states (Germany and Japan) that were bent upon upsetting the territorial status quo by threat and force.

Deriding collective security, which had been only partially applied in the case of Ethiopia, Mussolini in November 1936 said: "A virile people . . . refuses to confide its destiny to the uncertain hands of third parties." Continuing, he declared that Germany, "although surrounded and solicited, did not adhere to sanctions." Berlin, moreover, early recognized the conquest of Ethiopia. Consequently, the Germans and Italians could not but be sympathetic toward one another's aims. This new friendship, thundered Il Duce, was bolstered by common opposition to Bolshevism and was in reality "an

---

[2] In 1934 a Balkan Pact to maintain the existing "territorial order" in the Balkans was signed by Turkey, Greece, Romania, and Yugoslavia.

ALLIANCES AND PACTS, 1920 TO MID-1939

The dates indicate the year of signing of the treaties. Supplementary agreements
are listed only if exceptionally important.

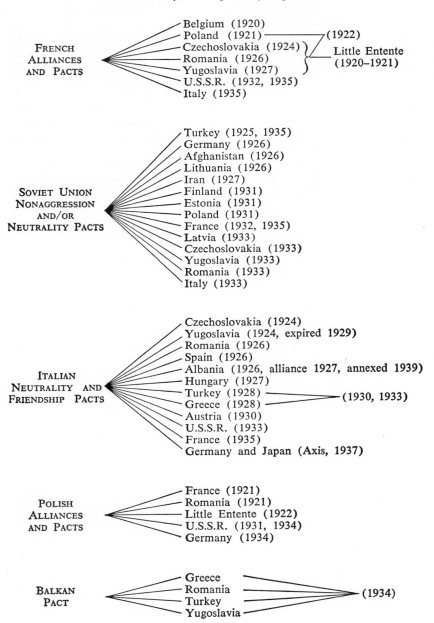

FRENCH
ALLIANCES
AND PACTS

- Belgium (1920)
- Poland (1921) ──────┐ (1922)
- Czechoslovakia (1924) ┐ Little Entente
- Romania (1926)   │ (1920–1921)
- Yugoslavia (1927)   ┘
- U.S.S.R. (1932, 1935)
- Italy (1935)

SOVIET UNION
NONAGGRESSION
AND/OR
NEUTRALITY PACTS

- Turkey (1925, 1935)
- Germany (1926)
- Afghanistan (1926)
- Lithuania (1926)
- Iran (1927)
- Finland (1931)
- Estonia (1931)
- Poland (1931)
- France (1932, 1935)
- Latvia (1933)
- Czechoslovakia (1933)
- Yugoslavia (1933)
- Romania (1933)
- Italy (1933)

ITALIAN
NEUTRALITY AND
FRIENDSHIP PACTS

- Czechoslovakia (1924)
- Yugoslavia (1924, expired 1929)
- Romania (1926)
- Spain (1926)
- Albania (1926, alliance 1927, annexed 1939)
- Hungary (1927)
- Turkey (1928) ──────┐ (1930, 1933)
- Greece (1928) ──────┘
- Austria (1930)
- U.S.S.R. (1933)
- France (1935)
- Germany and Japan (Axis, 1937)

POLISH
ALLIANCES
AND PACTS

- France (1921)
- Romania (1921)
- Little Entente (1922)
- U.S.S.R. (1931, 1934)
- Germany (1934)

BALKAN
PACT

- Greece
- Romania
- Turkey
- Yugoslavia

(1934)

axis around which all European states animated by the desire for peace might collaborate." Thus for the first time was the word *axis* used with a special political connotation. And thus also did Mussolini cede first place among the revisionists to the stronger Reich. Fascist Italy became content to follow where once she had led.

Soon after Mussolini made this speech, Germany and Japan drew together through the signing of an Anti-Comintern Pact (November 1936). The signatories agreed "to keep each other informed concerning the activities of the Third [Communist] International, to consult upon the necessary defense measures, and to execute these measures in close cooperation with each other.". One year later Italy adhered to this agreement and the Berlin-Rome-Tokyo Axis was an established fact. Referring to the ideological and practical differences of outlook of the Axis and non-Axis states, Mussolini announced: "The struggle between two worlds can permit no compromise. Either we or they!" Thus was the challenge of battle hurled at the British Commonwealth, France, the Soviet Union, China, and the United States.

National Developments, 1919–1939

Great Britain and Ireland | 4

THIRTEEN YEARS OF TROUBLE, 1918-1931

At the end of the war, in 1918, Britishers shared with others in the world the hope that the losses and sufferings of the conflict might convince men that they must find the way to a better world. In London, when the armistice was announced on November 11, there was dancing in the streets. People waved flags, blew whistles, and rang bells. The merry demonstrations eventually subsided into hopeful expectation that a happier society would be produced in Great Britain.

It was this hope for a better world that David Lloyd George used in gaining support for the idea that the wartime coalition government, which he had led, be reelected to office. The delirium of Armistice Day thus was replaced by preparation for general elections in December 1918. In these "khaki elections" Lloyd George appealed for support of the coalition on its record. He undertook, if endorsed, to advocate the trial of William II and the exaction of a large indemnity from Germany. A pledge was given to prevent the dumping of foreign goods and to protect the "essential industries." Finally, Lloyd George promised to care for the veterans, settle the Irish Question, and "reform" the House of Lords.

On this platform the coalition, which during the campaign was deserted by the Laborites, captured two thirds of the seats in the House of Commons. The Labor Party, with about sixty seats, became the official Opposition. The membership of the coalition was 70 per cent Conservative and hence, although the Prime Minister was a Liberal, the Conservatives predominated in the cabinet. Lloyd George at once went to Paris, but after the signing of the peace treaties his attention was absorbed by Great Britain's critical economic situation.

During the early postwar period British industry climbed to a peak of prosperity. Prices and wages rose, the number of people employed increased, and there was a tendency to shorten the work week. Unhappily, as 1920 drew to a close, conditions underwent a precipitate change. Numerous strikes broke out and unemployment increased so rapidly that by July 1921 there were 2,000,000 persons idle in a population of 42,000,000.

The reasons for this decline were many. The war had impoverished several of Great Britain's customers, including Germany, Russia, and the Danubian states. Then, while the British strove to reestablish the pound sterling at its prewar value, most of the continental governments resorted to inflation. In the world market this meant that the price of British goods was high, for British manufacturing costs exceeded those in countries where inflation resulted in relatively cheap labor. The fact that Great Britain's factories remained intact during the conflict was not an unmixed blessing, for now, although the country still had its machinery, much of it was outmoded. Competition with the more modern methods and implements in use in the United States and Germany became increasingly difficult.

During the war, the British had suffered a loss of markets, especially to the United States and Japan. The former acquired much of Great Britain's trade in Latin America; Japan secured much of it in China and India. Moreover, the tariff barriers erected by the new and strongly nationalistic continental states curtailed Great Britain's export trade.

In addition, Great Britain's war losses were heavy. About 750,000 of her men had been killed and twice that number wounded. Her total debt burden at the end of the war was ten times that of 1914. Much of her shipping had been destroyed. This last might have acted as a stimulus to shipbuilding, but the forced surrender from Germany of most of her ships checked any such development. By 1921 almost one-third of the men in the British shipbuilding industry were out of work. The unemployment problem was aggravated because the Britishers, unlike the French, could not fall back upon agriculture in time of industrial depression. Great Britain was primarily a manufacturing and exporting country. Hence the only solution for the crisis lay in a revival of trade and industry.

The government that first had to cope with the situation was the coalition under Lloyd George. In the beginning, resort was had to temporary expedients. One was the allotment of a "dole" to unemployed men and women. This involved an annual outlay of millions of pounds and was of transitory value; it was not a cure for chronic unemployment. Secondly, the government encouraged the emigration of jobless workmen to other parts of the empire, especially Canada. As the laborers generally were not eager to migrate and the dominions set up severe entrance qualifications, the scheme offered little relief.

In 1921 two specific attempts were made to get at the root of the trouble by reviving industry. First, Great Britain signed a trade agreement with Russia. Then there was passed a Safeguarding of Industries Act. This, deviating from traditional free-trade policy, levied a substantial duty to protect certain "unstable key industries."

Meanwhile the Conservatives had begun to weary of the dominance of Lloyd George. They disliked a treaty that had been signed with Ireland and they favored closer cooperation with France. They complained about the troubles Great Britain was having in the Near and Middle East, and they charged the government with extravagance. In October 1922, therefore, the Conservatives withdrew from the coalition. Thereupon Lloyd George resigned and the Conservative leader, Andrew Bonar Law, formed a ministry. Since the Conservatives controlled only a plurality of seats, new elections were set for November.

The Conservatives, waging the campaign on a platform promising "tranquility and stability," secured well over half the seats in Parliament. The Labor Party, which in 1900 had captured only 2 seats, now returned with 142. The Liberals formed a poor third. Bonar Law retained the Prime Minister's office, but illness soon forced him to resign and he was succeeded by the less experienced Stanley Baldwin. The new Prime Minister was an exbusinessman who had occupied several financial offices between 1917 and 1923.

Baldwin faced an unemployment situation that had become a "chronic malady." In his perplexity he was converted to the view that protection and imperial preference (preferential tariff rates among the several parts of the empire) were the only cures for the industrial depression. Since, however, Bonar Law had pledged the party not to change the tariff without a mandate from the people, Baldwin felt bound to dissolve Parliament and set new elections for December 1923.

This unexpected course of events stimulated the Liberals into renewed action. They campaigned vigorously for the continuance of free trade. If they could not oust the Conservatives from power, the Liberals hoped at least to recapture some of the seats previously lost to the Laborites. The Conservatives firmly defended their policy of erecting tariff barriers. The Laborites also favored free trade, along with the nationalization of mines and railways, and revision of the Versailles Treaty.

Although they polled nearly as many votes as in the previous election and still comprised the largest party in the House of Commons, the Conservatives now failed to command the necessary majority to control that body. The Laborites, on the other hand, increased their representation by more than a third, and the Liberals also registered a gain. When Parliament met in January 1924, the Liberals joined the Laborites in voting a lack of confidence in the

Baldwin Government. Liberal leaders Lloyd George and Herbert H. Asquith preferred to risk a coalition with the untried Laborites rather than encourage a continuance of Conservative rule. Hence, J. Ramsay MacDonald, leader of the Labor Party, became Prime Minister and Foreign Secretary in Great Britain's first Labor Government.

MacDonald was born in 1866, the son of a Scottish laborer. He acquired most of his education by attending evening classes and by avid reading. He chose the career of journalism and made frequent trips to various parts of the empire. He became active in bringing about a political fusion of the British intellectual socialists with the trade-unionists, and he helped found the British Labor Party.[1] An effective orator, he became secretary of the party and its leader from 1911 to 1914. As an avowed pacifist he was publicly denounced and defeated for Parliament in the "khaki elections" of 1918. Four years later he regained his seat in the House of Commons.

The first Labor Government worked under serious difficulties. There were rumors that radical legislation would become the order of the day. Some investors became panicky and some United States financiers withdrew their money from London. But aside from its avowed rejection of class warfare, the MacDonald Government had a practical reason for refraining from revolutionary methods and for tempering its program: it depended upon the support of the Liberals for its tenure in office.

The domestic accomplishments of the Labor Government were not striking, and unemployment grew worse. More spectacular were the exploits in the foreign field. The government played a prominent role in the acceptance of the Dawes Plan. MacDonald urged the admission of Germany into the League. He supported the Geneva Protocol of 1924, which aimed at ensuring peace by defining the term "aggressor nation." The Labor Government also made important disarmament gestures. Relations with France were improved. The Soviet Union was recognized and British goods were promised a better reception in the Russian market.

The Labor Government soon came under popular suspicion as being amenable to pressure from the Bolsheviks. The Soviet trade treaty was attacked, and much excitement ensued when the government dropped the prosecution of an editor of the communistic *Worker's Weekly* who was accused of inciting British soldiers to mutiny. Opposing a parliamentary motion to appoint a committee of inquiry on this action, MacDonald was defeated through the defection of the Liberals. He dissolved Parliament and ordered new elections.

During the campaign (October 1924) the cause of the Labor Party

---

[1] The British Labor Party grew out of the efforts of a Labor Representation Committee which adopted the name Labor Party in 1906.

was injured by rumors, generally unfounded, that it was friendly toward bolshevism. Many voters seemed to feel uncomfortable with the thought that the Labor Ministry might condone unbridled freedom for Communist propaganda.

The Conservatives won more than 400 seats in the election, whereas the Laborites and Liberals together had fewer than 200. MacDonald resigned as Prime Minister, Stanley Baldwin took the reins once more, and Austen Chamberlain became Foreign Secretary.

Soon after his resumption of office, Baldwin led the new Conservative Government in attempts to alleviate economic distress. Despite these attempts, however, the government was soon faced by a serious labor crisis.

Among the hardest hit of British enterprises was the coal industry. Before the war, Great Britain used millions of tons of coal annually in her own industries and sold additional millions abroad. But after 1920 the importance of coal as a fuel declined. Moreover, under the Versailles Treaty, Germany annually supplied large quantities of coal to France, Italy, and other regions which formerly had depended on British coal. Russia, because of domestic difficulties, bought substantially less coal in 1925 than in an average prewar year. Simultaneously, the general decline in British business lessened the domestic demand for coal. Consequently, conditions became so bad that many mines shut down. By June 1925 one-fourth of the insured men in the coal industry were without work. The Baldwin Government, in order to prevent the closing of all mines, undertook temporarily to subsidize the industry. The total cost of this subsidy, which checked the decline of wages while a parliamentary commission studied the coal industry, was $100,000,000.

The coal commission reported in March 1926 that the industry would have to be radically reorganized if it were to be kept alive. The report urged government ownership of the mines with private management under lease from the authorities. A continuance of the subsidy was declared preposterous and a decrease in wages was considered inevitable. This report satisfied neither workers nor management and, while the government tried to arrange further conferences, the operators gave notice that wages would be lowered. The workmen threatened to strike, and the General Council of the Trades Union Congress announced its intention to call a general strike unless the demands of the miners to maintain the subsidized wage rate were met by May 3. The owners refused to agree to the demands and the general strike began as scheduled.

The strike actually involved less than half of the trade-union membership and less than one sixth of the working population, but it frightened the government into declaring a state of emergency. Thousands of volunteers tried to keep the trains, buses, and industries going, and special constables were commissioned to protect the volunteers. But there was little violence. Rather, a gay humor was discernible, possibly because of the novelty of the situation.

Emergency bus- and tram-drivers vied with one another in displays of wit, and placards bearing inscriptions such as "Don't stop me! I can't start again!" were much in evidence.

After nine days the general strike came to an end. The Trades Union Congress called it off on the promise that further negotiations would be pushed by the government. Baldwin asked that there be no vindictiveness and that the men be taken back by their old employers.

The coal strike continued for six more months, until November. For a time, coal had to be imported from the United States and Germany to keep the factories and railways running. Meanwhile the plight of the miners became desperate. Their resources dwindled and winter was coming. Gradually the cold and hungry men drifted back to work on the owners' terms. The net result was the lengthening of working hours and the lowering of wages.

Politically, the strike weakened both the Labor and the Liberal parties. In the former, extremists pointed to the failure of the coal strike as proving the need for more direct action. MacDonald, however, succeeded in holding the party together. The Liberal Party was split once more when Asquith and Lloyd George disagreed on the question of supporting the strikers. The Conservatives were more solidly united than before and were determined to rid Great Britain by law of the possibility of a future general strike. In 1927 they put through Parliament the Trades Unions and Trades Disputes Act, which made general strikes illegal, forbade picketing, and protected union members who refused to join illegal strikes. The act also struck at the Labor Party by forbidding political levies by unions except where they had gained the member's written consent.

The Conservatives sought another advantage from the strike situation. They proposed to strengthen the House of Lords. By the Parliament Act of 1911, money bills became law within thirty days after their passage by the House of Commons regardless of the attitude of the House of Lords. The Conservatives, who never had approved of this arrangement, now believed that the "socialist peril" warranted a strengthening of the upper chamber. Then, even though public opinion might temporarily place a Labor Government in the saddle, the destinies of Great Britain would be safeguarded. In 1927 Baldwin introduced a plan to reorganize the House of Lords and increase its legislative power. But the scheme was so violently opposed in debate by the younger Conservatives, as well as by Laborites and Liberals, that it never was formulated into a bill.

The laws passed by the Baldwin Government included new provisions for widows', orphans', and old-age pensions, and the further extension of female suffrage. The electoral act of 1918 had limited the franchise to women over thirty, lest the women, who outnumbered the men, predominate in politics. This act, which simultaneously removed the few remaining property qualifications for male voters, was in line with a general European postwar tendency towards democracy. Not unnaturally, the women in Great Britain were dissatisfied with the age restriction and considered the arrangement a slur on their maturity. A decade of active campaigning was crowned with success in 1928 when Parliament extended the vote to all women over twenty one.

In foreign policy the Conservatives did not play a heroic role. War debt agreements with Italy and France were reached and the Locarno Pact was concluded. An equivocal part was acted during the negotiations for Germany's entrance into the League, and friendship with the United States was strained over naval disarmament. Most difficult were the dealings with the Soviet Union. Chamberlain unearthed a series of Soviet anti-British plots reaching from Great Britain to China, and in 1927 diplomatic relations with Moscow were severed. The Foreign Secretary was no more than lukewarm towards the Kellog Pact.

The chronic industrial depression proved to be as much a thorn to the Conservatives as it had been to Labor. Higher tariff rates, the establishment of some new industries (such as the manufacture of airplanes) in southern England, the active support given by the Government to foreign commercial advertising and propaganda, and the popularity of Great Britain with United States tourists, all failed to revive industrial strength. Irrational industrial organization and antiquated methods persisted.

To make matters worse, report had it that there was no future for British industry and that capital would bring in a greater return if invested abroad rather than at home. Hence, it often was difficult to raise sufficient funds for even urgently needed equipment. British exports in 1927 totaled only 79 per cent of those in 1913. From 1913 to 1927 British exports thus fell by 21 per cent, although the world's total export trade rose by 18 per cent in the same period. In January 1927 Great Britain had 1,500,000 unemployed.

Unemployment and industrial troubles loomed large in the regular parliamentary elections of May 1929. Baldwin, Lloyd George, and MacDonald took pains to appeal to the 5,000,000 women voters who would exercise a powerful influence in this, their first, opportunity to cast ballots. The Conservatives adopted as their slogan "Safety First!" and pointed with pride to their firm stand during the general strike. They advocated permitting industry to "save itself" without governmental interference, but urged higher tariff protection. They emphasized increasing cooperation between employers and workmen and prophesied that this would soon restore prosperity. They opposed recognition of the Soviet Union, stressed imperial defense, and objected to any additional peace commitments beyond the League Covenant, the Locarno Agreements, and the Paris Pact.

The Lloyd George Liberals recommended a stupendous public works program, reaffirmed their reverence for free trade, and advocated closer cooperation with the League and Germany. They favored friendship with the United States and the Soviet Union. The Laborites were particularly successful in their use of slogans and posters, many of which were especially designed to attract the younger voters. They advocated nationalization of the leading industries, an extensive public works program, longer compulsory education, and the development of natural resources. Promise was made of shorter working hours, higher direct taxes, additional social legislation, and the repeal of the Trades Unions Act of 1927. In foreign affairs the Laborites held about the same views as the Liberals, but stressed a determination to prevent war.

In the election, Labor captured 288 seats, the Conservatives 260, and the Liberals 59. In June 1929, MacDonald became Prime Minister for the second time, again depending on the Liberals to remain in office. The poor showing of the Liberals, incidentally, gave rise to a growing feeling that the mission of the party had been fulfilled, or at least that the days of Lloyd George's leadership were numbered.

The control of the Laborites became precarious when their Liberal supporters split into a left and a right wing. The former, led by Lloyd George, though not always in agreement with Labor's policies, still preferred Labor to any Conservative Government. The right wing, led by Sir John Simon, was ready to vote against the government at any time. The Labor Party itself suffered half a dozen defections when Sir Oswald Mosley and some friends became convinced that MacDonald was not striving sufficiently to remedy unemployment.[2]

The energies of the Labor Government soon were concentrated on foreign policy. Attempts were made to allay native disaffection in India, Arabia, and Egypt. Diplomatic relations with the Soviet Union were restored and the promise of a wide Russian market was secured. The Young Plan was accepted. MacDonald visited President Hoover in the United States and so prepared the way for the London Naval Conference of 1930.

In the domestic field the Laborites again did nothing spectacular. Agriculture was aided a little, the coal situation was slightly improved by the Coal Mines Act of 1930, which required a certain amount of collaboration in the marketing of the product, and reforms were effected in the motor transport system. Several important steps were taken in military matters, among them the restoration of the civil rights of conscientious objectors from the First World War and the abolition of the death penalty for desertion or cowardice in the army.

The most important campaign pledge of the Laborites remained largely unfulfilled—that of unemployment relief. There was no dearth of attempts to restore trade, but they were of little avail. The Prince of Wales made good-will tours, notably to Latin America,

[2] In 1932 Sir Oswald founded the black-shirted British Union of Fascists, whose slogan became: "Fascism is practical patriotism." After 1934, the British Fascists several times clashed with the police.

in the hope that he might be an effective social sales manager. When he returned he delivered some frank addresses in which he urged British businessmen to wake up to modern methods and to go out and look for trade rather than remain at home and wait for customers to come to their door. Negotiations were undertaken to get the continental states to reduce their tariffs in the interest of a general trade revival, but there was only failure to record, and the total value of imports and exports fell by more than a third from 1929 to 1931. Public works were inaugurated, but by the end of September 1931 the unemployed numbered 2,800,000. The people probably realized by this time that the situation was worldwide and not peculiar to Great Britain, but the Labor Government had promised more than it could perform. Labor lost a number of seats in by-elections.

In the summer of 1931 the government noticed with alarm that the country's gold reserve was shrinking rapidly. The general effects of the world depression, decreasing tax receipts, and heavy foreign withdrawals all combined to make the situation acute. A committee of financial experts suggested slashes in government expenses and recommended slight tax increases. But a majority of the cabinet refused to endorse the proposals, saying that they provided economy at the expense of the working people. In August 1931, therefore, MacDonald tendered the king the resignation of the entire ministry. One day later he reassumed control with a new "National Ministry" composed of members drawn from all three parties.

Soon after this startling development became public, the Labor Party expelled MacDonald and a few other leaders. Arthur Henderson was elected to succeed MacDonald as party leader, and the Labor Party officially went into opposition. These events were perhaps not so abrupt as they seemed. Whereas the rank and file of the party had been leaning increasingly toward the left, MacDonald and his close associates had become middle-class liberals. Though still concerned with the welfare of the people, they appeared to be content with the social status quo of the land. It seemed to them that they were placing loyalty to national welfare above loyalty to narrow party policies.

THE NATIONAL COALITION, 1931-1939

In September 1931 the National Cabinet pushed through Parliament a finance bill which embodied most of the proposals that had been suggested some weeks earlier. The government held that the law exacted equal sacrifices from all citizens, but the Labor Party insisted that most of the savings were made at the expense of the working people. When the act was published, thousands of teachers, postmen, and other government employees held protest meetings against the salary reductions. Riots had to be put down in most of the larger British cities.

Such incidents shook foreign confidence in the stability of Great Britain. The kingdom's credit fell rapidly and foreign withdrawals from the Bank of England rose steeply. The result was so great a depletion of the gold reserve that Parliament in September 1931 took Great Britain off the gold standard. Almost immediately the value of the pound fell by nearly a third. The chief consolation of this move was the belief that the cost of production would be lowered, thus giving British goods a sales advantage in the world market.

To enable the people to express their views on the policies of the National Government, Parliament was dissolved and elections were held in October 1931. The candidates who supported the National Government ran as Conservatives, National Laborites, and National Liberals. The opposition candidates retained their names of Laborites and Liberals. The Nationals asked for a vote of confidence and requested a blank check to do what they considered best for the country. The Laborites had their customary platform, but lacking their old leaders they seemed to find it difficult to make their points clear to the voters. MacDonald joined the Conservatives in prophesying disaster if the Labor Party were victorious.

The result of the election astonished even the most experienced political sages. The government won a majority over its opponents of nearly 500 seats. The Conservatives alone had a majority of about 325 over all the other groups and became the backbone of the next National Government. MacDonald, reelected as a National Laborite, formed another cabinet. Neville Chamberlain, a Conservative proponent of high tariffs, became Chancellor of the Exchequer. The Liberal Sir John Simon became Foreign Secretary.

Though MacDonald retained the prime minister's office for almost four years longer, his control was by leave of the Conservatives. In order to extend the life of the National Government and to maintain "national unity in the presence of the grave problems" that confronted "the whole world," the extraordinary step was taken of permitting individual members of the cabinet to express in Parliament "by speech and vote" views contrary to those held by the majority of the cabinet. Thus was broken a constitutional principle of 148 years' standing. In 1935 MacDonald resigned because of illness. Thereupon the Conservative leader, Stanley Baldwin, reconstructed the National Cabinet with himself as Prime Minister. The youthful Anthony Eden was added as "Minister for League of Nations Affairs," a post specially created for him.

Before the year was out, Baldwin decided to appeal to the country for support of his stand in the Italo-Ethiopian dispute which was then raging. Although some losses were sustained, the Baldwin Government was returned with a majority of about 250 seats. The Conservatives again formed the core of the coalition, having a sizeable majority over all other groups combined. There was little change in the cabinet except that Anthony Eden became Foreign Secretary.

In January 1936 King George V died and was succeeded by his oldest son, King Edward VIII. The new king soon became involved in a dispute with Prime Minister Baldwin. The difference grew out of the king's desire to marry a woman of American birth, Mrs. Wallis Warfield Simpson, who was about to procure a second divorce. The government resisted the king's wishes and on December 10, 1936, Edward abdicated. He left immediately for the continent as Duke of Windsor and some months later married the woman of his choice in France. The Duke of York now became George VI and was crowned in May 1937. He and his queen seemed to win the affection of their people quickly and were wildly acclaimed abroad.

Meanwhile, after the coronation, Baldwin retired from politics. He was succeeded as Premier by his Chancellor of the Exchequer, Neville Chamberlain. Aside from the perennial question of a budget, and that of rapid rearmament—itself a repercussion of the foreign situation—there was little in the way of domestic administration to which the new Premier could devote his energies. The Mediterranean activities of Italy, the exigencies of the Spanish Civil War, the territorial and military progress of Germany, the important relations with France—these demanded all Chamberlain's attention, particularly after the resignation in 1938 of Foreign Secretary Eden, who disagreed with his chief on further concessions to the totalitarian states. In explanation of his position, the Prime Minister told the lower house of his desire to find out "whether there was any common ground on which we might build up a general scheme of appeasement in Europe." This policy of appeasement he then steadfastly pursued until the very outbreak of the Second World War in 1939.

From 1931 through 1938 the several National Governments tried to revive prosperity. There was no definite program, but a series of measures was adopted so that Great Britain might once more "muddle through." The people were urged to help the government lessen a massive national debt by paying income taxes in advance of the date required, and to sell to the authorities their private gold possessions. Large quantities of gold were imported from India. To retain the foreign-trade advantages that presumably accompanied currency inflation, the government set up an Exchange Equalization Fund. The exact operations of this fund were secret, but its purpose was so to control the inflationary process and manage the currency that a fairly stable relationship might be established between sterling currency and gold.

At an Imperial Economic Conference at Ottawa (1932), Great Britain and the dominions sought to improve the economic situation within the empire by an exchange of trade concessions. A dozen bilateral trade treaties were signed, but they fell far short of accomplishing what had optimistically been hoped for from the conference. The sessions were characterized by a greater willingness to demand sacrifices than to make them, and gave evidence of the existence of serious intra-imperial economic rivalries. But some concessions were granted, especially by the mother country, and the empire trade gave signs of improving. Soon after the close of the Ottawa Conference, Great Britain also began to negotiate bilateral trade agreements with foreign countries.

Many observers felt that permanent recovery could come to Great Britain, with its economic structure "geared to the world market," only through the return of a prosperous foreign trade. Yet business was aided by a variety of immediate factors. These included a more vigorous trade with the dominions, and the enormous demands of the rearmament program. Though wages remained low and taxes high, and though strikes continued, the number of unemployed declined. British foreign trade in 1937 was the highest for any year since 1930. In 1938, moreover, there came to an end a six-year-old tariff and trade war with Ireland and there was signed with the United States a trade pact.

Thus, Britain was the scene in the 1930's of a grim struggle with the Great Depression, a struggle that barely lessened as the decade drew to a close. Yearnings for peace were heightened by Britain's economic troubles, and the nation manifested a spirit of pacifism during the interwar years. Out of this came general public agreement with Chamberlain's policy of appeasement. However, the time of tragic disillusionment with the policy lay just ahead.

IRELAND

In 1914 Parliament passed an Irish Home Rule Bill. This action, it was hoped, would end Irish agitation for autonomy, dating from 1801 when Ireland became an integral part of the United Kingdom. Had the provisions of the law gone into force, Ireland might have been rent by civil war. The six "Ulster" counties in the northeast, being industrialized and largely Protestant, were resolved not to submit to the control of an Irish parliament, the majority of whose members would be elected by the Catholic farmers in the twenty-six southern counties. The people in the south were equally determined that one parliament should rule the entire island. Upon the passage of the bill, both sides organized for armed conflict, but the outbreak of the First World War caused the British Government to suspend the operation of home rule. The Irish Nationalists in the south assured London that they would remain loyal during the war. The fealty of the Ulsterites was a foregone conclusion.

The British authorities now pursued ill-advised tactics in Ireland. The Ulsterites were permitted to form a military division of their own for overseas service, but the Irish Nationalists were denied a similar request, and south-Irish recruits were asked to enter English regiments. Beyond this, petty annoyances were multiplied until many people in the southern counties became indignant. In 1916 the discontent crystallized in an Easter Rebellion. This uprising was the work of some radicals who had left the Irish Nationalist Party, which still officially supported the British, and formed an Irish Republican Brotherhood. Most of the "Brothers" also were affiliated with a society known as *Sinn Fein* ("We Ourselves"), which had originally been organized for industrial betterment and for development of Irish national sentiment. In 1914 the association had entered politics and during the war it became identified with a republican movement. The republicans thus came to be known as the Sinn Feiners.

On Easter Monday, 1916, the Sinn Feiners seized some public buildings in Dublin and issued a proclamation in the name of the "Provisional Government of the Irish Republic." The British put down the rebellion within a week, shot a number of the leaders, and placed Ireland under martial law. Several thousand people were arrested and many were deported to Great Britain. By their harshness, the British turned the dismal failure of the uprising into a "moral" victory, and the ranks of Sinn Fein sympathizers swelled.

Throughout the war disorder increased, and a crisis was reached in 1918 when Parliament applied a conscription act to Ireland. The opposition to this measure was so strong that the authorities offered to suspend its provisions on condition that a sufficiently large number of Irishmen volunteered for service. The volume of enlistments, however, was small and the outlook for the future ominous. The signing of the armistice occurred in time to prevent disaster.

The British parliamentary elections of December 1918 assumed the form, in southern Ireland, of a contest between the Nationalists and the Sinn Feiners. The former stood for home rule, the latter for independence. In Ulster the Unionist group, which preferred close ties with England, was supreme. Of the 105 seats to which Ireland was entitled in Parliament, the Unionists got 26, the Nationalists 6, and the Sinn Feiners 73.

After election, the Sinn Fein deputies refused to attend the Parliament at Westminster, preferring to consider their election as a mandate to set up a separate Irish parliament. This they did, at Dublin, in January 1919. The deputies took the name Irish Republican Party and called their parliament *Dáil Eireann*. At the first meeting of this body, only twenty-nine men were present, since the rest were in prison or in hiding. Not daunted, the Dáil selected three delegates to attend the Paris Peace Conference and plead the cause of Irish self-determination. The assemblage, however, refused to recognize these emissaries. At a subsequent meeting the Dáil appointed a ministry and elected a New York born ex-professor of mathematics, named Eamon de Valera, President.

The defiance of the Dáil led to a state of war between the "Irish Republic" and Great Britain. The British military and police forces fought pitched battles with the Irish Republican Army led by the young and able Michael Collins. Cruelties were perpetrated on both sides, and late in 1920 the city of Cork was burned. Especially hateful to the Irish were the Auxiliaries sent over from Great Britain to aid the police. These men were recruited through advertisement in England and were mainly ex-soldiers. They soon were nicknamed Black-and-Tans, because their uniform consisted of a khaki outfit with black bands on hat and arm.

To end the strife, Lloyd George secured the passage of another Home Rule Act in December 1920. This law conceded more local autonomy to Ireland than the earlier one, but it set up separate parliaments for northern and southern Ireland. The Ulsterites proceeded to implement the law. The other Irishmen balked. They no longer were satisfied with home rule and they objected to a division of the island. When London ordered elections held in the spring of 1921, the Sinn Feiners captured 124 of the 128 seats allotted to the Parliament of Southern Ireland. At the opening session of this assembly, only four members were present. The body adjourned, never to meet again.

Still hopeful, Lloyd George invited de Valera to London to discuss an amicable settlement. A conference was arranged, but the British proposals were unacceptable to the Irish. Later a second conference was held. This time the Irish delegation was headed by Arthur Griffith, founder of Sinn Fein. On December 6, 1921, the plenipotentiaries signed a treaty which, in effect, was the birth certificate of a new Irish Free State. The treaty gave the Irish Free State the status of a dominion. Officials of the Irish Free State were to take an oath of allegiance to the king. The Crown was to be represented by a governor-general. The coasts of Ireland were to be protected by the British fleet, and Great Britain was to retain authority over some Irish ports as naval bases. The Irish Free State was to have its own military forces and eventually was to share in the coast defense. Northern Ireland might join the Irish Free State or continue the relationship established with Great Britain in 1920. Ulster chose the latter course, so that a boundary line remained to be adjusted.

When news of the treaty reached Ireland, there was a break in Sinn Fein ranks. De Valera denounced the document and resigned from the Presidency when the Dáil accepted it by a close vote. Arthur Griffith and Michael Collins led the movement for the organization of the Irish Free State, and a committee was appointed to draft a constitution. De Valera and his followers thereupon withdrew from the Dáil, boasting: 'We made it impossible for the British Government to rule Ireland, and we can also make it impossible for an Irish Government working under British authority to rule Ireland." When, in June 1922, elections for a provisional parliament were held, the chief issue was the acceptance or rejection of the treaty. The republicans interfered with the elections by tearing up railway tracks, intimidating voters, and assassinating speakers. Nevertheless, the friends of the treaty were overwhelmingly victorious in the balloting.

Republican "Irregulars" for some time continued their lawless activities with apparent immunity because many members of the provisional government were loath to deal harshly with the men who had been their comrades in the struggle against Great Britain. But in August 1922 the republicans killed Michael Collins from ambush. A few days earlier Arthur Griffith had died from overwork. William Cosgrave and Kevin O'Higgins took over the leadership of the parliamentary forces and determined to suppress the disorder. A struggle followed, fiercer than that with the British. Thousands were imprisoned and scores were assassinated or executed. Eventually the Free Staters triumphed, and in the spring of 1923 de Valera ordered his followers to lay down their arms.

From 1923 to 1927 de Valera and his followers abstained from violence. Organized as the *Fianna Fáil,* or Republican Party, they put up candidates for election to parliament, but when elected these delegates excluded themselves from office by refusing to take the oath of allegiance to the king as required by the constitution. For a time this was useful to Cosgrave, for it meant that there was no large opposition group in the legislature. In 1927, however, Kevin O'Higgins, Cosgrave's assistant, was assassinated. As Minister of Justice, O'Higgins had been active in repressing the Irregulars and he was generally regarded as the "strong man" of Ireland. Though de Valera and his aides denied complicity in the murder, the government determined to curtail the activities of the Fianna Fáil. A public-safety act empowered the authorities to deal vigorously with lawlessness, and the electoral law was amended so that any parliamentary candidate had to agree in advance to take the oath of allegiance if elected.

By this time popular opinion in Southern Ireland was decidedly averse to the methods of de Valera. Moreover, a number of Irish-Americans who had been assisting de Valera financially were alienated by his tactics. De Valera therefore announced his intention to head a constitutional opposition in the parliament, and the political atmosphere became calmer. In the elections of 1927, de Valera's party, having forsworn violence, became the second largest party in the parliament.

The provisional parliament, which in 1922 had elected Cosgrave president, also had adopted a constitution. This was republican in character and was accepted by the British Parliament without change. On December 6, 1922, King George V proclaimed the Irish Free State. Immediately thereafter the last British troops were withdrawn from the newest dominion.

An agreement of December 1925 settled the boundary between Northern and Southern Ireland, largely in the former's favor. Although fiercely opposed by de Valera's party, the agreement was ratified. Thereafter the two parts of Ireland agreed henceforth "mutually to aid one another in a spirit of neighborly comradeship."

It was to be expected that there would be a nationalistic reaction in the Irish Free State after the achievement of dominion status. The new country adopted its own flag and sent diplomatic represenatives abroad. In 1923 it was admitted to the League of Nations. There was a strong movement to make Gaelic the language of the people and many family and place names were Gaelicized. Irish coins and postage stamps were adopted, and the mailboxes were painted green in place of the former royal red. In the spring of 1929, Gaelic was made compulsory for lawyers as it previously had been for civil servants. The Irish delegate to the League Assembly delivered his speeches in Gaelic. The Irish Free State adopted a severe censorship system.

Yet the question of Irish destinies had not been finally answered, only deferred until the coming of the depression upset the normal economic order. As things grew worse in the early 1930's, de Valera's Fianna Fáil grew in strength. In the 1932 election the voting was close. De Valera emerged in control of the new Dáil by a narrow margin and was elected president of the Executive Council.

De Valera moved quickly to make changes. He rescinded the prohibition placed upon parades of the Irish Republican Army. He placed tariffs on a great variety of manufactured goods from England. One by one he moved to put aside the clauses of the treaty of 1921.

The increasing trend away from Great Britain was high-lighted in May 1937, when a new Irish constitution was enacted by vote of the people. The document declared the sovereignty and independence of Ireland, which was henceforth to be known by its old Gaelic name of *Eire*. There was no mention of king or commonwealth. There was to be a directly elected president, chosen to serve for seven years. In 1938 Dr. Douglas Hyde, a Protestant professor of literature who had never taken part in politics, was chosen first President under the new constitution. De Valera was designated Premier, and, in May 1938, Great Britain and Ireland signed a number of agreements settling some of the more troublesome financial and economic differences that had developed during the previous two decades. Meanwhile, Northern Ireland continued its British allegiance.

De Valera, following a victorious election in 1938, set out to establish "social justice." He encouraged plans for a redistribution of natural resources among the classes, fostered labor legislation, and tried to make agriculture more efficient. But there was opposition to such policies and particularly to the continued separation of Northern and Southern Ireland. When the opposition became violent, de Valera declared the Irish Republican Army illegal. But in 1939 the IRA renewed its activity, being charged with 130 bombings throughout the United Kingdom in the first eight months of that year. De Valera himself denounced the terrorist campaign and ordered the Irish police to assist in checking the illegal activities of the IRA. But when the Second World War broke out, Ireland alone of the commonwealth countries remained neutral.

GREAT BRITAIN AND THE COMMONWEALTH

The war and post-1919 periods witnessed some remarkable changes in the relationships within the British Empire. Beginning in 1907, and interrupted only by the war, numerous imperial conferences were held, attended by the premiers of Great Britain, Canada, Australia, New Zealand, the Union of South Africa, Newfoundland, and, for a time, the Irish Free State. At these gatherings the delegates discussed problems that confronted the empire as a whole and that affected the relations of the members one to another.

The exigencies of the First World War, the dependence of Great Britain on the help of the dominions, the independent signature by the latter of the peace treaties, and the circumstances that the dominions became members of the League of Nations, served greatly to alter the relations between the mother country and the colonies. Long before all the legal niceties involved in their new status were worked out, the dominions proceeded with a number of actions that usually were taken only by sovereign powers.

Canada, for example, in 1923 signed with the United States a Halibut Fisheries Treaty which bore the signature of only the United States and Canadian representatives. This precedent was followed in a number of later treaties between Canada and the United States and Canada and European countries. Some of the dominions appointed their own diplomatic ministers abroad. Australia, New Zealand, and South Africa administered mandates in their own names. In 1930 the Australians successfully contended that their choice for the governor-generalship, in this case a native, should be accepted. In 1931 the Irish Free State assumed a Great Seal of its own.

In principle, most of these actions had been affirmed by the Imperial Conference of 1926. In the Balfour Report this conference had declared: "They [Great Britain and the dominions] are autonomous communities within the British Empire, equal in status, in no way subordinate one to another in any aspect of their domestic or external affairs, though united by a common allegiance to the Crown, and freely associated as members of the British Commonwealth of Nations." It remained to enact this principle into imperial law, and in 1929 a committee representing Great Britain and the dominions was appointed to find a method of bringing the old legal restrictions and the new practice into harmony. The report of the committee was accepted by the Imperial Conference of 1930, and steps were taken in each dominion and Great Britain to give it the force of law. This was finally accomplished in December 1931 with the passage by the British Parliament of the Statute of Westminster.

The statute recognized the equal status of the dominions with the mother country and thus virtually accorded them independence. In future no law passed by a dominion parliament could be declared void "on the ground that it is repugnant to the law of England" or contrary to acts of Parliament. The dominion parliaments were recognized as having full power to pass laws applying to dominion citizens living abroad or traveling on the high seas. No law of the Parliament of Great Britain was to be applicable to any dominion unless the latter specifically consented to the extension of such law to its domains. No longer might the king on advice of his ministers "disallow" an act of a dominion parliament, and henceforth no alteration in the laws concerning succession to the throne or the royal titles might be made without the assent of the parliaments of the dominions as well as that of Great Britain.

Thus there was created a "British Commonwealth of Independent Nations," a group of separate political entities avowing allegiance to one and the same symbol of unity: the Crown. The king, a feeling of commonwealth citizenship, and perhaps a certain pride in descent from common stock, remained as the dominant ties between Great Britain and the dominions. But the latter, as long as they did not entirely break away from Britain, enjoyed the protection of a powerful navy which was paid for chiefly by the people of Great Britain.

France 5

POLITICS IN THE THIRD FRENCH REPUBLIC

The political structure of the Third Republic was somewhat different from that of other parliamentary states. There were a few parties, particularly radical parties, that had definite organization and party funds, and held periodic conventions. In addition, there were numerous political groups which, though they had none of these characteristics, were listed under special names and were entitled to representation on parliamentary committees, provided they had a certain minimum number of adherents.

In view of this situation, it was difficult for any one group to command a majority in the Chamber of Deputies. Hence the government functioned through a system of coalitions or *blocs*. Frequently the makeup of a bloc was based upon a few major issues and, when new issues arose, group realignments quickly followed. Consequently, the average life of cabinets in France was short. By the time of its expiration in July 1940, the Third Republic had had 110 ministries. Some degree of stability in governmental policies nevertheless was maintained by permanent undersecretaries and because the ministerial changes often involved merely a shuffling of portfolios.

During the war and until November 1919, France was governed by a bloc called Sacred Union. After the elections of 1919 the union split into two other coalitions, the *Bloc National* and the *Cartel des Gauches*.[1] The Bloc was made up of conservatives and moderates

---

[1] The conservative groups in the legislature, as in most continental parliaments, were seated to the right of the Speaker, the moderates in front of him, and the radicals to the left. Hence the designations "Right," "Center," and "Left" indicated the general political stand of any group or party.

led by Clemenceau, Poincaré, Alexandre Millerand, and Briand. It hoped to reduce Germany to economic bondage and make France secure, was opposed to socialism, and favored amicable relations with the papacy. The Cartel was led by Edouard Herriot. It was anticlerical, favored high income taxes and state social control, and, although fully as anxious as the Bloc to give France security, advocated friendship with Germany and Russia. Independent of these coalitions were the Socialists and Communists on the left and the Royalists on the right.

The powers of the French president were limited and he exercised far less control than the Chief Executive of the United States. Yet, if he happened to possess a dominating personality, the president might exert considerable influence on the course of politics. Poincaré, for example, was certainly more than a figurehead during his incumbency from 1913 to 1920.

In international affairs the attitudes of all postwar ministries in France were determined by a desire to make the republic secure against foreign aggression. French foreign policy, therefore, was an integrated foreign policy designed to maintain the status quo internationally, preserve the Versailles Treaty, and develop a favorable climate of world opinion for the French case as it developed in diplomatic confrontations. In carrying out this policy, some French leaders were unyielding; others were conciliatory. Nevertheless, since the same end always was kept in view, there was a marked degree of unity in French foreign policies. On domestic issues, however, and especially in economic and clerical matters, the various cabinets held divergent opinions.

FRANCE'S "ASPIRIN ERA," 1919-1939

When the war came to a close, France was in domestic chaos. The northern tenth of the country had been reduced to wasteland. Farms, factories, railways, and roads had been laid in ruins. In their place were barbed-wire entanglements, shell holes, and debris. Two million people had been forced to leave their homes. Little wonder, therefore, that the army was restless, urban workers were clamoring for bread, and the middle class was afraid of the spread of communism. The apprehension among peasants and the middle class of violence and disorder was so deep that the Bloc National won the elections of 1919, and moderate government thus was ensured at least until 1924.

Financial difficulties soon plagued the Bloc. Expecting Germany to pay the total cost of reconstruction, the government, without raising the tax rate, spent billions on restoration. Most of the total expenditure was raised through loans and the printing of paper money. Month after month went by, however, and the expected sums from Germany were not forthcoming. Late in 1921 Germany asked for a moratorium on reparation. The French conservatives, led by Poincaré and André Tardieu, now agitated for the downfall of Premier Briand, who had taken leadership of the national government early in 1921. They succeeded in their endeavors (1922) and Raymond Poincaré, noted for his steadfast devotion to the power and unity of France, assumed the premiership.

The new Premier floated foreign loans, introduced financial reforms, and raised taxes; yet the inflated franc continued to decline and the budget remained unbalanced. Poincaré's tactics in the Ruhr and his favorable attitude towards the papacy also were unpopular. The Left, consequently, hoped to overthrow him at the next election and promised the voters greater reliance on direct taxation, closer cooperation with the League, and a more conciliatory foreign policy. In the balloting of 1924 the Left won control of the Chamber of Deputies and ex-Professor Edouard Herriot of Lyon, leader of the Radical Socialists, became premier. Despite their name, the Radical Socialists were liberals and not Marxists. Self-proclaimed heirs of the French Revolution, they professed a firm faith in the republic and promised prosperity and security at home and abroad.

Sincere and honest, Herriot was inexperienced in national politics and for a time injured his reputation by his complete informality. In foreign affairs, the Herriot Ministry accepted the Dawes Plan, established more cordial relations with Great Britain, the Soviet Union, and Germany, and helped draft the Geneva Protocol. It was less fortunate in its domestic policies. Hence, when the Senate in 1925 refused to countenance further inflation, the ministry resigned.

In the months that followed, six ministries rose and fell. The franc continued to depreciate and by July 1926 was worth one-tenth of its prewar value. Because of the seriousness of the crisis, old group rivalries were set aside momentarily and a National Union Ministry was formed, headed by Poincaré and including six ex-premiers. The veteran Prime Minister now remained in office for three years, until July 1929. In these years he earned the title of "Savior of the Franc."

Poincaré informed the legislature that financial salvation could be obtained only through increased taxation and stringent economy. Since the deputies at last had come to be in a reasonably receptive mood, new taxes were voted and the French people had to submit to one of the highest tax rates in the Western world.

In 1926 the budget was balanced—for the first time in thirteen years. Consequently the franc rose in value and by December 1926 was worth double its value in July of that year. It was stabilized at this level in 1928. In the elections of 1928 the policies of Poincaré were upheld by vote of the people. Unfortunately for his successors, however, the power in the lower house was almost equally divided between Right and Left. Both groups supported him, but when illness forced his retirement a year later (July 1929) they fell to quarreling. Following Poincaré's resignation several short-lived ministries struggled with the financial and diplomatic problems. First came Briand and then two Tardieu governments.

Much was done by Tardieu as the leader of successive ministries. One achievement was the passage, after years of discussion, of a sickness, health, and old-age insurance law that went into effect in 1930. In addition, taxes were reduced, military service was cut from three years to one, and the size of the army was diminished. The war budget, however, was considerably expanded so that new fortifications might be built and maneuvers held on the Italian and German frontiers. Through the influence of Foreign Minister Briand the Young Plan was ratified, the evacuation of the Rhineland was completed, and a French scheme for a Pan-European federation was announced.

Now, in the German elections of September 1930 the nationalistic parties received an unexpectedly heavy vote. This caused a severe reaction in France because the German nationalists were the most determined opponents of the Versailles Treaty and the Young Plan. Many Frenchmen became panicky over what they called Briand's weak foreign policy. Poincaré emerged once more to complain that, though it was pleasant to listen to "international hymns to the divinity of peace," France also needed "other things" to give her a feeling of security. Hence, in December 1930 Tardieu's Government fell.

By this time it was apparent that the absence of Poincaré's strong influence in French political life had brought a return of the old instability. In addition, the world depression now made itself felt in France, bringing with it the hardships that accompany decreasing trade and increasing unemployment.

Eventually (1931), Senator Pierre Laval became premier, being supported chiefly from the Right. He reconstituted his cabinet three times in little more than a year in a futile effort to solve the republic's vexatious problems. Unemployment figures rose steadily and the volume of exports continued to decline. Important matters of international concern also arose to tax the patience of Laval. It was during his incumbency that France interposed against the projected Austro-German Customs Accord of 1931 and that she accepted, in modified form, President Hoover's plan for a moratorium on governmental-debt payments. A delegation was sent to participate in the Geneva Disarmament Conference. Early in 1932 Briand's place in the foreign office was taken by the Premier himself, because of the former's illness.[2] Soon thereafter Laval fell, over an electoral bill designed to aid the Right in the forthcoming elections. Tardieu now became premier for the third time.

The elections of May 1932 betrayed a decided leftward swing of popular sympathies. The Radical Socialists, still led by Herriot, became the largest group in the Chamber of Deputies. The Liberals

[2] Briand died in March 1932.

and Radicals had pointed out during the campaign that the rule of the Right had bequeathed the country an empty treasury and high unemployment.

After the election Tardieu was succeeded by Herriot. As had been his lot in 1924, Herriot once more came to power in a time of economic distress. The value of French exports in the month of the elections had been lower than in any month since the war. Unemployment figures were rising and income tax receipts fell rapidly. In external affairs, the cabinet had to consider the Lausanne Reparation Conference and the Geneva disarmament parleys. To meet the most urgent of these developments, the Herriot Government pushed through parliament a budget that once again reduced expenditures and raised taxes.

It appeared in the autumn of 1932 that Premier Herriot might continue for some time to hold the confidence of parliament. Yet he soon found it necessary to resign. The issue upon which the ministry fell was the war-debt question. Herriot urged that France meet the installment of about $19,000,000 due the United States in December; but the deputies disagreed. The Government's motion to make the payment was defeated and the cabinet resigned (December 1932).

In the next thirteen months France had five ministries. Each premier struggled to balance the budget while avoiding inflation. In addition, there were several financial and legal scandals that seriously embarrassed the government. Eventually there developed a growing demand that the executive authority be strengthened and that the lower house be deprived of some of its powers.

In January 1934 there was violence before the Palais Bourbon, where the deputies met. The participants were Royalists, Socialists, Communists, civil employees protesting against pay cuts, a group of "Young Patriots," and a Fascist war-veterans' association called Croix de Feu. On February 6, Premier Edouard Daladier attempted to protect the deputies from intimidation by placing troops around the Palais Bourbon. There was little excitement during the day, but at night the crowds became violent, property was destroyed, and conflict ensued between the populace and the guards. On the following day the fighting spread to other cities. Former President Gaston Doumergue was persuaded to leave his retirement and form a government that would place patriotism above politics and save the country from civil war.

Doumergue organized a cabinet of leaders from all groups save the Royalists, Socialists, and Communists. Among the members were Herriot, Laval, Tardieu, and Marshal Henri Phillipe Pétain of Verdun fame. There was a general belief that this ministry would restore order, strengthen the executive, and ensure security. Hence there was a lull in the demonstrations. The chastened deputies awaited the government's proposals.

A budget was adopted and the government was empowered to

reduce expenses by decree. Commissions were appointed to investigate various scandals. The burdensome number of civil servants was reduced and the salaries of the remainder were cut. Despite these accomplishments the Doumergue Government faced criticism. In the parliament, the Socialists, led by Léon Blum, voted against most of the cabinet's measures. Outside parliament, the Croix de Feu, led by Colonel François de la Rocque, threatened "action" if reforms in government were not soon forthcoming.

In September 1934 the Premier outlined his plans for constitutional reform. He proposed to give the cabinet exclusive right to initiate money bills and wanted power delegated to the prime minister to dissolve the Chamber of Deputies without the consent of the Senate. This latter suggestion was upheld on the ground that the deputies would be slower to upset ministries if there could be held over their heads the threat of a new election. To the Leftist groups in parliament these suggestions smacked of dictatorship. The cabinet, they said, must remain under the control of parliament, not parliament under the cabinet.

The heated discussions aroused by Doumergue's plans, the increasingly bad economic situation, the fears among Socialists and Communists that reactionaries were planning to seize the government, the recurrence of political riots, apprehension over the approaching plebiscite in the Saar, and then the assassination of King Alexander of Yugoslavia and Foreign Minister J. Louis Barthou (see Chapter 11), all made the position of the ministry insecure. Another crisis was precipitated when Doumergue, without letting the deputies see the new budget, requested that body to vote certain provisional funds for governmental use. Thereupon several members of the Cabinet resigned and the Doumergue Ministry fell.

Another coalition cabinet was formed (November 1934), this time by Pierre-Etienne Flandin. Its political complexion was less Rightist than had been that of its predecessor. Laval was appointed to carry on the foreign policies of the deceased Barthou. Flandin was more interested in tackling economic problems than in immediate political reform. But when, in the spring of 1935, he appealed to the deputies for power to do whatever he thought necessary to fight the depression, the answer was a vote of no confidence.

Pierre Laval then became premier in June 1935. Given extraordinary powers to take measures "in defense of the franc," he reduced governmental salaries and pensions, raised the tax on incomes and on munitions manufacturing, inaugurated new public works, lowered certain rents and the prices of some commodities, and studied ways of stimulating foreign trade. These acts relieved the financial strain but aroused opposition. There was an increasingly restless activity on the part of several antiparliamentary leagues, chief among which was the Croix de Feu. Laval dissolved several of the smaller leagues, but was unable to retain his ministerial control. In January 1936 he was succeeded by Albert Sarraut (Radical Socialist), who formed a stopgap ministry that lasted through the elections of April–May 1936.

For the fifth time since the war, France attempted the setting aside of party lines to follow a new "savior." The parties of the Left (Radical Socialists, Socialists, and Communists) combined in the election as the Popular Front. They denounced fascism, urged the nationalization of munitions manufacture, and promised to "break the power of the two hundred families who control the economic life of the nation." They undertook to stimulate production, were friendly to Great Britain and the League of Nations, and upheld a strong military program. The voters gave 62 per cent of the ballots to the Popular Front and the remaining ones to the candidates of the Right and Center. The Socialist Party formed the largest single group in the chamber. Its leader, Léon Blum, a well-to-do Parisian of legal and literary renown who first had entered parliament in 1919, organized a government in June 1936.[3]

During its year of office the Popular Front Government encountered many political storms. The first was an immediate epidemic of "sit-down strikes" in which 1,000,000 workers "occupied" their places of employment (standing with folded arms and later sitting and lying down) in factories and stores. Transport, lighting, and food services were, in general, unaffected, so that the public was not seriously inconvenienced. The real reasons for this demonstration were not clear; perhaps the proletariat wanted to make sure that the government would fulfill its election promises to labor. Certainly the authorities were impressed by the evidences of discipline in the strikes.

Blum called representatives of the employers and the workers to a conference and effected a temporary settlement. New legislation provided generally for a forty-hour week without pay reduction, collective bargaining, the closed shop, paid vacations, wage increases, and compulsory arbitration in labor disputes. These things brought some satisfaction to the workers but further alienated many worried businessmen.

By the end of 1936 the Popular Front had fulfilled its campaign program. Credit was provided for farm mortgagors and small-businessmen, and the public works program was expanded. The press (often corrupt) was required to publish its sources of revenue. Finally, the Bank of France was reorganized so that the government secured more control, whereas the so-called Regency Council, composed of the two hundred largest stockholders, was deprived of its power.

In defense and foreign affairs, the Polish and Yugoslav alliances were renewed, the armed forces were strengthened, and the lead of the British was followed in the Spanish situation. The sympathies of the voters who had elected the Popular Front, however, were evi-

---

[3] Blum emerged as a popular figure when a group of Royalists in February 1936 pulled him from an automobile and severely beat him.

dently with the Spanish "Loyalists." They could see no reason why France should imitate the British and not permit the legal sale of arms to the legally constituted Madrid Government. It therefore required all Blum's oratorical skill to convince his supporters of the advisability of following Great Britain's example—particularly in a Europe so full of powerful dictatorships.

In the beginning of 1937, it was apparent that the Popular Front Government, having achieved the aims which held it together, must simply "coast along," hoping that no great issue would arise to disturb its equilibrium. In the spring unemployment figures were down, labor temporarily was satisfied, and the conservative elements became less restive upon the promise of a legislative pause. The much heralded and oft postponed opening of the Paris Exposition occurred in 1937, and the exhibits attracted large crowds of natives and foreigners during the summer. The relative domestic quiet of the first half of 1937 produced a deceptive display of French brotherhood and quietude.

In the end, the financial situation proved to be the nemesis of Blum, as it had been that of so many of his predecessors. The interest on the public debt consumed more than one third of the government's income when Blum took office, and during his incumbency the situation had not improved. In June 1937 Blum requested broad powers to deal with the financial crisis. The Chamber agreed, but the Senate twice refused its assent. The Premier therefore resigned and was succeeded by Camille Chautemps, a Radical Socialist.

The Chautemps Government promptly raised taxes, import duties, and public utility rates. In the fall of 1937 the authorities frustrated a plot of an armed secret society, *Les Cagoulards* ("The Hooded Ones"), to reestablish a monarchy. The forty-hour-week law was modified, with greater consideration for seasonal industries. At the close of the year a strike of public utility employees in Paris was ended after one day, chiefly because of the government's threat to call the strikers to the colors and order them, as soldiers, to carry on their jobs.

When 1938 opened, France appeared to enjoy relative domestic calm. Then the Chautemps Ministry encountered opposition and fell, in March 1938, when the Socialists and Communists refused the Premier's request for renewed emergency financial powers.

Since the overthrow was caused by the Left, President Albert Lebrun asked Léon Blum to try to form another government. This he did, forming another Popular Front Ministry—without Communist participants. The second Blum Cabinet lasted less than a month. The Premier resigned when the Senate refused to follow the example of the lower house in voting him emergency financial powers similar to those that Chautemps had demanded one month earlier. Thus, again and again, the French Parliament, unable to cope with the country's financial difficulties, refused special powers to the premiers. Meanwhile Germany had absorbed Austria, and General Francisco Franco, with German and Italian aid, was extending Fascist influence along the southern borders of France.

Blum was succeeded (April 1938) by Daladier, who had risen above the popular ill will aroused during his premiership in 1934. It had not been lost on Daladier that, during the debate preceding Blum's fall, the upper house had indicated its readiness to give emergency financial powers to *a* premier, but not to *Blum*. It also had become clear, by this time, that the Senate was veering away from the principle of collective security and becoming reconciled to the idea of bilateral agreements with Hitler and Mussolini, in line with Chamberlain's policy of appeasement. Hence Daladier appointed a cabinet composed of Radical Socialists. There was not a Socialist or Communist in this "anti-Red" ministry, as it came to be called. Now the parliament granted its government plenary powers and adjourned.

Thereupon appeared a lively succession of governmental decrees. All taxes immediately were increased. Greater amounts of money were assigned to measures providing for national security. Over the objection of the General Confederation of Labor, the forty-hour week was modified and the army was enlarged. In the face of an approaching foreign crisis, these measures appeared to win popular approval.

In September 1938 the whole national life was caught in the web of events that accompanied the German demand for an immediate solution of the Sudeten problem in Czechoslovakia. The French people, in response to the orders of the government, faced both the prospect of war and the actual preparations for an armed conflict with a fatalistic resignation that must have astonished as much as it delighted the authorities. When the crisis had passed, the Chamber overwhelmingly endorsed the conduct of the cabinet, though this represented a virtual repudiation of France's whole postwar diplomacy.

This vote of confidence heralded the breakup of the Popular Front, for the Communists alone had voted against Daladier's conduct of diplomatic affairs. The split was widened when, in response to the Premier's demand for further plenary powers, the request was granted by the assembly. The Socialists had abstained and the Communists voted "no." In November 1938 the Radical Socialist Party specifically dissociated itself from the Popular Front, and the latter ceased to be a moving factor in French politics.

A series of strikes now broke out during which the police and workmen engaged in violent clashes. A one-day general strike was called, whereupon the government mobilized the workers and ordered them, as soldiers, to carry on with their jobs. This maneuver proved successful, and many men refused to obey the strike call. Although both sides claimed victory, the strike was not "general" and the Government did fine or imprison a number of persons who had quit work despite the mobilization order.

Meanwhile a fresh international complication had arisen. In November 1938 a demand was voiced in the Italian Chamber of Deputies for the acquisition of French-controlled Tunisia, Corsica, Savoy, and Nice. Despite its advocacy of appeasement, Daladier's government seemed as firmly determined as any Frenchman to resist Italy's demands for French areas. The Premier took the occasion to make a triumphal tour of France's Mediterranean and North African possessions, to be greeted everywhere with demonstrations of fervent loyalty.

Although he endorsed Chamberlain's policy of appeasement, Daladier became convinced, after the absorption of Bohemia and Moravia by Nazi Germany in March 1939, of the need to build up the military strength of France. Almost immediately thereafter Daladier asked parliament to pass a bill granting his Cabinet full power for eight months. The legislature quickly complied with his request, and the government proceeded to convert France into a "workshop of national defense."

Decree followed decree, and the Premier came to be looked upon as a new "strong man" on the European political stage. The press was placed under strict control. The army was further enlarged. The index of production went up, the national debt increased, prices rose, and unemployment virtually disappeared. The French people, in general, seemed content to have the government grasp affairs firmly, thus putting a stop to protracted debates. Even Blum endorsed Daladier's position, in principle if not on every point. When war came, in September 1939, France had the outward appearance of a well-functioning economic and military machine.[4]

THE PROBLEM OF ALSACE-LORRAINE

When, after the conclusion of the armistice of 1918, French troops crossed the Vosges Mountains into Alsace-Lorraine, they were greeted with banners, triumphal arches, and kisses. Most of the people appeared happy that the "lost provinces" were freed from German control and reunited with a victorious France.[5] Trouble, however, soon followed. The newly recovered provinces and their

[4] In September 1939 Daladier dissolved the Communist Party in France after some of its leaders objected to French military action against the recently formed Nazi-Soviet "Front." Meanwhile the life of the parliament had been extended to 1942, eliminating the prospect of a regular election in 1940.

[5] Between 1871 and 1914, several hundred thousand people migrated from Alsace-Lorraine to France, whereas many Germans came to settle in Alsace-Lorraine. There were further large movements of population in 1918–1919 and 1940.

motherland quickly found themselves at issue over questions of language, political rights, and economic opportunities.

When France regained the provinces, about one fourth of the natives spoke French; the remaining three fourths used German dialects. This situation had existed for centuries: under the rulers of the *ancien régime,* under Napoleon and his successors, and under the German emperors from 1871 to 1918. Yet, after the war, the French, feeling that only French-speaking people could be genuine patriots of the republic, tried to force their language on the provincials by barring German from all schools. The opposition to this attempt at Gallicizing the inhabitants was so great that a compromise had to be reached. Eventually it was agreed that children would have to learn French exclusively only during the first two school years. Thereafter they might receive three hours a week of German instruction, and German might be used in the periods devoted to religious teaching.

Meanwhile, the provinces were flooded with railroad and civic functionaries who spoke only French. This led to a Lorraine railway walkout in 1919, the strikers demanding the removal of all railway officials and foremen who could not speak German. Said one of the strike leaders: "It wasn't worth while to get rid of the Germans if the French come and take all the good jobs." The strikers won their point.

Under German rule the natives had enjoyed local autonomy. They had had a separate parliament since 1911, and Strasbourg had been governed by its own municipal council. This situation was respected for a time by the French, but in 1925 the local parliament and the municipal council were deprived of their powers and the whole administration was centralized in Paris. The Alsatians and Lorrainers were unaccustomed to, and became much annoyed by, the centralized French system. Even more painful to the natives was the abolition of the designations Alsace and Lorraine and the redivision of the provinces into the three new departments of the Upper Rhine, the Lower Rhine, and the Moselle.

Finally, there were economic grievances. From the material standpoint many of the inhabitants of the area had been better off under German control than they were under the postwar regime. Although this situation gradually changed with the passing years, the natural trade outlets and business connections of the provinces still were with Germany.

Annoyed by such a combination of political, economic, and social grievances, the natives often found it difficult to be loyal to France. In 1926 a *Heimatbund* or Home League was formed which, particularly strong in Alsace, demanded local autonomy and priority for German in the schools. In 1927 the French suppressed three German newspapers in Alsace on the ground that they were advocating reunion with Germany. The year 1928 saw fifteen Alsatians tried for conspiracy. An Alsatian butcher tried to assassinate the French state's attorney who prosecuted the alleged conspirators.

The situation became so critical that Poincaré in 1929 delivered a ten-hour speech on Alsace-Lorraine. He reviewed the history of the conflict between France and the provinces and intimated that the autonomist movement was receiving moral and financial support from "east of the Rhine." He admitted that France had made errors but promised better conditions in future.Upon the conclusion of his speech, the Chamber of Deputies overwhelmingly voted its faith in the patriotic attachment of Alsace and Lorraine to France. Despite this official vote of confidence in their fidelity, many Alsace-Lorrainers continued to feel unhappy. Although they were at first glad to be reunited with France, they soon became as restive as they had been under the German regime.

LES AFFAIRES SONT LES AFFAIRES

France emerged from the First World War tired, but capable of a quick return to power. Enjoying a balance of industry and agriculture, and with half of her population engaged in farming, France was virtually self-sufficient in food supply. Moreover, French industry made great strides after the war. The French had learned much from United States experts and greatly improved their methods and machines.

The French Government was noted for its intelligent business regulation. The state exercised considerable supervision over big business, and the commercial code required corporations to divert specified portions of their earnings to reserves. The bankruptcy laws "were so severe that they made the bankrupt business man an actual outcast." At times of labor shortage foreign workers, usually from Poland, Italy, Spain, and Belgium, were invited—but nearly always under contracts that required them to return home when there was no more work for them. In this way unemployment was kept to a minimum. Because of official restrictions and the temperament of the people, there occurred no such overexpansion of industry as in postwar Germany. The French preferred, on the whole, to build their large industries "brick by brick out of earnings" rather than on credit.

The Great Depression affected France later than most other countries and found her in an enviable economic position. The unemployment figures, though large for France, were small when compared to those in other lands. The Bank of France had a gold reserve second only to that of the United States Federal Reserve System. A sizable proportion of the wealth was manipulated to serve political as well as economic ends—to bind to France certain needy allies and to force political concessions from impoverished enemies.

No discussion of France could be complete without a word on the character of its people. To generalize about the French is difficult. George Meredith once spoke of them as "the most mixed of any European nation." Nevertheless, a few remarks may be risked. The Frenchman, particularly the French peasant and the shopkeeper, was thrifty, prudent, realistic, and individualistic. Economic self-sufficiency was his fondest dream. His hope was to have a little property and a modest income from investments—not much, perhaps, but enough for comfort. To gain this end he would work unceasingly and deny himself pleasures and even necessities. He was suspicious, jealous, and "astonishingly void of sentiments when his interests were at stake." And "when at last he considered himself independent, with enough for his own wants, he ignored with beaming self-satisfaction everything that did not appertain to his own community, almost to his own person." The Frenchman's character was a fundamental reason for the power of his country—and for its weakness. It remained for the exigencies of the Second World War to lay bare this weakness.

Fascist Italy | 6

VICTORY—AND UNHAPPINESS

The Italians were reasonably united during the First World War and, in their opinion, made a notable contribution to the Allies in the conflict's final stages. But as the din of battle faded, traditional political squabbles reopened and new ones appeared. Consequently, Italy was the only major power among the victors to experience a complete change in system of government soon after the war. This change, hastened by Italian disappointments at the peace conference, had its inception in the war years. There was considerable disagreement among Italians in 1914 as to what course Italy should pursue in the struggle. The government promptly issued a declaration of neutrality. But there were many who, for material or emotional reasons, favored intervention. These groups eventually brought about Italy's entry into the war in return for the offer of certain territories.

The Italians found the costs of the war, in terms of casualties and money expended, more exacting than they had anticipated. Moreover, a disastrous rout at Caporetto in 1917 made the final victory of 1918 all the more emotionally exciting. In the circumstances, Victor Emmanuel's subjects were sorely disappointed not to achieve their desires in Dalmatia, Albania, the Near East, and Africa.

Reference has been made to the problems encountered by the peace conference in dealing with Fiume on the east coast of the Adriatic. But when it appeared, after the war, that one of the Slavic ambitions was the acquisition of Fiume, the Italians were enraged. Fiume came to have an emotional importance out of all proportion to its economic or strategic value. Histrionic effects were added when the poet, Gabriele d'Annunzio, led a band of black-shirted

86

veterans to Fiume in a chartered boat and took the city by force—over the objections of the peace conference and the inhabitants. Giovanni Giolitti, who had become Premier in 1920, deprecated such artificial nationalist stimulations and negotiated with Yugoslavia the Treaty of Rapallo (1920), whereby the independence of the Free State of Fiume was recognized "in perpetuity." Soon thereafter Italian troops drove d'Annunzio's legionaries from their stronghold.

During the war, Italians had fought on Albanian soil. Italian troops continued to occupy the land for several months after the armistice. During this occupation the Italian delegates to the peace conference attempted to acquire Albania as an Italian mandate. The Albanians, however, desired independence. They resorted to guerrilla warfare to drive out the foreigners. By the summer of 1920 Giolitti, preoccupied with domestic problems, withdrew the Italian troops from all Albania except the island of Saseno. Italian nationalists bewailed this additional "inglorious page" in their country's history.

In the Near East, much of the territorial bait that had been held out to Italy by the Allies to draw her into the war either went to Greece or was retained by Turkey. The Italians received only some minor commercial concessions. In Africa, where Great Britain, France, and Belgium acquired the former German colonies, Italy got only small extensions to Lybia and Somaliland. Therefore, despite the acquisition in Europe of 8900 square miles of land and 1,600,000 people, the Italians accused their allies of "faithlessness." They were angry that "Italian achievements were being discounted and Italian imperialism denounced."

The nationalists flung uncomplimentary epithets at most of the diplomats at Paris. Then they turned against their own ministries, accusing them of weakly consenting to the "mistreatment" of Italy. They blamed their older statesmen for the debacle whereby "the war had been won and the peace lost." Fiery young patriots referred to the "old men" as "parasites on the better blood of the nation" and vowed that they would recreate Italy in such fashion that the world would be "forced to sit up and take notice."

Meanwhile the government faced a disheartening domestic situation. Millions of men had to be demobilized. It was impossible to find employment for all the returned veterans. Even the "safety valve" of emigration was shut, owing to lack of funds at home and the restrictive legislation of foreign countries. The price of food rose quickly, and there was the usual popular hatred of the war profiteers.

In the elections of 1919 the Socialists captured 156 parliamentary seats. These deputies consistently voted against government measures, thereby creating a parliamentary stalemate. Popular discontent soon took the form of strikes and riots. These were idly watched by the impotent authorities who feared to call upon an army that could not be trusted to restrain the people when they became restive. Socialism spread rapidly, owing in part to fantastic rumors regarding the marvelous changes wrought by proletarian rule in Russia and in part to the government's inaction. Shouts of "Down with the King!" and "Long live Lenin!" frequently were heard.

"Direct-action" schemes won increasing favor, and many communes were seized by Socialists. Peasant tenants refused to pay rent, large estates were broken up, former service men appropriated plots of ground, and numerous outrages, often economically unwise, were perpetrated. In some cities, when the employers announced their inability to continue in business, the workmen themselves took over the factories. In 1919 and 1920 there was talk of establishing a dictatorship of the proletariat. Even the formation in 1919 of a moderate Catholic People's Party failed to stem the "Red tide."

But the period of factory and land "occupation" did not last. The workers found it difficult to carry on without raw materials, without sufficient food, and without managerial experience. The peasants were illiterate and fundamentally conservative. The Socialists split into factions. The novelty of doing things as the Russians were supposed to be doing them wore off. A feeling arose that a proletarian state might be no more able to cope with Italy's problems than was the existing weak regime. If neither the parliamentary system nor a possible proletarian state could help Italy, then, wondered many, who should be entrusted with the government?

The strife of the war and postwar years had created bonds of sympathy among several important groups. Many landlords and property holders were much affected by the incidents of the reign of radicalism. They were determined that Italy should have a government strong enough to protect private property. Many university people and professionals were disgusted with the whole trend of events since 1914. They wanted to see a general governmental house-cleaning and the emergence of a strong and patriotic administration. The nationalists and ex-soldiers were angered by the thought that the net result of their participation in the war might be an anarchic Italy. They, too, wanted to see new men at the helm. At this critical moment Benito Mussolini came forward to seize control.

MUSSOLINI: FROM PRIVATE TO PREMIER

Benito Mussolini was born in Romagna in 1883. His father was a blacksmith, with socialistic leanings. His mother was a schoolteacher. Upon his mother's advice, Mussolini eventually became a teacher. Dissatisfied with his lot and by nature rebellious, he soon quit his position and went to Switzerland. There he eventually obtained work on a Socialist newspaper, but his activities in organizing labor and fomenting strikes led the Swiss Government to demand his departure. Returning to Italy for a time, Mussolini took up journalism, and then went to Austria. Once more his radical activities made it necessary for him to leave.

He came back to Italy, where he was kept under surveillance as a revolutionary. In 1912, after some able speechmaking at a Socialist congress, he became editor of *Avanti*, the official paper of the Italian Socialist Party. When the war broke out he favored Italian neutrality; but nationalism, and perhaps bribery, soon triumphed over socialism and he began to urge intervention. For this he was made to resign from *Avanti* and was expelled from the party. He then founded an interventionist paper in Milan, *Il Popolo d'Italia.*

When his class was called to the colors in 1915, Mussolini entered the army as a private, served on the Isonzo front, and rose to be a corporal. In 1917 he was wounded by the explosion of a trench mortar. Upon his recovery he was exempted from further military service so that he might return to the editorship of *Il Popolo d'Italia* and use its columns to combat the growing spirit of defeatism. Mussolini now displayed a dominating, magnetic personality. He was an effective orator, adept in the use of short, crisp sentences. Combined with his flashing black eyes, his determination, and his imagination, these characteristics enabled him readily to sway masses.

In 1919 Mussolini called a meeting of ex-servicemen and others who were interested in solving Italy's problems and defending her war record. The meeting was attended by many who earlier had been affiliated with societies known as *fasci d'azione*. These fasci had been organized as early as October 1914 by young "men of action," eager to have Italy join the Allies in the war. Within a few months more than 100 fasci had been founded, and vigorous methods of propaganda had been employed to win the country to the interventionist viewpoint. Mussolini had led the Milan fascio and his *Il Popolo d'Italia* had become the Fascist literary organ. Now, under Mussolini's guidance, these former interventionists reorganized themselves into *fasci di combattimento*.

The gathering adopted a program calculated to appeal especially to the returned soldiers, the "proletariat of the trenches." Said Mussolini: "It is we who have the right to succeed this government, for it was we who pushed the country into the war and led it to victory." Fascism was not a party but an antiparty, he claimed, an organ not of propaganda but of combat.

Despite the confidence of its leader, the cause of fascism progressed slowly. In the elections of 1919 the two Fascist candidates for office in Milan, one of them Mussolini himself, polled fewer than 5000 votes. During the period of the Communist factory occupation, the Fascist movement was dormant. With the end of the occupation, however, it took on a new life. Recruits came from property holders, sons of businessmen, unemployed ex-soldiers, and discontented students. The wealthier sympathizers made monetary contributions.

Filled with a hatred for Socialists and Communists, the Fascists embarked upon a campaign of terrorization known as "squadrism." Castor oil, clubs, and guns were used to convert or dispatch the radicals. Scores of "battles" were fought between the rivals from the summer of 1920 to that of 1921. The government watched the civil war with resignation, because it was too weak to intervene or because it hoped to see communism destroyed.

Eventually the Fascists emerged triumphant. The Left in Italian political life was divided and Leftists were at odds among themselves. At the same time, the Fascists had come under the domination of Mussolini's Milan group. Another factor in the Fascist victory was a vigorous propaganda campaign, involving the use of posters, books, and speeches in an attempt to convince patriots that they alone had saved the country from the horrors of Russian Bolshevism and that they alone could restore to Italy security, prosperity, and international respect. In 1921 the Fascists, now with thirty-five deputies in parliament, constituted themselves the National Fascist Party. By this time their program was much less radical than in 1919. During the fight against socialism the Fascists had given up their faith in the proletariat.

Following the lead of other patriotic organizations, the Fascists donned distinctive uniforms and adopted a ritual. Apparently because many of d'Annunzio's black-shirted followers had joined the Fascists, the latter adopted the black shirt. They patterned their ceremonial after old Roman customs and chose the Roman salute. The *fasces* or bundles of rods enclosing a battle-ax, symbolizing strength and power in ancient Rome, became the emblem of fascism.

Meanwhile the government was so unstable that there was talk of forming a coalition ministry and of inviting Mussolini to accept a post in it. But Mussolini refused, saying: "Fascism will not come into the government by the service entrance." Then, during the spring and summer of 1922, he hinted several times that the Fascists might overthrow parliament and substitute a strong nationalistic regime. In September 1922 he first raised the cry: "On to Rome!"; but he hastened to reaffirm his faith in the monarchical form of government, professing merely a desire to see the monarchy strengthened.

Then Mussolini presented the Chamber of Deputies with a set of demands. He warned parliament that failure to comply might lead to the use of force. The demands included a call for a strong Italian foreign policy and cabinet posts for Fascists. Although the recently organized Fascist Militia was gradually taking over control of the larger cities in the north, the deputies seemingly regarded the ultimatum as a joke. At a National Fascist Congress held at Naples in October 1922, Mussolini invoked force. Following a threatening speech he entrained for Milan, while thousands of armed Fascists began to concentrate on Rome.

Although it appears that the army could have been counted upon to meet this danger, King Victor Emmanuel III refused to sanction martial law. Instead, when the weak Premier Luigi Facta resigned, the king telephoned Mussolini, asking him to form a cabinet. Mussolini at once left Milan for Rome, and on October 30 a new and astonishingly moderate cabinet took office. The moderate composition of the government was attributed to Mussolini's desire to follow a policy of compromise, until he could be certain that popular opinion would support him in more venturesome measures.

MAKING ITALY FASCIST

The parliamentary opponents of fascism hesitated to express an immediate lack of confidence in Mussolini. They hoped that his inexperience would lead him into some tactical blunder that might serve as an excuse for his ousting. But Mussolini was wary. He secured a grant of virtually dictatorial powers until the end of 1923. Then he assured himself of the loyalty of the administrative branch of government by the appointment of Fascist prefects to govern the provinces. Control of the legislature was next assured by the Acerbo Election Law in 1923. In order to get parliament's consent to this law, Mussolini indicated to the legislators that he was ready to use force.

The law stipulated that the party polling a plurality was to have two-thirds of the seats in the Chamber of Deputies, and there could be no single opposition group. In the first elections held under the new system (April 1924), the Fascists gained a majority of the votes. They therefore had easy control of the new Chamber.

The chief opposition group was the Socialist Party, led by a young deputy named Giacomo Matteotti. In an anonymously published book and in speeches he enumerated Fascist outrages and threatened to expose as bribetakers certain members of Mussolini's new Cabinet. Before he had a chance to present his evidence, Matteotti disappeared. His body was found in a wood some weeks later. This murder (June 1924) aroused a storm of indignation, especially since it was only the most notorious of a number of excesses.

Since it appeared that Matteotti's charges had been well founded, Mussolini decided to bluff his way through the crisis and assumed full responsibility for the actions of his followers. As a sign of protest, most of the non-Fascist deputies withdrew from parliament, vowing not to return to their seats as long as fascism remained in power. This actually made it easy for Mussolini, for it left him in absolute control of parliament. In 1926 he deprived the secessionists of their seats. Meanwhile Mussolini, pledging law and order, dismissed from office nearly every one who had been connected with the Matteotti incident. But not until almost two years later were the murder suspects brought to trial; some were acquitted and the others given short jail terms.[1]

Having weathered the crisis of 1924, Mussolini proceeded to make himself supreme in Italy. In 1925 and 1926 municipalities, towns, and cities were deprived of their local political rights and placed under the control of appointed government officials. Parliament was deprived of the right to initiate legislation. Mussolini became solely responsible to the king, and was empowered to issue decrees with the force of law. The press was censored, and opposition papers were bought up or suppressed. Mussolini became commander of all armed forces, and new members of the Fascist Party had to swear "to follow without question the orders of Il Duce." Membership in the Socialist Party at first was made punishable with deportation, and then, in 1926, all opposition parties were abolished.

At the apex of the hierarchical party organization was the Fascist Grand Council, headed by Mussolini as *Il Duce*, "the Leader." The council included most of the high party and government officials. By virtue of his power to add to its membership at any time, Mussolini dominated the council. By law, the Grand Council of the Fascist Party was recognized as the "supreme organ, coordinating all the activities of the regime." The Fascist Grand Council, for all practical purposes, became the government of Italy.

The party base consisted of about 10,000 local fasci, which in each province were federated and controlled by provincial councils. The provincial secretaries appointed the secretaries of the local fasci. The organization exemplified well the theory of government stated in the constitution of the party: "The ordinances and hierarchies without which there can be no discipline of energies nor education of the people must be illuminated and guided from on top where there is a comprehensive view of powers, duties, functions, and merits."

Italy now was "purified." Anti-Fascist lawyers were disbarred, prominent opponents of the regime were imprisoned or exiled, the property of Italian emigrants who said anything adverse to fascism in foreign countries was confiscated, and the universities were staffed with Fascist professors.

A new penal code was completed in 1931. The death penalty, which had been abolished in 1888, was restored for those who attacked "the life or liberty" of the leaders of the government. Parents were forbidden to name their children after "Socialists or other rebellious people." The puritanical side of Fascism was shown by making swearing punishable by arrest and forcing cabarets to close at midnight. To help enforce such restrictions, a secret police force was organized and made directly responsible to Mussolini.

Mussolini attempted to secure a Fascist future for Italy by train-

---

[1] In 1947 three surviving murderers of Matteotti were retried and sentenced to thirty years' imprisonment.

ing and disciplining the youth of the nation. Several uniformed societies were organized to give their members military training and a thorough grounding in Fascist aims and achievements. A decree of 1934 subjected all males between the ages of eight and thirty-three to a definite schedule of military training, which thus became "an integral part of the national education."

A strong foothold had been gained among Italian workers before 1914 by a doctrine known as "syndicalism," which advocated government by economic groups. During the war many of the syndicalists became imbued with nationalism and fought loyally to defeat the enemy. In 1919 these nationalistic syndicalists united with the nationalistic Fascists in the struggle against communism. After the victorious outcome of this conflict, Fascist syndicates were organized as a counterbalance to the socialist trade-union movement. The Fascist syndicalists accepted "the capitalist class as socially productive" and preferred "class collaboration" to class warfare. In 1926 the federated Fascist syndicates had a membership of 2,400,000. Mussolini therefore determined to control them.

By a law of 1926, thirteen confederated Fascist syndicates were given legal status. The syndicates acquired the sole right to formulate collective contracts and were empowered to tax all persons engaged in their industry, regardless of whether or not the taxpayer was a member of the association. The syndicates became subject to the direct control of a Ministry of Corporations. (Mussolini was the first Minister of Corporations.) The same law prohibited strikes and lockouts, and established sixteen labor courts from which there could be no appeal. Only persons politically acceptable to the Fascist authorities might become members of the syndicates, but their decisions were binding upon all workmen and employers in the industry. Members were entitled to preference in employment over nonmembers.

In 1930, Mussolini inaugurated a National Council of Corporations composed of representatives of the syndicates and of government. The council was ordered to supervise the official employment bureaus, promote production, and settle intersyndical disputes. Thus the employers and employees were brought together into an organization which was at the same time an administrative agency of the state, controlled by the Minister of Corporations.

It had been hoped that the establishment of national syndicates under governmental supervision would lead to an improvement in conditions of labor. Progress, however, was slow. Hence, Mussolini in 1927 promulgated a "Charter of Labor." "The Italian nation," declared the document, "is an organism having aims, life, and means of action superior to those of the single or grouped individuals who compose it." Beyond its ideological lessons, the charter dealt mainly with guarantees to the workers, granting overtime pay and unemployment compensation. In addition, the state promised, and later enacted, a broad social-insurance program.

In 1928 a law was passed which made Italy the first Western state to have a national legislature representing economic divisions. The membership of the Chamber of Deputies was set at 400. These deputies were to be elected by the entire kingdom, acting as a single electoral constituency. In effect, the Fascist Grand Council would decide upon a satisfactory 400 candidates and then the approved list would be made public. On election day the voters would receive a ballot containing a single question: "Do you approve of the list of deputies designated by the Fascist Grand Council?" The answer had to be either "yes" or "no" for the entire list. No individual names might be rejected. If the majority of votes cast were "yes," the 400 were to take their seats. If the majority were ever "no," new elections under a complicated system were ordained.

Universal suffrage was abolished by this electoral law. The franchise was limited to those who paid a syndicate rate or met other restrictive qualifications. Women were excluded from the national franchise, while men, to vote, had to be twenty one, or eighteen if they were married and had children. The male electorate thus was reduced by approximately 3,000,000. The procedure was undemocratic, but the Fascists were proud of this very fact. They considered democracy to have been "a good method of government for the nineteenth century" but inadequate for the twentieth.

Early in 1929, the executive councils of the syndicates and some other institutions met to nominate 1000 candidates for the first elections under the new law. Mussolini's name came first on nearly every list. The Fascist Grand Council then selected 400 men of "reliable Fascist faith." The list was published, and the voters were permitted to accept or reject the entire list. Approximately 90 per cent of the qualified voters went to the polls, and the official list was endorsed by a proportion of 62 to 1. The second election under the law was held in 1934. This time the government's list of "deputies-designate" was accepted by an even greater majority.

In 1934 the Italian Government created twenty-two new corporations, each of which represented the state, capital, and labor. Three functions were assigned to the corporations, which covered agriculture, industry, and services: to advise the government, to settle labor disputes, and to regulate production, distribution, and prices. Under this system, said Mussolini, private initiative was transferred from the individual to the corporate sphere.

After several years of study, the Fascist Grand Council in 1938 decreed the organization of a new legislative body to take the place of the Chamber of Deputies. Called "the Chamber of Fasces and Corporations," this house was to be composed of about 700 "national councillors"—all to be appointed by Mussolini. This arrangement was promptly accepted by the "Suicide Chamber," elected in 1934; it dutifully voted itself out of existence. The first meeting of the Chamber of Fasces and Corporations was opened by the King in March 1939. Thus national elections were abolished in Italy.

FASCIST DOMESTIC POLICIES

Financial conditions improved during the first eight years (1922–1930) of the Fascist regime's dictatorial efficiency. The budget was balanced by 1926, after which the treasury generally held a surplus until the Great Depression. Many international debts were paid. After 1930, however, the government found it necessary to decrease the number of official positions and float large loans. The number of unemployed fluctuated between 400,000 and 1,300,000, and every available method was mobilized to combat the crisis.

Beginning in 1932 the outlines of a planned economy became evident. A board was established, without whose consent no new factories could be opened and no old ones expanded. New public works were launched, wages and prices were fixed, and overtime work was abolished. Efforts were made to reduce the country's dependence upon foreign imports and develop Italy's economic self-sufficiency.

Despite various material advances in the development of indigenous industries and agriculture, Italy remained dependent upon foreign capital and foreign coal, iron, oil, and phosphates. These deficiencies became especially apparent during Italy's venture in Ethiopia in 1935–1936. Although the limited League sanctions against Italy (see this Chapter, section entitled "Italian Foreign and African Relations") failed to prevent her successful completion of the war, they did place a severe strain upon her economic structure. The League's "siege," as Mussolini called it, marked "the beginning of a new phase in Italian history," one during which the government tried to secure "in the shortest possible time, the maximum degree of economic independence." Mussolini had decided that to carry out aggressive foreign policies his state must become self-sufficient.

Renewed energy therefore was put into the development of substitute products and the fullest exploitation of the resources that Italy did possess in some quantity. Restrictions were placed on the amount of money that Italian tourists might spend abroad. Patriotic citizens gave up wedding rings for iron bands to relieve Italy's shortage in foreign exchange, but the gold coverage for bank notes continued to fall and financial deficits were hidden in "extraordinary" budgets. In 1935 all foreign trade became "a function of the state," and steps were taken to deprive industries of their "private character." A law of 1936 converted private banks into state institutions. In 1937 shipbuilding became a government enterprise.

Among the leading obstacles facing the Fascists was the illiteracy of the people. In 1911 almost 40 per cent of the Italians were illiterate. The Fascists attacked the problem by voting increasingly large education budgets and by enforcing more strictly the laws for compulsory school attendance up to the age of fourteen. In order that the children might be reared "in a healthful spirit of Fascism," all textbooks were reexamined and those not meeting Fascist standards were dropped. Since the schools provided one of the best fields for propaganda, every teacher had to swear to uphold the existing government and refrain from anti-Fascist activity.

Two new cultural factors in Italian life under fascism were national discipline and anti-Semitism. Mussolini provided the theme for the first with his slogan: "Believe! Obey! Fight!" The Fascist ideologist Giovanni Gentile wrote: "Fascism means to take life seriously. Life is toil, effort, sacrifice, hard work; a life in which we know very well that there is neither matter nor time for amusement . . . . Even in our sleep we must give account of the talents entrusted to us." Then, in 1938, a group of Italian university professors published a report, apparently phrased largely by Mussolini, that outlined the "scientific bases" for an "Aryan" racial policy. The report contained ten propositions which became the platform for an Italian anti-Semitic campaign, although Italy had only 70,000 Jews.

The propositions held that a "pure Italian race now exists" whose racial conception must be "essentially Italian and Aryan Nordic in trend." Jews, it was declared, do not belong to the Italian race; henceforth, the "physical and psychological characteristics of Italians must not be altered in any way." Decrees followed in rapid order, barring Jews from Italian schools, ordering Jews who had entered Italy since the First World War to leave within six months, prohibiting new trade licenses to Jewish businessmen, and forbidding marriages between Italian "Aryans" and Jews. Thus Mussolini officially brought Italy into ideological harmony with Nazi Germany and launched a campaign of virulent anti-Semitism.

ALTO-ADIGE, THE FORMER SOUTH TIROL

For strategic reasons the Paris Peace Conference assigned to Italy not only that part (Trentino) of the South Tirol which was inhabited by Italians, but the portion that was inhabited by a quarter-million German-speaking Austrians. At the time of transfer, one of Italy's delegates to the conference made a parliamentary speech in which he assured the new subjects that "their language and cultural institutions would be respected." When the Fascists came into power, this promise was disregarded. Said Mussolini: "We shall make them Italians."

The process of Italianization was vigorous. The area was placed under a prefect appointed from Rome. Italian was made the official language of the courts and of all public services. Only Italian-speaking citizens could serve on juries, and decrees were published in Italian exclusively, even at a time when there still were many natives who neither read nor understood Italian. Most of the former officials were replaced by non-German-speaking Italians. Public inscriptions and signs had to be in Italian. Wherever towns, rivers, or mountains had German names, these were Italianized.

The name "Tirol" was abolished, and the area was renamed Alto-Adige. The use of the words "Tirol" or "Tirolese" was made subject to severe penalties. All German newspapers were suppressed, except for one that was edited as a Fascist propaganda sheet. The statues of such Tirolese idols as Walter von der Vogelweide and Andreas Hofer were torn down. German schools were closed. The teaching of German was forbidden—in Alto-Adige, but not in the remainder of Italy!

Most objectionable to the Tirolese was a decree of 1926 which ordered the "re-Italianization" of all family names that, in the opinion of the authorities, "had been translated into other languages." All citizens were ordered to watch the *Official Gazette* to see what their names henceforth were to be. Adherence to German forms of officially Italianized names was made punishable by heavy fines.

Such measures led to repeated protests from Austria and Germany. Mussolini eventually became "aroused" over these "interferences" and in 1928 declared: "The next time I shall make acts do the speaking . . . . A self respecting state does not tolerate such interference." He scoffed at the suggestion that the matter be referred to the League of Nations for settlement. Austria was worried by the tenor of Mussolini's speech and in 1930 signed a treaty of conciliation and arbitration. Thereafter, Austria refrained from officially championing the cause of the Tirolese. Germany, moreover, even after Hitler came to power, offered little in the way of concrete help to the "racial comrades" under Italian control. Instead, Hitler and Mussolini reached an agreement in 1939, whereby the Tirolese were given the choice of migrating to the Reich or remaining and becoming loyal Italians. Thousands thereupon left the land of their ancestors and settled in one or another of the regions that the Nazis rapidly were depopulating in pursuit of their wartime economic and social policies.

RELATIONS WITH THE PAPACY

In 1870 Napoleon III of France ordered the withdrawal from Rome, the pope's sole remaining temporal domain, of the French troops that had been stationed there to protect the Holy See against Italian territorial encroachments. When the French were gone, an Italian army marched on the Eternal City. Thus Rome became the capital of Italy, and thus was created the "Roman Question" which for fifty-nine years disturbed Italian national life.

Pope Pius IX considered himself a victim of unjust force and denounced the government. In order to appease His Holiness, the Italian Parliament passed the Law of Papal Guarantees (1871). This act guaranteed to the papacy perpetual possession of St. Peter's, the Vatican and Lateran palaces, and the Villa Castel Gandolfo. The Pope was granted sovereign rights within these possessions.

Pius IX ignored this statute. He would not recognize any unilateral arrangement devised by the Italian Government, for he believed it might at any time be abrogated by a succeeding parliament.
Moreover, if the status of the pope could be fixed by Italian law,
he would become an Italian subject and would be deprived of the
prestige inherent in his traditional position as the nonnational head
of an international religion. The Pope therefore retired to the
Vatican, called himself "the prisoner of a usurping power," and
directed Italian Catholics to abstain from participation in the political life of the kingdom. The successors of Pius IX continued his
policy, with the result that Italians who aspired to be both loyal
Catholics and patriotic citizens were confronted with a serious "conflict of conscience."

As time went on, the crisis became somewhat less acute. Intelligent Italians "did their duty by the state, and still called themselves
Catholics." The state tried in a number of ways to show that it
regarded the popes not as Italian subjects, but as foreign sovereigns.
Yet the Roman Question remained, in the words of Mussolini, 'a
thorn in the flesh of the nation."

When the Fascists came into control, they realized that so serious
a conflict between church and state materially weakened the power
of the nation. Religion, they felt, must be made to serve fascism, not
to combat it. Catholicism, because of its personal disciplining aspects, had special appeal for the Fascists. The government therefore
made some conciliatory moves. The crucifix was restored to class-
rooms. Religious instruction was made compulsory in the elementary
schools. At the same time Pope Pius XI, realizing that no help could
be expected from other countries, was equally prepared to end the
quarrel. Negotiations came to a successful conclusion on February
11, 1929. Three documents in all, collectively known as the Lateran
Accord, were signed.

The international status of the papacy was agreed upon in the
political agreement. The Pope regarded the Roman Question as defi-
nitively settled and recognized the kingdom of Italy under the house
of Savoy. Italy, in turn, through the establishment of Vatican City
under the "complete ownership" and "sovereign jurisdiction" of the
Holy See, assured to the latter "absolute" independence in international relations. The papacy declared its purpose to remain above
all "temporal disputes among nations" unless the contending parties
appealed to it as peacemaker.

A concordat established Roman Catholicism as "the sole religion
of the state." The selection of archbishops and bishops was to rest
with the Holy See, but before a candidate could be nominated his
name must be communicated to the Italian Government so that his
political views could be examined. Bishops, before taking office,
were required to swear loyalty to the state. The state agreed to pay
clerical salaries. The Catholic Church might freely exercise spiritual
power and jurisdiction in ecclesiastical matters and was promised

the state's assistance in the enforcing of the canon law among Catholics.

Religious instruction, formerly required only in elementary schools, was made compulsory in secondary schools as well. It was to be taught by state-paid instructors who were priests or other clerics "approved by ecclesiastical authority." The Catholic Action and other religious societies were recognized by the state on condition that they refrained from political activity and confined their efforts to the "teaching and practice of Catholic principles." The Holy See prohibited all ecclesiastics from taking part in any political party. A third agreement settled all outstanding monetary claims of the papacy against Italy.

Thus was terminated a conflict that had lasted for two generations. Henceforth, according to Mussolini, "the citizen is a Catholic and the Catholic is a citizen." Or, as the Pope remarked, "God has been restored to Italy and Italy has been restored to God."

Some differences of opinion regarding the respective spheres of influence of church and state caused renewed difficulty in 1931. In May of that year, Pius XI issued an encyclical on labor. The document deplored the circumstance that "the whole economic life has become hard, cruel, and relentless in a ghastly measure." The Pope urged a "just" wage and recommended that wage earners be made "sharers" in the profits of capitalistic enterprise. Pius lamented the "dreadful scourge" of unemployment and blamed it, in part, on the world's "extreme freedom of competition."

The Pope was careful, however, to make it clear that he was not endorsing the Fascist economic system. He added: "It is to be feared that the new syndical and corporative institution possesses excessive bureaucratic and political character, and that, notwithstanding [certain general advantages], it risks serving particular political aims rather than contributing to the initiation of a better social order." The Fascists quickly responded that the Pope had no right to pass judgment on economic and social matters. Pius, on the other hand, held that the church could not surrender its right to exert influence over the economic and social welfare of the family. An open break between church and state threatened. Before long, Fascist students started destroying church property, trampling the pope's portrait, and attacking priests. On the ground that they were engaging in political activity, Mussolini dissolved all Catholic societies not directly connected with the Fascist Party.

Pius denied that the Catholic Action was dabbling in politics and accused the government of violating the Lateran Accord. He called "illicit" the Fascist oath which "even little boys and girls are obliged to take, about executing orders without discussion," and deplored the setting up of a "true and real pagan worship of the state." He also complained that Italian children were being diverted from attendance at church service in favor of participation in military and athletic events. The Fascists replied by reminding the Pope that as sovereign of a foreign state he had no right to interfere in a purely domestic situation. Mussolini announced that "the child as soon as he is old enough to learn belongs to the state alone. No sharing is possible."

For a time it appeared as though the agreement of 1929 would be torn up, but eventually a compromise was effected. The Pope placed control of the reopened Catholic Action clubs in the hands of the bishop of each diocese rather than in those of laymen, as formerly had been the case. The Fascists agreed that in future their military and athletic programs would be so arranged as not to interfere with Sunday church services for the children. Differences, however, continued to flare up from time to time. The government was firm in its contention that, though Italy was Catholic, she was, above all, Fascist.

NATIONALISM, POPULATION, IMPERIALISM

The Fascists sounded warlike as well as nationalistic. They strove to revive the prestige of ancient Rome and glorified war as a symbol of national virility. One of their leading publicists, Mario Carli, wrote: "The warlike spirit is the fundamental character of Italians; it is not a Fascist invention or a post-bellum attitude. Find me a single moment of history in which we have not fought—for whom or what little matters." Mussolini himself, in an article on Fascism in the *Enciclopedia Italiana,* declared: "Only war carries human energies to the highest level and puts the seal of nobility upon peoples who have the courage to undertake it." A nation which thus glorified combat, and that was desirous of expanding territorially as the old Roman Empire had expanded, required a large population.

Because of Mussolini's belief that the population of Italy was not sufficient to carry out grand designs, the government began acting on the theory that "without quantity there can be no quality." Thus, the Fascist Government prohibited the giving of contraceptive information, restricted emigration, and placed a tax on bachelors. On the other side, encouragement was given to early marriage and large families. The legal age for marriage was fixed at sixteen for boys and fourteen for girls, and newlyweds were offered trips to Rome on the state railways at a fare reduction of 80 per cent. Such policies, however, did not achieve the "population explosion" for which Mussolini hoped.

The combination of extreme nationalism and an increasing population pressure in a country with limited resources became a disturbing factor in international politics. With an area of only 120,000 square miles and a population density of 375 to the square mile, every addition to Italy's population increased the margin of insufficiency. The kingdom's African colonies offered few attractions to immigrants, and even so large a reclaimed area as the Pontine

Marshes between Rome and Naples accommodated only 60,000 persons. Despite the variety of methods employed by the government to increase the country's food-supplying potentialities, the problem of feeding Italy became intensified. The only solution, in Fascist opinion, lay in territorial expansion. Fascism, according to Mussolini, regarded expansionism "as a manifestation of vitality."

ITALIAN FOREIGN AND AFRICAN RELATIONS

Expansionist in tendency, the Fascist Government in external relations strove to make amends for the "weaknesses" displayed by the pre-Fascist ministries. Mussolini adopted a bellicose front and inspired Italy with confidence in her position as a world power. Simultaneously, emphasis was placed upon the need for ever greater armaments. To explain to the people the necessity for further military preparedness and to exercise stricter control over the newspapers, a press and propaganda bureau was created in 1934.

The most threatening of Italy's foreign relations in the early postwar years were with France. Mussolini did not like to see thousands of Italians flocking to France in search of employment. He was the more vexed that France encouraged the immigrants to become naturalized. France also was hospitable to *émigrés* who had left Italy through dislike for, or fear of, fascism. Some Italians, moreover, maintained that Tunisia, Corsica, Savoy, and Nice, all in the possession of France, belonged rightfully to Italy. The Fascists placed chief blame on the French for the disregard of Italy's "legitimate" claims at the peace conference and her failure to acquire any mandated territory. The two countries competed for control of the western Mediterranean and for superiority in naval armament. On occasion, Franco-Italian relations became impaired because of quarrels between Italy and France's allies, especially Yugoslavia. Extensive military preparations thus were made on both sides of the Franco-Italian border but no incident occurred to precipitate armed strife.[2]

Meanwhile, soon after his rise to power, Mussolini attempted to consolidate Italian power in Eastern Europe. In 1923, Rome was confirmed in the possession of the Dodecanese Islands. Fiume was acquired by treaty in 1924. Treaties of friendship, neutrality, and commerce were signed with a number of the Central and Eastern European states.

In the 1920's there also developed a confrontation between Italy and Yugoslavia. The agitation was accompanied by violence, and relations between the two powers continued under high tension.

[2] France was not the only country with territory coveted by Italy. Mussolini once referred to British Malta as part of "Unredeemed Italy," and some Fascists urged the "restoration" of the Italian-speaking Swiss canton of Ticino.

The Italo-Yugoslav quarrel, which in essence was a struggle for control of the Adriatic, was further intensified by the establishment of an Italian protectorate over Albania (see this Chapter, section entitled "Italy and Albania"). After 1928, Italy attempted to consolidate her postwar orientation of friendships. While drawing away from France, Poland, and the Little Entente, she became increasingly friendly towards Germany, Austria, Hungary, Bulgaria, and Turkey.

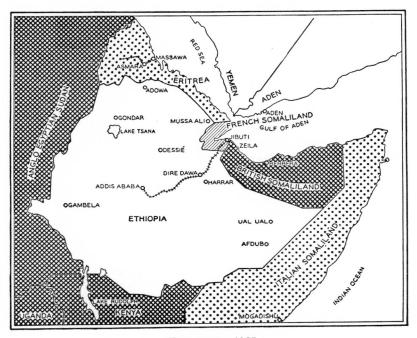

ETHIOPIA 1935

From Townsend, M. *European Colonial Expansion since 1871*, 1941.
Courtesy, J. B. Lippincott Co.

Italy also pursued African interests in the postwar period. Beginning in the summer of 1934, rumors were current that Rome was displeased with the efforts of the emperor of Ethiopia to modernize and enlarge his army. Emperor Haile Selassie was equally worried over the strengthening of the defenses of Italian Somaliland and Eritrea, both of which bordered on Ethiopia. Late in 1934 several incidents occurred, involving clashes of armed patrols at Ualual and other points along the incompletely demarcated boundary. Ethiopia appealed to the League for arbitration, whereupon Italy dispatched troops to Africa.

Before the League had time to study the Italo-Ethiopian dispute,

France and Italy signed a pact at Rome in January 1935. Because of the recent political changes in Germany and the rising danger to Austrian independence, Mussolini, for a brief period, sought a *rapprochement* with Paris. France, afraid of Nazi Germany, welcomed the opportunity to improve relations with her neighbor on the southeast. The result of these changed outlooks was the Laval-Mussolini Pact, wherein the countries settled some outstanding colonial differences and agreed to consult if Austrian independence were threatened. France ceded to Italy almost 45,000 square miles of territory adjoining Libya and a small piece of French Somaliland touching Eritrea. The Italians thus acquired an extra portion of the Sahara and an outlet on the Gulf of Aden. In addition, Italy was allotted a share in the French railway connecting Addis Ababa, the capital of Ethiopia, with French Somaliland. According to Mussolini, moreover, Laval secretly gave him a free hand to proceed as he wished in Ethiopia.

The Rome Government advanced many reasons to explain this particular colonial interest. The charge of unfair treatment in the matter of African colonies at the peace conference of 1919 was once more repeated. Italy's need for more room and more food for her growing population again was proclaimed. The constantly recurring incidents along the edge of their own and Ethiopia's possessions had at last "exhausted the patience" of the Fascists. A humiliating Ethiopian victory over Italian troops in 1896 had to be avenged. The Italian nation's "civilizing mission" in the world was reiterated and the "backwardness" of Ethiopia was graphically depicted. Furthermore, Italy expected to find in Ethiopia the natural resources which she so urgently needed.[3] Because of her newly cemented friendship with France and the weakened condition of the League caused by the recent withdrawals of Japan and Germany, the time appeared opportune to Italy for an imperialistic venture.

Early in 1935, Ethiopia pleaded for arbitration of the Ualual incident that was being used by Mussolini as justification for projected military measures in Ethiopia. Haile Selassie promised to abide by the award of an arbitration commission. Italy, after several months, agreed to this, but then further time was consumed in wrangling over the makeup and power of the proposed commission. Eventually the League Council ruled that the commission must fix responsibility for the clash of patrols without regard to the question of whether Ualual was in Ethiopian or Italian territory. The arbiters announced their unanimous decision in September that neither side was to blame since each believed itself to be fighting on its own soil.

In the meantime, at the Council's suggestion, representatives of Great Britain, France, and Italy met (August) to seek a settlement

[3] Ethiopia in 1934 had an area of 350,000 square miles, a population of 7,000,000, and a negligible foreign trade. There was reason to believe that the mineral and agricultural potentialities of the country were substantial, but reliable estimates did not exist.

of the whole Ethiopian problem. Now Great Britain and France agreed, subject to the consent of Haile Selassie, to give Italy extensive economic rights in Ethiopia. Mussolini, however, rejected this overture and announced his intention to annex the lowlands in eastern Ethiopia. The Rome Government had made such extensive war preparations and had so stirred up sentiment at home that it probably dared not forego the opportunity to create a "Fascist empire" through the "glory of Italian arms." The League therefore took up the matter once more. Italy refused to curtail her mobilization activities while a League committee deliberated.

The strongest anti-Italian stand by a great power now was taken by Great Britain. The British feared that the successful conclusion of Italy's Ethiopian venture would endanger British predominance along the Red Sea and in northeastern Africa and encourage the Fascists to contemplate further territorial expansion. France, on the other hand, was only mildly interested in the immediate Ethiopian controversy.

When the League's conciliation committee reported a plan for the international development of Ethiopia with a recognition of Italy's "special interests," Haile Selassie accepted the scheme in principle but Mussolini rejected it. Then, while the Council was at work preparing a report of the dispute, Italian troops advanced into Ethiopia from the north, east, and south (October 3, 1935). The pretext for beginning the invasion at this time was the Ethiopian *withdrawal* of its soldiers from the border. This "strategic move," according to Italy, "necessitated" an immediate advance in order to protect Eritrea and Italian Somaliland against further aggression. On October 7, the Council, except for Italy who was a party to the dispute, adopted a report which declared that "the Italian Government has resorted to war in disregard of its obligations under . . . the Covenant." Thus, for the first time since its establishment, the League designated the aggressor in an armed conflict. The Council's verdict was referred to the Assembly, where the representatives of fifty-one nations voted to invoke sanctions against Italy.

It was decided to make the sanctions effective on November 18.[4] The first "great experiment of the coercive powers" of the League was launched. But the experiment was not complete. Sanctions were not imposed on oil—Italy's greatest foreign need. When Secretary Anthony Eden proposed oil sanctions in 1936, French Foreign Minister Flandin insisted that there first be another attempt at ap-

---

[4] Acting under the terms of a recent neutrality resolution, President Franklin D. Roosevelt issued two proclamations announcing that Italy and Ethiopia were in a state of war, placing an embargo on arms shipments to both belligerents, and warning United States citizens against traveling on the ships of either warring country. Persons who traded with or traveled on the vessels of either Italy or Ethiopia did so "at their own risk."

peasement. Then, when Hitler remilitarized the Rhineland, all talk of an oil embargo was dropped.

While these events occurred in Europe, the Italian military advance continued at a moderate rate, although the Ethiopians had only primitive weapons to use against Italy's modern ones. The Ethiopians impeded the Italian advance without permitting themselves to be drawn into any large open engagement. At last, in May 1936, after seven months of warfare, Italian troops entered Addis Ababa. While Haile Selassie was on his way to Europe on a British warship, Italy formally annexed his country. King Victor Emmanuel took the title Emperor of Ethiopia. Recognition of Italy's new empire by the other powers followed slowly, although relations between Rome and Geneva continued to be strained after the lifting of sanctions. It occasioned no astonishment when Italy submitted her resignation from the League in 1937.

A decree of 1936 united Ethiopia, Eritrea, and Italian Somaliland into Italian East Africa, and in 1937 Mussolini took the post of Minister for Italian Africa. A six-year plan was announced, but never realized, to develop Ethiopia, and it was hoped to derive large quantities of cotton, coffee, meat, hides, wool, timber, and minerals from the new empire.

After the Ethiopian War, Italy drew ever closer to Germany and became further estranged from Great Britain, France, and the Soviet Union. Germany had not participated in the sanctions against Italy and had been quick to recognize the conquest of Ethiopia. Both the Nazis and the Fascists, moreover, supported General Francisco Franco in the Spanish Civil War that began in 1936. So Italy and Germany finally reached a general understanding, which Mussolini first called an Axis.

In 1937, Mussolini expressed a lessened interest in the protection of Austria against Nazi advances, endorsed the German claim for colonies, and subscribed to the German-Japanese pact against communism. In 1938 he made the best of what was an unpleasant surprise and acquiesced in the German absorption of Austria; soon thereafter he supported the Reich in the feverish negotiations over the Sudentenland. In 1939 he justified Germany's absorption of Bohemia, Moravia, and Memel. In that year, also, he concluded a formal military alliance with Hitler.

For a time, Italy obviously gained the less from Axis activities. Hence Mussolini in 1938–1939 made two efforts to swell the area of the "Italian Empire." Late in 1938, in the presence of a newly accredited French Ambassador and of Mussolini, a group of parliamentary deputies raised the cry of "Tunisia!," a cry that was rapidly taken up by the spectators and then by crowds in the streets. According to French figures, the number of Frenchmen and Italians in Tunisia was about equal, but Rome claimed that its nationals considerably outnumbered the French residents. Thus Italy began to plead the cause of an "oppressed nationality" in Tunisia much as the Germans had done in Czechoslovakia. In addition, Fascist voices were raised for Corsica, which France had bought from Genoa in 1786, and for Savoy and Nice, which had been ceded to France by treaty in 1860. On all these, however, France remained firm, and so Mussolini next turned his aggressive attention to Albania.

ITALY AND ALBANIA

One of the results of the Balkan Wars of 1912 and 1913 was the emergence of a new state: Albania. A German prince, William of Wied, was chosen ruler. William proved incapable of governing the mountainous state with its unruly inhabitants, and when the First World War broke out he returned to Germany. During the war Albania was officially neutral, but the Austrians, Italians, and Serbs used it as a battleground. At the peace conference the Italians sought an Albanian mandate, but Wilson objected and told the natives to form a government of their own. In 1920 a provisional government was established, which concentrated its efforts upon ousting the foreign soldiers who still occupied the country. At the end of the year Albania became a member of the League of Nations, but its final boundaries were not fixed until 1926.

The provisional government led a precarious existence, but out of the chaos emerged the conspicuous figure of a young Moslem chieftain, Ahmed Zogu. By January 1925, Albania had been declared a republic and Zogu was chosen president for seven years by a national assembly.

Zogu attempted to consolidate his power, but found himself obliged to turn to Italy for financial aid. Not long thereafter, Italy lent Albania money. Other transactions followed, and Italy stood in a fair way to dominate Albania. But Yugoslavia was vehemently opposed to any scheme that would endanger her freedom of access to the Mediterranean Sea. Precisely such a factor had constituted one of the grievances of the old Serbia against Austria-Hungary.

In 1926–1927 numerous internal improvements were prosecuted in Albania with Italian funds and under the supervision of an Italian development corporation. In addition, Italian officers reorganized the Albanian army. Faced by another rebellion in 1926, Zogu once more turned to Italy for aid. This Mussolini was ready to give—for a price. In November 1926 the two countries signed the Treaty of Tirana. By its terms "Italy and Albania recognized that any disturbance directed against" the status quo in Albania was not in their mutual political interests. An accompanying letter gave Italy the right to intervene in the external or internal relations of Albania whenever the latter requested aid.

Thoroughly alarmed at this turn of events, Yugoslavia took advantage of a frontier incident to make certain military preparations. In 1927, after an employee of the Yugoslav Legation had been arrested at Durazzo for espionage, diplomatic relations with Albania were severed. Italy championed the cause of Albania, and war seemed imminent. The matter was adjusted without recourse to arms, but Yugoslavia now eagerly turned to France for an alliance. Italy and Albania reacted by signing a twenty-year military pact.

In 1928 Zogu had himself proclaimed king, as Zog I. In the following year an Italian company secured an oil concession from the king, and in 1930 an arrangement was concluded whereby an Italian bank assumed supervision of Albania's coinage system. Thereafter, however, the Albanians displayed an increasingly anti-Italian feeling. Zog, late in 1932, rejected an Italian proposal for a customs union and in 1933 closed all Italian-controlled private schools. During 1934 Zog tried, though with little success, to lessen the influence of Italian officers in his army and to check Italian immigration. Apparently as a warning against such tendencies, an Italian fleet appeared in Durazzo harbor without previous notice and without firing the customary salute. Though these omissions were officially explained as an oversight, it was widely believed that the demonstration had political implications. The belief was strengthened when several new Italo-Albanian commercial agreements were announced.

At last, on Good Friday of 1939, Italian soldiers landed on the Albanian coast and on the next day entered Tirana. There was little resistance, for the natives were poorly equipped. Zog fled the country and Albania was joined to Italy in a personal union. Victor Emmanuel III added to his titles of King of Italy and Emperor of Ethiopia that of King of Albania. Germany appeared to have known in advance of Mussolini's Albanian plan; the other powers accepted the *fait accompli.*

The new Italian possession received from the king a constitutional statute. Italy took over Albania's diplomatic services and the Albanian army was absorbed into the Italian. Legislation was to be the function of a native council, but it could not act on any matters which had not first been authorized by the King of Italy. The puppet state was permitted to retain its own language.

Spain 7

SOME HISTORICAL BACKGROUND

Maps showed Spain as a united country from the time of the fall of Granada in 1492. By that date the reconquest had been completed by local Christian kings of the territories captured by the Moors between 711 and 718. Actually, the Spaniards had little unity of language, thought, or traditions, and were not a homogeneous people. The marriage in 1469 of Ferdinand of Aragon and Isabella of Castile, which foreshadowed the union of the two largest kingdoms in Spain, was opposed by some contemporary statesmen because of the difference between the two peoples. In reality, there was in Spain a proud provincialism, which was essentially the outgrowth of an obstructive geography. At times foreign invasions, such as that of Napoleon, brought to the fore an embryonic nationalism, but ordinarily patriotism in Spain seemed to be a local phenomenon reflecting the geographical division of the country.

The two most practical elements in the population of early modern Spain appeared to be the Jews and the Moors. The former were active in commerce and trading, and knew how to invest their capital in productive enterprises. The Moors were skilled in agricultural activities. The forcible expulsion of these peoples—the Jews in 1492 and the Moors in 1609—largely for religious reasons, left a population whose leaders tended to despise labor as dishonorable.

The very elements of the population, which in other countries became a productive middle class, in Spain often viewed labor as fit only for infidels and Jews. Since monasteries and nobles were ordinarily exempt from taxation, and since more and more land came into the possession of these privileged groups, the levies on surviving trade and industry necessarily were heavy. Whereas rulers of other lands curried favor with the middle class, most Spanish sovereigns blocked its rise. The army and the church were considered sufficient pillars of the monarchy.

Thus even during the years of her greatest apparent glory, Spain contained within herself the causes of decline. Supported in the sixteenth century chiefly by the efforts of a few energetic rulers and by the influx of silver and gold from the Americas, Spain's brilliance could not last because the authorities failed to adapt their economic outlook to the changing economic conditions of a modernizing world.

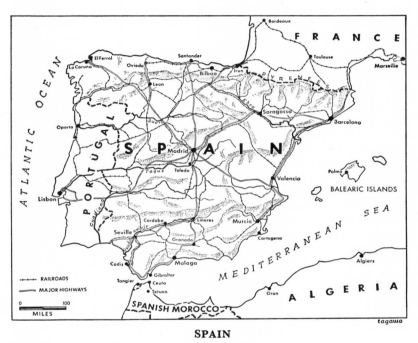

SPAIN

Courtesy, Foreign Policy Association, *Headline Series.*

The list of corroding influences upon Spanish development from 1500 to 1900 was long. Heavy military losses, the emigration of large numbers of colonial adventurers, the eagerness with which young men and women flocked to the monasteries and convents, the popular hostility towards foreign settlers, the relative poverty in mineral wealth, and the high per centage of illiteracy, all tended to weaken the monarchy. In addition, there was an uneconomic discrimination against agriculture in favor of sheep raising.

With this historical sketch in mind, it is understandable why the opening years of the twentieth century should have witnessed a sorry state of things in Spain. The decade and a half between the closing of the Spanish-American War of 1898 and the opening of the First World War saw the national stage almost continually occupied by disorders ranging from attacks on churches to attempts at political assassination. Not until the outbreak of war in 1914 was there a temporary cessation of these symptoms of instability—and then the question of what course to pursue during the struggle served to arouse further dissension among the people.

Although the choice of sympathies in 1914 was difficult for King Alfonso XIII (1886–1931), who had an Austrian mother and a British wife, the Spanish people readily fell into two opposing groups. Many intellectuals and, in general, liberals who possessed antimonarchical and anticlerical views favored the Allied cause. The conservative elements sympathized with the Germans. In the circumstances, the safest decision for the country was to remain neutral, and the *Cortes* (parliament) so voted. The wisdom of this policy became apparent when the belligerents began to send in orders for war materials. From 1915 to 1919 Spain for the first time in many years enjoyed an excess of exports over imports. After 1919, however, an adverse trade relationship reappeared.

Although it would seem that increased wartime industrial activities should have resulted in comparative prosperity and domestic quiet within Spain, such was not the case. No fewer than seven ministries held office during the period of the First World War, and ten more rose and fell within the next five years. Liberal, Conservative, and coalition cabinets alike failed for lack of stability. This unrest was traceable to four major developments: (1) the discontent and growing radicalism of the laboring classes; (2) the existence of strong regionalist and separatist movements; (3) interference in governmental affairs by military juntas or councils; and (4) continued military disasters in rebellious Spanish Morocco.

UNREST, COLONIAL DEFEAT, AND DICTATORSHIP, 1917–1930

Although labor unrest was general throughout Spain it was most conspicuous in Catalonia, where separatism was strongest and economic difficulty greatest.[1] In 1919 a general strike broke out in Barcelona. All constitutional guarantees were suspended and bloody street fighting occurred among the strikers, strikebreakers, police, and soldiery. Similar tragedies were enacted in other parts of the realm. At one time the Spanish Employers' Association threatened a nationwide lockout unless the government exercised moderation in its treatment of both employers and workmen. But the year 1920 brought, instead of moderation, a reign of terror. And in 1921 the Premier was assassinated.

[1] Catalonia consisted of four provinces in northeastern Spain, including industrial Barcelona.

The stability of the ministries, constantly endangered by the labor and regionalist crises, was further jeopardized by the activities of numerous military juntas. These councils of army officers criticized governmental policies, attempted to interfere in the civil administration, and pursued obstructionist tactics with regard to the Moroccan situation.

During these years the army was fighting a losing war against the rebellious Riffian tribes in Spanish Morocco. The more the troops were beaten, the heavier were the taxes imposed upon the people at home and the more oppressive became the weight of military service, censorship, and personal restrictions. A dramatic climax was reached in July 1921 when a force of Riffians routed a larger Spanish army. The indignation in Spain was so great that a parliamentary committee was appointed to investigate the government's conduct of empire.

While the army continued the campaign against the rebels, the committee examined evidence in Spain and Morocco. Its report to the Council of Ministers was immediately suppressed. When it became evident that the report not only was being withheld from the people, but that its recommendations might be disregarded, protest meetings were held throughout the kingdom. Full disclosure of the colonial situation was demanded by the public. In fear of a coup d'etat, the government dissolved the parliament and ordered new elections. The temper of the next national legislature, however, was quite the same as that of the old.

To add to the troubles of the authorities, there was another series of strikes and radical outbreaks. Regionalist agitation increased, and the news of the successful Fascist coup in Italy added to the general excitement. It was not surprising then that, in September 1923, Captain General Miguel Primo de Rivera, military governor of Barcelona, overthrew the national ministry, suspended the constitution, and set himself up as military dictator. Though it was evident that the coup was not directed against the monarchy, it was not known until some years later that the plan had been carried out with the consent of King Alfonso.

Primo de Rivera was born in Cadiz in 1870. Throughout his career in the military, he had several times come into conflict with higher authorities because of protests against what he regarded as the needless "butchery" of soldiers in Morocco. Upon assuming dictatorial control, Rivera dissolved the Cortes, suspended certain civil rights, and strengthened the position of the Catholic Church.

Rivera soon discovered how difficult it was to set up a government that was at the same time strong and satisfactory to a discontented people. Popular hostility to the dictatorship and, indeed, to the monarchy was increased by such incidents as the dismissal of provincial legislatures and the exile of several popular republicans. The extreme censorship antagonized the leading intellectuals, many of whom began to devote their literary abilities to fighting the regime.

Beginning in 1925, however, Primo de Rivera inaugurated policies calculated to win the support of public opinion. Martial law was abolished. The military directorate was replaced by a civil cabinet. Efforts were made to settle labor disputes by arbitration, to break up some of the large landed estates, and to expand educational facilities. The support of a portion of the working class was gained by the appointment to public service positions of some national labor leaders. As a concession to constitutionalism there was convoked a National Advisory Assembly (September 1927) to sit in place of the Cortes that had been dissolved four years earlier. The assembly, whose members all were nominated by the government, was given only consultative powers, but in 1928 it was directed to draft a new constitution to replace the one of 1876.

The backing of nationalists was sought by a vigorous foreign policy. In 1926, Spain and Italy signed a treaty in which each promised to maintain a benevolent neutrality if the other were attacked by a third party (presumably France). Then Spain served notice of intention to withdraw from the League of Nations because her demand for a permanent seat on the Council had been refused.[2] Finally, the Moroccan situation was brought under control as the French joined the Spanish in successful action against the Riffians.

Despite these developments there were continuing indications of popular discontent. In 1926 there was a mutiny in the artillery corps because men were promoted through influence rather than by seniority and merit. A plot, in the same year, to set up an independent Catalonia was frustrated mainly by the alertness of the French police, who arrested several Catalonian separatist leaders across the border. In 1928 a plot was unearthed in Barcelona to overthrow the dictator. Since the dictatorship generally was opposed in the universities, it was deemed necessary temporarily to shut the doors of all higher schools. During these years, frequent attempts were made to assassinate both the king and the dictator. Throughout all these manifestations there ran an undercurrent of republicanism that slowly but steadily was gaining in intensity.

In January 1930, after more than six years of difficult rule, Primo de Rivera resigned his powers as suddenly as he had assumed them. Illness, disagreements with the king, and constant disorders had induced him to give up his office.[3]

Upon his retirement, Primo de Rivera was succeeded by General Dámaso Berenguer. Berenguer inaugurated his regime by easing censorship and adopting a conciliatory attitude toward the universities. But he lacked leadership qualities and was unable, in the face of the world depression, to provide prosperity. Even before he had time to outline his plans there were renewed student riots and strikes.

[2] Before the required two-year notice of withdrawal took effect, Spain notified the League of her decision to retain membership. She did resign in 1941.

[3] He died in Paris a few weeks after his resignation.

A group of Catalonians began to agitate strenuously for democracy and republicanism.

The king and his council tried desperately in 1930 to regain the confidence of the people. New parliamentary elections were promised for 1931. To aid the farmers, a decree was issued suspending the further importation of wheat. Tariffs were boosted to protect manufacturers. Concessions were made to freedom of speech and meeting. The police were forbidden to search homes without warrants. But all this was in vain. The increased freedom of discussion only demonstrated how widespread the idea of republicanism had become. Many people demanded royalty's abdication. In September 1930 a large crowd, meeting in the Madrid bull ring, cheered wildly for a republic. December brought a mutiny in the aviation corps and a premature republican revolt.

By 1930, the continued existence of the monarchy rested upon three factors of uncertain strength: the loyalty of the army, the support of the great landowners and of the Catholic Church, and dissension within the ranks of the republican opposition (twenty-two republican parties had been organized). Opposed to the old regime were the regionalists, the Socialists, the "New Industrialists" who longed for a changed order corresponding to their interpretation of the needs of the twentieth century, the anticlerical intellectuals, and the republicans.

BIRTH AND PROBLEMS OF THE REPUBLIC

In February 1931, Premier Berenguer restored the constitution that his predecessor had suspended and ordered parliamentary elections. Contrary to the general's expectations, the people greeted the news with anger. Nearly all the antigovernment groups announced that they would refuse to vote in any election save one for a constituent assembly. They had no desire to participate in a resurrection of the document of 1876. Berenguer thereupon resigned, just one year after assuming power.

Municipal elections were ordered, preliminary to a national vote. These elections resulted in a republican landslide. A republican junta threatened revolution unless the king abdicated. Alfonso sailed for France without formally abdicating, leaving the people free to decide whether they wished to keep the monarchy. Prominent Republican Niceto Alcalá Zamora, however, immediately (April 14) proclaimed a republic, with himself as provisional president and with executive authority vested in a previously selected coalition cabinet of republicans and Socialists.[4]

---

[4] Zamora, the son of a poor southern landowner, earlier in his career had been a monarchist and three times had occupied ministerial posts in royal cabinets. During the dictatorship, however, he was converted to republicanism, and in December 1930, he led a premature revolt against the king.

The new government set the date for elections and pledged itself to bring about land and church reforms, personal liberty, and a fair degree of local autonomy. Although most of the political groups decided to await the results of the election before taking any further steps, the provisional government was kept busy the first ten weeks of its existence putting down anti-republican movements and Communist riots, imprisoning royalist officials, pleading with the Catalonian separatists not to impair the unity of the state, and passing urgent preliminary legislation.

Two other serious developments commanded the attention of the government prior to the elections. First, anticlerical riots were precipitated when church officials appealed to faithful Catholics to vote only for deputies who would defend their religion. Churches, monasteries, and convents were burned. The Zamora Government showed little sympathy for such disorders and proclaimed martial law in an attempt to restore order. Secondly, a group of Catalonians who regarded any Madrid regime as obnoxious, declared an antonomous Catalonia. It was obvious from the outset that Spain's "Irish Question" would disturb the harmony of the republic as it had that of the monarchy.

In June 1931, the people flocked to the polls in the first national election since 1923. The result of the balloting once more was a defeat for monarchy and a triumph for moderate republicanism. The Socialist Party became the largest single group in the Cortes. The Radical Party, which favored consolidation of the republic and liberal reforms, was second. Most of the representatives were young men, and only fourteen of them had had any previous parliamentary experience.

The Cortes voted to keep in power the provisional ministry that Zamora had appointed and then proceeded to the consideration of a republican constitution. While the document was being pieced together, the cabinet devoted itself to the solution of more immediate problems. Efforts were made to stabilize the currency and bring efficiency into government. It required all Zamora's persuasiveness to induce the Catalonian deputies to remain in the Cortes, for a plebiscite in Catalonia had resulted in an overwhelming endorsement for autonomy. It became necessary to dispatch soldiers to Barcelona to quell a radical regionalist uprising.

Negotiations also had to be carried on with the Vatican concerning both the property damage done in the early days of the revolution and the future policies of the republic. Inasmuch as the entire non-Catholic population of Spain was less than 30,000, the relationship between government and papacy was of unusual importance. When the Cortes resolved to abolish a state religion, expel the Jesuits and confiscate their property, and prohibit members of religious orders from teaching or engaging in business, Zamora resigned in protest against what he regarded as unnecessarily harsh terms.

The chief executive post was then entrusted to Manuel Azaña, a man who, as head of the war office, had stimulated great confidence by his ability and integrity. Consequently, he was invested with extraordinary powers for the suppression of disorder. One of the most spectacular acts of the assembly was to declare Alfonso XIII guilty of high treason. His property in Spain was confiscated and he was sentenced to life imprisonment should he ever return to Spain.

In December 1931, the Cortes proclaimed the new constitution. Spain was declared "a democratic republic of workers." Its government was to consist of a unicameral legislature made up of representatives elected by direct and secret vote of all citizens over twenty-three years of age. None of the president's acts was valid unless countersigned by a cabinet minister, and the cabinet was made directly responsible to parliament.

In social and cultural matters the break with tradition was wide. There was to be no state church; divorce was legalized; education was secularized; and civil liberties were guaranteed. All types of property, regardless of ownership, might be expropriated with due compensation. Work was made a social obligation. The constitution recognized the "compatibility" of autonomous regions within the centralized state.

The Cortes was empowered to elect the republic's first constitutional president. Zamora was chosen and Azaña became Prime Minister. Instead of dissolving itself now and ordaining parliamentary elections, the Constituent Cortes determined to continue sitting as a regular parliament. The deputies felt that the body which had drawn up the constitution should be permitted to launch the legislative program that would convert its principles into practice.

In 1932, then, the Jesuit Order was dissolved. Its corporate property was confiscated and ordered distributed for social welfare purposes. The individual Jesuits soon left the land. Later legislation nationalized all ecclesiastical property. The church schools were closed, and all educational matters were placed under the Minister of Education.

After the flight of Alfonso, the Pope had directed the clergy to accept the republic but to oppose by constitutional means the enactment of anticlerical legislation. The failure of these efforts led Pope Pius XI to issue an encyclical (1933) protesting the separation of church and state. Once more Catholics were urged to obey the civil authority, but only in matters that did not infringe the rights of the Catholic Church. The members of the government were informed that their actions brought upon them automatic excommunication. This did not appear greatly to worry most of them.

The closing of the church schools and the prohibition of teaching by clerics made worse the bad educational situation in Spain. The national illiteracy in 1931 was estimated at more than 45 per cent. Despite the shortage of funds, therefore, 9600 new state schools were opened from 1931 to 1933. Land reform proceeded slowly, but the Cortes provided for the distribution of several large estates.

It was not to be expected that autonomist groups would be satisfied with the home-rule concessions granted in the constitution. In April 1932 a meeting of Catalonians demanded the immediate recognition by Madrid of autonomy for Catalonia. Like the Sinn Feiners in Ireland, the Catalonians founded a society called "We Ourselves" (*Nosaltres Sols*) and continued turbulent demonstrations. In September the Cortes finally recognized a Catalonian Statute of Autonomy, which gave Catalonia the right to use its own language (Catalan), anthem, and flag. In addition, the Catalonians were permitted to establish a state government of their own and were granted the privilege of raising taxes, creating a school system, and enforcing the national laws in Catalonia. Other areas now became more insistent in *their* demands for similar grants of autonomy. To many Spaniards it seemed desirable that the republic should eventually become a federation of Spanish states.

Inevitably there appeared opposition to the continued dominance of the moderate republicans. To the right were the royalists, who favored restoration of the monarchy; the clericals, who abhorred the anti-Catholic legislation; and the landlords, who preferred to keep their large estates. To the left were the Communists, who desired a reconstitution of Spanish life on the Soviet model; the Syndicalists, who advocated "the erection of a society based on trade-unions alone;" and the anarchists, who favored the entire abolition of government.

The first serious revolt against the Azaña Government occurred in August 1932. A group of royalists seized Seville and a few small towns. A loyal army quickly crushed the movement. Then, in January 1933, a syndicalist-anarchist revolt broke out in Barcelona It spread rapidly to other cities, but once more loyal republican troops overcame the revolutionaries.

Less violent than these manifestations but equally indicative of the growing dissatisfaction were the results of two elections in the spring and summer of 1933. First, municipal elections throughout the country showed a definite trend to the right. Then, the government's candidates for a tribunal, created to decide on the constitutionality of laws, were defeated. Consequently, it was decided to hold the first national election under the republican constitution. As a result a moderate ministry (Right Center) was formed. Further closing of religious schools was stopped until sufficient lay teachers were available to meet the needs of the school population. Yet throughout the spring of 1934 the country was torn by strikes and disorders. Now leftists of various varieties rioted because the laws against the church and the landholders were not enforced quickly enough and because religious processions were tolerated during Easter Week for the first time since 1931. Despite the proclamation of a national "state of alarm" the violence continued and became worse.

Early in 1934 the government of the republic was forced to deal with the worst rebellion it had yet encountered. The occasion of the uprising was the offer by Premier Alejandro Lerroux of several cabinet posts to so-called Catholic Fascists, followers of José Maria Gil Robles, editor of the leading clerical paper. All radical groups cooperated in a general strike that soon became violent and merged with a desperate attempt by the Catalonian radicals to break away from Spain—indeed, the independence of Catalonia was declared. Again the Madrid Government was able to quell the rising, but only with the aid of the armed forces, and at a high cost in blood and money.

Meanwhile Lerroux, strongly backed by the Cortes (many of the radical members were either under arrest or refused to sit while martial law was enforced), entrenched the position of the Right. The Catalonian Statute of Autonomy was suspended. Madrid assumed responsibility for the policing of Barcelona and other centers of disturbance. The regular municipal elections were postponed.

CIVIL WAR AND "LITTLE WORLD WAR," 1936-1939

New elections early in 1936 brought to power a leftist Popular Front. Premier Azaña, however, led a cabinet composed entirely of Republicans, with no Socialist, Communist, or Syndicalist members. By April 1936 public disorders grew worse than ever, and numerous acts of violence were attributed to the partisans of both Left and Right.

The authorities imprisoned many Fascists and ordered the dissolution of the Spanish Phalanx, the most aggressive antigovernment group. The ministry was especially fearful of the restive army men. A decree therefore automatically pensioned all military officers who had participated in politics. Politically minded officers who already were on the retired list lost their pensions, and a general shakeup occurred in the high command. Suspected officers were dismissed or transferred to distant parts. General Francisco Franco, once commander of the Spanish Foreign Legion in Morocco, was "exiled" to the Canary Islands. Clearly, the controlling group of general officers was in danger of being rendered impotent. Quick action was necessary if the traditional power of the army was to be upheld.

It was evident, by this time, that the republic was approaching the decisive moment in its career. It had succeeded the monarchy in 1931 because the impoverished population was no longer willing to tolerate the rule of a small minority composed of army officers, estate owners, clerics, and big industrialists. The reforms of the republic were intended to break the power and wealth of this minority. But they were put into effect at a pace that seemed far too slow for the impatient laborers and peasants. While the tension between Right and Left therefore became ever greater, the government tried to continue along a middle course. In the end, the extremists of each side came to regard force as the surest means of reaching their objectives. It remained only for an "incident" more serious than the rest to precipitate civil war.

About the middle of June 1936, José Calvo Sotelo, a fiery monarchist, launched bitter verbal attacks against the government. He uttered warnings of the army's growing impatience with the inability of the authorities to check popular excesses. There were frequent rumors regarding impending coups of both monarchists and Communists. Each group, it was said, was working feverishly to forestall the plans of the other. Madrid was "a nervous city." When, in July, a leftist police lieutenant in Madrid was murdered, several of his comrades killed Calvo Sotelo. Gil Robles placed responsibility for his death at the government's door. On July 17 several regiments in Spanish Morocco revolted, and civil war began.

General Franco left the Canary Islands and flew to Morocco to head the rebellious forces. With the support of most of the regular army, the Foreign Legion, and some Moorish contingents, he quickly made himself master of Spanish Morocco. Simultaneously, garrisons in all parts of Spain mutinied. General José Sanjurjo, leader of the anti-republicans, attempted to fly to Spain from his exile in Portugal. The plane crashed and the general was killed. Franco then emerged as the leader of the new movement.

Most of the military as well as civilians of conservative, Fascist, monarchist, and clerical sympathies rallied around Franco's standard.[5] These were reinforced by thousands of well-trained "volunteers" from Italy and Germany and, for a time, from the Irish Free State. The established government could count on only a small part of the organized armed forces, including the military air force and a part of the navy. It had to seek additional aid from the radical labor and peasant groups. This popular militia included many women. Thousands of foreign sympathizers, especially from the Soviet Union, France, and the United States, fought for the Madrid Government in such units as the International Brigade, the Debs Column, and the Abraham Lincoln Battalion. Finally, there was a sizable contingent of anti-Fascist Germans, Italians, and Poles.

The rebels apparently envisaged rapid victory in three steps: seizure of Spanish Morocco, capture of the provincial capitals, and overthrow of the government in Madrid. The first step was successful, but the others were blocked by the rapid arming and determined resistance of the "masses." Nevertheless, by November 1936 the rebels reached the outskirts of Madrid, and the established government transferred its seat to Valencia. Germany and Italy, at this point, recognized the Franco Government.

In the meantime the established government's increasing depen-

---

[5] The followers of Franco soon were called Rebels, Fascists, Nationalists, and Insurgents. The supporters of the Madrid Government came to be called Loyalists, Marxists, and Reds. The only noncommittal terms from the point of view of international law seemed to be "rebels" and "established government."

dence upon left-wing support as the fighting was prolonged made necessary the admission of Socialists and Communists into the ministry. Once this process had started it was hard to go back. Indeed, after two months, Francisco Largo Caballero, the Premier, assigned several cabinet posts to Syndicalists in order to gain the fullest support of Catalonia. The established government thus became a truly leftist government, although it had not been so when the rebels first attempted to seize control.

Following a revolt of anarchists in Barcelona, the Caballero Ministry resigned (1937). It was succeeded by a more moderate one under Juan Negrín, a right-wing Socialist and former Finance Minister. Thereafter the established government, moving to Barcelona, followed a more conservative pattern, even the Communists agreeing that social revolution should be subordinated to the successful termination of the war.

The defense of the established government stiffened materially once the rebels reached the limits of Madrid. Thus far the Franco Government had been the chief beneficiary of military supplies, especially planes and tanks, sent to Spain from Italy and Germany. Now, however, the Loyalists also received considerable aid of a similar type, from the Soviet Union. The Madrid forces repulsed the rebel attack and during 1937 pushed the Nationalists back to a safer distance. The Italian troops with Franco were badly defeated on the Guadalajara front.

The year 1938 was definitely more favorable, from both the military and diplomatic viewpoints, to the Insurgents than the Loyalists. The air superiority and tank equipment, which Franco owed to the Italians and Germans, and the food shortage that affected chiefly the Barcelona Government areas, began to tell decisively. Just before Christmas 1938, Franco prepared what was to prove the major offensive of the war. Having as its objective the city of Barcelona itself, the campaign was bitterly fought for a month. Then the Loyalist capital fell. The end of February 1939 saw the recognition of the Franco regime by Great Britain and France. In March, Franco's soldiers at last entered Madrid and all remaining Loyalist strongholds capitulated. Franco had won, after more than thirty-two months of bitter fighting.

Besides the long-term task of reconstructing war torn Spain, Franco faced certain vital immediate problems. These included feeding the starving populace; getting rid of the thousands of Italians, Germans, and Portuguese who had helped him to victory; negotiating with France over the future status of about 300,000 refugees who had gone or been driven northward across the Pyrenees; "settling accounts" with Loyalist sympathizers and soldiers; and rebuilding public property as quickly as possible.

The foreign soldiers gradually departed, following the holding of a great "victory parade" in Madrid. Manpower for public works was procured through the imposition of labor service upon all males between eighteen and fifty and the use of concentration camp inmates. The council of the recreated Spanish Phalanx met under Franco's Presidency and drafted plans for the creation of a political and economic structure based on the Italian Fascist model. Wholesale arrests were instituted against the "enemies" of the civil-war days. There were executions and there were jail sentences.

The "we or they" attitude in international politics had become sufficiently crystallized by the summer of 1936 so that the outbreak of civil war in Spain threatened to precipitate another general war. The Fascist states, including Portugal, feared the rise of another "Bolshevik" state in Europe and hence determined to help Franco. Strategic reasons were as important as ideological ones. Italy and Germany believed that a Fascist Spain would strengthen their own international influence, whereas a radical Spain would have been of advantage to the Soviet Union. Finally, the triumph of a fascist government friendly to Italy might strengthen the latter's pretensions to control in the western Mediterranean.

To curtail Hitler's and Mussolini's rising influence in Spain, the Soviet Union decided to assist the established authorities. France and Great Britain attempted, at least in the beginning, to steer a middle course. Actually, neither country was united in opinion on the war. Thus, the aid that came from Britain and France was in the nature of private contributions of money, arms, and men, although the government policies were noninterventionist.

Eventually, twenty-seven European states, including all the great powers, agreed to set up in London an international nonintervention committee. The committee held frequent meetings and was kept busy examining charges by the Soviet Union against Portugal, Italy, and Germany, and reciprocal charges by these powers against the Moscow Government. Since the committee did little more than examine these charges, a steady flow of supplies entered Spain. When it became apparent that not merely supplies, but soldiers and pilots were being sent to Spain, France and Great Britain suggested the extension of the nonintervention agreement to cover foreign "volunteers" as well as weapons. In February 1937 such a ban became (theoretically) effective.

The nonintervention committee also took up the question of withdrawal of volunteers already in Spain. While the discussions were in progress, a series of submarine attacks on merchant vessels occurred. These vessels had been conveying cargoes destined for the Barcelona Government through the Mediterranean. Suspicion centered on Italy, and Moscow openly accused Italian submarines of having torpedoed two Soviet freighters. This new form of piracy led Great Britain and France to call a conference of powers in Switzerland. Germany and Italy refused to attend because the Soviet Union attended, but in September 1937 a Nyon Agreement was signed by nine states. A "piracy patrol" made up of several signatory states was assigned to Spanish waters and the submarine attacks ceased.

During the entire year of 1938, the nonintervention committee tried to find a satisfactory formula for the withdrawal of the foreign volunteers, but the last German and Italian fighters did not quit Spain until several weeks after the war was ended. Just before their departure, and coincident with Italy's occupation of Albania, Spain signed (April 1939) the Anti-Comintern Pact originally negotiated by Germany and Japan. Thus did the "Little World War" end in victory for the Axis.

Germany | 8

FROM EMPIRE TO REPUBLIC

World War I ended for Germany on November 11, 1918, with German acceptance of Allied armistice terms. On the previous day, Emperor William II had crossed the frontier into the Netherlands and permanent exile.

During the war the Social Democratic Party (SPD) gradually had split over the question of voting continuing war credits. The majority wanted to go on supporting the war, whereas the minority opposed the granting of further funds.[1] In November 1918 it was the majority, led by right-wing Socialist Friedrich Ebert, an ex-saddler, who proclaimed a republic amid a welter of demonstrations, strikes, and mutinies.

The birth of a German Republic was foreshadowed when General Erich F. W. Ludendorff's great drives of 1918 collapsed and the army appeared ready to quit fighting and go home. Prince Max of Baden, the Chancellor supported by a moderate coalition that came into being in October 1918, hoped to save the throne for the Hohenzollerns by rushing through a number of reforms which converted Germany into a constitutional monarchy. Max then began to negotiate with President Wilson for an armistice based on the Fourteen Points. He emphasized that the new German administration was a government "of the people, in whose hands rested both actually and constitutionally the authority to make decisions."

[1] Out of this dissatisfied minority came two new political parties. The more important was the Communist Party (KPD), which was known in the early years of the republic as the Spartacus League. It openly followed instructions from the Third (Communist) International and advocated policies originating in Moscow. The other was the Independent Socialist Party (USPD), which enjoyed a brief but influential existence.

122

From October 1918 it was widely held that the Emperor should abdicate, for Wilson insisted that as long as the imperial government was in power he would not discuss peace negotiations. On October 23 a demand was voiced in the Reichstag that the Emperor abdicate. The newspapers quickly took up the cry and on the evening of the 29th, Philipp Scheidemann, as leader of the Majority Socialists, requested Prince Max to secure William's abdication.

Meanwhile, at the Kiel naval base, the rumor spread that armistice negotiations would probably result in a surrender of the German fleet. The officers indicated a determination to seek an honorable death in an unexpected attack on the blockading British fleet. But the 80,000 sailors who would have been involved in this maneuver had no desire to become dead heroes. They refused to participate in a wholesale suicidal venture, and mutinied. The spirit of revolt spread to the workers at Kiel, where revolutionary councils demanded the abdication of the Hohenzollerns and amnesty for the leaders of earlier mutinies. Other cities followed the example of Kiel, and soon the demand for a republic was general along the German north coast.

The government hoped in vain to keep the remainder of the country ignorant of these developments. At a demonstration in Munich on November 7, an Independent-Socialist editor, Kurt Eisner, demanded the overthrow of the Bavarian dynasty. The Wittelsbach family fled and a "democratic and social republic" was set up in Bavaria with Eisner as its head. Similar republican proclamations were issued in Berlin and the chief industrial centers of the land. Indeed, the movement was so widespread as to be accompanied by relatively little disorder. The leaders of the Majority Socialists, fearing the loss of followers to the more radical Independents, now warned Prince Max that, unless the Emperor abdicated, they would resign from the government and declare a general strike. Max, still hoping to save the monarchy for the Hohenzollern family, labored to secure William's abdication in favor of the infant son of the crown prince.

William refused to listen. He expected the army to aid him in retaining the imperial crown. Eventually, however, the General Staff convinced him that the army would not fight the German people. At this point, Ebert promised Max to maintain order and call a constituent assembly. Max felt justified, in light of Ebert's apparent attitude of responsibility, in surrendering the government into the Socialist leader's hands.

Thereupon, early on November 10, William fled to the Netherlands. Not until November 28, however, did he send in a full abdication. By that time the empire had been converted into a federation of republican states, provisionally governed by a Council of People's Commissars. The commissars pleaded with the people to maintain order and protect private property. Most officials of the former imperial service continued to serve the new government, but the

Spartacists refused to cooperate. They were as much opposed to a social democratic republic as they had been to the empire. Through acts of terrorism they tried to prevent the calling of a national constituent assembly until their tactics should have cowed a sufficiently large number of citizens into accepting the idea of a Communist regime.

The question of an election date actually was settled by a national congress of councils. In imitation of organizations formed by soldiers and workers in Munich and Berlin, local councils appeared all over Germany. Frequently they assumed governmental powers. In December 1918 a national gathering of these councils was held. The congress excluded Communists and decided upon January 19, 1919, for the constituent elections. When force was used to subdue rebellious Communists, the Independent Socialists (USPD) withdrew from all official posts. This enabled the Majority Socialists to fill the vacancies, even in the Council of Commissars, with loyal supporters.

While awaiting election day, the commissars strove to control a restive Germany. The ingrained desire of many Germans for law and order, their patriotism, and their willingness to accept any government that gave promise of being able to function smoothly, rendered the problem of internal control less difficult than might have been expected. Yet, in anticipation of trouble from the Spartacists, the commissars held ready a well-equipped force of about 3000, commanded by ex-imperial officers.

The Spartacists, meanwhile, had formed armed bands that roamed the streets of the larger cities, ready for violence at any moment. The "voice" of these extremists was the writer, "Spartacus" Karl Liebknecht. The "brain" of the movement was the crippled Rosa Luxemburg. The Communists made their bid for power on January 6, 1919, when a vast crowd of armed workmen of Spartacist and Independent-Socialist sympathies assembled in the center of Berlin. The commissars, themselves recruited largely from the laboring classes, dreaded to use troops against their kind. One after another they refused the responsibility of dealing with the situation, until finally Gustav Noske accepted the task. "All right," he was reported as saying, "someone must be the bloodhound. I do not shirk the responsibility." An experienced strike organizer, Noske was not afraid to deal with the workers. With elements of the army and various Free Corps units he crushed the rebellion.[2] The Spartacist

[2] The Free Corps were paramilitary organizations made up largely of ex-soldiers who grouped around individual leaders. At the command of the leader they engaged in street fighting or open warfare. The creation of these Free Corps units among veterans was urged by important army officers immediately after the war. Eventually, some of them became involved in the Baltic area, fighting in the Russian civil war. Most of them were drawn to the political Right since they were nationalistic and antirepublican. Although antagonistic to the provisional government, they were ready to fight against whomever they considered the enemies of the

movement collapsed, and on January 19, 1919, elections for the national assembly took place in an atmosphere of relative quiet.

Thirty million Germans voted, on a basis of proportional representation. By the time of the elections the old political parties all had been reorganized. The Conservatives had been reconstructed on a monarchist platform as the German National People's Party (DNVP). The right-wing National Liberals, chiefly businessmen, had re-formed under Gustav Stresemann as the German People's Party (DVP), which somewhat grudgingly supported the republic. The Centrists (*Zentrum*), under Matthias Erzberger, favored a democratic republic and broad social legislation. A new Democratic Party (DDP) was formed in support of the republic and led by the banker, Hjalmar Schacht. The Majority Socialists readopted the name Social Democrats (SPD) and continued to urge the gradual socialization of industry and property, whereas the Independent Socialists (USPD) urged a more rapid nationalization process. The Spartacists took the name German Communist Party (KPD), but refused to participate in the elections.

When the returns were counted, the Social Democrats, with 163 of the 421 available seats, became the largest single group in the assembly. To protect the gathering against violence, Ebert convoked the assembly for February 6 in the peaceful city of Weimar.

The assembly met and adopted a previously drafted provisional constitution as its basis for government. Thereupon the commissars surrendered their powers and a "Weimar Coalition" of Social Democrats, Centrists, and Democrats became the official government. Friedrich Ebert was chosen President of the republic. Scheidemann became Chancellor.

The assembly faced the threefold task of putting down internal opposition, concluding peace with the Allies, and drafting a permanent constitution. Noske, Minister of Home Defense, attended to the first of these duties. There were violent strikes and there was much fighting. In Munich a Communist government was established after a nationalist had murdered Kurt Eisner. Noske decided once and for all to "settle accounts with the lunatics," and with the aid of the Free Corps crushed the radical movement by the summer of 1919.

The conclusion of peace proved to be more difficult. No group was prepared to accept the treaty as it was presented in May by the Allies. Scheidemann resigned the chancellorship rather than agree to the document. But in view of the severity of the punishment threatened by the Allies if the assembly rejected the terms, a majority of the delegates on June 23 agreed to the treaty.

The final task of the assembly was completed in July 1919 with

---

fatherland. Thus, in its hour of peril, the government of Majority Socialists was forced to ask for aid from elements which were to be attacking the republic not long after the suppression of the Spartacist uprising.

the adoption of a constitution. Its chief drafter was Professor Hugo Preuss, an opponent of states' rights. In the final balloting the SPD, Centrists, and Democrats voted for the constitution, whereas the USPD, the DVP, and the Nationalists voted against it.

The constitution defined the Reich as a federation of republican states called *Länder*.[3] There was a bill of rights, and the vote was accorded to all men and women over twenty on a basis of proportional representation. A president was to be elected by popular vote for seven years, and no action of his would be valid unless countersigned by the chancellor or appropriate minister. He might dismiss the Reichstag, although any particular basis for such action was not to be used more than once, and new elections had to be held within sixty days. In time of emergency the president, acting with the chancellor, might suspend certain constitutional guarantees and issue decrees with the force of law (Article 48).[4]

The chancellor was empowered to formulate policy and select the cabinet. Resignation of the cabinet had to follow only upon a specific vote of lack of confidence. A supreme court was instituted at Leipzig.

The chief legislative body was the Reichstag, with members elected for four years. After 1920, elections were held under the Baden system of proportional representation, whereby each party secured one deputy for every 60,000 votes polled. This system eventually resulted in the appearance of more than a score of parties and the consequent inability of any one of them, at least until the National Socialists accomplished the feat in 1933, to get a majority. The resultant inefficiency in legislation was grist to the mill of Nazi propagandists.

The less important upper house, representing the states, was labeled the *Reichsrat*. It might hold up, but could not veto, most laws passed by the Reichstag. Its consent, however, was necessary for the passage of any measure affecting the states as such. To prevent Prussia's securing a preponderant influence, the constitution provided that no state could have more than two-fifths of the total representation.

For some time after the adoption of the constitution, the republic was in danger. While the government had concentrated its energies upon suppressing the Communists, opportunity had been taken by

---

[3] In 1920 there were eighteen such Länder, but in 1929 Prussia annexed Waldeck, reducing the number to seventeen.
[4] Legally the Reichstag could demand the repeal of any such measures, but in practice this rarely was done. In its effort to fight the depression, the Berlin Government eventually issued several hundred emergency decrees. Indeed, from 1930-1933, Germany was ruled by a "constitutional dictatorship," for in that period presidential emergency decrees virtually replaced parliamentary legislation. Many historians have seen in Article 48 the fatal flaw in the constitution that later was to destroy the republic. Others have pointed out that the article was hedged with sufficient safeguards and that the Reichstag, had it had any abiding faith in the democratic process, might have prevented heads of government from utilizing it.

rightist die-hards to form strong ultranationalist organizations such as the *Stahlhelm* (Steel Helmet). These organizations had a long list of grievances against the republicans. It was rumored that cowardly republicans had made defeat inevitable by undermining the military power of the empire during the last months of the war.[5] The Weimar Assembly was attacked for accepting the "Versailles Dictate" and for permitting Allied commissions to "overrun" the country. Some individuals feared that the authorities might surrender "war criminals" to the Allies for trial.

In March 1920 a rightist *Putsch* was attempted. It had been planned by the New York-born banker, Dr. Wolfgang Kapp, who had gained some notoriety during the war for a fierce attack upon the policies of the then Chancellor Theobald von Bethmann Hollweg. Enlisting the aid of a Free Corps called the Ehrhardt Brigade, Kapp with 8000 men early one morning marched a dozen miles from the military barracks to Berlin. Noske had only 2000 men to oppose the plotters, and the government fled to Dresden.

President Ebert reacted by calling a general strike. Workmen throughout the land responded, and Berlin's public utilities and communications were tied up. Kapp fled to Sweden. He soon returned and surrendered to the authorities, only to die in prison while awaiting trial (1922).[6]

The Kapp affair did not end the attempts of reactionaries to avenge the "betrayal" of the fatherland. They instituted a reign of terror against persons connected with the signing of the peace treaty, persons who gave aid to the Allied commissions in Germany, and individuals prominently identified with socialism. The Centrist leader, Erzberger, who in 1917 had urged peace without annexations, was killed in 1921. In 1922 Walther Rathenau, successful industrialist, political philosopher, and efficient cabinet officer, was assassinated. The government replied to these acts by suspending the constitutional guarantees, but the agitation continued.

In November 1923 another coup, the Ludendorff-Hitler Putsch, was attempted from Munich. General Erich Ludendorff, of World War I fame, and Adolf Hitler, at this time a still somewhat obscure Austrian rabble rouser, planned to seize the government. The plot misfired and several leaders of this "beer-hall rebellion" were jailed. The harassed authorities once more turned to the other problems that confronted the state.

[5] This "Stab-in-the-back" charge held that the republic, in the days of its infancy, had stabbed the military in the back by signing Germany into defeat, even though the German army still had an excellent chance for final victory in the field. The assertion was patently false. Germany had lost the war and some generals were looking for a way to keep the onus of defeat from falling upon the General Staff.
[6] The Independent Socialists forced the dropping of Noske from the government, after the failure of the Kapp Putsch, by threatening continuance of the general strike. In 1922 the Social Democrats and Independent Socialists were reunited as the SPD.

INFLATION, DISILLUSIONMENT, HOPE

The German Government had been so confident of an early and successful conclusion of World War I that the conflict had been paid for through deficit financing. At the end of the war there were almost five times as many marks in circulation as in 1913.

This situation could not last long. When the laws that had established wartime price fixing lapsed, prices began to soar in proportion to the abundance of currency in circulation. The shortage of gold now became apparent. The Germans, in order to get the foodstuffs and raw products necessary to rebuild the economy, resorted to paper money. The circle of mounting deficits and further inflation became increasingly vicious with each passing month. By November 1922 a dollar, normally worth 4.2 marks, would purchase 7000 marks.

The crisis was heightened during the foreign occupation of the Ruhr. The seizure by the French of billions of Reichsbank notes and the attempt of the German Government to subsidize (through the printing press) the patriotically idle workers of the occupied region completely destroyed the value of the currency. Only a miracle could have stopped the "toboggan slide" of the mark, and no miracle occurred. By the end of July 1923 the mark fell to more than 1,000,000 to the dollar. The middle of November 1923 saw the mark quoted at 2.5 trillion to the dollar in Berlin. Milk sold for 250,000,000,000 marks a quart and was scarce at that price. Even private firms and individuals printed "emergency money."

The results of the financial debacle were terrible. The middle class suffered most, as formerly comfortable incomes from investments and savings became worthless. Many persons who had expected to live on their incomes found themselves forced to seek employment in an overcrowded labor market. Many industrialists, on the other hand, benefited by the cheap labor and cheap cost of materials and invested their financial surpluses in foreign securities. People hoarded goods and sought to exchange their marks for commodities having a more stable value, thus causing a "flight from marks to goods."

In the autumn of 1923 the German people virtually repudiated the mark, and conditions became worse than at any time during the war. Farmers refused to take their products to the cities and merchants closed their shops. Thousands of war cripples and persons who had expected to live on fixed incomes faced starvation. Hunger riots became common, and the chaos was made worse by the activities of foreign troops in the Ruhr, by separatist movements in the Rhineland and Bavaria, and by the rise to power of Communists in Saxony and elsewhere. National cabinets rose and fell with monotonous frequency, and the country appeared on the verge of collapse.

To prevent Germany's fall into complete dissolution, the authorities decided (October 1923) to launch one last, desperate program to aid the people in lifting themselves out of the mire. Dr. Hans Luther and Dr. Hjalmar Schacht, equipped with emergency powers, stabilized the mark by creating a new currency.

The printing of paper money was halted. A *Rentenbank* was opened and empowered to issue *Rentenmarks* with an assigned value equal to that of the prewar gold mark. Coverage was provided by a blanket mortgage on the national wealth of Germany. The Rentenmark was circulated along with the paper marks at a ratio of 1 to 1,000,000,000,000. Thus "there was created out of nothing . . . a currency which was kept stable by the confidence of the people."

The budget was balanced by ruthless measures. War claims were rejected, and thousands of public employees, many of whom had received lifetime appointments, were dismissed with little or no compensation.[7] The government raised tax rates and instituted a better system of collection.

Many of these acts had to be repealed or modified later, but not until they had served their immediate purpose—not until the budget had been balanced and inflation stopped. Conditions also became easier when the Dawes Plan went into effect in September 1924, Germany got a large foreign loan, and the Ruhr was evacuated. A new Reichsbank then was created to take the place of the Rentenmark, and a *Reichsmark* was substituted for the Rentenmark. Until mid-1925, paper marks were redeemable at the rate of one trillion to one Reichsmark. The distress was not yet over, but a measure of stability and confidence was restored, and the path to economic recovery was made less thorny.

Small wonder, in view of all this, that in the years immediately following the war a wave of pessimism swept over the German people. In their defeat it seemed to them that civilization was coming to an end. Many a thinker found refuge and solace only in metaphysical speculation and mysticism.

Strongly relevant to this air of pessimism was Oswald Spengler's *The Decline of the West*. Although this work was conceived before the outbreak of the war and completed late in 1917 while the German armies still were winning victories, it suited well the disillusioned, despairing Germany of 1919 and after. The book had for its theme the cyclic character of the historic process. History was regarded as a succession of civilization cycles, each with its birth in a spring and its death in a winter. The end of each cycle was as inexorable as its beginning. Three such periods had already come and gone: the Indian (beginning about 1800 B.C.), the Antique (from about 900 B.C.), and the Arabian (ushered in with the Christian and Moslem eras). The Western, dating from 900 A.D., now

---

[7] The Reich dismissed about 330,000 persons in all services, including the railway and postal systems; the states and municipalities dismissed 400,000 more. Many of these people later became Nazis, thus lending credence to the idea that the Nazi rise to power was in part a revolution of the economically disaffected.

was in its winter and was doomed to die before many more centuries passed. Then, wrote Spengler, "there will be no more Western culture, no more German, English, or French." *The Decline of the West* achieved a considerable vogue. In it, the gloomy found confirmation of their fears, and the disillusioned, proof of the futility of life.

Equally popular with books of pessimism and fatalism were volumes on the causes of the war, on how it might have been prevented, and on how it might have been won. There was a flood of memoirs, especially from officials who tried to justify their past actions and from persons who had been connected with the imperial household.

Descriptions of the war and of life at the front appeared in great quantities, and many went through numerous editions. Erich Maria Remarque's *All Quiet on the Western Front* (1929), and then his *The Road Back* (1931), took the country by storm. Psychological novels and psychoanalytical studies led the lists of best sellers; and plays, in order to be successful, generally had to be tragic and horrible. In art, too, this spirit was reflected, and "expressionism" or "direct action in art" was carried farther in Germany than elsewhere. Somber, geometrical, and bizarre representations of machinery, death, fate, and mental disorders were all the fashion.

The despair which was so characteristic of the middle-aged and older people in Germany—whose dreams of a settled future had been blasted by the war—was not common among the younger persons. Their plans had not been upset, nor their calculations destroyed. They merely reflected upon the hunger, the privations, the restraints of the war period, and they regarded peace as a cause for optimism. This group believed that its elders had brought on the war by a blind groping in the dark, the result of silly conventions and old-fashioned ideas. But the younger people were made of different stuff. They would not be led blindfold along the path of destruction. They would know how to handle themselves in a future crisis.

As after the humiliation of Prussia by Napoleon in 1806, German youth now believed that regeneration depended upon a higher mental and physical development of the nation. Some saw in the free, simple life of the ancient Germans the cure for despondency and national lethargy. Gymnastics, forest air, sunshine, song, these were needed to revive faith and hope. Accordingly, organized youth movements aroused widespread interest and attracted millions of recruits. Modern youth, in a traditionally Germanic manner, chose athletics as the outlet for its restless energies. In every field the Germans strove to achieve superiority over the athletes of other nations.

Sometimes freedom was confused with license. Eventually, moreover, many of the youth organizations became identified with political, religious, or class groups, and often strife ensued. The bad economic situation and the increasing ill will manifested among nations after 1929, led more and more of the young men and women to wonder if, after all, their optimism was justified. After a time, many of them turned willing ears to the blandishments of the new prophets in brown shirts, and swelled the ranks of Adolf Hitler's movement.

PARTIES AND POLITICS, 1924-1932

In 1924 the Reichstag that had been elected in 1920 was dissolved. During its session, four chancellors had striven to give stability to the republic. The two elections of 1924 eventually produced a Centrist-People's-Nationalist coalition under Dr. Hans Luther. A conciliatory foreign policy was assured when the portfolio of foreign affairs was left in the hands of Dr. Gustav Stresemann. Stresemann, indeed, remained in continuous control of the foreign office under every government from November 1923 until his death in October 1929.

A few weeks after the organization of the Luther Cabinet, President Ebert died (February 1925), and it became necessary to hold Germany's first popular presidential election. According to law, the president had to be elected on a national ticket, the candidate who received a majority of all votes cast, becoming the victor. In the event that no candidate got such a majority, a second election would have to be held. The second election would go to the nominee who received the largest number of votes.

Two elections had to be held in 1925, for in the first balloting no candidate was successful. For the second election, the parties supporting the Weimar Republic jointly nominated the Centrist leader Wilhelm Marx. The rightist parties also combined, nominating the aged and popular Field Marshal Paul von Hindenburg, hero of the Great War. The Communist Party renominated Ernst Thälmann. A spirited campaign ensued, each group striving to draw to the polls some of the millions who had neglected to vote in the first contest. The final returns (April) gave the seventy-seven year old Hindenburg almost a million votes more than the second-place Marx.

Hindenburg's election was widely regarded as a blow to the republic. The marshal, however, took the oath to support the republican constitution seriously, and his moderation soon won confidence at home and abroad.

In December 1925, after eleven months in office, the Luther Ministry resigned. It had fallen into disfavor with the Nationalists because of its sanction of the Locarno Pact. Six weeks' time and a threat of presidential dictatorship were required before another cabinet was formed, again by Luther. Soon this government, too, fell (May 1926), over a question regarding the national flag.

The succeeding Marx Ministry governed until 1928. In the elections of May 1928, the Nationalists lost heavily, whereas the Social Democrats considerably increased their parliamentary membership. The Marx coalition of Center and Right elements therefore resigned, and the Social Democrat, Hermann Müller, who nine years earlier had signed the Versailles Treaty, became the first Socialist chancellor since 1920. Müller's regime was not happy. Budgetary difficulties were immense. The acceptance of the Young Plan aroused nationalistic opposition. With the coming of the depression, the unemployment situation became critical. In March 1930, Müller resigned, and Dr. Heinrich Brüning, leader of the Centrist Party, formed a moderate coalition.

The new ministry desired to continue the policies of its predecessor, but was forced to continue in foreign affairs without Stresemann, who had died in October 1929. The government's tenure was shaky, and several times the Cabinet was saved merely because the opposition was divided among itself or because Hindenburg threatened to dissolve the Reichstag and rule as a dictator under Article 48 of the constitution if the bickering did not cease. In July 1930, after the Reichstag rejected a government budget, the President carried out his threat. The legislature was dissolved, and new elections were ordered for September.

The outstanding feature of the election of September 1930, for which twenty-seven parties nominated candidates, was the gain made by the Communist Party and the National Socialists (*Nationalsozialistische Deutsche Arbeiterpartei* or NSDAP). The Communist Party increased its membership in the Reichstag from 54 to 77 seats. The National Socialists raised their Reichstag contingent from 12 to 107, forming the second largest group in the lower house. They were led only by the Social Democrats with 143 seats. Before analyzing this success of the National Socialists or Nazis, let us consider the early history of the party and its leader, Adolf Hitler.

The future chief of the German Nazi Party was born on April 20, 1889, in Upper Austria, the son of a customs official. Against the wishes of his father, who wanted him to enter the civil service, Adolf Hitler indulged his marginal talent for drawing, eventually going to Vienna to study architecture. Failing to gain admission to the imperial art academy, he eked out an existence as a housepainter. His free time was spent in avid reading on the racial, moral, social, political, and economic problems confronting the German-speaking people in Austria and Germany. He argued with his fellow workmen, particularly over politics and economics, and he steadfastly refused to join the Austrian Social Democratic Party. On several occasions he fled before his irate fellow laborers. In the end he came to attribute his inability to get and hold a job to the machinations of the Socialists. Since he associated immorality and radicalism with Judaism, regarding socialism as a ruse of international Jewry to control the workers, the Catholic Hitler also became an anti-Semite.

In 1912 Hitler went to Munich, and when the war broke out, he requested permission to fight in the Bavarian army. Apparently he preferred not to join the Austro-Hungarian forces because he objected to the fact that the Dual Monarchy was a state composed of several nationalities rather than a truly Germanic state. He acquitted himself well in action on the western front, was wounded and gassed, and was decorated. The events of the German revolution of 1918 filled Hitler with bitterness. He remained in comparative obscurity until 1923, but then, with Ludendorff and others, participated in an unsuccessful attempt to overthrow the government. For his part in this, Hitler was sentenced to five years' imprisonment, but he was released after having served a few months.

Upon his release from prison, Hitler put new life into the National Socialist German Workers' Party, a political organization which he had joined in 1919 and which had suffered a decline in the period of his inactivity.[8] A party program of "Twenty-five Points" had been drawn up for the group by an engineer named Gottfried Feder, one of the half-dozen original colleagues of Hitler and later economic adviser to the Nazis. Eventually this outline of party policy was expanded by Hitler in a book written while he was in prison and entitled *Mein Kampf*.

According to the original pronouncements, the ultimate goal of the Hitlerites was a "third Reich,"[9] a greater Germany uniting all those of "German blood," including the Germans in Austria, Poland, the Netherlands, Czechoslovakia, and Alsace. Jews were regarded as having alien blood. The achievement of this "program for the ages" envisioned, among its most important items: abrogation of the treaties of Versailles and St. Germain; refutation of war guilt; revision of reparation; reacquisition of colonies; expulsion of all persons not of German blood; and parity with other great nations in armament. Several aspects of the program were modified in later pronouncements by Hitler, but the catchwords of the movement remained anti-Semitism and anti-Bolshevism.

A party organization was developed and the *Hakenkreuz* (hooked cross or swastika) became the Nazi emblem. As with the Italian Fascists, there was an elaborate ritual and a military ceremonial. Ordinary party members, who in 1932 numbered 700,000, paid monthly dues and were expected to be faithful attendants at meetings, to which there generally was an admission charge. Above this rank and file were the brown-shirted *Sturmabteilungen* (SA), or "Storm Troops," assigned to protect Nazi meetings and break up opposition political gatherings. There was also a smaller group of black-shirted "Elite Guards," the *Schutzstafflen* (SS), who were as-

[8]Hitler's Nazis were formed out of a political fringe group called the German Workers' Party (DAP). In 1918 Hitler was asked by some military men to investigate various groups and see if any might be useful to the army. Instead of "spying" on the DAP, Hitler lectured to it on several occasions and then joined it. Rapidly he rose to its leadership and, in 1920, renamed it the National Socialist German Workers' Party.
[9]The first Reich was the Holy Roman Empire; the second, from 1871 to 1918.

signed as bodyguards for Nazi leaders and to carry out especially difficult missions.

For purposes of agitation and organization the Reich was divided into districts and cells, each covered by trained speakers. Hitler was a highly successful orator, able to sway large audiences, but it appeared to be his manner of speaking more than the content of his speeches that produced an electric reaction among crowds. He became popular with German women and the nationalist youth, which later was organized in a Hitler Youth Society.

One of the pillars of the early Nazi movement was the white-collar section of the middle class. When judged by income and standard of living, many of the 3,500,000 individuals in this category fell into proletarian ranks. Yet, unlike the workers, they did not look to the Socialists for economic relief. Class pride made them seek aid elsewhere, and Hitler's movement promised help. Equally poor, equally unwilling to acknowledge a common interest with the working class, and equally ready to try Nazi remedies, were thousands of former army officers, soldiers' widows, and retired tradesmen.

There were numerous other Nazi enthusiasts. The anti-Semitism appealed to professional people who resented the competition of Jews in their areas of special interest. Much support came from debt-saddled peasants, particularly in southern Germany, who had no sympathy with Marxist attitudes towards private property.

University students and graduates formed another source of Nazi strength. The number of university students in the Reich increased by 60 per cent between 1914 and 1930, and thousands of unemployed educated persons had come to despair of any improvement in their lot under the existing system. Any program of revolution seemed promising to them. Finally, a number of industrialists, such as Fritz Thyssen, who feared Communism more than National Socialism, supported Nazism.

In the two weeks preceding the election of September 1930, the Nazis held more than 30,000 meetings. They constantly reminded their listeners of Germany's "enslavement" and of the Government's "subserviency" to the Allies. The "war-guilt lie" was furiously attacked, and reparation was denounced. Hitler's election manifesto urged the voters to "send the betrayers of their future to the devil." In protest against existing conditions and against the apparent inability of the groups in control to remedy them, the voters, as has been indicated, cast their ballots in unprecedented numbers for both the Nazis and the Communists. Yet Chancellor Brüning was able to muster sufficient moderate support in the Reichstag to remain in office until May 1932.

A presidential election was due in 1932. Both Hindenburg and Hitler were candidates. Ernst Thälmann again was the candidate of the Communist Party, and the extreme nationalists nominated Theodor Düsterberg. Hindenburg received 7,300,000 more votes than Hitler, and Thälmann ran a poor third. Because Hindenburg had not quite obtained the majority required under the Weimar constitution, there was a second election, which he won easily. The aging general began his second term in his eighty-fifth year.

A few weeks after the presidential contest, Brüning's Centrist-Socialist Government resigned. The Chancellor's system of government by emergency decree had accomplished little. Unemployment figures had risen to 6,000,000. Nationalists therefore clamored for more effective action. The President selected as the new Chancellor Lieutenant-Colonel Franz von Papen, the same man who, in 1915, had carried on espionage activities in the United States during the period of her neutrality. Papen chose for his colleagues a group of arch-conservatives. It was evident that the new government could not command a majority in the Reichstag; therefore that body was immediately dissolved. The resulting elections (July 1932) gave the Hitlerites 230 seats, an increase of 123 since 1930. They now had exactly as many deputies as the Social Democrats and Centrists combined. When the Reichstag convened, Captain Hermann Wilhelm Göring, one of Hitler's lieutenants, was elected Speaker. The house then adjourned until September. When it reassembled, the Chancellor immediately dissolved it and ordered still another election. Papen had the support of Hindenburg, but was denounced by the Nazis and the Communists as a dictator.

In the election of November 1932 the vote of the Nazis fell off by about 2,000,000, whereas the Communist Party gained 700,000 votes. No party or group of parties gained control of the Reichstag, and the Papen Cabinet therefore resigned. Hindenburg, apparently influenced by von Papen, now invited Hitler, as the leader of the largest political party, to form a government; but when the Nazi leader demanded dictatorial powers, the President turned to General Kurt von Schleicher. The new government lacked the backing in the Reichstag, which was necessary to ensure longevity. Eight weeks later (January 1933) Schleicher resigned and Hindenburg accepted Hitler as Chancellor—when the future dictator temporarily abandoned his demand for dictatorial power.[10]

[10] The coming to power of the National Socialists in Germany probably has aroused as much diverse opinion as any one historical question. Alan Bullock, in his *Hitler: A Study in Tyranny,* has emphasized the importance of Hitler's personality in National Socialist successes. Another school, finding the causes of the Nazi rise to power in the international political situation imposed upon Germany at Versailles, has been represented, among others, by French historian Maurice Baumont. A number of historians have seen the Nazi's taking control of the German state as a particularly German phenomenon based on German national characteristics and history, finding the roots of the National Socialist mind variously in Martin Luther, in nineteenth-century German romanticism, in the German philosopher Friedrich Nietzsche, or in a whole series of nineteenth-century writers who developed pseudoscientific racial theories. Among writers who have held this sort of view, the most important are the Frenchman Edmond Vermeil, the Englishman A. J. P. Taylor, and the American author of the best-selling *Rise and Fall of the Third Reich,*

GERMANY
before and after
World War I
Arrows indicate countries to
which Germany ceded territory
(blackened areas, incl. Danzig).

From Landman, J., *Outline History of the World Since 1914*, 1934.
Courtesy, Barnes and Noble, Inc.

ECONOMIC RECOVERY AND DECLINE, 1924-1932

The German Empire of pre-1914 days was a closely knit economic organism of great wealth and power. The First World War completely dislocated this intricate mechanism and made necessary widespread readjustments.

Not only did the war cause material damage and death or incapacity to millions of citizens, but the peace treaty deprived Germany of one tenth of her population and one eighth of her European land area. She lost two-fifths of her coal and substantial portions of her agricultural production, colonies, and foreign investments, most of her merchant marine, and nearly all foreign trade contracts. In addition, she had to face a hostile Europe and suffer temporary occupation of her chief industrial region, the Ruhr. In one respect Germany was fortunate: there was no need to reconstruct war-torn areas, since most of the fighting had been done on foreign soil.

William L. Shirer. Still others have called attention to the mass German overreaction to the threat of Communism, the impact of the Great Depression, the role of the German generals in preparing the way for Hitler, and the negative influence of the Prussian nobles (Junkers) on Germany. A later opinion is the thesis of David Schoenbaum that the Nazi revolution was launched against "bourgeois and industrial" society with "bourgeois and industrial" means by a party that was a natural by-product of a rapidly industrializing social order. See: David Schoenbaum, *Hitler's Social Revolution, Class and Status in Nazi Germany 1933–1939* (New York: Doubleday & Company, Inc., 1966).

During the years immediately following the war, Germany sank lower and lower in the economic scale until nadir was reached with the economic collapse of 1923. Just as dissolution seemed imminent, government and people united in a determined effort to save the fatherland and rebuild its economic structure. Thereafter an upward trend set in which continued for six years, until the middle of 1929. This boom period placed Germany in a position where her industrial development and standard of living seemed second only to those in the United States.

This "industrial efflorescence" was the result of many causes. The enormous foreign sale of German currency and notes, the inflation, and then the wholesale repudiation of the paper money added about $2,000,000,000 to the real worth of the country. Benefit also was derived from foreign capital, especially after the Dawes Plan went into effect. Another factor that helped recovery was the introduction of standardization and scientific management into German business and industrial life. Although this tendency sometimes was carried to extremes, it generally effected astounding savings and raised the average production per worker. This reorganization also raised the output of the coal mines. Added to the traditional renown of German chemists, the tendency toward greater efficiency made Germany the world's largest postwar exporter of chemicals.

In addition, the Germans, realizing the value of trust combinations for greater efficiency in production, perfected the "vertical" trust system, "uniting all stages and parts of the industrial process, such as coal mines, iron mines, steel mills, and shipyards." Moreover, the government supported this process of combination. Perhaps the greatest trust-builder was Hugo Stinnes. At the time of his death (1924), Stinnes was said to have had an interest in 1400 business undertakings and to have controlled a fifth of Germany's total production. The prewar tendency towards cartelization was perpetuated, although the general influence of the domestic cartel (an association of independent businesses formed to regulate prices, production, and markets for the benefit of the former) declined as international cartels became more important.

Germany's economic recovery, gained through all the avenues just listed, was not of long duration. Even while prosperity rode high, factors appeared that forecast approaching decline. It became increasingly difficult to secure foreign loans and reparation quarrels continued. The development of economic nationalism raised foreign tariff walls against German goods. Because of these and other adverse factors, there was a gradual but steady increase in the number of unemployed university graduates and workers of both the blue- and white-collar types. During the depression years following 1930, the situation became acute, and by 1932 Germany, with her population of 64,000,000, had an army of unemployed numbering 6,500,000. Unemployment-insurance schemes and doles seemed inadequate to meet the problem, and thus campaign material was provided for both Nazis and Communists.

The government of Chancellor Brüning (1930–1932) strove to deal with the crisis, but the international situation precluded any domestic solution of the difficulties. Germany had placed undue reliance upon foreign loans. Consequently, a crash was destined to come as soon as external conditions made further loans impracticable. Then Great Britain, suffering from a loss of gold reserves herself, found it impossible to continue making short-term loans to the Reich. Slight assistance was received from the Federal Reserve Bank in the United States, but Germany was so close to bankruptcy that only concerted international action could be of avail. The only such important international actions taken were the Hoover Moratorium of June 1931 and the Lausanne Reparation Conference of 1932. Neither helped to retard greatly the increasing stagnation of German economic life.

GERMAN FOREIGN RELATIONS, 1919-1932

From 1919 to 1932 it was the chief aim of German diplomacy to gain for the fatherland readmission into the family of nations. German statesmen, however, were divided on the question of whether the new orientation should look towards Soviet Russia or the Allies. The group that preferred to look eastward advocated alliance with the Bolsheviks and defiance of the treaty restrictions. Those who looked westward proposed the fulfillment of treaty obligations and reconciliation with former Allied enemies.

At first it appeared that the pro-Russian viewpoint might triumph. In 1922 the German and Russian delegates to a Genoa Economic Conference concluded a trade treaty at Rapallo. Four years later the principles of the Rapallo agreement were reaffirmed in a treaty of friendship negotiated in Berlin. Then the eastward trend of policy temporarily was halted by those who advocated "a policy of fulfillment and reconciliation." These men were led by Dr. Stresemann, who so dominated German foreign policy between 1924 and 1929 that the period often is called "the Stresemann era."

Born in 1878, in Berlin, the son of a beer merchant, Stresemann grew up to be a skillful industrial organizer. In 1907 he was elected to the Reichstag as a National Liberal, and ten years later he became head of this party of big business. During the war, he advocated the vigorous prosecution of hostilities, and after the revolution he reorganized his followers into the German People's Party, which favored a monarchy but was willing to support the republic to secure peace and business revival.

In August 1923, Stresemann became Chancellor, but the internal disorder and the foreign occupation of the Ruhr led to his downfall within a few months. Appointed Foreign Minister by his successor, Chancellor Joseph Wirth, he occupied this post until his death in October 1929. The cardinal points of Stresemann's foreign policy were reconciliation with France and Germany's re-entry into the community of nations as a respected partner. A gifted orator, honest and tactful, he soon acquired general trust, though he did have numerous enemies, both at home and abroad. In 1926 Stresemann, Briand, and Austen Chamberlain were awarded the Nobel Prize for their contributions (at Locarno) to the cause of world peace. Stresemann was seriously ill most of his days, and the strenuous duties of office eventually claimed his life.

As Foreign Minister, Stresemann was responsible for the discontinuance of passive resistance in the Ruhr. He eloquently urged adoption of the Dawes Plan, thus preparing the way for evacuation of the Ruhr, the restoration of foreign confidence in Germany, and the negotiation of commerical treaties. His greatest work was the negotiation of the Locarno treaties (1925) and the admission of Germany into the League (1926).

Since permanent peace in Europe was improbable as long as France was haunted by the specter of German recovery and revenge and as long as Germany feared French designs on the Rhineland, Stresemann several times suggested to France the signing of a guaranty pact. In 1925 his proposal met with favor. The result was the Locarno Pact, which was to go into force immediately upon Germany's admission to the League. The republic accordingly applied for membership and, in September 1926, after some irritating delay, Germany was unanimously elected to membership.

German membership in the League soon led to further favorable developments. In 1927 the last Allied commissions in Germany were withdrawn. In the same year a German was appointed to the Permanent Mandates Commission. In 1928, largely because of the efforts of Stresemann, Germany adhered to the Kellog Pact for the renunciation of war as an instrument of national policy. At the meeting of the League Assembly in 1928, the way was opened for a renewal of reparation parleys, which led to the adoption of the Young Plan (1929) and the complete evacuation of the Rhine territory (1930).

After Stresemann's death, his foreign policies were continued for a time, but in 1931 the conduct of foreign relations became increasingly difficult—largely because of the activities of the various nationalistic groups and the diplomatic intransigence of France. Although many of the postwar grievances that had irritated the Germans were removed by the close of 1932, there remained as disturbing factors the questions of Germany's eastern frontiers, union with Austria, reacquisition of colonies, repudiation of war guilt, equality with the other great powers in armaments, and further revision of the reparation schedule. Early in 1933 these problems were passed on to a wholly new German Government—a National Socialist Government.

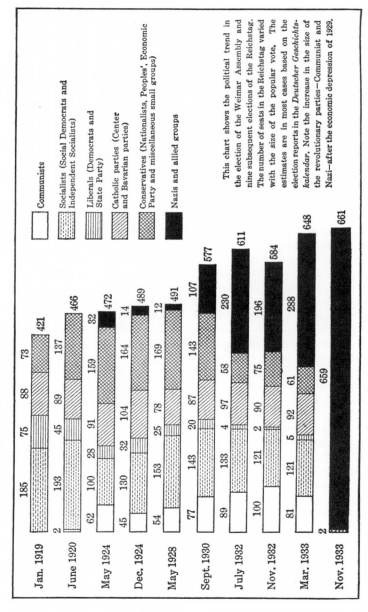

THE GERMAN ELECTIONS, 1919–1933

Reprinted with permission from Slosson, P. W., *Europe Since 1870*, 1935.
Published by Houghton Mifflin Co.

DER FÜHRER

On January 28, 1933, after an incumbency of only eight weeks, Chancellor von Schleicher resigned because of the President's refusal to allow the dissolution of a hostile Reichstag. Two days later the chief ministerial post went to Adolf Hitler, whose party held 196 of the 584 seats in the Chamber. Associated with Hitler in the Cabinet was a group of nationalistic conservatives, headed by Vice Chancellor Papen; Dr. Alfred Hugenberg, leader of the National People's Party as Minister of Commerce and Agriculture; and Konstantin von Neurath, nonparty nationalist, as Minister of Foreign Affairs. The inclusion of these conservatives, to check any "dangerous" Nazi experiment, apparently was made a condition of Hitler's appointment by Hindenburg.

Since the Nazis were in a minority in the Cabinet and in the Reichstag, Hitler demanded dissolution of the Chamber and new elections on March 5. During the pre-election weeks, the government instituted repressive measures against the Communist, Social Democratic, and Center parties. Papen, moreover, was appointed Reich Commissioner for Prussia, a post equivalent to that of Prussian Premier. He promptly brought about dismissal of the Prussian Diet and ordered new elections to be held simultaneously with those for the national legislature. Thus the Nazis, confident of victory, also hoped to gain control of a body that had been a stronghold of socialism.

A few days before the voting the Reichstag building in Berlin was nearly destroyed by fire. The followers of Hitler placed the onus for the deed upon the Communist Party. The Communists, however, pointed out that a subterranean corridor led from the residence of Nazi Reichstag President Göring to the basement of the Reichstag building, and they accused Hitler's followers of plotting the affair to discredit Communism. Further restrictions now were put on the electioneering rights of the antigovernment parties.[11]

In an atmosphere tense with excitement, 39,000,000 citizens cast their ballots on the 5th of March. More than 17,000,000 voted for National Socialist candidates, and an additional 3,000,000 supported the allies of the Nazis, the German National People's Party. The Nazis captured 288 of the 647 seats in the new Reichstag and the Nationalists 52. The Nazi-Nationalist coalition thus received ap-

---

[11] In December 1933 Marinus van der Lubbe, a young Netherlands Communist, was convicted of setting fire to the building. A German and three Bulgarian Communists who were held with him were acquitted. The Netherlander, who seemed to be in a stupor during the trial but who doggedly maintained that he had set the fire without the help of accomplices, was executed in January 1934. A recent study holds that van der Lubbe alone set the fire, as he had claimed at the trial, in the hope that it would trigger a rising against the Nazis. As it turned out, however, the blaze worked to the advantage of the National Socialists. See: Fritz Tobias, *The Reichstag Fire* (New York: G. P. Putnam's Sons, 1964).

proximately 52 per cent of the popular vote and a majority in the Reichstag.

On March 23, 1933, the new Reichstag, by a vote of 441 to 94, passed an "Enabling Act" called the Law to Combat the Misery of the People and Reich. In effect, it suspended the constitution and endowed the Hitler Government with dictatorial power.[12] To explain to the world this startling development became the function of a specially created "Ministry of Propaganda and Enlightenment" headed by Dr. Paul Joseph Goebbels.

It may be convenient now to recall some of the factors that underlay the Nazi rise to power. The war and the peace settlement left Germany crushed, spiritually and materially. The Germans could not easily forget the humiliation of the defeat and of the "dictate of Versailles." The continuing hostile attitude of France; the quarrels over the Ruhr, the Rhineland occupation, the Saar, and reparation; the wrangling over disarmament—all these fed the anger of many Germans. In such circumstances, the republic's policy of reconciliation and fulfillment, and its apparent inability to assert itself more strongly in international affairs rankled in the hearts of many, especially the younger war veterans and the youth that believed itself deprived of a glamorous and secure future by the "treachery" and "cowardice" of seemingly complacent republican politicians. During a temporary economic revival from 1924 to 1929, these factors remained somewhat in the background. But they continued to exist, and it required only a few years of hard times and increasing unemployment to bring them out in full force.

Many of the Germans, too, were weary of the manner in which the democratic parliamentary system functioned. Those Germans who could remember the days when order and discipline prevailed in the Reichstag, and many of those who had merely heard or read about such days, were impatient with the bickering and quarreling that characterized the republican lower house. Increasingly, many Germans became convinced of the need for a "strong man" to restore German prosperity and prestige.

The republic seemed unable to pay due attention to the inner feelings or psychology of many citizens. The official toleration of attempts to drag down the ideals and heroes of imperial Germany, and the abandonment of other traditions popular with large sections of the populace, alienated the young university students, the conservative peasants, the aristocrats, believers in Germany's "mission," and the rank-and-file war veterans who hated politicians. The Nazi leaders understood these grievances, and with their remarkable propaganda methods capitalized on them. Oratory, posters, uniforms, ritual, anti-Semitism, and the dynamic personality of Adolf Hitler

---

[12]The negative votes all were cast by the SPD members who attended the session. The remaining twenty-six Socialist deputies and all eighty-one Communists were abroad, hiding, or under arrest.

attracted millions of Germans at a time when the alternatives appeared to offer worse depression and continued foreign impasse.

Having surrendered its legislative powers, the Reichstag, elected in March 1933, adjourned, whereas Chancellor Hitler proceeded to coordinate under the Nazi aegis the political, economic, and cultural life of the nation (a process termed by the Nazis *Gleichschaltung*). The supreme and final authority in all matters was Hitler himself, later to be known officially as *Der Führer* (an appellation he had assumed some years before the Nazis gained control of the government). This principle of leadership (*Führerprinzip*) was calculated to emphasize the unity of purpose of the whole nation.

ANTI-SEMITISM

The most spectacular immediate consequence of the National Socialist triumph was a reign of anti-Semitism, and most prominent among the anti-Semites were Hermann Göring and Julius Streicher.[13] Göring was a World War I air ace and one of the most militant Nazis. He had participated in the Hitler-Ludendorff Putsch of 1923 and then had fled to Italy, where he had studied the Fascist system. Now Göring became Deputy-Minister of the Interior for Prussia, Commissioner of Aviation, and Reich Minister without Portfolio. Streicher had been a schoolteacher in Nuremberg and was the editor of *Der Stürmer,* the most violently anti-Semitic (and often obscene) newspaper in Germany. Under their leadership, the Storm Troops and other Hitlerites launched wild attacks upon the Jewish population. Göring explained the situation by saying: "We have been telling the people for years that they might settle accounts with the traitors. We stand by our word: accounts are being settled." After a time, and partly in response to foreign protests, physical violence against Jews lessened—only to reappear with greater fury in 1938.

The first far-reaching anti-Semitic legislation was a civil service law of April 1933. This act ordered the dismissal of all officials who were "non-Aryan" or whose previous political activity did not offer surety that they would "at all times act unreservedly for the national state." It also purged the professions of Jews.

A "non-Aryan" was defined as any person descended "from non-Aryan, particularly Jewish, parents or grandparents." It was sufficient if only one grandparent had "professed the Jewish religion." Later it was decreed that a person with a Jewish great grandfather or yet more remote Jewish ancestor, even if the far-removed predecessor had been baptized, might also be regarded as non-Aryan and ineligible for office. Aryans married to non-Aryans were placed under the same restrictions.

[13] According to the census of 1925, the Jews in Germany numbered 560,000 or 0.9 per cent of the total population.

Through this law and its successors, the civil services and professions were ruthlessly "cleansed" not merely of Jews, but of all elements objectionable to the Nazis. By the end of 1938 there were virtually no practicing Jews or anti-Nazi Aryans in the professions. Tens of thousands of these had been placed under "protective arrest" in concentration camps. From 1938, no Jews were admitted to German schools. Eventually the Jews were barred from any connection with the stage, musical performances, the cinema, and journalism. Jewish artists could appear only before Jewish audiences; they were forbidden to present the works of Aryan composers or authors.

Inasmuch as the program of the Nazis excluded Jews from the fellowship of "German people," the authorities altered the laws governing citizenship. In 1933, the government decided to withdraw German citizenship at will from "undesirables" who had been naturalized by the Weimar Republic and from individuals who, having fled abroad, conducted anti-Nazi propaganda or refused to return on the demand of the National Socialist Government. The property of such persons and of any other "antistate" elements was made subject to confiscation. In 1935 all Jews were deprived of German citizenship and classified merely as subjects (*Staatsangehörige*).

The actions of the government were supplemented by the anti-Semitic activities of private groups and individuals. Most firms eventually dismissed all Jewish employees. No books by Jews were to be published in the Reich. On May 10, 1933, bonfires were made in a number of cities and university towns of the works of about 150 writers whose volumes were regarded as Jewish, or in any other way "un-German."

Throughout 1936 and 1937 the Nuremberg or Ghetto Laws of September 1935 were put into effect. These forbade marital and extramarital relations between Jews and citizens of "German or kindred blood," deprived all Jews of German citizenship and political rights, and forbade any German female under forty-five to assist in a Jewish household. A decree of April 1938 required all Jews who possessed property worth more than 5000 marks ($2000) to render an itemized report of their belongings to the state, which could then confiscate the excess for use in a "Four-Year Plan" to revitalize the economy. Another order compelled every Jew who did not already have given names that were officially classed as Jewish to add "Israel" or "Sarah" to his or her name. Jewish children born in future might be given only such names as were to be found in a permissible list; and the names had to be "spelled in the Yiddish manner so as to stamp them as foreign and ridiculous in the eyes of the Germans." In the fall of 1938 there came a period of utter tragedy, during which the Jews were eliminated from the economic life of the Third Reich.

Following a report that Poland would refuse to readmit any Polish Jews living abroad whose passports were not validated by the end of October 1938, the Nazis rounded up thousands of Polish Jews who had long been resident in Germany, herded them aboard rail-road cars, shipped them to the Polish border, and there forced them to walk across into Polish territory. The Polish authorities strove to resist this wholesale dumping of freezing and panic-stricken unfortu-nates, and finally they threatened, in retaliation, to treat similarly Germans who were living in Poland. Official negotiations followed, the whole affair was labeled a "misunderstanding," and the deporta-tions ended—but not the tragedy.

One of the deported Polish Jews sent a postcard to his seventeen-year-old son in Paris, telling of his unhappy adventure. The boy, Herschel Grynszpan, brooded over the situation and then went to the German Embassy, apparently determined to kill the German Ambassador. When he arrived at the embassy, he shot the third secretary. Two days later the young diplomat died. In reprisal for the killing, a horrible attack on the Jews broke loose in Germany early in the morning of November 10. Propaganda Minister Goeb-bels maintained that the attacks were the spontaneous result of the "justifiable and understandable anger of the German people over the cowardly Jewish murder of a German diplomat," but the terror obviously was organized and directed. The government, after a time, "requested" the population to cease demonstrating and promised to give a "final answer" to the assassination "by way of legislation and ordinance."

The promised decrees soon appeared. Holding German Jewry collectively responsible for the act of a brooding Polish adolescent in Paris, the Berlin Government eliminated all Jews from the econ-omic life of Germany. The authorities imposed a collective fine of $400,000,000 on the Jews of Germany. The fine was assessed in the form of a capital levy of 20 per cent of the property of all Jews own-ing more than $2000 worth of goods. Further decrees eliminated Jews, in 1939, from the retail, mail-order, and handicraft trades, and "Aryanized," at bargain prices, the remaining Jewish businesses.

At this point, Jews were relegated to full ghetto life. In the cities certain districts were closed to Jewish dwellers and certain streets were barred to Jewish pedestrians. Jews were forbidden to drive automobiles. Those Jewish people who had fled the Third Reich, leaving much of their material wealth behind them, now appeared to be far more fortunate than those who remained behind in the hope that they could weather the storm and that life eventually would return to normal.

POLITICAL AND ECONOMIC "COORDINATION"

Soon after Hitler came to power, steps were taken to create a totalitarian state. A decree of March 1933 dissolved all provincial legislatures, except the newly elected one in Prussia, and ordered their reconstitution under Nazi control. The several state cabinets were empowered to promulgate laws, even laws contrary to the state constitutions, without consulting their respective diets. On the first anniversary of the Hitler regime (1934), the Reichstag unanimously adopted a measure abolishing the "popular representation of the states" and authorized the Reich Government to "determine new constitutional law." The unanimous acceptance of this bill on the same day by the Reichsrat, the direct parliamentary representative of the states, automatically made that body superfluous. Municipal diets were abolished on the second anniversary of the Hitler regime.

Meanwhile, an edict of 1933 had placed over each state a Reich Regent, chosen by the chancellor. In Prussia, where Hitler himself was Regent, he appointed Göring as Minister President. Göring thus became *the* ruler of the largest German state, responsible only to Hitler. Perhaps largely because Göring objected to a diminution of his power in Prussia, a plan to obliterate the old state boundaries and redivide the Reich into new administrative units of approximately equal population size was postponed indefinitely.

While the superiority of the central government thus was being established, the National Socialist Party became identified with the state itself. All other parties were abolished. Freemasonry was forbidden, and the trade unions were broken up, their leaders arrested and their buildings and funds confiscated. Simultaneously, veteran's organizations, such as the Steel Helmet, and conservative political groups, such as the German National People's Party, were absorbed into Nazi ranks. A law of July 1933 confirmed the fact that the Nazi party was "the only political party in Germany." Another law of 1933 followed the Italian example by connecting inseparably the Nazi Party with the state. Ernst Röhm, Storm Troop leader, and Rudolf Hess, deputy leader of the party, were made members of the cabinet. With the creation of a *Jugendführer* or "Youth Leader," and the subordination to its incumbent (Baldur von Schirach) of all German youth organizations, the state became politically totalitarian.

On the economic level, indecision and conflicting theories marked the Nazi economic way, but gradually there evolved a program of state supervision and planning. At first the largest industries were coordinated by the appointment of Nazi supervisors. Business, professional, labor, and peasant organizations were purged of "objectionable" members and reconstituted in accordance with the new National Socialist supervisors' schemes. In July 1933, however, the Chancellor warned his followers against unauthorized interference in private business affairs. Thereafter the Nazi supervisors, who often had been appointed because of party service rather than executive ability, gradually were removed from control.

To provide immediate relief for the unemployed some novel schemes to "make" work were advanced. Within a year, unemployment figures were reduced from 6,000,000 to 4,000,000. This was accomplished chiefly by requiring certain industries, for example, the Ruhr mines, to take on more men than production would normally warrant. In addition, several hundred thousand young men were enlisted in a "voluntary" labor corps. Members of the corps received food, shelter, and small wages in return for work on governmental projects and large estates.

To replace the trade-unions that were abolished in 1933 and the employers' associations that were dissolved in 1934, there was established the German Labor Front. Controlled by Dr. Robert Ley, this body was intended to coordinate all German employers and workers. Its prime function was the indoctrination of Nazi principles, but it was given some power to arbitrate in labor disputes. Associated with this Labor Front was a recreational organization called "Strength through Joy." It arranged inexpensive vacation trips for workers and their families.

Relations between capital and labor were regulated by laws of 1933 and 1934. Strikes and lockouts were prohibited. Employers with more than twenty workers were designated as "leaders" whereas their employees officially became "followers." The usual conflicts between labor and management were to be resolved by appointed "labor trustees."

In foreign trade and commerce the Nazis put into practice all the principles of economic nationalism. Every means was employed to create a self-sufficient balanced economy, that is, to make Germany an autarkic state. Pressure was exerted to decrease imports and increase exports. Raw materials were rationed. Tariffs were raised and citizens were urged to "buy home products." Important to this drive for international economic independence was the development of synthetics (*Ersatzmittel*).

Agrarian affairs were placed under Minister of Agriculture Richard W. Darré. Believing that Germany should in the future depend for her leaders upon a hereditary, Aryan, landholding nobility, Darré was instrumental in the promulgation (1933) of a novel Hereditary Farms Law. In order to create a new "farmer aristocracy," which would eventually be the chief source of strength of the German people, it was ordained that every farm of fewer than 309 acres must pass undivided, upon the owner's death, to the legal heir. The new owner was made responsible for the education and professional training of the immediate remaining heirs. Only the head of the homestead was to enjoy the *honorary title* of "farmer" (*Bauer*). Hereditary farms could not be sold, mortgaged, or attached for debt. Only those might be farmers who were able to prove their Aryan ancestry to 1800.

Economic conditions showed some improvement by 1935. The national income rose above that of 1932, and the official unemployment figure fell to 1,750,000. The national wealth seemed to be more equally distributed, and the specter of starvation was banished. Some of this development was attributable to the widespread official work-creation schemes and the establishment of labor camps for youths; some to intensive rearmament. This was true particularly after Hitler's repudiation (1935) of the restrictive military clauses of the Versailles Treaty. The conscription and equipment of a large army were of considerable influence in the further reduction of unemployment figures.

And then, in 1936, Germany really moved into a "war economy." The entire economic life of the Third Reich was subordinated to the demands of a Four-Year Plan. "In four years," said Hitler, "Germany must be entirely independent of foreign countries with respect to all those materials which can in any way be produced through German capability, through German chemistry, or by our machine and mining industries." The execution of the plan was entrusted to Göring, although Dr. Schacht was Minister of Economics. When Nazi arms production continued to replace traditional financial programs, Schacht resigned as Minister of Economics and was relieved as head of the Reichsbank. Dr. Walther Immanuel Funk, a long time friend and economic adviser of Hitler, took Schacht's place.

The late spring of 1938 found the government concentrating on three main domestic items. First, to repeat, there was the Four-Year Plan. The successful completion of this was all the more necessary because foreign countries were becoming less eager to trade with Germany on her own terms. Germany wanted raw materials but would pay for them only in goods or in special marks that had little utility, and often payment was long deferred. Trade could not flourish in such circumstances.[14]

Secondly, there was the desire to weld Germany's potentially great military might into an efficient whole. The army, in its mechanized units, was not functioning as smoothly as had been hoped. The speed and competence of the Czechoslovak mobilization in May 1938, when a crisis seemed to have been reached over the Sudetenland, convinced the Nazis that they had further preparations to make. Simultaneously, fortification work was pushed at a feverish pace along the western frontier, where the German complement of the French Maginot Line was to be made impenetrable.

To combat a growing labor shortage, a decree of 1938 made all state members subject to conscription for short-term labor service "on nationally urgent tasks." Compensation for such conscript labor was to equal that for similar private labor, and the Reich Labor Trustees were empowered to establish maximum wages for all work. The labor decree applied to every male and female capable of working. Thus did the Nazis, with their totalitarian politics and economics, prepare for the total war which they precipitated in 1939.

[14] The Germans were especially fond of paying their debts with razor blades and mouth organs, and in at least one case with a hippopotamus. See: D. Miller, *You Can't Do Business With Hitler*, 2 ed. (Boston, 1942).

CULTURE AND RELIGION

The coordination of German culture (literature, the press, music, painting, and so on) was entrusted to a Reich Culture Chamber under the direction of Joseph Goebbels. Through this body the Reich intended to "determine the intellectual course" and cleanse the national spiritual life of all that was non-Nazi or non-Aryan. An extreme censorship was established, and cultural activities came to be largely political and propagandistic. "Anyone who dares to question the National Socialist outlook," said a Nazi official, "must be branded as a traitor."

The chief task of the schools came to be "the education of the young for service . . . in the spirit of National Socialism." Objectivity in the teaching of history was discarded as "one of the numerous fallacies of liberalism." To students in the secondary schools and universities it was made clear that "a good examination record will be valuable only if accompanied by a good SA record." In the curricula, main emphasis was placed on the inculcation of Nazi racial theories and the development of strong physiques through athletics and through compulsory labor on farms and in camps. The traditional list of German heroes was extended to include Adolf Hitler, Leo Schlageter (killed while resisting the French occupation of the Ruhr), and Horst Wessel (composer of the Nazi party song and victim of a fatal brawl in 1930).

It could hardly be expected that the judicial system of Germany would remain unaltered. The legal system, based largely upon Roman law (which supposedly "served the interests of the materialist system of the world") was to be scrapped for a system resting upon German common law (*Volksrecht*). Thus justice would be brought in closer touch with "the German consciousness," and the strong forces of the nation would be protected against the weak elements. Since "the individual is nothing, while the people is everything," justice must be based upon the popular feeling of right as much as on legal texts. The new justice was exemplified in a decree that established tribunals called "People's Courts." These courts were, in general, to be composed of two judges and three laymen, all appointed by Hitler. Their jurisdiction was over cases of high treason, a term which was so defined that it might include even the distribution of a banned newspaper. Choice of defense counsel before these tribunals was subject to the approval of the court president, and there was no provision for appeal. The extreme penalty for treason was decapitation by an ax.

Coordination in the Third Reich encountered its most persistent opposition in the sphere of religion. Until 1933 German Protestantism comprised 29 groups. To achieve unity and control, a group of Nazi "German Christians" moved to establish a single Protestant Church under a bishop appointed by the Führer. To forestall such action, representatives of the various churches organized a German

Evangelical Church Union, to be presided over by a Lutheran bishop (for the Lutherans formed the majority of German Protestants). The first man chosen for this post was Dr. Friedrich von Bodelschwingh. Since he was prominent chiefly for social welfare work and had not been identified with any political faction, it was hoped that the government would refrain from interference.

But the German Christians were not content. This was particularly true of Dr. Ludwig Müller, Nazi chaplain and friend of the Chancellor, who wished himself to be national bishop. He and his followers refused to accept Bodelschwingh's election. In Prussia, moreover, Göring declared that the churches had no right to act without his approval. Accordingly, he appointed a lawyer, Dr. August Jäger, to be Reich Church Commissioner for Prussia. When Jäger proceeded to dissolve all local church councils, appoint German Christians to clerical offices, and use Storm Troops to enforce his edicts, Bodelschwingh resigned (June 1933). Strenuous efforts simultaneously were made to convert all pastors and theological students to the German Christian point of view. Parallel developments took place in other predominantly Protestant German states.

The strife led President von Hindenburg to plead for harmony within church ranks. As a consequence, Jäger was dismissed, and deputies of the Müller and Bodelschwingh factions met to draft a constitution. The completed document provided for a Lutheran Reich Bishop elected by a national synod. A July election was set for a vote by Protestant church membership. The government actively supported the German Christian position and hampered the opposition. As a result, the German Christians gained control of the national synod and elevated Müller to the office of *Reichsbischof*.

The strife was not yet ended. There was a division of opinion among Bishop Müller's followers. Extremists wished to do away with the Old Testament and end the split between Protestantism and Catholicism by eventually uniting all Aryan Germans in one national church. Led by a fiery wartime submarine commander, the Rev. Martin Niemöller, some thousands of anti-Müllerites now formed a Pastors' Emergency League. In January 1934, Müller, uneasy over the opposition and the growing membership of the Pastors' Emergency League, attempted by decree to make himself dictator. This only increased the ardor of the opposition, and the decree was rescinded.

The German Christians then induced several of the regional churches, in Saxony and Brandenburg, for example, to surrender their traditional autonomy and accept the full authority of Bishop Müller. But the opposition in other areas continued. The Pastors' Emergency League was disbanded, but its work was carried on by a Confessional Synod headed by Niemöller and the Protestant bishops of Bavaria and Württemberg. This synod refused to regard the Nazi revolution as a revelation of the Divine Will or to serve two masters:

their God and the Nazi's hand-picked leaders. The reply to this position was the arrest, suspension, transfer, or retirement of hundreds of pastors and the removal of the two southern German bishops. This last action led to widespread protest meetings.

Thus far, Hitler had taken little public part in the conflict with the church. He adopted the attitude that, as long as it remained loyal to the state, the church might settle its own difficulties. But in September 1935 he decreed the supremacy of the Nazi State over the Protestant Church. The Reich Bishop was shorn of his authority, and control of nondoctrinal church affairs was placed in the hands of Hanns Kerrl, Minister for Church Affairs. The new minister was placed in charge of the personnel, property, and finances of the Protestant churches. Henceforth, resistance to Nazi church policy would constitute lawbreaking.

In 1937, it was made a crime to collect or contribute money for Niemöller's Confessional Synod or any other church group not approved by the Minister for Church Affairs. Only church news that had the approval of Kerrl might be published, and he usually passed only information emanating from the German Christian movement, still led by Müller. Pastors who displeased the authorities were jailed without trial. Niemöller, incarcerated since 1937, was tried secretly in 1938 on charges of sedition. The court freed him on all major charges, but the police rearrested him and, without publishing any new charge, placed him in a concentration camp. The conflict continued briskly into the summer of 1939, but in the second month of the new war, the clerics agreed to a truce. In view of the national emergency, the Confessional Synod agreed to accept temporarily the administrative headship of Kerrl.

Meanwhile, a conflict had been in progress involving the Nazi State and the Catholic Church. Hitler was grieved that relations between the Vatican and German Catholics were regulated by three separate concordats—between the papacy on the one hand and Prussia, Bavaria, and Baden severally on the other. Accordingly, the Catholic von Papen was sent to Vatican City to negotiate a single concordat for all Germany's Catholics. It was hoped that such a treaty would end the unpleasant encounters between Storm Troops and Catholic organizations that occurred frequently in the early days of Nazi control.

In July 1933 a new concordat was signed. The Catholic clergy was forbidden to participate in Reich politics, and all future diocesan appointments were to be made by the Holy See after consultation with the government. The state sanctioned the continued existence of the Catholic Action organization as a nonpolitical society. Catholic schools, youth groups, and cultural organizations were not to be disturbed if they refrained from political moves. It was not long before friction developed over the interpretation of this instrument. Nazi political leaders strove to restrict the freedom of the Catholic Action, the Catholic Youth Movement, and the Catholic press. Quarrels arose over the control of education, and leading Catholic churchmen openly denounced Nazi policies. Perhaps the most outspoken cleric was the archbishop of Munich, Michael Cardinal von Faulhaber. Apparently to forestall his arrest, the Pope in 1934 conferred upon him the rank of papal legate, which brought with it diplomatic immunity.

In the ensuing years the struggle was marked by police action and resulting violence. A number of monks and nuns were imprisoned on the charge of smuggling money out of Germany. Membership in the Hitler Youth was made compulsory for boys and girls, who thus were removed more effectively from clerical influence. In 1937 most of the Catholic schools in Bavaria were converted into state institutions. When the Pope criticized Nazi interference in religious matters and accused the government of having violated the concordat, his protests drew intemperate replies from Nazi officials and precipitated a new series of trials of monks and lay brothers on charges of immorality and other violations. But even after the outbreak of the Second World War, Catholic clerics in Germany continued to denounce Nazi efforts to destroy the institutions of the church and the family.

Meanwhile Streicher's *Der Stürmer* printed more and more scurrilous references to Jesus Christ; and *Das Schwarze Korps*, organ of the SS commanded by Heinrich Himmler,[15] decorated its pages with blasphemous articles and cartoons aimed at making Christianity seem ridiculous. In 1937 Hitler awarded the National Prize, Germany's substitute for the Nobel Prize, to Alfred Rosenberg— outstanding philosophical foe of Christianity and spiritual leader of the Neo-Pagans, who advocated a return to old Teutonic rites.

POLITICS AND PURGES, 1933-1939

The Reichstag that was elected on March 5, 1933, was dissolved by the government in October of the same year, coincident with Germany's withdrawal from the disarmament conference and announced intention to resign from the League.[16] New elections were called for November, at which time the people were to elect deputies and register their approbation or disapproval of Nazi diplomacy. About 96 per cent of the qualified electors went to the polls. Of these, 93 per cent endorsed the government's policies. And 92 per cent of the ballots were in favor of the single (Nazi) list of candidates. Such an endorsement strengthened the hands of the government at home and abroad.

Yet, early in 1934, it became evident that there was dissatisfaction

[15] Himmler also was chief of the Nazi secret police (*Geheime Staats- Polizei* or *Gestapo*).
[16] The state legislatures also were dissolved, and no new ones elected.

within Nazi ranks. Particularly was this noticeable among the Storm Troops (SA), many of whom once had been Communists and still considered themselves revolutionaries. They apparently resented the circumstance that the "socialistic" items in the party program seemingly were being forgotten. Many men were still awaiting the jobs they had been promised, and the personal extravagances of a number of Nazi leaders added to the ill will and restlessness.

The leadership of the discontented Brown Shirts was assumed by Captain Ernst Röhm, their chief of staff. Röhm seemed eager, furthermore, to incorporate a large number of Storm Troops in the regular army or *Reichswehr*. To this, both the Reichswehr generals and Hitler were opposed, and in April 1934 it was announced that all SA men were to go on vacation during July. In June, Röhm himself was given leave of absence "for reasons of health," and it was rumored that his troops might be reduced in number since the Reichswehr had no faith in a large "people's army." Meanwhile, Vice-Chancellor von Papen also had raised his voice in opposition, denouncing the extreme censorship, the resort to terrorism, and the use of force in religious disputes. The apparent intent of the government to weaken the Storm Troops, and the fact that nothing happened to Papen for his temerity, seem to have induced the malcontents to consider an early seizure of power. Before their plans were completed, Hitler liquidated their leaders (and some other prominent anti-Nazis) in a purge on June 30, 1934.

It was not known how many persons were killed in the blood purge. Most prominent among the victims were, besides Röhm, former Chancellor von Schleicher and his wife; Erich Klausner, leader of the Catholic Action; and several of Papen's assistants. Papen himself was arrested by Göring but was saved by his closeness to Hindenburg. After Hitler had given the Reichstag his version of the affair, the legislature thanked him for his vigorous forestalling "of civil war and chaos."

Soon after the purge the government reduced the number of Storm Troops. The primary function of this semimilitary organization had been accomplished by the "winning of the streets" from the opposition elements. The membership, however, had continued to grow, and Röhm at one time claimed command of 2,500,000 men. Increase in size was accompanied by a decline of discipline, and neither Hitler nor the Reichswehr favored so large a private army. Consequently the SA was reduced in size and largely disarmed. Even the better-disciplined, black-shirted Nazi body-guards or SS were restricted in their activities. The Reichswehr emerged in 1935 as the supreme military organ of the Third Reich, particularly after the reintroduction of conscription and a large standing army.[17]

On August 2, 1934, the aged President von Hindenburg died. On

[17] In October 1935 the German General Staff, abolished by the Versailles Treaty, was publicly re-established.

the preceding night the cabinet had adopted a decree providing for the union of the offices of president and chancellor from the moment of Hindenburg's death. From August 2, therefore, Hitler ruled alone. Declining the title of President, he asked to be called only Der Führer. "In the next thousand years," he said, "no more revolutions will take place in Germany."

In the period 1935 to 1938, certain prominent leaders of the high command and of the foreign office fell into disfavor with Hitler. Some of these men were not actual members of the Nazi Party. Some continued to be opposed to many Nazi policies and actions. Hitler's displeasure was vigorously manifested early in 1938 when he reorganized both these branches of the national administration. Using the marriage of War Minister Werner von Blomberg to a lady of much lower "station" as a convenient time determinant, Hitler dismissed not merely this officer but also Commander-in-Chief Werner von Fritsch, Foreign Minister Konstantin von Neurath, and others of similar sympathies. They were replaced by men who were more closely attuned to Hitler's methods and views, such as the new Foreign Minister Joachim von Ribbentrop, and the political-minded General Wilhelm Keitel.

Another reorganization was effected in 1939. The SA, now under Viktor Lutze, was made responsible for the continued physical fitness and military preparation of nearly every German man before and after the completion of his required service in the army. The ground now was well prepared for the international aggressions of 1939.[18]

---

[18] One of the most tragic consequences of the Nazi policies was the fate of hundreds of thousands of persons who were driven from their homes and rendered "stateless." As an aftermath of the Bolshevik Revolution in Russia, a League refugee organization had been formed; then, in 1938, the League established in London an Office of the High Commissioner of the League of Nations for Refugees. The Commissioner for a time was aided by an Intergovernmental Committee on Refugees, also set up in 1938.

Central Europe | 9

A. Storm and Stress, 1918-1932

In November 1916 the aged Emperor Francis Joseph died. His reign of sixty-eight years ended, as it had begun, amid tumult and warfare. He was succeeded by his grandnephew, Charles. The new ruler was good-natured and courageous, but inexperienced in statecraft.

The events of 1916 to 1918 broke the morale of the Austro-Hungarian people. The entry of the United States into the war and the dissemination of Allied propaganda behind the lines helped to undermine the faith of the people in their government. Amid starvation, mutiny, and fears of Communist revolution, the German-speaking deputies in the parliament at Vienna proclaimed a separate German-Austrian state. On November 11, eight days after an armistice was signed with Italy, Emperor Charles renounced all share in the government.[1] He immediately left Vienna and soon afterwards went into Swiss exile.

Even before Charles had quitted Vienna, the Social Democrats, Christian Socialists, and German Nationals had set up a provisional government in German-Austria by an almost bloodless revolution. On November 12 this government issued a tentative constitution that declared German-Austria to be a republic and an integral part of the new German Reich. Meanwhile the non-German portions of the Dual Monarchy had gone to form the new states of Czechoslovakia and Hungary or to increase the territories of Italy, Romania, Yugoslavia, and Poland. In the interim between the creation of

[1] Two days later he renounced all share in the government of the Kingdom of Hungary.

German-Austria and the elections for a constituent assembly in February 1919, the provisional government watched over Austria's welfare.

Seeing after Austria's welfare was no small task. As a member of the Dual Monarchy, German-Austria had been the center of a relatively self-sufficient economic unit. All this suddenly was changed. The great industries were ruined because the raw materials now were located in foreign areas and tariff walls were raised by nationalistic neighbors. To make matters worse, the Allies maintained a food blockade of the Central Powers for four months after the armistices, and Austria could produce only a fraction of the food that she needed for her population. In addition, the postwar unemployment situation rapidly was worsening as returning veterans sought jobs that a malfunctioning economy could not provide.

The chaos gave rise to a general desire for the early restoration of order and economic stability. Hence the assembly elections of February 1919 resulted in a triumph for the moderate parties. The provisional government resigned its control into the hands of a coalition, consisting of the urban Social Democrats and the agrarian Christian Socialists. The Constituent Assembly confirmed the declaration by the provisional government that German-Austria was a republic and an integral part of Germany. Then most of the Habsburg family was banished and its property confiscated. Economic ties with the non-German portions of the old Dual Monarchy were permitted to lapse.

Then, to the shock of Vienna, the Allies forbade an Austro-German union! And the Treaty of St. Germain, which Austria was compelled to accept in September 1919, stipulated that union (*Anschluss*) might take place between Austria and Germany only with the (unanimous) consent of the League Council. Even the name "German-Austria" had to be changed to the "Republic of Austria." The assembly now had to proceed with the making of a permanent constitution. In October 1920 the assembly adopted an instrument establishing a state that resembled the federal system of Switzerland.

After the first parliamentary elections held under the new constitution, the Christian Socialists combined with the Pan-German Party to form a new government. The Federal Assembly elected Dr. Michael Hainisch, a man of considerable scholastic reputation, to be Austria's first president. In the same month (December 1920) Austria was admitted to membership in the League of Nations.

Almost fifteen months after the adoption of the constitution, the boundaries of the new republic finally were delimited (December 1921). Austria comprised nine provinces with an area of 32,369 square miles and an estimated population of 6,800,000—nearly a third of these in Vienna alone.

During 1921, economic conditions in Austria were terrible. The winter of 1920–1921 was particularly harsh, and thousands starved to death. Inflation set in and the Austrian crown soon stood at 3000 (instead of 20) to the dollar. Early in 1921 the despairing authorities appealed to the League for funds with which to purchase food. The reply of the League was to send a commission of investigation. International loans and charity provided temporary relief.

The economic situation gave added impetus to the movement for union with Germany. A bill for a plebiscite on the Anschluss was presented in the parliament. If the vote favored union, the government should petition the League for its consent. The Allied Powers, however, threatened to punish Austria if the bill were passed. The proposal was dropped.

From June 1921 to September 1922, the crisis and the calls for at least economic Anschluss with Germany continued. Chancellor Ignatz Seipel in September 1922, with the crown at 77,000 to the dollar, addressed an appeal to the League for economic aid.

The League Council submitted to Austria a plan whereby certain western governments would guarantee a loan of $130,000,000 for twenty years. Such Austrian assets as the government tobacco monopoly should serve as security and Austria was asked to pledge specific economic reforms. The parliament accepted the plan and began the demanded reforms. In 1924 a new monetary unit, the schilling, replaced the crown and financial progress was rapid.

Similar advances could not be reported in other fields. The general unrest was alarming, and in 1924 there was extreme social disquiet, accompanied by strikes and attempted political murder. By the close of 1925 the discontent and economic stagnation once more brought forth the idea of Anschluss. Demonstrations in its favor became so popular that Italy and the Little Entente warned the government to prevent any overt action. By July 1927 the government was faced with a situation approaching civil war. To understand this crisis it is necessary to consider the development of two powerful, rival, political organizations, the *Heimwehr* and the *Schutzbund*.

From the earliest days of the republic there existed a bitter feeling between the industrial and the rural interests in Austria. The workers of Vienna and of the Styrian mining districts formed an industrial proletariat with socialistic and anticlerical leanings. They formed the core of the Social Democratic Party. Most of the remaining Austrians were agrarian, conservative, and religious. They supported the Christian Socialist and Pan-German parties, and hated Marxism.

After the war Vienna fell into the hands of the Social Democrats and high property taxes were used to build apartment houses for workmen. The *Karl Marx Hof*, completed in 1930, was the largest apartment house in Europe, with 1400 units. The municipality also acquired control of the public utilities and of some private businesses.

Most of this was anathema to the peasants, and the bitterness between Vienna and the rural hinterland expressed itself in the organization of rival militant bodies: the agrarian Heimwehr and the

Socialist Schutzbund. The program of the Heimwehr called for the overthrow of the Socialists and union with Germany; in the early years of its existence, it associated itself with the Hitler movement in Germany. By 1931 the Heimwehr included 60,000 armed men.

The Schutzbund in 1931 counted a trained membership of 90,000 men, concentrated in the industrial regions. It possessed quantities of munitions, stored away in such places as the office buildings of socialist newspapers. Frequently the Heimwehr and the Schutzbund arranged for demonstrations in approximately the same place on the same day, and then the government had the problem of preserving order. Since, by the peace treaty, the army was limited to 30,000 men, the government had the smallest armed force in the country.

In July 1927, a jury acquitted three members of the Heimwehr who had been accused of the murder of two Socialists in Burgenland. Proletarian sentiment stamped the accused as guilty, and on the day following the verdict thousands of Viennese workmen went on strike, swarmed into the fashionable *Ringstrasse,* overpowered a small police force, and set fire to the beautiful Palace of Justice. Rioting continued for three days, during which scores were killed and hundreds wounded.

Following this crisis, clashes between the two organized factions occurred in alarmingly rapid succession. Several times during 1929 and 1930 the Heimwehr threatened to march on Vienna, as the Italian Fascists had marched on Rome, and put an end to what they considered a weak parliamentary government. In September 1931 there was an attempted, but unsuccessful, Putsch in Styria. The leaders were arrested—and acquitted by a jury in Graz. By 1932 it was clear that Austria could enjoy neither domestic nor foreign quiet so long as the Heimwehr and the Schutzbund continued to exist as private militias.

It seemed to many that the difficulties suffered by Austria could be eased by union with Germany, but the former Allies continued to object. The foreign objections to an Austro-German union were based on a variety of considerations. United with Austria, Germany's area would have exceeded that of France. The combined populations of Germany and Austria were one and three-fourths that of France. Anschluss would have made Germany, rather than weak Austria, the immediate neighbor of Italy. In other ways, too, the European states were aware that the combined strength of Germany and Austria would be formidable.

Not all the citizens of Germany and Austria favored Anschluss. Many German Protestants were not anxious to incorporate in the Reich 6,000,000 Austrian Catholics. On the other hand, devout Austrian Catholics feared the loss of influence of the church in case of union with Protestant Germany. Many Viennese feared that union with Germany might reduce their capital to the status of a second-rate provincial city.

At any rate, organizations were founded in both countries to agitate for Anschluss and the perennial question again assumed prominence in 1930, by which time the unemployment figure embraced one of every four Austrian workmen. Berlin and Vienna, however, dared go no farther than to sign a protocol for a projected customs union (1931). This immediately was opposed by France and the Little Entente, and financial pressure was brought to bear to make Germany and Austria renounce the document. This they did, two days before the World Court rendered an advisory opinion that the contemplated pact would have violated previous international agreements.

Though the renunciation eased the international tension, it left unsolved Austria's economic difficulties. In 1932 the world witnessed in Austria a sovereign state literally begging the League for a million dollars in order that the starving inhabitants might be fed. The republic strove frantically to secure favorable trade treaties with her neighbors, usually without avail. Chancellor after chancellor resorted to desperate methods in vain attempts to prevent further decrease in the country's gold supply. The leading banks crashed, and eventually no funds were left with which to pay doles.

During the summer of 1932, money was offered Austria—under political conditions that were unacceptable to her patriots. At length, however, economic need overcame all other considerations, and the parliament, by a vote of 82 to 80, ratified the Lausanne Protocol. This document, drawn up under League auspices, gave Austria a loan of $42,000,000 for twenty years in return for a promise that the republic would not enter into any political or economic union with Germany. The fight for acceptance of the protocol had been led by Chancellor Engelbert Dollfuss, a Christian Socialist.

B. Austria's Five-Year War Against Nazism, 1933-1938

The elevation of Hitler to the German Chancellorship in January 1933 moved the question of Anschluss to a different plane. A few years previously, a Nazi party had been established in Austria. The members wore the same uniform as their German colleagues and adhered to the same basic program. They were recruited mainly from the lower bourgeoisie and the peasantry, and they placed their chief hope in a political union with the Third Reich. The movement grew slowly, and no Nazi was elected to parliament in 1930. In the provincial elections of 1932, however, the Nazis won seats in several local diets. Upon the triumph of the Nazis in Germany, the Austrian National Socialists determined to bring about Anschluss.

In this endeavor they had the support of Germany. Although Berlin realized the danger of outright annexation of Austria, there appeared to be no serious obstacle to the accomplishment of this end by indirect means. Since the Austrian Nazis took orders from

Hitler, it was believed that a National Socialist victory at the polls would complete Austro-German union despite the objections of the former Allies. To force the Austrian Government to hold new elections and to ensure the winning of these elections, the German Nazis exported funds and agitators to the little republic. The radical activities of these agitators encountered the determined resistance of Chancellor Dollfuss, who until recently had himself favored Anschluss.

Dr. Engelbert Dollfuss was born on a small farm in 1892. Following studies in law and economics, he entered politics and in 1931 was appointed Minister of Agriculture; in the following year he was asked to form a cabinet of his own. His coalition of Christian Socialists, Heimwehr, and Agrarian League had a majority of one over the Social Democrats and Pan-Germans. Dollfuss' simplicity of manner, good nature, and religious fervor charmed those who came in contact with him. Because of his resolute spirit and because he was less than five feet tall, he was popularly dubbed "the Millimetternich."

In 1933 Dollfuss was invested by the president of the republic with emergency powers to cope with a worsening situation. He soon issued hundreds of decrees. Many of these decrees were aimed at the Nazis and at other political groups objectionable to the Government. Restrictions were placed on the freedom of the press and of assembly. Nazi propaganda was barred from Austrian radio broadcasts. German agitators were expelled. It was forbidden to wear the Nazi uniform or display any political emblem other than the Austrian flag. In June 1933, after bombs had been thrown at a detachment of auxiliary police, the National Socialist Party was outlawed. Meanwhile the authorities also had dissolved the Socialist Schutzbund and abolished the Communist Party.

As the struggle continued, German planes dropped propaganda leaflets over Austrian towns, and violent anti-Dollfuss speeches were broadcast from Munich. An armed Austrian Legion, consisting of Austrian Nazis who had fled to Germany, was organized in Bavaria. The Austrian Chancellor appealed to the world for moral and economic backing, and at the London Economic Conference he pleaded eloquently (June 1933) for increased foreign trade and tourist traffic, so that Austria might not be forced by economic necessity to submit to German domination.

Upon his return from London, and after conversations with Mussolini, Dollfuss turned from defense to attack. He wanted to build up a concrete alternative to Nazism—a Catholic, anti-Socialist, authoritarian, *Austrian* movement. He believed that the republic "could live alone," and he hoped to unify it on a basis of Austrian patriotism. To this end he created the Fatherland Front, which was to be above all parties. With its backing, Dollfuss moved against all political elements that opposed his authoritarian regime.

The authorities, in February 1934, dissolved all political parties and raided Social-Democratic headquarters in several cities. The Socialist leaders, sensing their last chance to fight back, called a general strike. The government retaliated by declaring martial law, outlawing the Social Democratic Party, and ordering the execution of any civilian caught with firearms. Civil war resulted.

Although the Austrian Nazis remained aloof, the government forces everywhere emerged triumphant. The city hall in Vienna was taken over almost immediately. The most serious fighting occurred in the Viennese municipal dwellings, especially the Karl Marx Hof. Here the workers held out for four days against machine-gun and light-artillery fire. Then, after a promise of amnesty for all but certain leaders, the Socialists capitulated. Vienna was deprived of self-government and was made subordinate to the mayor, an appointee of the chancellor. Thus the organized Austrian Social Democratic Party came to an end—and many bitter Socialists became Nazis.

A new constitution was provided in May 1934. The President was accorded unusually broad powers and the democratic republic was converted into an authoritarian state.

Meanwhile the activities of the Nazis again had become serious. An official announcement listed 140 bombings in the first week of 1934. Foreign tourists were frightened away, railroads were blocked, powerhouses were destroyed, and individuals were assaulted. Dollfuss, Dr. Kurt von Schuschnigg (Minister of Education and leader of his own *Sturmscharen* or "Storm Bands"), and the other cabinet officers fought back vigorously. The reaction to the German purge of June 1934 encouraged Dollfuss to proceed even more energetically than before, and he arrested hundreds of suspected National Socialists.

The increasing vigor displayed by the government induced the Nazi leaders to attempt an early Putsch, to avoid the fate of the Social Democrats. On July 25, 1934, a group of armed Nazis seized the government radio station in Vienna and forced the announcer to broadcast a statement that the Dollfuss Ministry had resigned. Shortly thereafter another group of Nazis, wearing Heimwehr uniforms, entered the chancellory and captured several members of the cabinet. Among the Nazi attackers was Otto Planetta, who shot Dollfuss twice.[2] The Nazis were able to seize the chancellory so easily because the Government, warned of a plot, had asked for a Heimwehr guard—and when the disguised conspirators arrived they were looked upon as the requested protectors. The real Heimwehr men arrived almost immediately afterward and laid siege to the building.

While the loyal troops withheld their fire lest harm come to the captive officials, Dollfuss slowly was dying. No physician was called,

[2] The Nazis wanted Dollfuss to make way for Dr. Anton Rintelen, Austrian Minister to Italy. Rintelen was sentenced to life imprisonment, but later became an official in Nazi Germany.

and his prayers for a priest went unheeded. Austrian President Wilhelm Miklas deprived the imprisoned cabinet of its authority and announced that no agreement forced from its members would be valid. Eventually the conspirators began to negotiate for their own surrender. With the aid of the German Minister to Austria they agreed to free their victims in return for a promise of safe conduct to the German border. In the evening the government forces entered the chancellory. The Nazis, contrary to their expectations, were arrested—because safe conduct had been promised only if none of the capitives were injured. Dollfuss' death had altered the situation.

The Heimwehr, loyal army, and police had to put down other Nazi uprisings throughout the state. The conspiracy was widespread, and the Austrian Legion had been ready to pour into Austria as soon as the news of Nazi success in Vienna should have arrived. Mussolini rushed troops to the Austrian border. Il Duce believed the German Nazis to have been implicated in the revolt and was ready to use force to uphold Austrian independence, particularly since he was fond of Dollfuss.

The Hitler Government denied any complicity, removed the members of the Austrian Legion to northern Germany, recalled the German Minister who had acted as intermediary for the plotters, and appointed Papen as its new envoy to Vienna. No connection was established between the Austrian conspirators and the German Nazis at the trial of the former, although Planetta and others who were executed for murder or treason shouted *"Heil Hitler!"* just before they died.

Before the end of July, Schuschnigg became Chancellor. His task was made somewhat easier by the reaction among Austrians to Dollfuss' murder. Relative quiet prevailed while he tried to follow the principles championed by his predecessor. Nazi activities diminished, and better relations with Germany were restored.

After 1934 there was an increasingly strong sentiment for revival of the Habsburg monarchy in Austria. The new constitution made no mention of the word "republic," and Schuschnigg had monarchist leanings. As the disorder and economic crisis had become progressively worse, more and more Austrians came to look upon a Habsburg restoration as the only remedy for Austria's troubles.

In April 1936, the government introduced compulsory military service, thus repudiating a provision of the Treaty of St. Germain, and thus also abolishing such private armies as the Heimwehr. An "armistice" in the struggle with Germany was sealed by an agreement in July 1936, whereby Germany promised to respect the sovereignty of Austria and recognized that National Socialism in Austria was entirely a problem of the Austrian Government. On the other hand, Mussolini, now an Axis partner, was beginning to show a lessened interest in Austrian independence.

In February 1938, Schuschnigg visited Hitler and received an ultimatum—which Mussolini later advised him to accept. Thereupon he formed a new cabinet, assigning the portfolios of justice, foreign affairs, and the interior to Nazis. After Nazi Minister of the Interior Arthur Seyss-Inquart visited Hitler, the Fatherland Front was opened to Nazis and a wide political amnesty was granted.

Suddenly, on March 9, 1938, Schuschnigg announced that a plebiscite on Austrian independence would be held on March 13. He hoped thus to prove wrong Hitler's argument that a majority of Austrians now wanted Anschluss. Two days before the plebiscite was to be held, Hitler threatened to act unless the poll was canceled. Schuschnigg thereupon "took leave of the Austrian people" over the radio, and on March 12 Seyss-Inquart assumed power. He at once invited Hitler to send in the German army to "preserve order," and by the close of the day the occupation of Austria was completed. Hitler in great emotion visited his native Braunau.[3]

The time chosen by Hitler for the coup was propitious from an international point of view. In Great Britain a pro-appeasement group was in control. In France there was a cabinet crisis. Italy, with many of her soldiers in Ethiopia, Spain, and Libya, accepted the fact and received Hitler's promise of eternal gratitude. Now Hitler announced the holding of a plebiscite, simultaneously with elections for the first Reichstag of Great Germany. Before the plebiscite was held, two laws legalized the "reunion" of Austria with the Reich and introduced the Four-Year Plan into the new province. Anti-Semitic decrees were quickly put into force in Austria and there was horrible cruelty.

The plebiscite was held on April 10, 1938, in all Great Germany. The ballot listed the single question: "Do you agree to the reunion of Austria with the German Reich carried out on March 13 and do you vote for the (Reichstag) list of our Leader, Adolf Hitler?" More than 99 per cent of the votes cast were in the affirmative. Thus about 7,000,000 more German-speaking people were added to the population of the Reich.

THE KINGDOM OF HUNGARY

A. Politics and Economics

The attitude of the ruling Magyars toward their subject nationalities did much to hasten the collapse of Hungary. Even in the darkest war days, the Magyars disregarded the demands of their minorities for liberal treatment. At the war's end the subject Romanians and Slovaks insisted on rights of self-determination. Moreover, when Wilson recognized the independence of Czechoslovakia and Yugo-

---

[3] President Miklas resigned and Schuschnigg was jailed. Seyss-Inquart became Governor of Austria, renamed Ostmark. Seyss-Inquart's "name might easily have become the synonym of fifth columnists in place of Quisling's had it not been so awkward."

slavia, the respective minorities in Hungary demanded union with their fellow-nationals.

On November 16, 1918, Hungary was declared a republic. A self-appointed National Council ordered the election of a constituent assembly by universal suffrage. Michael Károlyi, Premier since October 1918, drew up a platform promising widespread civil rights and reforms. However, the unfavorable foreign and internal conditions made it impossible to put this program into effect. The subject nationalities no longer were interested in "rights;" they desired complete separation from Hungary. The Allies tightened the blockade. Returning soldiers swelled the ranks of the unemployed, and foreign ex-prisoners of war ravaged the countryside. The conservatives objected to the proposed breaking up of large estates. Communistic ideas trickled in from Russia.

Soon supporters deserted Károlyi and there was an attempt to thrust him aside by electing him provisional president of the republic. The final blow to Károlyi came with the news that the peace conference had awarded Transylvania to Romania. The President thereupon resigned and went into exile (March 1919). Now, in anticipation of Károlyi's exit, plans already had been drawn up by Sigmund Kunfi, a Socialist member of the government, and Béla Kun, an imprisoned Communist, for a union of Hungarian Social Democrats and the recently formed workers' and soldiers' councils. The coalition was prepared to take the reins at any time. When Károlyi departed, Kun was released from prison to become head of a new government.

Béla Kun, former journalist and politician who had served as an officer in the Austro-Hungarian army, had been taken prisoner by the Russians and in a prison camp absorbed Marxist doctrines. After the war, he returned to Hungary and edited a subversive newspaper.

The People's Commissars, as Kun's cabinet officers called themselves, ousted all political opponents and formed a well-disciplined "Red Army." Soon the Social Democrats were ousted from the government and then private property was nationalized. A radical constitution was adopted, and preparations were made for the spreading of Marxist doctrine into neighboring states. While Kun led his "Red Legions" against Czechoslovakia, the opposition at home was put down with ferocity.

The Communist regime was doomed to early failure. The refusal of the peasants to accept a new currency for their foodstuffs and the maintenance of the Allied blockade brought the cities to starvation. Thousands of counterrevolutionists, or "Whites," led by Archduke Joseph, Stephen Bethlen, and Nicolas Horthy, vice-admiral in the former Austro-Hungarian navy, gathered at Szeged in an area occupied by French troops. Withdrawing from Czechoslovakia lest the wrath of the Paris Conference be converted into military measures against him, Kun now led his legionnaires against a

Romanian army that was marching toward Budapest. This time Kun was defeated. In August 1919 he fled to Vienna—there to be placed in a mental hospital. Eventually he made his way to Russia.

For a few days after Kun's flight, a Social Democrat took charge of the government, but soon Archduke Joseph, who had been proclaimed regent by the returning counterrevolutionaries, appointed a monarchist premier. This return of Habsburg influence so frightened Hungary's neighbors that they insisted upon Joseph's withdrawal from the government.

Elections at last were held early in 1920. No party received a majority, but most of the delegates had monarchist leanings. The assembly virtually restored the former monarchical constitution, but since an Allied note precluded the return of a Habsburg to the throne, Horthy was designated Regent. The next twelve months witnessed a wave of reactionary legislation. Not until April 1921, was order restored.

In the circumstances, Charles was encouraged to return to Hungary and reclaim the throne on Easter Sunday 1921. Horthy, however, refused to surrender his powers without the prior consent of the assembly. Besides, the Allies protested and Czechoslovakia threatened military action unless Charles left Hungary immediately. The disconsolate Habsburg returned to Switzerland. In October he came to Hungary once more and led a hastily gathered force on Budapest. Horthy attempted unsuccessfully to dissuade Charles from this enterprise and, when Czechoslovakia and Yugoslavia began to mobilize, the Regent sent troops to dispute the royal contingent's entry into the capital. Charles was captured and taken to a British war vessel in the Danube. (He died of pneumonia in 1922.) The Little Entente then forced Hungary to adopt a dethronement act, deposing the Habsburgs and making the kingship elective.

The real head of the government and virtual dictator of Hungary from April 1921 to August 1931 was Premier Bethlen, the "Sphinx of Europe," scion of a wealthy and noble family from Transylvania. When the Bethlen Ministry came into office it was confronted with two urgent tasks: the freeing of Hungary from fear of interference by the Little Entente and the financial and economic reconstruction of the kingdom. The worry over the Little Entente was reduced when Hungary became a member of the League of Nations in 1922, since Hungarian sovereignty and integrity were simultaneously guaranteed. Her new status, moreover, entitled her to assistance in the settlement of her financial difficulties.

Hungary promptly appealed to the Reparation Commission for financial relief. The commission drew up a plan which was adopted by the League Council late in 1923. The plan provided for an international loan and the payment of reparation in twenty moderate annual installments. The reparation plan functioned smoothly and the budget was balanced. Thereafter, the budget continued to show a surplus until 1930.

Economic reconstruction was more difficult to achieve than financial rehabilitation. The Hungary that had been partitioned by the peace treaty had been stripped of two-thirds of its area and three-fifths of its population, leaving the new rump state without a sea coast and with only negligible industrial resources.

Attempts to foster a new industrial life were partially successful, but Hungary remained predominantly agricultural. Although more than half of the population continued to earn its livelihood directly from the soil, Hungary was still a land of large estates. In 1930 one-third of the agricultural area was concentrated in about 1500 large holdings.

Because of its importance as an exporter of foodstuffs and an importer of manufactures, Hungary occupied a strategic position in any move to bring about a Danubian federation. Numerous conferences were held during the Great Depression among the Little Entente, Austria, and Hungary, at which an economic league was the chief topic of discussion. Each time the same obstacles to union were encountered. The states displayed so much jealousy of their sovereignty that concession and compromise were difficult. The question of what form to give the projected union was another stumbling block. Also, the great powers, fearing a loss of markets because of the privileged position that the industries of Austria and Czechoslovakia would have in federation, were lukewarm toward any effective unification schemes.

B.   Restoration and Revisionism

Hungarian foreign relations after 1920 were shaped primarily by the questions of the kingship and the peace treaty. The lenient attitude of the Hungarian courts toward monarchist agitators, combined with the royalist sympathies of Bethlen, might have led to an early solution of the monarchical complication, but for a split among the royalists themselves. The Legitimists insisted upon the coronation of the youthful Archduke Otto, eldest son of Charles. The "Awakened Magyars" rallied around Archduke Albrecht, popular and wealthy Hungarian Habsburg. The disagreement lasted throughout the 1920's, much to the satisfaction of the Little Entente powers.

But there was renewed nervousness in the Little Entente with the approach of the day in 1930 when Otto would reach majority. On this day, the headship of Otto was acknowledged by all members of the family, including Albrecht who, having in the meantime married a commoner, was no longer a rival for the throne. The government was prepared to meet a coup, but nothing exciting transpired. Otto, studying at the University of Louvain, disclaimed any desire to endanger the peace of Europe.

The agitation for boundary revision was more ominous than that for monarchical restoration. The peace treaty not only greatly reduced the size of Hungary but assigned almost 3,000,000 Magyars to neighboring states. Upon its publication in Budapest the treaty was printed with black bands around it, and an irredentist movement was precipitated that became intensified with each succeeding year. In churches, in all public places, everywhere were displayed maps of the old Hungary with the lost territories in black and the whole surrounded by a crown of thorns. On these maps was printed the question, "Can it remain thus?" and the answer, "No! No! Never!" These three words appeared on envelopes, postcards, and other objects. The propaganda was worldwide and was especially successful in Great Britain and Italy. Various societies were active in obtaining foreign sympathy for revision.

A treaty of friendship was signed between Italy and Hungary in 1927, which was soon followed by a shipment of arms from Verona to Hungary. The shipment, labeled "machine parts," was in open violation of the Treaty of Trianon. It was exposed by Austrian customs officials. The Little Entente asked the League to act, but, lest Italy be upset, Geneva merely rebuked Hungary. Soon after, Mussolini began expressing himself in favor of revision of the Treaty of Trianon.

In 1931 and 1932 the agitation for revision and restoration suffered a temporary decline. The reason was the need for foreign financial aid in the midst of the world depression. Some loans were made, but the financial situation worsened and, unusually for Hungary, Julius Gömbös, a commoner, became Premier. The Gömbös Government emphasized agrarian change and continued agitation for revision of Trianon. But, despite strenuous counter efforts, unemployment increased.

The most spectacular developments of the Gömbös Administration grew out of revisionism. To Gömbös, the rectification of Hungary's boundaries was urgent. Several times it appeared as if economic necessity might lead to a *rapprochement* between Hungary and the Little Entente, but on each occasion the negotiations failed because the Entente first demanded a cessation of revisionist agitation and Gömbös refused any such condition.

Throughout the remainder of 1933 and in 1934 Italo-Austro-Hungarian relations became constantly closer. A personal friendship developed among the respective premiers, Mussolini, Dollfuss, and Gömbös. In 1934 these men signed the Rome Protocols and negotiated several trade agreements. The arrangements brought no appreciable upswing in the economic life of any signatory.

In the spring of 1934 Hungary and Yugoslavia accused each other of fomenting trouble along their mutual boundary. The bitterness of the Magyars further increased when new political and business restrictions were imposed on the minorities in Romania. By this time, too, the Hungarians had begun to complain of the military provisions of the peace treaty that kept them in a state of virtual disarmament, although permitting the neighboring countries (except Austria) to arm at will. The atmosphere in east-central Europe therefore was tense as the summer of 1934 drew to a close. Into this atmosphere burst the news of the assassination (October 9) at Marseille of King Alexander I of Yugoslavia and Foreign Minister Barthou of France.

The King had arrived in France for an official visit, and was being driven through Marseille when a bystander leaped on the running board and fired into the car. Alexander died almost instantly; Barthou died within a few hours. The assassin, Vlado Gheorghieff Chernozemsky, was trampled to death by the crowd. He was a Macedonian émigré in league with Croatian émigrés from Yugoslavia, organizers of a terrorist society with training camps in Italy and Hungary. The terrorists hoped that the death of the King would lead to a breakup of the Yugoslav State and the "freeing" of Croatians, Magyars, and Macedonians from Serbian control.

The whole situation so closely resembled the events of 1914 that Europe was gripped by a fear of war. But as it took several days for the police to identify the assassin, Yugoslav feelings had time to subside. After burial of the King, Yugoslavia appealed to the League Council to fix responsibility for the deed. The appeal was couched in general terms, but the finger of blame was pointed at Hungary. The Council unanimously adopted a resolution which was accepted as a settlement of the controversy. "Certain Hungarian authorities" were declared responsible, "at any rate through negligence," for some of the "acts having connection with the preparation of the Marseille crime." The Budapest Government therefore was asked to seek out and punish these authorities. Thus Yugoslav sentiment was appeased, Hungary's dignity was upheld, and peace was preserved.

Throughout 1935 and 1936 Premier Gömbös continued to foster friendship with Italy and Germany and advocated treaty revision. Following his death in October 1936 the cabinet was reconstituted by Kálmán Darányi.

Hungary repudiated the Treaty of Trianon in 1938 when Darányi announced rearmament as one of the main features of a five-year plan of economic development. Darányi further outlined a scheme to curb Jewish economic and professional activities and a project to speed up land reform in favor of the peasant masses. These proposals were intended to "steal the thunder" of the various Nazi groups that had begun to spring up, but there was a feeling in parliament that more vigorous measures should have been taken in this connection.[4] Darányi, consequently, was overthrown and succeeded (1938) by Béla Imredy, a respected conservative Catholic financier.

[4] The most prominent Nazi group was organized in 1937 by Major Ferenc Szalasi. In 1938 Szalasi was imprisoned, but he soon was released and reorganized various Nazi groups into the Arrowcross Party.

Under Imredy and his successor, Count Paul Teleki, anti-Semitic activities continued in a further attempt to take support from the Nazis by following a Nazi-like policy. Eventually, the state was empowered to expropriate, with compensation, Jewish farms of more than half an acre.

The German annexation of the Sudeten areas in 1938 and the consequent weakening of the Czechoslovak state led to a political crisis in Hungary, where the revisionist element demanded the immediate occupation of Slovakia and Carpatho-Ukraine. In March 1939, Carpatho-Ukraine was annexed and Hungary's population rose from 8,000,000 to 11,000,000.

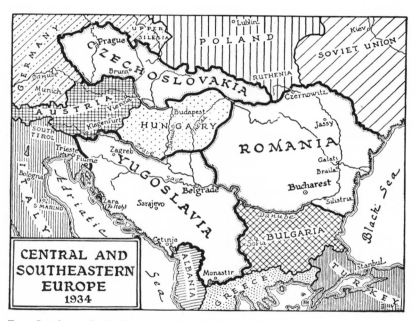

From Landman, J., *Outline History of the World Since 1914*, 1934.
Courtesy, Barnes and Noble, Inc.

As the year 1939 wore on, Hungary signed the Anti-Communist Pact, severed diplomatic relations with the Soviet Union, and announced her withdrawal from the League of Nations. Thus, by itself moving toward the radical right, the Hungarian Government managed to keep the Nazis from controlling the new parliament in 1939. Soon after the election, former Premier Bethlen announced his retirement from political life, explaining his action by saying: "Nowadays only those who breakfast on Jews, lunch on aristocrats, and after dinner hand out fortunes and properties that do not belong to them are national heroes."

CZECHOSLOVAKIA

A. Problems of Independence

The strongest state to emerge from the Dual Monarchy was Czechoslovakia. The republic enjoyed an economic stability and a foreign respect unusual for one of the newer states of Europe. Credit for this achievement belonged largely to two former college professors: Thomas Garrigue Masaryk and Eduard Beneš.

Masaryk was born in Moravia in 1850, the son of a Slovak coachman. Despite poverty, he got an excellent scholastic training and eventually became a professor of philosophy at Prague. During World War I he worked rigorously in the Allied states to arouse sentiment for Czech independence.

Beneš was born in 1884 near Pilsen. He studied law and philosophy and became a prolific writer. He was also a professor of philosophy and sociology in Prague and an admirer of democracy. When war came, Beneš first remained at home in order to keep Masaryk informed; eventually he found it necessary to flee. After arriving in Paris, his ability helped secure hearings for the Czech national cause.

The tasks confronting the revolutionaries were difficult. Sentiment was divided on what course to pursue to gain freedom. Some prominent leaders advocated relying for support on Russia and Pan-Slavism. Masaryk and Beneš preferred to seek help from the democratic states of the West. The first intimation of success for Masaryk's and Beneš' cause came in 1917 when the Allies listed as one of their war aims an autonomous Czechoslovak area. Then, when Allied victory seemed assured, Masaryk issued a declaration of independence. A Czech National Council in Prague reiterated the declaration of independence and took over the administration from the imperial officers. A Slovak National Council voted for union with the Czechs in a single state. The overturn was almost bloodless, and on November 14, 1918, a provisional assembly proclaimed the republic. Masaryk was elected President, Dr. Karel Kramář became Premier, and Beneš was appointed Foreign Minister. Kramář and Beneš represented the republic at the Paris Peace Conference.

In February 1920 the provisional assembly adopted a constitution providing for a democratic parliamentary regime with separation of powers among the ministry, a lower house, and a senate. There soon appeared numerous political parties. The political alignments were based in the first instance upon ethnic divisions and then subdivided according to economic and religious interests. Thus there grew up both Czechoslovak and German parties labeled Agrarian and Social Democratic. Similarly, there were Czechoslovak and Slovak People's Catholic parties, and German and Hungarian Christian Socialists. Communistic and independent groups also took root. With such party splintering the cabinets necessarily were based on coalitions.

The most pressing domestic problem was that of land reform. Throughout the new state most of the land was in the hands of a very small minority made up of the former ruling classes. Now, lands belonging to the Crown or to the Habsburg family were expropriated without compensation, whereas in other cases compensation was fixed at a level below the real value of the property before 1914. The land thus acquired by the state was sold on easy terms to landless persons who were willing to till the soil. In no circumstances were more than 37.5 acres to be assigned to any one individual. Eventually hundreds of thousands of citizens became "middle-class farmers."

The breakup of the large estates precipitated a quarrel between the government and the Roman Catholic Church, for many of the estates had been church property. Popular opinion supported the government, although most of the population was nominally Catholic. Friction developed on other grounds, too, as secularized education was instituted and compulsory religious education in the schools abolished. Some members of parliament demanded an absolute separation of church and state, and early in 1920 a Czechoslovak National Church was established, which proclaimed its independence of the papacy and abolished the requirement of celibacy for the clergy. The new church gained few members.

The quarrel between the two authorities came to a head in 1925 when the anniversary of the burning of John Hus, fifteenth-century heretic, was proclaimed a national holiday. After a deadlock of two years and a half, both sides agreed to compromise. Harmony was restored by an agreement of 1927, which gave the state satisfaction on many of its demands at the price of continued payment of clergy salaries.

From an economic point of view Czechoslovakia was fortunate. A splendid system of railway lines was inherited from the Dual Monarchy, along with approximately 80 per cent of its industries. And on the agricultural side the situation was equally favorable, Czechoslovakia being virtually self-sufficient in food supply. In addition, the soil was rich in mineral resources. From 1919 to 1931 Czechoslovakia enjoyed a consistently favorable balance of trade. Her chief economic handicap was her landlocked position, but this was mitigated by provisions in the peace treaties that granted her access through foreign territory to the sea.

Since the country had an industrial equipment that originally took care of the needs of a large empire, the existing population could not absorb the entire manufactured output. Consequently, Czechoslovakia depended for her economic prosperity upon foreign trade. Her best customers until 1933 were Germany, Austria, Great Britain, and Hungary, in the order named, whereas her purchases were made chiefly in Germany, Austria, and Poland.

B.   Foreign Affairs, Minorities Problems, the Munich Agreement

Business was not the only incentive for harmonious foreign relations. The republic's access to the sea depended upon the upholding of the peace treaties. Five countries, most of them at one time or another hostile, completely surrounded the state: Germany, Poland, Romania, Hungary, and Austria. For half the length of her boundary she was surrounded by a pincers formed by the German and Austrian borders, and her frontiers offered little natural protection.

Masaryk and Beneš pursued four main lines of policy: (1) support of the League as the protector of small states and the mainstay of peace; (2) support of the peace treaties to which the republic owed its life; (3) endorsement in larger European affairs of the policies of Great Britain and France, especially France; and (4) united action, through the Little Entente, with Yugoslavia and Romania in Central European matters.

Between 1923 and 1927 it appeared that the bonds of the Entente might be loosed. But then a series of events gave new life to the Entente relationships: the continuing Anschluss agitation in Germany and Austria; the conclusion of a treaty of friendship between Italy and Hungary, followed by arms shipments from the Italians; the vigor of Magyar irredentist agitation; and the consideration during the depression years of a Danubian federation to improve the economic standing of the countries concerned. In 1934 and 1935 the crisis resulting from the murder of King Alexander of Yugoslavia appeared to offer a successful test of the strength of the alliance bonds. But then the problem of minorities helped bring ruin to all three members of the Entente.

Czechoslovakia, according to the census of 1930, had 15,000,000 inhabitants, of whom two-thirds were Czechs or Slovaks. The remaining third was made up of 3,300,000 Germans and other minorities. At the peace conference of 1919, Czechoslovakia signed a minorities treaty for the protection of these nonnational subjects, and the constitution guaranteed legal equality without distinction as to race, language, or religion. In accord with these promises, schools were provided for the minorities, official business was conducted in a minority language where one-fifth of the population used that tongue, the printed matter on bank notes was repeated in three languages, and a voice in the government was assured the minorities through proportional representation in parliament. Despite these concessions, difficulty was experienced with the subject peoples.

First, the population question was greatly complicated by the antagonism of the Czechs and Slovaks themselves. The Czechs, who outnumbered the Slovaks two to one, were more Westernized and better educated than their compatriots, who were essentially farmers. The Czechs thus tended to dominate the governmental partnership. Disagreements and quarrels, sometimes violent, soon arose. The Slovaks accused the Czechs of monopolizing the desirable offices and violating the Pittsburgh Pact of 1918, wherein Masaryk, in order to get the support of the Slovaks in the United States, had promised Slovak autonomy. The Slovak People's Catholic Party especially was anxious to secure autonomy for the province and thus gain freedom from governmental interference with the school system. Between 1926 and 1930 dissention lessened somewhat, but then agitation intensified again. The Czech-Slovak controversy thus remained a potential danger to the unity of the state.

The most serious minority problem in the long run proved to be that of the millions of German-speaking people in Bohemia and Moravia. These had, on the whole, comprised the upper class in pre-1914 days, and they now formed a powerful opposition unit. At first they boycotted the elections, but gradually they realized that more might be gained by active participation in politics. Masaryk encouraged this attitude, and in 1926 two Germans were appointed to the cabinet. Naturally there were irreconcilables on both sides, and in 1930 some Bohemian nationalists damaged theaters in which German films were being shown. The triumph of Hitlerism in the Reich in 1933 gave the problem a dangerous international aspect.

The Czechoslovak Government took energetic measures to limit Nazi propaganda, but the *Sudetendeutsche Partei*, headed by Konrad Henlein, polled more votes than any other party in the parliamentary elections of May 1935. A coalition of the democratic parties succeeded in retaining control of the cabinet, but before the end of the year the new president, Beneš, and the new premier, Milan Hodža, faced the worst situation in Czechoslovakia's history. Germany conducted a vigorous diplomatic and press campaign against its neighbor to the south.

The Czechoslovaks were accused by the Goebbels propaganda machine of mistreating the Germans and of being in league with the Soviet Union to spread "Semitic Communism." Beneš and Hodža defended their minorities policy, denied any intent to spread abroad doctrines of any kind, explained that strong measures were made necessary by the dangerous activities of Henlein's followers, and promised the German-speaking subjects more cultural autonomy. But the Sudeten-German Party demanded political autonomy and staged a huge demonstration near the German border in October 1937. In reaction, Prague forbade all political meetings and postponed some forthcoming municipal elections. When the elections finally were held, in May and June 1938, the Henleinists captured 90 per cent of the vote in the German districts, whereas in 1935 they had polled only 67 per cent.

It is impossible here to give a detailed account of the happenings between March and October 1938 which broke up Czechoslovakia. Briefly, after Neville Chamberlain refused to commit British arms to France in the event of a war provoked by German action against Czechoslovakia, the Henleinists presented Prague with an Eight-Point Program. The program demanded complete autonomy, ideologically as well as politically. Despite pressure from London and Paris, Prague rejected the demands, and when troop movements were observed in Germany the Czechoslovak army was mobilized. The crisis then subsided temporarily, and the Czechoslovak Government agreed to accept unofficial British mediation in the minorities dispute.

On September 15, 1938, while Chamberlain was trying to find out from Hitler at Berchtesgaden what he really wanted, Henlein issued the first public statement demanding annexation of the affected area to Germany. Although the Sudeten areas never had belonged to Germany (rather to Austria), he cried: "We wish to be home in the Reich!" Meanwhile, it had been made clear to Prague that in the event of armed resistance to German military action, the Czechs could not count on the support of any great power. The Soviet Union agreed to fight if France did, but France would not act without the prior commitment of Great Britain, and such a commitment was not forthcoming. Czechoslovakia therefore announced acceptance of certain Franco-British proposals for the cession of territory to Germany.

Chamberlain, on September 22, flew to Godesberg to confer with Hitler and was disturbed by the increased severity of new German demands. Nevertheless, he had a British diplomat transmit them to Prague without comment, Czechoslovakia meanwhile having ordered general mobilization. Beneš protested that the demands went far beyond the scope of the Anglo-French proposals earlier accepted by his government. While Great Britain and France half-heartedly declared their determination to fight if Germany attacked Czechoslovakia, Hitler threatened military force unless all his demands were accepted by October 1.

President Roosevelt and Mussolini now appealed for further negotiations, and on September 29 Chamberlain, Daladier, Mussolini, and Hitler met in Munich. They signed the Munich Agreement. By this agreement and some supplementary documents, Germany gained 11,000 square miles of Czechoslovak territory rich in industry, electric power, and military installations, plus 3,500,000 inhabitants, including several hundred thousand Czechs.

An annex to the Munich Agreement contained the promise of an Anglo-French "guarantee" of Czechoslovakia's new rump state, but left a door open in the matter of the Polish and Hungarian minorities in Czechoslovakia. For while the Sudetenland was being given to Germany, Poland and Hungary began to clamor for the return of lands originally taken from their territories to form Czechoslovakia.

When the Munich Agreement was announced, Warsaw sent an ultimatum to Prague requiring the surrender of industrial Teschen and three neighboring districts. On October 1, 1938, Prague yielded and Polish troops occupied an area of 400 square miles with a population of 225,000. Of these, only 80,000 were Poles and more than 120,000 were Czechs. Now Poland supported the claims of Hungary, with whom she wanted a common frontier. Italy approved, but Germany, though willing to enlarge Hungary at Czechoslovak expense, had no desire to see a relatively strong Polish-Magyar front established between herself and the east. When Hungary and Czechoslovakia requested Germany and Italy to arbitrate their dispute, the German and Italian foreign ministers met in Vienna, and on November 2 they announed their decision. The Vienna Award did not establish a common Polish-Magyar frontier but assigned to Hungary a part of Ruthenia and southern Slovakia. The area of the cession was 4600 square miles and the population 1,000,000. Altogether, Czechoslovakia lost to her neighbors more than one-fourth of her area and almost one-third of her population.

C. The Collapse of "Czecho-Slovakia"

Within Czecho-Slovakia, as the diminished republic now spelled its name, great changes meanwhile had been taking place. On October 5, 1938, feeling that German pressure might be relaxed if he left the scene, President Beneš resigned. The National Assembly thereupon chose as his successor Dr. Emil Hácha, president since 1925 of the supreme court.

Partly as a reaction to the "desertion" of her allies and partly because of German pressure, the republic completely reversed a number of her traditional policies. Officials who had been identified strongly with the earlier regime were dismissed. Monuments to Masaryk and Beneš were taken down. The Communist Party was suppressed and Masonic lodges were encouraged to dissolve themselves. Close economic relations were established with Germany, for Czecho-Slovakia had become a relatively poor agrarian state. Anti-Semitic outbreaks became frequent, especially in Slovakia where the Hlinka Guards, named after a nationalistic priest, pursued tactics similar to those of the German Brown Shirts. Upon Andrew Hlinka's death, his followers came under the leadership of another Catholic priest, the separatistically minded Father Joseph Tiso, Premier of autonomous Slovakia.

To quell the mounting disturbances in Slovakia, the Czech Government in March 1939 dismissed Tiso. The latter then conferred with Hitler in Berlin, and on March 15 German troops occupied what was left of Masaryk's republic. Czechia was declared (March 16) a German "protectorate," named Bohemia-Moravia, under the nominal presidency of Hácha but the actual control of a "Reich Protector." Slovakia, too, became a "protectorate," and was required to "conduct its policy in close cooperation with the German Government." At Hitler's command, Father Tiso was installed as head of the puppet Slovak state. Meanwhile, through military occupation, the Carpatho-Ukraine (formerly Ruthenia) was incorporated in the Hungarian Kingdom, which thus gained a common frontier with

Poland and brushed aside a major section of the Treaty of Trianon. Czechoslovakia, for the time being, was no more.

German action in 1938–1939 with respect to Austria, the Sudeten areas, Czechia, Slovakia, and Memelland[5] added about 77,000 square miles and 20,000,000 people (including several hundred thousand soon-to-be-persecuted Jews) to the area and population of the Third Reich. Population pressure within Germany thus was increased rather than decreased, and the areas in question (except Slovakia) "were actually more dependent upon foreign sources of food supplies and raw materials than was the German Reich."

POLAND

A. Political and Economic Affairs, 1919–1939

Throughout the nineteenth century a Polish national spirit continued to grow, although Polish territories were ruled by others. At last, in 1914, many patriotic Poles thought they discerned in the war the long-sought-for opportunity to set up a Polish national state. Thanks to the friendship of the Allies and the efforts of Joseph Pilsudski, founder of the non-Marxist Polish Socialist Party, this hope was realized.

Pilsudski and his followers hoped to use Austria "as the sword against Russia and the shield against Germany." They wished to take advantage of Austria's relatively liberal Polish policy to organize a Polish army as the instrument of eventual independence. Not all Poles shared this view. A considerable group preferred to fight on Russia's side in the belief that Polish unity depended on the defeat of the Central Powers. A third group wanted to achieve Polish independence unhampered by the restrictive aid of either Russia or Austria. This view was the most popular among the Poles who lived abroad. Their ablest representative was the famed pianist, Ignace Jan Paderewski.

Eventually the Poles became convinced that, insofar as Russia and Austria were concerned, they could expect as little disinterested help from one side as from the other. Thus it seemed that salvation lay in independent action. Encouraged by Wilson's speech of January 1917, in which he held that "statesmen everywhere are agreed that there should be a united, independent, and autonomous Poland," and heartened by the Russian evacuation of Poland in the same year, Pilsudski told his followers: "Russia is beaten now; next we must fight Germany." Berlin replied by arresting Pilsudski.

At the close of the war Pilsudski was released by the Germans

---

[5] After 1933 there was considerable strife between Memel Nazis, supported by the Reich, and Lithuanian officials. On March 22, 1939, Lithuania acceded to German threats and surrendered Memelland to the Reich.

and went to Warsaw. He took command of the Polish soldiery as "Chief of State" and on November 16, 1918, announced an independent Polish Republic. But Polish national leadership also was claimed by others, and eventually the major political differences had to be reconciled by Paderewski, who was held in esteem by his own country and had won the confidence of the Western nations. In January 1919 he became Premier and Foreign Minister, and Piludski continued as Chief of State. The cabinet included leaders from all important political and geographical groups in the country. While Pilsudski set out to establish wide frontiers for Poland by force of arms, Paderewski went to the Paris Peace Conference to render the same service around the diplomat's table.

Filled with a desire for natural frontiers, the Polish leaders sought to incorporate the reborn state of Lithuania, the Ukraine, Galicia, part of the new Czechoslovakia, and large parts of Germany and Russia. Poland now actually engaged in war with Lithuania, the Ukraine, and Russia; threatened war on Czechoslovakia; and disregarded the admonitions of the Allied Supreme Council—only to end by accepting frontiers which gave her an area of 150,000 square miles rather than the 282,000 square miles that her spokesmen had demanded.

Paderewski resigned as Premier in December 1919, largely because of popular dissatisfaction with his accomplishments at the peace conference. Pilsudski remained as Chief of State until after the adoption of a constitution and the election of a president.

The constitution of 1921 provided for an upper house and a more powerful lower house, established universal suffrage, and ordained proportional representation. Because of the resultant large number of parties, government came to be carried on through the bloc system.

During the four years after 1922, political conditions in Poland were reminiscent of the days of the decadent kingdom. Conservatives and radicals in the parliament were deadlocked, land reform lagged, the financial situation was critical, and corruption prevailed.

Pilsudski, who temporarily had retired from politics and army leadership, became more and more irritated at what seemed to him the dilatory tactics of the politicians and the lack of legislative accomplishment. In May 1926, when one of his bitterest enemies, Vincent Witos, became Premier, Pilsudski denounced the government for its weakness and corruption. When it appeared that the authorities might institute judicial proceedings against him, Pilsudski led three regiments in a march on Warsaw. After a three day's battle Pilsudski entered the capital, and the President and Premier resigned and fled (May 14). The marshal refused to set up a formal dictatorship. Instead, he brought about the election as president of his friend, Professor Ignace Mošcicki, a successful chemist. He himself was content to become Minister of War.

In the next few months a bitter conflict developed between

Pilsudski and the lower house (*Seym*), for the Marshal forced through the legislature several constitutional changes. These amendments gave the president broad powers, and extended the authority of the cabinet to include some legislative functions. When the Seym attempted to reassert its authority and defeated the ministry on two motions, Pilsudski requested the President to appoint him Premier.

From October 1926 until June 1928 (with a slight interruption because of illness) Pilsudski was Premier. He was able to rule through parliamentary channels because the national legislature did not dare to oppose him. Hostility to this veiled dictatorship increased, however, and in June 1928 the Marshal resigned on the grounds of illness and disgust with the corruption and inefficiency of the Seym; he reassumed the office of Minister of War.

Parliamentary difficulties did not cease with the reorganization of the ministry. On the contrary, Pilsudski continued to attack the politicians as unworthy intriguers who had "purposely framed" the constitution "so that the greatest shame which savage ignorant brains could devise would be placed on the nation's most popular men." As Minister of War, he continued to dictate Polish policies and urged a revision of the constitution to increase still further the power of the national executive. But such a constitution was not promulgated until 1935, as the Seym, under eight different ministries, employed diverse tactics to block its institution.

As supplemented by a later electoral law, the 1935 constitution put an end to parliamentary democracy in Poland.[6] The president was made largely independent of parliament and given a suspensive veto power. He was empowered to appoint or dismiss ministers and summon or dismiss the houses of parliament at his discretion.

Thus did Pilsudski arrange for a continuance of the "constitutional dictatorship" even after his own strong hand should have been withdrawn from the control of affairs; for the marshal's health was rapidly failing and he had found it necessary to take frequent vacations abroad where the climate was more favorable to him. On the ninth anniversary of his attack on Warsaw, Marshal Pilsudski died (1935).

Early in 1937 it appeared that Poland might join the group of totalitarian states. Marshal Edward Śmigly-Rydz, friend and comrade-in-arms of Pilsudski, was recognized as "Leader of the Nation." Ignace Paderewski thereupon issued a warning against the trend towards authoritarianism, and several liberal and labor groups petitioned the president for a more liberal electoral law. During 1938 certain Fascist, anti-Semitic elements were expelled from the government by friends of the late Pilsudski. Believing that neither democracy nor fascism would suit Poland's national genius, they hoped to lead her to a "lawful and disciplined democracy." In the parlia-

---

[6] Political parties as such could not be represented in the Polish Parliament, but they continued to exist outside parliament.

mentary elections of 1938, the candidates—representing districts rather than parties—were nearly all government supporters. But before another year passed, Poland disappeared from the map as an independent state.

On the economic side, Poland, like her neighbors, suffered in the postwar years from inflation and instability. The ravages of the war and a series of bad crops constituted a grave threat to the republic. Eventually, in 1923, a coalition cabinet of experts was appointed and entrusted with emergency powers to stabilize the finances.

The cabinet checked the depreciation of the Polish mark. Economy was introduced into government departments and other emergency measures were taken as well. But these changes ended in failure. They seemed too drastic and bore too heavily on the people as a whole.

When the new currency unit, the zloty, fell to one-half of its par value, the government invited the American Professor Edwin W. Kemmerer to study financial conditions in Poland and make recommendations for their improvement. This invitation was confirmed by the Polsudski dictatorship that came into being in May 1926. The Kemmerer Commission made sweeping recommendations, many of which promptly were adopted by the Polish Government. The application of sound monetary principles bade fair to inaugurate a period of economic prosperity. A foreign loan was obtained in 1927, and at the same time Charles S. Dewey, Assistant Secretary of the Treasury of the United States, was engaged as financial adviser. From 1927 to 1932 the Pilsudski regime kept the zloty stable and balanced the budgets. When Dewey resigned in 1930, Poland seemed well on the road to financial equilibrium.

The economic depression that affected the world after 1930 naturally made itself felt in Poland. After 1933 the situation went from bad to worse, and by the end of 1934 the unemployed totaled 300,000 in a population of 32,000,000.

In addition there was a constantly increasing landless proletariat that demanded land reform. A working compromise between radical peasants and the large-estate owners was reached in 1925. Before long, however, the newly created group of farmers was hurt badly by the Great Depression.

B. Minorities

Since fewer than three-fourths of Poland's 27,000,000 inhabitants in 1919 were of Polish nationality, the Paris Peace Conference required the republic to sign a minorities treaty guaranteeing equality of rights to all citizens. Minority nationals were to be given the choice of becoming Polish citizens or leaving the country, and in no case might they be deprived of property, the right to establish their own schools, or the free exercise of religion.

The largest minority group in Poland was the Ruthenians or Ukrainians in the east and south, who formed, according to Polish figures, one-seventh of the total population. A second vocally dissident group was the Germans, located in the Polish Corridor and Silesia.

A law of 1922 granted local autonomy to eastern Galicia, but the Ukrainians complained of Poland's governmental policies, which appeared to involve the enforced Polonization of the eastern provinces. In 1924, the Soviet Government protested to Warsaw and brought the matter to the notice of the world. Moscow claimed a direct interest in the treatment of these people because of the large number of Ukrainians in the Soviet Union.

Though Poland replied defiantly to the Soviet notes, laws were passed concerning the use of minority languages in administrative offices, courts, and schools. Polish was confirmed as the state language, but the parallel use of Ukrainian, Lithuanian, and White Russian was permitted in the conduct of official and judicial business. Instruction in the Polish language in history and geography remained compulsory.

Even when these laws eventually were enforced, relations remained inharmonious. The Ruthenians continued to complain of mistreatment, and some of them formed a Ukrainian Military Organization to fight for an independent Ukrainian state. The Polish Government took severe repressive measures. In 1930, the laments of the minority reached the ears of the League Council, which remitted them to a committee for consideration. While the committee investigated, the situation in Poland became aggravated. The Ukrainian peasants stopped paying taxes, and the government dispatched soldiers to arrest the leaders and compel obedience to the laws. The League Committee eventually upheld the policy of the government.

Late in 1935, the government and the Ukrainian leaders arrived at a "gentlemen's agreement" wherein the minority was promised greater consideration of its demands. Before long, a specially created Ukrainian Congress expressed dissatisfaction with the operation of the compromise. The authorities, on the other hand, placed responsibility for several political murders on Ukrainian nationalists. The matter threatened to become serious at the time of the Munich Agreement in 1938 when Germany, Hungary, and Poland expanded their possessions on the ground that Czechoslovakia had been unjustly ruling *its* minorities; but no overt act took place. In 1939, after the outbreak of the Second World War, the Soviet Union occupied that part of Poland which was inhabited by the Ukrainians.

The German minority problem involved two quarrels. There was, first, the question of the farmers, who with the aid of the Hohenzollern Government had colonized Prussian Poland. The Poles attempted to evict these colonists, who held land under contracts from the German Government, without compensation. Germany took up the case of her nationals and appealed to the League

Council. Poland denied the competency of this body, and the dispute was placed before the World Court. The court upheld the jurisdiction of the Council and handed down an advisory opinion that Poland must respect the private rights of the German nationals. In consequence, the Warsaw Government eventually agreed to compensate the evicted Germans.

The second difficulty concerned the Germans in industrial Upper Silesia. Here the minority protested against Polish mistreatment and discrimination, particularly in educational opportunities. A *Volksbund* was organized to agitate for better conditions, and the sympathy of the Reich was solicited. It was alleged that the Poles exerted every form of pressure from censorship to terrorism in order to intimidate the German minority. Berlin several times brought the Silesian troubles to the attention of the League but got little satisfaction. In 1937 the German and Polish governments exchanged guarantees of cultural and religious autonomy for their respective minorities, but the dispute really involved the broader problem of a general revision of Germany's eastern frontiers. As such, it was a constant threat to peace.

C.   Danzig and the Polish Corridor

The Paris Peace Conference provided for the conversion of the German port of Danzig into a free city under the economic authority of Poland and the general supervision of the League. Although nearly all inhabitants of the city at the time were Germans, it was decided that such an arrangement would best solve the problem of giving Poland access to the sea. The League accordingly asked the Danzigers to draw up a constitution and make an arrangement with Poland. By 1922, it was established that Poland would control the economic and diplomatic life of the free city, whereas the inhabitants would enjoy political autonomy.

Relations between Danzig and Poland soon were strained. Through 1927 "there was hardly any session of the [League] Council at which Danzig affairs did not appear on the agenda," and even the World Court was called upon to settle disputes. The difficulty of drawing a line between economic and political matters and the traditional hatred between the two peoples made the situation dangerous.

In order to diminish the dependence of Polish merchants and shippers upon the Danzig harbor facilities, Warsaw, with the aid of a French syndicate, pushed the development of a port at Gdynia, a few miles west and north of Danzig. Naturally the Danzigers were concerned over this enterprise, which deflected their chief business, shipping, to the neighboring city. Although Warsaw pointed out that Danzig's volume of trade consistently exceeded the prewar figures, the Danzigers with equal truth indicated that by 1933 Gdynia's trading volume had surpassed that of the free city.

The Germans of the Reich frequently expressed sympathy with the Danzigers, and the Nazis declared their determination to right what they called a glaring wrong of the Versailles Treaty. When the Nazis came to power in Germany, there was fear in Poland regarding future German official policy. This was increased when, in the elections of May 1933, the Danzig Nazis gained control of the free city's parliament. However, the Nazi president of the upper house, Dr. Hermann Rauschning, advocated conciliation with Poland. Two agreements were signed, wherein Poland promised Danzig more freight traffic and Danzig agreed to the establishment of special schools for the children of Polish residents. During 1934, Polish-Danzig affairs continued to reflect a general improvement in Polish-German relations. Rauschning's retirement late in 1934, however, and his replacement by a more militant Nazi, once more clouded the outlook.

West and south of Danzig was a stretch of territory 260 miles long and ranging in width up to 80 miles, which formerly comprised in part the provinces of West Prussia and Posen. Through it flowed the Vistula River, one of the main arteries of commerce in east-central Europe. The Versailles Treaty assigned this land to Poland, with a consequent division of Germany into two unconnected sections.

Through the creation of this Polish Corridor, Poland became an economic unit. Germany was weakened economically and militarily and found it harder to exert her influence in the Baltic region as well as to communicate with her province of East Prussia. These grievances were aggravated by the belief that the Poles were mistreating the German minority in the corridor. The exact ratio of Germans to Poles in the region in 1918 never was determined, but the latter soon came to comprise a large majority of the inhabitants. The Warsaw Government induced many Germans to leave and encouraged the colonization of the land by Polish settlers. In 1934, the resident Germans numbered perhaps 100,000.

The Polish Corridor, therefore, was one of the prime factors in the mutual ill will manifested by Germany and Poland. A commercial treaty between the two powers was held up for nine years because of disputes over the corridor and the minority difficulties. In 1925, at Locarno, Germany refused to subscribe to a guarantee of her Polish frontiers. Thereafter, official reference often was made to the urgent need for a revision of the eastern boundaries. Poland's claim that her economic life depended upon the retention of the corridor was consistently supported by France. A ten-year nonaggression pact signed by Germany and Poland in 1934 eased the tension, but conditions remained sufficiently upset so that H. G. Wells, writing in 1933, could prophesy that the next great war would begin over the Polish

Corridor in 1940. He was wrong only in setting the date a few months late.[7]

D. Foreign Affairs

The external relations of Poland were shaped largely by her geographical proximity to a number of unfriendly powers. To the east there was the Soviet Union; to the north, Lithuania and East Prussia; to the west, Germany. Poland, accordingly, placed her hope for security upon military alliances and arbitration agreements. In 1921 alliances were formed with Romania and France, and a treaty of neutrality was signed with Czechoslovakia. In 1922 friendly relations were established with the Little Entente. Three years later, arbitration treaties were negotiated with Finland, Latvia, Estonia, Czechoslovakia, and Austria; and the Locarno Agreements were accepted. In 1931 Poland reached a nonaggression accord with the Soviet Union.

Several efforts were made by Poland to create a Baltic Union of Poland, Latvia, Estonia, Finland, and Lithuania. There were obvious advantages to such a confederation, but little progress was made in its direction. Moscow opposed any plans that might create a Polish hegemony in the Baltic; Lithuania harbored no friendship for Poland; and Finland leaned towards a Scandinavian rather than a Baltic orientation.

During 1933, Poland gradually drew away from France and sought closer relations with Germany and the Soviet Union. The Poles no longer were content to be regarded as satellites of France. For a time Warsaw hesitated between accepting the friendship of Berlin or of Moscow, but in the end amicable arrangements were made with both parties. The new orientation of Polish foreign policy aroused considerable opposition in the Seym, lest it lead to a loss of French protection and ultimate diplomatic isolation, but such opposition was discounted by the foreign office.

For a time, indeed, it appeared as though Hitler and Foreign Minister Colonel Joseph Beck would bring about a genuine improvement in German-Polish relations. In October 1938 Poland, largely because of Germany's aggressive actions, was enabled to enlarge her territory and population at the expense of Czechoslovakia. Warsaw's wish to achieve a common boundary with Hungary was fulfilled in March 1939, through the Hungarian annexation of Ruthenia. During a 1939 visit to Warsaw by Nazi Foreign Minister Joachim von Ribbentrop, the spirit of the German-Polish agreement of 1934 was called to mind through cordial speeches. But before the year was out, Nazi boots pounded on Polish soil in the opening stages of the Second World War.

[7] H. G. Wells, *The Shape of Things to Come*, 1933.

The Soviet Union | 10

OLD REGIME AND REVOLUTION

Nicholas II, from 1894–1917 "Emperor and Autocrat of all the Russias," ruled an empire that comprised almost one sixth of the land surface of the globe, stretching eastward from Central Europe to the Pacific Ocean, and southward from the Arctic to the Black and Caspian seas and China. The inhabitants numbered 180,000,000, about half of whom were Russians proper, or Great Russians. The remainder consisted of scores of other nationalities.

Although serfdom had been abolished by Alexander II in 1860, the social order remained highly stratified. Freed serfs were given farm allotments, but the increase in available lands failed to keep pace with the rise in peasant population. An unduly large portion of each year's income was absorbed by taxes imposed by the village (mir), the province, and the state. The regulations of the village authorities were strict, and peasants generally were not allowed to migrate to cities without their approval.

These evils were somewhat mitigated after the revolutionary outbursts of 1905. Edicts reduced the power of the mirs over their members. With control over their freedom of action relaxed, the peasants began to compete with one another to obtain larger shares of land through saving their earnings to buy up neighboring holdings. But, in the process, some failed and ended by working for wages on the farms of more successful landowners or by going to the cities in search of work. Hence, conditions did not improve sufficiently to create a satisfied peasantry; 1914 still found millions of farming households living in poverty and greedy for additional land.

The plight of Russia's 2,500,000 industrial workers was deplorable. They suffered from the ills usually associated with the beginnings of industrial revolutions and were prevented from expressing their grievances. Some unions were broken up, strikes were suppressed, and there was relatively little social legislation. As a consequence, the industrial proletariat listened eagerly to apostles of reform, and, since the workers were herded together in factories and slums, it was easy to agitate among them and reach them with propaganda. During the Revolution of 1905, the workingmen demonstrated their temper by strikes and riots in the larger cities, and by 1914 they seemed ready for another violent outbreak.

The percentage of illiteracy among the Russians was one of the highest in Europe. The masses, on the whole, feared and hated the upper classes. The state-controlled Orthodox Church wielded considerable influence over the peasantry, but it was a loyal supporter of the tsarist regime and did little to raise the people from their low cultural level.

Political conditions in the empire were unstable. The censorship was notorious and the police administration ruthless. Nicholas II was ill suited to the exercise of autocratic power over a vast domain. Though well intentioned and patriotic, he was swayed easily by the arguments of whatever person happened to be with him at any particular moment. He was especially dominated by the Tsarina Alexandra, who herself was under the influence of a Siberian "monk" named Gregory Rasputin. Rasputin's origins and life were shrouded in obscurity, but he appeared to have hypnotic powers. He acquired his control over the empress because he alone seemed to be able to soothe the hemophilic and cranky young Tsarevich Alexis. It was said that a word from Rasputin was sufficient to bring about the appointment or dismissal of a minister or general, and his authority was not always wielded for the good of the nation. The autocracy required firm leadership. It could not endure under a weak-willed imperial family and an illiterate adventurer.

After the uprising of 1905, Nicholas had granted his people a parliament (*Duma*) with limited powers. The electoral law rendered certain a conservative majority in this Duma, and the government continued its traditional policies. In 1914 parliament, with the exception of five deputies, upheld the administration in its decision to go to war. The dissenting legislators, who were sent to Siberia, belonged to an organization called the Bolshevik faction of the Social Democratic Party.[1]

[1] The radical groups in pre-1914 Russia were the Constitutional Democrats, intellectuals and businessmen who favored responsible government of the British type; the Social Revolutionaries, chiefly peasants led by middle-class reformers, whose aim was the transfer of land to the peasantry and who resorted to terrorism to bring about collectivization of agriculture; and the Social Democratic Party, which found its strength among the industrial workers and advocated the abolition of private property and the control of production by the masses.

    At a meeting of Social Democrats in London in 1903, opinion was divided on party discipline, organization, and cooperation with non-

Despite some military victories in the first weeks of the war, it soon was evident that Russia would experience difficulty in any extended prosecution of the conflict, as the country was ill prepared for war. The German armies soon inflicted disastrous defeats upon the Russians, which further weakened the morale and disorganized the industrial structure of the land.

In the first three years of the struggle, the Tsar called out 15,000,000 men—far more than suitably could be equipped and fed. Millions of hands thus were withdrawn from the fields, where they should have been engaged in planting and harvesting, and millions of men had to be fed at public expense. Since the soldiers' rations in many cases exceeded the average consumption of the individual peasants in peacetime, food was required in greater quantities than during normal periods.

The railway system was incapable of handling the wartime traffic. The empire in 1914 had one-sixth as many miles of track as had the United States, for an area three times as great. It was impossible to forward supplies expeditiously to the front. Rumors of terrible conditions and enormous casualties among the fighting men leaked back from the lines, and woeful tales of misery at home filtered out to the trenches.

The pressure of wartime demands for goods and the success of several strikes made prices soar. Eventually, extreme inflation set in. The bad conditions notwithstanding, little heed was paid by the authorities to the numerous demands for a more liberal policy. The officials discouraged voluntary popular movements, even when these were motivated by a desire to aid the war effort, lest they become revolutionary. Thus, the groups in control simultaneously betrayed their fear of the lower classes and maintained an uncompromising attitude. Nicholas himself wavered and hesitated, undecided on any course of action. The assassination of Rasputin in December 1916, by a group of aristocratic conspirators, did little to help the situation.

The doom of the old regime was heralded by a general strike in Petrograd in February 1917. The unplanned and unorganized walkout led to street demonstrations by the war-weary proletariat. The city garrison refused to fire on the demonstrators and fraternized with the people. Had the Tsar quickly called in troops from outside the city to suppress both the mobs and the Duma, which also was displaying a restive spirit, or had he agreed to the demands of the liberals for a new cabinet and responsible government, he might

---

proletarian revolutionaries. One group, led by N. Lenin, favored strict discipline, a centralized organization, and independence from bourgeois support. The other preferred a looser party organization and the admission of nonproletarian sympathizers. A vote was taken on these views, and the majority indicated a preference for the Leninist ideas. The partisans of the latter came to be known as Bolsheviki, from *bolshinstvo,* meaning *majority,* while the others were called Mensheviki, from *menshinstvo,* meaning *minority.*

have postponed the approaching crisis. Nicholas, however, could not act with decision. Unwilling to grant concessions, too irresolute to take swift action, he simply did nothing.

The vacillation of the ruler goaded liberal-minded men both within and outside the Duma into a revolutionary stand and supplied the more radical agitators with propaganda material. Early in March 1917, there were mob attacks in the larger cities and some peasant riots. The Tsar ordered the Duma to go home and the workingmen to cease striking and return to work. These decrees precipitated the March Revolution.

The legislative chamber refused to disperse. Instead, it elected a committee to lead a revolution against the decadent autocracy. Simultaneously, the radical elements outside the Duma organized a Petrograd Soviet (Council) of Workers' and Soldiers' Deputies, which invited all factory and army units to send delegates to its deliberations. The Duma committee and the soviet agreed to cooperate, and on March 14 a provisional government, headed by Prince George Lvov, came into being. The cabinet included a majority of Constitutional Democrats. Its most radical member was the Social Revolutionary, Alexander Kerensky, vice-president of the soviet's executive committee.

On March 15, Nicholas recognized the new government and abdicated in favor of his brother, Grand Duke Michael. The latter refused to accept the crown until an assembly, chosen by universal, secret suffrage, should have decided upon the future form of government. Six days later, Nicholas and his immediate family became prisoners in the imperial palace near Petrograd. Thus the rule of the Romanovs, founded in 1613, came to an abrupt end.

The provisional government immediately issued decrees easing the press censorship, freeing political and religious prisoners, and recognizing the right of workmen to unionize and strike. The Allied countries, following the example of the United States, accorded prompt recognition.

Despite these favorable omens the Lvov Cabinet, dependent upon a misalliance between the parliamentary revolutionaries and the Petrograd Soviet, was destined to have a short existence. The Duma had desired the overthrow of the Tsar, for one reason, because he failed to prosecute the war with sufficient vigor, whereas the workingmen had been motivated partially by a wish to end the war. The soviet wanted a thorough revision of the property-holding system, a program with which most of the moderates in the Duma had little sympathy. Finally, the two groups favored differing courses of action to achieve their ultimate goals.

By a famous "Order Number One" of March 14, the Petrograd Soviet instructed the army and the navy to disregard any commands of the provisional government that conflicted with the soviet's regulations. Local revolutionary committees were set up by soldiers and sailors, which assumed control over the auxiliary military weapons.

Disposition of the latter was to be entrusted to the officers only when the respective local committees were certain that such action would not jeopardize the interests of the revolution. Army discipline thus was shattered, for the soldiers enjoyed their newly gained "responsibilities" and unceremoniously shot those officers who could not grasp the "significance" of the changed situation. There also resulted bitter quarreling among the men, for some desired to remain loyal to their officers, whereas others refused to fight and started marching home.

In June 1917, at the initiative of the Petrograd Soviet, there met the first All-Russian Congress of Soviets. The thousand delegates included Social Revolutionaries, Mensheviks, and Bolsheviks, the last in a small minority. The gathering indulged in fervent speech-making against imperialism and in favor of peace without annexations, although the chief practical accomplishment was the appointment of an All-Russian Central Executive Committee of the Soviets. This body was to act as a sort of soviet parliament.

As it gradually became apparent that the Lvov Ministry was unable to cope with the difficult situation, one after another of the moderate members resigned from the cabinet. By July only three of the original appointees, including Kerensky, remained. Kerensky had risen to be head of the government, and used eloquence and skillful parliamentary procedure in an attempt to restore domestic order while continuing the war. By this time, however, even a Social Revolutionary Government was unsatisfactory to the masses, who craved peace and whose leaders demanded direct control over the means of production. Kerensky's postponement of elections for a national assembly weakened the confidence of many people in his ultimate motives.

In the fall of 1917, Russia was at the threshold of another revolution. The soldiers were staging the greatest mutiny in history. The peasants rose and seized what land they could. Many workers in the towns sought to take over control from private owners of factories and plants. In order to give more force to their ideals, they formed local soviets and organized themselves into "Red Guards." The subject nationalities, notably the Ukrainians and Finns, took advantage of the general confusion to establish their independence, and the armies of the Central Powers were swarming over the western portions of the country. In the face of these conditions, Kerensky's grant of seemingly modest reforms failed to satisfy any considerable portion of the people.

The Bolsheviks, overwhelmingly outnumbered in the All-Russian Congress of Soviets, organized local soviets and agitated against Kerensky. Everywhere they shouted the slogan "Peace! Land! Bread!" and promised freedom for oppressed nationalities. The campaign was ably directed by Lenin, the "father of Bolshevism," who had been aided by the Germans in his return to Russia from Switzerland. The Germans had helped the revolutionaries not out of any sympathy for their ideals, but in order to undermine the Russian state system and end the war on the eastern front. The cause of the Bolsheviks and other radical antigovernment groups received a setback in July, when Kerensky put down a premature uprising that had been opposed by Lenin.

In September, however, an equally futile reactionary coup under General Lavr Kornilov, commander-in-chief of Kerensky's armed forces, enabled the Bolsheviks to recapture lost ground and enhance their reputation. Momentarily posing as the defender of the established order, the Bolsheviks contributed their "Red Guards" to help suppress the rightist attempt to overthrow the Provisional Government. Such an action was not without other advantages for the Bolsheviks, since a more rightist government would not have tolerated them to the extent that did the Kerensky regime.

At last, at a party meeting of October 1917, the Bolsheviks decided upon a coup d'état. On November 6 and 7, Petrograd was seized by force, and the members of the government were arrested, only Kerensky managing to escape. The date for the event had been chosen so as to precede the meeting of the Second All-Russian Congress of Soviets, which had been called for the 7th. When this body assembled, therefore, it was faced with a *fait accompli*. Since the gathering contained a Bolshevik majority, it received the announcement with glee and constituted itself the supreme authority in Russia. (By the Russian calendar, this was the October Revolution.)

The spirit of this second revolt soon spread, and everywhere in Russia the local soviets seized power. The Congress meanwhile appointed a Bolshevik-controlled central executive committee and an administrative board called "the Soviet of People's Commissars." The chairman of this cabinet was Lenin, and Leon Trotsky became Commissar for Foreign Affairs, Alexei Rykov for the interior, and Joseph Stalin for nationalities.

To indicate the good intentions of the new government, the long-postponed elections for a constituent assembly were held on November 25. To the chagrin of the Bolsheviks, this first Russian election in which the suffrage was universal, secret, and direct, resulted in an overwhelming victory for the Social Revolutionaries. Had the government been of the responsible type, the Bolsheviks now would have resigned their authority into the hands of the majority party. Having no intention of jeopardizing their control, they postponed the meeting of the assembly until January 1918 and strove in the meantime to consolidate their strength and intimidate opponents.

Despite these tactics the assembly, when it met, elected a Social Revolutionary president and voted down a Bolshevik proposal to disarm all classes of the population save the workmen. The Bolsheviks thereupon dissolved the "reactionary" assembly by force. Local soviets that betrayed anti-Bolshevik sympathies were likewise dissolved and their leaders imprisoned or exiled. A working class dictatorship replaced the short-lived democracy. It may be interesting, at this point, to survey the careers of the two most prominent commissars.

Vladimir Ilyich Ulyanov, alias N. Lenin,[2] was born in 1870. The Ulyanov family, though it belonged to the lower nobility, was known for its radical tendencies. Vladimir's brother, Alexander, was hanged for complicity in a plot to kill the Tsar and Vladimir himself was expelled from a university for participation in a student riot. A few years later he was permitted to enter another university and eventually got a degree in law. In the meantime he had become absorbed in the study of Karl Marx's *Capital.* He joined a radical group and soon became one of its most active members, paying for this temerity with an involuntary sojourn in Siberia. In 1900 he went to Switzerland and, except for a brief visit during the Revolution of 1905, remained outside Russia until 1917. During these years he edited radical newspapers and traveled extensively in Western Europe, making the acquaintance of outstanding agitators. In 1903 he became the leader of the Bolshevik faction of the Social Democratic Party.

Lenin was unprepossessing in appearence : short, thickset, bald, and bearded. He never knew poverty, but he led a simple life. A dedicated revolutionary, capitalism appeared to him as evil incarnate and world revolution as the highest goal. To achieve the destruction of the former and the attainment of the latter, he regarded all means fair.

In 1917 the Germans, hoping that the most prominent Bolshevik might agitate effectively for Russia's withdrawal from the war, permitted Lenin to return to Russia in a sealed car to conduct subversive propaganda. He carefully planned the overthrow of the provisional regime and took note of the widespread peasant and worker movements which, after the first outbursts of violence, now aimed at consolidating the social and economic results of the overturn. After several months of activity he decided that the time had come to strike, and in October he converted his followers to the same view.

One of Lenin's ablest lieutenants was Lev Davydovich Bronstein, alias Leon Trotsky, born in 1879 of prosperous peasant parentage. Trotsky enjoyed little formal schooling but was an avid reader and grew up to be a man of literary culture. The inequality and injustice which he saw about him in his childhood made lasting impressions upon his sensitive mind, and while still young he came under the influence of radical thinkers. Between 1898 and 1917 he spent four years in prison, was twice exiled to Siberia, and lived abroad for twelve years.

Like Lenin he traveled widely in Europe, lecturing and writing. When the break between the Bolsheviks and the Mensheviks occurred, he for a time led a middle group of Trotskyites and did not go over to Lenin's side until 1917. During the war he was expelled from France and Spain and deported to the United States, living in

[2] Lenin sometimes used the initial "N.," but not the name "Nikolai."

New York for a time in 1917, but then managing to return to Russia. Trotsky was an indefatigable worker and an able organizer. A strong believer in discipline and system, he laid the foundations for the powerful and efficient Red Army.

THE END OF FOREIGN AND CIVIL WAR

The conclusion of a separate peace with the Central Powers was accomplished through the signing of the Treaty of Brest-Litovsk (March 3, 1918).[3] By the terms of this and some supplementary pacts, Russia gave up 500,000 square miles of territory and agreed to pay a heavy indemnity. The conclusion of this peace, harsh though it was, permitted the Bolsheviks to concentrate upon domestic affairs. Most urgent among these was the need to deal with numerous counterrevolutionary movements. From 1917 to 1920 the Bolsheviks were engaged in a life-and-death struggle with an opposition variously led by nobles, clergymen, republicans, adventurers, ex-tsarist officers, and champions of local rights. For a time, several groups of counterrevolutionaries were aided by the German invaders. Later the Allies sent men, money, and munitions to be used against the Reds.

The Allies hoped by restoring bourgeois control to rebuild the eastern front against Germany. They wanted to keep from German or Bolshevik hands the war supplies at Murmansk and Archangel, which they earlier had placed at the disposal of the Russians. They were angered by a Bolshevik repudiation of all Russian debts. The Allied blockade therefore was extended to Russia; Allied and United States military contingents were sent to Murmansk, Archangel, and Vladivostok; and, when Turkey quit the war, the French captured Odessa and the British attacked Baku.[4] Thousands of Czech and Slovak soldiers, who previously had deserted to Russia from the Austro-Hungarian armies, likewise turned against the Bolsheviks. Nationalists in the Baltic states and the Transcaucasian areas declared their independence, and Romania stepped into Bessarabia.

Wherever they were sent, the foreign troops cooperated with anti-Bolshevik natives to set up "White" governments. In the beginning it appeared that the Bolsheviks would be overwhelmed by all these foes. The few Red Guards could not cope with enemies who outnumbered them several times. At one stage the followers of Lenin were in control only of Petrograd, Moscow, and a few provinces surrounding these cities.

---

[3] Late in 1917, the Bolsheviks denounced and published the texts of the wartime Secret Treaties to which Russia had been a party. Negotiations for a separate peace were undertaken only after the Allies had refused a proposal of Trotsky to consider a general peace, with self-determination for all subject peoples and "no annexations and no indemnities."
[4] The Japanese dispatched thousands of soldiers to Siberia.

Two factors, nevertheless, played into the hands of the Bolsheviks. First, the intervention of foreign soldiers in a domestic matter induced a number of patriots, especially young officers, to aid the Reds in repelling the outsiders. Secondly, many peasants, although they did not understand the theories of the Bolsheviks and did not like their policies, were even more opposed to the restoration of the Whites. Of the two evils the peasants apparently preferred the Reds. Consequently, the Russian masses in general obstructed the progress of the counterrevolutionaries as much as they dared.

While the Red-White conflict was at its height, it seemed dangerous to the Bolsheviks to keep the ex-imperial family confined near Petrograd, where it might become a rallying point for reactionaries. Hence, the Romanov prisoners were sent to the Ural town of Ekaterinburg (Sverdlovsk). It was planned to subject the former emperor to a public trial, with Trotsky as state prosecutor; but when, in the summer of 1918, the Whites under Admiral Alexander Kolchak fought their way to the neighborhood of Ekaterinburg, the local soviet officials became panicky and ordered the shooting of Nicholas, Alexandra, their son, and four daughters.

As the months rolled by, the Bolsheviks gradually developed two weapons with which to cut short domestic and foreign opposition. To crush the counterrevolutionaries there was created an Extraordinary Commission to Combat Counterrevolution, Speculation, and Sabotage, known from its initials as the Cheka. Trotsky declared that "terror, as the demonstration of the will and strength of the working class, was historically justified." Thus, the Cheka arrested and executed at will, and then merely presented reports of its activities to the commissars and the central executive committee. There were no reliable statistics on the number of lives taken by this revolutionary tribunal, but it broke the backbone of the opposition and almost obliterated the bourgeoisie and intelligentsia.

The tsarist generals and foreign troops were dealt with by the Red Army, which, by 1919, had become a well-drilled force of 100,000 men, led largely by ex-imperial officers loyal to Russia. As the Bolshevik army grew, the Allies became less anxious to continue their armed intervention. Besides, the actions of the Whites alienated the sympathies of Western labor and of some Western diplomats, who eventually contented themselves with contributing supplies and a few officers to the cause of restoration. In the summer of 1920, Great Britain, the United States, and Italy raised the Russian blockade.

The Red Army fought until late in 1920 to restore internal peace. Its first successes came in the neighborhood of Petrograd and then in Siberia. Between July and October 1920, peace treaties were signed with Lithuania, Latvia, Finland, and Poland. A compromise boundary with Poland was established. By November 1920, the last important White leader had gone into exile. After six years of continuous warfare, Russia was at "peace".

This "Russia" of 1920 comprised only a fraction, if a large one, of the former empire of the Tsar. Indeed, there remained as Russia only an association of autonomous regions known, since the spring of 1918, as the Russian Socialist Federated Soviet Republic (R.S.F.S.R.). Gradually, however, neighboring areas were regained until, in 1922, a treaty of union was signed among a number of separate Bolshevik states. This treaty went into effect in 1923, and the new federation was termed the Union of Soviet Socialist Republics (U.S.S.R.) The word *Russian* was omitted from the official title since it was hoped that other countries, inhabited by non-Russians, eventually might join the U.S.S.R.

By 1936 there were eleven Soviet republics, including Asiatic territories. Soviet acquisitions in 1939–1940 increased the number of republics to sixteen, as shown in the accompanying map. Despite the supposed equality of the republics, the R.S.F.S.R., comprising the larger part of the area and population of the union, dominated the combination. The members of the federation, in theory, retained considerable autonomy and "the right freely to leave the union."

GOVERNMENT AND THE COMMUNIST PARTY TO 1939

To the older Bolsheviks, communism was both a philosophy and a method. Philosophically, it aimed at the building of a classless society through the abolition of private property and the common ownership of all means of production and distribution. Its method involved first a national, and then an international, social revolution under a dictatorship of the working people. These principles, traceable to the *Communist Manifesto* published in 1848 by Karl Marx and Friedrich Engels, underlay the Soviet constitution.

The constitution of the R.S.F.S.R., model for all others in the U.S.S.R., proclaimed Russia a socialist republic of workers and peasants, with authority vested in soviets. National resources were declared the property of the state. Labor was made the duty of every citizen. Workingmen were guaranteed freedom of religious and atheistic opinion, and the enjoyment of education. Oppression of national minorities was forbidden, and foreign workers who came to dwell in Russia were to have the same status as native laborers.

Supreme authority was lodged with an All-Russian Congress of Soviets. The congress, until 1936, was composed of 1 deputy for every 25,000 *voters* in the cities and 1 delegate for every 125,000 *inhabitants* in the provinces. Since the resulting body was unwieldy, the congress empowered an All-Russian Central Executive Committee to act as the effective directing agency.

This committee was given power to issue decrees, coordinate legislation and administration, and appoint a cabinet known as the All-Russian Council of People's Commissars. The importance of the committee increased proportionally with the declining influence of the congress. The congress at first met infrequently, then annually,

REPUBLICS OF THE SOVIET UNION 1940

and eventually biennially. Eventually also, it merely approved whatever the committee had ordained. Since even the committee soon was regarded as too large for efficient work, it came to meet only a few times a year, leaving the conduct of affairs and the supervision of the commissars to a presidium of about forty. Under the watchful eyes of this body, the Council of Commissars or *sovnarkom* carried on the actual work of governing the state. All decrees of the sovnarkom required eventual submission to the central executive committee for ratification or annulment.

Local authority was given to local soviets, closely supervised by

Courtesy, Foreign Policy Association, *Headline Series.*

the central government. The cities were to be governed by soviets elected on a basis of 1 deputy for each 1000 of the population. Representation was based upon vocation rather than geographical division, and the people in the various occupations were to vote separately—generally by show of hands.

Representation in the soviets above the local councils was made indirect. The village soviets until 1936 sent delegates to district congresses of soviets and these in turn to regional congresses. From these last were chosen the All-Russian Congress.

The franchise was accorded to all men and women over eighteen who were workers, soldiers, or sailors. This rule applied equally to Russians and to foreigners living in Russia. The following groups in general were deprived of the suffrage and the right to hold office: (1) persons who hired labor for profit or who lived on an income not derived from their own direct labor; (2) businessmen, traders, commercial agents, monks, and clergymen; (3) members of the former dynasty, police, gendarmerie, and secret service; and (4) individuals and the children of individuals who opposed the process of farm collectivization. In 1934, citizenship and suffrage rights were restored to those former landlords, members of the bourgeoisie and wealthier peasantry, priests, and former White policemen and soldiers who had been engaged for at least five years in "socially useful work" or who had served faithfully in the Bolshevik army. According to Soviet figures, only 2.5 per cent of the adult population now remained disfranchised.

The supreme organ in the U.S.S.R. was the All-Union Congress of Soviets, elected, until 1936, by the city and regional soviets in each of the republics. Since the Congress contained more than 1500 delegates, it met only biennially, for about a week, to approve the work of the Union Central Executive Committee and the Union Council of Commissars.

Until 1936 the Union Central Executive Committee consisted of two bodies, a Union Soviet and a Soviet of Nationalities. The Union Soviet was elected by the All-Union Congress and represented the republics in proportion to their population. The Soviet of Nationalities was elected by the local central executive committees in the various republics, subject to confirmation by the All-Union Congress. The creation of this council of nationalities emphasized the fact that the Soviet Union included scores of distinct national groups and encouraged the perpetuation of cultural and linguistic differences among these groups. Until 1936 the whole committee met three times a year, its two branches sitting and voting separately. Between sessions, the committee's powers were delegated to a Union Presidium, which supervised the work of the Union Council of Commissars, the cabinet of the U.S.S.R. Subordinated to the Union Central Executive Committee was a Union Supreme Court.

The soviet governmental system had four distinguishing characteristics. First, although the U.S.S.R. was a federal state, the central government had unusually broad powers. The member republics might legislate freely only on affairs of definitely local importance. Secondly, since the Bolsheviks believed that the individual's attitude towards political questions was determined by his occupation, representation rested upon a vocational rather than a geographical basis. Thirdly, the electoral system, until 1936, was highly indirect. The peasants were six steps removed from the Union Council of Commissars and the urban workers four steps. Thus many non-Communist deputies were weeded out in the successive elections, and the supreme authority was free of popular control. Finally, there was no separation of powers. The Union Central Executive Committee had supreme legislative, administrative, and judicial control in the land.

In December 1936 the All-Union Congress of Soviets adopted a new constituion. The economic basis of the U.S.S.R., according to this charter, was "formed by the socialist system of economy and the socialist ownership of implements and the means of production." Socialist ownership had "the form" of state ownership in the cities and collective-farm ownership in the rural areas. Every peasant household on each collective farm was to have "for its own use a small piece of land attached to the homestead and . . . a dwelling house, productive livestock, poultry, and minor agricultural implements." Legal protection was extended to "the right of personal property of citizens in the income from their toil and savings . . . as well as the right of inheritance of personal property." Thus there would be "realized the principle of socialism: 'From each according to his ability, to each according to his toil.' "[5]

The new constitution ended the unequal weighting of town and country votes. Since by this time most of the rural households were collectivized, the authorities felt it safe to equalize the political weight of peasantry and industrial proletariat and to end the indirect method of building up the governmental hierarchy. Final authority now was given to a Supreme Soviet of the U.S.S.R., which contained two equipowerful houses: the Union Soviet and the Soviet of Nationalities. Members of both houses were to be elected every four years. All citizens over eighteen were permitted to take part in elections on an equal basis and voting was made secret. The directive organ of the Supreme Soviet was to be the Presidium of about forty; this body also was to keep watch over the Union Council of People's Commissars. The first election under the new constitution was held in 1937. It represented a total victory for the Stalinist candidates—there being no others.

The All-Union Communist Party was the foundation stone of the soviet governmental structure and the source of its power. Without directions from the party "no important political or organizational problem was ever decided by the soviets." The roll of the party in 1939 included 2,500,000 members and probationers.[6] In addition, there were several junior Communist societies, such as the *Komsomol* or Alliance of Communist Youth. New members of the party came to be recruited chiefly from among the graduates of the Komsomol,

[5] This represented a considerable modification of the original Bolshevik maxim: "From each according to his ability, to each according to his needs."

[6] Soon after they came into power, those Bolsheviks who had been active in the days of tsardom formed a Society of Old Bolsheviks. Intelligent and well educated, these persons for some time monopolized the important party and state offices. They lived under a rigid code of discipline and morals. In 1935 the society was reported dissolved.

but not every graduate was admitted. From 1939, an applicant for membership had to be endorsed by three party members of at least three years' standing. It was impressed "on the mind of every candidate that there must be a complete subordination of all personal feelings to the welfare of the party." Communists had to be at the disposal of their superiors, obey orders implicitly, go without question wherever and whenever they might be sent, devote their spare time to preaching communism, and be ready to defend the revolution with their lives.

Each year a committee purged the party of some of its members. The percentage of expulsion varied, affecting 2 per cent of the membership in one year and 25 per cent in another (1934). The grounds for expulsion were broad, including drunkenness, church attendance, and utilization of party standing merely to advance one's personal career. Lenin was said to have likened such politicians to radishes—"red" outside but "white" at heart.

The organization of the Communist Party was outlined in a constitution of 1925, amended in 1934 and 1939. At the base of the pyramid-like party structure were thousands of local cells. These elected representatives to a party congress which, being too large for efficient work, merely approved the decisions taken by its smaller committees.[7] Of these the most important were a Central Committee and a Commission of Party Control. The latter was charged with consolidating the unity of the party and maintaining discipline and loyalty among the adherents.

The Central Committee—the actual directive agency of the party —was composed of about seventy members with almost as many alternates. Although it met frequently, its functions were carried on through two small bureaus and a secretariat. An organization bureau (Orgbureau), consisting (1939) of nine regular members, was responsible for fixing the conditions of membership in the party, for promotions and demotions, and for supervising the propaganda. It was subordinate to the political bureau (Politbureau) which, with nine members, determined the general policies of the party and, through it, of the state.

The chief officer of the party was the Secretary-General of the Central Committee. Joseph Stalin, as incumbent of this office and at once a member of the Politbureau, the Orgbureau, and the secretariat, was for almost three decades the most important factor in the determination of the party's policies. Inasmuch as the party was "the helm of the government," he became the dictator of the Soviet Union. In 1941, he took the title of President of the Council of People's Commissars or Premier.

---

[7] Originally this congress met every two years, but gradually its gatherings became even less frequent. In addition to the local cells and the congress, the party hierarchy included county, provincial, city, and regional committees. There were no separate parties representing the federated republics in the union.

To uphold its class dictatorship during the transitional period in which the U.S.S.R. was presumably to be prepared for thorough-going communism, the party resorted to a variety of means. It was the only organized political group in the land. Since the number of available party candidates was limited, the village soviets some-times were made up largely of non-Communists. However, at least until 1936, the indirect process of selection for the higher offices invariably led to the elimination of the nonparty deputies from the superior governmental agencies. The strict censorship, the propa-ganda, the open voting (until 1936), and the disfranchisement of the naturally hostile groups, all were of help to the Communist candi-dates in the cities.

In the early days of Bolshevik control, criticism of the party's policies was not entirely prohibited. Conservative suggestions in line with Communist policy were accepted, though they had to come from within the party, not from organized opposition groups. Stalin, however, holding that "the party is not a debating society," re-pressed all opposition. Suppression originally was enforced by a Unified State Political Administration, known from its initials as the OGPU. This secret police agency was the heir of the Cheka, which was abolished in 1922. In 1934 the dread OGPU, which had inflicted many summary death sentences, was replaced by a Commissariat (later Ministry) for Internal Affairs. The latter, whose initials spelled NKVD (later MVD), might inflict penalties, without public trial, as severe as exile at hard labor for five years.[8]

---

[8] The advent of the Bolshevik Revolution and Communist totalitarianism in Russia has been another major problem troubling historians. In William Henry Chamberlin's *The Russian Revolution,* published in 1935, the author saw the first upheaval, in March 1917, as a spontaneous uprising of "the anonymous host of workers . . . and soldiers." John Maynard, in his *Russia in Flux,* which appeared in 1958, observed that the demands of the peasantry were the initiating factor in March. Merle Fainsod, in 1953, in *How Russia Is Ruled,* found the iron hand of Lenin, brilliant tactician and organizer, behind the second or Bolshevik Revolution in 1917. Isaac Deutscher in his *Stalin,* published in 1949, indicated that the Bolsheviks as a group led the Russian workers toward radical revolution. In addition, several writers sought to place blame on Alexander Kerensky as the be-trayer of Russia, who knowingly passed the country into the hands of the Bolsheviks. Kerensky, who survived the troubled days of 1917 to come to the United States, defended himself vigorously in many writings. Recently historians have attempted to take a broader view. The signi-ficance of the Russian Revolution, indicated one of the more recent authors, does not lie in the Bolsheviks' seizure of power, but in the overall struggle for political, social, and industrial modernization that convulsed Russia, beginning with the first industrial expansion at the close of the nineteenth century and continuing through the First Five-Year Plan. Through it all, too, indicated this writer, runs the continuous thread of a deeply felt desire to replace the West as a model for formerly backward but develop-ing nations. See: Theodore H. Von Laue, *Why Lenin? Why Stalin?* (New York: J. B. Lippincott Company, 1964).

ATTEMPTED PURE COMMUNISM
AND "NEP," 1917-1928

The Soviet Government, soon after coming into power, decreed the nationalization of the land, the natural resources, and the means of production and distribution. The immediate goal was to permit the peasants to use the land according to their needs, and to place the factories, mines, and transportation facilities under control of the workers. The products of industry and agriculture were to be turned over to the state for distribution among the people on a basis of need. Thus, crops raised by the peasants in excess of their own wants were to be used in feeding the industrial proletariat, whereas the manufactured output of the latter was to be distributed among the peasantry. A Supreme Economic Council was charged with keeping the factories supplied with raw materials and fuel, providing food for the laborers, and making available to the peasants such manufactured goods as they might require.

It had been planned to devise a schedule of nationalization and to confiscate at first only the large trusts, allowing the smaller businesses temporarily to carry on under the old forms. Actually, the early process of nationalization was haphazard, taking on the character of a punitive rather than an economic measure. The workers were impatient to oust their bosses and managers and to run the factories under the supervision of elected committees; but since few of the men were trained in management, there was little discipline and less efficiency.

For a while it seemed as if even the most radical transformations might be successful. As long as the Whites' counterrevolution and the intervention of the Allies continued, many of the changes were regarded by the workers and peasants as phases of a transient "War Communism" dictated by military emergency. With the return of peace, however, the procedure began to appear impracticable and conducive more to chaos than to the increased welfare of the masses. The chief opposition to the Communist regime came from peasants. At first even these, in fear lest the landlords come back, had offered little resistance to the emissaries of the state who came to requisition their surplus crops. But when the danger was past, the peasants anticipated a new-found prosperity, for they interpreted the abolition of landlordism as the end of rents and taxes and the right to an extra strip of land. By 1920, indeed, they had occupied more than 96 per cent of the arable soil in European Russia. They had no inclination to listen to theories concerning state ownership of land or the desirability of sharing their produce with the urban proletariat.

In return for their grain, the peasants wanted money or manufactured goods, neither of which was available in quantity. There was little hard money in circulation, and the peasants wanted none of the worthless paper. There was a dearth of manufactured goods because importation had dwindled to a trickle. The factories were short of raw materials, equipment had broken down, management was poor, and transportation facilities were almost nonexistent. The peasantry began to hoard its crops and plead poverty whenever the government requisitioners appeared.

To enforce requisitions, the state organized the poorer peasants into committees to denounce the wealthier peasants and make them surrender their surpluses. This added the bitterness of intravillage strife to the other difficulties and did little to increase the grain supply for the cities. The war and devastation, and the fact that the counterrevolutionaries for a time controlled southern Russia, added to the grain shortage. Despairingly, the state armed the workmen, enrolled them in a Food Army, and sent them into the villages to force the peasants to disgorge their hoardings.

It now was the turn of the peasants to despair. In self-defense they resorted to passive resistance. Since everything above their barest needs was to be taken from them, they would raise only enough to keep alive. Then, in 1920 and 1921, the country suffered a severe drought. Famine resulted—one of the worst in the history of Russia. Several million persons starved to death in city and country. More might have perished but for the generosity of foreign, especially United States, relief contributions.

Meanwhile, the Supreme Economic Council was unable to carry out its functions. Despite the issuance of official decrees lengthening working hours and establishing rewards for production, the industrial output in 1920 was but 13 per cent of that in 1913. Cries of "Down with the Soviet Government!" were heard during 1920 at popular meetings, and Tambov witnessed a military outbreak. In 1921 the sailors at Kronstadt, once the very hotbed of Bolshevism, mutinied. Although most of the mutineers were recent recruits of peasant background, the uprising convinced the government that a change in policy was urgent. Lenin decided to effect a strategic retreat.

At the tenth party congress, in 1921, the Communists voted to adopt a New Economic Policy (NEP). They now realized that their enthusiasm had carried them too far, that they had pushed ahead with insufficient regard for the obstacles that an agrarian Russia offered to an industrial dictatorship. The realities of the situation indicated that if the political changes that had been effected were to be maintained, it might be necessary to make economic concessions. Such a course would involve retreat, but it need not be a rout. The Communists might retain control of the government, certain key industries, and major economic elements, while granting minor concessions in such things as local trading and graduated wage scales. Lenin recommended that the party change its tactics from "assault to siege," retaining "as much communism as the exigencies of the situation would permit, and no more."

It appeared for a time as though the NEP would cure the major economic ills of the country. In 1925 the state permitted the renting of land for short periods and the employment of a limited number of farm laborers. Thereupon some of the more enterprising peasants leased their neighbors' lands and hired extra hands. As a result, the peasantry again fell into three classes: the poor, those who were fairly well off, and the well to do. In 1928 the authorities decided to burden heavily the more prosperous *kulaks* or "fists," who constituted about 12 per cent of the total peasantry.

The state had no intention of allowing the kulaks to develop into a strong class, holding large stretches of land. They were tolerated for a time because their enterprise was needed to increase the production of grain, but they were given to understand that the government contemplated their eventual downfall. As one means of combating the kulaks and simultaneously increasing the grain output, the Bolsheviks elaborated an earlier program for the creation of collective farms. Every effort was made to secure modern machinery and ambitious workers for the enterprise, but little progress was made before 1928.

In the industrial sphere the state continued its virtual monopoly of manufactures. Several hundred state trusts were created. Each was placed under a committee of managers responsible to the Supreme Economic Council.

For the first few years after the introduction of the NEP, private trading flourished. In the fiscal year 1923–1924, three-fifths of the retail trade was handled by private merchants. Individuals who took advantage of this opportunity to gain profit, however, generally were unpopular and came to be called Nepmen. The government fought the Nepmen, especially through consumers' cooperatives, societies that eventually handled about half of the state's retail trade.

Although the NEP did much to heal the ravages of the early Communist experiments and gradually brought production back to the prewar level, considerable hardship was caused by the disparity between the prices of grain and of manufactured products. The state allowed grain to sell at the world market price, but manufactures could be bought only at figures arbitrarily set by the state trusts. Thus, in 1928, the cost of grain was half again as great as in 1913, but the price of manufactured goods was three times as high.

While the NEP was in force, state bureaus gathered statistical information on every phase of the union's economic life. The data thus accumulated were used in the projection of a five-year plan for the further increase of production. In October 1928 the First Five-Year Plan was inaugurated. Before considering its details, it is necessary to relate the story of a quarrel among the leaders of the Communist Party.

THE SUPREMACY OF STALIN

Until the spring of 1922 Lenin, chairman of the Politbureau of the Communist Party, was dictator of the Soviet State. With his prestige he was able not only to shape governmental policies, but to prevent any outward appearance of disharmony among the lesser party leaders. The tremendous strain of the work gradually began to tell on Lenin's health. In 1922 he suffered a stroke and temporarily lost the use of his right arm and leg. Upon his recovery he once more applied himself to his work, but soon found it necessary to entrust many administrative duties to others. In 1923 he suffered a second stroke. He lived in agony for months and finally, during an evening in January 1924, he died. To the rank and file of the Communists, his tomb in Moscow became a shrine; to the party leaders, his passing signalized a struggle for control.[9]

Outstanding among the candidates for leadership of the party and government were two men: Leon Trotsky and Joseph Stalin. Firebrand, organizer of the Red Army, prominent member of the most important party organs, Trotsky was, after Lenin, the best known of the Bolsheviks. He had many enemies. Some Communists were repelled by his aggressiveness, rudeness, and vanity. His impatience to inaugurate a world upheaval regardless of the difficult domestic situation, and his disdain for the peasantry as being too backward to be of any aid in the firm establishment of communism, antagonized others. The Old Bolsheviks had not yet forgiven him for his opposition to Lenin, up to the very year of the successful revolution. Finally, his opponents made effective capital of the trenchant epithets which he and Lenin had hurled at each other in the early days of their acquaintance, and of his failure to attend Lenin's funeral.

The main opposition to Trotsky came from three men: Stalin, Leo Kamenev, and Gregory E. Zinoviev.[10] The chief of this triumvirate was the Georgian peasant Stalin, really Joseph Vissarionovich Dzhugashvili, who was born in 1879, the son of a shoemaker. Inspired by a decree of Alexander III, which made it possible for poor men's sons to enter the priesthood, Joseph's parents sent the boy to a theological seminary. The burly youth, however, had little desire to become a priest and displayed greater acquaintance with Marx than with the Bible. He soon was expelled from the clerical institution and became actively affiliated with the Social Democratic Party. Fearless, unscrupulous, and taciturn, Dzhugashvili proved adept in the execution of dangerous missions. Of all the aliases which he found it expedient to assume, none seemed to fit him better than

[9] Soon after Lenin's death the name of Petrograd was changed to Leningrad. Moscow had become the capital in 1918.
[10] Kamenev, a close friend of Lenin, once had studied law in Paris. Zinoviev, a cruel but able organizer, was director of the association charged with promoting the world revolution.

that of Stalin, meaning *Steel*. In 1903, he was one of the first to follow the lead of Lenin as a Bolshevik.

Stalin, despite his cunning, was six times arrested and exiled between 1902 and 1913. Five times, through sheer physical prowess, he managed to escape, but in 1913 he was sent to the Arctic Circle and remained a prisoner until released after the March Revolution. It appeared that the tsarist police on no occasion recognized him as a previous offender, else one or another of his sentences might have been death instead of exile. In disregard of the danger, Stalin preferred to agitate from within Russia rather than from the safety of an office abroad. He worked incessantly, writing, organizing revolutionary circles, forging bank notes, and "expropriating" money to finance the cause.

After the November Revolution he won distinction as a military leader, particularly in the successful defense of Tsaritsin (later Stalingrad) against the Cossacks. When the government of the R.S.F.S.R. was organized, Stalin, already Secretary-General of the party, was made Commissar for Nationalities (1917–1923). He was instrumental in the unification of the Transcaucasian Republic and in the organization of the U.S.S.R. Himself a member of a national minority, he saw to it that the rights of the lesser national groups were protected.

The rival leaders, both of whom professed to be loyal Leninists, expressed antithetical views on several major points. Stalin believed capitalism to be so firmly entrenched in the West that any effort to bring about its immediate overthrow would be futile. He preferred to concentrate on "socialism in one country" rather than upon uncertain attempts to dislodge capitalism from the West. Trotsky, on the contrary, was intolerant of any letup in the world revolutionary movement.

Further, Stalin, the peasant, was aware that the welfare of the U.S.S.R. in the last analysis depended upon the cooperation of the country's food producers. Hence, he advocated the establishment of better relations between the government and the peasantry, even though this entailed a prolongation of the compromise with petty capitalism. Trotsky had no desire to wait until the peasants became reconciled to communism. Revolution in the capitalistic West appeared to him far more important than economic prosperity in the U.S.S.R. He would simply force the agrarians in all lands to bow to the rule of the "enlightened proletariat." Finally, whereas Stalin was convinced of the necessity of hiring foreign capital and technical assistance to hasten the industrialization of the U.S.S.R., Trotsky looked upon any deal with Western financiers or experts as treason.

The duel for supremacy began immediately after Lenin's death, and from the outset Stalin seemed to have the advantage. During his long tenure as Secretary-General he had had ample opportunity to see that a majority of the important party posts, especially those on the Central Committee, were filled with his adherents. Elevated to succeed Lenin as Chairman of the Politbureau, he quietly worked with Kamenev and Zinoviev to oust Trotsky, the Commissar for War and Member of the Council of Labor and Defense. Early in 1925 this was accomplished, and soon thereafter Trotsky's followers were removed from the war and navy departments. The fallen leader temporarily was exiled to the Caucasus "for his health," and then given only a minor job in Moscow.

With Trotsky out of the way, Stalin sought compromise with the peasants and the foreign concessionaires. So great was his apparent retreat from communism that his erstwhile supporters, Kamenev and Zinoviev, turned against him. Stalin skillfully got the approval of the party congress of 1925 for his actions and saw to it that his latest antagonists were demoted and ordered to cease their opposition. He also recruited a new circle of supporters on the council of commissars, the secret police, and the staff of the party newspaper, *Pravda* (Truth).

Trotsky, seeing in the changed situation an opportunity to retrieve his position, joined forces with Kamenev and Zinoviev in an effort to oust his enemy from control. Once more the party backed Stalin, for he had made his policies appear as a fulfillment of the wishes of the congress, whereas Trotsky persistently strove to bend the party to his will. The "deviationists" received another admonition to cease their opposition and submit to party discipline. When they persisted in anti-Stalinist agitation, the dictator ordered the OGPU on their trail. Every move of the dissenters was watched, and they were given no chance to express their views in speech or press. Driven to meet in secret, the Trotskyites eventually were charged with the illegal organization of an opposition group. Late in 1927 Trotsky, Kamenev, and Zinoviev were expelled from the Communist Party, and in 1928 the trio was sent to outlying parts of the union.

For a brief period Stalin's leadership seemed unchallenged. Kamenev and Zinoviev recanted and were reinstated in the party. Trotsky, however, from Central Asia, continued to agitate against the man whom he regarded as "the outstanding mediocrity of the party." Experienced revolutionary that he was, Trotsky managed to keep in touch with a considerable number of dissatisfied working men who shared his distrust of Stalin and the peasants. When, in the winter of 1928–1929, his activities inspired several disturbances, the OGPU was ordered to stamp out opposition. Wholesale arrests were made, and Trotsky was accused of "preparing for an armed struggle against the Soviet power." Promptly deported, he settled down near Constantinople and soon produced an autobiography, an account of the Bolshevik Revolution, and innumerable attacks on Stalinism.

All Stalin's actions against Trotskyism were upheld by later party conferences. During 1929 and 1930, Stalin was equally successful in crushing a "rightist deviation." In 1934 Zinoviev once more was ousted from the party, for "Trotskyist deviation," and in 1935 he was sentenced to prison for ten years.

Slowly but surely Stalin pushed ahead. Never openly forcing his views on anyone, carefully giving the impression of merely carrying out the mandates of the party, the "man of steel" appeared, in 1935, to be one of the most firmly entrenched of continental dictators. Then, in August 1936, a startled world was informed by the Soviet press that Zinoviev, Kamenev, and five others were accused of having formed terrorist groups to assassinate eight Soviet leaders, including Stalin, and of having carried out the "foul murder" of Stalin's aide, Sergei Kirov, in December 1934. Nine other men were charged with "being members of the underground Trotskyite-Zinovievite organization" and with having participated in "the preparations to assassinate" the seven marked officials remaining after Kirov's death. All defendants were linked with Trotsky (who had since gone to Mexico) and with the Nazi secret police. They were charged with having planned a fascist dictatorship.

The public trial was held before the Union Supreme Court and, to the astonishment of the world, the accused vied with one another in their eagerness to confess guilt and to implicate others not yet on trial. All but two pleaded guilty to the whole charge and verbally castigated themselves for having betrayed Stalin. Within five days the defendants were declared guilty and sentenced to be shot. Twenty-four hours later the press reported that the executions had been carried out. Trotsky and his son also were "convicted by the evidence" and made subject to "immediate arrest and trial" if ever discovered on Soviet soil.

Meanwhile the Government had investigated other highly placed personages, and another sensational trial occurred in 1937. The alleged Trotskyite conspirators now included Karl Radek, former editor of *Izvestia*, Grigori Sokolnikov, former ambassador to Great Britain, and Grigori Piatakov, former Assistant Commissar for Heavy Industry. They were charged with having agreed to support Germany and Japan in a war against the U.S.S.R. and with promising the two states "a large number of political and economic privileges and territorial concessions." All seventeen defendants pleaded guilty, and thirteen were sentenced to be shot. Four, including Radek and Sokolnikov, were given prison terms on the ground that their crimes had been "political" rather than "terroristic."

A specific enumeration of undisputed facts in the Moscow trials yielded meager results. Several prominent Old Bolsheviks were indicted for plotting against the Stalin regime. They were accused of conspiring to assassinate high officials, form alliances with enemies of the Soviet Union, ensure an industrial breakdown in the event of war, and substitute a fascist state for the existing setup. The defendants were brought to court, confessed guilt, and were condemned to punishment. Trotsky, in exile, was linked to all charges and denied connection with any of them. Nothing else was definitely known, although the partisans of each side speculatively elaborated upon these facts.

Throughout 1937–1938 and into 1939 there were numerous additional purges and trials, and, apparently, hundreds of executions of civil, military, and church officials. Marshals, commissars, and vice-commissars were demoted, dismissed, imprisoned, or shot, and entire branches of the administration were reorganized.

Inefficiency, sabotage, and conspiring with foreign agents were the usual charges. The need to replace so many officials in short order led to the appointment of numerous young and inexperienced Soviet-reared executives under whose direction it was difficult to achieve efficiency and discipline. Hence a vigorous campaign was launched, in 1939, against lazy, tardy, and irregularly attending workers. At the end of the year, Stalin again was undisputed head of the Soviet Union.[11]

THE FIVE-YEAR PLANS

It was under the watchful eye of Stalin that the First Five-Year Plan, which supplanted the NEP, entered into operation (1928). The plan was a complete forecast of the economic and cultural life of the Soviet Union for the period 1928–1933. It was formulated, inaugurated, and directed by a State Planning Commission or *Gosplan*. No major step in industry, agriculture, transportation, or finance might be undertaken without the prior consent of the Gosplan.

Under the plan it was hoped within half a decade to increase the industrial output of the U.S.S.R. by 136 per cent and the agricultural output by 55 per cent. Technical schools were to be established and foreign experts hired. The cost of production was to be lowered by a third and the productivity of labor doubled.

One-fifth of the peasant holdings were to be collectivized. Illiteracy was to be virtually wiped out, the number of books published greatly increased, and music and dramatic performances made available to every village.

To make possible the proper distribution of raw materials, foodstuffs, and manufactures, the Russians strove to improve their motor-transport facilities and railways. Technical assistance agreements were signed with foreign companies and individuals, and generous terms were offered to skilled foreign workmen who would agree to come to the U.S.S.R.

An effort was made to secure for the plan the fullest cooperation of the citizenry. That the program would bring hardship was no secret, particularly after the reintroduction in 1928 of a food-rationing system. By all avenues of public communication, the people were stirred to a fever of excitement. "Shock brigades" of young Communists vied in the accomplishment of production tasks. The

[11] In 1940 Trotsky was killed in Mexico by a former disciple.

spirit of competition was systematically exploited and prizes were awarded when production quotas were exceeded.

The plan in operation seemed actually to outstrip the plan on paper. Industrial projects were dedicated ahead of schedule and production goals were surpassed in some areas. In agriculture the results for a time appeared equally gratifying, and so encouraging were the results that the date for the ending of the plan was advanced to December 1, 1932.

Nevertheless, the plan lagged in two important items: a lowered cost of production and an increase in the productivity of labor. Moreover, quantity was being produced at the expense of quality. The automobile works at Nizhni-Novogorod (Gorki), which had been expected to turn out 144,000 cars per year, was closed three months after its much celebrated opening. In 1932 there was a shortage of grain and livestock. Why?

So comprehensive a plan would have been difficult to fulfill in any country. It was especially hard in the industrially backward U.S.S.R. For a time, the projected schedule actually was exceeded, particularly in construction work and in the setting up, with foreign help, of foreign machinery. But once the factories were built and the machines installed, it became evident that the untrained native workmen were more likely to ruin than operate complex engines. There was a shortage of technical labor, and the factories were staffed largely with inexperienced ex-peasants.

A further check to efficient production resulted from the reservation of numerous privileges to the workers. Whereas the successful direction of large-scale industry demanded a fairly rigid discipline and a certain minimum of regimentation, the U.S.S.R. permitted workmen to delay carrying out an order of management until after they had met to discuss its propriety.

To make matters worse, the Gosplan had failed to provide for an extension of transportation facilities adequate to meet the needs of expanding industry. Consequently, freight piled up in the depots, perishable goods rotted at the terminals, and the factories ran short of raw materials.

In order to maintain the feverish enthusiasm that the official propaganda created among the people and to enable the laborers to work at top speed over a period of years, a plentiful food supply was essential. Yet the government found it necessary to curtail the sustenance allowances of its workers. Since neither the U.S.S.R.'s credit nor her rubles enjoyed much standing abroad, and since she was in desperate need of foreign machines and goods she had to export and sell at any price huge quantities of products badly needed at home. To obtain this surplus for export the state drastically reduced worker's rations.

To induce farmers to pool their interests, the state extended tax reductions and easy credit to the members of collectives. Persistent nonjoiners were subjected to a crushing tax, were ordered periodically to surrender specified quantities of grain, and were deprived of their farms if they failed to meet the quotas. It was chiefly the kulaks who suffered. They had little desire to merge their property with that of their poorer neighbors, to get in return merely a share of the profits proportionate to the amount and quality of labor which they would contribute in the fields. The state then attempted to "liquidate the kulaks as a class" by inciting the poorer against the richer peasants. In each collective a liquidation committee was formed to select the victims for the local "drive." The hounded kulaks banded together for self-defense, attacked the property of the collectives, and destroyed their own crops and livestock lest these fall into the hands of the hated opponents. Thousands were exiled to Siberia, or the north, to build roads and other public improvements. Some of the less courageous kulaks entered the collectives, but first slaughtered their animals, preferring to eat them rather than surrender them. Altogether, more than a third of the country's livestock was killed, with a resulting meat shortage in 1931 and 1932.

The net result of these stringencies and of the continued export of badly needed supplies was a lowering of the standard of living beneath that which had prevailed in the later years of the NEP period. There was a parallel decline in the efficiency and enthusiasm of labor and in the progress of the Five-Year Plan. The authorities took steps to counteract these adverse influences. Thus, between 1930 and 1932, the work day was lengthened, discriminations against non-Communist skilled workers were lessened, and the control of factory managements over employees was increased.

In agriculture the process of collectivization was slackened. The abler members of the collectives were given managerial posts. Five per cent of the net income of each collective was set aside as a fund to reimburse members for the animals and machinery that they contributed to the association. Peasants and petty craftsmen were allowed to exchange food and manufactured goods. These dispensations came too late to prevent famine in 1932–1933. Unfavorable climatic conditions, heavy requisitions, and the drive on the kulaks, all contributed to an agricultural crisis that was especially severe in the Ukraine, the Caucasus, and Central Asia. Here the proportion of kulaks and dissatisfied members of the collectives was relatively large, and the government decided to enforce complete submission by means of what has been called "organized famine." The censorship was tightened so that news of the resulting starvation might not escape. Foreign correspondents were refused access to the affected regions until the famine was over. In 1933 the people, weak and submissive but aided by favorable weather, produced a bumper crop.

The plan had important repercussions on the union's foreign relations. Because Russian goods were placed on the world market at prices below the cost of production, the Soviets were accused of "dumping" their products in order to demoralize the capitalistic system and prepare the way for world revolution. But the chief object of the Bolsheviks probably was to secure certain urgently needed manufactures. Although willing to negotiate reciprocal trade agreements with any states that cared to solicit her business, the U.S.S.R. was determined to dispose of her requisitioned surpluses under any conditions. Meanwhile the Gosplan compiled figures for a second five-year plan, hoping to avoid the mistakes of the earlier program.

In 1933 the Gosplan announced that the "achievements of the First Five-Year Plan made it possible to set, in the Second Five-Year Plan [January 1933 through December 1937], the task of finally abolishing the capitalist elements and classes generally . . . ; it has also permitted the raising of the great question of . . . securing the technical and economic independence of the U.S.S.R."

The new plan stipulated that the industrial output in 1937 was to be more than double that of 1932. The agricultural output was to be doubled and collectivization completed. The capacity of production in many industries was to be increased greatly. The kulaks, all remaining "capitalist elements," and any still existent "private property in production," were to be "liquidated." Illiteracy was to be ended.

Several general differences between the first and second plans were evident. The second plan placed more emphasis on quality and paid greater attention to transportation facilities and consumers' goods. The later program allocated the new industries in greater proximity to the raw materials and forecast an eastward trend in the future establishment of manufacturing plants—this being important from the viewpoint of military protection.[12]

The estimates of the Second Five-Year Plan generally appeared on the road to fulfillment in the opening years of the program. On the other hand, the advances in transportation once more lagged, and neither the cost of production nor the price of goods fell so rapidly as had been anticipated. Hence the avowed goal to "overtake and outstrip America" was far from realization when the Second Five-Year Plan gave way to the Third Five-Year Plan in January 1938. Nonetheless, by the time of the war in 1939, much economic progress had been made under the several plans.

EDUCATION AND RELIGION

Through its persecution of the intelligentsia, the professionals, and the well-to-do-people whose patronage supported these groups, the government inflicted upon the state a serious cultural loss. It was the middle and upper classes that had supplied most of the

[12] The wisdom of this step became apparent after the German invasion of the U.S.S.R. in 1941.

empire's famed aesthetic and professional leaders; but, with the death, exile, or suppression of these individuals, the country was left with a cultural vacuum. Worse still, a majority of Russians were illiterate, for the war and revolutions had interfered with a program of the Duma to establish compulsory education by 1922.

The Bolsheviks, however, were determined to "liquidate the bourgeois ideology" and build up a new culture. Every "toiler and toiler's child" was to be given the right to schooling. Wholesale illiteracy would hamper the material development of the state and make impossible the effective spreading of the Marxist-Leninist ideology. Unless the people were literate and able to absorb instruction in the principles of Marxism, they would fail to understand, or misinterpret, every policy that the authorities inaugurated. To the schools, therefore, was assigned the threefold task of enlightening the adults, preparing enthusiastic young Communists to carry on the revolution, and developing new technicians.

As far as possible, the schools were staffed with Communists. The fall of 1938 saw 33,000,000 children in elementary and secondary schools and more than a million persons in the higher institutions of learning. According to official figures, 81 per cent of the population was literate in 1939.

In their efforts to shape a new ideology the authorities relied not merely upon schools and teachers but upon the stage, movies, art, literature, music, and radio. There was constant official direction of and curb on creative accomplishment, but the U.S.S.R. soon did produce some outstanding personalities in literature, science, and art. Boris Pilniak, author of *The Bare Year,* an account of the famine and war years, and of *The Volga Flows to the Caspian Sea,* became perhaps the best known of the younger writers. The work of Sergei Eisenstein in the production of films aroused admiration in Europe and the United States. Other prominent members of the new intelligentsia included the physicist, Abram Joffe, and the biophysicist, Petr Lazarev. Of the prerevolutionary intellectuals who continued to serve Russia, perhaps the best known were the dramatist, Maxim Gorki, and the physiologist, Ivan Pavlov. The works of a young Soviet composer, Dmitri Shostakovich, were widely acclaimed at home and abroad.

Since the followers of Lenin looked upon religion as an "opiate for the people," they resolved to banish the influence of the clergy. The Orthodox Church was disestablished, its properties were confiscated, and many of its edifices were torn down or converted into clubhouses and museums. The clergy was deprived of control over education, marriage, cemeteries, and the registration of births and deaths. At first religious instruction was forbidden, but eventually the teaching of religion to small groups was permitted outside school or church buildings.

Since the Communists at first aimed their shafts specifically at the Orthodox Church and raised the ban on the free propagation of other faiths and of atheism, various religious groups, such as the Lutherans, Baptists, and Methodists, by dint of considerable social welfare work, won converts from Eastern Catholicism. This situation spurred into renewed activity the Orthodox Church, which had continued to exercise some influence over the peasants. The state, quick to observe this, promptly limited the activities of all clerical bodies to preaching in churches. The fight against religion was made an aspect of the struggle against counterrevolution, and "godless societies" sprouted in profusion.

Although attendance at church was not prohibited to the mass of citizens, it was forbidden to members of the Communist Party. Such anniversaries as Christmas and Easter continued to be observed, not as religious holidays, but as "traditional days of rest." An effort was made to substitute for them such revolutionary holidays as Lenin Day. Religion, clericals, and worshippers were held up to ridicule, and some of the most famous churches and monasteries became antireligious exhibition halls.

THE U.S.S.R. IN INTERNATIONAL AFFAIRS TO 1939

The ultimate mission of communism lay in four steps: (1) the overthrow of the existing order; (2) the temporary establishment in all countries of a dictatorship of the proletariat; (3) the creation of a world federation of soviet republics; and (4) the achievement of a universal Communist society. To launch this program was the self-imposed task of an international gathering of Communists in Moscow in March 1919. Assured of the support of the Bolshevik Government, the congress organized itself as the Third (First Communist) International or Comintern,[13] drew up a plan of action, and elected Gregory Zinoviev as its first president.

At the Comintern headquarters in Moscow came to be represented most of the Communist parties of the world, but the Russian Communist Party dominated the proceedings. In its periodical congresses the International laid down rules of discipline for individual and national members, outlined a program of anticapitalistic activities, and encouraged the organization of new national branches. From the International, agitators were sent out to stir up the discontented of the world against the established orders. The Communist International regarded itself as the "general staff of the world revolution."

[13] The First (Socialist) International, really the International Working Men's Association, was organized in 1864 by Karl Marx and held annual sessions until 1876. The Second International, with which were affiliated most of the Socialist and Labor parties of the world, was established in 1889. Its activities were checked by the First World War, but it came to life again in 1919. The Second and Third Internationals remained hostile to each other. The Red anthem was called the *"Internationale."* Its words were written in 1871 by Eugene Pottier.

The Comintern caused great annoyance to foreign governments. The authorities in Germany, Hungary, and the Baltic states bitterly resented the aid rendered by the body to the radicals who, in the postwar years, set up or tried to set up local soviets. Eventually, many governments extended to the Communists freedom of speech, press, and assembly, provided there was no violence and no incitement to direct action. In eastern and southern Europe, and in many of the colonial regions of Africa and Asia, agitators continued to be arrested upon identification as Communists.

At the outset, the Third International and the Soviet Government worked in close harmony. From 1918 to 1921 the policy of the Soviet Government in foreign affairs was to promote world revolution, use Russia as a base from which to launch the onslaught against capitalism, and aid Bolshevik uprisings wherever they might occur. Efforts were made to convert the masses of Asia to communism in the hope that they might then be united, under Russian leadership, in a gigantic "crusade against capitalism and imperialism."

Despite energetic Communist activity on a worldwide basis, capitalism in the West, as 1921 drew on, seemed more solidly entrenched than ever, whereas attempted pure communism had failed in Russia. Hence, coincident with the adoption of the New Economic Policy, the Soviets, convinced of the need to consolidate their power at home and improve the economic situation, were ready to enter into a truce with the bourgeois world. They realized that they were dependent upon the capitalist world for manufactures and technical advice, and they knew that these essentials would be available only if they could promise in return a cessation of Bolshevik propaganda. Consequently, the supply of funds to the Comintern was curtailed, and efforts were made to convince other countries of the independent status of the government and the International.

For the sake of trade and other concessions, the Soviet Government, over the objections of the International, occasionally ordered its representatives abroad to check Bolshevik propaganda. Sometimes the Comintern scolded the state for its domestic and foreign compromises with the bourgeois system, but these reprimands were lightly treated by the leaders who, like Stalin, claimed that the only worthwhile Communistic propaganda was the success of the Russian experiment. Meanwhile the bourgeois states, made confident by successful resistance to radical propaganda and anxious to "do business" even with the Bolsheviks, were equally willing to negotiate.[14]

The first fruit of the new attitudes was an Anglo-Russian trade

[14] Gradually, especially after the rise of Nazism, the Comintern, while still working for world revolution, transformed itself largely "into an international body whose chief and immediate goal was the defense of the Soviet Union." In 1935 the Comintern permitted the various national Communist parties to cooperate with the liberal bourgeois elements in a fight against fascism, while simultaneously continuing to "bore from within" in order to "create a united proletarian front."

agreement of 1921. This provided for the resumption of normal trade relations, subject to the mutual renunciation of propagandist activities. Before the end of the year the Russians had completed similar trade pacts with eleven other states. Although Russia automatically was accorded *de facto* recognition[15] by the countries that thus signed conventions with her, full diplomatic relations were not yet restored. Most of the treaty signatories merely exchanged commercial representatives with Russia, for they still resented the fact that the Bolsheviks had repudiated all foreign debts accumulated during the tsarist years. Finally, through the Treaty of Rapollo with Germany in 1923, the U.S.S.R. received *de jure* recognition by a great power and sufficient economic help to lessen its dependence on London and Paris.

However, by the end of 1923, Russia had received *de jure* recognition only from Germany and a few minor states. She therefore announced that, henceforth, unconditional recognition would be expected from any country that desired to discuss trade or debts. A "prize" in the form of an especially favorable commercial treaty was offered to that great power which first accorded recognition. Mussolini at once arranged for conversations with Bolshevik representatives. While the Italo-Soviet talks were in progress, British elections resulted in the elevation of Ramsay MacDonald, leader of the Labor Party, to the prime minister's office. In February 1924, the MacDonald Government extended to the U.S.S.R. unconditional *de jure* recognition. This news spurred the Italians to quicker action, and Rome formally recognized the Soviet Union a few days later. Russia, thereupon, opened negotiations for commercial treaties with both Great Britain and Italy. Before the close of 1924, nine other countries recognized the Bolshevik Government.

The fortune that attended Soviet foreign endeavors in 1924 did not last into the following year. A proposed treaty with Great Britain, respecting a debt settlement and credits, was thrown out by the Conservative Government that succeeded the Labor Ministry. Efforts to negotiate a trade agreement with France were unsuccessful, chiefly because the Bolsheviks frowned upon the importation of luxuries—the main items in French exports. Even the link with Germany seemed to be weakened when the latter signed the Locarno Pact, which was regarded in Moscow as a conspiracy against the U.S.S.R. Fearful lest a European bloc be formed against her, the Soviet Union concluded nonaggression pacts with several nearby countries.

Anglo-Soviet friendship further was strained when the Bolshevik trade unions contributed funds to aid the participants in the British general strike of 1926. In 1927, Chamberlain warned Moscow that

---

[15] *De facto* recognition means recognition of a government as actually existing, with no implication as to its legality. *De jure* recognition implies recognition of legal existence.

diplomatic relations once more would be severed unless anti-British propaganda in Europe and Asia ceased. Then, unexpectedly, the British police raided the private offices of Arcos, Ltd., the Soviet trading corporation in London. The police believed that the Bolsheviks possessed secret documents that recently had disappeared from the British War Office. Although the papers were not found, Downing Street declared that sufficient evidence of illegal activities had been uncovered to warrant the termination of diplomatic relations with the U.S.S.R. Parliament so voted. Not until 1929, when a second Labor Government was in power, was Anglo-Soviet diplomatic intercourse resumed.

The same year that witnessed the rupture in Soviet-British relations saw a crisis in Soviet-French affairs. The French, despite their official recognition policy, adopted an unfriendly attitude towards Moscow. They were vexed by Moscow's continued ban on the importation of luxuries and by their inability to redeem the Russian bonds that had been purchased prior to the summer of 1914. The Soviet-German *rapprochement* frightened them, and they interpreted as an affront a remark of the Soviet Ambassador to Paris that he would regard it as his duty, in case of a foreign war against the Soviets, to encourage the soldiers and workers of the bourgeois states to join the Red Army. In 1927, Poincaré rejected a Soviet offer regarding debts and credits and demanded the recall of the ambassador. In this year, also, the Chinese Nationalists raided the Soviet Embassy in Peking, and the Soviet Ambassador to Poland was assassinated by an exiled White.

Such incidents caused uneasiness in Moscow, and further attempts were made to ensure security against united European action. Non-aggression treaties were negotiated with Persia and Latvia, the Kellogg Pact was signed, and several of the U.S.S.R.'s neighbors in 1929 signed with her the Litvinov Protocol. Moscow also helped to bring about a reconciliation between Fascist Italy and Turkey, and made an arrangement with Germany, whereby the Reich guaranteed to German industry a large Soviet credit.

It was now the turn of France to become worried. Paris was alarmed at the growing Russian-German-Italian-Turkish friendship and disgruntled over France's inability to capture a profitable share of Soviet foreign trade. In 1930, therefore, France raised the cry that the Bolsheviks were "dumping" their goods upon foreign markets in order to break down the Western economic system, and she advocated the formation of a Pan-Europa minus the U.S.S.R. Soviet imports into France were placed under a licensing system that made it possible for the government virtually to abolish such imports. Soon thereafter Belgium inaugurated a similar measure. The cry of dumping quickly was taken up in other countries, notably the United States and Great Britain. In 1931 interested parties who objected either to Soviet sales competition or to the Soviet system agitated for embargoes on Soviet shipments.

Then there came about another change in the attitudes of the U.S.S.R. and the European states towards each other. Moscow became suspicious of the anti-Communist tactics of the Nazis in Germany, who pronounced a Soviet-German war inevitable. Germany suffered severely from the world depression and, hence, was growing less valuable as a Soviet customer. It therefore was felt that greater efforts might be made to gain the advantages of increased trade with France and the United States. The states of Western Europe, on the other hand, now regarded prosperity as more important than prejudice.

The path to a reorientation of international policies seemed cleared at a Geneva conference of 1931, which deliberated upon the feasibility of a European union. At this gathering Maxim Litvinov, Commissar for Foreign Affairs, created a favorable impression and aroused some enthusiasm for a plan to negotiate an economic non-aggression pact between capitalism and sovietism. Although this suggestion was not adopted, the door was opened for further individual developments. France, especially, seemed to reverse her former stand. She was anxious to destroy the solid front of those states—Germany, Italy, the U.S.S.R., and Hungary—which advocated a revision of the peace treaties. As a first sign of the new development, a Franco-Soviet treaty of neutrality and nonaggression was signed in 1932.

As 1933 opened, the United States remained the only major power that refused to recognize the U.S.S.R., for Washington wished to have no dealings with a government that neglected to fulfill its international obligations and that attempted to subvert democracy in other lands. But when, in 1932, the value of American sales to the U.S.S.R. dropped to $13,000,000—one-third as much as those of Great Britain and one-tenth as much as those of Germany—an important section of American businessmen came to favor closer relations with the Soviet Union. The latter, meanwhile, had found new cause for worry in Eastern Asia, where Japanese and Soviet interests threatened to clash in Manchuria and Mongolia. In 1933, therefore, Moscow welcomed the invitation of President Roosevelt to discuss the resumption of diplomatic relations. Litvinov thereupon journeyed to Washington, and diplomatic relations between the two states were reopened in November 1933.

Each government agreed to respect the territorial integrity of the other and to prohibit "the formation or residence on its territory of any organization or group" which aimed at "the overthrow of, or bringing about by force of a change in, the political or social order" of the other.[16] All United States-Soviet financial questions were left to future settlement through regular diplomatic channels. The

[16] A literal interpretation of this provision seemingly would have required the Soviet Government to expel the Comintern unless the latter withdrew all support from the Communist movement in the United States.

U.S.S.R. waived her claims for damages arising out of United States intervention in eastern Siberia from 1918 to 1920, although reserving the right to claim damages in connection with United States military activities at Murmansk and Archangel in northern Russia.[17] Those in the United States who had expected recognition to lead to an enormous increase in trade with the U.S.S.R. were disappointed, for Soviet purchases in the United States remained at a low figure.

Fear of a Japanese imbroglio and of the ultimate aims of Nazi Germany not only induced the U.S.S.R. to welcome the opportunity for United States recognition and for strengthening the ties of friendship with her smaller neighbors, but led her to view the League of Nations with an almost kindly regard. At first the Soviets would have nothing to do with the League, considering it a superweapon of capitalism. By 1927 they had been ready to participate in an economic conference held under League auspices, and in 1928 and 1929 they sent representatives to preparatory disarmament gatherings. In 1932 the U.S.S.R. took part in the Geneva Disarmament Conference. Hence it caused little astonishment when, in 1934 (the year after Japan and Germany submitted their resignations), the Soviet Union was admitted to League membership with a permanent seat on the Council.

In 1935 the growing *rapprochement* with France, stimulated by mutual fear of German rearmament measures, led to the signing of a Franco-Soviet pact of mutual assistance that was in some ways reminiscent of the Franco-Russian Alliance of 1894. Then, while sympathizing actively with the established government during Spain's civil war and plainly showing displeasure over the Anti-Comintern Pact, the U.S.S.R. strove to keep strong its diplomatic connections with Paris and Prague. However, it refused to come alone to the defense of Czechoslovakia against Germany in 1938. The Franco-British acquiescence in Germany's demands at Munich, indeed, marked another turning point in the relations of the Soviet Union with the great powers of Europe.

After the signing of the Munich Agreement and then the Anglo-French acceptance of a German protectorate over Czechia and Slovakia, Moscow openly mistrusted the leadership of London and Paris. The first concrete evidence of a new Soviet orientation was the "resignation" (May 1939) of Foreign Commissar Litvinov, leading Bolshevik advocate of collective security in cooperation with Britain and France. He was succeeded by Viacheslav M. Molotov, close friend of Stalin and advocate of a nationalistic Soviet foreign policy.

[17] The United States had made no attempt to appropriate territory in eastern Siberia; rather, she had exerted a restraining influence on Japan.

Southeastern Europe | 11

ROMANIA

Long "the sore spot of Europe," the Balkans continued, in the period 1919–1939, to be characterized by restlessness and instability. To the turbulence and corruption, that were the heritage of centuries of Ottoman misrule, the more recent decades added the conflicting Near Eastern policies of the great powers and the rivalries of half a dozen Balkan nationalisms. National lines were not clear cut in Balkania and each racial group had, or thought it had, proud traditions and heroic legends, and a mission to fulfill. Often these missions clashed.

The restive Balkan peoples had suffered severe hardship during the First World War and occasioned bitter tilts at the Paris Peace Conference. After 1918 the confusion and disorder abated little. Nationalist demands sometimes became more unreasonable, irredentisms grew fiercer, governments were overthrown at record rates, new chains of alliances were formed, and intrigue and violence appeared as common as they had been before the war.

Romania chose her side well in the war and was rewarded in the peace negotiations. When the boundary lines finally were adjusted, the kingdom comprised an area more than twice the prewar figure. Land was acquired from the former ally, Russia, and the ex-enemy, Austria-Hungary. The Soviet Government refused to recognize the Romanian annexation of Bessarabia, and the fear of a possible Soviet attack drove Romania into defensive alliances with Poland and France. Not until the two claimants signed a nonaggression pact in 1933 was the war danger in Bessarabia diminished.

The problem of minorities was serious, especially since the Romanians had a long record of discrimination against non-national elements. In 1919 Romania signed a minorities treaty only after the Allies had presented, as an alternative, the surrender of some of her recent territorial gains. Despite the treaty, complaints of injustice were frequent and loud, notably among the 1,500,000 Magyars.

Particularly objectionable to the Hungarians was the land legislation. In 1914, about half of the arable land in Romania was held by a few thousand proprietors. To appease a discontented peasantry, legislation was passed between 1917 and 1921, providing for the expropriation of several million acres from large holdings. Compensation was provided and the land acquired by the state was to be distributed among the peasants on easy terms. In Transylvania, the Magyars were the chief losers, as most large estates had been in their hands.

So rapidly were the land laws put into effect that, by 1932, 90 per cent of the farm land was controlled by small peasant proprietors. Progress simultaneously was made in the organization of co-operatives for the improvement of cultivation and the purchase of tools, seeds, and livestock.

In addition to the loss of Magyar estates, the treatment of the Magyars who wished to retain their Hungarian citizenship aroused the government of Hungary. By the terms of the Treaty of Trianon, Magyars who lived in Transylvania were to be permitted to keep their Hungarian citizenship; now their estates were expropriated by Bucharest. This situation heightened Hungary's desire to recover Transylvania and prevented the establishment of friendly relations between Romania and Hungary.

In 1923 Romania adopted a new constitution. The former three-class system of voting was abolished and universal suffrage was granted. A chamber of deputies was to be elected for four years, but the senate was to have *ex-officio* as well as elected members The king might appoint and dismiss members without regard to the wishes of parliament; he also was given a suspensive veto.

Before the war there had been two principal parties in Romania, the Liberal and the Conservative. The Conservatives represented the wealthy, landed, pro-German aristocracy. The Liberal Party advanced the interests of the banking and industrial groups, and was opposed to foreign economic influence. Although pro-Allied, the Liberals, who happened to be in power, postponed Romania's entry into the conflict until Allied chances of victory seemed good and until a satisfactory bargain had been struck. This same Liberal Party ruled the country with few interruptions from 1866 to 1928. After the war the Liberals seemed exceptionally firmly entrenched. Not only had they led the country to victory, but the rival party had disappeared: the landed aristocrats had been discredited by their pro-German sentiments and crushed by the breakup of the large estates. Yet the Liberals soon were challenged by a new opposition group, since the assignment of property and the extension of suffrage to the peasants brought about a political revolution.

The Liberal leadership antagonized many people by its extreme economic nationalism, which deprived the country of necessary foreign capital; by the high tariff policy, which hurt the agrarians; and by the indirect taxation schemes, which placed the heaviest burden on the poorer classes. Further opposition came from the newly acquired territories. For the first eight years after the war the government was controlled by groups representing the "old kingdom," although it included less than half the population of the new Romania. This was caused by King Ferdinand's arbitrary choice of ministers. When the opposition showed signs of becoming strong, an electoral law was passed (1926), which gave control of parliament to the party that polled 40 per cent of the votes.

In protest against these acts a National Peasant Party was formed. It advocated international friendship and agrarian reform at home. The party's great opportunity came with the deaths of King Ferdinand and Liberal leader Jon Bratianu in 1927. Premier Vintila Bratianu was not able to exert the same degree of control as had his brother, and antigovernment demonstrations were held throughout the kingdom. Eventually, Bratianu's inability to negotiate a foreign loan led to his resignation (1928). In the new election the National Peasant Party elected 322 of the 387 deputies.

Under the leadership of Premier Julius Maniu, an attempt now was made to place Romania "on the constitutional basis which brought prosperity to the Western states." Censorship was lifted, anti-Semitism suppressed, and foreign capital sought. Railways and public works were built, educational opportunities were extended, a foreign loan was floated, and the currency was stabilized. But in 1931 the party was forced out of power by King Carol II.

Crown Prince Carol first had stirred Romania in 1925 by renouncing his right to the throne, deserting his second wife, and going to Paris to live with his mistress. Since Carol was disliked by government leaders, his elopement caused the passage of a law which disbarred him from the throne, designated his five-year-old son Michael as crown prince, and provided for a council of regency in the event that Ferdinand should die before his grandson came of age. When Ferdinand died in 1927, Michael became king. Late in 1928, however, the National Peasants came to power and they favored Carol's return and accession to the throne.

It was not astonishing, therefore, that Carol should have returned to Bucharest in June 1930 and have been proclaimed king. Michael again became crown prince.

After October 1930 it became apparent that Carol was not inclined to be reconciled with his wife, Princess Helen of Greece, preferring a continuing association with his mistress. Although the army remained loyal to the king, the National Peasant Party frowned upon his actions. In 1931, accordingly, a new government was organized, under Carol's former tutor, Professor Nicolae Jorga. The latter, a prominent historian and prolific writer, ordered new elections and placed himself at the head of a National Union ticket. Thanks to violence and the electoral law of 1926, the National Union secured three fourths of the seats in the new chamber.

During the next year, Carol and Jorga ruled under a dictatorship thinly disguised behind the veil of a parliamentary majority. Both men were impulsive, fond of publicity, and strongly partisan. Conditions rapidly went from bad to worse. The world economic depression added to the nation's woes, and the government deficit increased at an alarming rate. This situation brought a return to power of the Liberal Party in 1933, under Jon G. Duca.

Duca followed a policy of moderation and attempted to curb the activities of a Fascist, anti-Semitic organization called the Iron Guards. In retaliation, a student assassinated Duca, and soon a Fascist plot was disclosed for the establishment of a military dictatorship. The new (1934) Liberal Government of George Tatarescu met the threat with energetic countermeasures. The Tatarescu Government then tried to concentrate on improving Romania's economic situation, but soon found itself concentrating instead on the rising tide of fascism. The anti-Semitic Romanian Fascists, who received encouragement from the German Nazis, were especially angered by the government's friendship with France, Czechoslovakia, and the Soviet Union. An example of foreign encouragement came in 1937 when the German and Italian ministers to Romania took part in an Iron Guard demonstration during the funeral of two members who were killed while fighting for Franco in Spain.

Worldwide interest centered on the parliamentary elections of December 1937. It was expected that a three-cornered fight would develop among the Liberals, the National Peasant Party, and the Fascist Iron Guard. Great was the general astonishment when it was announced that the pro-French peasant party would ally itself for electoral purposes with the anti-Semitic, pro-German Iron Guard. It was explained that the purpose was merely to present a united front against the personal rule of Carol, and that this move involved no compromise of principles. When the returns were counted it appeared that the Liberals would not have a majority, and the ministry therefore resigned. Shortly thereafter, in February 1938, Carol proclaimed a new constitution. Traditional politicians were dropped, political parties and secret societies were banned, and the King indicated his determination to rule as he thought best for the country.

Carol's actions were motivated by fear that if he did not establish a firm government of the type he wanted, the Fascist elements, with foreign backing, would take all power into their own hands. The absorption of Austria by Germany increased his suspicions, and he proceeded with energy against all those who seemed a menace to his throne. Government officers raided Fascist hide-outs and seized records which, it was said, showed that the Iron Guard was conspiring to seize the King and overthrow the regime. As a result, the Fascist leadership was imprisoned. The revolutionary movement now quieted down and the King issued numerous decrees designed to lessen the tensions caused by economic and social ills.

The autumn of 1938 saw a renewal of Fascist outbreaks. The police took quick action to check the outbursts, and many Iron Guard leaders were shot by prison guards on the ground that they had tried to escape. Although further plots of Iron Guard sympathizers were uncovered throughout 1939, Carol seemed to have the situation under control. However, on the eve of the Second World War, the Iron Guard once more became active. An attempt on Carol's life failed, but his premier was murdered.

BULGARIA AND MACEDONIA

Under King Ferdinand, Bulgaria entered the war on the side of the Central Powers and paid for this misstep in the Treaty of Neuilly. The treaty deprived the country of considerable territory, limited its army, and burdened it with reparations. Because of the poor economic condition of the kingdom, the indemnity was several times reduced until, in 1930, a "final" amount was set at $84,000,000.

Bulgaria was populated largely by a hard-working peasant class anxious to develop the country. Possessing relatively poor land, having little industrial life and no outlet to the sea, the Bulgarians still fulfilled the treaty requirements. In 1927 the last vestiges of inter-Allied control were removed.

In 1918 Ferdinand abdicated and was succeeded by Boris III. The new and popular ruler followed a general policy of noninterference with his ministers. Until 1934 Bulgaria continued to be governed under her constitution of 1879, which provided for a unicameral assembly (*Sobranye*) elected for four years by universal suffrage.

Perhaps the most remarkable postwar development in Bulgaria was the rise of the "Green" Socialists, agrarians who favored state aid to farmers and social legislation, but opposed the confiscation of private property. Prominent among the leaders of the Greens was Alexander Stambulisky, a peasant who had spent three years in prison for threatening King Ferdinand with personal violence if Bulgaria joined the Central Powers. Coming into office after the war, he signed the peace treaty and then devoted himself to the introduction of political and economic changes.

Policies of internal economic, agrarian, and social reform were gradually fulfilled between 1919 and 1923, but Stambulisky's methods created numerous enemies. He was interested solely in the welfare of the peasants, and in order to carry out his plans, he manipulated elections, arrested opposition leaders, closed universities, defied the church, and established censorship. The opponents of the regime included leading representatives of the military, the bourgeoisie, and the intelligentsia, as well as some of the more moderate

Agrarians. In 1923 Stambulisky was assassinated, and a government of professors, lawyers, and generals came into power. For the next two years and a half the middle-class government, employing many of the methods that had made the leader of the Greens unpopular, undid much of his work. When the peasants resorted to reprisals and assassinations, the government struck back with vigor and crushed the opposition.

A new bourgeois ministry took office in 1926 and remained in power for more than five years. Thousands of political prisoners were released and the censorship was lifted. Although political murders now ceased, much discontent remained. The moderate Agrarians adopted constitutional opposition tactics, being joined, shortly, by several other groups. Together they formed the National Bloc which, in the elections of 1931, came to power.

From October 1931 to May 1934, the government attempted to follow a moderate course, only to be troubled by mounting economic problems and the consequent rise of the spectre of communism. As a reaction to the relatively lenient treatment of Communists, a military dictatorship was established in May 1934. All political parties were abolished, and it seemed as though the military clique aimed at the abolition of royal political influence. Boris thereupon (November 1935) set up a new civil government under George Kiosseivanov.

The new government tried to steer a middle course. Both Fascists and radicals, however, grew in number. The Fascists demanded that the lost portions of Macedonia be recovered from Yugoslavia and Greece, but the King preferred a policy of conciliation with all Bulgaria's neighbors. In May 1938 a Bulgarian Parliament met for the first time in several years. The elections had been held on the King's orders and with a restricted suffrage. The candidates based their campaigns on personal issues, since they were forbidden to represent parties. And the assembly's powers by now had become mainly advisory. In 1939 an embryonic Nazi movement was suppressed.

Bulgaria's foreign relations were determined chiefly by the Macedonian question. Macedonia was a fertile region of indeterminate boundaries, situated partly in Greece, partly in Bulgaria, and partly in Yugoslavia. For centuries the area had been under Turkish rule, but it long had been claimed, on historical and linguistic grounds, by the three states mentioned. Each of these states carried on a vigorous campaign in Macedonia to convince the inhabitants that they really belonged to this or that nation. The Bulgarians appeared to enjoy the greatest success in these efforts, but as a result of the Balkan Wars of 1912 and 1913, they secured only a small northeastern corner of Macedonia. During the First World War they conquered some more of the area, but the Paris Peace Conference assigned most of it to Greece and Yugoslavia. Thereafter, thousands of Macedonian refugees began to pour into Bulgaria, using it as a base from which agitation for Macedonian independence might be carried on.

The unification and independence movement was directed by the Internal Macedonian Revolutionary Organization, founded in 1893. The IMRO comprised armed bands of *comitadjis*, whose methods were terrorism and guerrilla warfare along the international frontiers. The Bulgarian army was so small that the comitadjis could act with virtual impunity, while keeping the government in constant dread of unpleasant border incidents.

In 1922 Greece, Yugoslavia, and Romania warned Bulgaria to check the disorders along the frontiers with Greece and Yugoslavia. Two years later Athens complained of the mistreatment of Greeks in the Bulgaro-Macedonian village of Voden. The protest apparently had the wrong effect, for soon thereafter the Greek mayor of the village was murdered. By way of reprisal a Greek army officer ordered the shooting of seventeen Bulgarians. A crisis was reached in October 1925, when a clash between frontier outposts resulted in the dispatch of a Greek army that occupied seventy square miles of Bulgarian territory. Sofia offered no military resistance and appealed to the League for protection.

The League Council ordered the Greeks to recall their troops from Bulgaria, and sent a commission to investigate the origin of the conflict and recommend action. This body reported that neither party to the dispute had appeared to act with premeditation, but that Greece had been hasty in ordering the invasion without prior investigation of the circumstances. The commissioners therefore suggested that Greece pay Bulgaria $220,000 for material and moral damages. The Council accepted these decisions as did the disputants, and Greece promptly paid the fine. The peaceable outcome of the affair not only was a victory for the League, but it paved the way for a better understanding between Bulgaria and Greece. The Greeks came to realize that the government of King Boris was not to blame for the border incidents, and Greco-Bulgarian treaties of commerce and friendship were signed.

Meanwhile, in 1926, some comitadjis had crossed from Bulgaria into Yugoslavia where they attacked a town. This triggered a whole series of incidents, with increasing bitterness and the closing of the frontier by the Yugoslavs. The bad feeling was lessened only when the royal dictatorship that was established in Yugoslavia in 1929 began to regard the boundary difficulties in a less serious light and reopened the frontier. This action opened a path for further negotiations, and in 1930 the two countries regulated the control of the borders and agreed that future disagreements would be settled by peaceful arbitration.

The signing of Bulgarian treaties with Greece and Yugoslavia lessened the danger of international war, but the internal situation in Bulgaria was made worse when the Macedonians themselves split into two hostile groups. The Macedonian antagonists used such violent methods against each other that in 1933 the government proclaimed a state of siege in Sofia, and placed in concentration camps a large number of suspected Macedonian terrorists. All Macedonians were ordered to surrender their arms, and the IMRO leaders were imprisoned or removed to other parts of the land. In 1934 the two groups dissolved, but Macedonian nationalist propaganda continued to be carried on, both at home and abroad.

The Sofia Government used the Macedonian situation as the basis for a request to the League to permit a larger army than was stipulated in the Treaty of Neuilly. Success in this endeavor was not achieved until 1938, when Bulgaria and the Balkan Entente (Greece, Turkey, Yugoslavia, and Romania) signed a treaty at Salonika. In the document, Bulgaria's right to rearm was recognized by the Entente. Soon thereafter, Bulgaria got a loan for rearmament purposes from an Anglo-French banking group. The partition of Czechoslovakia reminded the Bulgarians of their own irredentist grievances with respect to their neighbors, and on the nineteenth anniversary (1938) of the signing of Neuilly, the government found it necessary to proclaim martial law in order to prevent rash acts that might lead to international complications.

GREECE

In 1917 Premier Eleutherios Venizelos, with the aid of the Allies and against the wishes of King Constantine, had led Greece into the war. At the Paris Peace Conference he secured for his country numerous territorial awards. He expected a cordial reception upon his return from Paris but, for a variety of reasons, had come to be generally disliked. It was common knowledge that his advent to power in 1917 had been based on forceful Allied support, and his action in compelling the king to abdicate in favor of the young Alexander had not made Venizelos popular. Venizelos' policies already had plunged the people into three wars, in 1912, 1913, and 1917–1918, and they were not desirous of waging a fourth conflict in order to protect the land acquired in Asia Minor by the Treaty of Sèvres. To make things still worse for Venizelos, King Alexander died in 1920, whereupon his father, Constantine, immediately announced his readiness to return from exile.

Hence the Venizelists were defeated in the elections of 1920, and a plebiscite resulted in the recall of Constantine. The premier discreetly left the country, passing on to the returned ruler a war against the Turks. Not only was Constantine forced by circumstances to continue this struggle, but his position was made precarious when the Allies refused to recognize his government and cut short the flow of supplies that had been made available to Venizelos. Constantine was blamed for a resulting Greek debacle at Smyrna, the threatened loss of Thrace, and the coldness of the Allies. This led him to abdicate a second time (1922). The throne went to his son, George II.

Venizelos was recalled to salvage what he could at the peace conference of Lausanne (1923). He had to give up Smyrna and eastern Thrace, and agreed to a compulsory exchange of populations with Turkey. As a result of the exchange of peoples, a million refugees were "dumped" into Greece from Turkey, bringing the population to 6,500,000. The lot of the refugees was miserable, because Greece found it difficult to provide the necessities of life for the incoming hundreds of thousands.

One of the most difficult diplomatic problems arising from the enforced uprooting of so many people was the liquidation of the ensuing property disputes. This controversy between Greece and Turkey was not resolved until 1930, at which time the two countries reciprocally renounced the claims that their exchangeable refugees had against each other and agreed to permit the Turks in western Thrace and the Greeks in Constantinople to remain where they were living.

The early reign of George II was marked by confusion and unrest. An extreme censorship prevailed; there were frequent military executions; and quarrels between the royalists and Venizelists, a majority of whom had republican sympathies, became more and more vindictive. In 1923, after a Venizelist victory at the polls, the king and queen were requested to leave the country while parliament decided upon the future form of government. In March 1924 the national legislature deposed the dynasty and declared a republic. This action was upheld in a plebiscite by a vote of more than 2 to 1.

Political life under the republic was no less turbulent than under the monarchy. In 1929 Alexander Zaimis, who had been Prime Minister eight times, became President. Since the new executive was chosen by parliament, it appeared that the republic was on a tolerably firm footing. In 1934 Zaimis was reelected by parliament for another five-year term.

Meanwhile Venizelos, who had retired to his native Crete, once more returned and in 1928 led the Liberal Party to victory in an election that resulted in his becoming Premier. He remained in power, with brief interruptions, for almost five years, until March 1933, and achieved a number of important acts. The result of his policies was a restoration of order and improvement of the public condition. Friendlier relations were established with the neighboring states. Venizelos appeared to be much in favor of a Balkan federation as a step toward the fulfillment of Briand's Pan-Europa scheme, but nationalist jealousies blocked progress in this direction.

After 1930 the appearance of the Great Depression in Greece again damaged foreign trade and led to increased unemployment. The Premier tried a number of remedies, all of temporary value, and then retired, without having solved the economic riddle. His successor was Panagiotis Tsaldaris, leader of the Popular Party.

Shortly before Tsaldaris celebrated his second anniversary in office, there broke out a widespread military and naval revolt. The rebels doubted the sincerity of Tsaldaris' devotion to the republic and wanted to place the ministerial power back in the hands of Venizelos. After ten days of fighting, General George Kondylis, the war minister, reported victory over the insurgents. Venizelos went into exile, and the victorious government arrested the leaders of the revolt, confiscated the property of the Venizelos family, dismissed Venizelist sympathizers from office, and abolished the Greek upper house, which had been controlled by Venizelos' Liberal Party. Kondylis was named a marshal and Deputy-Premier.

In an election of June 1935 the Tsaldaris-Kondylis government party won 287 of the 300 deputies' seats. This parliament authorized a plebiscite in which the people should choose between republicanism and monarchism. Before the vote, the Premier and his deputy quarreled. Tsaldaris was willing to restore the monarchy if the people expressed such a wish through an honest plebiscite. Kondylis, irritated by Tsaldaris' determination to be strictly neutral in the plebiscite and tired of the uncertainty of the situation, engineered a coup d'etat and forced the Premier to resign. In rapid order the republic was abolished, the monarchical constitution of 1911 was restored, and Kondylis was made Premier and Regent pending the return of former King George II.

George, in London, was informed of these events and expressed an eagerness to return to Greece; but he decided to await the result of a plebiscite in which the people were given the opportunity to confirm the coup. Meanwhile President Zaimis quietly passed into the political background, and Regent Kondylis ousted all leading republicans from office. The plebiscite resulted in an overwhelming endorsement of Kondylis' measures and of royal restoration. King George II therefore returned to continue his interrupted reign (November 1935). Because the King and Kondylis found it difficult to cooperate, Professor Constantine Demerdjis became Premier in the same month.

In January 1936 no group could win a majority in the election. Hence a nonpartisan cabinet, including General John Metaxas as war minister, was formed. Within three months after the election, death removed many of the important Greek politicians. Metaxas, who became head of the cabinet, displayed impatience with the rise of radicalism caused by the bad economic conditions, and induced the King to dissolve parliament and suspend the constitution (August 1936). Then he abolished all political parties, imposed a strict censorship, and announced that the country had been saved from communism. Metaxas overcame attempts to oust him and, in July 1938, made himself Premier for life.

The foreign relations of Greece were troublous. The difficulties with Turkey and Bulgaria have been mentioned. Contacts with Italy and Yugoslavia were equally disturbing for a time. Italian control of the Dodecanese Islands in the Aegean since the close of the Turco-Italian War in 1912 gave rise to a Greek irredentist movement, since the islands were inhabited largely by Greeks. More serious was a rupture in the relations between the two countries when some Italian army officers aided in the delimitation of a boundary between Albania and Greece.

It seemed to the Greeks that most of the disputed points were being decided in favor of Albania. In 1923 the Italian general who headed the boundary commission, three other Italians, and an Albanian interpreter were killed on Greek soil. An ultimatum immediately was forthcoming from Rome. It demanded an official apology, an indemnity of 50,000,000 lire to be paid within five days, and permission for the Italian military attaché to help in the apprehension of the assassins. The time limit for acceptance was twenty-four hours. Greece rejected a number of demands as contravening her national sovereignty and appealed to the League for help.

Before this body could act, Italy bombarded and occupied the island of Corfu, inflicting casualties mainly upon some Armenian refugees who had been collected there. At the same time the Italians indicated their displeasure at the apparent intention of the League to interfere in the controversy. Hence the League turned the matter over to a Council of Ambassadors in Paris. These diplomats decided that Greece had been at fault in the murders, but that the ultimatum had been too harsh. It was recommended that Greece apologize, seek out and punish the murderers, and pay the demanded indemnity; Italy should evacuate Corfu. The suggestions were accepted, and relations between Italy and Greece gradually underwent an improvement. In a sense, the outcome was a League victory, but it also demonstrated that the League could not proceed as readily against a large state as against a small one.

The chief Greek quarrel with Yugoslavia arose out of a treaty of 1913 between Greece and Serbia, wherein the former had promised the latter a free zone in the port of Salonika. The First World War forced the postponement of the final arrangements, but in 1923 a convention was signed, whereby Yugoslavia was given a fifty-year hold on a Salonika free zone. The area was to remain under Greek police surveillance but was to be under Yugoslav customs administration. The accord did not work well and disputes developed as the Yugoslavs claimed that the dual control of the zone hampered trading activities.

The ill will between the two peoples increased perceptibly, until Venizelos returned to power in 1928. He visited Belgrade, and in 1929 negotiated a compromise that proved satisfactory to both sides.

Thus, Greece hurdled the last serious obstacle to cordial foreign relations. Venizelos concluded treaties of friendship with Italy, Yugoslavia, Bulgaria, and Turkey. The premiers who succeeded Venizelos generally continued this foreign policy, and by 1939 Greece seemed to have achieved relative stability.

YUGOSLAVIA

In 1917 a group of Yugoslavs or Southslavs, from Serbia and the Southslavic provinces of Austria-Hungary, signed a pact at Corfu to form a new constitutional monarchy, to be known as the Kingdom of Serbs, Croats, and Slovenes. These peoples had never been united in one state, and each group was anxious to reserve certain rights. It was agreed that the Serbian dynasty should rule the kingdom and that a national flag should be adopted. The equality of all major religions in the new state was to be guaranteed. As soon as possible, a constituent assembly was to be elected by universal secret suffrage. The pact was silent as to whether the government should be unitary or federal, and this omission later caused difficulty.

The new state was formed according to these precepts in 1918–1919 under King Peter I of Serbia. The actual ruler was Peter's son, Alexander, who had been Regent since 1914 and who became sovereign in his own right in 1921.

From the beginning, the people of the Serb-Croat-Slovene Kingdom were split on the kind of central government to establish. One group, regarding the new state as a Greater Serbia, favored a centralized government with all authority emanating from Belgrade. The leading advocate of this view was the aged but energetic Premier Nicola Pashich, who had been head of the Serbian Government when the war broke out. The chief opposition to centralized control came from the Croatian Peasant Party led by Stefan Radich, a fiery and prodigious speaker, who was ready to give up his life in the cause of Croatian autonomy.

Pashich argued that the backward situation of some of the regions acquired from Hungary made local autonomy preposterous. Moreover, he said, the Serbs, by sheer weight of numbers, would dominate the government anyway, and the fact might as well be recognized officially. Finally, the problem of reconstruction was so grave as to require united action, directed from one central point, Belgrade. Radich turned a deaf ear to these pleas. He explained that the Croats had enjoyed autonomy under the Habsburgs and, hence, had every right to continue in control of their own affairs. He pointed out that the Croats as a group were more advanced culturally than the Serbs and, consequently, should not be made subordinate to them.

For two years the question raged, and the king refused to call elections for a constituent assembly until all boundary disputes were adjusted. Late in 1920 the call for elections was issued. Radich's Croatian Peasant Party elected 50 (out of 417) deputies, but in compliance with his instructions they refused to take their seats. The assembly was dominated by the moderate Democratic Party and Pashich's Serbian Radicals. In 1921 the Radicals, bitterest opponents of federation and advocates of *conservative* domestic policies, secured the adoption of a document that fulfilled their fondest hopes. The constitution provided for a centralized form of government. There was to be a single national parliament the unicameral *Skupshtina*, elected by universal suffrage. Local officials were made responsible to the central authorities.

After the adoption of the constitution, the most urgent domestic problem became revision of the document because, until 1924, the Croats refused to take part in the political life of the state. Radich spent much of the time in jail or exile, but by 1924 he decided that obstructionist tactics might be carried on more effectively within parliament. Hence he permitted the Croatian deputies to take their seats. The Pashich Government, in consequence, was forced to resign, and thereafter one short-lived ministry after another rose and fell. In despair the King recalled Pashich, who crushed the opposition by having Radich arrested for high treason and ordering new elections in 1925. The opposition remained strong enough to defeat most of the government's bills.

After a brief stay in prison, Radich once more decided to change his methods, this time letting it be known that he would recognize the constitution of 1921 and cooperate in parliamentary activity, provided his party were given representation in the government. The Cabinet accepted this offer, and Radich was released to become Minister of Education. But meanwhile the personal element had entered the quarrel to such an extent that Radich seemed unable to refrain from bitter verbal attacks on Pashich and other ministers. Before long the partnership was dissolved. The death of Pashich in 1926 failed to end the controversy but deprived the proponents of centralization of their ablest leader.

Confusion soon was transformed into chaos, both within parliament and among the people. On several occasions the police had to end fighting among the deputies, and riots became common in the streets. A climax was reached in June 1928 when Radich in parliament launched an especially bitter attack against the government because it proposed ratification of a commercial convention with Italy. He complained that the convention was an Italo-Serbian compromise drawn up at the expense of the Croatian peasants. Angered by these denunciations, a progovernment deputy drew his pistol and fired directly into the group of Croatian deputies. Two of the latter died instantly and several, including Radich, were wounded. Radich soon succumbed to his injuries, and the dead leader became a martyr.

The Croatian deputies withdrew in a body from the Skupshtina and met separately. They resolved to disregard any laws of the "rump" parliament in Belgrade. Then the Croats threatened to set up their own legislature and act independently of the central authorities. In December 1928 the Croatian people refused to participate in the celebration of the tenth anniversary of the kingdom.

Unable to foresee an end to the parliamentary deadlock and fearful of the growing separatist spirit, King Alexander in January 1929 dismissed parliament, abolished the constitution, and established a royal dictatorship to function through a cabinet responsible solely to him. The King, now an absolute monarch, announced that the restrictions would be removed as soon as domestic order had been reestablished and friendly relations with the outside world restored.

Alexander, an energetic man and an able military officer, appealed to his subjects to forget their local prejudices and their Serbian, Croatian, or Slovene origin, and to remember only that they were all Yugoslavs. To give emphasis to this plea, the official name of the country was altered by royal decree to Kingdom of Yugoslavia. The old administrative divisions were wiped out and replaced by nine new districts.

In 1931 the King promulgated a new constitution. It restricted the formation of political parties,[1] recognized the equality of the three major languages, and set up a bicameral parliament, consisting of a *Senat* in addition to the Skupshtina. Half of the senate membership was to be appointed by the king and the other half elected. The lower house members were to be elected by all men and women over twenty-one. In the first elections under the new system, the only voting list was that of the Yugoslav National Party, formed through a combination of the chief former parties. In the next two years and a half, the premiership was occupied in turn by several leaders of the Yugoslav National Party.

The Croats steadily resisted all attempts at "Serbifying" the government and the people. Despite the strictest surveillance, their discontent was manifested on frequent occasions. A climax in the struggle was reached in 1934 when, as has been discussed, King Alexander was assassinated in Marseille, apparently as the result of a Croatian-Macedonian conspiracy. While the League Council busied itself with preventing the crisis from leading to war, since Yugoslavia accused Hungarian irredentists of connivance in the murder, Alexander's eleven-year-old son was proclaimed King Peter II. A council of regents was established, headed by Prince Paul, a cousin of Alexander.

The new ruling group was conciliatory, and an amnesty was granted to Croats who had been jailed under Alexander. In the parliamentary elections of 1935 the authorities permitted opposition candidates to stand for office, but then adopted the customary methods for ensuring a government victory. Most of the opposition deputies who were elected were Croats, and they refused to enter the new parliament. A somewhat more hopeful sign appeared when

[1] Parties might not be based on regional, religious, or class divisions.

Dr. Milan Stoyadinovich, a Serb who had never approved of the dictatorship, became premier (1935).

Stoyadinovich attempted to win the good will of the minorities by including in his cabinet several Croats, Slovenes, and Bosnian Moslems, in addition to the customary Serbs. He then organized the Yugoslav Radical Union, which advocated a gradual transition from dictatorship to democracy, but which also was pledged to maintain a strong central government. Several Croats in the cabinet thereupon resigned, holding that Croatia favored federalism and would be satisfied only when she had acquired a status similar to that enjoyed by Hungary in the old Dual Monarchy. Stoyadinovich attempted various measures to win over the Croats, but was unsuccessful and in 1939 resigned. Control over the "nation of three nations" passed to one of his former aides, Dragisha Cvetkovich.

During Cvetkovich's administration, external danger succeeded in accomplishing what years of internal pressure had failed to do, namely, bring about a Serbo-Croat compromise. In August 1939, an agreement was signed that set up a self-governing district of Croatia with autonomy in certain areas (for example, health and education), and with partial fiscal autonomy. The new government was constituted on a broader base, with a cabinet that included Serbs, Croats, one Slovene, and one Moslem Bosnian.

Nationalist difficulties were not the only problems confronting Yugoslavia. The peasants, who formed 80 per cent of the population, were dissatisfied with the size of their holdings despite efforts by the authorities to break up large estates. The country lacked adequate outlets to the sea and suffered from a poor system of internal communications, which made it hard to develop the mineral resources. The kingdom was heavily burdened with debt, having assumed the prewar and postwar obligations of all its component parts.

The foreign relations of Yugoslavia have been considered in other connections. It needs to be added here only that, while remaining loyal to the Little Entente and to her alliance of 1927 with France, Yugoslavia, from 1937 to 1939, drew ever closer to the Rome-Berlin Axis. The increasing *rapprochement* of Belgrade with Italy and Germany, especially after the Anschluss, was justified by the government as "making new friends while keeping old ones." In mid-1939, less than two years before he invaded Yugoslavia, Hitler declared that the German-Yugoslav borders were fixed "for all time."

Turkey for the Turks

12

Had the Treaty of Sèvres, drawn up by the Allies and signed in 1920 by representatives of Sultan Mohammed VI, gone into effect, the once resplendent Ottoman Empire would have been reduced to an insignificant region of desert and mountains in Asia Minor. But Fate, acting through the person of a young army officer named Mustapha, decreed otherwise.

Mustapha was born in Salonika in 1880. At the Military Staff School in Constantinople, in recognition of his superiority as a student of mathematics, one of his professors bestowed upon him the name of *Kemal*, signifying Perfection. Military life appealed to Kemal, and he developed into an excellent soldier; but he also became an inspired reader of French Revolutionary literature and an antagonist of the autocratic Turkish Government. Kemal's revolutionary tendencies were known to the agents of Sultan Abdul Hamid II, but the police did not arrest him until his graduation. Then he was banished temporarily by being assigned to a cavalry regiment in far-off Damascus. There the young officer found time to muse over the evils of misgovernment and to organize a secret political society called "Fatherland".

During the Young Turk Revolution of 1908, Kemal acted as chief of staff to the commander of the army that marched on Constantinople and forced Abdul Hamid to grant a constitution. The muddled tactics and political intrigues of the Young Turk ruling body induced Kemal to devote his attention entirely to military affairs, and in 1910 he went to France to study Western army maneuvers. Stopping for a while in Paris, he was deeply impressed by what seemed to him the progressive nature of French life.

Kemal returned to Turkey and continued to fight in the army as the Turks moved through the Balkan Wars into World War I. He played a conspicuous part in the defeat of the Allies at Gallipoli in 1915, and then was chagrined when the Allies imposed on Turkey the Armistice of Mudros (October 1918). The terms of this document were so drastic that the Young Turk leaders, who popularly were held responsible for the disasters of the war, fled from the capital. Kemal in anger laid down his command in Palestine and hastened to Constantinople, only to be ordered into Anatolia by the Sultan, to supervise demobilization in an out of the way area. He went, but used his commission to gather around him the nucleus of a new political party, the Turkish Nationalist Party.

Meanwhile, following a decision by Great Britain and France to forestall Italian imperialist enterprises in Anatolia, Greece was encouraged to land troops at Smyrna. The pillaging of this port so aroused patriotic Turks that Kemal seized the opportunity to attempt to unite nationalists throughout the country. He called two congresses, in 1919, to discuss the future policy of the Nationalist Party. At these meetings the basis was laid for the Turkish National Pact, a statement of principles adopted in January 1920 by a Constantinople Parliament that, elected late in 1919, contained a Nationalist majority.

The first three articles of the statement dealt with the principle of self-determination, referring to all those areas of the old Ottoman Empire that contained large numbers of Turks. The fourth article demanded the security of Constantinople. Article 5 assured the rights of minorities in Turkey, and the last article demanded the abolition of foreign extraterritorial rights.

The Nationalists were expecting too much if they thought that the Allies would permit them to follow the principles outlined in the pact. Soon after the document's adoption, an Allied army marched into Constantinople, proclaimed martial law, and deported some of the Nationalist deputies. Most of the Nationalist delegates who had escaped arrest hastened to Angora in north-central Anatolia, where they set up a "rump" parliament called the Grand National Assembly. When the Sultan now convened another parliament at Constantinople, the country had two governing bodies: one, subordinate to the sultan and maintained by Allied troops; the other, supported by Turkish national sentiment and protected by the desert and mountains separating Angora from the Allied forces.

The Angora Assembly, in April 1920, elected Mustapha Kemal to be its president as well as commander-in-chief of the Nationalist Army. Then the body undertook to draw up a new instrument of government. In January 1921, such a document, called the Law of Fundamental Organization, was adopted. This law vested the sovereignty of Turkey in the people and in their representatives sitting as a Grand National Assembly at Angora. The document outlined an elaborate program of social change.

While the assembly was engaged in lawmaking, Kemal, at the head of the Nationalist forces, launched a campaign to clear the country of foreign soldiers. In this undertaking he covered himself with glory and won the title of *Ghazi* or Conqueror.

Meanwhile Greek armies, with British naval support, had driven the Nationalists out of Thrace and pushed eastward into Anatolia. These victories, however, were counteracted by some unexpected diplomatic developments. The Greek Premier, Venizelos, who was chiefly responsible for Greece's attempts to take the territories assigned to her by the unratified Treaty of Sèvres, was defeated in the parliamentary elections of November 1920. British support was becoming less enthusiastic. The French began openly to favor the Turks out of dislike for the Greek King and for British policy. Italy, finally, who herself coveted Smyrna, had never sympathized with the Greek venture. Accordingly, an attempt was made at London to revise the Sèvres Treaty, chiefly at the expense of Greece. When it appeared that the demands of the Turks and Greeks could not be reconciled, Athens, against the advice of the Allied Supreme Council, determined to enforce the original treaty on its own account. In May 1921 the Allies proclaimed their neutrality in the Greco-Turkish War, and the Turks, by September 1922, had driven the Greeks out of Smyrna itself.

When Kemal, in the flush of victory, proposed to cross the Straits and drive the Greeks out of eastern Thrace, he once more came into conflict with the British. At the time of the Allied proclamation of neutrality it had been stipulated that a specified area on each side of the Straits was to be considered as a neutral zone in which no fighting would be permitted. Now, fearing for control of the Dardanelles, Lloyd George announced his determination to enforce this provision and prevent the Turks from fighting the Greeks in Thrace. Neither the French nor the Italians, however, cared to back the British Premier, inasmuch as the Kemalists had concluded favorable agreements with France and Italy. Lloyd George therefore had to act alone, and British reinforcements were sent to prevent a Greco-Turkish clash in the zone of the Straits.

For a time war seemed imminent, but the British commander eventually induced Kemal to attempt a peaceful settlement of the controversy. In October 1922, an armistice was signed. The Greeks had to evacuate and restore to Turkey all Thrace as far as the Maritsa River, and invitations were issued to several of the former Allies to meet at Lausanne for revision of the Treaty of Sèvres to meet the new conditions. Shortly before the first Lausanne Conference met, the Grand National Assembly deposed (November 1922) Sultan Mohammed VI. But not until a year later, in October 1923, did the legislature declare the nation to be a republic and unanimously elect Kemal as Turkey's first President.

At the Lausanne Conference the Turkish delegates refused to sign any treaty that restricted the economic or judicial freedom of their country. In consequence, the negotiations dragged on until July 1923, and then ended only because the Turks had been able to secure virtually everything that they had demanded in their National Pact.

Under the terms of the Lausanne Treaty, Turkey recovered eastern Thrace as far west as the Maritsa River. Constantinople was restored as an integral part of the Turkish State, but the zone of the Straits was demilitarized and opened to the ships of all nations in time of peace and, when Turkey was a neutral, in time of war. In the event of Turkey's belligerency, enemy vessels might be kept out of the Straits. A number of islands in the Aegean were distributed among Turkey, Greece, and Italy.

Turkey gave up all claims to North African and Arabian areas and recognized Great Britain's annexation of Cyprus. When the Turks agreed to recognize the rights of minorities, all Allied claims for reparation arising out of the First World War were renounced, the foreign control of customs was lifted, and no restrictions were placed on Turkey's military, naval, and air forces. A supplementary Greco-Turkish convention provided for the compulsory exchange of Turkish subjects in Greece for Greek subjects in Turkey. At peace with the world for the first time in many years, Turkey proceeded to set her house in order.

THE TURKS, THE GREEKS, AND THE KURDS

The Turkish Nationalists were eager to oust from the republic all groups of peoples who were not Turks. Since the largest group of nonnationals in 1923 consisted of Greeks, the Angora and Athens governments had agreed at Lausanne upon a wholesale exchange of populations on the basis, primarily, of religion. The exchange occasioned untold suffering. It frequently was difficult to decide whether a family should be considered as Turkish or Greek, particularly where the original migration had taken place long ago. Besides, there were Orthodox Christians in Anatolia who knew only Turkish, and there were Moslems residing in Greece who spoke no Turkish. Mismanagement, cruelty, and neglect often were in evidence, for the racial and religious antagonisms did not always permit humanitarian treatment.

Altogether about 1,000,000 people were sent to Greece and 400,000 to Turkey. The property disputes arising from the exchange embittered Greco-Turkish relations until 1930. Then, as has been indicated, a compromise was reached, which was followed shortly by the signing of a treaty of friendship. In the meantime the Turks had passed a law forbidding the immigration of any large group of foreigners.

After the ousting of the Greeks, the chief remaining obstacle to Turkish national homogeneity was the million or more Kurds inhabiting the eastern part of the republic. These tribesmen, speaking a language more akin to Iranian than Turkish, continued to be imbued with the spirit of clan allegiance rather than that of Turkish nationalism. The Kurds long were among the most unruly of the sultan's subject, and they continued to be restless under the new Turkey, especially since the Lausanne Treaty shattered hopes of autonomy that had been held out to them by the Treaty of Sèvres. In 1925, when the authorities arrested a few Kurds on a charge of sedition, the discontent crystallized into open revolt. The uprising quickly was put down, and the rebel leader was executed.

The incident appeared to increase the solidarity of the state as a whole. Loyal Turks rallied to the support of the central government, and the latter seized the opportunity to strengthen its control of national life. Further Kurdish uprisings occurred in 1930 and 1937—to remind the Turks of their one remaining minority problem.

KEMAL, THE DICTATOR

As president, Mustapha Kemal determined to abolish outworn institutions and to raise his country to the level of Western civilization. In bringing about this transformation he adopted an admittedly dictatorial policy, and a number of executions accompanied the march of reform. On the other hand, one of the chief reasons for Kemal's success was the fact that he customarily took just one big step at a time. Reforms succeeded one another at moderate intervals, and in this way the opposition rarely became so formidable as to crystallize into open resistance. Although there were some antirepublican assassination plots, eventually a majority of the people appeared to endorse the dictator-president's policies.

In Turkey, as in some Western states, nationalism seemed to transcend the desire for liberty or democracy. So powerful was this spirit that there generally was only one political party, the Nationalist People's Party. Its first president-general was Kemal who, in 1927, was given the right to name all its electoral candidates for the assembly. In 1930 Kemal permitted the organization of an opposition Liberal Republican Party; it was dissolved in the fall of 1930 because of lack of support.

Kemal was unanimously elected president four times, but in 1938, after several months of illness, he died at the age of fifty eight. It was a tribute to the skill and success with which he had welded the Turkish Republic that, on the day after his death, the National Assembly unanimously, and apparently with popular approval, chose as his successor, General Ismet Inönü. The new president had won fame as a general in the Turkish "wars of freedom," and had demonstrated diplomatic ability.

Inasmuch as Inönü had been chosen only to finish Kemal's unexpired term, it was necessary to hold another presidential election in 1939. Inönü again was selected, and Turkey's second president used his powers not merely to continue along the path that his predecessor had outlined, but to reconcile some of the elements in the country that had been more or less disregarded by Kemal.[1] In domestic as in foreign affairs, the Turkish Government pursued one straightforward policy: a pro-Turkish policy. Thus it happened that, by 1939, the once "sick man of Europe" was being courted by all the great powers which, a quarter century earlier, eagerly had been anticipating his early demise.

RELIGIOUS, SOCIAL, AND CULTURAL CHANGES

When the Grand National Assembly abolished the sultanate in 1922, it did not abolish the caliphate—that is, the sultan's spiritual leadership of the Mohammedan world. Mohammed VI continued to be caliph for some days after his deposition as sultan. Then, upon his flight from the country, the assembly elected his cousin, Abdul Mejid, to be caliph in his place. The new Commander of the Faithful had no direct political power, but it was virtually impossible for devout Moslems to dissociate his office from its traditional political implications. A caliph, therefore, was an incongruity in the new Turkey. Accordingly, in 1924, the assembly abolished the Turkish caliphate and exiled the former ruling family.

The abolition of the caliphate had a wide significance in the Moslem world. By depriving themselves of a caliph, the Turks at the same time deprived most Mohammedans of a spiritual leader. It was true that even before the war many non-Ottoman Mohammedans had ceased to recognize the caliphate; yet the office and its prerogatives were not shadows. Indeed, it was evident soon after the Turkish pronouncement that there was no lack of aspirants for the vacated honor. But the general scramble for the title produced no successor and the caliphate remained an unappropriated dignity.

In conformity with Kemal's policy of enacting only one major reform at a time, the constitution of 1924 still assigned to Mohammedanism the place of a state religion. Then, in 1928, the assembly unanimously deleted from the constitution the article that declared Islam to be the state religion. Henceforth, Mohammedanism officially was tolerated in Turkey in the same way that any other religion was tolerated. Generally, there was no extensive opposition to Kemal's action, indicating how strong a hold the Turkish dictator had over the minds of his people and how ardently the Turks desired to become modernized. However, a serious religious outbreak did occur in the winter of 1930–1931 near Smyrna, where a group of dervishes unsuccessfully attempted to restore the caliphate.

Second in importance only to the changed attitude toward religion, and really but a phase of this modified outlook, was the altered

[1] Inönü was reelected in 1943 and 1946.

status accorded Turkish women. Laws of 1925 abolished legal polygamy, required the registration of marriages, and gave the president the power to grant divorces. Now Turkish women were given marriage rights similar to those of women in most Western countries.

In 1926 civil marriages were made obligatory, though these might be supplemented by religious ceremonies. The wearing of the veil was made optional, and Western clothing was introduced. This was followed by a whole series of changes, so that by 1934, with the granting of the franchise, women could take a full role in the national political life.

The changed conditions of life in Turkey made imperative the scrapping of the old law codes, the *Sheriat* or Holy Law included. Parliament therefore adopted new civil, penal, and commercial codes, based on Western models.

One of the most difficult problems confronting the Turkish Government was that of educating the people. School attendance was made compulsory for children from seven to sixteen, but the shortage of money, teachers, and school buildings prevented the full enforcement of the law. Nevertheless, by 1932 the national illiteracy was said to have fallen from 85 per cent to 42 per cent. Within a few more years, the latinized alphabet was in general use.

Severe restrictions were placed on the teaching of religion in public and private elementary schools, and in 1928 a United States girls' school at Brusa was closed for disregarding the law prohibiting attempts at religious conversion. As a "symbol of intellectual liberation" the wearing of the fez or turban—the distinguishing mark of pious Moslems—was prohibited. During 1934, Turkish families generally were occupied with the task of providing themselves with family names, which had to be registered with the authorities by the end of the year. Mustapha Kemal accepted the surname suggested to him by the assembly, namely, Atatürk or Father of the Turks.

"EFFICIENT TURKS FOR TURKEY"

Asked his opinion of the leaders of the Turkish Republic a Bulgarian diplomat was reported to have said: "They are working as we never thought Turks could work." During the days of the sultans, relatively few Turks concerned themselves with trade, commerce, or industry. The masses, when not in military service, generally labored in the fields. Hence business, as such, came to be almost a monopoly of the resident Greeks, Jews, and Armenians. But with the advent of the republic a new spirit became evident. The Nationalists wanted to have in Turkey nothing but Turkish labor, capital, ownership, and production. The obstacles to the fulfillment of such a program were enormous, but the pressure of circumstances soon led to the rise of a commercial middle class, whose nucleus was a group of refugees from Greece, where some of them had been engaged in trade. By 1950, one-fourth of the population lived in cities. Since, however, a majority of the people continued to be engaged in agriculture, the government also took pains to make efficient farmers of the Anatolian peasants.

Commerical treaties were signed with many countries. Extensive farm areas were settled with governmental aid in Anatolia. State departments were created to study agriculture, commerce, shipping, and industry. The government subsidized agriculture by the free grant of cattle, plows, and even houses to deserving families. Like Mussolini, Kemal had his own model farm on which he worked with rolled-up sleeves, driving his own tractor.

In 1929 the National Assembly voted a public-works program to extend over twelve years, and Swedish engineers were employed to supervise the completion of these works. Infant industries were stimulated by means of a protective-tariff system. A considerable amount of the necessary machinery had to be imported.

There was a tendency in Turkey, in the interest of efficiency, to establish state control over important industries. The government secured ownership of the railways and a large portion of the mercantile marine. It possessed several monopolies, and established factories to supply the clothing needs of the army and navy. Concessions were granted to foreigners, chiefly for the sake of additional capital and expert advice, but the authorities were careful in each case to safeguard Turkey's political and economic independence. In 1934 a five-year plan was adopted for the building of state and private factories, hydroelectric development, and the exploitation of mines.

A number of Turkish cities rapidly increased in size. Angora, for example, whose name was changed in 1929 to Ankara, had a population of 5000 in 1918; in 1932 its population was 80,000, and in 1940 it was 157,000. Naturally the increase in this instance was stimulated by the new political importance that the city assumed. Kemal connected the capital with the sea by rail, tried to annihilate the mosquitoes in the surrounding swamps, instituted reforms in sanitation, roads, and police protection, and in general supervised the beautification of the city. Even statues, hitherto considered idolatrous, were erected—chiefly of Kemal.

Despite these advances, Turkey, by 1939, had not yet learned to know the meaning of prosperity. A succession of poor crops, the inertia of some of the people, and the hesitancy of the Government to borrow from foreign bankers retarded material progress. When the harvests improved, the decline in the price of agricultural products in the world market had an equally unfortunate influence. From 1931, civil service staffs and salaries were cut, and drastic import quotas were fixed on foreign products. Attempts were made to mobilize the whole nation for a campaign of thrift, and all citizens were urged to avoid imported goods. Kemal himself set an example by wearing Turkish homespun clothes and drinking linden tea instead of coffee.

INTERNATIONAL RELATIONS

The harsh treatment meted out to Turkey after the First World War, and an adverse decision of the League in a Turco-Iraqi boundary dispute, made the Nationalists highly suspicious of the West. This was in part responsible for the close relations that early developed between Turkey and the U.S.S.R., Russia being the only power with which Turkey had a treaty of friendship prior to 1928. But the communistic activities of the Russians eventually caused an unfavorable reaction in Turkey. In 1929 some Turks were sentenced to prison for having carried on communistic propaganda, and Kemal threatened "destruction" to all persons engaged in subversion.

The resulting estrangement from the U.S.S.R., combined with the friendly attitude now adopted by some of the Western powers, who were eager to weaken Bolshevik influence in Turkey, gradually induced Ankara to look with increasing favor upon membership in the League. Beginning in 1927, when the Permanent Court rendered a favorable award to Turkey in a dispute with France over responsibility for the collision of a French steamer with a Turkish ship, there developed a gradual amelioration in Turco-Western relations that caused the Turkish Republic, in 1932, to accept an invitation to join the League.

The relations between the United States and Turkey after the war were peculiar. Although the two countries never had declared war upon one another, diplomatic and commercial relations had been severed, and a new treaty arrangement had to be effected. A Turco-United States Treaty of Amity and Commerce of 1923 was debated for several years in the Washington Senate and finally rejected, although the opponents of ratification had mustered only doubtful arguments.

In the meantime, Turkey had placed an especially high tariff on imports from all countries with which she had no treaty agreement. Economic interests eventually outweighed diplomatic considerations, and a Turco-United States *modus vivendi*, providing for restoration of diplomatic and consular relations, was concluded 1927. Soon thereafter the high commissioner, who had represented United States interests in Turkey since 1919, was replaced by amabassador. Commercial treaties followed in due course.

During the early 1930's, Turkey became anxious to refortify region of the Straits, demilitarized under the terms of the Lausanne Treaty. Finally, in 1936, Ankara did lay before the Lausanne tories and the League a request for revision of the appropriate terms. Partly because of the general feeling against Italy's venture and her apparent aims in the eastern Mediterranean partly out of gratification over the legal rather than method employed by Turkey to gain her ends, the Allies promptly agreed to consider her wishes. The result was reux Straits Convention, permitting the refortification of the zone in question. In time of peace the Straits were to be open equally to all commercial ships and to a limited tonnage of war vessels. In war, Turkey might close the Straits to belligerents, unless these were acting under League authority. The Ankara Government now lost no time in refortifying the strategic area connecting (and separating) the Black and Mediterranean seas.

Meanwhile Turkey had continued her policy of cementing friendships with all her neighbors, north, south, east, and west. Treaties of nonaggression and mutual cooperation were signed with Near Eastern neighbors. In 1939 Turkey, occupying a strategic international position, signed treaties with Great Britain and France, providing for mutual assistance in case of attack. A few weeks later the Second World War began.

The Arousing of Asia and Africa   13

THE TWAIN DID MEET

The huge conservative Asiatic mass, containing one-half of the population of the world; tied to age-old cultures; weighed down by autocracy, caste systems, and ancient traditions; torn between a rising nationalism and a vigorous imperialism in some sections, but never yet visited by Westerners in other sections; with little linguistic unity, and full of conflicting and often fanatical religious beliefs —this Asia was profoundly stirred by its contact with the West, especially during the twentieth century. The very fact that Europeans and Americans strove to impose a foreign culture upon the Asiatics drove many of them into a greater veneration for their own traditions and customs. They held to their accustomed ways tenaciously. Into such an environment the Westerners tried to introduce modern technology.

Before Europe had reached its 1914 stage of civilization it had passed through a Renaissance, a Protestant Revolt, a century of religious wars, and an Industrial Revolution. But in Asia, the aim was at remaking a much vaster continent nearly instantaneously.

The attempted hasty industrialization of his continent was not the only bewildering phenomenon that the Asiatic was forced to witness. He was made to look at a confusing and terrifying series of contrasts. How startling it must have been to him on occasion to hear almost simultaneously the pacific words of a missionary and the sputtering of a machine gun; to hear about self-determination and at the same time to see foreign gunboats or troops violating his country's territory. He must have been amazed by the facility with which so many Westerners mixed idealism and materialism. He heard his autocratic systems of government denounced, and he wit-

243

nessed the setting up of even more autocratic regimes. Still more was he puzzled, after the war, to hear from some Europeans about the wonders of industrialism and the advantages of the capitalist order, and from others about the evils of capitalism and imperialism and the supposed glories of an international Communist system. With his own condition, moreover, he was dissatisfied. What was he to do?

It was one of the unfortunate aspects of the situation that most of the people in Asia did not know exactly what they wanted. They often were discontented, poor, and oppressed people, who groped in the dark. Their great stumbling block appeared to be the paucity of adequate leadership. Frequently such leaders as did arise were inexperienced visionaries with grandiose but impractical dreams. Interested groups generally found little difficulty in counteracting the influence of these leaders by holding them up to ridicule or else throwing them into prison. Generally, it was oratory and curse against blast furnace and armored tank. To this rule, however, there were a few conspicuous exceptions, notably the "Chinese George Washington," Dr. Sun Yat-sen.

The hundreds of millions of people who comprised the mass population of Asia found their course of life little altered as a consequence of the military aspects of the First World War. Even India and China were affected only slightly by the actual fighting, although the Indians did have forces aiding the British.

More important were the economic and psychological effects of the war. Many moderate Indian leaders who had hoped that a loyal India would be rewarded after the conflict with political autonomy became radical and bitter in their eventual disappointment. At the same time a few leaders added considerably to their experience and prestige by participating in the Paris Peace Conference and in some of the postwar British Imperial Conferences. During the war, moreover, India's iron and steel industries were stimulated, and new commercial contacts were established with Japan.

In China, the passing of Kiaochow from German to Japanese control caused a renewed flaring up of a young nationalism that strove to assert the right of the Chinese to their fatherland. Interested foreign groups, however, soon brought pressure to bear on the nationalists, and local chieftains were encouraged to set themselves up as war lords in various parts of China. It thus appeared to many Chinese that, whereas nationalism was exalted in the West, the same spirit, when it appeared in so-called backward countries, was to be crushed by Western and Japanese imperialists.

Persia, whose sovereignty had been impaired by Anglo-Russian agreements of 1907 and 1915, and on whose neutral soil Russians, Britishers, and Turks had fought some of their battles during the First World War, national resentment was strong enough in the postwar years to accomplish unexpected things. An Anglo-Persian treaty of 1919, that would have converted Persia into a British protectorate, was denounced because of an aroused nationalist opinion.

The government that had consented to the treaty was overthrown in 1921 by Riza Khan, an able soldier who rose from the ranks to become eventually the hereditary ruler, Riza Shah Pahlevi (1925).

Under its nationalistic government Persia made rapid political and economic headway. Foreign officers were dismissed, the army was converted into a well-drilled unit, and most of the hitherto autonomous desert tribes were brought under the central authority. Able foreign financial advisers were employed to straighten out the monarchy's fiscal difficulties, to improve the conditions of health and education, and to give counsel on other reforms. Then the Persian Government forced the Anglo-Persian Oil Company, a majority of whose stock was owned by the British Government, to accept a revised lease concession (1933). The new agreement gave Persia better financial terms than she previously had received and curtailed the company's sphere of interest. The outcome of this incident, which for a time threatened to precipitate a dangerous quarrel, constituted a triumph for a state that only a dozen years previously had been regarded as a legitimate field for aggressive exploitation. In 1935 the official name of Persia became Iran.[1]

Although the two main aspects of the Asiatic revolt—resentment of European domination and discontent over the changes resulting from the "Westernization" of Asia—expressed themselves in a variety of ways, the most effective weapon that the natives for a time were able to use against Western machinery and arms, was the economic boycott. Uprisings could be crushed, bombs and tanks were more destructive than lances and fanaticism—but the only way to beat an Oriental boycott seemed to be by making concessions. More than once Japan was forced to give way, when her demands on China were too unpopular, by the power of a Chinese boycott that threatened to cripple Japanese trade and commerce. Great Britain several times felt the force of Indian boycotts and preferred not to have to deal with that unpleasant phenomenon. But here again the absence of effective native leadership precluded the unity necessary to support a successful demand for equality.

For a time after the First World War, the universality of unrest in Asia gave rise to talk of a Pan-Asia movement. It was feared in some quarters that the Asiatics might attempt to set up a counterpoise to the League of Nations and thereby definitely divide East and West into two powerful hostile combinations. Yet remote as a Pan-Europa seemed, a Pan-Asia appeared to be even more distant. It was said that the psychological differences between India and China, for example, were greater than the corresponding differences between Western Europe and China. The groups so loosely termed Asiatics by Europeans and Americans really were widely separated

---

[1] Somewhat similar events occurred in neighboring Afghanistan, whose able ruler, Amanullah Khan, secured British recognition of independence in 1922.

from one another by political, economic, social, and religious gaps.

Of more immediate importance were the relations of Asia with the League of Nations. Japan for a time was a leading member, with a permanent seat on the Council and an influential voice in affairs. China was elected to a temporary seat on the Council. Iran, India, Iraq, Afghanistan, and Siam all were admitted to membership and took active part in the workings of the League. These relationships appeared the more remarkable because the League was conceived fundamentally to deal with antagonisms arising ouf of the developments of European, not Asiatic, life. But since much of Asia's future confidence in the League depended upon the latter's help to such countries as China—countries that were striving to absorb the shock of the clash of West and East and to reach a working compromise between the two—it seemed unfortunate to some that the Geneva body failed to intervene more actively in the Sino-Japanese dispute of 1931 and after.

From a material standpoint, much of Asia continued to require friendly assistance and needed to learn about Western advances. Millions of people needed to be educated, stable governments had to be established, and advanced industrial and agricultural procedures needed introduction. But this could not be achieved overnight nor by forceful imposition upon unwilling recipients. All Asiatic traditions did not need to be discarded and replaced by European traditions. Instead, Asiatic traditions required gradual modification to fit modern world conditions. First it was necessary to introduce new viewpoints and attitudes, then new methods—that seemed to be the most effective approach in a region where custom played so important a role.

Let us now turn to a more detailed study of developments from 1919 to 1939 in certain Asiatic countries.

PALESTINE (ISRAEL) AND SYRIA

In 1922 the League approved the assignment of Palestine to Great Britain as a Class A mandate. The Moslems in the Holy Land were disappointed that the terms of the mandate confirmed the Balfour Declaration of 1917, wherein Great Britain had promised to establish in Palestine "a national home for the Jewish people." The Arabs found little consolation in the parallel promise that "nothing shall be done which may prejudice the civil and religious rights of existing non-Jewish communities."

The first British High Commissioner, Sir Herbert Samuel, promptly promulgated a constitution (1922). It provided an appointive executive council and a legislative body in which Moslems, Christians, and Jews would be represented. The Moslems refused to vote at elections for this council, and Samuel was obliged to govern with an appointed advisory body. In 1940 the legislative process still consisted of the promulgation of decrees.

The discontent of the Arabs crystallized in a violent anti-Jewish outbreak in 1929, during which many Jews were killed. The Mac-Donald Government rushed armed forces to the scene and soon restored order. A British commission established as the cause for the rioting "the Arab feeling of animosity and hostility toward the Jews." The League Mandates Commission, however, claimed that the outburst was directed as much against Great Britain as against the Jews and blamed the British for failure to provide adequate military and police protection.

The Arabs did enumerate specific grievances against both the authorities and the Jews. They complained that the land legislation enabled the Jews to buy up large portions of the limited arable soil and threatened the existence of thousands of Arabs. They objected to the government's favorable attitude towards Jewish immigration. Also, they claimed that most of the entering Jews, coming from Poland, Russia, and Romania, were poor and, frequently, radical.

Another Arabian-Jewish dispute involved the Wailing Wall in Jerusalem. At this wall, supposedly a relic of Solomon's Temple, the Jews had been accustomed to worship and to mourn. Since the wall adjoined a sacred Mohammedan shrine, the Mosque of Omar, there was opportunity for strife whenever religiously excited Jews and Moslems appeared for worship simultaneously at the neighboring holy spots. So serious did this Wailing Wall situation become that the British Government in 1930 appointed a neutral commission to find a solution for the problem. The commission reported that the wall and its adjoining pavement were Moslem property, but that, with certain restrictions, the Jews should be granted free access to it. The report was promptly implemented by the high commissioner.

Meanwhile the British Government had come into conflict with the World Zionist Organization and the Jewish Agency for Palestine. In May 1930 the authorities indefinitely had suspended immigration permits already issued to more than 2000 prospective Jewish immigrants. The ban was imposed pending a study of Palestinian economic conditions by a commission under Sir John Hope Simpson. The commission issued its report in October 1930, and simultaneously the British Colonial Office published a White Paper that announced a new official policy in the future administration of the mandate.

The White Paper maintained that too much haste had been shown in the upbuilding of the Jewish homeland and that, as a result, the future welfare of the Arabs had been jeopardized. The report indicated that rapid immigration by the Jewish peoples had caused available land to diminish and that little fertile land remained for further colonization.

Obviously, close cooperation between Arabs and Jews was impossible so long as the Arabs felt that Jewish immigration was depriving them of land, work, and political power. For, as the Simpson Report pointed out, the Jewish Foundation Fund, which leased land to Jewish colonies, had forbidden Arabian labor on its soil, and the General Federation of Jewish Labor had adopted a policy of importing Jewish workmen rather than employing landless Arabs. In these circumstances Great Britain felt justified in continuing the suspension of immigrations.

The declaration of this new British policy was gratifying to the Arabs. But the Jews, both within and without Palestine, were angered and the British Government was accused of the "cruel and unfair betrayal" of a "harassed people." The MacDonald Government, however, insisted that it was simply striving to carry out the threefold task of giving the Jews a national home in Palestine, of dealing fairly with the large Moslem majority, and of preparing the land for self-government.

In 1932 the government of Palestine eased its restrictions against further immigration and permitted free entry to any farmer, merchant, or businessman who possessed a minimum capital of $2500. Each month, also, a quota of Jewish laborers was admitted, for the economic progress of the land was remarkable. Capital to the extent of many million dollars flowed into the Holy Land, and scientific methods were applied to agriculture and industry. There was little unemployment, and the Palestinian budget showed a surplus. The rise to power of the National Socialists in Germany, however, brought a new wave of Jewish migration to Palestine and again agitated Arabian leaders.

In 1936 the triple conflict among Arabian nationalism, Zionism, and British imperial interests once more became violent. The Arabian leaders, late in 1935, had presented a list of demands asking for many items, among them a suspension of Jewish immigration. The refusal of the authorities to adopt this proposed program led to renewed anti-Jewish riots in 1936. London thereupon appointed a commission under Earl Peel to ascertain the underlying causes of the disturbances.

The Peel Commission conducted hearings and listened to Jews, Moslem Arabs, and Christian Arabs. It then returned to London to prepare its report on the basis of a "small mountain" of evidence, plus the knowledge that Palestine was strategically important to Great Britain. The British also had to consider the effect of any decision upon the attitude of Jews throughout the world and of the Moslems scattered throughout the British Empire.

The report was approved by the British Cabinet and made public in 1937. The commissioners declared that "the obligations Britain undertook toward the Arabs and the Jews some twenty years ago . . . have proved irreconcilable, and as far ahead as we can see, they must continue to conflict . . . . We cannot—in Palestine as it now is— both concede the Arab claim to self-government and secure the establishment of the Jewish National Home." Inasmuch as "neither race can fairly rule all Palestine, each race might justly rule part of it . . . . Partition offers a chance of ultimate peace. No other plan does."

It therefore was proposed to end the mandate and divide the country into three parts: a new Jewish state occupying about one-fourth of the area of Palestine, an Arabian section including most of the remainder of Palestine in union with Trans-Jordan, and an area under British administration including Jerusalem, Bethlehem, and other holy places.

The plan aroused protests from all sides. The Jews raised the cry of betrayal. The Arabs claimed that "the richest zone is to be given to the Jews, the holiest to the British, and the most barren to the Arabs." Some Arabs again became violent, stimulated by Italian encouragement. Italian radio sets were distributed among the Arabs, and anti-British broadcasts emanated from the Italian sender at Bari.[2] Moderate Arabs who pointed to the advantages in the Peel Plan were the victims of murderous attacks, and a British district commissioner was assassinated. Scores of Arabian leaders were jailed or deported. Meanwhile the unrest had damaged economic life, with much attendant suffering for the population.

The British Government had declared its purpose to carry out the plan, but in the face of so much criticism the House of Commons ordered the submission of the whole matter to the League for further consideration. The League recommended another study of the entire Palestinian affair. Hence, in 1938, another commission, headed by Sir John Woodhead, was directed to draw up a "more precise and detailed scheme" for solving the Palestine riddle. The Woodhead Commission unanimously opposed the partition proposals because it appeared impossible to recommend boundaries for the suggested areas that would afford a reasonable prospect of the eventual establishment of self-supporting Arab and Jewish states. The British Government thereupon decided that "the surest foundation for peace and progress in Palestine would be an understanding between the Arabs and Jews," and hence invited to a Conference at London representatives of the disputing parties.

This news came at a time when Great Britain had found it necessary to send many more soldiers to Palestine. For months Palestine had been the scene of political murder and guerrilla warfare. Arab extremists attacked moderate Arabs who were willing to seek a compromise solution as fiercely as they attacked Jews or British guards. During the period of the European crisis over Czechoslovakia the rebel campaign was intensified, and the misery of the masses became worse. At last, in February 1939, the London conference on Palestine was opened by Premier Chamberlain. But because the Arab delegates refused to sit in the same room with the

---

[2] In 1938 the British Broadcasting Company inaugurated Arabic programs to counteract the Italian broadcasts.

Jews, Chamberlain had to extend his official greetings in two sections.

The Arabs demanded the formation of an independent Arab state tied to Great Britain by treaty only, proportionate representation for Arabs and Jews in the parliament of the new state, denunciation of the Balfour Declaration, prohibition of Jewish immigration, and stoppage of land sales to Jews. The Jews took an opposite stand on each point. The British tried to find a compromise position, but to no avail. The conference soon closed in failure. In the midst of further violence came the news of the outbreak of the Second World War.

The experiences of France in her Syrian mandate, an important silk-producing area, were almost as troublous as those of Great Britain in Palestine. For convenience and perhaps to prevent the development of any strong national feeling, the land was divided into five (later four) administrative areas, each with a different name and law system, but all subordinate to one high commissioner. Martial law and censorship were established and French became the language of the law courts. Trouble soon developed as the Moslems, who comprised a majority of the population, believed that the French were favoring the Christian minority.

In 1924 High Commissioner General Maxim Weygand, a conservative Catholic, was removed at the insistence of the anticlericals in the Chamber of Deputies. He was replaced by General Maurice Sarrail, who antagonized the Christians as well as the Moslems and who crowned his administrative efforts in 1925 by inviting the leaders of some discontented Druse tribes to Damascus for a parley and then putting them in prison when they accepted the call. Thereupon the Druse tribesmen broke into open revolt. The French captured some of the rebels and, as a warning to others, displayed in the public square of Damascus the corpses of twenty-four persons whom they had shot. When the city populace thereupon became enraged and attacked some French troops, the latter were withdrawn from Damascus and the city was bombarded. Part of the city was destroyed, many people were killed, and a severe fine was imposed on the city's inhabitants.

Later policies were little more enlightened and, early in 1926, hostilities were resumed. Damascus again was bombarded. The Mandates Commission reacted by criticizing French policy and condemning recourse in mandates to expedients involving bombing civilian populations from the air.

In 1928 a Syrian Constituent Assembly was convened to draw up an instrument of government. When the nationalist delegates, who were in a majority, insisted on the establishment of an independent republic, the gathering was suspended. In 1930 the commissioner himself, Henri Ponsot, issued a constitution, setting up a republic restricted only by the mandatory powers of France and by French control of its foreign affairs. The document provided for a parliament and for a president who always was to be a Moslem and was to be chosen by the parliament for five years.[3] The first elections under this constitution were held amid great disorder in 1932, and an assembly was elected, which contained a majority of Moderate Party deputies. This caused the minority Nationalists, who opposed the French Mandate, to claim that the French had influenced the course of the election.

In 1933 the French were unsuccessful in an attempt to get the Syrian Parliament to accept a treaty which would have assured that, for the next twenty-five years, France would continue to supervise Syrian foreign, military, and financial matters. In September 1936 France and Syria signed another treaty, this one providing for Syrian independence after three years. Turkey thereupon requested that an autonomous regime be set up in the new Syria for the district of Alexandretta—including the city of Antioch—which was inhabited by a large proportion of Turks. The matter was referred to the League Council, which proposed that Alexandretta should remain under the sovereignty of Syria, with the latter controlling its foreign relations and customs. The district was, however, to have its own local legislature, with Turkish as the official language. These principles were incorporated in a statute, and a League commission was dispatched to Alexandretta to prepare for elections in 1938.

The Turks objected to the commission's methods, which, it was claimed, would give them a minority in the local assembly. Rioting occurred and the League commission was forced to retire from the area. The critical situation in Europe in 1938 induced Paris and Ankara promptly to sign an agreement in the Turkish capital. The document provided that Alexandretta should become "an autonomous State under Franco-Turkish administration, with French and Turkish troops as a joint defense force." The territory then, in September 1938, became the Republic of Hatay.[4]

The new state had a short life. As the European situation became more critical in 1939, both Great Britain and France became more interested in gaining assurances of Turkish friendship in the event of trouble in the eastern Mediterranean. The British negotiated an accord with Turkey providing for mutual assistance in case of attack. A similar treaty was signed by Turkey with France, but the French had to pay a price: they ceded to Turkey most of Hatay.

Syria protested the cession, claiming that France had no right to give away mandated territory. Nazi Germany and Fascist Italy joined in the protest (on the ground that the treaty violated the League Covenant!), and the Permanent Mandates Commission censured France. But Paris remained firm. When renewed rioting

---

[3] This constitution did not apply to the administrative unit called Lebanon, which, in 1926, had been given a republican charter of its own.
[4] Hatay, the Turkish name for the district, bore an obvious relation to Hittites, whom the Turks looked upon as ancestors.

broke out in Syria, the mandate's constitution was suspended and the French High Commissioner assumed full control. Such was the situation when the Second World War began.

INDIA

Within three months after the outbreak of the First World War, Indian troops were fighting on the western front. The government of India presented Great Britain with a gift of $500,000,000. But the fact that she made it unnecessary for Great Britain to quell serious native revolts, was India's greatest contribution to the Allied cause.

The political life of India long had been characterized by unrest. Conditions had been troubled under the regime of the British East India Company (1600–1857), and there had been only slight improvement under the administration of the British Government from 1858. A number of leaders, through their travels and studies in the West, had come to look upon representative government as an urgent goal. During the war, therefore, Indian leaders made it clear that they hoped to win concessions as a reward for their loyalty. Their hands were strengthened by a *rapprochement* that the war brought about between the Moslems and Hindus in India. The Mohammedans refused to heed the Ottoman Sultan's call for a Holy War against Great Britain, and instead, they united with the Hindus in aiding the British and demanding political change. In 1916 the Indian National Congress, organized in 1885, and the All-India Moslem League, founded in 1906, met together for the first time. The fraternization of Moslems and Hindus resulted in the presentation to Great Britain (1916) of a political plan known as the Congress-League Scheme.

With their attention centered upon the war, the British at first paid little heed to the scheme. Eventually, however, the growing unrest made some action imperative. In 1917 a survey was made, and the consensus of British officials in India was that any diminution of British power would lead to disorder and caste warfare. This view was upheld by the European merchants in India and by some Moslems who feared Brahmin rule. Nationalist spokesmen, on the other hand, heaped up charges of extravagance and waste against British rule.

Following these interviews and a resultant report, parliamentary committees in 1918 framed legislation. Meanwhile an increasing discontent in India, manifested by strikes and agitation, led to the decreeing of the Rowlatt Acts. These laws empowered the government to suspend jury trial, curtail the right of appeal, and inflict severe penalties. Later all public meetings were forbidden. In 1919 the conflict between the authorities and the natives reached a climax at Amritsar.

Here the rioting had cost the lives of some British persons. Brigadier Reginald E. Dyer was called upon to restore order, and, on one occasion, British troops killed about 400 people. Popular indignation was so great that Parliament appointed a commission to investigate the "massacre." The report of the commission whitewashed the affair, though it did censure Dyer. The Indians were indignant over the report, and their anger was not appeased when Dyer, though re-called from India, lost neither rank nor pension.

The Indians, therefore, were in no happy mood when Parliament passed the Government of India Act (1919). This act, which applied only to the provinces comprising British India and not to the 600 Indian States, increased the number of voters in *provincial* elections from 30,000 to 5,300,000, thus enfranchising 2.2 per cent of the population. In central affairs the viceroy was to be assisted, as before, by a Council of State and a Legislative Assembly. Laws generally required the consent of the assembly, although in some instances the assent of the council was sufficient. In case of emergency the viceroy might issue decrees with the force of law, and to him was left full control of finances and defense. Further change, it was pro-vided, would be considered after ten years.

The most remarkable feature of the law created a dyarchy or double government in provincial matters. In each province such matters as police, law, and administration were "reserved" to the provincial governor. The governor was appointed by the viceroy, himself an appointee of the Emperor of India. Affairs such as sanita-tion, education, agriculture, and health were "transferred" to the supervision of the provincial councils, a majority of whose members were elected.

The Indian Nationalists, now organized as a party, were not con-tent with these concessions. They complained that the viceroy still would be supreme through his control of the purse strings; that the act, which in effect was India's constitution, ought to be subject to revision in less than the prescribed decade; and that the franchise was too restricted. A movement to secure further concessions from the British at once was inaugurated, the leading agitator now being a fifty-year-old lawyer named Mohandas Karamchand Gandhi.

Gandhi was born in 1869 of a prominent family. After an un-happy youth, he went to England to study law, under the threefold vow of celibacy, vegetarianism, and abstention from alcohol. "Shy, retiring, awkward, uncouth in dress and speech, bewildered by strange manners, and nearly starving in a country where people took little pains to provide for vegetarians, he suffered pitiably. In time, however, he located a vegetarian restaurant; and with regular and ample meals his health improved." Following his admission to the bar, Gandhi returned to India to practice law. He was not particu-larly successful and was delighted when an opportunity came in 1893 to handle a case in South Africa.

For the next twenty years, Gandhi remained in South Africa, up-holding the rights of immigrant Indian laborers. He rose to eminence as a pleader, and the British Government usually supported his endeavors to establish the equality of Indians with other subjects of the empire. For this aid Gandhi was grateful, and from 1914 to 1918 he was active in securing Indian military enlistments. After the return of peace, however, the Rowlatt Acts and the Amritsar incident turned him against British policy.

Personally, Gandhi seemed an enigma, being labeled, in turn, a prophet, a madman, and a politician. A small wizened ascetic, he spent much time fasting and praying and appeared little interested in riches or pleasure. His followers called him *Mahatma*, the Great Soul or the Holy One.

Gandhi strove fervently to secure home rule for India. He professed abhorrence for violence, and when Great Britain hesitated to grant autonomy, began preaching passive resistance. His followers were urged to adopt a policy of material and spiritual noncooperation. Before long the Hindus effectively boycotted British schools and disregarded the Rowlatt Laws, all in hope of gaining home rule. During 1920 and 1921, several incidents aided Gandhi's movement. Moslems flocked to his standard because of the harsh Allied treatment of Turkey in the peace negotiations at Sèvres. Additional recruits were gained when the British Parliament restricted the area in the African colony of Kenya in which Hindus might settle. The harshness of the police in dealing with the Indian crowds also reacted to the Mahatma's advantage.

Gandhi, however, was not capable of preventing some of his followers from resorting to violence. A visit of the Prince of Wales to India was made the occasion for serious strikes and riots, and in 1922, Gandhi was sentenced to six years' imprisonment for inciting the populace to violence.

With Gandhi in prison the anti-British agitation subsided, and the Moslems and Hindus fell to quarreling again. Noncooperation apparently had proved a failure. Some Nationalists decided to abandon the boycott and run candidates for election to the Legislative Assembly. Here, as members of a newly formed Swarajist (Home Rule) Party, they could at least air their views in public debate. From 1922 to 1927 the home-rule agitation was confined chiefly to the legislative chambers. In these circumstances the government considered it safe to free Gandhi in 1924. He remained in retirement for five years after his release.

Meanwhile, a committee of the assembly had voted the dyarchic system a failure. Both the British and the Indian members were in agreement on this point. In 1925, Pandit Motilal Nehru, leader of the Swarajists, asked for full responsible government in the provinces and responsible government in all national spheres, save defense and foreign affairs. A commission was appointed in 1927 and, although there were no Indians on this body, Sir John Simon, its chairman, invited the leading native statesmen to work with the group "in joint conference." The Nationalists, however, resented their official exclusion and boycotted the delegation when it arrived in India. Several attempts were made to dynamite the commission's special train. The investigation ended in 1929, and a report was published in 1930.

While the Simon Commission was at work, the tide of Indian nationalism rose once more. Gandhi emerged from retirement, and at an All-India National Congress of 1929, which represented Moslems as well as Hindus, a resolution was passed demanding dominion status for India. In 1930, Gandhi demanded immediate British acquiescence in the resolution.

When his demand was rejected, Gandhi launched a new civil-disobedience campaign. Choosing as the target for his passive resistance the government's salt monpoly, he determined to violate a law that forbade natives to make salt from sea water. He and a band of volunteers marched 170 miles to Dandi on the Gulf of Cambay to make salt. His first violation of the law was the signal for a general defiance of laws throughout India. In the cities, natives obstructed railway and street traffic by lying down on the tracks or in the path of vehicles. Gandhi again cautioned his followers to abstain from violence, but much blood was shed. The authorities for a time refrained from arresting the Holy One lest he be regarded as a martyr; but eventually the situation became so bad that he and other prominent Nationalists were jailed.

The resulting anger of the people was heightened when the recommendations of the Simon Commission became known. The report aimed at increasing the powers of the Viceroy and the provincial governors. It avoided even a reference to dominion status, and it hurt educated Indians by the curt manner in which it proposed making the provincial legislatures a school wherein the natives might secure "primary instruction and training in government." Now more and more members of the National Congress began to demand independence, but the incarceration of the leaders and the approach of the rainy season checked the outbursts as 1930 drew to a close.

Meanwhile, Prime Minister MacDonald had called a Round Table Conference in London as a possible means of arriving at some Indian compromise. This Round Table Conference achieved a number of results. The Native Princes announced their willingness to enter a federation with British India. It was agreed that Burma should be separated from India. The high-caste members approved political equality for the untouchables in the projected constitution. But the greatest quandary that faced the conference was the Moslem-Hindu controversy. The Moslems feared their treatment under an autonomous government since they formed only 22 per cent of the population. The problem of their protection was not settled by the conference.

When the Indian conferees returned from London to explain their accomplishments, the extremists at home, many of whom now were released from confinement, denounced the gains as no more than

"a cup of milk for a hungry lion." Gandhi renewed his civil-disobedience campaign until March 1931, when a truce was reached.
The Nationalists promised to refrain from civil disobedience, and
the government granted some amnesties. Neither side fully observed
the terms of the truce, and disorder was rife throughout the summer.
London therefore proposed a reassembling of the Round Table Conference in September 1931. Gandhi, after much hesitation, accepted
an invitation to attend.

The second Round Table Conference was a disappointing affair.
Not only were the proceedings made difficult by the conflicting
views of the Indians and Britishers on the extent of self-government
to be accorded, but the delegates from the Native States and from
British India could not agree on a form of federation and the Moslems and Hindus were farther apart than ever on the question of
political safeguards for the former. Much to the annoyance of
Gandhi, Prime Minister MacDonald informed the Indians that a
new constitution would have to wait until they themselves could
reach a compromise on communal (religious) electorates and minority safeguards. After several months spent in fruitless wrangling,
the British adjourned the conference and most of the Indian delegates went home feeling that the gathering had been a failure.

Throughout 1931[5] the anti-British manifestations had repeatedly
taken the form of attempts on the lives of officials. Now the unsuccessful conclusion of the Round Table spurred the natives to
further violence. Conditions became so bad that the viceroy issued
strict ordinances. Gandhi, upon his return from Great Britain, sought
to induce the viceroy to rescind the decrees, but when his request
was disregarded the civil-disobedience campaign was renewed and
the Mahatma once more was jailed.

Incidents of violence and civil disobedience were not conducive
to a settlement of the controversies laid bare at the Round Table
Conference. Not only did Anglo-Indian relations become bitterer
than at any previous time, but the Moslem-Hindu rift widened
rapidly. Bloody religious outbreaks occurred in several large cities.

The impasse sorely tried the patience of the British, and eventually
Sir Samuel Hoare, Secretary of State for India, announced that the
British Government itself would devise a solution for the minorities
question and submit its decision to Parliament. This news was
greeted in India with more riots, but London proceeded according
to plan. A third Round Table met in London late in 1932, but
Gandhi, whom the viceroy refused to release so long as the civil
disobedience campaign lasted, was not a member. Before its adjourn-
ment, the conference drafted a constitution to replace the instrument of 1919. The document, after some amendment, became law as

---

[5] In this year British exports to India were one-third less than in 1930. The
economic depression added greatly to unrest and turmoil in India.

the Government of India Act in 1935. It did not establish dominion status.

India's new constituion was inaugurated in 1937, although not all provisions were made effective at once. Many of the vocal groups in India expressed bitter opposition to the document. Some wanted independence. Others had hoped for dominion status. There was general discontent over certain "reserved powers" that left the viceroy in control of foreign affairs, defense, and finance. Many objected because the franchise had not been widely extended.

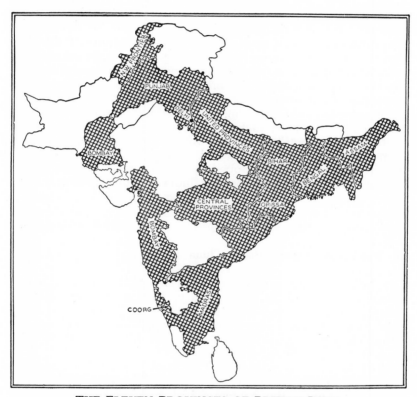

THE ELEVEN PROVINCES OF BRITISH INDIA

From Tschan, F. J., Grimm, H. J., and Squires, J. D. *Western Civilization*, 1942. Courtesy, J. B. Lippincott Co.

The lead in opposition was taken by the Indian National Congress, whose members now had a choice of two leaders. Gandhi still retained his influence with the moderate elements. The more impatient group followed the young Pandit Jawaharlal Nehru, who believed in independence to be obtained through obstructionist tactics. Nehru, the president of the congress, had also come to be

politically radical. In 1936 he informed his colleagues that he regarded socialism as the only solution for India's ills. This stand
resulted in a further split among the Indians, for Nehru's attitude
appealed to many among the masses, but alienated the sympathies
of others who hitherto had supported anti-British campaigns.

In the voting of 1937 the National Congress Party gained control
of six of the eleven provincial assemblies. This apparently induced
Gandhi to take a more radical view. He endorsed the Delhi Resolution, which bound members not to accept ministerial posts in provincial assemblies in which they had a majority unless the governors
gave advance assurance that they would not set aside any legislative
decisions—as had been done in the past.

In 1939, India witnessed increasing tension among three contending elements. The viceroy favored the gradual application of the
India Act of 1935. Gandhi's followers advocated continued negotiation with the British for dominion status. Some nationalists demanded a radical independent state. The stalemate among the three
groups persisted until, following the outbreak of hostilities in Europe,
the viceroy announced that the final settlement of India's status
must await the outcome of the war. Once again the provincial
assemblies under congress control resigned (October 1939), and
Gandhi threatened civil disobedience until an acceptable British
declaration of war aims respecting India was forthcoming.

CHINA AND JAPAN

A.   The Course of Revolution in China

In 1912, the Western world received the startling news of a suc-
cessful revolution in the largest and perhaps most conservative of
Asiatic empires: China. The Manchu dynasty, which had ruled
China since 1644, was ousted from power, and the empire was con-
verted into a republic, bearing, at least outwardly, the earmarks of a
European parliamentary system.

China long had been in a state of "backwardness," whereas the
West had been advancing towards world supremacy. China's
government under the emperors had been corrupt; her social
development retarded. Education had been confined to the few and
had been out of tune with the requirements of a modern age.
Famines, pestilence, and floods had wreaked havoc. Foreign "barbarians" had been exploiting China's natural resources.

Between 1898 and 1900 there had occurred two unsuccessful
movements to remedy the abuses of the Manchu regime and curtail
the activities of foreigners. In 1898 a group of patriotic intellectuals
influenced the young Emperor Kwang Hsu to launch a sweeping
reform program. But because of their very radicalness the reforms
were foredoomed to failure. China was too backward to be moder-

nized overnight by edicts, and turmoil and reaction followed the sudden attempt at widespread reform. Then, during the period of reaction, the authorities, inspired by the Dowager Empress Tsu Hsi, turned the popular dislike of "foreignism" into a concerted move to oust the "barbarians." The resulting Boxer Rebellion brought on an international punitive expedition.

As the twentieth century wore on and the Chinese became aware of the remarkable transformation wrought by the Westernization of Japan, an increasing number of Chinese students went abroad to study. At first, thousands of students went to Japan, which was relatively close and had a language similar to Chinese. But eventually many students preferred to seek education elsewhere. Some of them came to the United States, particularly after Washington arranged generous scholarship funds.

Their foreign contacts and observations inspired these young people with a fervent national spirit. China's defeat by Japan in the war of 1894–1895 and the aggression of the foreigners helped to disseminate this spirit among the business classes and the professionals. The Manchus had never entirely lost their foreign aspect in the eyes of the Chinese intelligentsia, and from the late 1890's a powerful secret agitation worked for the overthrow of the conquerors.

Sensing this widespread discontent and spurred by the example of Japan, who in 1904–1905 astonished the world by her stand against Russia, the Manchu Government inaugurated another reform program (1905). A plan of constitutional reform was outlined, and provision was made for the calling of a national assembly. Before much progress in this direction was registered, the throne fell (1908) to Pu Yi, a boy not yet three years old. The regent was a conservative politician who attempted to halt the reform movement.

The reformers now renewed their activities, and a national assembly was convened at Peking in 1910. It soon was dismissed, and the year 1911 witnessed troop mutinies, movements for local autonomy, and violent reactions to the continued granting of foreign concessions. In despair the Manchus abdicated in February 1912, after almost 270 years of power.

Meanwhile, on January 1, 1912, a revolutionary assembly at Nanking had elected Dr. Sun Yat–sen president of a provisional republican government. Dr. Sun was a patriotic and capable scholar who had been forced to spend a considerable portion of his life in exile. As one of the founders of the *Kuomintang,* or Nationalist Party, he had spent most of the period since 1895 organizing Young China into an energetic association bent on achieving political and economic change. Sun believed that his country, with its massive resources of people and materials, was destined to play a leading part in human affairs. He wanted to arouse the Chinese people from the national lethargy into which they had fallen under Manchu control, and to allow no new oppression to take the place of the old. In 1924, he summed up his ideas in a series of lectures entitled *The Three Principles of the People (San Min Chu I)*. These principles, for which the new China was to strive, were Nationalism, Democracy, and Livelihood (economic equality).

At the time of his election Sun agreed that, for the sake of unifying the country, he soon would retire in favor of Yuan Shih–kai, well known as China's ablest military organizer, who had come into control of northern China. This arrangement was completed in February 1912, and Yuan thus became the first president of a united Chinese Republic. Friction soon developed between the northerners led by Yuan and the southerners under Sun when it became apparent that Yuan had dictatorial ambitions.

The Kuomintang deputies in the parliament that convened in 1913 persistently voted against Yuan and his policies. The mutual ill will increased steadily, and eventually an attempt was made to oust Yuan. This "second revolution" failed and Yuan commenced a dictatorial rule that lasted until his death in June 1916. Following Yuan's death, the country was split over the questions of participation in the First World War and the further granting of foreign concessions. The central authorities found it virtually impossible to collect taxes, and hence China's mineral and industrial resources were being given outright to foreigners in return for loans that promptly were squandered.

Late in 1917 the Kuomintang set up a southern government at Canton in opposition to a northern government at Peking. The confusion was increased by the activities of a dozen military governors, who did most of the tax collecting and who used their armies to further private ambitions. The Canton Government claimed to be the legitimate representative of the people, but Peking obtained both recognition and funds from foreign powers seeking further privileges.

B. The Twenty-One Demands

Japan declared war on Germany in August 1914 and soon thereafter captured the area about Kiaochow, which Germany in 1898 had leased from China. To carry out this project, Japan had violated China's neutrality by landing troops on her territory more than a hundred miles from the German leasehold. When, after the fall of the German strongholds, the Chinese asked the Japanese to retire, the latter presented to President Yuan a list of twenty-one demands (1915). These demands were calculated to make China a Japanese protectorate. The preoccupation of Europe with the war afforded Japan, in the words of one of her publicists, "the opportunity of a thousand years" with respect to China.

In answer to inquires from abroad, the Tokyo Foreign Office denied that any demands impairing China's sovereignty had been formulated and published an expurgated list that contained only an outline of eleven of the points. When the Chinese Government revealed a full list of the demands, Japan announced that the omitted demands had been only "wishes." No such distinction, however, had been made to China.[6]

The United States and other powers protested that they would not recognize any Sino-Japanese arrangement that violated their own treaty rights, but in May 1915, after a threat of war by Japan, China signed two treaties. The documents embodied a modified version of the original demands and contained clauses, granting economic concessions, which provided for their enforcement on the date of signature. Since the Chinese Parliament never ratified them, the treaties consistently were regarded as invalid by the Kuomintang.

C.   China, the War, and the Washington Conference

From the outset of the European conflict, China had feared that Japan would take advantage of the situation to establish her control in China. The Peking Government therefore thrice attempted to join the Allies, but each time the Japanese prevented such action. Japan had no desire to see China recruit an army, mobilize her resources, and participate in a peace conference. Only in 1917 did Japan reverse her policy. The military position of the Allied Powers in 1917 was critical; hence, they made special efforts to secure additional help, from the United States and from the Far East.

In 1917, then, a secret treaty was signed between Japan and Great Britain. The former promised to dispatch some war vessels to the Mediterranean, and the latter agreed to support the claim of Japan to Shantung and the German Pacific islands north of the equator at the peace conference. France agreed to similar pledges in return for Japan's promise to encourage China's participation in the war. Russia and Italy followed suit. Upon the conclusion of these bargains, Japan urged China to break off relations with Germany. The United States, after her entry into the war, likewise suggested to China that relations with Germany be severed. Peking, moreover, was annoyed at the unrestricted submarine warfare and the drowning of several hundred coolies through the sinking of a French ship that was transporting them to France to work in war-material factories. In August 1917 Peking and Canton declared war on Germany and Austria-Hungary.

China's participation had little effect on the outcome of the war. After the struggle, however, China was entitled to representation at the Paris Conference. Sino-Japanese difficulties developed as soon as Japan presented her claims to all former German rights in Shan-

[6] The parallel texts of the demands as originally handed to China and as furnished by Japan to foreign governments may be found on pages 307–311 of S. K. Hornbeck, *Contemporary Politics in the Far East*, 1916.

tung. To this the Chinese delegation strenuously objected. President Wilson for a time upheld the Chinese view, but Lloyd George and Clemenceau insisted that they were bound by the secret treaties to back Japan. Eventually the Japanese had their way, acquiring Shantung and mandatory rights over all former German colonies north of the equator. Thereupon China withheld her signature from the Versailles Treaty and became a member of the League of Nations by adhering to the Treaty of St. Germain with Austria.

When news of these events reached China, it was greeted with violent demonstrations; and the demonstrations soon were followed by China's most powerful weapon—the economic boycott. The resulting decline in her foreign trade seriously worried Japan, and she started negotiations for the return of Shantung to China. The latter rejected the offers that were made and appealed to the world for financial and diplomatic help. Foreign loans, however, seemed out of the question, for China had no credit standing. At this point (1921) President Harding of the United States invited eight powers to attend a conference in Washington on the limitation of naval armaments and the settlement of international problems in the Pacific and Far East. It was hoped that the conference, too, might forestall any united Anglo-Japanese action injurious to the interests of the United States.

The conference in 1922 concluded seven treaties. Two of these dealt with naval disarmament; the remaining five, with Pacific and Far Eastern questions. Two additional treaties, one dealing with Shantung and the other with the island of Yap, were signed outside the conference, but by powers represented there.

It was difficult to evaluate the work of the Washington Conference. Regarding China, the principle of the Open Door once more was subscribed to by the great powers, no new disabilities were imposed, and a certain amount of lost autonomy was restored to the republic. Shantung was reacquired, and China was given a breathing spell during which, if she had the capacity, she might rebuild her weak national structure. The signing of the Sino-Japanese conventions was followed by the adoption in Japan of a so-called friendship policy towards China, which lasted until the spring of 1927. Moderate Japanese leadership attempted to harmonize the interests of China and Japan without force. However, when the moderates were replaced in power at Tokyo by expansionists, aggressive imperialistic methods appeared once more. The naval arrangements concluded at the conference temporarily lessened a growing naval rivalry among the United States, Great Britain, and Japan.

D. Education and Nationalism in China, 1919–1931

The internal history of China from 1919 to 1927 was conspicuous chiefly for administrative confusion in every province. Scores of generals ravaged country and town and laid waste much of the natural wealth of the republic. There were catastrophic floods and famines, fanatical antiforeign outbursts, and political quarrels between republicans and Communists. Out of the turmoil, however, there emerged two definite phenomena: progress in education and an organized nationalist movement.

Under the old regime, education had been reserved for a small minority. After the revolution numerous efforts were made to increase literacy. A movement was launched to substitute in literature the colloquial language of the country for the ancient literary forms. In order to popularize the vernacular as a literary medium it was utilized in the composition of a variety of works of high literary merit.

Another expression of the educational reform spirit was a Mass Education Movement aimed at familiarizing the people with 1000 of the most commonly used Chinese ideographs. Easy and inexpensive readers were devised, and the lessons were so arranged that the information could be mastered by spending one hour a day on them for four months. Within a few years, millions of persons learned to read.

The advances in education were accompanied by the emergence of students as an important factor in the agitation for liberation from foreign restrictions and the shackles of tradition. In 1919, for instance, the most serious attacks on the Versailles Treaty and on the officials who proposed to endorse it were led by students. The spirit displayed by the emancipated young people was encouraging, but it required mature leadership. Some direction was given to the students' movements by the Kuomintang.

The Kuomintang Government at Canton opposed most of the moves undertaken by the government at Peking, which continued to function under the guidance of interested foreigners. Led by Dr. Sun, the Nationalists worked for several years to bring the north under the sway of the Kuomintang and unify the country, through the use of force and propaganda. Support for this endeavor was forthcoming from Soviet Russia, which meanwhile had surrendered most of the privileges acquired in China in tsarist days. An able diplomat, Michael Borodin, was dispatched to China to win the confidence of Sun and his associates—a mission he fulfilled with eminent success. Simultaneously, Moscow had an ambassador at Peking.

In 1924 a Kuomintang Congress at Canton extended party membership to all Chinese Communists who were ready to accept the Kuomintang principles. Soon thereafter Peking signed an agreement with Moscow whereby the Russians gave up extraterritorial rights in China and agreed that the Chinese Eastern Railway in Manchuria, a Sino-Russian enterprise conceived in 1896, should remain under the joint control of the two states until China could redeem it "with Chinese capital." In 1924, also, Sun established a military academy and Soviet military officers were invited to train the Nationalist forces.

With the approach of 1925 there developed a rift in Kuomintang ranks. The right-wing members of the party were out of sympathy with the aims of the Communist left wing and wanted to end the close relationship with the Soviet Union. Dr. Sun was able to hold the two camps together, but after his death in March 1925 the breach widened. In 1927 Chiang Kai-shek, who had succeeded Sun as leader of the Nationalists, broke off relations with the Russian Communists and discriminated against the Communist members of the Kuomintang.

Just prior to the break with the U.S.S.R., the Nationalists, led by Chiang, had succeeded in extending their control over nearly all China. The fruits of the victory, however, were spoiled by the fierce struggle that had developed among factions in the Kuomintang.

The Communists tried to discredit Chiang by committing excesses, the most serious instance being the Nanking Affair of March 1927. After the capture of the city by the Nationalists, left-wing elements attacked the foreign residents. The powers demanded restitution, and Japan sent soldiers to protect her extensive interests. In the end, the actions of the Communists reacted to the advantage of Chiang, whose support came increasingly from the commercial and industrial groups.

Chiang was born in 1888 and obtained a military education at the Tokyo Military College. During 1911 and 1912 he commanded revolutionary soldiers and from 1913 to 1920 was secretary to Dr. Sun. By 1924 he had become director of the National Military Academy and soon thereafter succeeded Sun as leader of the Nationalists. As a result of his successes, Chiang was able in 1928 to establish a Nationalist Government at Nanking. The northern government was abolished and Nanking became the new national capital.

In October 1928, the Kuomintang promulgated an Organic Law for the National Government of China. The law was to be executed under the supervision of the party's executive committee, which thus virtually became the government of the republic. The highest administrative unit was to be a State Council, and the committee elected Chiang to be chairman of the first such council, an office equivalent to that of the president of China. The Nationalist Government promptly secured recognition from most of the Western states and Japan.[7]

Chiang faced a difficult task as chief executive of China. He invited United States and German experts to assist in the reorganiza-

[7] The organic law, with some revisions, remained in force to the end of 1946. From 1931 there was a regular President of the National Government, who had little power; more important was the president of the Executive Yüan or cabinet, and this post went to Generalissimo Chiang Kai-shek.

tion of the country and strove to weld the Chinese nation into a powerful state. However, the continuing need to lead troops in battle interfered with Chiang's plans. The constant disorder and the ravages of floods and famines had enabled the Chinese Communists greatly to increase their numbers, and now they massed all their strength against the Nanking regime in an attempt to replace it by a soviet system. Chiang waged almost uninterrupted warfare against the Communists and against rival military leaders, who hoped in the confusion to acquire control of individual Chinese provinces.

Besides its domestic difficulties, the Nationalist Government in 1929 had a quarrel with the Soviet Union. The dispute grew out of Bolshevik propagandist activities in northern China and an attempt by the governor of Manchuria, Chang Hsueh-liang, to gain control of the Chinese Eastern Railway and to oust the subjects of the U.S.S.R. from the territory under his jurisdiction. Soviet consular offices in Manchurian cities were raided, and hundreds of Soviet officials and employees of the Chinese Eastern Railway were arrested. The U.S.S.R. retaliated by arresting Chinese merchants who happened to be in the Soviet Union. Diplomatic relations were severed, troop movements were begun, and some minor battles occurred.

At the height of the crisis, forty-two cosignatories of the Kellogg Pact, which included the U.S.S.R. and China, reminded the disputants of their obligation to settle the dispute by peaceful means. Eventually (1929) the parties concerned did reach agreement, and the *status quo ante* was reestablished. A conference to settle all other causes of dispute was in the planning stage when a Sino-Japanese conflict occurred over Manchuria in 1931.

E. Economics in Manchuria and in Japan

China was a tempting field for Western and Japanese investments and business enterprises, and billions of dollars were poured into the land. Among the most promising economic sections of China was Manchuria. Situated in the northeast, this region, with an area in 1931 of 380,000 square miles, a population of 29,000,000, and 4000 miles of railways, came to assume a tremendous importance in international affairs. The land grew numerous crops in abundance, and there were substantial subsoil resources. In 1928, Manchuria was responsible for almost one-third of the commodity exports of China and about one-fifth of the imports.

The Kuomintang Government regarded Manchuria as a vital outpost of Chinese culture. Between 1923 and 1929, 4,000,000 Chinese were reported to have entered Manchuria to take advantage of the fertile land and the relative freedom from domestic turmoil. Many of the immigrants returned southward after they had accumulated savings, but perhaps half of them became permanent settlers. Nanking encouraged this latest of "people's wanderings" and was anxious to restrict the encroachments of foreigners in the area.

Most of the world's industrial powers, however, had interests in Manchuria. The U.S.S.R. and Japan felt that they had special rights. The Soviet Government was half-owner of the Chinese Eastern Railway, which offered the most direct route from the west to the Siberian port of Vladivostok. The Bolsheviks, moreover, exercised considerable authority in Outer Mongolia, a wild region just west of Manchuria. The Japanese had control of the South Manchuria Railway, which terminated at the Japanese-controlled port of Dairen, through which passed more than half of the foreign trade of Manchuria. Moreover, the foreign banking business of Manchuria was almost a monopoly of Japanese firms. Large as were her financial holdings in Manchuria, Japan advanced additional reasons for desiring recognition of her paramount interests in the territory. For an understanding of these it is necessary to survey the economic position of the empire.

In the mid-nineteenth century Japan was a medieval country, cherishing feudal traditions and anxious to avoid contact with the West. Before the close of the century Japan had been "opened" by importunate Westerners seeking new trade outlets, and the Nipponese soon were imitating the intruders' methods and adopting their business views. With the coming of modern industry to the islands, the same pressing needs developed that earlier had induced the Western powers to seek overseas expansion. Industrialized Japan wanted sources of cheap raw materials, markets for surplus manufactures, fields for investment of accumulated capital, food for workers, and outlets for surplus population.

During the First World War, economic conditions in Japan took an unusually favorable turn. The Allies bought enormous quantities of war materials; new trade contacts were established in Asia, Africa, and the Americas; and Japanese ships were chartered to handle a considerable portion of the world's ocean commerce. However, after the war there came a gradual slump. The former belligerents reengaged in the manufacture of peacetime goods and competed once more for foreign markets. Since foreign trade by this time had come to be the backbone of Japanese prosperity, normally accounting for one-third of the total commerce, any appreciable decline in exports was sure to have a serious effect on the economic condition of the country.

For some years after the armistice, Japan's export figures remained at a relatively high level because the United States, in her new-found prosperity, became a heavy purchaser of silk. Then silk substitutes were developed (rayon, for instance) and the world depression appeared. There was then a decline in the demand for silk and other products of Japanese manufacture.

In 1930 the area of the Japanese Empire, including Korea (Chosen), was 265,000 square miles, or about that of Texas. Its population was estimated at 92,000,000. In Japan proper (area 148,700 square miles; population, 65,000,000), more than 40 per cent of the people derived a meager existence directly from the soil, only one-sixth of which could be cultivated. The unemployed numbered 1,000,000, and the national debt stood at $3,000,000,000. Hence Manchuria, with its plentiful resources, undeveloped opportunities, geographic nearness, and strategic location, tempted Japan. The work which was begun in 1915 with the presentation of the Twenty-one Demands, it seemed to her statesmen, must now be completed. The year 1931 appeared favorable for this undertaking.

F. China, Manchoukuo, Japan

Conditions in China in 1931 were turbulent. The right- and left-wing members of the Kuomintang exchanged accusations of self-interest and treachery, and sent military forces against each other. Famines and floods deprived millions of food and shelter. Communist propaganda was rife, and local chieftains revived their bandit activities.

Elsewhere in the world, faced with the great depression, governments were preoccupied with equally numerous problems. With Westerners distracted, Japan, pressed by many of the same problems, felt the moment ripe for the realization of long-held expansionist dreams in Manchuria. There seemed little likelihood that the Western powers would interpose forcefully even if they disapproved of Tokyo's plans. For a variety of reasons, the Japanese army took the lead in the Manchurian venture.

In Japan the army and navy departments were virtually independent of the civil authorities. Their leaders might approach the emperor directly, without regard for cabinet procedure. The army long had been suspicious of the civil government. It saw little good in the custom of ministerial responsibility, which dated from 1918, or in the universal manhood suffrage that had been proclaimed in 1925. The military professed to be interested in the well-being of the farming and laboring classes, from which came most of their recruits, and they believed that the country's difficulties easily might be alleviated by the conversion of Manchuria into a great agricultural and industrial colony. The army, moreover, worked hand in hand with an influential group of bankers and industrialists who had financial stakes in Manchuria.

During the years 1930 to 1932, the military wrested much political control from the civil government. A section of big business feared possible Western economic retaliation against Japanese aggression, but millions of the people were induced by national pride and personal poverty to side with the army. Numerous Fascist societies appeared, political murder became frequent, and there was a popular demand for the achievement of economic security through the use of force.

Unfortunately for China, there occurred in 1931 two incidents that provided the Japanese military with a pretext for entering Manchuria with armed forces. First, the "honor" of the army was "violated" by the murder in Inner Mongolia of a Japanese captain; and then a short stretch of the South Manchuria Railway line was damaged by explosives. The Japanese troops who guarded the railway accused Chinese soldiers of the deed. Without prior notification to the Tokyo Foreign Office, the Japanese military machine was set in motion, and a wide area of Manchuria was occupied.

The Chinese withdrew before the advancing Japanese, and the Nanking Government appealed to the world for help. The diplomats at Tokyo supported the military by pointing out that the governor of Manchuria had violated an old Sino-Japanese treaty by building a railroad paralleling the South Manchuria Railway. Japan had said nothing about this while the line was being built, but now complained that the road constituted a military and economic threat to Japanese interests.

While China appealed her case to the League, the Japanese rapidly extended the area of occupation. In September 1931 Japan had been in direct control of 1400 square miles of territory. By January 1932 the area of control included 200,000 square miles of land. Efforts were made to encourage local separatism. Loyal Chinese officials were replaced by friends of Japan.

In February 1932, some Manchurian leaders at Mukden (which was in Japanese hands) issued a declaration of independence. The new state was named Manchoukuo. The newly instituted government was patently under Japanese tutelage.

Japan's activities, as was to be expected, exerted a unifying influence upon Chinese politics. In December 1931 a reconciliation was effected between the Nanking authorities and a rival government that had been set up in Canton by left-wing members of the Kuomintang. Anti-Japanese outbreaks became frequent occurrences, and Chinese residents in foreign lands sent home money to bolster the nation's defense against the invaders. The Chinese people once more resorted to their most powerful weapon, a nationwide economic boycott. Since China normally took one-fourth of Japan's exports, the boycott caused havoc to Japanese industry.

In January 1932, the Japanese residents of Shanghai, the chief foreign-trade center of China, called upon Tokyo to suppress the anti-Japanese movement by naval force. The navy welcomed this opportunity to follow the army in the pursuit of glory. War vessels and marines were dispatched to Shanghai as a means of forcing the Chinese to buy Japanese goods. Economic warfare was to be combated with naval warfare. The marines clashed with the local Chinese garrison, and the Battle of Shanghai was precipitated. The resistance of the Chinese to the invaders was labeled aggression by

Tokyo. The rainy season put a stop to the battle, and in May 1932 negotiations were completed for the withdrawl of the Japanese forces and the ending of the boycott.

Meanwhile, in December 1931, the League Council had appointed an international commission, under the chairmanship of Lord Lytton, to investigate the Sino-Japanese situation and recommend possible solutions. While the commission was at work, Secretary of State Henry L. Stimson announced that the United States henceforth would refuse to recognize the legality of any situation or treaty resulting from action taken in violation of the Kellogg Pact. This Stimson Doctrine, as it came to be known, failed to elicit endorsements from the European powers.

In September 1932, shortly before the report of the Lytton Commission was made public, Japan affronted the League by recognizing the State of Manchoukuo. The motive presumably was to confront the League with a *fait accompli,* and the procedure called forth a sharp rebuke from the president of the Council, who happened to be the Irish Eamon de Valera. Recognition was accorded through a Japan-Manchoukuo Protocol, wherein the former Chinese domain, in return for an endorsement of its "independent" status, promised Japan a long series of favors, including the right to station troops at any desired point in Manchoukuo. (The Japanese yen dropped during these months to less than half of its par value.)

The Lytton Report expressed doubts whether a government-inspired boycott was a "legitimate weapon of defense against military aggression by a stronger country;" it suggested that China set up an autonomous government in Manchuria that would acknowledge Chinese suzerainty, and it proposed widespread internal Chinese reforms. The League Council referred the report to the Assembly, which referred it to another committee.

During 1933 Japan suffered diplomatic defeats at Geneva and won military victories in China, pushing south of the Great Wall under the pretext of preventing further Chinese "raids" into Manchoukuo territory. Since Japan paid no heed to the pleas of various League committees, China finally accepted an armistice. Under this agreement the Japanese were to return north of the Great Wall, and China consented to the creation of a demilitarized zone south of the wall, to be administered by Chinese officials friendly to Japan.

Meanwhile (March 1933) Japan had informed the League of her intention to withdraw from membership. Two years later, when Japan officially ceased to be a member of the League, Manchoukuo had been legally recognized by only her protector and El Salvador.[8]

The U.S.S.R. offered to sell its half-interest in the Chinese Eastern Railway to Manchoukuo, which had appropriated the half-interest of China. Negotiations among representatives of Moscow, Tokyo,

[8] Later Germany, Italy, Spain, Hungary, and Romania followed suit. Japan simply retained her mandates upon quitting the League.

and Hsinking were concluded in 1935, transferring all Russian rights to Manchoukuo in return for $52,000,000. Japan guaranteed the payments, "in view of the close relations existing between Japan and Manchoukuo."

Renewed friction meanwhile had developed between Japan and other states over the assignment of a Manchoukuo oil-sales monopoly to a firm under Japanese control. The United States, British, and Netherlands Governments protested this action as a violation of the Open Door policy guaranteed in the Washington Nine-Power Treaty and previously confirmed by the puppet government of Manchoukuo. Tokyo replied by saying (1) that the Open Door had not been violated; (2) that the Manchoukuo Government's promise could not be invoked since the government was not recognized by the complaining powers: and (3) that Japan could do nothing about the matter anyway since Manchoukuo was an independent state. The Western nationals thereupon prepared to withdraw from the oil business in Manchoukuo.

G.   Toward a "New Order" in Eastern Asia

Japan specifically enunciated the doctrine of a "new order" in eastern Asia in 1938. The trend in this direction had been foreshadowed in a declaration of 1934 by the Tokyo Foreign Office. Having broken with the West by withdrawing from the League, having declared herself to be "the principal protector" of stability in the Far East, and desirous of accommodating her rapidly increasing population, Nippon announced that she would continue to foster Sino-Japanese "friendship" and oppose "any attempt on the part of China to avail herself of the influence of any other country in order to resist Japan." Then Tokyo promoted "friendship" with her neighbor by encouraging separatists in northern China to set up an autonomous state under Japanese tutelage (1935) and by disarming the customs guards along the Great Wall so that Japanese goods readily might be smuggled into China (1936).

The increasing aggression of Japan on the Asiatic mainland for a time led to more serious difficulty with the Soviet Union than with any other third power. During the winter of 1935–1936 there were several border incidents along the Soviet-Manchoukuo, and the Manchoukuo and Outer Mongolian, frontiers. Outer Mongolia, or the Mongolian People's Republic, declared its independence of China after the First World War and had gradually come under the influence of the Soviet Union. U.S.S.R. advisers guided the policies of the Mongolian People's Republic and nearly all Outer Mongolia's foreign trade was with the Soviet Union. A commission appointed to demarcate a boundary between Manchoukuo and Outer Mongolia soon abandoned its efforts, and in 1936 the U.S.S.R. and Outer Mongolia signed a pact for mutual assistance in case of attack.

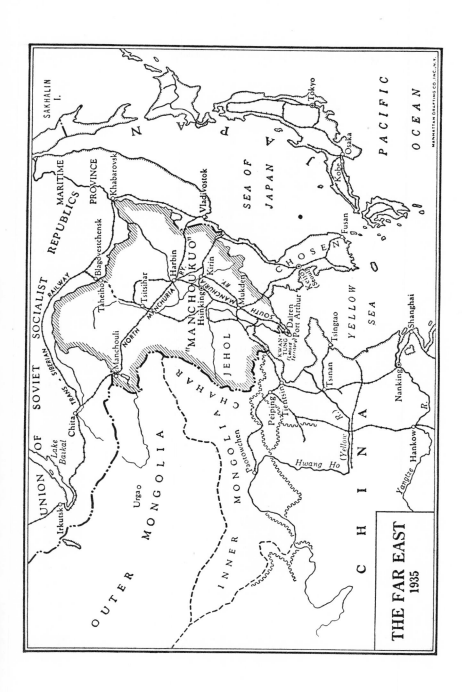

THE FAR EAST
1935

Meanwhile, several clashes occurred along the Manchoukuo-Siberian border. In 1937 Japanese artillery shelled Soviet gunboats in the Amur River, and one year later a Soviet-Japanese battle was waged over the border heights of Changkufeng. The incident had its origin in the occupation of the heights by Soviet soldiers for the construction of defense works. Tokyo protested that the area was in Manchoukuo territory. A map, appended to a Russo-Chinese frontier agreement of 1886 and now produced by the Soviets, failed to impress the Nipponese, and a Japanese force unsuccessfully attacked Changkufeng. The two governments then agreed to appoint a commission to demarcate the correct boundary. Establishment of the border commission was delayed, and in 1939 fighting was renewed. There were further disputes—some involving fishing rights—and, although the Mongolian-Manchoukuo border eventually was defined, the Siberian-Manchoukuo frontier remained vague.

In China itself, meanwhile (1936), certain nationalistic leaders had warned the Nanking Government to resist further Japanese aggression, lest there be a civil war. For in that year Generalissimo Chiang Kai-shek was the only outstanding military leader who still hesitated to adopt a strong anti-Japanese policy—probably because he felt that China must wait until she was more thoroughly unified and better prepared for war before risking an all out conflict with Nippon. Chiang disregarded the warning, continued to order the suppression of anti-Japanese demonstrations, and proceeded to Shensi in the north. There General Chang Hsueh-liang, bitter foe of Japan, supposedly was acting under orders of Nanking; but he was lukewarm in his campaign against the Chinese Communists. The Commander-in-Chief wanted more energetic action against the Reds.

Suddenly (December 1936) Chiang Kai-shek was seized by some of Chang Hsueh-liang's generals and held prisoner for two weeks. A growing number of northern soldiers had become reluctant to fight their own countrymen, even though these were Reds, while the Japanese were penetrating farther and farther into China. Chang Hsueh-liang made his superior's release conditional upon the latter's promise to readmit the Communists into the Kuomintang, and thus make possible a united Chinese front in a war against Japan. Chiang refused to make any commitments until released, and eventually he returned to Nanking with Chang Hsueh-liang in the role of voluntary prisoner. There the offending general received a full pardon. Then, prolonged negotiations between the national and Communist leaders took place. The Communists agreed to modify their social program and fight under Chiang Kai-shek in return for a promise of political reform and a war of resistance against Japan.

Meanwhile, in Japan, following an electoral victory by the Liberal Party, there occurred a military rebellion. Early one morning in February 1936 a group of young officers led about a thousand soldiers from their barracks to the center of Tokyo. While the troops seized a number of official buildings, designated officers murdered several of the nation's outstanding liberal statesmen. The rebels held their position for three days, disregarding even the Emperor's command to surrender. Then they yielded, and some of the officers were condemned to death. The population remained relatively calm in the face of the army's seeming inability to control its younger officers—who were determined to set up a dictatorship.

The conflict between the civil and military branches of the government was manifested continuously in the difficulties of the Japanese cabinet throughout 1936. It was aired in public when several parliamentary deputies bitterly attacked the army and its policies. The military, evidently unable to reply convincingly, precipitated additional cabinet crises until a new election was ordered for April 1937. The moderate elements won an overwhelming victory—which was promptly disregarded by the advocates of force. In July the advance into China was begun in earnest.

The Nanking Government now announced its readiness to fight "to the death." The fighting spread, and Japan declared a blockade of Chinese shipping. Thousands of civilians and refugees were killed by Japanese bombs in areas far removed from the fronts, and the Japanese army advanced steadily against the stubborn opposition of the Chinese soldiers. There were rays of hope for China in September 1937 when the Communist armies in the north finally prepared to march against the Japanese invaders and when the League of Nations referred a Chinese appeal to its Far Eastern Advisory Committee. This committee, on which the United States was represented, unanimously condemned Japan's tactics and urged a meeting of the signatories of the Nine-Power Treaties of 1922. Fifty League members endorsed the committee's findings, expressed moral support for China, and called a parley of the interested parties to meet in Brussels. The Brussels Conference sat for three weeks, condemned Japan, and then adjourned indefinitely.

In the meantime, the Chinese Government had moved to the inland city of Chungking, because of the Japanese advance on Nanking. As the mechanized Japanese forces pushed on, Chinese sympathizers in many Western countries organized boycotts against Japanese goods, but these boycotts had no influence. In December 1937 Japanese soldiers poured into Nanking, celebrating their victory with a reign of terror.

On the day preceding the fall of China's ex-capital, Japanese planes sank the United States gunboat *Panay* and some Standard Oil Company ships in the Yangtse Kiang. Several Americans were killed and many wounded, and the survivors reached safety under the greatest difficulty. The Japanese Government at once apologized, promised to punish those responsible for the crime, and indicated that there would be no future attacks. Washington was not satisfied, and Japan presented a second apology. The attack was called "entirely unintentional," assurance was given of full indemnity, and it was pointed out that the responsible officers had been disciplined severely. The United States accepted this explanation, and the incident was closed.

In 1938 Japanese military victories in China continued, with occasional setbacks. Despite their defeats and staggering losses of people and territory, the Chinese continued to resist the invasion of the Japanese. Foreign sympathy China appeared to have in abundance, but little foreign aid. Supplies did reach the Chinese, chiefly from the Soviet Union and through Indo-China, but not in the desired quantities.

The domestic situation in Japan was not improved during 1938. There were frequent clashes between the government and the parliament, for many members of the latter, like the public at large, wanted to know the ultimate purpose of the costly campaign in China. There also were frequent reorganizations of the cabinet, but always in the interest of a more vigorous prosecution of the undeclared war.

During her advance in China, Japan frequently performed acts which aroused the protests of the Western powers, acts that did much damage to foreign property and trading interests. To these charges the Japanese replied by declaring their purpose to extend to all China the status "enjoyed" by Manchoukuo.

Throughout 1939 the Japanese continued the struggle in China, extending their occupation, further impairing their own diplomatic relations with the West, bombing more open cities, striving to set up a puppet government for China corresponding to that in Manchoukuo, and failing in their efforts to break down the morale and the resistance of the Chinese. As the Japanese stripped, insulted, and slapped British subjects in the presence of Chinese (to impress the latter with the new importance of Japan), and advanced challengingly close to Hong Kong, the British enlarged their credit advances to China and warned Tokyo of the future consequences of its acts. As United States property was being destroyed through Japanese air attacks in various parts of China, Washington gave the required six months' notice of its intention to terminate the United States and Japanese Treaty of Amity and Commerce that had provided Japan with its much needed United States market and supplies. In Japan itself, prices rose steadily, consumers' goods began to run short, and casualty lists mounted; nevertheless, the military leaders ordered a further tightening of the people's belts and persisted in their conviction that the new order in Asia was close at hand.

BLACK AND WHITE IN AFRICA

Shortly after the outbreak of the First World War, Germany proposed to the Allies that the neutrality of the African colonies be maintained during the conflict, on the ground that the preservation of Europe's ascendancy in Africa depended upon the solidarity of the white race on that continent. Perhaps the knowledge that she could not defend her overseas possessions against Allied attack stimulated Germany to advance this thesis. At any rate, the suggestion was disregarded, and the war was carried into Africa. Then, after the war, the general disorganization following a long period of armed conflict combined with other factors to produce great unrest from Morocco to the Cape of Good Hope. Among the most provocative of these factors were the following: the reaction against a long period of subjection; the influence of some of the religious teaching; the increasing competition for work between blacks and whites in such relatively well-developed regions as South Africa; and the effect on the blacks of Western education.

When the Western peoples in the nineteenth century contemplated the partitioning of Africa, they were aware of their moral obligation towards the Africans. In 1885, in the General Act of the Berlin Conference, the representatives of the leading Western countries had agreed for the sake of humanity "to protect the natives in their moral and material well-being; to cooperate in the suppression of slavery and the slave trade; to further the education and civilization of the natives;" and to preserve freedom of religion.

Neither the agreements nor the wishes of the conference were observed fully, and for years a thriving slave trade was pursued. Although there was considerable talk about what soon came to be known as the "white man's burden," relatively little was done before 1914 towards shouldering this burden. Indeed, in order to earn sizable dividends on their investments, white concessionaires frequently employed questionable tactics. The natural wealth of Africa and the physical powers of the inhabitants were exploited until some natives were driven in despair to rebel against the "black man's burden."

In Kenya, the former British East Africa, for example, the unrest reached a climax in 1921 when, as a result of economic depression, the white employers announced a reduction of wages for all black workers. The blacks at first were helpless, but eventually a native government clerk named Harry Thuku founded an East Africa Native Association and organized protest meetings. Thuku's speeches assumed an increasingly violent and anti-European tenor, and his meetings sometimes were attended by several thousand natives. In 1922 he was arrested for sedition, and, when crowds tried to interfere with the police at the jail where he was being held, the guards discharged their rifles and killed some of the rioters. Thuku was deported, and now the leaderless natives consoled themselves by forming a harmless sort of trade-union, which they hoped would protect their common interests.

Although the religious doctrines disseminated by the missionaries in Africa frequently tended to make the natives satisfied with a position of inferiority relative to their white masters, some of the teachings had an opposite effect. The blacks were stirred by assurances that all human beings were God's children. Gradually there appeared so-called prophets and performers of miracles who attracted large native followings. Frequently such movements became violently anti-European.

The most threatening of these manifestation occurred in 1921 in the Belgian Congo. There the carpenter, Simon Kimbangu, who had become a Baptist, dreamed that he was divinely directed to go forth and heal the sick. His following increased tremendously in a relatively short span of time. The Kimbangists established their own native chapels, churches, and schools, and eventually stopped working in the fields to be near their Prophet. Kimbangu quoted passages from the Bible and boasted that his enemies were powerless to harm him. Gradually this movement grew more revolutionary, and the white inhabitants of the Congo became alarmed. Kimbangu was arrested, tried, and sentenced to death, though he never had advocated violence against the whites. Eventually his sentence was commuted to life imprisonment. Thereafter, it was forbidden for any native to preach or teach without a certificate from some Christian missionary organization.

In the Union of South Africa it was increasing labor competition between blacks and whites that led to unrest. Here the blacks, who out-numbered the whites three or four to one, gradually were becoming more and more skilled in the various occupations that previously had been monopolized by the whites. So active did the challenge to white supremacy become that, in 1918, the white trade-unions threatened to call a strike unless the black engineers were dismissed from a particular job.

The supreme court of South Africa took a hostile attitude towards regulations tending to discriminate between equally competent persons solely on the ground of color. But the trade-unions agitated strenuously until the South African Labor Party came into power. Then, in 1926, a Color-Bar Bill was passed, definitely excluding blacks from certain occupations. Because whites were paid from five to ten times as much as were blacks for identical services, some employing groups preferred black labor. But the more costly white labor managed to maintain its preeminence.

Educated African leaders eventually perceived that African conditions were in need of improvement, and that a determined stand must be made for fairer treatment. In 1919 black delegates from Africa and America met in Paris, under the auspices of a Pan-African Congress, and drew up a charter of liberties for the black men. Among the demands were those for political, economic, and educational equality; the restoration of confiscated native lands; the checking of economic exploitation; and the appointment by the League of Nations of direct representatives with powers of investigation in the mandated areas. Similar African conferences later were held in other large cities.

These meetings, though they failed to lead to any immediate improvement in conditions, laid the basis for a growing race consciousness and served notice that the blacks were cognizant of the economic value of their continent with its large population and abundant natural resources. An increasing number raised the cry of "Africa for the Africans."

But it was not only the blacks in Africa who adopted a new attitude in the postwar years. The whites, too, changed their views on several aspects of the native situation. During the war the traditional policies had been reflected in the secret wartime dispositions made by the Allied powers of the German colonial possessions. But at the Paris Peace Conference, as has been noted, President Wilson's idealism clashed with these imperialistic aspirations. A compromise was effected, and in the Covenant of the League the "well-being and development" of backward peoples was designated "a sacred trust of civilization." Hence, instead of becoming outright owners of the lands that were taken from Germany, ostensibly on the ground of her mistreating the natives, the Allied countries became trustees or stewards of the League in the administration of affairs in these territories.

A cynical view of this arrangement often was taken, particularly since the assignment of the mandates followed almost exactly the lines of the secret agreements. Yet, the written reminder of trusteeship and the creation of a Permanent Mandates Commission continuously recalled to the white administrators their moral obligations to educate the colonials and develop mandated areas for the benefit of the natives as well as the Europeans. This realization was responsible for the introduction of a number of colonial reforms.

Eventually the whites came to realize that the continued abuse of native labor and the decimation of the population were out of accord with their own economic interests. The concessionaires began to realize that rubber plantations and mines were worthless without the necessary people to work them. Thus, the fear of economic loss was responsible for the better treatment of the natives in some sections.

From 1920, France made special efforts to stimulate the economic development of her overseas areas. She hoped to derive a larger proportion of her imports, particularly raw materials, from the colonies. Progress was slow, however, and after more than a decade of effort, most of France's colonial imports continued to come from other countries' possessions. The French authorities also began to pay more attention to the spread of vocational and professional education in their African territories. By way of encouraging assimilation, French citizenship was offered to all natives who had served with distinction either in a civil capacity or in the armies during the war. But military conscription was introduced into all French African colonies, and the beneficent influences of education and economic improvement sometimes were overshadowed by the harsh tactics of punitive expeditions.

A British Parliamentary Commission, which visited East Africa in 1925, declared its conviction that "the status of trusteeship involves an ethical conception," imposing moral duties upon the trustee. Although the British authorities failed to abide wholly by the spirit of this report, the punishments for minor infractions of rules were made less severe in a number of the British-controlled areas. Educational opportunities for the black men were increased and the government liberally assisted in the upkeep of native churches. Yet the whites usually were careful to retain the upper hand whenever the interests of natives came into conflict with their own.

In other regions the actions of callous exploiters frequently reached the ears of groups that were able to force reform measures. Thus, a report published by the United States Professor Frank A. Ross, on conditions which he witnessed during a trip through Portuguese Africa in 1925, was brought to the notice of the League, and in 1926 the Portuguese Government was constrained to set up a committee of protection in each colonial district. Similar improvements took place elsewhere on the continent.

The problems of Africa, and of Europe in Africa, after the First World War, appeared, in short, to be these: given a certain amount of education and economic opportunity, many black men came to desire autonomy, if not independence; kept in subjection, without education and without the opportunity to better themselves, the natives were considerably less useful in the development of the natural resources. Although renewed humanitarian and altruistic considerations served as stimuli for the extension of both spiritual and practical schooling, the limited amount of enlightenment actually spread was responsible for the appearance of a clamor for more equitable treatment. Obviously, the Western world soon would have to seek a workable solution for the African dilemma. Africa would continue to learn from Europe, and it would be the white man's duty to teach Africa in as friendly a way as possible.

EGYPT

When Turkey and Great Britain went to war in 1914, Egypt was placed in a unique position. Though occupied by the British since 1882, Egypt still was under the technical sovereignty of the Ottoman Sultan. In December 1914, however, Great Britain announced that "the suzerainty of Turkey over Egypt is terminated" and Britain then extended a protectorate over Egypt. The British elevated the nephew of the former ruler to the throne as sultan of Egypt.

Egypt soon began to seethe with discontent. Contrary to earlier pledges not to seek Egypt's help in making war, the British organized Egyptian units to aid their armies in Palestine and Syria. Service was made voluntary at first, and good wages were paid; but as the war continued, the treatment of the men became poor, and in the end forced recruiting was used. Because of the bad accommodations, some Egyptians froze to death during the cold Palestine winters, and some of the conscripts were made to fight. The British also requisitioned Egyptian livestock and grain at their own prices. In addition to these material grievances, the Egyptians experienced the general hatred of patriots for foreign rule and the traditional dislike of Moslems for Christians. The desire for independence, too, was quickened by President Wilson's talk about self-determination. Yet open revolt did not occur during the war years, probably because British troops were quartered in the land.

After the armistice, Egyptian leaders were amazed to find that, although Indian rajahs and Arabian sheikhs had been invited to attend the peace conference, no such privilege was accorded them. The leader of the Nationalist Party (*Wafd*), Saad Zaghlul Pasha, placed himself at the head of a delegation to embark for Paris to present Egypt's case for independence. The British arrested the delegation and shipped it to Malta. This act precipitated an insurrection (1919), which then was followed by other disorders until, early in 1922, Egypt was proclaimed "an independent sovereign state" by the British. But independence was not complete, for the following points were "absolutely reserved to the discretion of His Majesty's Government": the defense of Suez, the defense of Egypt, the protection of foreigners and their interests in Egypt, and the control of the cotton-rich Sudan. Coincident with this termination of the British protectorate, Sultan Ahmed Fuad, who had come to the throne in 1917, changed his title to that of king. The new arrangement irked the Nationalists, but they were powerless to resist it. A constitution was promulgated in 1923, and parliamentary elections were held. The Wafdists were overwhelmingly victorious at the polls, and Zaghlul became premier.

Another crisis occurred late in 1924 when Sir Lee Stack, Governor-General of the Sudan, was murdered in Cairo. Both Fuad and Zaghlul expressed their horror at the crime and promised swift prosecution of the assassins. But, inasmuch as this was merely the worst in a series of outrages, the British demanded an official apology, the punishment of the criminals, the suppression of political demonstrations, a cash indemnity, and the immediate withdrawal of all Egyptian soldiers from the Sudan. They further announced the indefinite extension for cotton cultivation of the Gezireh irrigation area in the Sudan, thus threatening Egypt's water supply.

Zaghlul accepted all the terms save those relating to the Sudan. The British thereupon occupied the customs house at Alexandria, and Zaghlul resigned. He was succeeded by a more tractable premier, who agreed to the British demands. Subsequently, London promised to use only the Blue Nile for Sudanese irrigation projects and to leave the White Nile for Egypt, but the Egyptians continued to be alarmed by successive British dam projects. The Egyptian

Parliament appealed to the League of Nations for redress; but Great Britain maintained that the affair was not international, and hence no League member brought it up for discussion.

The return to power of a Labor Government in Great Britain in 1929 raised Egyptian hopes for independence. Egyptians rejoiced when Foreign Secretary Arthur Henderson announced the draft of a new treaty to be presented to the parliaments in London and Cairo. Although acceptance of this treaty would have been a further step in the direction of independence, it did not satisfy the new Wafdist leader, Mustapha Nahas Pasha, and was rejected. The people became restless again, and parliament was suspended for the fourth time in five years. Ismail Sidky Pasha thereupon became dictator and in 1930 promulgated a new constitution.

Sidky retained dictatorial control of the land for several years. Parliament was convened and prorogued at his will, and repressive measures were taken against over-enthusiastic Wafdists and Communists. Considerable economic distress was experienced in these years, largely because of a decline in the price of cotton. In 1933 a series of anti-Christian outbursts was precipitated by the alleged attempt of a British schoolmistress at Port Said to coerce a Moslem girl into accepting Christianity. The latent anti-Christian sentiment grew into an organized Moslem campaign against missionaries and mission schools. There was some violence, and the government was petitioned to withdraw all subsidies from the missions, to tax missionary institutions, and to establish Moslem orphanages, schools, and clinics so that poor Egyptians might not be dependent upon Christians for education and medical attention. Only the last of these requests was acted upon. The violent outbursts eventually subsided, but the campaign to uphold Islam against the "lure" of Christianity continued.

Because of illness and the interference of the king in administrative affairs, Sidky resigned in September 1933. After fourteen troubled months, Mohammed Tewfik Nessim Pasha, a popular and patriotic man of independent political views, came to the helm. He persuaded King Fuad to abolish the undemocratic constitution of 1930. The sovereign was to govern by decree until a new instrument could be promulgated. The Nationalists expected that the constitution of 1923 would be restored, but month after month went by without such action. The situation became dangerous in the autumn of 1935 because of the Mediterranean crisis precipitated by Italy's Ethiopian venture.

When Great Britain, concerned over Italian military measures, took special military and naval precautions in the Egyptian zone, sensitive natives were hurt at the apparent disregard for the views of the Egyptian Government. Some natives feared lest they be drawn into an Anglo-Italian conflict, whereas others regarded the time as opportune for exerting pressure on London. The Wafdists warned Great Britain to expect no help from Egypt except on a basis of "cooperation between equals." Britain promised that Cairo would be informed of every development that affected Egypt, but indicated that the time was not ripe for treaty negotiations. Anti-British riots broke out in several cities, and late in 1935 all Egyptian political parties, save one, formed a United Front.

Thereupon, the high commissioner announced Britain's readiness to negotiate as soon as Egypt had a government representing all parties. The king restored the constitution of 1923, and new elections were held in 1936. The returns gave the Wafdists almost 80 per cent of the seats in the chamber, and Nahas again became premier. Meanwhile King Fuad had died (1936) and had been succeeded by his sixteen-year-old son, Farouk I.

The treaty negotiations lasted for months and several times appeared on the verge of breaking down. But Italy's aggressive tactics in eastern Africa had a sobering effect on both parties and made them more willing to cooperate, lest a common enemy be the gainer. At last an Anglo-Egyptian Treaty of Alliance was signed in London, and ratifications were exchanged just before Christmas 1936.

The treaty, of indefinite duration, provided that each signatory would aid the other in case of war. Great Britain was given the right, in the event of war, to utilize all Egyptian facilities. The British promised to support Egypt's candidacy for admission to the League of Nations, agreed to an exchange of ambassadors, and undertook to confine their troops in Egypt to a zone at the northern end of the Suez Canal. Joint rule over the Sudan was to be reestablished, with the right of unrestricted immigration for Egyptians.

In accordance with another treaty promise, Great Britain helped arrange for a meeting of those powers with extraterritorial rights in Egypt at Montreux in 1937. There the Montreux Convention was signed, providing for the complete abolition of extraterritoriality in Egypt by 1949, with certain steps to be taken at once. Shortly thereafter Egypt became a member of the League, and Farouk was invested as the first king of independent Egypt.

The Nahas Government, which had negotiated the treaty of 1936, soon found itself at odds with the young King. There was trouble when Farouk insisted upon a traditional religious investiture ceremony. There was disagreement regarding the King's role under the constitution. Eventually, at the end of 1937, the King dismissed the cabinet and appointed the moderate Mohammed Mahmoud to the premiership. When the latter dissolved a Fascist organization called the Wafdist Blue Shirts, there were more riots, and Great Britain dispatched additional troops to Egypt.

The spring of 1938 witnessed an exciting election campaign. Premier Mahmoud upheld the principles of liberal government and warned of the autocratic temper of the Wafdist leader, Nahas. The latter stood on his record of diplomatic achievement, but had to face a split within his own ranks when certain dissidents demanded a return to the original and democratic Wafdist principles. The poll represented an easy victory for the government coalition under Mahmoud over the dissension-rent Wafdists. Mahmoud continued at the head of the Egyptian Government until, in August 1939, illness forced his retirement. Upon the outbreak of war in 1939, a military government with wide powers was instituted.

During 1938 and 1939, Egypt—Mediterranean power and neighbor to Italian-controlled Lybia—felt the need to increase her armed strength. The King therefore urged relatively heavy arms expenditures upon his parliament. The increasing gravity of the Palestinian situation also interested the Egyptians, who in 1939 joined Iraq and Saudi Arabia in an expression of sympathy with the cause of the Arabs.

Latin America 14

THE WAR AND ITS AFTERMATH

The Latin American nations took little active part in the First World War; but the conflict worked significant changes in them all, since Latin America played an important part in the struggle as a supplier of materials. In supplying demands for foodstuffs and minerals, Latin America saw new industries arise, and new commercial and industrial centers spring up. A consequent shift in population to the industrialized and commercialized areas followed, as did an expansion of wealth, an increase of foreign investments, and a more active participation of the middle and laboring classes in politics.

At the outbreak of the war, Latin America suffered a temporary reduction in foreign trade because of the unsettled world conditions. From 1916, however, Europe's needs brought about a swift expansion. The total export-import trade more than doubled from 1913 to 1920, fluctuated as a consequence of the depressions of 1922 and 1932, and rose again after 1939.

Latin American economic development was greatly aided after the First World War by foreign capital. This was not a new phenomenon—European capital had flowed freely into Latin America during the nineteenth century—but the rate of capital imports increased rapidly. By 1940, the United States supplied the bulk of the credits, having gradually displaced the earlier European creditors.

Following the outbreak of the Second World War, Latin America, as in the previous conflict, was again cut off from some of her best markets. If anything, her position was more critical than on the earlier occasion, since her foreign commercial ties now were more numerous. The United States and Great Britain, however, took steps to lessen the economic stringency. Great Britain needed all the food and raw materials she could get. The United States needed raw materials, was anxious to prevent purchases by the Axis Powers, and was ready to put into effect a policy of inter-American trade cooperation that had been carefully worked out by her economic experts.

Because of defaults on many loans during the depression of the early thirties, some Latin American nations found it difficult to borrow when the time came for renewed expansion. To meet this

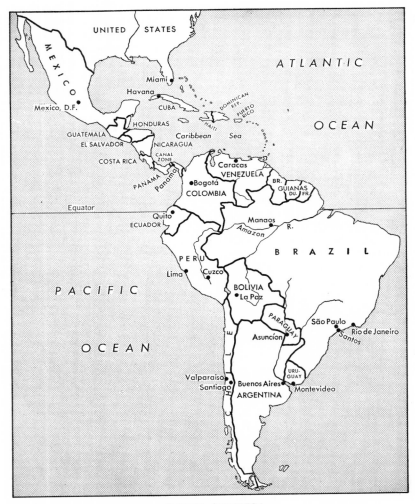

LATIN AMERICA

Courtesy, Foreign Policy Association, *Headline Series.*

situation and to promote inter-American commerce, Washington in 1934 organized an Export-Import Bank to "create" trade. Further stimulus was provided by a number of reciprocal trade treaties, whereby each signatory made special concessions regarding the importation of certain products of the other. Finally, the United States negotiated agreements to take all the exportable surpluses of specified products from a number of Latin American states.

The stimulation of foreign investment during the 1930's led, in Latin America as a whole, to the firm establishment of local industries, which supplied consumer goods to the domestic markets. The considerable industrialization, then, brought about intensive urbanization, a phenomenon that was of particular significance in social and political developments. Although there was a distinct tendency, as far back as colonial times, to form cities at the administrative seats of the provinces and in the mining districts, the recent rapid growth of such cities gave rise to the same problems of a mixed urban and rural society as was found in many other parts of the world. Buenos Aires, for instance, came to hold about one-fifth of Argentina's population, and Montevideo more than one-third of that of Uruguay. Not infrequently, one large city dominated a vast rural area, with important social and economic results.

In light of Latin America's industrial advances, the importance of communication and transportation facilities was obvious. The topography presented troublesome international barriers and made even internal communication difficult: the mountain passes of the Andes are from 9000 to 15,000 feet above sea level. There was continuing need for more railway mileage and hard-surfaced roads, since shipping by way of rivers and oceans offered only a partial solution.

Among the important results of the modern economic development in Latin America was the rise of the middle and laboring classes. A merchant class and unattached laborers had existed throughout colonial times, but even in the nineteenth century their political influence was greatly inferior to that of the landed aristocrats. A gradual change became evident when an increasing dependence of Latin America on world markets shifted farming little by little to a capitalistic basis and stimulated the growth of cities. In many countries the peasant thereupon became a hired laborer with no right to the soil. Or he migrated to the cities and mining districts to become, if fortunate, a member of the middle class; or, if less fortunate (and this was the rule), a worker. A distinction must be made, moreover, between the relatively small group of well-to-do middle-class people and the relatively large number of such bourgeois-oriented but economically marginal people as professionals, petty merchants, and white-collar workers.

The upper middle class came to be composed largely of landed aristocrats, who were forced by competition to manage their farms as capitalistic enterprises. Often they also invested in commerce, industry, and mining, and acquired new economic concepts to fit their new interests. In some of the countries, where no strong local middle class appeared, the influx of foreign capital created interests that affected political developments as much as, and often more than, local forces. As the traditional political policies of the landed group changed, the middle class, by virtue of its increasing numerical and financial strength, its congregation in the cities, and its educational advantages, came to wield political power. The illiterate masses, on the other hand, exerted little positive force on political happenings. In these circumstances the growth of a professional and white-collar group and a small-merchant class assumed special importance.

Argentina furnished a good illustration of middle class and labor growth in an agricultural and commercial country. The characteristic land-holding unit in 1940 was still the large *estancia*, comprising from 25,000 to 500,000 acres. Before the First World War nearly a third of the province of Buenos Aires was owned by ninety-three proprietors, and the situation did not change materially in the next quarter-century. The large estates were worked by tenants and hired laborers, often immigrants from Europe. On the industrial side, the city of Buenos Aires in 1913 contained 400,000 workers, an increase of 240 per cent since 1895, but only half as many as in 1935. Chile, on the eve of the Second World War, presented a similar picture. About half the population was urban, and some 500 large estates made up half of the country's agricultural area.

In Uruguay, where the principal industry was stock raising, the great ranches were owned by a few individuals—but Montevideo contained a numerous proletariat. The major cattle and sheep raising sections of Argentina, southern Chile, Brazil, Mexico, Paraguay, and Venezuela offered a similar view. The land was customarily held in enormous blocks, and the packing plants generally were controlled by United States or British packers. The coffee plantations, the sugar estates, the cotton fields, and the banana groves of Latin America were nearly all in large holdings. Some of the owners were local inhabitants, but many were foreign absentee owners. The wage-workers formed an Indian, black, or white proletariat.

The industrialized areas of Latin America further illustrated the simultaneous rise of the middle and working classes in the decades before 1940. A numerous laboring class had existed even in pre-1914 days in the mining regions of Latin America. The mines usually were located in otherwise barren areas, to which food to sustain the miners had to be brought from hundreds of miles away. The agricultural regions, in turn, depended upon these industrial areas to furnish markets for their food products. The economic structure was further complicated by the fact that most of the mineral output had to be marketed abroad, and, if the foreign market failed, unemployment, depression, and social disturbances often followed. A parallel situation obtained in the petroleum-producing regions.

Latin America between the two world wars thus offered a scene in which the comparatively recent rise of an upper middle class of industrialists, a lower middle class of white-collar workers, and a landless proletariat, was a dynamic factor. About three-fourths of the Latin Americans lived under conditions characteristic of the Western economic structure. At the same time there still existed among the large Indian populations of Mexico, Guatemala, Ecuador, Peru, Bolivia, and Brazil, a semibarter economy.

The accumulation of local and foreign capital and the rise of the middle and laboring classes furnished the background for important political, educational, and social changes. The middle class demanded and received a greater voice in political affairs and brought about a revision of the educational system. Out of the universities, now attended by many students of middle-class origin, came new currents of thought and agitation for change of the social structure. The laboring class obtained partial recognition of its demands through political action or revolution. A few examples will demonstrate the trend of these events.

The discontent aroused by the domination of the *estancieros* in Argentina led to the organization of the *Unión Cívica Radical* late in the nineteenth century and the eventual passage (1912) of reforms that made possible the election of this party's candidate, Hipólito Irigoyen (1916–1922), to the presidency. Since the election of Irigoyen was a triumph of the middle class in cooperation with the workers, the new executive faced the problem of satisfying both supporting groups.

Radical agitation was sufficient to force Irigoyen and his successor, Marcelino T. de Alvear (1922–1928), to enact some social legislation. However, notably lacking among the reforms was any serious attempt to bring about a broader division of the land.

Irigoyen again was elected to the presidency in 1928, but a revolution by conservatives, anti-Irigoyen radicals, and army men unseated him in 1930. Henceforth, Argentina was governed by a conservative coalition that enjoyed army support. The international policies of this government seemed at times to favor the Axis Powers.

In Chile, where the upper middle class had shared power with the landed aristocracy since 1891, the post-1920 depression effected a change comparable to the election of Irigoyen in Argentina. A coalition of middle-class and labor votes brought the liberal-minded Arturo Allessandri into power in 1920. He was responsible for a limited amount of labor and social legislation and the adoption, in 1925, of a new constitution. This document increased the powers of the president, gave greater autonomy to the provinces, widened the suffrage, and separated state and church. Many changes suggested by Alessandri were delayed until General Carlos Ibáñez became dictator-president in 1927. Supported by the army, Ibáñez became the agent of further change. At the same time he fought his political enemies in a manner that won him the reputation of a tyrant.

When Chile began to feel the effects of the depression of 1930, Ibáñez tried to solve his problems by borrowing and by stringent economy measures, but this failed to stem a rising tide of opposition, and his regime collapsed in 1931. Chile's economic position became desperate and her politics chaotic. Several ephemeral administrations held power before an election in 1932 again brought Alessandri into the presidency for a six-year term.

His administration saw the rise of a strong Communist Party, a further growth of the Socialists, and a general shift to the left in politics. Eventually (1938) a coalition of leftists came into control of the government.

The influence on social legislation of the middle and working classes was exceptionally strong in Uruguay. The executive power came into the hands of the liberal Colorado Party in 1872 and was still there seventy years later. Traditionally progressive, this party was reorganized at the beginning of the twentieth century and became an instrument of middle-class and workmen's interests. The chief opposition group represented the large-estate owners and the Catholic Church. To retain the support of the laborers and to limit the growth of the Socialists, who over the years gained an increasing number of seats in the legislature, the Colorados consistently fathered social legislation, democratic governmental reform, and some nationalization of industry.

The depression precipitated a crisis in 1933, which Uruguay found it peculiarly difficult to meet because of the division of administrative powers. The framers of a constitution enacted in 1919 had hoped to prevent dictatorship by creating an executive council with powers independent of the president, but the system was unwieldy. In 1933 President Gabriel Terra assumed dictatorial authority on the ground that the economic dilemma made strong action imperative. A new constitution in 1934 strengthened the hands of the president. But the special prerogatives granted the minority later were to cause difficulty, since it was made possible for the minority to control at least one-third of the legislature regardless of the vote it had polled. When the Nationalist Party prevented legislation that Terra's successor, President Alfredo Baldomir, deemed vital for national defense, the executive dissolved the congress early in 1942 and created a Council of State.

Colombia, too, made notable progress after the opening of the twentieth century. After many years of Conservative rule, the Liberals came into office and remained in control through World War II. Under their direction Colombia achieved the reputation of one of the stablest states in the Americas. Among the chief acts of the government, though one not widely publicized, was the quiet but efficient redistribution of Colombia's agricultural wealth.

Peru wrote much social legislation into her constitution during the dictatorship of President Augusto B. Leguía (1919–1930), and continued this tendency under President Oscar R. Benavides (1933–1939). Much of Benavides' reform work coincided with what his political opponents advocated, but his dictatorial policies and harsh treatment of those who opposed him, plus a pro-Axis leaning in international affairs, turned many liberals against him. He was succeeded by Manuel Prado, who freed most of the political prisoners and adopted a policy of definite friendship with the United States.

Bolivia, Ecuador, the Central American and Caribbean countries, and the other nations of Latin America also enacted extensive codes of social legislation. The Andean states outlined programs to improve the living conditions of the Indians, who comprised large portions of their respective populations, but no marked success was achieved in this connection by 1940. Several Indian congresses were held under the auspices of the Pan-American Union, but, except in Mexico, the lot of the Indians remained backward.

Before the twentieth century, education was confined principally to a small upper class and the clergy. The curricula usually were based on classical studies and were ill suited to either the new scientific and social developments or the needs of the classes born of industrialization and urbanization. The task of setting up a modern educational structure was complicated by a variety of factors. The rural communities were hampered by bad transportation facilities. Governmental funds, never plentiful, tended to be spent on soldiers rather than school children. The leaders of Latin America were slow to adjust to the idea of education for the masses rather than for the classes. Whereas the percentage of illiteracy in some regions remained high, others presented a creditable record in schoolwork. Many Latin educators went to the United States or Europe for training, and educators from foreign countries were invited to Latin America to aid in the reorganization of old, and the founding of new, systems of instruction.

In the universities, the progress after 1918 was characterized by broadening curricula, an improvement in the quality of instruction, a lessening of outside political influences, and the greater participation of students in the government of the schools through seats on the university councils. To the students themselves belonged much of the credit for these changes. The students soon discovered that reform in the government-controlled universities depended first upon certain general political changes. Accordingly, the students of more and more states began to participate wholeheartedly in political upheavals against the old regimes. By way of example, a word may be said of the student agitation in Peru.

In the midst of Peru's first postwar depression, President Leguía inaugurated reforms that improved the material condition of the country. His eleven-year dictatorship, from 1919 to 1930, however, was marked by political corruption and persecution, and the students who sought educational changes beyond those which the government was willing to concede were among the chief sufferers. The students eventually founded the radical *Alianza Popular Revolucionaria Americana* (APRA), which became especially active after the downfall of Leguía. Within a few years it became one of the best-organized parties in Peru, with a nationalistic program that called for closer cooperation with the neighboring states, the division of the large landed holdings, liberal educational reforms, and a general reorganization of the national economy.

Because it was the local situations in all these countries that produced the issues which were taken up by the students, there was no one Latin American student policy or attitude. Allied with the workers in some states and with the middle class in others, students, on occasion, furnished the intellectual leadership in radical labor movements, arrayed themselves against the landlords and the clericals, and fought against the continued domination of foreign economic groups. But, whether they were Democrats, Communists, or Fascists, the students became an important influence in the life and development of Latin America.

BRAZIL

Brazil was colonized by Portugal, not Spain, as were the other nations; hence Portuguese became the official language. Brazil was about three times the size of the next largest Latin American country, Argentina, and larger than the contiguous United States with an extra Texas. All but 7 per cent of the inhabitants came to live along the seaboard, the regions of greatest concentration and wealth-production being the states of Bahía and Pernambuco in the north and Río de Janeiro, São Paulo, and Minas Geraes in the south.

Political developments in Brazil were influenced strongly by economic factors and the grouping of people in a few areas. Prior to 1912, when rubber was a highly important Brazilian product, the northern states exercised some political power; but with the decline of the rubber industry, political influence became almost a monopoly of the coffee-growing and industrial southern states. The struggle for control of the federal government came to be largely among São Paulo, Minas Geraes, and Río Grande do Sul—the chief producers of coffee and cattle, and the centers of trade and manufacturing. The key to Brazilian politics could be found in the rivalries of these states and especially in the efforts of São Paulo to control the national government in order to protect her coffee interests. National political parties did not exist. There were, instead, separate state parties.

The scene was further complicated by the extensive autonomy of the individual states, their independence of the federal government being far greater than that of the commonwealths in the United States. They could levy tariffs, and their police forces were, in effect, armies, which on occasion opposed the federal government itself. The political machines in the states nominated the candidates for political office and then formed combinations in their support. Of the fourteen presidents chosen between the establishment of the republic in 1889 and 1940, ten were from the three southern states named in the previous paragraph.

To speak of the political control exercised by these states meant, in reality, to speak of the influence of the great coffee growers and cattle raisers plus the middle class that had grown up in the industrial centers. The "people" of Brazil had little voice in politics, since three-fourths of them were illiterate and only the literate could vote. Thus, illiteracy was politically significant. The practical workings of the state political machine system could be seen in the events that transpired after 1930.

In 1930 Julio Prestes, governor of São Paulo, was elected president in a manner that his opponent, Getulio Vargas, governor of Río Grande do Sul, alleged to be fraudulent. Vargas was the candidate of a coalition composed of the old political machines and a variety of liberal and left-wing forces. His program promised wide social changes. When it became evident that Prestes would be credited with a majority of the votes cast, the coalition, with the aid of part of the army, placed Vargas in power. He derived further support from the mere fact that Río Grande do Sul believed it was the turn of one of its own men to be president. Vargas thus was supported by a heterogeneous group, and Brazil was plunged into prolonged unrest.

Out of industrial growth had come labor unions, on the one hand, and capitalists, on the other. Both had supported Vargas, and both expected rewards. The army men wanted domestic order and respect for the military corps, an aristocracy all its own. Vargas moved slowly and skillfully through the conflicting political currents. When the state of São Paulo rose in revolt in 1932, using Vargas' earlier promise to grant a new constitution as a pretext, he was able to crush its forces. He kept his promise to appoint a minister of labor, but deprived the unions of their autonomy by placing them under federal control. He broadened the system of social insurance and framed minimum wage laws; but the minimum wages were so low that the standard of living was affected only slightly.

In 1934 a new constitution was promulgated, which incorporated many of the campaign promises, but the government in reality appeared to be moving in a rightist direction in both domestic and international affairs. The position of the president and the army as arbiters of a very delicate situation became clearly apparent. In 1935 Vargas' opponents again revolted, the rebels this time including elements of every political color, from Communists to capitalists. After the revolt was put down, Vargas ruled through martial law for almost two years. Then, by 1937, the political situation was again at the breaking point. Although many of the Communists and left-wing leaders were in jail, their followings still were numerous.

Since, under the constitution, new presidential elections were to be held in 1938, opposing candidates were nominated, and an intensive campaign was in full swing by midsummer of 1937.

In the meantime a new factor, fascism, had entered the scene. In 1932 there was organized a Fascist *Integralist Action.* Taking the Guaraní Indian greeting "Anaue" as their equivalent of "Heil," the Greek letter *sigma* as their substitute for a swastika, and the green color of the Brazilian flag for their shirts, the Integralists grew rapidly. No Brazilian village was too small to have an Integralist center. Their program was frankly based on the Nazi-Fascist pattern. The Fascists boasted that through their "control of the teaching staffs of schools throughout the nation" they held in their hands "the future of Brazil."

Simultaneously, the German Nazis and Italian Fascists had formed strong organizations in Brazil. They owned newspapers, carried on a vigorous propaganda, were directed and financed from abroad, and had the support of many Brazilians. They also maintained close contact with the Integralists and participated with them in parades and demonstrations. By the summer of 1937 street fighting between the Fascists and their opponents became a frequent occurrence. The Fascist leader, Plinio Salgado, became a candidate for the presidency, and on several occasions the Integralists held "practice mobilizations," in preparation, they said, for the day when they would take over the country.

But President Vargas had other plans. Using the disorders as an excuse for canceling the forthcoming elections, he staged another coup late in 1937 and issued a previously prepared constitution of a more authoritarian character than had been the one of 1934. Among other things, the new document continued the incumbency of Vargas until such time as a plebiscite might determine otherwise. In 1938 all political parties were abolished. For some time thereafter Vargas assumed an attitude in international affairs that to many foreign observers seemed to be of a proaxis nature; but in 1942 he brought his country into the Second World War on the side of the United Nations.

MEXICO

During the long dictatorship (1877–1911) of Porfirio Díaz, economic progress came to Mexico. Foreign trade increased, internal peace was maintained, and industries were built up. But some of these improvements occurred under conditions that were destined to cause trouble. Petroleum fields and mines were largely foreign owned. The land was in the hands of relatively few people. Labor was meagerly paid, thousands of peons were "debt slaves," and the Indians in many cases had been driven from their lands.

In 1919–1921 a political revolution led to the overthrow and flight of Díaz. Then the demand for land by the rural workers, and for better working conditions by the urban laborers, gradually converted political revolution into social revolution. During the next ten years, to the beginning of 1920, the fighting was almost continuous, but in 1917 a new constitution was adopted. It aimed at securing a "Mexico for the Mexicans." The document, containing numerous social and economic reforms, was nationalistic, antiforeign, anticlerical, pro-labor, and pro-Indian. The realization of this constitutional program began during the administrations of Álvaro Obregón (1920–1924) and Plutarco E. Calles (1924–1928) and continued thereafter at a steady pace, despite the opposition of the formerly privileged.

The government, by the end of 1934, had nationalized 34,000,000 acres of privately held land, and by 1935 more than 700,000 heads of families, who hitherto had been landless, were settled on plots of their own. Then, during the administration of General Lázaro Cárdenas (1934–1940), the amount of land redistributed was greater than the total distribution from 1911 to 1934. Nevertheless, some large landholdings remained.

Industrial working conditions were likewise bettered after 1910. Minimum-wage laws were put into effect, the government, on occasion, cooperated with strikers and aided them in securing the fulfilment of their demands, and the living conditions of millions were improved. The Mexican unemployment figure remained comparatively small.

Cárdenas was succeeded in 1940 by General Manuel Ávila Camacho. Generally regarded as more conservative than Cárdenas, Camacho took the railroads under government management and inaugurated a new landownership policy. The agrarian revolution of Mexico long had been based on a program of restoring the *ejidos,* or communal village landholdings, characteristic of pre-Cortesian and colonial times; the tendency under Camacho was to substitute individual farm ownership.

THE CHURCH IN LATIN AMERICA

In all stages of Latin American history, the position occupied by the Catholic Church and its relations with the state were of paramount importance. During the colonial period and the first years of Latin American independence, the Roman Catholic Church was everywhere the established church. Religious toleration did not exist except in Argentina, the remaining nations having forbidden the public exercise of any but the Catholic religion. Education, charity, and hospitalization were monopolies of the church, whose wealth comprised half of the real estate of Latin America. The clergy, in general, seemed opposed to liberty of religion, press, speech, and assembly. The church claimed the right to maintain its own courts and to keep numerous *fueros* or privileges.

Gradually, however, the position of the church was weakened, sometimes, as in Ecuador, Colombia, and Mexico, to the accompaniment of civil war. A specific, though varying, state-church relationship existed in 1940 in Venezuela, Colombia, Peru, Bolivia, Paraguay, Argentina, Haiti, the Dominican Republic, Nicaragua, and Costa Rica. In Cuba and Panama the status of the church resembled that in the United States, whereas in Brazil the Catholic Church was accorded a preferred, but not an established position. Uruguay completed the separation of church and state in 1917, as did Chile eight years later.

In Mexico the conflict over religion was especially fierce. The constitution of 1857 deprived the church of many privileges it had enjoyed in the first years of Mexico's republican existence. Díaz, however, allowed it to regain most of the former rights, in practice if not in theory, by 1910. Hence, the church opposed the revolt against Díaz; and hence, in turn, the constitution of 1917 contained anticlerical provisions.

Education was secularized, monastic orders were outlawed, and religious liberty was guaranteed. The church was forbidden to hold property and lost many of its traditional prerogatives. Up to 1925, the federal government made little effort to enforce these provisions. Then, however, several state legislatures moved to carry out the constitutional terms.

In February 1926, an open conflict between the church and the civil authorities was precipitated by a clerical denunciation of the disputed constitutional articles. President Calles answered this protest by urging their immediate strict enforcement. Church property was nationalized, foreign priests were deported, and all schools, asylums, and convents where religious instruction was given were closed. The teaching of religious subjects in primary schools was prohibited, clergymen of any creed and members of religious orders were forbidden to teach, and schools were warned against the use of holy pictures for the inculcation of religious ideas.

These measures encountered strong opposition. A boycott was launched by faithful Catholics "to create in the nation a state of intense economic crisis." All priests were withdrawn from the churches, and religious services were suspended. The civil authorities thereupon took over the churches and kept them open for worship. When it became apparent that the economic and religious boycott would fail, various organizations resorted to armed violence. Using the battle cry: "*Viva Cristo, rey!*" (Long live Christ, the King!"), the *Cristeros* or Church Party participated in serious disturbances from 1926 to 1929.

A truce was reached in 1929 and, amid popular rejoicing, church services were resumed for the first time in three years. But the agreement satisfied neither side, and the conflict was reopened in 1931 when the state of Vera Cruz limited the number of priests to 1 for each 100,000 of the population. Similar action soon was taken by other states. In 1932 the papal legate was deported.

The struggle became particularly bitter when the government proposed to make socialistic instruction compulsory in all schools and universities. It was the avowed goal of the authorities to imbue the children with "a love for the exploited masses" and to analyze religions for them "in the light of reason and science." When Catholics were ordered not to permit their children to attend school under pain of excommunication, the attorney-general of the republic was instructed to take action against all Catholic clerics who were "fomenting rebellion." Eventually, however, in 1936, state-church relations began to improve. The Cárdenas regime permitted the Catholic Church gradually to regain some of its lost privileges. Camacho continued this policy after 1940, thereby establishing another uneasy truce during which the church continued to press its claims.

The United States | 15

In the election of 1916 Woodrow Wilson defeated Charles E. Hughes for the Presidency of the United States by a narrow margin. With the war's end there was a reaction, on the one hand, against the domestic policies fostered by the first Wilson Administration and, on the other, against the wide powers that the Government had exercised during the war. In the congressional election of 1918 the Republicans obtained control of both houses.

The blame for the high cost of living that followed the war was placed upon the Democratic Administration. The end of the conflict and the cancellation of government contracts running into billions of dollars partially disrupted the economic system of the country. Yet many manufacturers, accustomed to large profits, refused in the early postwar years to be satisfied with moderate returns. Profiteering continued and, for a time, became worse. Labor was equally insistent upon keeping wages up to and above the inflated war level. The consumer was the loser, for the purchasing power of the dollar was 52 per cent lower in 1920 than in 1913. The class that suffered the most from these circumstances was the salaried group—the professionals and clerks whose pay was fixed for long periods in advance. To make matters worse, numerous major strikes after the war (3000 in 1919) prompted a "Red Scare."

In addition, many citizens were dissatisfied with the Paris Peace Conference. Some felt that the treatment accorded Germany was too severe. Others believed that Great Britain was reaping most of the benefits of the war. Yet others were dissatisfied with the treatment of various nationalities from which they themselves had sprung. There was opposition to the League of Nations, and some

Republicans resented their exclusion from the Paris Conference. Hence, when Wilson placed the Versailles Treaty before the Senate (1919) for its consent to ratification, the prospects for acquiescence were slight. Among the opponents of the treaty were Henry Cabot Lodge, chairman of the Senate Foreign Relations Committee, who insisted upon sweeping amendments, and the "irreconcilable" Republicans, led by William E. Borah of Idaho, who opposed America's entering a league in any form.

The main public attacks on the treaty were directed against the League Covenant. The President tried to make clear that all League obligations were "moral" rather than "legal." His antagonists, however, would not listen, and the treaty failed of acceptance when brought up for vote.

In June 1920 the Republican National Convention met in Chicago and nominated Warren Gamaliel Harding of Ohio, a "genial standpatter" and advocate of a return to normalcy. Harding also seemed to be the one man at the convention who had no national enemies. The Democrats met in San Francisco. Governor James M. Cox of Ohio eventually secured the nomination.

The outcome of the campaign of 1920 was influenced by all the political and economic factors already mentioned, and by a seemingly general feeling that the time had come to relax and avoid crusades or reforms. The League seemed to play a relatively minor part in the campaign, being overshadowed by a general feeling that "our own yard is enough to worry about." Wilson recommended that the election be made "a great and solemn referendum" on the League, but Harding straddled the issue, saying, in effect, that he opposed *the* League but favored *a* league, a "free association of nations." The Republican candidate won by a plurality of 7,000,000 votes. The most obvious political sentiments displayed in this vote were a repudiation of Wilson and the desire for a move toward an isolationist position, which Harding termed "triumphant nationalism."

HARDING AND THE "RETURN TO NORMALCY"

President Harding entrusted the State Department to the experienced Charles E. Hughes. One of the new secretary's first tasks was to bring an end to the technical state of war that still existed between the United States, on the one side, and Germany, Austria, and Hungary, on the other. Wilson had vetoed a joint resolution to end hostilities without the formality of a treaty agreement. In July 1921 Congress passed it again and Harding signed this resolution, which declared the war "to be at an end." A few months later the treaties of Berlin, Vienna, and Budapest were signed and ratified, the United States in each case being guaranteed "all the rights and advantages stipulated" for her benefit in the German, Austrian, and Hungarian treaties with the Allies.

Once in office, Harding, realizing that the members of the League of Nations would hardly disband that organization and form a new one, dropped all talk of his "free association of nations." So completely did the administration try to forget the League that for almost six months no reply was sent to the communications which its secretary-general forwarded to Washington. The American Ambassador in London was "instructed to inform the League's authorities that as the United States had not joined the League, she was not in a position to answer letters from it." Not until the situation was exposed in *The New York Times* did the State Department send even formal acknowledgment of League notes.

Beginning in 1922, the government sent "unofficial observers" to conferences "where matters of concern to the United States were under consideration." Despite his indifference to the League, Harding urged membership in the World Court on condition that the United States be given an equal voice with other countries in the selection of judges. This proviso was necessary since the United States had no representation in the League bodies that elected the judges. The President died before the Senate acted on his suggestion.

Equally frigid during these years were Washington's relations with Russia. Secretary of Commerce Herbert Clark Hoover held that under the Bolshevik economic system Russia could expect "no real return to production" and hence little international trade of benefit to the United States. In these circumstances it was felt that there existed no motive for making diplomatic arrangements to facilitate the exchange of goods with Russia.

There were two spheres, however, in which the United States did not remain aloof: naval construction and Pacific and Far Eastern relations. The naval rivalry between Great Britain and the United States, inaugurated by a National Defense Act passed by Congress in 1916, threatened harmonious relations between the two peoples. The matter was made more serious and broader in scope by the Anglo-Japanese Alliance, which, it was feared, might become a menace to United States Pacific interests. The status of all Far Eastern territories might, therefore, profitably be discussed. Accordingly, a nine-power conference was held in Washington in 1921–1922, and agreements were reached on the limitation of naval armaments and on Pacific and Far Eastern problems.[1]

In domestic matters, President Harding by "a return to normalcy" meant a return to policies favoring business. For example, in 1921, Congress repealed a wartime excess-profits tax, lowered the surtax maximum on the largest incomes to 50 per cent, and passed a high-tariff law.

---

[1] See Chapter 13. The United States in 1921 made it plain to Great Britain and France that United States oil companies were not to be excluded from a share in the oil concessions of the Near Eastern mandates.

Meanwhile Congress was becoming acutely aware of the economic plight of the farmers. During the war the process of farm industrialization had advanced at an unprecedented rate. The wartime food needs had made it profitable to devote every available acre to cultivation, and the farmers, consequently, had borrowed heavily in order to buy more land and more machines. After the war, however, the farmers found themselves saddled with extensive mortgages.

Even in the heyday of war prosperity the average farmer had realized little more than 6 per cent on his total investment. Hence, when the prices of farm products declined in the business slump that followed 1919, the farmers were in a desperate situation. Though they had developed marketing and purchasing cooperatives, they had no organization for regulating production or fighting deflation. Farmers were faced with interest payments that had to be met, or their mortgages would be foreclosed.

In despair, the farmers turned to the government for relief. A congressional Farm Bloc was created (1921) to represent the interests of the western farmers, who cared little about the concerns of eastern legislators. Several farm-relief measures were passed between 1921 and 1923, but none could solve the country's agricultural problem.

In 1923 the Hardings started on an ill-fated tour across the country, including a visit to Alaska. Harding was not well when the trip began, and he became seriously ill in Alaska. He was returning home when death overtook him in San Francisco, on August 2, 1923. Probably his mind had been troubled and his illness aggravated by certain deeds of official corruption in the years 1921 to 1923.

One of the first scandals to be uncovered grew out of the practices of Charles R. Forbes, director of the Veterans' Bureau. According to a Senate investigating committee, the record of Forbes' activities was one of "almost unparalleled waste, recklessness, and misconduct," costing the government $200,000,000. For his misdeeds, Forbes was sentenced to a term in Leavenworth Prison. Another investigating committee discovered that Attorney-General Harry M. Daugherty had surrounded himself in the Department of Justice with disreputable characters, and failed to prosecute grafters and leading bootleggers. When Daugherty denied the committee permission to search his department files for further evidence, President Calvin Coolidge dismissed him (1924).

The greatest scandal involved the leasing of some government oil reserves. It appeared that Harding had signed an order permitting Secretary of the Navy Edwin Denby to transfer to Secretary of the Interior Albert B. Fall the administration of the petroleum reserves earlier set aside at Elk Hills in California and Teapot Dome in Wyoming for the use of the navy. Fall was prominent as an opponent of Mexico and as a man "who affected a cowboy pose and a fine contempt for reformers and conservationists." In 1922, without calling for competitive bids, he leased the Teapot Dome reserves to

Harry F. Sinclair and the Elk Hills reserves to Edward L. Doheny. In each case the government was to obtain a small royalty on the oil secured.

Soon the smell of oil was detected on official garments, and a senatorial committee of investigation discovered a trail of corruption. It developed that Doheny had "loaned" Fall $100,000 without security and without interest in 1921; that Fall also had received a loan of $25,000 from Sinclair; and that he had accepted valuable gifts from other oilmen. Then he had resigned early in 1923, before the scandals were made public, and had retired to a large ranch purchased with the "loans."

In 1924 the government instituted judicial proceedings against Fall, Doheny, and Sinclair. It asked for the cancellation of the leases and the conviction of the defendants for bribery and conspiracy. The Government won its first point in 1927 when the Supreme Court voided the leases and ordered the return of the reserves. Both Doheny and Sinclair were able to convince juries that they had acted out of patriotic motives. They maintained that the oil was being drained away by people who had sunk wells near by, that the terms were favorable to the government, and that, after all, undeveloped oil reserves were not much good to the navy. Sinclair, however, blundered by hiring private detectives to shadow his jurors and by refusing to answer certain questions of the Senate committee. For this contempt he had to serve a three months' jail term. Fall was convicted in 1929 and sent to jail.

This crime wave in the years following the war was not confined to officialdom. Private crimes came to be everyday topics of conversation, and the official misdeeds merely reflected on a large scale what happened privately on a smaller scale. In 1921 there was said to have been one major bank robbery per day throughout the country, and one automobile out of every twenty-two in Chicago and every thirty in New York was stolen. "Burglary-insurance rates in American cities were from fifteen to twenty times as high as in England," and "the homicide rate of the United States was sixteen times that of England and Wales." Machine guns and sawed-off shotguns were among the weapons employed by postwar criminals. Racketeering or the custom of levying tribute under threat of violence was revived as a widespread source of illegal income.

COOLIDGE AND "SAFE AND SANE" POLITICS

Calvin Coolidge, who took the oath of office as Harding's successor, was born in Vermont. A graduate of Amherst College, his brevity of speech became famous, and, having sternly put down a Boston policemen's strike in 1919 during his term as governor of Massachusetts, he had come to be hailed as "the silent man of iron" and nominated as Harding's running mate. He believed that "the business of America is business," and he "thoroughly approved of the Ten Commandments."[2]

President Coolidge retained his predecessor's cabinet and made economy his goal. He saw his function as the prevention of "crime" and the preservation of "contracts." He believed that economic systems were governed by natural law and that nothing could go wrong in the financial order as long as it was not disturbed by the intemperate actions of ignorant men. The remainder of Harding's term was directed under the influence of these basic ideas, and no one had reason to believe that a future Coolidge administration would institute any radical departure from such guidelines.

Coolidge easily secured the Republican nomination for the presidency in 1924. General Charles G. Dawes, of reparation fame and first director of the National Budget Bureau established in 1921, was selected as his running mate. The Democratic candidate was John W. Davis, a "dark horse" conservative from West Virginia who had achieved success as a corporation lawyer in New York. Coolidge won easily over Davis and the Progressive Party candidate, Senator Robert M. ("Fighting Bob") La Follette of Wisconsin.[3]

In the second Coolidge Administration the national debt was reduced, the surtax was lowered to 20 per cent, and slight reductions were made in the tax on lower incomes. A few laws to aid agricultural production and marketing were passed, although the Republican return to high protective tariffs had hurt the farmers by making it more difficult for foreign nations to buy American products. Thus the crops that America produced in overabundance could not readily be sold abroad. The McNary-Haugen Bill, which proposed a fixed domestic price for grain, was vetoed as being economically unsound. The enforcement of Prohibition, based on the Eighteenth Amendment and the Volstead Act of 1919, continued to be one of the government's most difficult tasks. Much profit was derived from violations of the law by bootleggers and smugglers, and a leading racketeer boasted that in one year his organization had spent $30,000,000 to check law-enforcement activities.

In the summer of 1928, the customary presidential nominating conventions assembled. When the President made it clear that he was not to be considered a possible candidate for another term, it soon appeared that Herbert Hoover, who had served in both Hard-

---

[2] In his biography of Coolidge, entitled *A Puritan in Babylon* (1939), William Allen White noted what seemed to him the odd situation that the riotous, high-living "golden twenties" should have been presided over in Washington by a frugal Yankee, who firmly believed in the restrictions imposed by a Calvinistic background.

[3] The years from 1924–1926 witnessed a clearing of the political stage through the deaths of several of the older leaders. Theodore Roosevelt had died in 1919. Wilson, Lodge, and long-time labor leader Samuel Gompers died in 1924. Death claimed La Follette and William Jennings Bryan in 1925, and Socialist leader Eugene V. Debs and "Uncle Joe" Cannon, long the leading conservative in the House of Representatives, in 1926.

ing's and Coolidge's cabinets, would be selected. A successful mining engineer and Secretary of Commerce for two terms, he had worked closely with the business community, and his administrative ability was well known. He was nominated on the first ballot. Senator Charles Curtis of Kansas, Republican leader in the Senate, was chosen as vice-presidential candidate. The platform promised a continuation of "safe and sane" Republican policies.

The Democratic nominators adopted a platform that stressed the corruption under Harding. The colorful Alfred E. Smith, four times governor of New York and well known as an able politician and administrator, was selected as the party's standard-bearer.

The campaign was exciting and attracted a large vote. The extensive use of radio for speech-making and the presence of religious and Prohibition issues roused millions from their normal political apathy. Hoover, a Quaker who considered Prohibition a "noble experiment," was backed by the Protestant and temperance organizations of the country. Such bodies as the Ku Klux Klan—which had come into renewed prominence after the war as an association for upholding the supremacy of white Protestants over black men and "foreign" elements—aligned themselves against the Catholic Democratic candidate.

Hoover was victorious by a plurality of more than 6,000,000 votes over the man from "the sidewalks of New York." Smith carried only six southern states, along with Massachusetts and Rhode Island. He lost his own state, New York, although the Democratic candidate for governor, Franklin D. Roosevelt, won easily.

HOOVER: "THE ENGINEER IN POLITICS"

The new President was a hard worker and a man with a high sense of duty. During his occupancy of the White House he gave ample evidence of his abilities as an administrator, but he soon showed himself to be less apt as a leader. It was said that "he could run a department or set of departments with great skill; he could organize forces to meet an emergency; but he could not direct a party ... or guide public opinion." Impatient of criticism, he placed his chief trust in commissions of experts, appointing more such bodies than any of his predecessors. In politics he was conservative, and in economic theory a neo-mercantilist, favoring high tariffs and big business.

At the outset it appeared as though the Hoover Administration might be highly successful. Both houses of Congress contained substantial Republican majorities, the cabinet was able, the political appointments generally were acceptable, and the country seemed to enjoy prosperity. Yet the President was immediately confronted by some problems of overwhelming magnitude and was induced to call Congress in special session without allowing himself sufficient time to formulate legislative recommendations of his own. In his inaugural address Hoover had pointed out the need for "limited changes" in the tariff, early farm relief, and stricter enforcement of the laws. The first two of these problems were referred directly to Congress for action (April 1929). As a preliminary step in dealing with the question of law and order, the chief executive appointed a Law Enforcement Commision, under the chairmanship of former Attorney General George W. Wickersham, to make a thorough survey of the crime situation.

By 1929, the "crime industry" had become so well organized that municipalities, and even states, confessed inability to cope with it. The annual cost of crime to the nation in 1931 was estimated at $100 per capita. A major portion of the crimes was connected with violations of the Volstead Act, but the racketeers, able to "buy protection," extended their activities to numberless other fields. Relatively few major criminals suffered arrest, and fewer still, conviction. Eventually the Federal Government itself found it easier to imprison racketeers for falsifications of their income-tax returns than for violations of the alcohol or homicide laws.

The Wickersham Report, therefore, was eagerly awaited, but when it was published (1931), the document was vague on some of its most important revelations. The net result of the labors of the commission was disappointing, although two definite gains were made: it was clearly established that some sort of Prohibition reform was desirable; and on the advice of the commission, Congress transferred the enforcement of the liquor laws from the Department of the Treasury to the Department of Justice.

In the matter of the tariff, Congress disregarded the President's advice concerning limited changes and quickly engaged in log-rolling. The Hawley-Smoot Tariff lowered the rates on some 250 items, but raised them on about 900 items. Against the advice of more than 1000 economists and of numerous experts representing both political parties, Hoover signed the bill (1930), trusting to the tariff commission to uncover any injustices in the act. There was a storm of opposition to the President's decision, and foreign countries generally resorted to one or another form of retaliation. The foreign-trade situation became worse instead of better.[4]

The method adopted by the administration to provide farm relief was equally unsuccessful. Congress rejected several plans designed to aid the farmers through subsidies on agricultural staples. Instead, a Federal Farm Board was created (1929), equipped with a revolving fund of $500,000,000 to fight overproduction. The board was empowered to form stabilization corporations for the several crops with power to buy and sell surpluses in these grains. The measure, based

---

[4] The resulting higher prices for manufactures and a combination of good farm crops and foreign boycotts of American grain continued the trend of economic grief for the American farmers.

on the hope that the surpluses would be temporary, was expensive and in reality fostered rather than discouraged overproduction.

Meanwhile, in October 1929, the stock market in Wall Street had crashed. On the twenty-fourth of that month uneasy speculators dumped almost 13,000,000 stock shares on the exchange market. The origins of the crash would seem traceable, at least in part, to the economic upheaval wrought by the First World War. During the period of hositilities there had been a great inflation of prices. Except for a brief depression soon after the war, the United States continued to prosper in the 1920's, chiefly because of the wartime depletion of goods and the readiness of Europe and Latin America to place orders there, as long as credits were available and people in the United States were willing to invest in foreign bonds. In consequence, a speculative mania developed during which prices remained artificially inflated and paper fortunes were made. Prices rose, industry expanded, and production increased with little plan or precaution.

Yet, at the same time, tariff walls were raised still higher, nations everywhere placed obstacles in the way of world commerce, and the questions of reparation and war debts continued to embitter international relations. It was inevitable that postwar deflation eventually would occur. A financial break was almost certain to come when United States investors became uneasy about their holdings and when foreign purchases diminished. After the crash in the United States, disaster quickly attacked Europe's weak financial structure. First came collapse in Austria, then elsewhere, and finally the economic depression became worldwide.

The President's first public comment on the stock-market situation characterized it as merely the result of a wave of uncontrolled speculation in securities. Hence the difficulty was depicted as temporary and recovery was said to be close at hand. But when conditions became worse, Hoover explained that the crisis was of global magnitude and was caused by factors beyond the control of the United States. In order to speed economic revival, the President, as has been indicated, proposed an international moratorium from mid-1931 to mid-1932. This action only emphasized the seriousness of the world's predicament and did little to restore confidence.

Energetic measures were taken to deal with the situation at home, for unemployment figures rose rapidly and by 1932 were estimated at 7,000,000. Congress appropriated large sums for the construction of public buildings and highways. Unemployment-relief committees were appointed by cities, states, and the nation, and funds were collected from charitably inclined persons throughout the land. Employed citizens were encouraged to "share their work" with less fortunate neighbors, and there was an increasing demand for the five-day week. Banks in difficulty were permitted to borrow from the Federal Reserve System on joint promissory notes.

Another act created a Reconstruction Finance Corporation with the power to issue loans for industrial or agricultural projects. Later the corporation's lending powers were extended to include loans to states, for by this time financial disaster threatened not only companies, but municipal, county, and state governments.

Among other incidents that illustrated the extent of the economic emergency was a march on Washington (1932) by unemployed war veterans from all over the United States. The march was organized to dramatize the soldiers' demands for a cash bonus based on twenty-year prepaid endowment policies they had received in 1924. Having been told that they could, when in need, borrow on these policies, many veterans now asked for cash redemption of their certificates.

Congress disregarded the soldiers' plea, since payment of a cash bonus would have placed an enormous strain on the already weakened financial system of the country. The Bonus Expeditionary Force (BEF), as it came to be called, threatened to remain camped in Washington until its demands were met. The government eventually used troops to clear the city of petitioners. Public opinion generally condemned this handling of the BEF.

In this atmosphere the country prepared for the election of 1932. The Republicans renominated President Hoover and Vice-President Curtis. The Democrats eventually chose Governor Roosevelt of New York over Alfred E. Smith. John N. Garner of Texas, Speaker of the House (which had come under Democratic control after the elections of 1930), was selected for the vice-presidency. The chief plank in each platform dealt with Prohibition.

The Democratic candidate carried forty-two states and secured a plurality of more than 7,000,000 votes. Both branches of Congress also went to the Democrats, the House of Representatives by more than a two-thirds majority. The Republicans, as the party in power, had taken credit for the prosperity of the 1920's and now were blamed for the depression. One of Hoover's earlier campaign slogans had been "a chicken in every pot and two cars in every garage." In 1931 there appeared a cartoon in a New York newspaper depicting two chickens scratching for food in an empty garage.

SOCIAL TRENDS

The 1920's have offered an unusually fertile field of investigation to the social historian. Various terms have been used to describe that time: the era of "speak-easies," the days of "flaming youth," the Jazz Age, and the hey-day of installment buying. In literary history it has been usual to speak of the "lost generation" of disillusioned writers, who pessimistically sought meaning in the aftermath of the World War. Certainly it was an era of rapid social change, marked by the appearance of societal patterns that sometimes were shockingly new.

In spectator sports, great enthusiasm was lavished on boxing and football. Thus, the Dempsey-Tunney championship prize fight in 1927 drew $2,625,000 in gate receipts; a college football game for the first time attracted 100,000 spectators.

The gangsters' great empires, built on alcohol and murder, lent a somewhat macabre atmosphere to the time. Henry L. Mencken, the Baltimore writer, described the current scene as "the greatest show on earth," depicting, with exaggeration, a society of bathtub-gin makers and flagpole sitters. To many citizens, the era appeared as one without serious issues and with unlimited money to spend.

Behind the frenzy of "good times" powerful America demonstrated what many foreign observers regarded as an unnatural fear. There was a Red Scare, even though the elections showed fewer than one American in every 2000 had any sympathy with Communist doctrine. The tendency to see subversion in many areas reached a dramatic climax in the Sacco-Vanzetti trial in which two Italian anarchists, Nicola Sacco and Bartolomeo Vanzetti, were convicted of a robbery-murder near Boston (1920). The belief has persisted among some historians that the judge and jury, influenced by the general hysteria against radicalism, were prejudiced against the defendants.

There were other fears. Popular books warned of the Asiatic "Yellow Peril." Some indicated that the country was in danger from a Jewish conspiracy and, if not that, a Catholic conspiracy, or even an atheistic plot. Perhaps the most important manifestation of such attitudes was to be found in the revival of the Ku Klux Klan, an organization first founded in the post-1865 days, which now became very strong in the South and the Middle West. A revived Klan meant a renewal of racial violence in the South, but it also meant the spread of racial and religious bigotry to other parts of the country.

Although intolerance was an aspect of the period, as were interest in sports and the flaunting of Prohibition, there were deeper changes. Mass production, as one French visitor observed, meant that the average American could obtain luxuries "reserved for the privileged classes anywhere else." The United States developed a worldwide reputation, still maintained, as a land of industrial miracles, with a high standard of living for almost everyone.

The Jazz Age was often irresponsible, generally exciting, and usually creative.[5] Perhaps most important for the future of American life, the abolition of poverty, through mass production and mass employment, became a fixed national dream.

---

[5] Merely to list the important American writers of the postwar period would require considerable space. Let it suffice to note the names of Sinclair Lewis, Ernest Hemingway, William Faulkner, and John Dos Passos.

FOREIGN AFFAIRS, 1923-1933

During the Harding Administration the foreign policies of the United States were concerned chiefly with a liquidation of the immediate political problems raised by the country's participation in the First World War and rejection of the Versailles Treaty. After 1923, the trend of foreign affairs was shaped by a realization among Americans of certain recent and vital changes in their national financial position in the world.

Up to 1914, Europe had been the world's banker. As a consequence of the war and its aftermath, the situation underwent a striking transformation. By 1930 the United States had become a creditor nation and Europe the debtor. The European war debts to the Washington Government amounted to $11,000,000,000. United States foreign trade in the five-year period 1924-1928 averaged $9,000,000,000 annually. The citizens expected their government to protect these foreign interests, and Washington, in general, was ready to assume the obligation.

American foreign policies toward Latin America also were altered. Harding had criticized an earlier Wilsonian intervention in the Caribbean, and in keeping with that criticism had withdrawn American marines from the Dominican Republic in 1924. Coolidge had followed this policy by calling back American marines from Nicaragua in 1925. But political disturbances in Nicaragua endangered American life and property, and several thousand sailors and marines again were dispatched. There was widespread disapproval of this action throughout the Latin American countries and among anti-imperialist groups at home. Coolidge finally sent Henry L. Stimson, a former secretary of war, to arrange a compromise. This was done by the working out of an agreement between the two leading factions, providing for the general demobilization of the antigovernment rebels and for American-supervised elections.

Simultaneously with intervention in Nicaragua came a Mexican imbroglio. The Mexican constitution of 1917 had vested ownership of land and mineral rights in the Mexican nation, but permitted the state to transfer its rights to private Mexican citizens or to foreigners if the recipients agreed not to call on their governments for protection in any dispute over such rights. In 1926 the president of Mexico decreed that all owners of land who had secured their titles prior to the promulgation of the constitution of 1917 must exchange these titles for new fifty-year "concessions." A number of United States oil companies, fearing for their interests, organized an Association for the Protection of American Rights in Mexico to carry on propaganda against the land decrees.

The State Department denounced the decrees as infringements of United States property rights, and the Senate voted to arbitrate the questions in dispute. Coolidge maintained that United States property rights required no arbitration, and Secretary of State Frank B.

Kellogg, who had succeeded Hughes in 1925, accused Mexico of spreading Bolshevik propaganda in the United States and Central America, and of aiding the Nicaraguan revolutionists. But no overt action was resorted to, and the administration appointed the tactful Dwight W. Morrow to be ambassador to Mexico, following this by other good-will overtures.

Morrow tried to see the viewpoint of the Mexican officials and as a result was able to convince them that the United States had no desire to disrupt the amicable relations that earlier had been established between the two governments. Both sides compromised. The companies agreed to lay their cases before the Mexican Supreme Court, and the latter declared unconstitutional (1927) some of the more obnoxious land and oil laws.

After the Morrow mission, the United States became increasingly conciliatory in its dealings with Latin American states. Indications of this trend could be found in Coolidge's opening of the Pan-American Conference of 1928 and Hoover's good-will tour to South America in the fall of the same year.

In 1927, Washington became concerned over the safety of American lives and property in China. The activities of both the Chinese nationalists and the Communists were a source of danger to foreigners, and the United States, following the example of other countries, dispatched armed forces to Nanking. When the nationalists appeared to have established control and promised adequate protection, the United States forces were withdrawn.

In the relations between the United States and Europe, the question of the Allied war debts already has been discussed. Pending final settlement of this problem, the United States was faced with the dilemma of whether or not to collaborate with Europe along general political lines. In 1923 Coolidge, following the example of Harding, asked the Senate for its consent to the ratification of the World Court Protocol. After considerable executive persuasion, the Senate, in 1926, agreed, but with five reservations. The most sweeping condition was in the fifth reservation. The court should not, it read, "without the consent of the United States, entertain any request for an advisory opinion touching any dispute or question in which the United States has or claims an interest." The members of the court substantially accepted all reservations except this one, which would have given the United States a privileged position. Here the matter rested until, in 1929, the League Council charged a committee of jurists, which had been appointed to revise the court statute and of which Elihu Root was a member, simultaneously to consider the question of United States accession to the tribunal. Out of these beginnings the Root Plan evolved, which appeared acceptable to the members of the court and to the State Department.

The plan stipulated that the United States might withdraw from the court "without any imputation of unfriendliness" if ever the court should persist in entertaining a request for an advisory opinion even though the United States was "not prepared to forego its objection" to such procedure. Upon this basis a protocol for American adherence was signed by fifty-four states, including the United States—but it never was ratified.

In spheres other than that of the court, the United States, during the Coolidge and Hoover administrations, cooperated increasingly with the League. All the League's disarmament and economic conferences were attended by United States delegates. Usually, unofficial observers were sent to take part in the discussions and make suggestions, but the United States never bound herself to accept any of the decisions reached.

The United States during these years also collaborated with Europe in efforts to establish world harmony. In 1924 and 1929 United States financial experts played a leading, though unofficial, part in the formulation of new reparation arrangements. In 1927 the Geneva Conference on the limitation of naval armaments was held at the suggestion of President Coolidge. In 1928 Washington adhered to the Paris Pact for the renunciation of war as an instrument of national policy. In 1930 the United States became a party to the London Naval Treaty. Efforts were made to aid disarmament at the Geneva Conference of 1932. There was, finally, a steady exchange of notes with the League on Manchuria. Thus, in the 1920's, America's contribution to the cause of world peace lay chiefly in its participation in disarmament conferences and pacts.

Yet, the most significant characteristic of United States diplomacy in this decade was the attempted withdrawal from Europe. One historian has indicated that "no less than in Cleveland's day, Americans in the twenties insisted on the unique mission of the United States, the need to maintain independence of action and avoid permanent alliances. . . ."[6] But, this neo-isolationist position, this return to the pattern of foreign relations that had been interrupted briefly by America's European adventure of 1917–1918, was not to endure. The new technology, the new politics, and new social currents at work in the world created powerful forces that drew the United States inexorably back into the arena of world power.

ROOSEVELT AND "NIRA"

On March 4, 1933, Franklin D. Roosevelt, a man who, because of his personality and approach to politics, has been either violently disliked or greatly admired by many, took the oath of office as President. By this date the United States for two years and a half had been sinking lower and lower into economic depression. The unemployed numbered 13,000,000, the national income had fallen

[6] Thomas N. Bonner, *Our Recent Past* (Englewood Cliffs, N.J.: Prentice-Hall, 1963), p. 248.

to half that of 1929, approximately 40 per cent of the farms were mortgaged, strikes and violence had become common occurrences, and virtually every state had found it necessary to place some restriction on banking operations. The President, however, prophesied that the nation would "revive and prosper." He promised a "New Deal," thus permanently labeling his administration, and declared his intention to ask Congress for "broad executive powers to wage a war against the emergency."

The people rallied to the President's support. Roosevelt's cheerful informality, his cordial attitude towards the press, and his "heart-to-heart" talks with the citizenry over the radio, won him much confidence. Congress, too, backed the executive, passing important bills in record time. On occasion, Congress did demur and show jealousy of the growing executive power, but the President so skillfully won over public opinion that he generally had his way. As the pattern of his "new deal" became apparent, it proved to be similar to the demands that many farmers and laborers had been making since the Civil War.

On March 5, 1933, Roosevelt declared a nationwide bank holiday and called for a special session of Congress on the ninth. On the very day of its meeting, Congress passed an act giving the President power to regulate currency and credit transactions, penalise the hoarding of gold, assist the national banks whose assets were endangered, and issue Federal Reserve notes against government obligations. Then Congress passed an Economy Bill; a Beer Bill, modifying the Volstead Act so as to legalize the sale of beverages with an alcoholic content of 4 per cent by volume;[7] and a bill establishing a Civilian Conservation Corps (CCC), to provide employment for several hundred thousand young men on public works. Federal salaries were cut, the Federal Farm Bureau was abolished, all agricultural credit matters were placed in the hands of a Farm Credit Administration, and most of the banks were reopened.

The drive of administrative action continued with equal vigor in April and May. An executive order reduced the pension and benefit payments to war veterans; another took the United States off the international gold standard. The Agricultural Adjustment Act empowered the government to compensate farmers who curtailed their production. A gradual but controlled inflation was stimulated to make more money available.

The Wagner-Lewis Emergency Relief Act appropriated $500,000,000 for direct relief. The Tennessee Valley Authority (TVA) Act gave the government authority to develop power and natural

---

[7] This law was adopted pending state action on a proposed constitutional amendment, passed in February 1933, repealing the Eighteenth Amendment and forbidding the transportation or importation of intoxicating liquor only in those areas that retained dry laws of their own. Ratification proceeded swiftly, and on December 5, 1933, the Twenty-First Amendment, repealing the Eighteenth, became effective.

resources. This was advocated by Roosevelt to stimulate industry, relieve unemployment, and check the waste of resources resulting from lack of planning.

This sweep of legislative accomplishment was eclipsed by even more extensive lawmaking in June 1933. Federal credit was extended to save small-home owners from eviction by foreclosure. A Federal Deposit Insurance Corporation was established to guarantee depositors against loss in case of bank failure. Railroad workers were protected against loss of employment. On June 16 the President signed the National Industrial Recovery Act.

The NIRA, in effect, empowered the President to set up machinery for "a great cooperative movement throughout all industry in order to obtain wide reemployment, to shorten the work week, . . . and to prevent unfair competition and disastrous overproduction." The act permitted the suspension of the antitrust laws, provided for codes of fair competition in industry, contained protective clauses for labor, and outlined a public works program involving an expenditure by a Public Works Administration (PWA) of $3,300,000,000.

To integrate the recovery measures the President created an executive council composed of the cabinet and the heads of the agencies recently established by Congress, including General Hugh S. Johnson, administrator of the National Recovery Administration (NRA), the agency responsible for the preparation and enforcement of the codes. To expedite matters, a "blanket code" was developed, which, for example, abolished child labor under fourteen, established a work week of thirty-five hours for industrial laborers and forty hours for white-collar groups, and set a minimum wage.

Specific codes soon followed, but criticisms of the NRA system soon were advanced. It sometimes was difficult to get the employers and workers to agree on the proper length of working hours. The American Federation of Labor took the opportunity to appear as a champion of labor, to increase its efforts to unionize all industry, and to fight the formation of company unions. Often the employers themselves in an industry found it impossible to agree, and then the government acted as arbitrator. Strikes continued and made the problem still more complex. Thus there was opposition to the NRA from both capital and labor, but, for the time being, popular sentiment backed the Democratic Administration.

To the London Economic Conference of 1933, Roosevelt made it plain that, in his opinion, the immediate removal of trade barriers was far more urgent than any immediate stabilization of currencies (as proposed by France). In view of this fundamental difference, the conference achieved little or nothing. Meanwhile prices, especially on farm products, once again had begun to fall, with consequent farm strikes and violence in many parts of the West. There was a growing demand for inflation, and the President authorized the Reconstruction Finance Corporation to purchase freshly mined domestic and foreign gold. Thus the dollar might be progressively cheapened and price levels "restored." The RFC began buying gold, but the increase in commodity prices did not keep pace with the drop of the dollar. Roosevelt therefore ordered the treasury, during the next four years, to purchase all silver mined in the United States at 50 per cent above the (December 1933) market price.

In the meantime, a Civil Works Administration had been organized to finance public works projects and thus remove names from the relief rolls. In some cases surplus food, clothing, and fuel were allotted directly to distressed families—thus reducing some of the commodity surpluses that had forced down prices. Another PWA allotment went to an emergency Housing Corporation, organized to purchase slum sections in the larger cities and erect on the sites low-cost apartment buildings.

Another avalanche of New Deal legislation was started in the 1934 Congress. Government loans to farmers were facilitated. The reorganization of bankrupt corporations was made easier. Money was made available for home-repair loans, and protection was offered to building-and-loan associations. A national board was created to mediate labor disputes growing out of the NIRA. Direct loans to industry were authorized.

All this and more was done to pave the road to recovery between January and June 1934. In the midterm elections held later in the year, the Democrats gained seats not only in the congressional, but in most of the state elections. In the Seventy-Fourth Congress, Roosevelt's party had a two-thirds majority in each house.

By the beginning of 1935 it was possible to estimate some of the effects of the New Deal legislation. Industrial production had reached 90 per cent of the average for the period from 1923 to 1925. About 4,000,000 persons had been reemployed. The banking system had been somewhat improved, and unfair practices in business had been curtailed. Certain results, however, were on the debit side. Thus, the imbalance between agricultural and industrial prices had not been adjusted. The cost of living had gone up without a commensurate rise in wages. And the national debt had risen steeply.

Roosevelt, nonetheless, informed Congress of his conviction that "the fundamental purposes and principles of the (NIRA) were sound" and that their abandonment was "unthinkable." He then asked for a two-year extension (until June 1937) of the act in somewhat modified form. While this proposal was being discussed, a new work-relief bill was voted, which appropriated $4,880,000,000 to be spent for recovery and "made-work" projects. Roosevelt dispensed the money to existing organs of administration and to newly created instruments, such as the Works Progress Administration (WPA).[8]

July 1935 saw the passage of the Wagner or National Labor Relations Act. This law required employers to bargain collectively with

---

[8] The WPA was involved in many projects, among them school building and rural electrification.

their workers and forbade them to do anything that might interfere with the full realization of the objectives of trade unionism. A National Labor Relations Board (NLRB) was created to enforce the provisions of the act, "which was frankly class legislation, in that it spoke only of industry's duty to labor."

In August 1935, finally, there was adopted a Social Security Act. This provided federal participation in insurance measures covering old age, unemployment, needy dependent children, and the destitute blind. The Social Security legislation was perhaps the most far-reaching reform to come out of the Roosevelt years. Although it was too late to be of significance in the thirties, it eventually became fixed in American life. With other government programs, it had the effect of giving the aged an increased purchasing power.

Meanwhile, in 1935, the Supreme Court shocked the government and delighted the opposition by declaring unconstitutional the whole NIRA establishment. The judges handed down three unanimous decisions, which declared unconstitutional much of the New Deal legislation.

The President was angry and declared that the decisions took the country back to the "horse-and-buggy days of 1789," but opponents of the New Deal held that the Constitution and country, after narrow escapes, had been saved. As the Administration busied itself with plans for continuing certain features of the NIRA project without contravening the Constitution, spokesmen for capital and labor issued contradictory statements on nearly every phase of past and proposed recovery legislation. Neither the leading employers nor the labor leaders seemed agreed among themselves as to the actual benefits or dangers of the NIRA. Hence the electoral campaign of 1936 gave promise of excitement.

A SECOND TERM, AND A THIRD

The Republican Party shelved its older leaders in 1936 and nominated Governor Alfred M. Landon of Kansas, a middle-of-the-roader. Landon had no national enemies and was expected to attract a large Western vote. The platform accused the Democrats of waste and of prolonging the depression, but it was vague on substitute proposals for recovery. The Democrats unanimously renominated Roosevelt and pledged a continuance of New Deal policies.

Much name-calling and bitterness characterized the campaign. The Roosevelt ticket was called communistic and Roosevelt "the Kerensky of the American Revolutionary movement." The followers of Landon were labeled economic royalists. And these were only the mildest epithets that were current. An American Liberty League, founded by Republican industrialists, backed Landon, and a newly organized American Labor Party gave its support to Roosevelt. In the end, the Democratic leader captured the electoral votes of every state except Maine and Vermont. His popular vote was 27,700,000 to 16,800,000 for Landon. Various minor parties together were able to win only 3 per cent of all votes cast.

Following the election, Roosevelt determined to reap the advantage of his popular endorsement. He believed himself in position to demand that Congress consolidate the changes of the New Deal. For this purpose he wanted further changes in three fields: in the judicial (where the Supreme Court had nullified important New Deal laws), in the administrative (where there was much waste and inefficiency), and in the legislative (where, in Congress, there still were many anti-Administration senators and congressmen).

Claiming that he consistently was opposed by five conservatives on the Supreme Court and supported only by four liberals, the President, in 1937, asked Congress to make possible an increase in the number of judges to fifteen. Such action was not without precedent, but Roosevelt's request aroused a storm of opposition, both within and without Congress, and it was charged that the Chief Executive was attempting to "pack" the court. The national legislature refused the President's bidding and merely permitted judges to retire at seventy at full pay. Though he was defeated in Congress, Roosevelt soon won a practical victory. One after another of the "nine old men" retired or died until, by 1941, the executive had had the opportunity to make seven appointments. The judicial verdicts, meanwhile, had come to be much more frequently favorable to the Administration.

During the midterm elections of 1938, Roosevelt tried, through promise of further changes, to get the solid backing of labor, agriculture, the unemployed, and the middle class. He specifically asked these voters to rid Congress of the "Bourbons" who opposed his policies; but this attempted purge of his political antagonists was almost a complete failure. Although the Democrats still controlled Congress, they lost a number of seats in both houses and several governorships. The voting doubtless was affected by an economic recession that had begun in 1937—perhaps because federal outlays were curtailed faster than private industry picked up—and by an increasingly widespread belief that the New Deal objectives were essentially inimical to basic property rights. The Republicans, with the aid of conservative Democrats, now could block further New Deal legislation. By 1939, the growing threat of war in Europe forced domestic affairs into the background and the main thrust of New Deal legislation expired.[9]

---

[9] Many American historians have attempted to assess the meaning of the New Deal in the history of the United States. Most agree that Roosevelt and his followers brought about a shift in economic power in American life, transferring considerable portions of available wealth to workers, farmers, and businessmen who had not previously shared in the nation's affluence. The questions arise over whether the New Deal represented a sharp change of direction or a logical continuity of the historical past. In

Although government efforts through the thirties had aided many, unemployment still was 10,000,000 in mid-1939. At that time, however, in view of the growing number of foreign and domestic armament orders, Congress provided for the gradual reduction of the relief rolls. By the time of the Second World War, Congress had voted $13,000,000,000 for relief, a sizable proportion of which was for defense measures.

The volume of relief expenditures, the increasing cost of administration caused by the many new agencies, and the added outlays occasioned by the numerous new federal functions, all combined to bring about a steady increase in taxes. There were those, too, who feared the rising power of the central government. These circumstances, plus the disturbing events of the Second World War, entered into the brisk contest which was the presidential election of 1940.

The Republican delegates in 1940 sidetracked the preconvention favorites and nominated a "dark horse": Wendell L. Willkie of New York and Indiana. Willkie was a former Democrat who, as president of the Commonwealth and Southern Corporation, had become an outstanding foe of New Deal policies, particularly as these concerned rural electrification under the TVA. A corporation lawyer by profession, he never had held public office. In foreign affairs he advocated maximum aid to Great Britain. From the time the balloting for candidates began, the gallery sitters chanted and shouted "We want Willkie" until, on the sixth ballot, they got him.

President Roosevelt refrained from commenting on a number of preconvention moves to draft him for a third term. But when the delegates gathered, he won nomination on the first ballot—partly because of the well-oiled state of the New Deal machinery and partly out of a fear that no other candidate would beat Willkie. Inasmuch as Vice-President John N. Garner and President Roosevelt no longer were on good terms, the convention nominated Secretary of Agriculture Henry A. Wallace to complete the ticket.

The platforms of the two parties bore many resemblances. Both advocated keeping the United States out of the war and rendering all possible aid short of war to Great Britain. Both promised to build up national defense, provide further economic relief, and pass legislation favorable to agriculture and labor. The Republicans con-

---

Louis M. Hacker's *The Shaping of the American Tradition,* the thesis is presented that the New Deal changed things so greatly that it actually constituted a "third American Revolution." On the other hand, historian Henry Steele Commager described it as the normal evolution of tendencies found in earlier American reformist traditions established by the Progressives and Populists. More recently, Richard Hofstadter, in his *The Age of Reform,* moved away from the idea that the New Deal was a "return to the preoccupations of Progressivism." Hofstadter observed that "the New Deal as a whole" was a "drastic new departure" in American history, which differed from Progressivism in "its ideas and its spirit and its techniques."

demned the extravagance of the New Deal and promised friendliness to business.

Both candidates were able, courageous, and popular. The third-term issue engendered heated discussions. In view of the situation in Europe, there was much talk about the advantage of keeping an experienced man in the White House. Party lines were widely crossed, so that there were Democrats for Willkie and Republicans for Roosevelt.

In the end, Roosevelt won. He captured the electoral votes of thirty-eight states to Willkie's ten; but in popular votes the count was 27,200,000 to 22,300,000. Willkie congratulated the winner and cooperated with him in seeking solutions for the problems facing the country. Having once more proved itself at home, American democracy soon found itself forced to fight for its existence against foreign enemies.

FOREIGN RELATIONS UNDER ROOSEVELT

The pressure of domestic affairs for a time absorbed most of the government's energies, but foreign questions soon demanded their share of official attention. To supplement domestic recovery efforts, the government by 1939 had negotiated reciprocal trade treaties with twenty-one foreign countries. To ease tariff bargaining, the President was authorized to lower or raise by not more than 50 per cent any existing duties on imports. The importance of these items became apparent when it was realized that "by 1938 some 380 bilateral special agreements were known to exist that excluded United States products." The secretary of state headed a delegation to the ill-fated London Economic Conference of 1933, and diplomatic relations with the Russians were reestablished in the same year—partly for business reasons.

In 1934 the United States became a member of the International Labor Organization. Four years later Washington ratified its first international labor convention. Like his predecessor, moreover, Roosevelt brought up the question of adherence to the World Court. The time seemed propitious since the Senate contained a large Democratic majority but, after a heated debate, the Senate in 1935 refused its consent to ratification.

The first Roosevelt Administration witnessed the collapse of the Geneva Disarmament Conference in 1934 and the expiration of the Washington and London naval-limitation agreements. A Japanese demand for naval parity with the United States and Great Britain was rejected by both of these powers, and Tokyo renounced the restrictive treaties. The congressional appropriations for the War and Navy Departments rose rapidly with each passing year, and additional sums for defense were forthcoming from work-relief funds. A committee headed by Senator Gerald P. Nye of North Dakota investigated (1934–1936) the munitions industry with a view to diminishing the possible influence of munitions makers on international disharmony and on the defeat of armament-limitation proposals. The reports of this committee, combined with the appearance of a large number of war novels of disillusionment and the stoppage of war-debt payments from the former Allies, all helped to spread a spirit of isolationism. This made it hard for Roosevelt to get public opinion aroused over the threat to the American way of life posed by totalitarianism.

The change in Latin American policy that had appeared during the Hoover Administration was carried further under Roosevelt. In his first inaugural address Roosevelt declared that he "would dedicate this nation to the policy of the good neighbor." Later, affirming that "the definite policy of the United States from now on is opposed to armed intervention," he said: "The maintenance of law and the orderly processes of government in this hemisphere is the concern of each individual nation within its borders first of all. It is only if and when the failure of orderly processes affects the other nations of the continent that it becomes their concern; and . . . in such an event it becomes the joint concern of the whole continent in which we are all neighbors."

The new official policy promptly was implemented and the deliberate cultivation of good relations with Latin America received almost universal approbation. The last United States marines were withdrawn from Haiti. A more liberal recognition policy as applied to Central America was inaugurated with the recognition of a de facto government in El Salvador. The United States reduced its controls over the internal affairs of Cuba. Similarly, improved relations were developed with other Latin American states. Late in 1936, when Roosevelt visited Buenos Aires and Río de Janeiro, he was received with ovations.

Out of these actions grew closer general relations among all the American republics. In 1936 these republics signed at Buenos Aires an American Collective Security Convention, which provided for the obligatory arbitration of disputes and consultation in the event of a threat to the peace of the Western Hemisphere. The Eighth Pan-American Conference at Lima in 1938 affirmed these principles in a Declaration of the Solidarity of America. Thus, twenty-one nations, not the United States alone, became the interpreters and executors of the Monroe Doctrine.

For some time after 1933 the international affairs of Europe filled United States citizens more with "distaste than alarm." Hence, many were confirmed in the isolationist views that they had built upon the foundations mentioned earlier. One result of this widespread feeling was a change in the traditional neutrality policy of the United States —that is, in the historic contention that there must be freedom of the seas and no interference with neutral trade in noncontraband goods with warring countries. The change was expressed in joint resolutions of Congress in 1935, 1936, and 1937.

These Neutrality Acts required the President, whenever he found that a state of war existed between foreign states, to proclaim the fact. Thereupon he also had to declare it unlawful to sell or transport war materials to any belligerent, purchase the securities of a belligerent, travel on belligerent ships, or arm United States merchantmen. Then, at his discretion, he might forbid: (1) the transportation on United States ships of *any* commodities to belligerents; (2) the shipment of goods until after they had been paid for and unless they were carried away in foreign bottoms (this cash-and-carry provision might be applied only until 1939); and (3) the use of United States ports to armed belligerent vessels. None of this applied to American republics if they were engaged in war with non-American states.

The President wanted the right to apply these restrictions only against the belligerent whom he might regard as the aggressor, but this concession Congress refused to make. Thus it happened that during the Ethiopian War and the Spanish Civil War the restrictions had to be applied to both sides, regardless of United States sentiment in favor of one or the other. This reacted to the advantage of Mussolini in one case and to that of Franco in the second. In the Far East, on the other hand, the President was able to refrain from declaring the existence of a state of war, and merely forbade government-owned ships to carry arms to either combatant and warned private shipowners that they transported war materials at their own risk. Thus it was possible to extend credits to China; but enormous quantities of scrap iron went to Japan.

Through this legislation Congress hoped to prevent a repetition of such incidents as the *Lusitania* sinking, which had helped to bring the United States into the First World War. But the exigencies of the Second World War soon led to further revision of the neutrality laws. Meanwhile, as has been indicated, the war played an important part in the Presidential campaign of 1940. From 1939, Roosevelt had warned of a war that might come to wrap the world, including the United States, "in flames." In 1941, with the disaster at Pearl Harbor, this prophecy was fulfilled.

The Second World War and After III

Return to War | 16

HOW WAR CAME AGAIN

The delegates of the Allied and Associated Powers who met at Paris in 1918–1919 to frame a peace settlement theoretically had a choice among several alternatives. They might have made the treaty with Germany so crushing that an early and powerful come-back would have been out of the question. Or, had they possessed a super-human detachment, they might have drafted a settlement so concili-atory as to provide little basis for the future growth of a movement in Germany sworn to nullify the treaty. As it happened, the Allied leaders adopted a middle course and drew up an instrument that was severe enough to make the Germans vengeful and moderate enough to enable the Reich to experience a great military revival within twenty years.

Germany's efforts to nullify the Versailles Treaty—on which it placed the blame for many difficulties that grew out of the war itself —were made easier by the fact that France and Great Britain, de-sirous of maintaining the status quo, both pursued the same end along divergent paths. As the former Allies drifted ever farther apart diplomatically, it became the easier and safer for Germany to revise the terms unilaterally—especially since the peace settlement had largely surrounded her with relatively weak neighbors. Instead of practical and effective Anglo-French cooperation in the enforcement of most treaty terms and the legal revision of others, there was an individualistic pursuit of diverse foreign policies conditioned by the disparate international needs of the ex-Allies. As a consequence, many of the worst postwar Franco-German quarrels developed into Franco-British quarrels, to the obvious advantage of Germany.

The French, no matter whether the Right bloc was in power or the

Left, sought with few exceptions to uphold the settlement of 1919. The Versailles Treaty became for them an object of high esteem. It represented to a harassed nation the only tangible guarantee of security. Each concession from its terms was looked upon as weakening the whole structure. Its general maintenance came to be regarded as the strongest protection against renewed evil from without—especially since the Guarantee Treaties that had been signed in 1919 by the representatives of the United States and Great Britain never came into force. To prevent, or at least minimize, treaty revision, the French, until 1935, gave active and directional support to the League of Nations and simultaneously sought military security according to a formula of their own making.

At League and disarmament conference meetings, the French repeatedly proposed the creation of an international police force and regularly maintained that their existing state of armament was the minimum permissible vis-à-vis Germany's existing state of disarmament. Great Britain and other states did not agree with these views, and so it happened that successive gatherings were devoted chiefly to quibbling. Paris therefore drew tight lines of alliance with Belgium, Poland, Czechoslovakia, Romania, and Yugoslavia. But in cementing friendships with these countries through political treaties and financial advances, France apparently did not realize that each of her allies also represented a strategic liability. Every one of these allies was relatively weak and surrounded by numerous past and potential enemies. When the test at last came, when Czechoslovakia needed French help in 1938, France found it inadvisable to fulfill her alliance pledges. For by that time France had decided to follow the lead of Great Britain in appeasing Germany.

Following traditional lines of British foreign policy, Great Britain had steadfastly refused, from 1919 to 1935, to assume any universal commitments for the preservation of peace. Believing that imperial considerations imposed special duties on them, the British, at least up to the Italian venture in Ethiopia, preferred to retain freedom of action in defense matters. Without the support of Great Britain, effective plans of collective security had little chance of success.

The British, feeling safe in the possession of a large fleet and content to rely on French armed might to shield them from any land attack, were interested chiefly in the revival of the world trade to which their economy was geared. With the passing of the years, British businessmen came to realize that, whereas Germany had been Great Britain's chief commercial and naval rival before 1914, she also had been one of Britain's best customers. Great Britain, therefore, not only tolerated but welcomed steps that might assist German economic recovery. Because the continuing quarrels over reparation, war debts, Rhineland occupation, armaments, and boundaries were harmful to the revival of trade, they were irritating to London. So the British, feeling relatively secure and anxious to foster world trade, and the French, feeling worried over the warlike activities east of the Rhine and preferring to see Germany weak and disorganized, failed to agree in their foreign relations and often acted at cross purposes.

It was only after the axis had demonstrated its nuisance value and after Italy had precipitated the Ethiopian crisis that Britishers in official circles seemed to recognize the dangers inherent in Britannia's unprepared position. Now that Nazi Germany was vigorously nullifying treaty terms, the British found that they simply dared not interpose what could only be inadequate armed resistance. The Chamberlain Government temporized and made concessions until such time as armament could be procured in sufficient quantity to back up British positions in international affairs. The French, unwilling to injure Italian *amour-propre* in the absence of outright British guarantees of help against German aggression, and torn by internal dissension occasioned by recent legislation, followed where the British led. The Paris Government, retiring behind the imagined impregnability of the Maginot Line, joined the British in appeasing an aggressive Germany.

Meanwhile, in Germany, the Weimar Republic had lost its fight for existence. In power, the Nazis first concentrated on the "coordination" of Germany's internal life and then embarked on a vigorous foreign policy. According to Nazi racial theory, if the superior Teutonic race wished to live on a high level it had to have inferior races to work for it. In Nazi opinion, Europe was filled with decrepit people who must be harnessed to serve the supposedly young master race.

At first the Nazis proceeded with relative caution, taking only one forceful step at a time and following each accomplishment with some form of pledge to make this achievement the last of its type. But as success followed success, with only verbal interference from the defenders of the status quo, the Nazis became bolder. They saw no point in stopping when it was so easy to go on. Only then, when the ultimate European aims of the Nazis became clear beyond a doubt, did the British and French realize that danger threatened not merely the little states of Central and Eastern Europe but the entire Western way of life.

Although it remained for Hitler to translate the challenge between the totalitarian and democratic ways of life into military action, it was Mussolini who first formulated that challenge. "The struggle between two worlds," he exclaimed, "can permit no compromise. Either we or they!" Basically, the distinction between the two ideologies lay in their differing conceptions of the position of the individual in the state. Under the democratic conception, as it was understood in the Western democracies, the individual was regarded as the creator and the rightful beneficiary of all state activity; he might be interfered with only when his doings reacted to the harm of his fellow individuals. The totalitarian conception was wholly anti-individualistic.

The dominant powers of the two camps were divided along economic and territorial as well as spiritual lines. The nations that upheld the political and territorial status quo were sometimes, in over-simplification, labeled the "Haves." The axis states were the "Have-nots." For reasons of economics, strategy, and prestige they demanded additional territory, old and new. In Germany and Japan, moreover, there were the additional incentives of political or religious philosophies which contemplated a world revolution culminating in the final hegemony of the respective "master race." Those who advocated totalitarian control had confidence in the power of a disciplined will to overcome the "spiritually weak" democracies. By the end of 1938, however, following wholesale German treaty repudiations, the democracies, if spiritually weak, had begun to show a determination to be militarily strong.

The British, for example, had outlined a costly arms program and drafted a plan of conscription to be put into effect immediately in the event of war. The French, too, had taken action, by oversub-scribing successive defense loans and strengthening the ties among the members of the French Empire. In the United States the Administration's campaign for increased armament was so energetically fostered that it evoked shrill protests in the overseas totalitarian press.

Meanwhile, in 1936, Germany had startlingly denounced the Locarno Pact of 1925. The Germans claimed that a new Franco-Soviet Pact, presented to the French Parliament for ratification early in 1936, had deprived the Locarno agreement of its "inner meaning." On the very day of Hitler's announcement, German soldiers re-entered the hitherto demilitarized Rhineland. The action was denounced in the Western press, but no official effort was made to apply sanctions or take reprisals.

The Belgains demonstrated worry over the self-confidence of the Nazis and the disinclination of London and Paris to cooperate strongly in the face of German and Italian challenges to the status quo. In 1936, therefore, Brussels announced that henceforth Belgium would pursue an exclusively Belgian policy. Britain and France endorsed this stand and bound themselves to preserve Belgium's integrity and release her from all obligations under the Locarno treaties.

The faith of the small states in the promises of their powerful allies was, however, severely shaken in 1938 and 1939 by the events accompanying Germany's absorption of Austria, the Sudeten areas, Czechia, Slovakia, and Memelland, and Italy's occupation of Albania. It was only after all these things had happened, that Great Britain and France discarded the policy of appeasement. Germany's next aggression precipitated war.

In summary, then, the war of 1939 was caused by these circumstances: The disillusionment and humiliation following military defeat in the First World War filled many Germans with a desire for revenge. Then, the awkward tactics of the Weimar Republic, the unhappy policy of alternating intransigence and concession on the part of the former Allies, and the effects of the world depression brought to power in Germany a group whose impelling philosophy called for the establishment of its hegemony over the continent and eventually beyond the confines of Europe. Meanwhile the British and the French, both intent on maintaining conditions as they were, followed divergent international policies. They drifted apart diplomatically at a time when, from a realistic point of view, they should have cooperated to implement by force of arms the system which they had established by force of arms. As time went on, there developed a great game of diplomatic bluff, with Germany and Italy on one side and Great Britain and France on the other. The Soviet Union sat by as an interested observer, leaning now to one side and then the other, determined not to be drawn in no matter how the game progressed. When, at last, one side called the other's bluff, the consequence was war. Poland was the unhappy victim of the critical move in the ghastly game played in the spring and summer of 1939.

1939: THE END OF TWENTY YEARS' ARMISTICE

Success having followed success in their unilateral revision of Versailles, the Germans in March 1939 centered their attention on Danzig and the Polish Corridor. By way of psychological preparation, they launched a press campaign against alleged anti-German excesses in Poland. This time the British were quick to grasp the Nazi strategy: stirring up minorities within neighboring states to disorder and then intervening to restore order. Hence, Prime Minister Chamberlain announced that Great Britain and France would aid the Poles if their independence were threatened. Hitler defied the British warning and threatened the Poles with dire consequences if they remained "obstinate." In April Germany denounced her naval agreement of 1935 with Great Britain and her nonaggression pact of 1934 with Poland. Simultaneously she demanded the return of Danzig and the right to maintain a rail and motor road across the Polish Corridor to East Prussia. Poland denied the German demands early in May.

An Italo-German alliance was signed in May 1939, which made it apparent that Italy was content to cede first place among the revisionists to the stronger Reich, and to follow where once she had led. When Great Britain and France agreed on mutual assistance with Turkey, Germany signed nonaggression pacts with Denmark, Estonia, and Latvia. In June Hitler began to speak of a new British plan to "encircle" Germany, and in July, Chamberlain indicated that any unilateral effort to reunite Danzig with the Reich would bring into operation the British guarantee of Polish independence. Hitler, however, continued to insist on territorial cession by Poland.

While military conversations were being held in Moscow among Soviet, British, and French officers, the German and Polish press began to carry atrocity stories, and there were clashes bringing death to both Germans and Poles. Hitler acted infuriated at the reports brought to him concerning the alleged mistreatment of his "racial comrades" in Poland. Some of his advisers, confident that London and Paris would not fight to save Warsaw, convinced him of the soundness of their analysis.

In August 1939 Germany and the Soviet Union, through Foreign Ministers Joachim von Ribbentrop and Viacheslav M. Molotov, signed a nonaggression pact. The ten-year agreement provided that the two parties would not resort to war against each other, would not support any third power in the event that it attacked either signatory, would consult on all matters of common interest, and would each refrain from associating with any grouping of powers aimed at the other. A secret protocol, made public in 1948, divided Eastern Europe into eventual German and Russian spheres.

The announcement of the Nazi-Soviet Pact struck many persons like the proverbial bolt from the blue. It seemed incredible that, after all the Nazi attacks on Bolshevism and the Soviet charges against Nazism, Stalin and Hitler should have become diplomatic partners. Yet the signing of the treaty really was not so astonishing. Germany did not want to have to worry about an immediate eastern front in the event that Britain and France came to Poland's support. Later, when the western states had been defeated, it would be easy to draft charges of broken faith against Moscow—preferably after the invasion of the Soviet Union had begun. The U.S.S.R., weakened by military purges and uncertain of the intentions of Britain and France, wanted all the time she could get to carry forward the military industrialization contemplated in the Third Five-Year Plan. The Nazi-Soviet Pact represented *Realpolitik* as much for one as the other.

After the signing of the Nazi-Soviet Treaty, events moved swiftly to a violent conclusion. On August 29 Germany demanded from Great Britain, who hoped that direct discussions might yet preserve peace, that she arrange to have a Polish delegate with full powers reach Berlin on the thirtieth. On the thirtieth the British explained that such a procedure was unreasonable and the time limit impracticable; London therefore urged that Germany follow the usual diplomatic procedure of transmitting her demands to Poland through the Polish Ambassador. When German Foreign Minister Ribbentrop received these advices from the British Ambassador at midnight, he replied by reading in German "at top speed" a sixteen-point proposal for the settlement of all German-Polish differences. But when Sir Nevile Henderson asked for a copy of the proposals, Ribbentrop "asserted that it was now too late as (the) Polish representative had not arrived in Berlin by midnight."

On the next day, August 31, the German Government broadcast the sixteen points; but when the Polish Ambassador tried to communicate the terms officially to his foreign minister, he was unable to do so because Berlin had cut all communications between the two countries. The Nazis then interpreted as a rejection of their overtures, the Polish Government's inability to send a representative on twenty-four hours' notice to accept a quasi-ultimatum, which had not yet been communicated to Warsaw. At 4:45 a.m. in the morning of September 1, Germany, without declaring war, sent its war planes to rain bombs on Polish cities and sent its soldiers to invade the Polish countryside.

Fifty hours later, on September 3, after Germany refused to withdraw from the territory it already had occupied and attend an international conference, Chamberlain informed the House of Commons that "this country is at war with Germany." The French Government adopted a similar view of the situation. Italy, as in 1914, declared her intention to remain neutral. Thus, twenty-five years and one month after the outbreak of the First World War, Europe entered the Second World War.

The Polish army had little opportunity to prove its worth. It was overwhelmed in less than a month by the mechanized might of Germany. Because Warsaw hesitated to order general mobilization until the last stage of political negotiations with Berlin; because Germany was informed by sympathizers of the day-by-day state of Polish preparations; because the Nazis disregarded the customary legal formalities preceding the opening of armed combat; and because the Germans had for some time been preparing for a drive on Poland, the Nazis were able to overwhelm the Polish defenders before the republic's armies were fully mobilized or properly concentrated.

The German forces, commanded by Colonel General Walther von Brauchitsch, were equipped with all the weapons of modern mechanized warfare. Preceded and accompanied by planes in coordinated attack, the armored units and infantry entered Poland simultaneously at four points. The suddenness of the onslaught enabled the invaders to destroy most of the Polish air force on the ground within two days. The loss of her air arm deprived Poland of necessary reconnaissance, and the Germans, aware of Poland's military dispositions, disrupted communications, interfered with formations, and terrorized the municipal populations and the refugees on the cluttered roads. On the first day of the fighting, the Nazi leader of Danzig, Albert Forster, proclaimed the reunion of the Free City with the Reich.

Poland hoped for aid from her allies in two forms: aerial assistance and a major attack on the Reich's western border. But aid in neither form was forthcoming. German air superiority and the destruction of Poland's air fields made it little short of impossible to send French or British planes to Poland's support. The French army, with its psychology of supposed security behind the Maginot Line and its belief in the equal impregnability of the German West Wall, did not launch any large-scale attack.

Meanwhile the partially mobilized Polish infantry and cavalry retreated steadily before the advancing enemy. Within two weeks, most of Poland's western provinces were occupied and Warsaw was virtually surrounded. Then, while the capital gallantly defied bombings and bombardments for three weeks, several Polish armies withdrew to the south and east, hoping to establish a new line along the Dniester River and there await Anglo-French aid through Romania. But then soldiers of the Soviet Union poured into eastern Poland, ostensibly to protect the resident Ukrainian and White Russian minorities. The Polish Government fled to Romania, there to be interned. When battered Warsaw surrendered, the fighting virtually came to an end.

On September 28, 1939, Foreign Ministers Ribbentrop and Molotov partitioned Poland formally. The Soviet Union acquired slightly more than half the territory and substantial oil resources. Germany secured more of the people and the major share of industry and mining. Thus was completed the fifth partition of Poland, following those of 1772, 1793, 1795, and 1815.

The Poles, however, did not quit the war. A Polish Government, having been accorded British and French recognition, set itself up at Angers in France, where it received extraterritorial privileges and the right to receive foreign representatives. After the defeat of France, the government moved to Great Britain, where sizable Polish forces were reorganized to continue the fight against Germany.

About 36,000 square miles of Poland were incorporated directly by Germany, and a process of "Germanization" was begun at once. The place names were Germanized so that Gdynia, for example, was renamed Gotenhafen. The incorporated area was converted into a *Gouvernement-Général,* with its capital at Cracow and Dr. Hans Frank as its administrative head.

The territory was used as a depository for Poles and Jews who had been or were to be gathered from their homes and herded into this one crowded area. The lands thus vacated were to be converted into homesteads for the 1,500,000 "Germans" still living in the Italian Tirol, the Baltic states, and former eastern Poland. The task of organizing these transfers of population was assigned to the much feared head of the secret police (Gestapo), Heinrich Himmler. He planned to exterminate the Jews and many Poles and force the remainder of the Polish population to act as servants for the Germans.

The lot of the German-speaking people compulsorily transferred from the Tirol and from the Baltic regions, where their families had lived for centuries, was bad; official sentiment towards them, however, was summarized by a Nazi paper in the words: "Baltic Germans will not have the leisure to look backwards, but will be put straight into their new surroundings." But the lot of the non-Germanic victims of this policy was terrible. Western Poles, for example, either were forced into the Gouvernement-Général, where the cities rapidly became overcrowded, or were carried off by the thousands to work in German fields. At best, they could expect orders to raise on their own farms specified crops and then to surrender portions of them to the conquerors.

The usage of Polish peasants was the least cruel of any; the harshest treatment was reserved for the clerical, professional, and

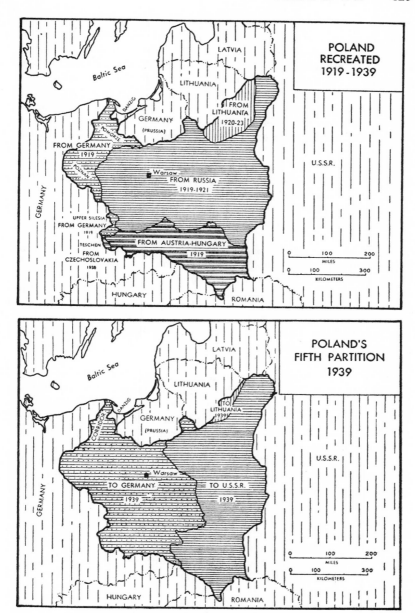

POLAND: RECREATED AND REPARTITIONED

From MacFadden, C. H. *An Atlas of World Review*, New York,
Thomas Y. Crowell Company, 1940. Reprinted by permission.

commercial classes. The Germans regarded these as the leaders and the ones most likely to keep alive the flame of Polish nationalism. Thus, they were marked for annihilation. Polish participation in the trades and the professions was reduced to a minimum, and inter-marriage or even "comradeship" between Poles and Germans was forbidden. The cruelties perpetrated on the Jews were beyond belief. Jews from all German-controlled territories in Europe were forced into one huge Polish ghetto. There several millions were gassed or burned to death at such extermination camps as that of Auschwitz.

SOVIET AGGRESSION, 1939-1940

The occupation of eastern Poland marked only the beginning of the Soviet Union's policy of erecting buffers between herself and Germany. Shortly after Germany and the U.S.S.R. partitioned Poland, Moscow signed pacts of mutual assistance with Estonia, Latvia, and Lithuania. The Soviet Government had summoned each foreign minister to Moscow and convinced him of the desirability of acquiescence. The Soviet Union acquired bases in each of the Baltic republics but promised not to interfere with their political, eco-nomic, or social systems. Soviet garrisons promptly were dispatched to all three states, and the Nazi Government began the repatriation of Baltic citizens of German descent. Apparently Berlin had given prior approval to the Soviet Union's tactics.

Keeping pace with German victories and gains, the Soviet Union in 1940, on the day on which Nazi soldiers entered Paris, presented an ultimatum to Lithuania. The document contained complaints of the violation by Lithuania of the pact of mutual assistance and demanded the replacement of the government by one that would "enjoy the confidence" of Moscow. Two days later similar ultimata were sent to Latvia and Estonia. In all three cases the governments resigned, the territories were occupied by the Red Army, and newly chosen Russian-oriented governments requested admission into the U.S.S.R. Moscow obliged in August 1940.

In June 1940 Moscow also presented an ultimatum to Romania, demanding the immediate "return" of Bessarabia and the cession of northern Bukovina, whose inhabitants were said to be "connected" with the Soviet Union through a "community of historic destinies." Bucharest appealed to Berlin and Rome for advice—and was told to meet the Soviet demands. The Soviet Union also made further terri-torial gains in the north, but for these she had to fight against Finland.

The Soviet Government professed uneasiness over the circum-stance that the land and sea approaches to Leningrad (via Finland and the Gulf of Finland) were in foreign hands. Moscow therefore adopted the same tactics vis-à-vis Finland that she so successfully pursued with Estonia, Latvia, and Lithuania. In October 1939 the

Soviet Government invited Helsinki to send a negotiator to the Kremlin.

The Bolsheviks presented a specific set of demands. Most important among them was the requirement that a Finnish port be given to the Russians for use as a naval base. Finland was prepared to acquiesce in most demands, but firmly refused to lease a site for a foreign military base. The negotiations broke down in the middle of November, and the Red press began to heap abuse on Helsinki. Ignoring a proposal to renew negotiations, the Soviet Government on November 30, 1939, ordered its airplanes and soldiers to cross the frontier for war. On the next day Moscow recognized a puppet "People's Government," set up near the Soviet border. While the legal government moved to defend Finland's borders and appealed to the League of Nations for help, the puppet regime granted the Soviet territorial demands.

The League acted with unwonted speed. Within two weeks the Soviet Union was declared the aggressor and expelled from the League. The Secretariat was authorized to coordinate whatever assistance the individual League members might lend Finland. Thus left to their own devices, many League members sent foodstuffs, medical supplies, and implements of war. Volunteers flocked to the Finnish colors, and even Italy sent some airplanes. But any really effective accretion of fighting power was denied Finland by the stand of her neighbors, Norway and Sweden. Permitting almost unlimited private help, the two Scandinavian kingdoms denied the right of passage for the soldiers whom France and Great Britain were willing to send to Finland's aid. Thus Finland, with her population of 4,000,000, was left to fight it out with the Soviet Union and her 180,000,000.

Soviet strategy called for an invasion of Finland at five points along its borders. The Finnish defense was entrusted to the experienced anti-Bolshevik fighter, General Baron Karl Gustav von Mannerheim. For weeks, the Finns fought stubbornly, while the Soviet Command made several mistakes. It launched its offensives with inadequately trained men; neglected to provide transportation security for supplies; and failed to ensure coordination among the armies.

Eventually the Russians decided to take firmer hold of the situation. They brought into the battle more and better troops, provided better weapons, and placed the energetic General Gregory Stern in charge of operations. Finnish cities were subjected to frequent bombings. At last, on March 12, 1940, the Treaty of Moscow brought a silencing of the guns.

The terms of the treaty were more exacting than the original demands of the U.S.S.R. Finland ceded considerable territory. No Finnish war vessels or military aircraft might be stationed in or adjacent to the republic's Arctic waters. The U.S.S.R. was permitted for thirty years to lease the port of Hangö for conversion into a Soviet naval base.

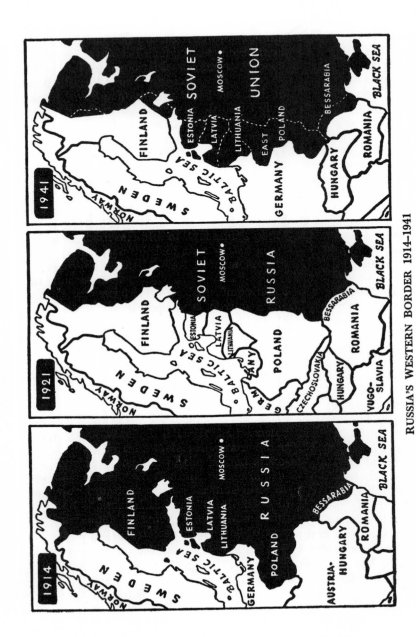

RUSSIA'S WESTERN BORDER 1914–1941

Courtesy, Foreign Policy Association, *Headline Series.*

The Soviet Union organized the new territories into the Karelian-Finnish Socialist Federated Soviet Republic and thus added another to the constituent republics of the U.S.S.R. But most of the 400,000 former inhabitants of the area packed their movable belongings and wandered back across the new border into Finland. It was not the least difficult reconstruction problem of the Helsinki Government to find new homes for these loyal subjects. Thus did the military preoccupation of the other great powers of Europe make easy the path of Soviet aggrandizement from the Arctic Circle to the Black Sea.[1]

[1] An important historical argument surrounds the beginning of World War II in Europe. The problem of fixing guilt for the war has dominated the writings of many, just as it did after World War I. First, there was the judgment, handed down at the Nuremberg War Trials (see Chap. 20), that Germany's Nazi leaders had deliberately started the war. This view began to be modified by some in 1948. Their opinion was influenced by the development of the "Cold War" and the consequent disappearance of agreement among the former allies.

In 1948 the United States Department of State published a collection of captured German documents, not used at Nuremberg, indicating the full nature of the Nazi-Soviet Pact of August 23, 1939, which, in effect surrendered Poland to Nazi designs. Out of this knowledge developed an obvious historical question: How long had such an alliance of opposites been part of the Soviet's long-range planning? Leonard Schapiro, in his *The Communist Party of the Soviet Union,* held that Stalin nurtured the idea of an eventual bargain with Hitler as early as 1936. The Soviet Union countered such charges by publishing its own series of documents, charging in accompanying comment that the British and French leaders of the 1930's had designedly appeased Hitler. This view has not been widely accepted, but is upheld in D. F. Fleming's, *The Cold War and Its Origins, 1917–1960.*

There have been those on the extreme Right in the United States, as well as the Communist Left, who have sought to fix blame on American leadership, particularly Roosevelt, for the outbreak of war. The best known example of this view was Charles Callan Tansill's *Back Door to War* (1952), in which it is argued that Roosevelt encouraged Poland, Britain, and France to resist Hitler's demands. Tansill saw Roosevelt culpable of remaining antagonistic, although unprovoked by Nazi actions, toward Hitler between 1933 and 1939. The Tansill book has been thoroughly criticized by scholars. By far the majority of historians in the West have continued to see Hitler as the one most responsible for the outbreak of hostilities. There is one important exception to this rule.

In 1961, the British historian A. J. P. Taylor touched off controversy by stating that Hitler's aims in 1939 were modest and that he had not schemed to start war. Taylor's staunchest opponent was the British historian R. Trevor-Roper, who suggested that Taylor was critical of the 1939 failure fully to appease Hitler because he wished to popularize the idea of appeasing Russia in the sixties. The more common interpretation of Taylor's work can be noted in this quotation from the writings of the United States historian, Arthur J. May: "On many counts a talented historian, Taylor glories in heterodoxy and often appears to indulge in controversy for controversy's own sake."

Most Western historians continue to regard Hitler as the one most responsible for the outbreak of hostilities. The number of important revisionist studies appearing after World War I has not been equaled for the Second World War.

The First Year of the War in the West   17

FROM SEPTEMBER 1939 TO MARCH 1940

Following the close of the campaign in Poland, Hitler addressed the Reichstag, saying: "Why should this war in the west be fought? ... Poland of the Versailles Treaty will never rise again." Following the technique used in earlier speeches, he then declared that Germany had no further "demands," save that "for the return of German colonies." If this peace offer were refused, "then we shall fight." Understandably, France and Great Britain decided to carry on until more effective guarantees against aggression were forthcoming than Hitler's "unsupported word."

Benefiting by some costly lessons of the First World War, the Allies[1] in 1939 quickly created unified military, naval, and air commands. British officers were placed in charge of the Allied sea and air forces, and General Marie Gustave Gamelin became commander of the Allied armies. In the first five weeks of the war 158,000 British soldiers were transported to France.

For a time there was little military activity on the western front. Neither side cared to risk the disproportionate casualties that presumably would accompany an offensive against "impregnable" defenses. Certain French leaders, in particular, were so steeped in a "Maginot psychology" that they vowed the enemy would be worn down in a war of attrition. Hence, while the Germans conquered Poland, the Allies were content to capture a few advance posts inside the western German border. Then, when thousands of Germans, freed from duty in the east, were sent to the West Wall, the Allied soldiers were withdrawn from German soil and put to work improv-

[1] All British Dominions save Ireland promptly joined the mother country in the war.

ing French defensive positions. The Germans, too, temporarily confined their land activities to bringing more troops to the French border, and to those of Belgium and the Netherlands. There were several "scares" in both monarchies lest the Germans invade them in an effort to outflank the Maginot Line; but the threat did not materialize until the spring. So it happened that the only *Blitz* or lightning of the winter of 1939–1940 was that provided by the weather—the severest in half a century. Thus, this period in the conflict was dubbed by journalists *Sitzkrieg* or "sitting war."

British activities at this time were designed essentially to spread propaganda in Germany and carry on reconaissance. The naval aspects of the war, however, were spectacular, even in 1939. The combined British and French fleets had a tonnage almost nine times that of the German. But there were tens of thousands of miles of sea lanes that had to be guarded against German raiders and submarines, for the German naval commander, Grand Admiral Erich Raeder, put into immediate practice unrestricted submarine warfare. Once again it was to be British blockade versus German submarines, with the surface units of the German fleet generally remaining in the protected waters adjacent to the mainland. As in the First World War, also, Winston Churchill became Britain's First Lord of the Admiralty.

Considerable British and French merchant shipping was destroyed in the first seven months of the fighting. To speed up their campaign, the Germans also torpedoed neutral ships and then resorted to indiscriminate sowing of mines. Meanwhile the oceans virtually had been cleared of German merchant shipping.

A final item to be noted about the first seven months of the war was a change in the French Government. Daladier, reputed to be a "strong man," seemed to enjoy general confidence in the fall of 1939. His measures against the Communists in the early days of the war— the suspension of Communist municipal councilors and the unseating of most of the Communist parliamentary deputies—were generally approved, even by the Socialists, who seemed to have lost their faith in Moscow after the signing of the Nazi-Soviet Pact. But this popularity waned as the public became increasingly dissatisfied with the leisurely prosecution of the war and with the failure to give direct aid to Finland. The unfavorable peace imposed on Finland soon was followed by the resignation of Daladier. He was succeeded (March 1940) by his Minister of Finance Paul Reynaud.

Reynaud eventually promoted to brigadier general, the leading French advocate of mechanized warfare, Charles Joseph de Gaulle. Reynaud, who shared de Gaulle's views, now brought him into his cabinet as Under-Secretary of War. Unfortunately for the French, the two men were not in position to cooperate effectively until it was too late. Too late, because the German mechanized advance was about to begin.

THREE MONTHS OF BLITZKRIEG,
APRIL-JUNE 1940

The *Sitzkrieg* in the West ended when German forces, moving in concert over a thousand-mile front, began the occupation of Denmark and Norway. The Germans claimed to know that the Allies had planned to seize Norway, and that Allied aggressive intentions were indicated by the fact that the British had begun placing mines along the Norwegian coast. The mining of Norwegian coastal waters actually was designed to impede the passage of German ships bringing vital ore from Sweden.

The occupation of small, poorly armed, and unsuspecting Denmark was a simple matter. Shortly before five o'clock in the morning of April 9, 1940, the Danish Government received a German note stating that Berlin had "indubitable evidence" of Allied plans to use Scandinavian territories as a battleground. To forestall such action, Germany intended to "protect" these regions, for they obviously could not adequately defend themselves. Any and all resistance would be "crushed" by German military power. Actually, German forces entered Denmark before Copenhagen had time to reply. King Christian X and Premier Thorvald Stauning accepted the situation under protest.

In Norway the story developed differently. There, too, the presentation of a note demanding the surrender of the kingdom to German administration, in order to forestall supposed Allied designs, was accompanied by the landing of Nazi troops at half a dozen ports. King Haakon VII and Premier Johan Nygaardsvold rejected the German demand and prepared to fight. Because the Germans readily got control of Oslo, the government had to flee; the King indeed, had to flee from place to place, hunted by German airplanes.

The Germans met relatively little resistance in their simultaneous landings because Norwegian "Fifth Columnists,"[2] collaborators in the army and government, combined with the attacking forces to paralyze any effective resistance. Most conspicuous among these fifth columnists was Major Vidkun Quisling, head of the Norwegian Nazis, who in the parliamentary elections of 1936 had failed to elect a single member. But as Minister of War for a brief period in 1932–1933, Quisling had appointed a number of garrison commanders who now surrendered their charges to little bands of Nazi troops. It was to him that the Germans turned when they sought a native chief for a puppet government.

While the Germans were extending their control against the re-

---

[2] This phrase usually was credited to General Emilio Mola, a supporter of Franco during the Spanish Civil War. He was reported to have said, on approaching Madrid, that, besides the four military columns then advancing on the Loyalist capital, a fifth column of Nationalist sympathizers already was inside the city, ready to cut off the Republican retreat.

THE SCANDINAVIAN REGION 1940

sistance of isolated Norwegian units, the Allies promised "full aid" to the Scandinavian kingdom. Some ships were sent, and 12,000 soldiers were landed, but the Allied effort was a failure. The Germans, through control of the best ports and with air superiority, were able to frustrate several Allied plans for reconquest. In June, with a German advance into France under way, the Allies left Norway and took King Haakon to London with them. The King at once issued a proclamation to his people to cease active resistance, and so another phase of the war ended in German victory. The Germans now tried to win support for their cause in Norway by turning the civil administration over to the native Quisling. The major failed to convert his countrymen to the new doctrines and eventually was removed from office, though he did stay on as head of the local Nazis, the only party permitted by the Germans. To his discomfort and the Germans' irritation, the Norwegians showed great ingenuity in their resistance, both passive and active.

Through the Scandinavian venture, the Nazis gained several advantages. They now had additional air, naval, and submarine bases, some of them closer to northern Britain than they had had before.

They no longer had to worry about the possibility of attack through the northern countries. They acquired the gold reserves of Denmark and large stores of oil, foodstuffs, and munitions. They could divert from Britain and France and steer toward Germany all the surplus products of the conquered areas. Even Swedish exports could now be counted almost wholly for the German side.

The Allies, despite a loss of prestige, also made some gains. They got the use of about sixty Norwegian war vessels and most of the Norwegian merchant fleet, the fourth largest in the world. These thousand ocean-going vessels helped keep Britain supplied with the oil and food without which she could not have continued the war. Eventually the people in the conquered regions formed resistance movements and greatly hampered the German war effort. British and Canadian forces occupied the Faroe Islands, Iceland, and Greenland, all formerly tied to Denmark.

For some time, there had been apparent a growing British dissatisfaction with the conduct of the war. Finally, the Scandinavian situation brought about a political crisis culminating in Chamberlain's resignation. As the Finnish troubles led to the resignation of Daladier in France, so in Great Britain the Norwegian invasion was "the culmination of other discontents." The people of Britain now wanted vigor and imagination in their government, and Chamberlain seemed to possess neither of these qualities. Hence, on May 10, 1940, a few hours after German soldiers had begun to swarm into Luxembourg, Belgium, and the Netherlands, Neville Chamberlain tendered his resignation to the king. On the following day Winston Churchill crowned a long and forceful political career by becoming Prime Minister. Fearless, energetic, and possessed of a vivid imagination, he gave promise of infusing a new spirit not only into the cabinet, but into the whole conduct of Britain's greatest war.

The Churchill Cabinet included both Chamberlain and some of the former prime minister's outstanding critics, such as Anthony Eden. There were also several Laborite leaders, particularly Clement Attlee and Minister of Labor Ernest Bevin, who distinguished himself for his energy and organizing ability. Chamberlain at last retired in October 1940, dying shortly thereafter. But now to return to the German invasion of Luxembourg, Belgium, and the Netherlands.

Late in the evening of May 9 the Netherlands Intelligence Service warned the government of impending attack. The authorities took certain precautionary measures that earlier had been agreed upon and then tensely awaited some notice of German intentions.

Meanwhile, unknown to the Netherlanders, in the darkness before dawn on May 10, Hitler had instructed the *Wehrmacht* as follows:

The hour has come for the decisive battle for the future of the German nation. For three hundred years the rulers of England and France have made it their aim to prevent any real consolidation of Europe and above all to keep Germany weak and helpless. With this your hour has come.

The fight which begins today will decide the destiny of the German people for a thousand years. Now do your duty.

At four o'clock in the morning of May 10, without notice of any sort, German soldiers poured into the Netherlands, as German airplanes dropped bombs on sleeping cities and German parachutists took over Netherlands' airports. Only then did the Netherlands Government ask Great Britain and France for help. For even after the German occupation of Denmark and Norway, the Netherlands, relying partly on German promises and partly on its own strength, had hoped to remain neutral.

Not until two hours after the attack began did the German Minister to The Hague explain the grounds for Germany's action and demand the submission of the Netherlands. Once more Berlin untruthfully claimed to have "irrefutable evidence of an immediately threatening invasion by British and French forces in Belgium, the Netherlands, and Luxembourg, prepared a long time beforehand with the knowledge of the Netherlands and Belgian governments." The Netherlands Government responded by accepting a state of war with Germany.

Again, as the Nazi armored columns poured into the Netherlands, the conquest of the country was speeded by the aid of local helpers. Some of these fifth columnists were Netherlanders. Others were Germans who earlier had entered the Netherlands as "tourists," "salesmen," or "students."

The slaughter was so great that, after five days of fighting, General Henrik Winkelman ordered the Netherlands army to cease firing. The victorious Germans, however, were unable to achieve one major objective, namely, the capture of Queen Wilhelmina and the members of her family and government. After passing through many dangers, the royal family and several prominent officials escaped to Great Britain and remained free to command the vast Netherlands colonial possessions on the side of the Allies. Meanwhile the kingdom itself, with its largest cities partially in ruins, was placed under the commissionership of Arthur Seyss-Inquart, the same man who two years earlier had helped to hand his native Austria over to the Third Reich. He found his new task difficult, for the Netherlanders proved stubborn and unbending. The staunch burghers were remarkably skillful in thinking up forms of passive resistance.

The fall of the Netherlands rendered easier the conquest of Belgium.[3] Here again, the recent policies of the government had reacted to German advantage. In 1936 King Leopold III had declared that henceforth the kingdom must pursue a policy "exclusively and entirely Belgian," without any alliances. The request for release from the obligations of the Locarno Agreements had been endorsed by Great Britain and France in 1937. Six months later Berlin had prom-

[3] Luxembourg, with a population of 300,000, fell in a day. Grand Duchess Charlotte escaped first to France and then to North America.

ised to respect Belgium's "inviolability," unless she took part in a military action aimed at Germany. Thereafter Belgium had resisted all efforts at military cooperation with its former allies, preferring to trust the pledges of Germany and the strength of its own defenses.

Crossing into Belgium at the same time that they had entered the Netherlands, the Germans again withheld notice until after the fighting had begun. With a larger and better-equipped army than that of the Netherlands and in better geographic position to receive Allied aid, Belgium was expected to put up stiff resistance. But once again the Nazis rushed ahead, investing cities, driving a wedge between the Belgians and their Allied reinforcements, and breaking up the opposing armies and enveloping their sections one by one. Within a week the Germans were in Brussels, and Hitler reincorporated into the Reich the districts of Eupen, Malmédy, and Moresnet, lost to Belgium by the Treaty of Versailles.

Meanwhile, aware that the French had weakened the defensive system behind Sedan by moving soldiers from there to assist the Belgians, the Nazis struck in full force across the Meuse River. The Maginot Line was weak at this northern end, for the French had counted (in vain) on a Belgian extension of the line to the Netherlands borders, and the Germans broke through with relative ease. Within four days they created a sixty-mile gap in the French defenses. A few more days, and the Germans had smashed their way westward to the coast and driven the main French forces south of the Somme River. To the north, the British and Belgian armies were reduced to dependence for supplies and help on the Channel ports alone.

Driving along the French coast, the Nazis simultaneously pounded away at the Belgian army to the northeast of Dunkirk. Generalissimo Maxim Weygand, recently appointed to Gamelin's place, flew to the headquarters of Leopold, who had taken personal command of the Belgian forces. The King warned Weygand that only "substantial new assistance" would enable the Belgians to continue the fight. When no such aid was forthcoming, Leopold, against the pleas of his entire government, asked the Germans for terms. The Nazis demanded unconditional surrender. On May 28, 1940, the King complied and ordered his soldiers to stop fighting.

The Belgian Cabinet, some members of the Belgian Parliament, and many soldiers repudiated Leopold's action and fled to France and then Great Britain, there to continue the fight against the Germans. Whatever the verdict of history on Leopold's act, the end of Belgian resistance placed approximately 400,000 British and French soldiers, who had been sent to help Belgium, in a terrible predicament. Harried by the Germans on the south, and now with their northern flank exposed, they were pushed into a corner of Flanders, in the vicinity of Dunkirk, with only the sea at their back.

Yet, successful as they thus far had been, the Germans failed in their effort of May 29–June 4 to "annihilate" the enemy. On June 4 they did enter the ruins of Dunkirk, but during the preceding days 335,000 of the supposedly doomed Britishers and Frenchmen had been returned from there to England. Disaster had been averted through the gallant stands of a small Anglo-French force in Calais to the south of Dunkirk and of a French tank unit around Lille to the east of Dunkirk; through the tireless work of the crews of about 220 Allied war vessels and 650 other craft of every size and description; through the ability of the Royal Air Force to achieve air superiority in the limited sphere above Dunkirk; and by foggy weather, which apparently helped the Allies as much as it hampered the Germans.

On the other hand, the Germans, after twenty-five days of fighting, were in occupation of Luxembourg, the Netherlands, Belgium, and northern France. Indeed, from Abbeville northward to the Arctic Circle, every mile of European coast was under German domination. The strategic basis for German victory again had been a combination of meticulous preparation, perfect coordination, surprise, the fullest use of mechanization, and the aid of persons behind the enemy lines.

In front of the German advance the roads had become cluttered with refugees, who hampered the soldiers' movements and who therefore were machine gunned from German airplanes. For the Germans also had given false evacuation orders as part of their battle plan, thus adding to the welter of confusion that helped bring them easy victory.

While the fighting at Dunkirk was in progress, Generalissimo Weygand tried to create a new line south of the Somme and Aisne rivers. On June 5, the Germans launched a terrific attack along more than 100 miles of this hastily constructed Weygand Line. Thus began the Battle of France.

Eager to put France out of the war before the British could send another expeditionary force across the Channel, the Germans used their full might in the new campaign. The French fought courageously, but could not check the Nazi drive. Aside from man power, the greatest French deficiency was in planes, and this deficiency the British could make up only in small part. On June 10, the French Government, taking Weygand's advice, left Paris. On this same day Italy entered the war. Mussolini, "who had been becoming more and more bellicose with each advance of the Germans," informed a crowd in the Piazza Venezia that "a declaration of war already has been handed to the ambassadors of Great Britain and France."

Unable now to get replacements from the soldiers stationed on the Italian border, the tired French fighters in the north continued to fall back, and the Germans began an encirclement of Paris. Lest that city be made to suffer the fate of Warsaw and Rotterdam, the French Government decided to surrender it without a fight. German soldiers entered Paris on June 14, finding the French capital only slightly damaged, but with streets deserted and deathly still.

The fall of Paris had an adverse effect on the morale of the French leaders, the more so since Weygand informed a cabinet meeting that "all is lost." In this view he was supported by the aged vice-premier, Marshal Pétain, the "hero of Verdun." A number of highly placed Frenchmen and Frenchwomen now urged Reynaud to ask for an armistice.

Reynaud held out for a time. He could not believe that France had collapsed, and he did not want to desert his British allies. Supported by de Gaulle, he pleaded with Churchill and asked Roosevelt for "clouds of planes." But such aircraft were not available. Roosevelt sent words of encouragement, and Churchill offered a constitutional Franco-British Union with common citizenship and joint ministries, but neither of these was of immediate help. On June 16, 1940, finding a majority of his cabinet and advisers in favor of "peace," Reynaud resigned. President Albert Lebrun called on the eighty-four-year-old Pétain to form a new government.

Pétain quickly appointed a cabinet, the most conspicuous member of which was Pierre Laval, former premier and long advocate of collaboration with Italy and Germany. With equal speed the new Premier requested Spain to act as intermediary in asking Germany for an armistice. He gave no satisfactory reply to the British officials, who were sent to remind him that the British Government had informed Reynaud of its readiness to release France from her pledge not to conclude a separate peace only on condition that the "French fleet were dispatched to British ports and remained there while negotiations [between the French and Germans] were taking place."

The Germans, meanwhile, easily had continued their march. By June 16 they were in occupation of about one-fourth of France. Hence Hitler was in no hurry to answer the French request. He held a meeting with Mussolini to talk over prospective terms and did not receive the French armistice delegation until June 21—in the same railway coach and in the same Compiègne Forest to which German delegates had been summoned on a similar mission twenty-two years earlier. The Frenchmen accepted the armistice terms and then flew to Rome, there to receive the Italian armistice demands. These also were accepted and firing ceased officially at 12:35 A.M. on June 25, 1940. At this time the Germans were in occupation of more than half of France and claimed to have taken 2,000,000 prisoners. The Italians were in occupation of a narrow strip of French territory, which they had conquered in an offensive begun on the day after France had asked Italy for an armistice.

The Franco-German armistice terms were calculated to prevent a French renewal of hostilities and to enable the Reich to continue the war against Britain without interruption. Germany was to occupy more than half of France, including most of the industrial regions, all the Atlantic ports, and Paris. Except for a small number of men to maintain order, all French forces were to be demobilized.

The French fleet, except for ships needed to protect the colonial empire, was to be brought together in specified ports and disarmed under German-Italian control. Germany "solemnly declared" its intention not to use such naval units during the war, save for coast surveillance and mine sweeping. No Frenchman might serve against Germany in foreign units, and no airplanes might leave from unoccupied France. France must pay the costs of the occupying forces, repatriate the inhabitants who had left the occupied area, and release all German prisoners of war. The armistice might be denounced "at any moment" by Germany if France were delinquent in fulfilling her obligations. The Franco-Italian armistice terms were similar to the German ones.

THE INVASION OF FRANCE 1940

Now Hitler had ridden the wave of victory to the English Channel. Seven states had fallen to Nazi arms, and all the continent from the English Channel to the Russian border was dominated by the Germans. Only England remained. But before the Battle of Britain is examined, a brief survey of France's situation under a new administration will serve to illustrate the nature of Hitlerian occupation.

THE END OF THE THIRD REPUBLIC

The Third French Republic died in July 1940, when the National Assembly invested Pétain with power to promulgate a new constitution. Its epitaph might well have read: "Born and died in military defeat, inflicted by German armies." But such an epitaph, while stating a fact, would hardly explain the demise of the republic. Even the hundreds of books and thousands of articles that have been written on the fate of France fail to give a clear picture of the fundamental causes of the disaster. These causes obviously are difficult to isolate, but it is possible to survey some contributory factors in the decline and fall of the Third Republic.

The collapse of France was not caused by the Nazi invasion alone. The very ease with which the Germans advanced offered circumstantial evidence of internal weakness. There was, indeed, a long list of corroding influences: the division of the country, ever since the French Revolution, into two Frances, bitterly divided one against another, was of singular importance.

An excellent description of the "two Frances" was given in 1934 by a sympathetic observer in these words:[4]

The French Revolution irrevocably divided the internal policies of France; since that time there have been twin Frances, mortal enemies. The residual bitterness of the American Civil War is still a measurable political factor, yet in America the geographic solidarity of the two sides has been an incomparably softening influence. The French Revolution was a Civil War in which, over large areas, the lines were drawn on a social rather than a geographic basis; when it was over, no softening distance mitigated the bitterness of the ex-combatants. As the completeness of the democratic victory, with the passage of time and the coming reaction, became less complete, two Frances emerged to confront each other — authoritarian France, founded on the ideological trinity of monarchy, army and church, in later years particularly the church, and democratic France, founded on the ideological trinity of liberty, equality and fraternity between individual citizens. All through the nineteenth century these two were locked in an uncertain struggle for supremacy, with now one the victor, now the other .... The Third Republic has now lasted some sixty years, but its stability has more than once been highly doubtful .... Certain recurrent issues have never exhausted their dynamite.

The national cleavage was responsible, at least in part, for the attitude taken in 1939–1940 by some French officers. They were

[4] Helen Hill [Miller], *The Spirit of Modern France,* New York; Foreign Policy Association, 1934, p. 14. Reprinted by permission.

royalist by tradition and in sympathy, and they found it difficult to put spirit into the fight for a system that they abhorred. They, and with them a sizable portion of the privileged class, were not pro-German and not necessarily pro-Fascist, but they were anti-Third Republic. To this group the speeches of Hitler and the blandishments of his well chosen agents sounded much more attractive than did, for example, the demands of French labor leaders for shorter hours and more pay.

Closely related to this attitude was that of many Frenchmen who never had forgiven the republic for its separation of the church and state early in the twentieth century. It was one of the founders of the Third Republic who in 1877 had rallied republicans with the cry: "Clericalism! That is the enemy!" And as late as 1939, a leading native authority on French politics (later a Pétainist official) held that "perhaps the surest criterion" of difference between the Right and Left was the matter of opinion on the position of the church in the state and relations with the Vatican.[5] There were, then, men and women in the France of 1940 who expected more freedom to set up the church-state relation which they desired through collaboration with Hitler than under the existing regime.

A second weakness in the French political structure was the character of the constitutional laws of 1875. Under the terms of the Franco-Prussian armistice of 1871, the French people were to elect a national assembly that should decide whether or not to continue the war begun in 1870. When the assembly met it included some 200 republicans and about 400 monarchists. This membership reflected the attitude of the voters towards the war rather than their domestic political wishes, for the monarchist candidates had promised peace and the republicans had advocated the renewal of hostilities.

The selection of monarchy as the permanent form of government became unlikely when the monarchists divided into factions, favoring either a Bourbon or an Orleans candidate. Prolonged deadlock resulted, during which more and more liberals, tired of monarchist bickering, veered to the republican side. Finally, in 1875, because it seemed futile to wait any longer for the monarchists to resolve their difficulty, three organic laws were passed, which eventually came to be the French Constitution. The first law, which defined a method for electing future presidents, was adopted by a majority of one. And it was this one vote that, in effect, established the Third Republic. In the circumstances, it is not astonishing that the republican form of government should have collapsed after sixty-five years. The wonder, rather, is that a sketchy and presumably temporary political instrument, despised by unreconciled opponents, should have endured as long as did the laws of 1875.

Republican France, in the third place, had only a few political

[5] Barthélemy, J., *Le gouvernement de la France*, 3 ed., Paris 1939, p. 44.

parties with a definite organization, party funds, and periodic conventions. But it had numerous political groups, and usually there were from ten to fifteen such groups in the lower house at one time. Hence it was virtually impossible for any one of them to get a majority, and government had to be by the bloc system. Sometimes the defection of one small group on a minor point brought the loss of a majority and the need for a reorganization of the government. This literal *ministerial* responsibility was largely to blame for the frequency of cabinet change in France. Unlike the experience of ministries in democracies operating under the two-party system, the average life of a French cabinet was about six months. Eventually, particularly in the hard years after 1930, this administrative fluctuability gave rise to a growing demand for a "disciplined," that is, authoritarian system.

A fourth contributory cause to the French overturn was the Bolshevik Revolution. When the Bolsheviks repudiated the foreign debts incurred by Russia under the tsarist regime, France was one of the heaviest losers. This circumstance, plus the Bolshevik attacks on private property and religion, aroused the implacable enmity of many influential Frenchmen. There was implanted in them a dread of communism and a readiness to do almost anything to avert a Bolshevik upheaval in France. Although the Third Republic, until 1931, was officially among the most consistent opponents of the U.S.S.R., this hate remained more or less in the background—though even then it was regularly fed by the many Russian *émigrés* who had found a refuge in France. But when, after the rise to power of the German Nazis in 1933, the Third Republic began to draw closer to the Soviet Union, the dissidents in France were filled with yet greater aversion to the existing government.

The formation of a Franco-Soviet Alliance in 1935, and the joint sympathy of Moscow and the Blum Government for the Spanish Loyalists after 1936, seemingly turned the fear of these groups into terror. In this emotional state they listened willingly to the honeyed words of German agents who convinced them that only a totalitarian French regime cooperating with Nazi Germany could save them from the loss of all they held dear. In the end, many French army officers adopted the attitude: "If there is to be a war, then let it be against the Bolsheviki." Such officers hardly could lead their men to victory against the Germans.

Mention must be made, next, of a French psychology of defense. The people generally had fallen under the spell of the high command's preachments regarding the supposed safety of the country behind the Maginot Line. Thus, the French believed they needed only to remain behind their "impregnable" defences to be safe. The French attitude well substantiated the view of a British historian that nations tend to idolize a military technique which, revolutionary in its inception, helped them to win a previous war. Believing that during the First World War they had discovered in attrition a new way to beat Germany, the French regarded this wearing-down process as being still the latest development in modern warfare. There were, to be sure, persons who realized the delusion of this view, particularly de Gaulle and Reynaud, but they were laughed at or disregarded by the "experts," until it was too late.

Finally, the French nation, for much of the period between 1919 and 1939, enjoyed a condition of relative complacency. Least affected of any great state by the depression, enriched by the lavish spending of tourists, France wanted only to be left alone in a world which, at Paris in 1919, she had helped to create. Out of the despair of the First World War and the ecstasy of glorious survival and revival, a generation grew up who measured success by financial standards, looked on political and journalistic corruption as part of the normal national life, and maintained a cynical attitude towards spiritual values. Such a state of things was grist to the mill of Nazi sympathizers, who spread propaganda calculated to ruin France through hypocritically singing of its glorious destiny in a new and totalitarian order. Thus French democracy, after a sixty-five-year fight for existence, gave way to another system.

The Pétain Government, having established itself at Vichy in unoccupied France, and having concluded armistices with Germany and Italy, wished to change the republic's constitution. In July 1940, accordingly, the National Assembly, composed of both parliamentary houses, conferred on Pétain the power to draft a new constitution, which would have to be submitted to a plebiscite for approval. In no hurry to draw up such a document, the government contented itself with issuing numerous statutes and "constutitional acts." Thus was the Third Republic converted into the Vichy Dictatorship.

By means of constitutional acts Pétain made himself Chief of the French State, gave himself "full governmental powers," designated Pierre Laval as his successor, and required all high officials to swear fidelity to his "person." With a cabinet that included only persons who were acceptable to the Germans, Pétain then issued law after law, all aimed at replacing the spirit of "Liberty, Equality, Fraternity" by the new one of "Labor, Family, Fatherland." The government was watched and directed in its actions by German military and civilian agents.

In December 1940 Pétain announced that Laval no longer formed "part of the government." There were rumors that the dimissed official, who advocated closest collaboration with Germany, had arranged with the Nazis to execute a coup d' état. For a time Laval was placed in confinement but, upon German representations, he was released. Then, in April 1942, the Nazis prevailed upon the eighty-six-year-old Pétain to take the pro-Axis Laval back into the government. This time the former delivery-wagon driver became Chief of the Government, leaving to Pétain the now empty title of Chief of the State. Collaboration with Germany henceforth proceeded more rapidly, and Laval obediently announced plans to draft

French factory workers between eighteen and fifty and ship them to Germany. Before this scheme could be put into effect, against the widespread opposition that it aroused, the Germans occupied all France, following the United Nations' landings in French North Africa.

Meanwhile, the Vichy Government had overhauled the country's legal codes. The new laws were anti-Semitic and suppressed secret societies. Many persons were deprived of their acquired French citizenship, and refugee Jews were forced back to Germany. Every phase of the nation's economic life was regulated. The press agencies were taken over by the government. In short, unoccupied France rapidly approached totalitarianism, with Nazi legislation as its model.

German influence went so far that legal proceedings were instituted by Vichy against such former leaders as Daladier, Blum, Gamelin, Reynaud, and Georges Mandel, former Minister of Interior. The Nazis wanted the accused convicted of causing the war, so that France actually would place upon herself the responsibility for the Second World War. But when the accused were brought to public trial in 1942, they were charged by Vichy with having failed to prepare France properly for the approaching war. The defendants were brilliant in handling their own cases, despite unfairness in the judicial procedure. Indeed, they came so close to proving things that neither Vichy nor Berlin wanted proved that the trials soon were suspended. But the accused remained under arrest and in 1943 were transferred to German soil lest they escape.

Many Frenchmen were not in accord with the views and policies of the Pétain Government. General de Gaulle, who had gone to London after the collapse of the French army, called on all dissidents to rally behind him as leader of a Free French Force and continue the fight against Germany. A French military court tried de Gaulle *in absentia* and condemned him to death for treason and desertion, but the British Government made a formal military agreement with him. This regulated the conditions under which Free French resistance would continue, in cooperation with Britain, and excused the Frenchmen from ever having to take up arms against France itself.

When it appeared that some commanders in French West Africa and French Equatorial Africa were unwilling to follow Vichy in its submission to Germany, de Gaulle decided to go to Africa. Eventually de Gaulle gained the adherence of French Equatorial Africa and some island possessions of France. In 1941 and 1942 his Fighting Frenchmen joined British and American forces in the North African campaign.

Immediately after the fall of Reynaud, it had seemed that French North Africa, Syria, and Indo-China might refuse allegiance to the Pétain Government and continue the struggle. This would have been of great help to the British, particularly in the Mediterranean region, where it now was necessary to fight Italy. But through prompt action the Vichy Government was able to prevent this defection. A new governor was sent to Indo-China who observed the wishes of Pétain. Weygand flew to Syria and there persuaded the military commander to abide by the armistice conditions. In Morocco the resident-general followed suit, and then Weygand himself arrived to assume supreme command over the French African forces. By 1941, however, Weygand had become so disillusioned with the new order in France that Pétain recalled him as being "unsafe."

DAUNTLESS BRITAIN, 1940

On the eve of what came to be called the Battle of Britain, Hitler advanced a second peace proposal. Stating no terms, he merely indicated that if the war continued it could "end only with the complete annihilation of one or the other of the two adversaries." Britain's concrete response to this vague proposal was an all-time-high budget for war. The public welcomed its announcement.

When the Germans turned their attention to Britain, they faced a new situation. Had Great Britain been another continental state, the problem for the Nazis presumably would have been simple: one more application of Blitzkrieg technique. But Great Britain, despite Hitler's dictum that there were "no more islands," *was* an island. The English Channel was a formidable barrier to mechanized land units. A second was the British navy, more powerful than those of Germany and Italy combined. Not only would the main part of this fleet risk destruction to keep an invading army from the shores of Britain, but the sea arm once more effectively blockaded the German area from the west and south. Furthermore, it made possible the delivery to the embattled kingdom of foodstuffs and supplies from the rest of the world. German submarines, surface raiders, and airplanes did considerable damage to British shipping, but the losses were replaced by building, seizures, and purchases.

The British also had better planes than the Germans—who built theirs hurriedly—and better, more carefully trained, pilots. Since the Germans did not begin large-scale air attacks on Great Britain until the second week of August 1940, the British had more than two months in which to recover from the effects of Dunkirk; two months that were used to speed up military production, training, and defensive measures at an amazing rate. Finally, there was the astonishing spirit displayed by the Britons, from king through clerk. The British citizen emerged as the outstanding hero in the first eighteen months of the war.

On June 19, 1940, Hitler made a speech in which he offered Great Britain peace:

In this hour I feel it to be my duty before my own conscience to appeal once more to reason and common sense in Great Britain as much as elsewhere. I consider myself in a position to make this appeal, since I am not a vanquished foe begging favors, but the victor, speaking in the name of reason. I can see not reason why this war need go on. . . .

Three days later London brushed aside the German offer and Winston Churchill told the British people:

The Battle of France is over. I expect that the Battle of Britain is about to begin. Upon this battle depends the survival of Christian civilization. Upon it depends our British life . . . . The whole fury and might of the enemy must very soon be turned on us. Hitler knows that he will have to break us in this Island or lose the war. If we can stand up to him, all Europe may be free and the life of the world may move forward into broad, sunlit uplands. But if we fall, then the whole world . . . will sink into the abyss of a new Dark Age . . . . Let us therefore brace ourselves to our duties, and so bear ourselves that, if the British Empire and its Commonwealth last for a thousand years, men will still say, "This was their finest hour."

Since Germany could hope to invade Britain only after achieving air superiority, the Nazis in mid-June 1940 started daily air raids over Great Britain. The British sent up fighting planes to disperse the German bombers, and Royal Air Force bombers to seek out targets on the continent. In the first few weeks neither side used many planes at a time, and both tried to limit destruction to military objectives. With the coming of July, the air warfare became more intense. The Germans, having improved the fields in the conquered regions, now sent over larger squadrons, day and night. In addition to their other objectives, they tried to establish a counterblockade by attacking shipping and wharves, and to soften British resistance by lowering the morale of the people. The British, having to carry more fuel and therefore lighter bomb loads, similarly increased their activities, especially in night attacks. To the evident astonishment of the Nazis, the British people did not become terror-stricken. The greater the danger, the more determined in its resistance democratic Britain seemed to become.

August ushered in mass daylight raids involving hundreds of German bombers coming over in waves. Neither side had yet devised a really effective air defense, but the British had built more and better antiaircraft guns, found effective ways of spotting enemy planes, and developed faster fighters that were relatively easy to handle and well designed to disperse enemy bombers. Large, vulnerable airfields were replaced by small, camouflaged, hidden fields with only a few planes each. Balloons rose thousands of feet into the air, connected by cables. From them hung long stretches of piano wire to catch low-flying planes. The Germans, in an effort to "erase" London, now dropped explosives indiscriminately and used time bombs to shatter the nerves as well as the housing of the population. Then came incendiary bombs and attacks on midlands industrial towns, and coastal ports. As the air raids continued, the British worked out a skillful system of civilian defense.

While the Germans continued their fierce raids, the Royal Air Force, watching for German invasion preparations, wrecked railway lines, factories, and plants; blasted French airfields and ports; ruined industrial works in the Rhineland; raided northern Italy; dumped explosives on Norwegian and Danish ports; and broke up barge concentrations. The coasts of Great Britain simultaneously were made as inhospitable as possible for invaders. Gun emplacements were provided, tracks were laid for heavy armored trains with special cannon, barbed-wire entanglements were stretched, land mines were planted, and a constant lookout was kept by the military and civilian volunteers. Simultaneously, a large conscript army was whipped into shape and a home guard was trained in auxiliary functions.

These must have been the things that Winston Churchill had in mind when he told the Commons, in his first speech as prime minister (May 1940): "I say to this House, as I said to the Minsters who have joined the Government, I have nothing to offer but blood and toil and tears and sweat."

The Spread of the War – to 1943   18

WAR IN AFRICA, THE BALKANS, AND THE NEAR EAST

The withdrawal of France from the war left the British in a precarious position in the Mediterranean and in eastern Africa. Formerly, Italian East Africa and Libya had been hemmed in by Allied units on all sides; now the British found themselves with exposed flanks wherever they had relied on French support. Accordingly, in August 1940, the Italians seized British Somaliland. Italy rejoiced in this rounding out of her East African empire, but in reality she had gained little. Italian East Africa was cut off, except by air, from contact with the mother country or her other possessions. To alter this situation, and to wrest from Great Britain control of the Mediterranean, the Fascists next turned their attention to Egypt and the Suez Canal.

Before the outbreak of the war, Fascist leaders several times had proclaimed Italy's destiny to remove British influence from the Mediterranean. But when war came, the Italian navy avoided any major engagement with the British fleet. Whenever British and Italian squadrons sighted each other, the Italians rushed to the protection of the nearest shore batteries. Even the Italian airplanes and submarines did relatively little damage to the British fleet, which continued to patrol the entire sea and successfully convoyed merchant vessels carrying troops and supplies. From 1941, however, German planes took off from Italian airfields. The Nazi aviators were less shy than their colleagues and did much damage to British shipping.

The task of approaching Suez by land was entrusted by Mussolini to Marshal Rodolfo Graziani, an experienced desert fighter.

To reach Suez from Libya, it was necessary to march through the desert which was western Egypt, and this Graziani set out to do in September 1940. His opponent, with far fewer men at his command, was General Archibald P. Wavell. Wavell's Army of the Nile was composed mainly of Australians.

In the early stages of the campaign, Graziani's men advanced rapidly, soon reaching Sidi Barrani, about sixty miles within the Egyptian border. There, however, the attack halted, while the Italians accumulated fresh supplies and developed security for transportation lines. In December, Wavell's forces began a well-planned counterattack. Aided by Free French forays from French Equatorial Africa, the British pressed their offensive into 1941. By March the last remaining Italian posts in Cyrenaica fell.

Meanwhile, in January 1941, the British, cooperating with Haile Selassie, who earlier had flown from Britain to the Sudan, renewed operations in eastern Africa. Striking from both the Sudan and Kenya, they readily penetrated East Africa. Eritrea was conquered, and Italian Somaliland, and finally Ethiopia. In May 1941, five years almost to the day since he had fled, Haile Selassie reentered his capital at Addis Ababa. For the time being, Suez was safe from both west and south; but in the meantime new dangers threatened from the Balkans and the Near East.

Almost from the beginning of her unified existence, Italy had displayed interest in the Balkan Peninsula as a field for the extension of her influence. This sentiment appeared in the terms of the Triple Alliance agreement into which she entered in 1882 with Germany and Austria-Hungary. It reappeared in the provisions of the Secret Treaties which she signed with the other Allies during the First World War, in her difficult relations with Yugoslavia and Greece after that war, and in the history of Italian relations with Albania, from the little kingdom's creation in 1913 to its absorption by the Fascists on Good Friday of 1939. Hence it was not astonishing that Rome, dissatisfied to have gained control of only a few miles of France and French Somaliland, while Germany had extended her rule over most of Northern and Western Europe, should have cast longing eyes at Greece.

In the late summer of 1940 Italy accused Greece of surreptitiously aiding the British navy and blamed her for terrorist activities on the Albanian frontier. Then Italy seized Greek merchant vessels, bombed Greek destroyers, and massed Italian troops on the Albano-Greek border. Athens protested these actions and hurriedly strengthened its defenses. But at three o'clock in the morning of October 28, 1940, the Italian Minister presented a three-hour ultimatum to the Athens Government.

The document resembled those which Germany had presented to *her* victims in the previous spring. It complained of terrorist activities "against the Albanian nation," and charged Athens with having promised to put naval and air bases at the disposal of Great Britain.

Therefore, in order to "avoid" hostilities between Italy and Greece, Rome demanded permission to occupy several strategic Greek areas for the duration of the war. Any resistance would be "broken." To the evident astonishment of Italy, Greece decided to resist. When Italian soldiers crossed the Greek frontier, Athens called on Britain for help, and Churchill pledged prompt assistance.

THE CENTRAL MEDITERRANEAN AREA 1940–1941

The outbreak of the Italo-Greek war astonished few; its course amazed many. The Italians, after a brief advance, not only were halted by the Greeks, but were thrown back across the border. The Greeks carried the fighting into Albania and steadily pushed the Fascists back toward the Adriatic coast. By January 1941 the Greeks were driving toward Valona, chief port of entry for Italian supplies and reinforcements. The Italians had expected little resistance and were unprepared to meet determined opposition. They were not successful in their attempts to use mechanized equipment in the rugged Pindus Mountains, where poor roads were made worse by rain, snow, and ice. The military ability of Premier John Metaxas and Marshal

Alexander Papagos also played a large part in the Greek victories, whereas the Italian generals seemed unable to inspire their men with confidence or the determination to win. The British fleet and bombers, seconded by Greek planes and submarines, hampered the shipment of Fascist supplies and men across the Adriatic, even though Italy controlled both sides of the narrow Strait of Otranto.

The entry of Greece into the war appeared of material help to Britain not only because it diverted some Italian energies, but because Britain now had several new bases, particularly on Crete, from which to undertake operations against the Fascists. Naples and other southern Italian cities frequently were bombed, and in November 1940 the air arm of the British fleet inflicted a severe blow on the Italian navy at Taranto. Soon thereafter Marshal Pietro Badoglio resigned as chief of the Italian General Staff, and a number of generals and admirals followed suit. In January 1941 there were riots in northern Italy over the presence of increasing numbers of German soldiers in the peninsula. Jealousy of the successes of the northern Axis partner and mistrust of its eventual goals made the Italians restive. Meanwhile Romania, too, had suffered at the hands of the Axis.

The partitioning of this kingdom in 1940 was only a bitter climax to twenty years of misfortune and unrest. Emerging from the peace settlement of 1919–1920 as the largest and presumably strongest Balkan state, Romania was almost constantly torn by internal strife growing out of her minorities problems, the poverty of her peasants, and violent personal rivalries. The acquisition by the Soviet Union of Bessarabia and northern Bukovina in 1940 already has been discussed; the next territorial beneficiaries were Bulgaria and Hungary.

In 1913, as a result of the Second Balkan War, Bulgaria had ceded to Romania the southern part of Dobruja province. Now, in 1940, Bulgaria asked for the return of this "Quadrilateral," a majority of whose inhabitants were Bulgarians. Under Axis pressure, Romania acquiesced in the demand, and the neighborhood kingdoms signed the Craiova Agreement. This permitted Bulgaria to reabsorb the southern Dobruja and provided for a partial exchange of populations.

More difficult of settlement was the Hungarian demand for the return of Transylvania. Since the time it was acquired by Romania in 1920, this area was among the most troublesome of Europe's sore spots. With Magyars now insisting on the return of the entire region, and Romanians opposed to any cession, negotiations between the two countries accomplished nothing. After weeks of fruitless discussion, the Hungarian and Romanian diplomats were summoned to Vienna, where the German and Italian Foreign Ministers in August 1940 simply handed down the Vienna Award. Romania was forced to cede to Hungary the larger part of Transylvania. Those inhabitants—and they formed a majority—who were of Romanian origin were permitted within six months to opt for Romanian nationality and to leave the ceded area. Germany and Italy guaranteed the "integrity" of what was left of Romania.

THE PARTITION OF ROMANIA 1940

The Vienna Award satisfied neither disputant, but whereas the Budapest Government at least could point to an extension of Hungary's frontier to the Carpathian Mountains, the Bucharest authorities had to admit territorial loss. The Fascist Iron Guards in particular were vehement in their renewed attacks on King Carol II who, in an effort to strengthen his position, appointed the nationalistic General Jon Antonescu as Premier with full powers. Antonescu then induced the King to bow to the Iron Guard's clamor for his abdication, and in September 1940 Carol passed the crown to his son, who now for the second time became King Michael I. The ex-king fled the country. Antonescu then announced that Romania was entering the political sphere of the Axis Powers and appointed Horia Sima, Iron Guard leader, as Vice-Premier. The import of all this became evident when German soldiers began to pour through Hungary into Romania, there to garrison strategic zones, guard the oil fields, and train Romanian forces. Antonescu, meanwhile, brought Romania's internal life into harmony with Nazi principles.

In March 1941 the Premier of Bulgaria signed a document in Vienna, whereby his country joined the Axis system. This action grew, at least in part, out of Bulgaria's desire to regain from Greece some land that she had been forced to cede to the Athens Government after the First World War. Within a few hours after the ceremony was completed, German forces were in occupation of the Bulgarian capital, Sofia.

Following the occupation of Bulgaria, Nazi armies were poised all along the northern and eastern frontiers of Yugoslavia. On the northwest and southwest, moreover, Yugoslavia bordered on Italy and Italian-held Albania. This situation boded ill for the South-Slavic State, whose economic life had come more and more under German domination. In the Greco-Italian war, Yugoslavia sympathized with her Balkan neighbor, but Belgrade maintained official neutrality. This attitude was inspired both by a fear of Germany and by uncertainty regarding the loyalty of the Croats and Slovenes—long dissatisfied with Serbian predominance in the triune kingdom.

Early in 1941 Berlin had demanded of Yugoslavia an alliance and permission for the passage of German soldiers to the Yugoslav-Greek border. The Regent Paul had secured a scaling down of the demands to a nonaggression pact and permission for the transit of only munitions and hospital trains. But when Paul recommended this compromise to his advisers, they warned that its acceptance would mean the collapse of the government. Simultaneously Britain and the United States promised military supplies to help stiffen potential resistance to German pressure. Paul, however, decided that the possibility of Italo-German invasions was more dangerous than that of civil war. In March he went to Vienna to conclude an agreement with the Germans. But before the document could be ratified, a military coup drove Paul into flight. King Peter II, though not yet eighteen, assumed full royal authority and chose as his premier General Dushan Simovich, popular chief of the air force and organizer of the coup. The Simovich Government offered continued friendship and economic cooperation with Germany, but refused to ratify the pact or demobilize the Yugoslav army. Thereupon the Nazi press trumpeted forth the same atrocity stories that earlier had been used against the Czechs and Poles. In April 1941 Nazi soldiers entered Yugoslavia and Greece.

The outright war in Yugoslavia lasted only twelve days—partly because Yugoslav mobilization had not yet been completed, partly because of aid given the invaders by discontented Croats and Slovenes, and partly because of the usual careful Nazi preparation. Peter and his government fled to London, and Yugoslavia was partitioned. Italy, Hungary, and Bulgaria all were rewarded territorially. The Germans themselves held on to Belgrade and created a new puppet state of Croatia-Slavonia.

The official end of the war found large units of Serbian fighters in possession of their arms and imbued with a fierce desire to continue the struggle against the Germans. Eventually, thousands of these collected under the leadership of General Draja Mikhailovich, who for years had studied the possibilities of organized mountain fighting. Now he and his *chetniks* carried on an amazingly successful mountain warfare that harassed the enemy without letup. In January 1942, when the Yugoslav Government-in-Exile was reorganized, Mikhailovich was appointed Minister of War.

Meanwhile, the fate of Greece also had been sealed. Three days after the collapse of Yugoslavia, the Athens Government gave up the struggle—to avoid the useless massacre of its people. Great Britain had tried to help by sending veterans from the Libyan Front, but this move, undertaken more out of political than military considerations, proved futile. The reinforcements were too weak to keep back the Germans, and their withdrawal from Africa paved the way for a new British retreat in Libya. Crete, too, fell into German hands.[1] Henceforth, until the Nazi invasion of the Soviet Union, Britain carried on the war without an ally or a foothold on the continent of Europe.

Thus far in the war the initiative on land had lain almost entirely with the Germans. From May to September 1941, however, the British forestalled German coups in Iraq, Vichy-controlled Syria, and Iran. The first and last of these states were of vital importance to Great Britain because of their geographic relation to the Persian Gulf and India, their oil resources, and their potential value to Germany as bases from which to drive through Trans-Jordan and Palestine into Egypt. Syria in unfriendly hands obviously was a constant threat to Britain's whole position in the eastern Mediterranean area.

In April 1941 a military coup in Baghdad brought into power a pro-Nazi regime under Rashid Ali Beg Gailani. Axis propaganda and agents now flooded the country. Britain therefore exercised her rights under a treaty of 1932 to send additional troops to certain strategic points in Iraq. Rashid Ali resisted and appealed to Berlin for help. Germany was unable to do more than send a few planes via Syria and to induce the Vichy authorities in Syria to give Rashid Ali some war materials. None of the other Arabian states chose to intervene, and the pro-Nazis were driven to flight (May). A pro-British regency returned, and Britain now was ready—not a day too soon—to act in neighboring Syria.[2]

Nazi penetration in Syria was far advanced. The German armistice commission and German technicians had done efficient work, and the Vichy commissioner, General Henri Dentz, had been cooperative. The direct aid given by Vichy to the pro-Nazi Premier of Iraq, Rashid Ali, and to the Nazi planes sent to help the Iraqi dictator made British action urgent. In June 1941 British and Free French columns entered Syria from Iraq, Trans-Jordan, and Palestine. The invaders tried to keep casualties to a minimum despite

[1] For a time the Nazis allowed Italy to occupy conquered Greece; but when this led to trouble, the Germans themselves resumed control. King George II set up a government-in-exile in London.
[2] Iraq declared war on the three chief Axis powers in 1943.

Dentz's determination to fight, and so the campaign proceeded slowly; but in July hostilities were concluded. Those Frenchmen who preferred not to join the Gaullists were repatriated, and Syria was safe from Nazi clutches.

Allied attention next was focused on Iran. With the German invaders in the U.S.S.R. approaching the Caucasus, it became essential to keep open feeder lines to the Russians via the Persian Gulf and Iran. Riza Shah, however, had been receptive to German influence in Iran and permitted the influx of numerous Nazi technicians and "tourists." London and Moscow requested the expulsion of the German agents, and when the Shah evaded action, British and Russian soldiers entered Iran in August 1941. They seized the oil centers and the one strategic railway line, whereupon Tehran agreed to expel the Nazis and permit the transit of supplies across Iran to the Soviet Union. When the Shah again adopted dilatory tactics, additional Allied soldiers were sent into the country. This encouraged certain tribesmen in the southwest, who had been treated harshly by Riza, to threaten revolt. The Shah thereupon abdicated in favor of his son, Mohammed Riza. With the new ruler's consent, a regular transport service to carry British and United States supplies to Russia was organized.

These Allied successes in the east occurred simultaneously with a renewal of the seesaw campaigns in northern Africa. After Wavell had driven the Italians out of Cyrenaica, the Germans shipped men and materials to Libya for another drive. The new leader of the Axis forces was an experienced tank commander, General (later Field Marshal) Erwin Rommel. In March 1941, shortly before some British African units were sent to the aid of Greece, Rommel began a well-planned push with his specially trained desert fighters, the *Afrika Korps*. Within less than a month the Allies were ousted from Libya, except that the garrison in Tobruk, supplied by British ships, held out until relieved in November by a British counteroffensive. This was launched by General Sir Claude Auchinleck, successor to Wavell.[3]

Auchinleck's offensive regained all Cyrenaica, but the retreating *Afrika Korps* was not destroyed. Indeed, after getting reinforcements, Rommel in May 1942 embarked on a new full-scale offensive. (Meanwhile several Australian divisions had been withdrawn from Africa to the new theater of warfare in the Far East). Rommel drove ahead so furiously and with such skill that he now captured Tobruk in a single day's assault, and the British retreated to El Alamein, seventy miles west of Alexandria. Here they prepared to make a last stand in the Egyptian desert—a site flanked on the north by the

[3] In the fight to keep the Mediterranean open for British ships and to hamper Axis shipments to Africa, the British island base of Malta played an amazing role. It became the world's most bombed area, experiencing an average of three air raids per day over many months.

sea and on the south by the treacherous sands of the Qattara Depression. By this time, moreover, fresh Australian and other troops had arrived, as had large numbers of planes and much mechanized equipment from the United States.

In July 1942 Rommel assaulted El Alamein and made a breach in its defenses. But British reserves closed the gap, and Rommel was checked. By the narrowest of margins he had failed to win the Battle of Egypt. For the next few months the British held against repeated assaults by Rommel, meanwhile building up strength for an offensive that should drive the Axis forces not merely out of Egypt but out of northern Africa.

THE WAR IN THE FAR EAST—TO 1941

It was inevitable that the war should have strong repercussions in the Far East, where the Japanese some years earlier had embarked upon a policy designed to create a new order in eastern Asia. The continued resistance of the Chinese, however, spoiled the Japanese plans. Under Chiang Kai-shek the Chinese armies remained in the field, fighting well according to the tactics for which their limited equipment and the terrain best suited them. The Chinese people, expert at passive resistance, helped the cause with guerrilla warfare, boycotts, and "scorching" of the earth.

In the hope of causing a rift among the Chinese, Tokyo in March 1940 recognized a puppet "Chinese National Government" at Nanking under the nominal headship of Wang Ching-wei, who recently had been expelled from the Kuomintang. The results of this move were disappointing to Japan. The non-Axis states continued relations with only the Chungking Government, to which came material aid from the Soviet Union, Great Britain, and the United States. Eventually, seeking consolation and compensation for its Chinese reversals, Tokyo turned its attention to southeastern Asia.

After the withdrawal of France from the war, the Japanese looked with increasing concentration at the rubber, oil, tin, and rice in the European possessions located in southeastern Asia. The longing for control over this richly endowed portion of the Far East was expressed in the phrase Greater East Asia, first used officially by the Japanese in August 1940. With France in collapse and Great Britain fighting Germany, the chief obstacles in the way of fulfillment of this ambition, aside from China herself, were the Soviet Union and the United States.

As events proved, Japan was strong enough to overpower the defenses of French Indo-China, Singapore, and the Netherlands East Indies. But there also existed in Japan a traditional suspicion of Russia; hence, at least until after the Nazi invasion of the Soviet Union, some Japanese leaders feared lest a gathering of power in southeastern Asia sufficient to conquer that region would leave Japan open to sudden attack by the U.S.S.R. Besides, the United States, through official utterances and through a concentration of naval forces in Pacific waters, made it clear that she was vitally interested in preventing any violent change in southeastern Asia.

In view of these circumstances, Japan in September 1940 concluded a tri-partite pact with Germany and Italy, changing the 1936 Anti-Comintern Pact into a military alliance with the Axis. Germany and Italy acknowledged Japan's prerogative to establish a "new order in Great East Asia." The alliance clearly was aimed at the United States.

Meanwhile, Japan successfully had made demands on the authorities of Indo-China, who were loyal to the Vichy Government. In September 1940 Tokyo got the right to land some soldiers and use some airfields in that French colony, thus enabling the Japanese to strike at China from the south. Simultaneously, the Indo-Chinese Government found itself embroiled with the neighboring state of Thailand. Thailand regarded the time as opportune for demanding from stricken France a return of some of Thailand's territory occupied by the French during the nineteenth and early twentieth centuries. Eventually Japan, already in occupation of a sizable portion of Indo-China, took a hand in the quarrel. By a treaty signed in Tokyo in March 1941, Indo-China ceded 21,000 square miles of territory to Thailand.

It was fairly obvious, even in the spring of 1941, that Japan was seeking a foothold from which to extend her influence southward through Indo-China and Thailand to the long and narrow peninsula at whose tip lay Singapore, adjudged the strongest naval base in the world. Lying in the path of any Japanese campaign against the Netherlands East Indies or Australia, Singapore's defenses from the land side were weaker than those facing the sea. But the big Japanese push southward did not come until after Germany had brought the U.S.S.R. into the war.

NAZI INVASION OF THE SOVIET UNION

In August 1939 Germany and the Soviet Union had signed an agreement of neutrality. Hitler wished to ensure Soviet neutrality until he should have disposed, in battle, of France and Great Britain. Then, he believed, he would be free to enforce any demands upon the U.S.S.R. Stalin, doubtful of the precise intentions of Paris and London, grasped at the opportunity to win some time for the military industrialization that was the essence of the Third Five-Year Plan. Meanwhile, in 1939–1940, the Soviets extended their western frontiers, thus placing additional mileage between the German border and Moscow.

Hitler, however, could only hold to such bargains temporarily. In August 1940 he gave orders to prepare invasion plans. His motives

THE FAR EAST 1937 AND 1940

Courtesy, Foreign Policy Association, *Headline Series*.

were many. He nursed an intense hatred of Bolshevism, deriving from a multitude of earlier political confrontations with Communists. He distrusted Russia's traditional expansionist designs on Europe. And he was imbued with a concept rooted deeply in the German historical experience, namely, a "drive to the east" (*Drang nach Osten*) to secure living space (*Lebensraum*) for the rapidly multiplying German people.

By the spring of 1941 there were unmistakable signs of growing tension between Moscow and Berlin. The eastward march of the Nazis, particularly the occupation of Bulgaria and Yugoslavia, led to outbursts in the controlled Soviet press. In April Moscow signed a neutrality pact with Tokyo, thus presumably leaving herself freer to act in the west. In May, Stalin assumed the premiership of the Soviet Union, thus for the first time openly taking the political leadership into his own hands.

Meanwhile the Nazi leaders concluded that Britain could not be defeated as long as it was necessary to keep German planes and soldiers in the east, because of uncertainty regarding Moscow's course. Hence the U.S.S.R. had to be defeated in another lightning campaign, and then full attention could be centered on Britain. In addition, direct access to the raw materials of the Soviet Union would be satisfactory compensation for the aid being rendered to Britain through growing United States lend-lease activities. Finally, a German war on Bolshevism might lead to an ideological split in both Great Britain and the United States, and thus weaken the democracies' determination to smash Hitlerism.[4]

At dawn on Sunday, June 22, 1941, Nazi soldiers without warning launched an attack across the Soviet frontier. Some 135 divisions raced forward on a 1500-mile front. The Russians, though not fully mobilized, had far more soldiers immediately available than the Nazis had anticipated. Churchill at once pledged full aid to the U.S.S.R., and Roosevelt two days later made a similar declaration. On the other hand, Italy, Romania, Hungary, Slovakia, and Finland all entered the war against the Soviet Union before the end of 1941. The Finns, thinking only in terms of revenge, soon found themselves closely tied up with the Axis Powers in their global war against the United Nations. In July, London and Moscow signed a military pact.

By December 1941—after six months of the fiercest kind of warfare—the invaders were in occupation of 500,000 square miles of Soviet territory, including all the regions annexed by Moscow in 1939–1940 and most of the rich Ukraine. But, by adopting a scorched-earth policy and guerrilla tactics, the Russian people

[4] In May 1941 Rudolf Hess, deputy leader of the Nazi Party, made a solo flight to Scotland, hoping to meet the British leaders and induce them to negotiate a peace, largely in Germany's favor. He was placed in confinement and later sentenced to life imprisonment as a war criminal. Hitler denounced the flight as the act of an unbalanced man—and the British did indeed treat Hess for mental illness.

greatly curtailed the economic value of the area to the conquerers. The Germans, moreover, had failed in three prime objectives. They had surrounded, but had not captured, Leningrad. They had come within thirty-one miles of, but had not taken, Moscow. And they had not "annihilated" the Russian armies.

The main reason for this failure of the Nazis was "General Space." Perhaps because they themselves had come to believe in their invincibility and were conditioned by earlier *Blitzkrieg* victories in relatively limited areas, the Nazis invaded the U.S.S.R. all along a front stretching from the Baltic to the Black Sea. Instead of concentrating their power and striking at a few vital points, they overextended themselves. As a result, they encountered not merely the Russian armies and spirit, but Russian spaces and distance. With sufficient manpower and space for counterattacking, the Soviets often wiped out enemy motorized spearheads before the infantry could come up to occupy the intervening terrain. No matter how far back they were pushed, the Russian armies still had room to maneuver; they could always retreat before they were destroyed, offering a fluid resistance to fluid attack.

There were other reasons, too, for the determined fight put up by the Reds. Little Nazi propaganda was spread in the U.S.S.R. before the invasion began. In most countries which the Nazis overran with relative ease, they first had "softened" the population by psychological warfare. This propaganda invariably stirred up internal quarrels, spread fear and terror, and created treacherous fifth columns. But in the Soviet Union the propaganda staffs of Goebbels had little opportunity to spread subversive ideas, for in Russia the censorship was as strict as in Germany itself. There could be few psychological preliminaries of the type that had helped bring about the collapse of France. The Nazis, for their part, knew little about the true state of Soviet preparedness or about the readiness of the Russian people to fight any invader to the death. It puzzled German soldiers that "hopelessly surrounded" Russian units refused to surrender, as had troops elsewhere, but fought all the harder and often hacked their way out of encirclements.

The Russians, in addition, had long been preparing for a war against any Western enemy. The "liquidation" of many technicians in the early days of Bolshevik control made this process an awkward one at first, but in the successive Five-Year Plans, provision was made for the rapid increase of the country's military strength. More and more with each passing year the Bolsheviks built their new plants to the east, first in the neighborhood of the ore-rich Ural Mountains and then in the raw-material-studded vastness of Siberia. A Western enemy might occupy most of European Russia, and still the mechanized war could go on. Besides, the Russians showed ingenuity in the eastward removal, piece by piece, of entire manufacturing plants, so as to keep them out of reach of the advancing Germans. Workers, too, were shifted, women and men alike, for in the Soviet Union women from the beginning of the war took a prominent part on the battlefields and in the factories.

Mechanized warfare was not novel to the Russians; they were pioneers in experimenting along such lines. They knew what to expect and how to meet it. They also found in their Cossack cavalry units an effective weapon against parachute attacks. The horsemen were of little use against tanks and armored cars, but they were effective against troops dropped from the sky. They could ride anywhere at any time, cut down the parachutists before they were free from their ropes, and dash off to the next place of danger.

The staff work and strategy of the Russians were good. The recently reported military purges had led many foreigners to believe that Stalin had lost his best officers and would be helpless against German attack. But the Red High Command appeared to make few mistakes, and such general officers as Semyon K. Timoshenko and Gregory K. Zhukov, although they had to retreat, did so in a way that kept their main forces intact and full of fighting spirit. When the time came, they led them in well-directed counter offensives.

With the coming of the cold winter of 1941–1942, the Soviets were better equipped to fight than were their enemies. The natives knew their winters and took the necessary precautions to keep their fuel fluid and their wheels turning despite the icy mud. The Germans, having expected the war to be over before winter set in, were greatly hampered by the prolonged subzero temperatures. The Nazi soldiers began to speak of fighting against "General Winter." One German later told of fighting in "unearthly cold" in which "the breath froze and icicles hung from nostrils and eyelashes all day long." If a German soldier sank weakly into the snow and was noticed by his officers he was "kicked and slapped." Those who responded to this treatment and got to their feet were hurried back to their positions. Others, who did not respond, were left to die.

The Bolsheviks took advantage of this weather, to which they were accustomed. The Red armies took the offensive and drove the Germans back in a number of places. But, except for Rostov, the Reds were unable to recapture any great strongholds. These held firmly and were used by the Nazis in their new campaigns of 1942.

This time the Germans did not repeat the mistake of overextension. Without straining themselves to take either Leningrad or Moscow, they concentrated their efforts in the south. The goal was to conquer the remainder of the Ukraine and to drive forward to the Volga River and the Caspian Sea. Success in this endeavor would bring tremendous advantages.

The Russian forces in the Caucasus would be cut off from the main Russian armies to the north. The Soviets, already deprived of much economic wealth and with a fourth of their population in German-occupied areas, would be deprived of additional industrial and food-producing areas, of raw materials, and of railway lines. The Germans would be able to use the oil resources of Baku. They could check the flow of United States and British goods to Russia via Iran. They could bypass Turkey and fan out into the Arabian Peninsula—heading on the one side for the Persian Gulf and a possible meeting with the Japanese allies in India, and on the other side for the Suez Canal. With these prizes beckoning, the Germans began a restricted offensive in May 1942 with a drive on the Crimean Peninsula. When, after two months of intensive fighting, the objective was taken, the Nazis launched a full-scale drive toward the Volga River and the Caucasus. The defensive task of the Russians was to preserve the main Red armies and so prolong the campaign as to leave the Nazis still short of their objectives at the beginning of the next winter.

Relentlessly the Nazi machine rolled forward. Russian resistance was stubborn, but relatively light, for the Bolshevik Command had withdrawn large forces from the Caucasus and the Ukraine in order to make a determined stand near Stalingrad, on the Volga River. In late August 1942 the Nazis made the first direct attack on Stalingrad. For three months a terrible struggle raged over one city. Stalingrad seemed to become a symbol in the clash of iron wills. No sacrifice of men or materials appeared too great for the Nazis in their effort to take the city; none seemed too great for the Soviets in their effort to hold fast. Eventually the capture, not of miles but of yards, not of suburbs but of individual buildings, became headline news. In late November the Russians began a new winter offensive of their own. Attacking in force on the central and southern fronts, they gradually pushed the Germans back to the west of Moscow and in the Ukraine and the Caucasus. Although a large Nazi army remained encamped outside Stalingrad, the Bolsheviks encircled this force and drove on beyond it. By January 1943 the Germans were in full flight along a front of many hundred miles, and in February the last of the Stalingrad besiegers were killed or captured. Meanwhile, with the attack of Japan on the United States, the war had assumed global proportions.

ENTRY OF THE UNITED STATES

The news of the European war in 1939 was not nearly so startling to the public in the United States as had been the similar news in 1914. During the intervening quarter-century, the people had come to know more about world affairs than at any previous time. Thousands had acquired familiarity with Europe through travel. Hundreds of thousands read the reports of newspaper correspondents who covered every scene on the European stage. If the Americans were astonished that war came in 1914, many were astonished in 1939 that the coming of the war had been so long deferred.

Other contrasts there were, too, with the situation in 1914. In the early months of the First World War there appeared to be a general indifference in the United States as to who might win; and among those who *were* strongly partisan, there was no overwhelming majority on one side or the other. Probably only few envisaged the possibility of eventual entry into the conflict. Such was not the case in 1939. The people generally seemed convinced that the war was the direct outcome of Nazi principles and techniques and that Germany was the aggressor.

The chief differences of opinion in 1939 came not over the question of where to place United States sympathies, but over the specific form in which the general sympathy should be manifested. Should the United States try to "isolate" herself and be content to pray for an Allied victory, or should she render all aid "short of war" to the upholders of her own preferred way of life, or should outright military aid be given to the enemies of authoritarianism? The decision became all the more urgent after the collapse of France in 1940. To some this catastrophe was a warning that full support must soon be forthcoming; to others it served as an argument for appeasement.

Meanwhile, on September 5, 1939, President Roosevelt had issued a proclamation of neutrality resembling those issued during previous international conflicts. Simultaneously, under the terms of the Neutrality Act of 1937, the President placed an embargo on the shipment of implements of war to belligerents. Having performed his duty under the law, the President then appealed to Congress to revise the neutrality legislation, because it seemed unrealistic. Since the British fleet in any case would make it impossible for Germany to buy United States warstuffs, the embargo was hampering only the Allies. Hence its retention would be "very nearly equivalent to presenting Germany with an Atlantic fleet." The inevitable application of the act to Canada, when that dominion entered the war, became another potent argument for its repeal.

In November Congress passed a new law called the Neutrality Act of 1939. Under its terms the president was required, in the event of international war, to enumerate the belligerent states. United States vessels and aircraft were forbidden to carry passengers or freight to any state so named. The president was further empowered to define specific "combat areas" and exclude from them all United States citizens, vessels, or planes. United States citizens were forbidden to travel on belligerent vessels (to prevent a repetition of the *Lusitania* incident), and her merchantmen might not be armed. Thus was instituted a cash-and-carry policy which, it was hoped, would enable the Allies to buy supplies without exposing the United States to the risk of having its public aroused to war fever by the acts of German submarines. On occasion, the Administration also asked manufacturers of war supplies to place a "moral embargo" against countries which, like Japan, while not engaged in the European war, were bombing open cities.

The entrance of Italy into the war, the rapid extension of German control, and the result of the election of 1940 led Washington to concentrate on three main defensive policies: the strengthening of the military might of the United States; cooperation in hemisphere defense with the other American countries; and the provision of all possible aid "short of war" to Great Britain, combined with economic warfare against the Axis.

The process of building up defenses required the cooperation of President, Congress, and people. Funds were voted to expand the armed forces. Fifth-column activities were searched out by the Federal Bureau of Investigation. Advocates of rapid rearmament and substantial aid to Britain—former Secretary of State Henry L. Stimson and Frank Knox, publisher of the *Chicago Daily News*—were made secretaries of war and of the navy, respectively.

To check a threatening skyrocketing of prices owing to increases in wages, housing shortages in defense-manufacturing areas, and declines in stocks of consumer goods, the President created the Office of Price Administration (OPA). Then there came into being an Office of Civilian Defense (OCD), whose job it was to establish and coordinate protective and morale-building services throughout the country.

Meanwhile the President had approved the selective Service Act of 1940. It was the first United States law to prescribe compulsory military service in time of peace. The act set an upper limit of 900,000 to the number of selectees who might be called to service at any one moment. The National Guard might be called to federal service whenever the national security demanded a strengthening of the regular army, and manufacturing establishments were required to give government defense orders precedence over all other contracts.

The gradual establishment of German control over European countries that had possessions in the Western Hemisphere brought sharply to the fore the need for clarifying Washington's stand on the Monroe Doctrine. In June 1940, several days before the publication of the Franco-German armistice terms, Secretary Hull sent identical notes to Germany and Italy informing those powers that the United States "would not recognize any transfer and would not acquiesce in any attempt to transfer any geographic region of the Western Hemisphere from one non-American power to another non-American power."

The vague reply which Germany sent to this note, the evidences of increasing Nazi fifth-column activities in several Latin American states, and the growing economic difficulties of many of the republics —because of the British blockade of Europe—made desirable even closer economic and political ties between the United States and Latin America. There was obvious advantage in the adoption of one Pan-American policy on the vital issues of the day. Hence the foreign ministers of the twenty-one republics met at Havana (1940). The conference adopted a Convention on the Provisional Administration of European Colonies and Possessions in the Americas. It entered into force early in 1942.

The document recommended certain measures to restrict fifth-column activities in the Western hemisphere. It proposed the organization of a permanent committee to help settle any disputes that might arise among the American states. It defined as aggression against all signatories any attempt on the part of a non-American state to infringe the territorial or political sovereignty of any one of the republics. This "continentalization" of the Monroe Doctrine was accompanied by the setting up of a provisional cooperative administration for the governance of any foreign-owned possessions "in danger of" a forceful "change of sovereignty."

Having thus arranged for cooperation with Latin America, Washington turned to Canada. President Roosevelt and Premier Mackenzie King in August 1940 set up a Permanent Joint Board on Defense, representing the public and the military services of each country. Meanwhile a related defense "deal" was being negotiated between the United States and Great Britain. After it was consummated, in September, the President told Congress what he had done, appending to his message an opinion of the Attorney-General supporting his authority to make the arrangement. The President informed the Congress that he had acquired the right to lease naval and air bases in various British possessions (the Bahamas, Trinidad, etc.) in return for fifty destroyers which were promptly handed over to Britain. The United States then prepared to fortify and garrison its new outposts.

As a further step in hemisphere defense, Secretary Hull in April 1941, after German air activity had been noticed over Greenland, signed an agreement with the Danish Minister, whereby that colony was placed under the temporary protection of the United States. The German-controlled Copenhagen Foreign Office declared the agreemen void and recalled the minister, but Washington continued to recognize him "as the duly authorized Minister of Denmark." In July 1941, after the United States freighter *Robin Moore* had been sunk in the Atlantic by a German submarine, United States forces began to replace the British garrison on Iceland.[5] The move was designed to forestall German occupation and to make easier the patrolling of the Atlantic.

The third aspect of Washington's policy in relation to the war concerned material aid to Britain and other opponents of totalitarian aggression. The British in particular needed much more help than they were getting or than they could pay for. Hence, to make possible full assistance short of man power, an Administration bill "to promote the defense of the United States" was introduced in Congres in January 1941. It was popularly known as the Lend-Lease Bill. The bill authorized the president to make or repair any implements of war for a friendly power whenever he deemed it necessary for the national defense.

[5] Following the German occupation of Denmark in 1940, Britain had sent men to both the Faroe Islands and Iceland (an independent state with the same sovereign as Denmark).

Congress plunged into lengthy debate on the bill. The public, too, hotly debated it. Opponents saw in it a ruse for getting Congress to resign all its powers into the hands of a dictatorially inclined president who desired war. Proponents regarded it as the only feasible way to meet and destroy the Axis threat while this still was confined to continental Europe by the British fleet. The bill, with some modifications, became law in March 1941. Roosevelt immediately ordered the shipment of stores from the "arsenal of democracy" to the remaining bulwarks holding back the tide of totalitarianism.[6]

While supplies in increasing quantity were dispatched to the peoples resisting Axis pressure, and while the relations with Germany were going from bad to worse, the disagreement between the United States and Japan over the Far Eastern situation became ever more serious. In July 1941, Japan obtained from Vichy France the right to set up naval and air bases in Indo-China; at the same time Japanse assets in the United States were frozen. In August the United States announced that any Japanese action against Thailand would cause her great concern, and Roosevelt and Churchill issued a joint declaration of general aims, soon to become famous as the Atlantic Charter. Throughout September Tokyo unsuccessfully tried to induce the President to meet Premier Fumimaro Konoye somewhere in the Pacific, rather than on the American mainland, for an airing of the conflicting views of the two peoples. In October, Konoye resigned to make way for an advocate of aggressive action, General Hideki Tojo.

Churchill promised, in November, that "should the United States become involved in war with Japan a British declaration will follow within the hour," and Secretary Knox warned that the United States was "faced with grim possibilities on the ... far side of the Pacific." Mid-November saw the arrival in the United States of "trouble shooter" Saburo Kurusu, who ostensibly came to help the Japanese Ambassador iron out the differences with the Washington Government; actually, his mission was to cover up preparations for the imminent Nipponese attack on United States possessions. The Neutrality Act of 1939, meanwhile, was amended so as to permit vessels to be armed and to carry cargoes to any belligerent port.

On December 6, President Roosevelt addressed a personal plea to Emperor Horohito to help him maintain peace, and on the following day Kurusu and Tokyo's Ambassador requested a conference with Secretary Hull so that they might transmit the official reply to some Washington proposals of the previous month. While the Japanese delegates were proffering the document, on Sunday, December 7, 1941, word reached the President that Japanese planes, carrier-

---

[6] The total value of lend-lease aid (to its end in August 1945) was $48,500,000,000, of which the British Empire and the Soviet Union were the chief beneficiaries. Lend-lease was not entirely a one-way affair, since the Allies provided United States forces with supplies and services valued at $7,800,000,000.

based and, therefore, of necessity en route for some days, had bombed the naval base at Pearl Harbor, Hawaii, where a large portion of the United States' Pacific Fleet was at anchor.

A few hours after the attack, Japan declared war "on the United States of America and the British Empire." On December 8 the state of war was recognized by a vote of 82 to 0 in the Senate and 388 to 1 in the House of Representatives. On December 11 Germany and Italy also declared war on the United States. Congress immediately and unanimously made a reciprocal declaration.[7] The war had become global.

GLOBAL WARFARE, DECEMBER 1941—APRIL 1943

The military and naval commanders at Pearl Harbor were caught off guard, despite recent and urgent warnings from Washington to remain continually on the alert for precisely the sort of thing that happened. Ironically, a detector's alarm of the approaching enemy aircraft was passed off by a junior officer as indicating the presence of merely friendly planes. The losses included several thousand casualties as well as destruction of or damage to 8 battleships, 10 other war vessels, a floating drydock, and about 250 planes.[7]

Over a period of months, during which the Nipponese continued to hold the military initiative, much of the damage was repaired; and in the meantime there had emerged two developments of advantage to the Allied cause. First, Tokyo's treachery and early victories brought to the people of the United States unity of spirit and a gradual realization that total effort would be needed to win the total war. Secondly, the anti-Axis states were drawn more closely together in the conviction that only global cooperation could be effective in the fighting of a global war. Among the first manifestations of this understanding was a reaffirmation of the principles of the Atlantic Charter in a Declaration by United Nations, signed by twenty-six powers on January 1 and 2, 1942. The charter, as announced on August 14, 1941, after a meeting of Roosevelt and Churchill aboard ship off the coast of Newfoundland, indicated that neither Britain nor the United States was interested in territorial aggrandizement. The joint pronouncement also reaffirmed the principle of self-determination. It was vowed that the United States and Britain would work ceaselessly, until the enslaved of the world had been freed and the war ended in victory for the Allied cause.

The United Nations then prepared a declaration indicating its support of the principles set forth in the charter. The twenty-six original signatories also pledged cooperation to all other states (nineteen in all during the war) who affixed their signatures to the United

---

[7] Eventually Romania, Hungary, Bulgaria, and Thailand also declared war on the United States.

Nations' document. The United States, Great Britain, and the U.S.S.R. obviously were the most important signatories.

With the passing of time, inter-Allied cooperation increased steadily. In various theaters of the war inter-Allied armed units were placed under single commanders, chosen for ability and knowledge of local fighting conditions rather than nationality. Roosevelt and Churchill met three times in the first thirteen months following the attack on Pearl Harbor—twice in Washington and once at Casablanca in Morocco. The United States and British general staffs cooperated as the Combined Chiefs of Staff, with Soviet and Chinese representatives present at their meetings. By the close of 1942 more than 1,500,000 United States fighting men had been sent overseas, to cooperate in every part of the globe with their colleagues from other powers among the United Nations.

There was also an increasing preoccupation with the subject of postwar collaboration among the United Nations.[8] Aside from official activity in this connection, there were hundreds of organizations and thousands of individuals in the United States and Great Britain who busied themselves with thoughts of peace aims. The discussion of postwar goals was made the more animated by Roosevelt's enunciation in January 1941 of the "four freedoms"—"freedom of speech, freedom of religion, freedom from want, and freedom from fear"— to which he held that all men were entitled.

In contrast to these developing concepts of political and social justice in the Free World, the Nazi leaders deliberately identified the whole German people with their activities. This fitted in with their claim to embody the national will and tended to discourage the belief that a defeated Germany might get better treatment if the Nazi leadership were surrendered to Allied justice. For this reason, and in order to force collaboration from the peoples in the occupied zones, the Nazis also pursued a policy of terrorism against civilians. The wholesale execution of "hostages" reached a horrible climax after the assassination of "Hangman" Reinhard Heydrich, who, as Himmler's chief assistant, had been sent to cow the people of Bohemia-Moravia into submission. His death was avenged by the Nazis through the massacre of hundreds of innocents and the destruction of the village of Lidice. Charging that Heydrich's killers had found refuge there, the Nazis admittedly murdered every adult male inhabitant of Lidice and dispersed the women and children throughout Central Europe (June 1942).

Meanwhile the fighting spread rapidly. For some months Japan had enjoyed a military success that, to her foes at least, was astonishing. Tokyo had planned a clever campaign to gain control of the

---

[8] In November 1942 Roosevelt appointed Governor Herbert H. Lehman of New York to be Director of Foreign Relief and Rehabilitation. In this capacity Lehman was to supervise the furnishing of "relief and other assistance to the victims of war in areas reoccupied by the forces of the United Nations."

Western Pacific area before the United States or Great Britain could bring any large forces to the scene of conflict. Time after time, the Nipponese had superior numbers at the critical points, for the Japanese were only hundreds of miles from their bases and the United States had to move its fighting forces thousands of miles. The Japanese Command regarded no sacrifice too great to achieve an objective, and, over a period of years, Tokyo had converted its scattered island possessions and mandates into a "fleet of anchored aircraft carriers."

The Japanese soldiers were hardened and tough, generally preferring death to surrender. Their leaders developed a skillful method of jungle fighting by dispersal and infiltration.[9] Their opponents at first underestimated their fighting qualities—partly out of a feeling of superiority to the "little yellow men" and partly out of the mistaken idea that Japan's inability to subdue China was owing to Nipponese weakness rather than Chinese inner strength. Japan also was the beneficiary of fifth-column activity, particularly in Vichy-controlled Indo-China, Thailand, and Burma. By their successful advances, the Japanese soon deprived the Allies not only of most of the island bases they did have in the Western Pacific, but of the tin, oil, and rubber that they had been obtaining from the southeastern Asiatic mainland and the Netherlands East Indies.

Simultaneously with their attack on Pearl Harbor, the Japanese struck at the United States island bases of Guam, Wake, and Midway. After stout resistance, the first two fell, so that by Christmas 1941, Midway remained the only United States stepping stone between battered Hawaii and the embattled Philippines. Meanwhile several British Pacific islands also were occupied, and Japanese land-based planes sank two of the largest British battleships off the eastern coast of Malaya. Their loss left the immediate naval defense of the Southwestern Pacific to cruisers and destroyers inadequately supported by aircraft.

Thereafter the Japanese swept ahead. By June 1942 the Nipponese had taken Hong Kong, Sarawak, Malaya, Singapore, Burma, the Philippines, the Netherlands East Indies, much of New Guinea, the Solomon Islands, and even some of the Aleutian Islands off Alaska. After six months of warfare Japan had control of the Western Pacific area "between India and Hawaii, and between Siberia and Australia." In this period there did occur some episodes to bolster United States spirits—episodes such as heroic stands on Bataan and at Corregidor, the bombing of Tokyo in a daring raid led by Lieutenant Colonel James Doolittle, the appointment of General Douglas MacArthur of Bataan fame to supreme command in the Southwestern

---

[9] Realizing the difficulty of taking Singapore from the sea side, the Japanese penetrated the "impenetrable" jungles to the north of that base and again appeared at the critical fighting point with an overwhelming superiority of men and planes.

Pacific, and a naval victory over Japan in the Battle of the Coral Sea in May—but the tide of Japanese advance was not checked until the summer of 1942.

The eventual call of halt to Japan came after arduous preparation by the United Nations. While the damage sustained at Pearl Harbor was being repaired, and while Australian defenses were being strengthened, United States forces built up bases on various Pacific Islands. United States reinforcements also were sent to New Zealand, Australia, the New Hebrides, and other Pacific regions, and United States and British supplies were poured into the Far Eastern war theater. The firm stand of the Soviet Union against Nazi armies helped give the United Nations a much needed breathing spell, as did the continued resistance of China.

The United States won an important naval victory over Japan in the Battle of Midway Island (June). The Japanese sought to take this island, from which they believed Doolittle's raiders had come and, at the same time, remove the last guardian of Hawaii. Midway, indeed, was the decisive naval defeat for the Japanese, since it proved to be the turning point of the war in the Pacific. Another positive note was sounded by the British when they occupied Vichy-controlled Madagascar. This occupation not only forestalled a possible Japanese-Vichy bargain similar to the one whereby French Indo-China had become a Nipponese base of operations, but kept open the vital sea route from the United States and Great Britain around Africa to the Orient.

Eventually, in August 1942, the first step toward retrieving lost territories was taken when United States forces, operating from New Caledonia, seized a number of small islands commanding Tulagi harbor. Probably the most important land operation of that phase of the war was "Operation Cactus," the establishment of a beachhead that included an almost completed new Japanese airfield on Guadalcanal in the Solomon group. In and above the jungles of Guadalcanal transpired some of the most ferocious fighting of the war in the Pacific. Most important, Guadalcanal taught American marines how to fight the war in the jungle.

During the winter of 1942–1943 Allied gains were consolidated against reinforced opposition, and an Australian and United States counterattack was launched on New Guinea that gradually drove the Japanese invaders back to the bare footholds in the north. In the process Japan suffered further important naval losses in a battle off the Solomon Islands during November 1942. Thus was begun the process of Allied reconquest of bases which, it was expected, would eventually become steppingstones on the route to Tokyo.[10]

[10] It was fortunate for the Allies that Japan did little commerce raiding in the Pacific, for throughout 1942 and 1943, the German U-boat menace in the Atlantic became ever more serious. The United Nations met the danger by building ships faster than the Germans could sink them, developing

The Japanese occupation of Burma, meanwhile, had given renewed importance to Anglo-Indian relations. There was widespread dissatisfaction in India based upon the fear that Great Britain was using the war as a reason for postponing indefinitely any further step in the direction of Indian self-government. Eventually, spurred by evidences of disloyalty to Britain and aid to Japan in Burma, London in the spring of 1942 suggested that, "immediately upon the cessation of hostilities," there be created a fully self-governing Indian Dominion. Any province that preferred to remain outside the Indian union would be permitted to attain a dominion status of its own. During the war, however, Indian's defense would have to remain the responsibility of the viceroy and his councils.

Most Indian groups found reason to treat the proposals cooly. The largest single group, the Indian Nationalists or Congress Party, insisted on immediate self-government; when this was not forthcoming, Gandhi preached a new campaign of noncooperation with Britain and nonresistance to Japan. The obstructionist tactics of the leaders—who advocated passive resistance against Britain's war effort and objected to the presence of United States aviators and technical troops in India, while Gandhi made anti-British speeches —led to a period of violence. In August 1942 Gandhi and other leaders were arrested, and order gradually was restored. India continued to fight the Axis with men and materials, far surpassing her contributions to the Allied cause in the First World War. The moderate natives appeared to find satisfaction in the belief that after victory the Indian demand for self-government would be supported by public opinion in all the United Nations. As the Indian situation gradually faded from the newspaper headlines in the West, North Africa surged back into the limelight.

In the summer and early fall of 1942 there was a noticeable increase in the number and intensity of British and United States air raids on Nazi-occupied Europe. Lend-lease aid was stepped up to China and the Soviet Union. Simultaneously the British were building up a powerful army behind El Alamein in Egypt, an army strengthened by United States bombers, tanks, and tank-destroyers. Meanwhile their augmented air strength in Egypt enabled the Allies to check several projected eastward drives by Rommel and partially to close his supply routes from the European continent and Libya.

Late in October 1942 the British Eighth Army, commanded by Lieutenant General Sir (later Field Marshal Viscount) Bernard L. Montgomery, began a campaign to drive Rommel out of both Egypt and Libya. The British apparently believed, as Rommel himself had indicated, that the Afrika Korps held "the gateway of Egypt." Mont-

---

additional antisubmarine bases, setting up air-ferry routes, and improving the convoy system. Convoys plied the North Atlantic to the U.S.S.R., the Middle Atlantic to Great Britain and Iceland, and the South Atlantic to and around Africa.

gomery had been quoted as saying, as if in direct reply, "Give me a month and I can chase him [the German] out of Egypt." Thus began the Battle of El Alamein with a British attack on October 23. It ended with the Axis forces in headlong flight. In January 1943 Montgomery's forces entered the city of Tripoli, having pushed westward 1300 miles in three months. One week later a British vanguard followed the remnants of the Afrika Korps across the border into Tunisia. Italy's African empire was no more. Meanwhile it had become clear that Montgomery's offensive was intended to be only the eastern jaw of a vise whose western jaw was a United States army driving through French North Africa, and whose closing would mean the expulsion of the Axis from Africa.

Operation "Torch" had been launched after almost half a year of preparation and the United States army was landed at selected points in Vichy-controlled French North and West Africa early in November 1942. The objects of the occupation were to forestall similar German action, tighten the anti-Axis blockade, make safer the South Atlantic and Mediterranean routes, and set up a possible invasion base against Southern Europe. Some British military units participated in the landings, but the entire expedition was commanded by Lieutenant General (later General of the Army) Dwight D. Eisenhower, hitherto chief of the United States forces in Europe. It was anticipated that a United States army would find less opposition in the French territories than would one composed largely of British soldiers.

Although there was some fighting, Morocco and Algeria soon were brought under Allied control. Pétain ordered resistance and broke off diplomatic relations with the United States, but General Henri Honoré Giraud, who some months earlier had duplicated a feat accomplished by himself during the First World War by escaping from a German prison fortress, promptly appeared in Algeria and urged cooperation with the Allies. Eisenhower placed him in command of the French North African forces, an appointment soon confirmed by Admiral Jean François Darlan. Darlan, who had gone to Algeria on secret orders from Pétain, was permitted by the Allies to assume authority over North Africa on November 11; he ordered all French resistance to end. By these arrangements Eisenhower hoped to avoid the casualties that might result from a protracted struggle between French and United States forces and to concentrate on the conquest of Tunisia, where German and Italian troops had begun to establish themselves. Meanwhile, also on November 11, Eisenhower appealed to the French fleet at Toulon to join the United Nations, and Hitler ordered his armies to march into hitherto unoccupied France, ostensibly "to repel an American and British landing." Italy assisted the German operation and occupied Corsica. Thus were the armistices of 1940 scrapped.

The Axis troops completed the occupation of France within a day, although, for the time being, they avoided Toulon. While Darlan now announced that he would speak for Pétain since the Vichy leader no longer was free to make his sentiments known, the Fighting French proclaimed from London that they would participate in the new campaign against the Axis but would not accept any political arrangement concluded between the Allies and the "Number Two traitor of France." On November 23, Darlan persuaded French West Africa, with its powerful base of Dakar, to go over to the anti-Axis side, and four days later the larger part of the French fleet at Toulon was scuttled. The wholesale sinkings were carried out according to prearranged plan when Nazi soldiers entered Toulon and Nazi planes appeared over the harbor.

The difficult political situation took an unforeseen turn on December 24, 1942, with the assassination of Darlan by a youthful French patriot, who was executed two days later. Thereupon Giraud, with Eisenhower's approval, assumed control. The Gaullists preferred Giraud to Darlan, although they were disappointed when the new commissioner kept some former Vichy officials in high position.

Meanwhile, on November 15, United States troops had crossed into Tunisia, where a hard fight was in progress. The Axis had the advantage of shorter supply lines, a factor that became the more important with the onset of bad weather. The Allies, moreover, still had to consolidate their gains and positions elsewhere in Africa. Hence, while Laval in France declared that German victory would save "civilization," the campaign in Tunisia was marked chiefly by local engagements, air attacks, and supply-ship sinkings in the Mediterranean. Early in 1943 the Germans withdrew what remained of the Afrika Korps from Libya into Tunisia, there to join the fresher forces recently arrived from Europe. Allied efforts to prevent a union of the two groups were unsuccessful, but by April the Axis forces had been pushed into a corner of northeastern Tunisia.

While Tunisia became more and more important as a battleground, there occurred another Roosevelt-Churchill meeting, this time at Casablanca in Morocco. For ten days, from January 14 to 24, 1943, the two leaders met, each accompanied by the supreme fighting commanders of his country. Stalin and Chiang Kai-shek, though not present, were kept informed of all developments. Giraud and de Gaulle also attended the meeting, and had an opportunity to agree "on the end to be achieved, which is the liberation of France." Both recognized the need for full military cooperation of all Frenchmen on the side of the Allies, but neither was prepared to accept the leadership of the other in the interest of political unity. The major conferences laid plans for the campaigns of 1943, and at a press conference on January 24, Roosevelt declared that the United Nations would fight until the Axis was ready to cry "unconditional surrender."

Allied Victory **19**

FROM NORTH AFRICA TO NORMANDY

At Casablanca, in January 1943, Roosevelt and Churchill not only agreed that the enemy must surrender unconditionally, but planned the next military blows to fall on Italy. First, however, it was necessary to drive the Axis forces out of Africa. This objective was attained by the middle of May 1943. After some temporary setbacks, all that was left of the Afrika Korps was captured in Tunisia. This victory marked the proverbial beginning of the end. The Italians were disturbed, and the Fascist structure gave signs of cracking. Nazi leaders, for their part, belittled the happenings in Tunisia as a successful delaying action during which they had been able to make Fortress Europe invincible. But this boast in reality was a sign that the "Maginot-line psychology of defensive warfare which had bedeviled the French in 1940 had in turn affected the Nazis."

"Operation Husky," the invasion of Sicily and Italy, though well planned, was not to be an "all out" effort. The Allies did not intend to dissipate their resources for a later invasion of France in an Italian "vacuum." But from Italy as a base, they could more readily bomb Germany and the Balkans; and by invading Italy they would cause diversion of some German divisions from the eastern front and thus bring relief to the still hard-pressed Russians. In July 1943, following heavy air attacks on the areas concerned and the capture of the strategically important islands of Pantelleria and Lampedusa, came the assault on Sicily. The Italians offered little resistance and surrendered in large numbers. The Germans fought hard, but, except for one savage Nazi counterattack, the beachhead was established with relative ease. Few Germans surrendered, however, and many were able to retire across the Strait of Messina to the Italian mainland.

The conquest of the island took thirty-nine days. Meanwhile Mussolini himself had fallen.

A few days after the initial Allied landings on Sicily, Mussolini visited Hitler and asked for more German reinforcements. The Führer denied the request and berated his friend for Italy's lagging support. Mussolini returned crestfallen, summoned a meeting of the Fascist Grand Council for July 24, 1943, and urged continuance of the war by abandoning southern Italy and establishing headquarters in the country's industrial north. The meeting was bitter. Mussolini's lieutenants pointed out that under the Duce's leadership Italy was disintegrating. Her colonies were gone. Her armies were largely destroyed or in flight. Her fleet was in hiding. Her industries were crippled by air raids, lack of fuel, and shortage of raw materials. Her people existed on meagre rations because of the blockade, and because food was being sent to Germany. For all this, blame was showered upon the Duce. At the close of the session the council passed a motion, by a vote of 19 to 7, asking the King to take direct command.

On July 25, 1943, Victor Emmanuel III dismissed Mussolini. Marshal Badoglio was appointed to head a new government, and Mussolini was placed in custody; his power had lasted twenty years and nine months. It widely was believed that Badoglio promptly would take Italy out of the war. But he delayed asking for an armistice, partly because the Germans were in virtual control of the peninsula and partly because he and the King were not yet ready to cast their lot with the Allies. His hand was forced by the increasing severity of Allied air attacks and by popular peace demonstrations. Secret armistice negotiations were held in Lisbon, and on September 3, 1943, Italy surrendered unconditionally. On the same day, the Germans took over Rome, and the Allies crossed from Sicily to the Italian mainland.

The Nazis had made good use of the interim to clear out the unreliable Italian forces and strongly emplace themselves in the mountainous terrain of southern Italy. Only slowly and at great cost were they pushed northward. In bitter weather, the Allies were held up for months in some of the fiercest fighting of the war at "Monastery Hill" on Monte Cassino. Here the Monastery of St. Benedict provided the Germans with a perfect observation post from which to spot every Allied movement in the valleys below and fire on it. Eventually, Allied bombers leveled the historical abbey, and in the spring of 1944, Cassino was taken. The Allied armies then pushed north to join an Allied garrison that had been held up on a beachhead at Anzio, but at last had broken out. Allied columns next converged on Rome.

Meanwhile, some Nazi paratroopers had freed Mussolini from prison and taken him to temporary safety behind the German lines. He set up a puppet neo-Fascist republic and rallied about him some Fascists who had all to lose and nothing to gain from an Allied

THE ALLIED CONQUEST
OF ITALY
1943 - 1944
Scale of Miles
0   25   50   75   100

victory. Since the Badoglio Government in October declared war on Germany, the Italians found themselves, if not always fighting, then at least leaning, on both sides.

At last, on June 4, 1944, Allied forces entered Rome. Thereafter, while some of the troops were withdrawn in preparation for the invasion of France, the remainder progressed steadily up the peninsula as far as Rimini. There they came to a halt before the German Gothic Line in the mountains south of Bologna. Another winter of warfare lay ahead in the struggle for control of the rich Po Valley.

The Axis defeats in Italy were paralleled on the eastern front by the liberation of Russia. Early in 1943, following the victory at Stalingrad, the Russians continued to push the Germans back to the west of Moscow, in the Ukraine, and in the Caucasus. Aided by equipment from the United States and Great Britain and by ceaseless western air attacks on German factories and material, the Russians gradually reconquered most of the territory lost to the Axis during 1942. Eventually, in July 1943, the Germans began in central Russia what proved to be their last great offensive on the eastern front. They made some initial gains, but these soon were lost in a Russian counteroffensive.[1] The Russians, showing skill in the use of artillery, in the encirclement of enemy spearheads, and in the development of pincers movements, pushed forward until, by March 1944, the Axis forces were expelled from most of the Ukraine. Meanwhile, in the north, Leningrad had been freed after a siege of nearly two years and a half; and by mid-May 1944 the Crimea once again was in Russian hands.

If, for a time, it seemed that the resultant shorter defense lines might make things safer for the hard-pressed Nazis, this illusion soon was dispelled. They were harassed by air raids from the west, south, and east and thus were unable to keep war production at the level required for the defense of Fortress Europe. The German leadership was disturbed more and more by the inefficiency of forced foreign labor and by underground resistance activities. Internally, the Nazi High Command was torn by strife and jealousies between civil and military authorities, especially after the failure of an attempt on July 20, 1944, against Hitler's life. To many, with the setbacks in the war, German life now seemed to be dominated by the notorious Minister of the Interior Himmler, who made "the terror from within transcend the terror from without." Perhaps most important to command circles, Germany, fearful of an imminent invasion blow from the west, could not long hope to retain control over the soil of Russia or of Russia's neighbors.

In June 1944 new Russian drives began against the Germans on

[1] In Russia the Nazis were estimated to have suffered 1,250,000 casualties in 1942 alone. The Russians admitted a loss of 4,500,000 killed and wounded in the first year of the war. Yet the Russians could replace their losses and the Germans could not. Thus, gradually, the Russians grew relatively stronger and the Germans weaker.

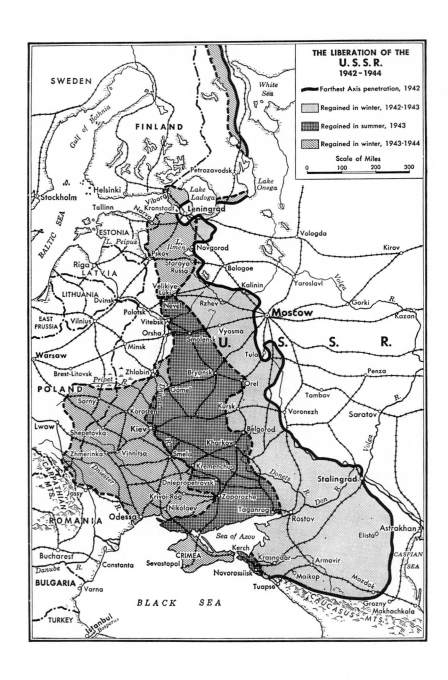

THE LIBERATION OF THE
U.S.S.R.
1942–1944

▬ Farthest Axis penetration, 1942

▦ Regained in winter, 1942–1943

▦ Regained in summer, 1943

▨ Regained in winter, 1943–1944

Scale of Miles

0   100   200   300

the central front and against the Finns behind their Mannerheim Line. Soviet soil was cleared of German armies before the year ended. By October the Russians had reentered Latvia, Lithuania, Estonia, Poland, and Romania, were in Bulgaria, Czechoslovakia, Hungary, and Yugoslavia, and had penetrated East Prussia. Romania and Bulgaria were induced to declare war on Germany, Finland was granted an armistice, and at Lublin in Poland a Soviet-sponsored government was set up in disregard of the Polish Government-in-Exile in London. Meanwhile British troops had helped the natives reconquer Greece, and Turkey had broken off diplomatic relations with Germany.[2] By the close of 1944, Eastern Europe was "liberated."

During these months there had begun the process of liberating France. From the beginning of her own invasion, and especially after the entry of the United States into the war, the Soviet Union demanded the opening of a second front in Western Europe so that the Nazis would be simultaneously engaged on two sides—though Moscow had shown no interest in opening a second front from 1939 to 1941, when the Nazis were winning in the West. London and Washington early agreed in principle that the main blow must be delivered across the English Channel; but the implementation of the strategy was successively delayed by the events in North Africa and by the insufficiency of resources for a French invasion. In late 1943, however, at conferences in Cairo and Tehran, the Allied leaders gave "Operation Overlord" top priority. On December 24, 1943, General Eisenhower was appointed Supreme Allied Commander and ordered to "enter the continent of Europe."

During the next six months the search for greater resources for Overlord continued. Eventually the target date, D-Day, for an attack on Normandy was set for early June 1944. Another landing, in southern France, was planned for some time later, so that the available "landing craft could be used first in the Channel, then rushed to the Mediterranean to do double duty." Meanwhile the Channel virtually was swept of mines, the skies were cleared of the Luftwaffe, strategic bombing of the continent reached a new intensity, and an average of 150,000 men per month was transported from the United States to the British Isles. By air attacks on bridges and rail centers, the invasion coast was isolated and the enemy's ability "to shift resources to the critical area was severely restricted."

V-E DAY

The invasion time, or D-Day, was early in the morning of June 6, 1944. According to the report of the United States Chief of Staff,

[2] In February 1945 Turkey declared war on Germany and Japan. Ankara was stimulated by an Allied decision not to invite to the forthcoming San Francisco meeting on the organization of the United Nations any power that had failed to declare war on the Axis by March 1, 1945.

General of the Army George Catlett Marshall, "the beaches of Normandy were chosen for the assault after long study of the strength of German coastal defenses and the disposition of German divisions. The absence of large ports in the area was a serious obstacle, but was offset in some measure by the relative weakness of the German defenses and elaborate construction in Britain of two artificial harbors to be emplaced off the beaches. The selection of target dates and hours for the assault required an accurate forecast of the optimum combination of favorable weather, tide, and light conditions. Moonlight was desirable for the airborne operations. D-Day was scheduled for 5 June; this date was changed to 6 June because of unfavorable but clearing weather . . . . The final forecast for the attack day predicted high winds; the sea was still rough, but rather than accept a delay of several weeks until tide and moon provided another favorable moment, General Eisenhower made the fateful decision to go ahead."[3]

An armada of more than 4000 ships carried the Allied men across the Channel. Aerial cover was provided by 11,000 planes. The undersea and land obstacles prepared by the Germans were ingenious and took a terrible toll of Allied lives. The resistance of the Germans was stubborn. Rommel, having been placed in charge of the Channel defenses, had warned that "the war will be won or lost on the beaches." Thus, the Nazis counterattacked fiercely and made skillful defensive use of the Norman hedgerows—"horse-high, bull-strong, hog-tight." The weather was unseasonably bad and almost destroyed one of the two artificial port installations. But the Allies controlled the air, handled an average of 30,000 tons of supplies and 30,000 additional troops every day, and by June 12 held eighty miles of the French coast between Cherbourg and Caen.

Cherbourg fell on June 27. A month later General Omar Bradley's men broke out at St. Lô. Lieutenant General George Smith Patton, Jr., and his United States Third Army, aided effectively by the French underground or French Forces of the Interior (FFI), pursued the fleeing Germans without letup. Paris fell to the Allies on August 25, by which time "the Germans had suffered at least 400,000 casualties, of whom more than 200,000 were prisoners of war." It still was necessary, however, to clear several enemy garrisons that had been left behind to prevent the Allies from using the harbor facilities in such critical seaports as Brest, Dieppe, and Le Havre.

Meanwhile, on August 15, 1944, the United States Seventh Army, under Lieutenant General Alexander McCarrel Patch, Jr., and including many French soldiers, had landed near Cannes on the Riviera. Within two weeks beachheads were firmly established in

---

[3] German surprise was heightened by the fact that the Nazi commanders expected the invasion to come across the Dover Straits to the Pas de Calais, which provided the shortest route into Germany. The choice of Normandy was unexpected.

southern France, and a rapid advance was begun up the Rhone Valley. Lyon fell on September 3, and eight days later the two Allied invasion forces effected a junction northeast of Dijon. The Germans fled to the shelter of the Siegfried Line or West Wall, and Allied forces, having crossed the Belgian frontier, streaked through Luxembourg and entered Germany on September 11, 1944—ninety-seven days after D-Day.

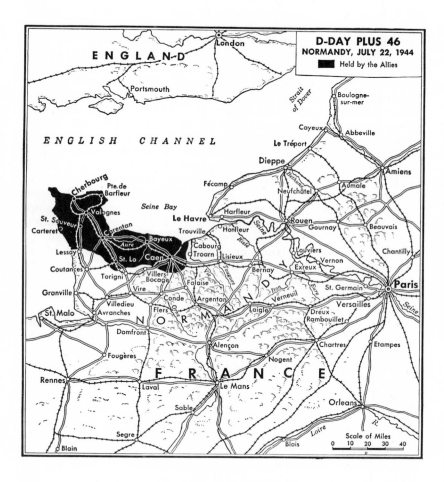

The reaction of these events on Berlin was sharp. On June 15, 1944, the Germans sent over from France to London the first of 8000 robot bombs called *Vergeltungswaffe* (V-1) or "vengeance weapon." Although they were inaccurate, these pilotless, jet-propelled bombs were independent of weather conditions and were hard to intercept or shoot down. The 2300 that got through to

London interfered with its efficiency as a war center, killed or injured more than 20,000 persons, placed a great strain on the nerves of Londoners in general, and diverted Allied planes to shooting down the missiles and bombing the launching ramps in the Pas de Calais region of France. But the bombs were of no value in determining the outcome of the war and served chiefly as a vent for Hitler's personal hate of Britain. The liberation of France involved the capture of the launching sites, and in the beginning of September 1944 the V-1's ceased to trouble London. However, the Nazis meanwhile had developed a V-2 which, launched from a greater distance, shot through the stratosphere at supersonic speed. With their explosive-filled noses, these rockets caused death and destruction in London until the spring of 1945.

A further reaction in Germany to the defeats was the development of conspiracies to kill Hitler. The one that came closest to success was a Generals' Plot to assassinate the Führer on July 20, 1944. Acting on behalf of several members of the General Staff, Count Claus Schenk von Stauffenberg placed a brief case containing a time bomb against the leg of a table in Hitler's conference hut at Rastenburg in East Prussia. The bomb exploded, but Hitler, though dazed and bruised, remained alive. Several General Staff officers thereupon were executed, some in disgusting fashion. Others, such as Rommel, perhaps because of their standing with the German people, apparently were induced to commit suicide. Hitler, moreover, placed Himmler, already in charge of internal affairs, in command of the Reserve Army. Soon Himmler also was given command of all prisoner-of-war camps and eventually of the Army Group of the Vistula, fighting against the Russians east of Berlin. "I am beginning to doubt," exclaimed the irate Führer, "whether the German people is worthy of my great ideals."

In the autumn of 1944, began a triple assault on what had shrunk to be Fortress Germany. The western Allies were poised for assaults along the Gothic Line in Italy and the West Wall in Germany; the Russians, along a line extending from East Prussia southward across Poland and Hungary. The Allied command in Italy launched an offensive against the transpeninsular Gothic Line on September 10, 1944. The weather was bad, the terrain was difficult, the fighting was bitter. Both sides utilized Italian soldiers—the Nazis using Mussolini's new Fascist Republican Army, the Allies using anti-Fascist Partisans. For several months the Allied advance was slow. The opposing ground forces were of nearly equal strength, the margin of Allied advantage being represented by air power. But in April 1945, the Po was crossed in force, and the armies of General Mark W. Clark, aided by Partisans, rushed onward. Mussolini, seeking escape to Switzerland, was caught by Partisans. On April 28, he was shot, and then hanged by the heels in Milan—scene of his first successes. Meanwhile, largely through the efforts of Allen Dulles of the United States Office of Strategic Services (OSS), secret negotiations had begun for the surrender of the shattered Nazi army in Italy. The negotiations ended in Nazi capitulation on May 2, 1945.

On September 17, 1944, the Allied western offensive had begun with an airborne attack on the Netherlands flank of the Siegfried Line. The operation achieved only partial success and was followed by a frontal assault farther south. Aachen fell in October, and the Metz and Strasbourg areas were conquered by late November. With more than 3,000,000 troops on the continent, General Eisenhower now launched a "charging offensive to penetrate the Siegfried Line and place himself in position to cross the Rhine." In order to gather strength at his chosen points of attack, he decided to hold the seventy-five miles between Monschau and Trier with comparatively weak forces. It was precisely here that Field Marshal Karl Rudolph Gerd von Rundstedt, acting on Hitler's personal direction, on December 16, 1944, launched a counteroffensive with the port of Antwerp as its objective.

The resulting Ardennes Counteroffensive, or Battle of the Bulge, made some progress. Aided by heavy fog of several days' duration and an intelligence lapse on the part of the Allies, Rundstedt was able unobservedly to assemble large forces in the heavily forested area. He broke through the United States position and at the point of extreme penetration drove more than fifty miles into the Allied lines. The United States forces defending Bastogne were offered an honorable surrender by the Nazi forces, but they refused and continued to fight until their colleagues came to their rescue. By the end of January 1945 the salient was eliminated. The Nazi offensive only "imposed a delay of about six weeks on the main Allied offensive in the north," and did this at the price of irreparable damage to "the principal element of Germany's strategic reserve" and of widespread disillusionment within Fortress Germany.

It was time for the diplomats to meet once more, and early in February 1945 President Roosevelt, Prime Minister Churchill, and Marshal Stalin gathered with their chiefs of staff at Yalta in the Crimea.[4] Here the general plan for the destruction of Nazi Germany was approved, and the German people were warned not "to make the cost of their defeat heavier to themselves by attempting to continue a hopeless resistance."

Soon the final campaigns were launched on all fronts. In the west, Cologne fell to the United States First Army on March 7, 1945. On the same day a platoon of this army found a Rhine bridge south of Cologne intact. The platoon leader daringly exploited the windfall by crossing the Ludendorff Bridge at Remagen and developing a small, albeit the first, Allied bridgehead east of the Rhine. The army commander promptly redirected his moving columns and sent strong elements across the river. General Patton's units reached the Rhine at

---

[4] Two months after the conference, on April 12, 1945, President Roosevelt died of a stroke. He was succeeded by Vice-President Harry S. Truman.

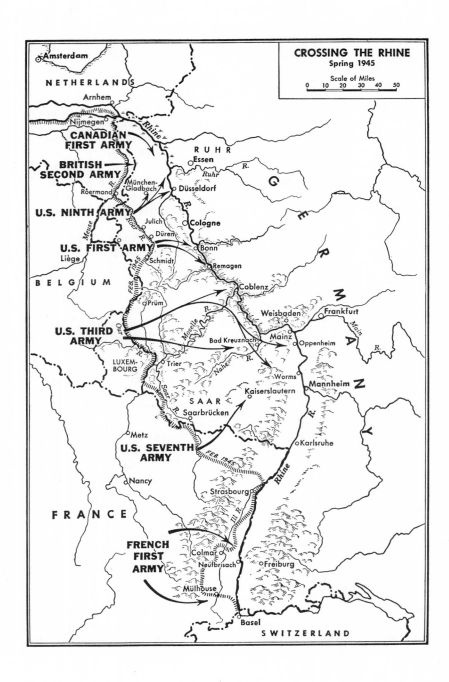

CROSSING THE RHINE
Spring 1945

Scale of Miles
0   10   20   30   40   50

Coblenz soon thereafter and on March 22, 1945, crossed the Rhine at Oppenheim.

All along the front the Allies rushed forward, astounding the Germans by blithely bypassing formidably garrisoned pockets, particularly those in the Ruhr Valley. Whereas the Canadians and British passed on through the Netherlands and northern Germany to the Baltic, and the French thrust eastward from Mülhouse into the Black Forest, the Americans drove, on the one hand, toward and into Czechoslovakia and Austria, and on the other, toward the Elbe and eastward to Torgau, near Leipzig. Here, at Torgau, the juncture with the Red Army occurred, on April 25, 1945. Meanwhile, from behind the Allied forward positions, three United States armies had taken the Ruhr—and with it, 300,000 prisoners.

While these events transpired in the west, the Russians were delivering sledgehammer blows in the east. Stripped of strategic reserves through the outcome of the Ardennes Counteroffensive and subjected to heavy strategic bombing, the Germans had neither the man power nor the resources to withstand the drives launched by Soviet forces at the start of 1945. A mass of men, reputedly 4,000,000 in number, advanced along a 750-mile front. They crashed into East Prussia, pushed through western Poland and into Silesia, and smashed their way across Hungary into Austria. Then, while some Russians met the Americans near Leipzig and in Czechoslovakia, others, under Marshal Gregory K. Zhukov, fought their way into the outskirts of Berlin on April 22, 1945. The fighting was fiercest at the Reich Chancellory, in whose underground defenses Hitler had set up his last headquarters. When all obviously was lost, Hitler and his bride of three days (Eva Braun) presumably committed suicide on April 30 in a Berlin Chancellory bunker.[5] He is believed to have shot himself through the mouth, after having designated as his successor Grand Admiral Karl Doenitz.[6] Doenitz assumed power as Hitler's successor, but could do nothing to avert disaster.

On May 5, 1945, the commander of all German forces in northeastern Germany, the Netherlands, and Denmark surrendered unconditionally. On the next day, the Nazi forces in Austria followed suit. On May 7, in a little schoolhouse in Reims, an emissary of Doenitz surrendered unconditionally "all land, sea, and air forces of

[5] Goebbels died in the same bunker, probably having himself shot by an orderly. Himmler hid in Flensburg for some days and then committed suicide by poison after walking into a British control post. Göring, as will be seen, lived to be captured and tried as a war criminal, along with Ribbentrop, Rosenberg, Seyss-Inquart, and others.

[6] If what was said to be Hitler's testament may be believed, then the Führer, shortly before his death, expelled Göring and Himmler from all their offices and from the Nazi Party. "Göring and Himmler," he reputedly wrote, "by their secret negotiations with the enemy . . . and by their illegal attempts to seize power in the state . . . have brought irreparable shame on their country." Feeling betrayed by the army, the SS, and the politicians, Hitler decided that his successor should be a navy man.

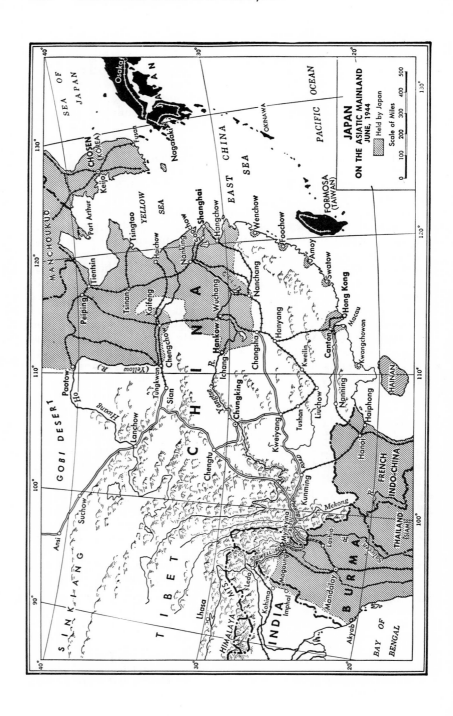

JAPAN
ON THE ASIATIC MAINLAND
JUNE, 1944

▨ Held by Japan

Scale of Miles
0 100 200 300 400 500

the Reich." A second capitulation was signed with the Russians in Berlin on May 9. Five years and eight months after the Nazi invasion of Poland, and eleven months after the Allied invasion of Normandy, came Victory-in-Europe or V-E Day (May 8, 1945).

V-J DAY

Despite the intensity of the warfare in Europe, the Allies simultaneously were forging victory in the Pacific area. Here the major responsibility fell on the United States, cooperating with Australia, New Zealand, Britain, Fighting Frenchmen, Chinese, Netherlanders, and, toward the end, Russians.

The successful attack on Guadalcanal, whose conquest was completed by February 1943, marked the inauguration of an island-hopping strategy, whereby enemy island outposts were isolated, conquered, converted into Allied bases, and used as springboards for further attacks—each one striking closer to Japan proper. At the same time, efforts were made to supply China via India with the necessary material to keep her in the war. Otherwise the Tokyo Government might have been free to exploit the tremendous Chinese resources and, indeed, in the event of a successful Allied invasion of the Japanese homeland, to continue the war from China as a base. The process, as directed by General MacArthur, was slow but steady. As United States strength in the Pacific gradually was built up, the pressure on the Japanese was intensified until, finally, they succumbed.

Between May and August 1943, the Japanese were dislodged from their holds on the Aleutian Islands, thus removing a potential threat to Alaska. By November 1943 the Gilbert Islands, including Tarawa and Makin, were in Allied hands. Three months later Kwajalein in the Marshall group and Eniwetok fell. From these bases, United States planes and ships were able to neutralize the fortress island of Truk and open the way to Saipan and Tinian in the Marianas, and to Guam by July 1944. The first major strike on a Japanese home island, Honshu, came from Saipan and Guam in November 1944. It is difficult to visualize the ferocity of combat that accompanied these advances. Generally, according to Marshall's report, "the enemy was concentrated within restricted areas, heavily fortified in pillboxes, and protected by mines and beach obstacles. Landing forces faced intense crossfires. The enemy could be dislodged only by shattering bombardment and powerful hand-to-hand infantry assault."

The autumn of 1944 saw two great Allied campaigns launched in the Far East. The one, under Rear Admiral Lord Louis Mountbatten, aimed at the reconquest of Burma and the reopening of adequate communications with China. Dependent on airborne deliveries, and thus "maintained at the end of the most precarious supply lines in history," these operations were completed successfully by May 1945. The other campaign, led by General MacArthur, involved the reconquest of the Philippine Islands between October 1944 and June 1945. For this enterprise the ocean path had been cleared largely by the naval and air victories of Admiral William Halsey and his United States Third Fleet. The first landings were made at the island of Leyte, and Japanese fleets that had hoped to intercept the landing armada were defeated in the Battle for Leyte Gulf (October 23–26, 1944). In January 1945 MacArthur made another surprise landing, this time on Luzon. Manila fell on February 23, 1945, and by the close of June organized resistance in the Philippine Islands was at an end.

The campaigns in southeastern Asia and in the Philippines did not check the island hopping of the Allies. Iwo Jima, one of the Bonin Islands and fewer than 800 miles from Tokyo, was bombarded for several months by the superfortresses (B-29's) based on Saipan. Then it was taken by storm in February–March 1945. On April 1, the initial landing on Okinawa began, and after three months of fighting this "doorstep" of Japan in the Ryukyus was won.[7] Meanwhile the Australians had landed on Borneo and completed "the chain of mutually supporting strategic bases from which Allied air and naval forces could cover the Asiatic coast from Singapore to Shanghai." By July 1945 an Anglo-American squadron was able to sail along the Japanese coast and drop shells on Honshu, while B-29's hurled destruction on the empire's cities.

The time therefore seemed propitious for another meeting of the heads of the Allied Governments, all the more since Tokyo already had extended peace feelers in Moscow—at this time still neutral with respect to Japan. On July 17, 1945, such a meeting was convened at Potsdam in Germany. Present were Truman, Chiang Kai-shek, Stalin, and Clement R. Attlee—who during the conference succeeded Churchill as prime minister of Great Britain following a Labor Party victory at the polls. Among other things, the Potsdam Conference confirmed an occupational division of Central Europe and called upon Tokyo "to proclaim now the unconditional surrender of all Japanese armed forces . . . . The alternative for Japan is prompt and utter destruction." Since the Soviet Union was not at war with Japan, Stalin did not participate in this declaration. But he did agree to implement his earlier promise made at the Yalta Conference (February 1945) that the U.S.S.R. would enter the war against Japan within three months after the close of armed hostilities in Europe.

Japan declared through Premier Kantaro Suzuki that it would

---

[7] During this campaign the Japanese made effective use of "suicide planes" from the Kamikaze Corps. Altogether, according to Fleet Admiral Ernest Joseph King, the Japanese at Okinawa hit from the air "about 250 vessels of all classes, from battleships and cruisers down to destroyers and landing ships, . . . by far the greatest proportion of them in suicide crashes."

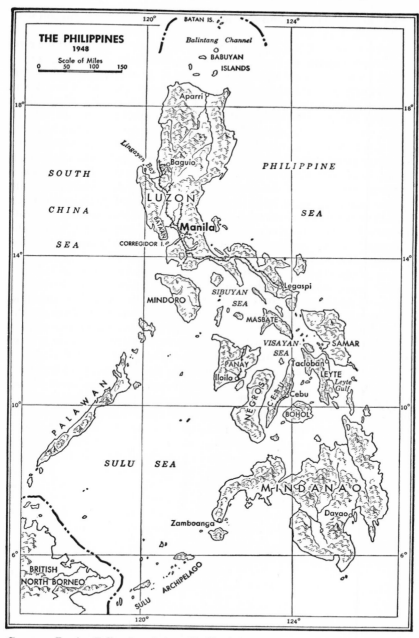

THE PHILIPPINES
1948

Scale of Miles
0   50   100   150

BATAN IS.

Balintang Channel

BABUYAN
ISLANDS

Aparri

Lingayen Bay

Baguio

SOUTH

CHINA

SEA

PHILIPPINE

SEA

LUZON

BATAAN

Manila

CORREGIDOR I.

Legaspi

MINDORO

SIBUYAN
SEA

MASBATE

VISAYAN
SEA

SAMAR

PANAY

Tacloban

LEYTE

Iloilo

Leyte
Gulf

NEGROS

CEBU

Cebu

BOHOL

PALAWAN

SULU   SEA

MINDANAO

Davao

Zamboanga

BRITISH
NORTH BORNEO

SULU
ARCHIPELAGO

Courtesy, Foreign Policy Association, *Headline Series.*

ignore the ultimatum and continue the fight. Thus a fateful die was cast.

On August 6, 1945, a B-29 flew over the militarily important city of Hiroshima and dropped a small bomb which, working through atomic fission, wiped out more than half of the target area. The decision to utilize the bomb if Japan did not capitulate had been made at the Potsdam Conference in the expectation that its employment would shorten the war. It also was believed that the use of the awesome atomic weaponry would make unnecessary the employment of a two-fold invasion plan of Japan that had been prepared by MacArthur and Fleet Admiral Chester William Nimitz. Two days later, on August 8, Moscow declared war on Tokyo. Red offensives were begun into Manchuria and into the southern or Japanese half of the island of Sakhalin. The Japanese forces still in Manchuria at this time were not so strong as the London and Washington governments believed, and the progress of the Soviet troops was swift. On August 9, a second atomic or A-bomb was dropped on Japan, this time on Nagasaki.

On August 10, Tokyo sued for peace through the Swiss and Swedish governments. Agreement was reached on Allied terms, but because of the need to take proper precautions against possible Japanese trickery and because of exceptionally bad weather conditions, the surrender document was signed only on September 2, 1945 (V-J Day), aboard the battleship *Missouri* anchored in Tokyo Bay. General of the Army MacArthur signed as Supreme Commander for the Allied Powers. Six years and a day had elapsed since the outbreak of the bloodiest and costliest war in history. For the second time within twenty-seven years there fell upon men the grave responsibility of so settling conditions that the loss in lives and goods should not have been entirely in vain.

"When There Is No Peace" | 20

VICTORY—AND DISILLUSIONMENT

During the war, in face of mortal peril from the Axis, Great Britain, the Soviet Union and the United States maintained an outward unity that was encouraging to those who looked forward to a postwar world of peace. Churchill, Stalin, and Roosevelt seemed to like each other personally. The respective chiefs of staff appeared to be in major disagreement only over the question of the timing of the invasion of France. From the many Big Three Conferences emerged communiqués that reflected seeming unanimity on all major points of discussion. Sometimes there were indications of French or Chinese displeasure over the triune assumption of world authority. But these were regarded as relatively unimportant, since the three strongest powers so obviously were dominant in the task of beating the common enemy. The optimists were certain that future peace would be assured by the continuance, after hostilities ceased, of the unity that characterized the difficult war years.

Disillusion, however, followed close upon victory. Actually, all was not harmony even during the war. There was much, albeit secret, wrangling at the top-level conferences. Often the disagreements were resolved only through the adoption of policy statements so broad and general that they later could be given widely differing interpretations. When the time came for implementing the policies, these widely differing interpretations led to dispute and trouble.

Implementation of the announced policies meant solving the critical postwar international problems. The more important of these included: the disposition of the millions of displaced persons (DP's) moved about by the Nazis; the status of millions of refugees from both the Axis countries and the Soviet Union, with its budding satel-

395

lites; the economic, cultural, and social rehabilitation of Europe and Asia; the capture and trial of war criminals and the process of de-Nazifying and "reeducating" Central Europe; the creation of an atmosphere conducive to the development of democratic institutions in Germany and the neighboring areas; the drafting of peace treaties with all former enemy states; the question of the atomic bomb and its influence on international relations; reparations; the restoration of world trade; territorial readjustments amidst continuing fear, rampant nationalistic spirits, and revived or newly aroused and often conflicting national ambitions. If the solution of such problems was avoided, as it was, by the Big Three when, under wartime conditions, they could act in secrecy and largely in disregard of public opinion, how much more difficult it would be to solve them after the war, without the restraints imposed by a life-and-death struggle against a common military enemy.

Arrival at generally accepted solutions was made harder by additional complications. There were clashes between several governments-in-exile and the respective local leaders, who had emerged as heroes from the underground resistance movements. The division of Germany and Austria into occupation zones, and the requirement of unanimous agreement among the occupying powers, where general decisions were involved, often resulted in a stalemate and a consequent worsening of conditions that needed prompt action. On-the-spot proof that the actual atrocities committed under Nazi sponsorship at the concentration camps of Dachau, Buchenwald, and Auschwitz surpassed in horror many of the incredible stories circulated during the war, often caused, understandably, hot blood to take precedence over calm judgment. In the victorious countries there were strong reactions against rationing and other wartime prohibitions and restraints. The fiercer and stronger national spirits that emerged from the conflict made ludicrous some experts' earlier talks regarding the supposed unimportance of political boundaries in the future.

Finally, the situation was made worse by ideological considerations. Almost everywhere in Europe, but especially in the areas closest to and most readily overawed by Moscow, there was a movement to the political left. Poland, Yugoslavia, Romania, Bulgaria, Hungary, Albania, Czechoslovakia, and Finland all came within the Stalinist orbit. In Western Europe the electorate as a whole rejected communism, but the Leninist-Marxist elements displayed strength and did much to hamper reconstruction. At the same time, most European countries looked to the United States for financial help. Since such aid was forthcoming, United States dollars became an important bulwark against the further spread of communism.

We now come to a more detailed discussion of how some of these well, attended by a seemingly harmonious relationship among the situations developed out of a war that appeared to be proceeding great powers winning it.

THE YALTA OR CRIMEA CONFERENCE
(FEBRUARY 1945)

The shape of the world after World War II basically was determined by the war itself. To one who has not lived through a major war, such as World War II, it is difficult to explain the almost total concentration of an embattled nation, its people, leaders, and officials upon the winning of the conflict. Hence it has seemed to some that the Allies, knowing by 1944 that eventually they would be victorious, might well have begun to plan for peace in a way that would avoid the mistakes of 1919. But such was not the case, largely because the defeat of the Axis overrode all other considerations.

There had, indeed, been some earlier indications of postwar aspirations for a better world. Thus, there was the Atlantic Charter of August 1941, which was endorsed by most of the countries at war with Germany. But the Atlantic Charter, idealistic and vague in content, provided few specific plans for shaping the world after victory. Then, too, there had been several summit-level conferences, at Casablanca, Quebec, Cairo, and Tehran. But all these concentrated on what seemed the most important immediate goal, namely, the defeat of the Axis Powers. Only in 1945 when victory seemed close at hand, were the problems of the peace-to-come given serious consideration near Yalta on the Crimean Peninsula.

Two miles from the Russian resort city of Yalta in the Crimea, the three most influential leaders in the Allied world sat down to lay a foundation for a new world order. Each of the leaders, Churchill, Stalin, and Roosevelt, sought a new ordering of world affairs, and each eventually was at least partly disappointed. Churchill wished, among other things, to preserve the British Empire; in this he failed. Stalin wished to extend westward a buffer zone to protect the U.S.S.R. and, at that time, to maintain viable relations with Western Europe; in the latter endeavor at least, he too failed. And Roosevelt, who apparently hoped for continuing friendship between Washington and Moscow, had sensed before his death two months later that the U.S.S.R. would become the focus of much trouble in the postwar world.[1]

Such good feeling as came out of Yalta soon was dissipated by rapidly changing international situations. Ten years after Yalta, amid deep antagonism between the United States and the Soviet Union, it was difficult even to imagine the atmosphere in which Western and Soviet statesmen had sat down as seeming friends to plan the total destruction of the Axis and the creation of a strife-free world.

---

[1] Some of the United States representatives, believing they had got a full Soviet commitment to help maintain the future peace, returned from Yalta in a jubilant mood. Harry Hopkins, Roosevelt's most important advisor at the conference, wrote later that he and his colleagues looked upon Yalta as "the dawn of a new day," and that Stalin was "reasonable and understanding."

The major decisions reached at Yalta concerned Germany, Poland, the Far East, and the United Nations. The Russians came to the Yalta Conference with an attitude of retribution, signs of which had been noticeable earlier, particularly at the Quebec Conference of August 1943. Stalin did not disguise his desire for a punitive peace that would deindustrialize and dismember Germany. In earlier discussions, Churchill and Roosevelt had gone along with this notion, but at Yalta they began to express doubt as to the wisdom of such a course. The firm Western position at Yalta therefore was to postpone talk regarding Germany's eventual fate. Thus the only important decision reached on Germany was an agreement to divide the country into four zones of occupation, to be administered, respectively, by the United States, the Soviet Union, Britain, and France. The Soviet Zone was to encompass Berlin, the captial of Germany. Actual administration of the city was to be a cooperative project of the occupying powers.[2]

The matter of Poland's postwar boundaries and the related border question of the future of all Eastern European nations occupied most of the statesmen's time at Yalta. Churchill, indeed, called Poland "the most urgent" item on the agenda of the conference. Churchill proposed that in the postwar settlement Poland be made "captain of her own soul." Stalin countered by restating the traditional Russian fears of a hostile Poland and demanding a "safe" buffer area adjacent to the Soviet Union. The Russian dictator was willing to agree to an independent Poland, provided its friendship for the U.S.S.R. could be assured. After much argument, it was decided that Poland should start with a provisional government. The establishment of a provisional government, however, was made difficult by the fact that there were two important claimants to such control. In London there still existed the Western-style democratic government-in-exile that had been established with Allied help after the fall of Poland. In Lublin, meanwhile, there had come into being a "government" of Polish Communists who claimed the right to determine the future of Poland. Eventually, it was agreed that the provisional government would be a coalition formed of both groups, until elections based on "universal suffrage" could be held to determine the permanent nature of the Polish Government. It also was indicated at Yalta that the Soviet Union would be granted territory in eastern Poland, with Warsaw compensated in the west at the expense of Germany.

Shortly after Yalta, as the armies of the Soviet Union raced toward Germany and overran Eastern Europe, it became apparent that the elections promised at Yalta probably would be held according to Soviet design. Later on, in fact, little attention was paid to the Yalta promises of "free and unfettered elections on the basis of universal

---

[2] Unhappily for future harmony, the question of Western access routes to the territorial island of Berlin was not considered at Yalta.

suffrage" and of a "secret ballot" for the inhabitants in any of the states bordering the U.S.S.R. on the West.

Those discussions at Yalta that dealt with the Far East seemed to arouse the least controversy. Roosevelt was anxious that the weight of Soviet arms be brought to bear upon Japan to speed the conclusion of the war. He had good reason to expect such action, since Stalin had pledged military help several times since Pearl Harbor, but had not yet given any. In return for a commitment from Stalin to enter the conflict against Japan as soon as victory against Hitler was won, the United States, without consulting China, agreed that the U.S.S.R. would recover harbor and railway privileges in Manchuria lost to Japan in the Russo-Japanese War of 1905. Roosevelt also agreed with Stalin that Outer Mongolia, still claimed by China but under Soviet tutelage as the "Mongolian People's Republic," should be recognized as "independent." Finally, it was agreed that the Soviets would be allowed to reclaim from Japan the southern part of Sakhalin Island, to lease the Port Arthur naval base, and to take the Kurile Island chain.

Decisions relating to a new international organization to preserve peace also were made at Yalta, and these were of great moment to the United States. There had been preliminary talks of a United Nations organization as early as 1941. At a Dumbarton Oaks Conference in Washington in 1944, a draft charter had been produced. At Yalta there was further delineation of several points: (1) it was decided that in the proposed Security Council, on matters of substance rather than mere procedure, any one among China, France, the Soviet Union, the United Kingdom, and the United States would have the right to exercise a veto; and (2), since some of the dominions of the British Empire would have votes of their own, the Soviet Republics of the Ukraine and White Russia also would get votes in the General Assembly.

The Yalta Conference ended on February 11, 1945, on notes of good will. It seemed, at this point, that a friendship born of the wartime alliance between Russia and the West could not but exert a positive influence in the making of the postwar world. At first, much of the Western world rejoiced at the apparent agreement on many important issues of war and peace. By the end of the war, however, there was widespread criticism of Stalin in the United States press and, in light of developing Russian tactics on the international scene, Western diplomats became increasingly apprehensive of Soviet aims.

But public opinion, especially in the United States, was not ready to turn against the Russians at the time of Yalta; there was no general shift in opinion until about 1947. Instead, most Americans in late 1945 and early 1946 seemed intent on getting the armed forces home as rapidly as possible.[3] Thus it happened that many people in the

---

[3] In discussing democratic public opinion, a prominent political theorist wrote that liberal democracies cannot be aroused to "the exertions and

Western democracies and those who represented them at the conference tables still admired Russia for her wartime sacrifices when the San Francisco Conference convened in late April 1945.

FORMATION OF THE UNITED NATIONS

It became increasingly clear, as the Second World War wore on, that some form of effective international organization was necessary if humanity wished to avoid the specter of an even more disastrous third global conflict. Among Western Europeans the conviction grew that new machinery must be created, of a type more likely to be utilized than was the League of Nations. Among United States citizens of both large political parties there developed a belief that American isolationism in the post-1919 period probably had helped prevent the creation of an effective international security system. President Roosevelt emerged as leader of those who believed that the United States would "have to take the responsibility for world collaboration" or else "bear the responsibility for another world conflict". In this stand he was seconded by Wendell L. Willkie, unsuccessful Republican presidential candidate in 1940.

Seeking to apply the lesson of experience, the Allied leaders decided to keep the matter of a new world organization distinct from the drafting and early enforcement of any peace treaties. Hence strenuous effort was made to bring a United Nations organization into existence while the wartime cooperation was still strong "and before the great coalition was weakened by disagreements which were bound to make their appearance at the peace table."

From the time of American entry into the war, much preliminary studying and planning, official and private, was done in both the United States and Great Britain. This bore fruit first in congressional resolutions of 1943 endorsing the principle of United States participation in appropriate international peace machinery.[4] Then came a Moscow Declaration of Four Nations on General Security issued in November 1943 by the United States, United Kingdom, U.S.S.R., and China. The declaration, among other things, stated that the powers concerned "recognize the necessity of establishing at the earliest

---

sacrifices" necessary to a struggle, such as a world war or the "Cold War" that followed World War II, until they are "frightened" by the opening disasters and thus "incited to a passionate hatred." The Western democracies, he held, must of necessity have the enemy portrayed as evil incarnate before public opinion can be mobilized against a country or ideology. Thus, there is bound to be a time lag in the major switching of democratic public opinion. See: Walter Lippman, *Essays in the Public Philosophy* (Boston, 1955), pp. 19–21.

[4] The Fulbright Resolution in the House and the Connally Resolution in the Senate were the two resolutions. Both major-party platforms in 1944 supported the substance of the resolutions, as did presidential candidates Roosevelt and Thomas E. Dewey of the Republican Party.

practicable date a general international organization, based on the principle of the sovereign equality of all peace-loving states, and open to membership by all such states, large and small, for the maintenance of international peace and security."

The next step was taken at the Dumbarton Oaks Conference in 1944. Here a general outline was drawn up providing for United Nations organs that resembled those of the old League. It already was apparent at Dumbarton Oaks that the views of the U.S.S.R. and other great powers would clash on some points. Moscow seemingly envisioned a world organization that could be used as a medium for getting general acceptance by all nations of the big powers' decisions. Probably, the publicity potential of the new body as a sounding board for Soviet propaganda also entered Stalin's considerations. The resulting arguments over a number of items at Dumbarton Oaks were shelved for later settlement—some of them coming up again at Yalta.

As already indicated, further progress was made at the Yalta Conference. Here the dominant leaders agreed that an organizational conference of the United Nations should be held in San Francisco to fill out the skeletons constructed at Dumbarton Oaks and Yalta. Fifty nations then participated in the San Francisco Conference, from April 25 to June 26, 1945, and fifty-one became original signatories of the resulting United Nations Charter.

The main purpose of the United Nations, according to this Charter, was to be the maintenance of international peace and security. The UN was to develop friendly relations among nations on the bases of equal rights and the self-determination of peoples. It was to achieve international cooperation in the handling of worldwide economic, social, cultural, and humanitarian problems. It further was designed to promote respect for human rights, dignity, and freedom. In pursuit of these ends, the members accepted the principle of the sovereign equality of large and small states, the obligation to settle international disputes by peaceful means and to refrain from the use or threat of force in their international dealings, and the duty to assist in any United Nations action against a violating state. The organization was not to intervene in matters that were essentially within the domestic jurisdiction of any country.

Beyond the fifty-one original signatories of the United Nations Charter, new members were to be admitted by a two-thirds vote of the assembly. The requirements for membership appeared simple. Applicants had to satisfy the UN membership that they were "peace-loving," would accept the obligations of the Charter, and were capable of carrying out these responsibilities. But the fact that any one of the Big Five could veto an application in the council made each membership appeal a potential opportunity for dispute, or at least for diplomatic bargaining.

Early in 1946, Trygve H. Lie (pronounced Lee), a Norwegian Labor Party leader and former foreign minister, was appointed Secretary-General by the assembly. After seven years of hard and effective work he resigned, largely because of Russian opposition to his policies. The financing of the organization was supervised by the assembly, which determined the financial contributions of members. Until permanent buildings were constructed in Manhattan, on land contributed by John D. Rockefeller, Jr., temporary headquarters were maintained at Lake Success on Long Island.

The Charter provided for six main organs: the General Assembly, the Security Council, the Economic and Social Council, the Trusteeship Council, the Secretariat, and the International Court of Justice. A group of subsidiary and specialized agencies was to operate under the general coordination of the Economic and Social Council, itself supervised by the assembly.

The General Assembly was the only instrument of the United Nations consisting of all members. Each member state might have five delegates but only one vote. The assembly was to meet every year beginning in September, but special sessions might be called by the Secretary-General at the request of a majority of the members of the Security Council. Decisions on "important questions" required a two-thirds vote; others only a simple majority. The "important" matters were recommendations as to peace and security, the admission or suspension of members, trusteeship items, and elections of members of other organs.

The assembly could discuss any matter "within the scope of the present Charter." It had to formulate plans for eventual disarmament and could make recommendations to the member states and, in most cases, to the Security Council. The assembly adopted the UN budget and was expected to receive, study, and discuss reports from all other organs. It elected its own president and vice-president for each session.

The assembly was empowered to elect the nonpermanent members of the Security Council, and all members of the Trusteeship Council and the Economic and Social Council. The last two bodies definitely were made to function under authority of the assembly. The General Assembly was well characterized as a "town-meeting of the world," as essentially a "deliberative organ, an overseeing, reviewing, and criticizing organ." With the Charter coming into force on October 24, 1945, the assembly opened its first meeting in London on January 10, 1946.

The Security Council, operating in effect as the executive body, was required to function continuously. It was made up of five permanent and six (later ten) nonpermanent members, each with one vote. The nonpermanent members were chosen by the General Assembly, three each for two-year terms. They were ineligible for immediate relection. The permanent members were China, France, the Soviet Union, the United Kingdom, and the United States. Decisions of the council required seven of the eleven votes. The concurring votes of the five permanent members had to be included in the majority of seven except on matters of procedure. Thus was established the principle of the veto of council decisions by one of the five permanent members. The principle came to be applied most frequently by the U.S.S.R.

To the Security Council was entrusted "primary responsibility for the maintenance of international peace and security." It was empowered to "investigate any dispute, or any situation which might lead to international friction or give rise to a dispute." To aid in this task the UN Charter provided, in the event that other sanctions failed, for an "international police force" to be constructed under special agreements, from the armed forces of the member nations. There was no permanent UN military force, but UN military forces were organized on a temporary basis on several occasions, including the Korean War that began in 1950, the Suez crisis of 1956, and the conflict in the 1950's and 1960's over Cyprus between Greece and Turkey.

The Security Council did not always work effectively. For its first few years it scored some major successes in areas where the interests of the great powers were not involved. But the Soviet Union by use of the veto increasingly restricted the council from acting in major international crises. Consequently, in such cases as those of the Korean War and the Suez crisis, the handling of major crises came to be assumed by the General Assembly.

In order to bring about the "conditions of stability and well-being" necessary for a peaceful international scene, and in order to promote higher standards of living everywhere, the Charter created an Economic and Social Council. This council was to be composed of eighteen members, elected by the General Assembly. The Economic and Social Council was empowered to prepare studies and reports on appropriate matters, make recommendations in the economic and social areas to the General Assembly, and coordinate the specialized intergovernmental agencies created by members of the UN. The UN eventually established many commissions—dealing with problems such as overpopulation, human rights, the drug traffic, and communications. One of the most important of the agencies created by the UN in this general area was the United Nations Educational Scientific and Cultural Organization (UNESCO).

The constitution of UNESCO came into force in 1946, at which time the General Assembly approved the transfer to UNESCO of the property of the League of Nations' International Institute of Cooperation. The purposes of UNESCO were to advance mutual knowledge and understanding of peoples through all means of mass communication, give fresh impulse to popular education, and increase and diffuse knowledge throughout the world.

The Charter established a trusteeship system "for the administration and supervision of such territories as might be placed thereunder by subsequent individual agreements." These regions were to be called "trust territories." Categories open to trusteeship were existing mandates, areas detached from enemy states as a result of the war, and any regions voluntarily turned over by their governments for administration. The Trusteeship Council was composed of all members administering trust territories, any of the five permanent members of the Security Council not already included as administrators, and as many other members as might be needed to give the Trusteeship Council an equal number of administering and nonadministering countries.

The chief administrative officer of the United Nations was the Secretary-General, appointed by the General Assembly upon recommendation of the Security Council. He acted as secretary-general at all meetings of the General Assembly, Security, Economic and Social, and Trusteeship councils. He was required to make an annual report to the assembly and was empowered to bring to the attention of the Security Council any matter that in his opinion might threaten international peace and security. He and his staff were international officials ineligible to seek or receive instructions from any authority outside the organization of the UN.

The International Court of Justice functioned under a statute based upon that used by the earlier World Court. Every member of the UN was automatically a member of the court. Nonmembers of the UN might join the court, on conditions to be determined in each case by the General Assembly and Security Council. Each member of the UN undertook to comply with the decisions of the court in cases to which it was a party. In the event of noncompliance, the aggrieved party might appeal to the Security Council for help. The court might render advisory opinions on legal questions submitted to it by the General Assembly, the Security Council, and other UN organs. Only states might be parties to cases before the tribunal. The court was composed of fifteen judges, all from different nations.

By the fall of 1970, there had been three Secretaries-General of the United Nations. After Lie, in 1953, Dag H. Hammarskjöld, a Swedish financial expert, took the post and impressed observers with his wisdom and patience. Following Hammarskjöld's tragic, apparently accidental, death in a plane crash in 1961 while he was en route to the Congo area, his office was assumed by U Thant, who had been the Burmese delegate to the UN.

THE POTSDAM CONFERENCE

As has been indicated, the general aims of the Allies for Germany had been outlined during the war. A Berlin Declaration on June 5, 1945, whereby the major Allies assumed supreme authority over the Reich, reaffirmed these aims. Finally, in July and August 1945, Germany's future was the main subject of discussion among representatives of the victorious powers meeting at Potsdam, just outside Berlin. Of the wartime Big Three chiefs of state who had met at Yalta, only Stalin remained to go to Potsdam. A Labor Party victory in Great Britain brought Clement Attlee to the conference as the British representative, and President Harry S. Truman represented the United States. Nearby, in war-devastated Berlin, the bewildered German survivors, who had believed in the infallibility of Hitler, searched the rubble of ruined houses to avoid starvation.[5]

At one time, serious consideration was given to the dismemberment of Germany. At Potsdam, however, the Western Powers wished to define the boundaries of Germany to coincide with those of December 31, 1937—as they had existed before Hitler's Reich began its career of expansion. But Truman and Attlee were faced with a *fait accompli* since the Soviet Union, without notifying Britain and the United States, already had entrusted to Poland the administration of German territory east of the Oder-Neisse rivers. Thus the Western Powers had little choice, short of outright military intervention, but to recognize the "temporary" Polish administration east of the Oder-Neisse Line, "pending the final determination of Poland's western frontier." The Western Allies, also, grudgingly gave approval to the eventual transfer of the northern half of East Prussia to the Soviet Union.

The remaining area of Germany (about 137,000 square miles) was divided into four zones of occupation. Each was to be controlled by an Allied zone commander under an overall Allied Control Council. The United States Zone consisted mainly of Bavaria, Hesse, and sections of Württemberg-Baden. In addition, a United States enclave was established at the port of Bremen, to facilitate its supply services. The British occupied an area including Schleswig-Holstein, Lower Saxony, Hamburg, and a new state called North Rhine-Westphalia (the former Lower Rhineland, Ruhr, and Westphalia). The Soviet Zone comprised Brandenburg, Saxony, Mecklenburg, Pomerania, and Thuringia. The smallest zone was turned over to France, consisting of the Palatinate and the Upper Rhine Valley, including the Saar Basin.

Berlin was given a special status. It was to be divided into four sectors, each to be occupied by troops of one of the four powers. As was Germany itself, the city was to be administered by an inter-Allied organ. Bilateral agreements, not part of the Potsdam arrangement, then were drawn up between the Western powers and the Soviet Union to allow the former free access to Berlin by automobiles, airplanes, canal boats, and trains. Berlin thus became a microcosm of the German macrocosm. (Similar arrangements were decreed in respect of Austria and Vienna.)

German denazification, demilitarization, and the trial of war

---

[5] By this time it was becoming apparent that Moscow would follow a policy of her own design in Eastern Europe. The Russians, for example, showed no signs of preparing for elections in Poland as promised at Yalta. President Truman, it should be noted, too, came to the conference with the knowledge that in the deserts of New Mexico an atomic bomb had been detonated successfully. Understandably, the atmosphere of the conference was a mixture of caution and tension.

criminals were considered at Potsdam. The Potsdam Decrees aimed at decentralizing the German administration and preventing the revival of Nazism and German militarism. Many former military and all paramilitary organizations (such as the SA and SS) were abolished. All Nazi laws and institutions were removed from the German scene, and Nazi office-holders were dismissed. War criminals were to be placed on trial in order that all Germany might learn the details of the "chaos and suffering" caused by Hitler's Third Reich.

It was decided that Germany must be divested of most of its heavy industries and of other plants that had produced war material. It was agreed that the German living standard would not be allowed to rise above that of other European countries. Tied in with this latter statement of intent was the matter of reparation, though no final decision was reached at Potsdam on the total amount of damage to be paid by Germany. Stalin, however, demanded $10,000,000,000 worth of industrial equipment already within the Soviet Zone and certain German foreign assets. Moscow also desired industrial equipment in the Western zones, and the powers eventually fell to bickering over how much of such machinery should be given to the Russians and how much was necessary for Germany's own postwar economy. The Potsdam Commitment that Germany would be treated "as a single economic unit" was virtually disregarded in practice. For the rest, the Potsdam Decrees became the writ for Allied Military Government and the basis of Germany's administration for several years.

At Potsdam, also, there was created a Council of Foreign Ministers representing the Big Four and China. Its duties were to draft the peace treaties with the smaller defeated states and to prepare a final German settlement.

THE NUREMBERG TRIALS

A direct outgrowth of the Allied assertion at Potsdam that German leaders should suffer for their war crimes was the Nuremberg Trials.[6] Beginning in the fall of 1945, twenty-two individuals and seven Nazi organizations were tried by an inter-allied tribunal at Nuremberg in Bavaria, a city that once had been the site of Nazi mass meetings. They were charged under four classes of indictment: crimes against peace (violation of treaties, and so on.); war crimes in violation of the developed customs of warfare; crimes against humanity (genocide, deportation of populations, and so on); and conspiracy to launch aggressive war.

Of the organizations tried, three were acquitted: the SA, the Reich Cabinet, and the Army General Staff and High Command. Four were adjudged guilty: the SS, the Security Police, the Gestapo, and the leadership corps of the Nazi Party. It was stipulated, however, that

[6] Actually, the Allied Governments had asserted as early as 1942 that, after the war's end, they would punish Nazis for specific crimes.

membership in these condemned organizations did not automatically make a man a criminal in the eyes of the law. Lower courts were to consider the circumstances of individual accusations before passing judgment.

Of the persons tried by the tribunal, only three were acquitted: Hjalmar Schacht, who had been dismissed from his post as president of the Reichsbank in 1939; Franz von Papan, who had incurred Hitler's disfavor as early as 1934; and Hans Fritsche, a radio propagandist. Twelve of the defendants, including Field Marshal Hermann Göring, were sentenced to hang. Göring, however, cheated the hangman by committing suicide in his cell. The Foreign Minister of Nazi Germany, Joachim von Ribbentrop; the party's "intellectual," Alfred Rosenberg; Arthur Seyss-Inquart of Austrian infamy; and Hans Frank, former Reich Commissioner for Justice, were among the ten actually hanged. Martin Bormann, who had left Hitler's bunker and disappeared, was convicted and sentenced *in absentia*. Rudolf Hess, Walther Funk, and Grand Admiral Erich Raeder were sentenced to life imprisonment. The remaining four were given sentences of from ten to twenty years' duration.

A number of the judges at the trial believed it to have been a success. Robert H. Jackson, an American Supreme Court Associate Justice who had sat on the tribunal, regarded the trials as a considerable improvement over the past approaches to the problem of war criminals. He declared that the Nuremburg Trials had set "a civilized legal precedent." Other judicial and political figures echoed Jackson's sentiments. But there also were negative assessments of the trials' worth. German critics pointed out that the judgments of Nuremberg rested upon victory in war and not upon basic law and fundamental concepts of justice. United States Senator Robert A. Taft, Sr., of Ohio, declared that "the trial of the vanquished by the victors cannot be impartial . . . ." Some suggested that it might have been wiser to make up a court of judges from countries (Switzerland, for example) that had been neutral during the war. Moreover, several of the crimes charged to the Nazis were not covered by existing international law. Thus, the tribunal was accused of creating a new international legality without the concurrence of all nations.

As the controversy diminished, the lesser war crimes trials were permitted to drag on, and public interest gradually turned away from them. In 1958, however, a Central Office for Nazi Crimes was set up by the Federal Republic of West Germany in Ludwigsburg. This was West Germany's answer to complaints by both Germans and foreigners that individual state governments in Germany were lax in seeking out war criminals. The new agency became active, and numerous new clues, and hence new criminals, were unearthed. The relevant statute of limitations was extended, and by 1970 some 5000 convictions had been added to the original Nuremberg list.

In 1961, interestingly, the former Nazi official Adolf Eichmann was run down by Israeli intelligence agents in Argentina, captured, and brought to Israel for trial. He had been chief of the Jewish Office of the Gestapo and carried out many of the genocidal orders issued by Nazi leaders. Eichmann was condemned to death on the basis of the international legal precedent set at Nuremberg and was executed in 1962.

THE PEACE TREATIES OF 1947

To the Council of Foreign Ministers, established at the Potsdam Conference, was assigned the task of preparing the treaties with the five Nazi satellites—Italy, Hungary, Bulgaria, Romania, and Finland. The council understandably ran into a maze of difficulties, but presented draft treaties to a Paris Conference of Twenty-One Nations in late July 1946. Unlike the case at the Paris Peace Conference at the end of World War I, the defeated powers after World War II were given an opportunity to plead their case. Unfortunately, much of the time was spent in arguments between the Soviets and the West, as the U.S.S.R. sought to impose a strongly punitive treaty on Italy and to gain more favorable terms for those former Axis allies who now had fallen within the Soviet sphere of influence. The ever widening chasm that separated Moscow's position from that of the West made it remarkable that the conference reached any conclusions at all—as it did in 1947.

The treaties with Italy, Romania, Bulgaria, Hungary, and Finland were signed in February 1947 in Paris and became effective in the following September. Yugoslavia and Italy promptly lodged protests against the treaties, and cries for revision soon were heard from all former enemy states except Finland.

Italy, considering her long and close association with Hitler's Germany, was treated moderately in the peace settlement, though she herself did not think this to be the case. The Italians were required to accept the creation of a Free State of Trieste, under the protection of the UN Security Council.[7] The frontier between Italy and Austria remained unchanged, and the Brenner Pass remained in Italian possession. Italy did lose some small pieces of territory to Yugoslavia, France, and Greece. Ethiopia and Albania already had regained their independence, and Italy's African colonies were taken under temporary trusteeship by Great Britain; their ultimate fate was to be decided at a future conference of the powers. Italy's armed forces were reduced greatly (the army, for instance, was not to exceed 250,000 men), and she agreed to pay reparation in the amount of $360,000,000, mainly to the Soviet Union, Greece, and Yugoslavia.

The other Axis satellites (including Finland) had to pay reparation

---

[7] Yugoslavia, supported by the Soviet Union, had put forth and continued to put forth vigorous claims to Trieste. Eventually, in 1954, an Italo-Yugoslav Agreement gave the larger part of the city and port to Italy and slightly adjusted the general frontier in favor of Yugoslavia.

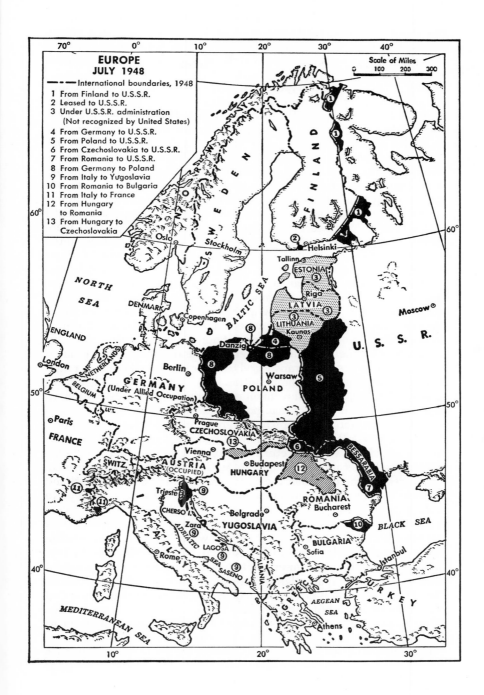

EUROPE
JULY 1948
- - - International boundaries, 1948
1 From Finland to U.S.S.R.
2 Leased to U.S.S.R.
3 Under U.S.S.R. administration
  (Not recognized by United States)
4 From Germany to U.S.S.R.
5 From Poland to U.S.S.R.
6 From Czechoslovakia to U.S.S.R.
7 From Romania to U.S.S.R.
8 From Germany to Poland
9 From Italy to Yugoslavia
10 From Romania to Bulgaria
11 From Italy to France
12 From Hungary
   to Romania
13 From Hungary to
   Czechoslovakia

Scale of Miles
0   100   200   300

as well, mostly to the Soviet Union. They, too, were made to reduce the number of men under arms. Since all these states, except Finland, in effect soon came under Russian control, the nature of the reparation agreements between the U.S.S.R. and Romania, Bulgaria, and Hungary, respectively, had little meaning.

Under the Finnish treaty, the borders existing between Finland and the U.S.S.R. as of 1940 were confirmed, giving the Petsamo Province and several other areas to the Soviet Union. Thus the Soviets regained the common frontier with Norway that had existed for a period of centuries prior to 1918.

Romania confirmed her earlier cession of Bessarabia and Northern Bukovina, inhabited largely by Ukrainians, to the U.S.S.R. Romania was compensated for her loss, however, by having Transylvania— gained from Hungary after World War I and restored to Budapest under Nazi pressure in 1940—returned to her. Hungary was restored to its 1938 frontiers except that some villages near Bratislava were ceded to Czechoslovakia. Bulgaria lost no territory and regained possession of southern Dobruja, but failed in an attempt to claim Western Thrace from Greece.

Once again world war brought in its train major population displacements, this time even more extensive than those following the war of 1914. The Nazis had begun the shifting of populations by putting their racial theories into practice on the eastern plains of Europe. In one way or another, they moved out non-German elements in order to create more *Lebensraum* for Germans; and, on occasion, isolated German minorities were transferred to other locales, where they might live in "pure" Germanic communities.

After the war, a mass movement of Germanic population westward was stimulated by the political policies of the U.S.S.R. and her satellite states. Western Europe was sought as a haven, too, by numberless "Displaced Persons" (DP's) who had been uprooted by Hitler and now did not wish to return to a place of origin that had fallen within the Soviet area of influence. As Germans left, or were driven, from areas, some of which they had occupied since medieval times, the place names were changed to Slavic, in a Russian attempt to obliterate the past.

One last word on the peace making remains to be mentioned here. Discussions concerning peace treaties with Germany and Austria were stalemated for several years (See Chapter 25). Meanwhile, in the Far East, the United States, who had borne the brunt of the war against Japan, claimed control over the defeated country. An Allied Council was established in Tokyo, representing the Big Three and China; but Japanese affairs were ordered by a Supreme Commander for the Allied Powers, a post held for almost six years by General of the Army Douglas MacArthur. Since the Soviet Union had entered the war (albeit near its close), Moscow promptly took the territories promised to her at the Yalta Conference (see page 399). But no final treaty was concluded with Japan until 1952.

THE BEGINNINGS OF THE EAST-WEST SCHISM

With the might of the German Reich and Japanese Empire in ruins, power vacuums were created in Europe and the Far East. But, since nature and international politics abhor vacuums, other powers quickly were drawn in. The United States, already heavily committed in the Far East, assumed temporary responsibility for the former area of Japanese hegemony. In Europe the United States faced special problems because of the traditional stance of large segments of the population. There was the usual postwar cry in the United States to bring home the fighting men, yet participation in the occupation of defeated Germany and Austria inevitably kept the United States involved in Europe. Therefore Washington's European policy this time could be only one of partial withdrawal.

This, however, did not mean that the United States Government fully realized the extent of the power vacuum that had come about in Europe with the fall of the Third Reich. There seemed to be no real comprehension of the fact that the "great powers" of the European past, France and Great Britain, were no match for the potential might of a Soviet Union, strengthened and tempered in the struggle against Hitler's Germany. Gradually at first, and only more rapidly later, did Washington recognize that the strength of the Soviet Union could be balanced only if the United States actively aided Western Europe. The catalyst that speeded Washington's realization of the new nature of world politics after 1945 was provided by the frustration of trying to achieve a German peace.

As the former Allies pursued a German settlement, more and more points of contention arose. Moscow's continuing demands for German industrial machinery gradually were resisted by the Allies. The Western Powers, to Moscow's ire, began putting money into the West Germany economy, so that it once more might start to function normally. At the same time, quarrels developed over the nature of the future German governmental structure; the U.S.S.R. favored a centralized state (hopefully to make easier its eventual communization) and the Western allies preferred a federal union. There developed fierce disputes over the Polish frontier of Germany, which Russia, but not the Western Powers, claimed was settled. The French reawakened memories of the 1919 settlement by proposing that the Ruhr Valley and its substantial industrial assets should be placed under international control, and that the Rhineland might well be detached from Germany. These, and other issues upon which the East and West could not agree, eventually led to the division of Germany into two separate states.

The Soviets, indeed, closed their zone and began to apply communist principles and procedures to industry and agriculture within East Germany. Soon the entire economy was nationalized. The Russians moved quickly in the political area as well, forcing the Socialists within East Germany into an unnatural merger with the Communist Party to produce a dominant "Socialist Unity Party" (SED). As the Russians began to move in a direction that obviously would mean the communization of East Germany, the United States and Great Britain reacted (December 1946) by agreeing to combine their zones into a "bizonal" economic union.

In March 1947, the Big Four Council of Ministers met in Moscow. The meeting revealed the strained nature of relations between East and West, for it took place in an atmosphere of mutual distrust and suspicion, one that was heightened by the recent expression in Washington of the Truman Doctrine. Consequently, the Moscow Conference adjourned without accomplishment.

Another important step was taken by the United States in June 1947. In that month, General George C. Marshall, United States Secretary of State, called for far-reaching economic assistance to European nations and indicated that the United States would do "whatever it is able to do" to speed the world on its way to recovery. Large-scale economic aid programs to help Europe for at least three or four years were announced. The idea of the "Marshall Plan" or "European Recovery Program" was simple: help Europe to help itself and thus bring about an economic and political recovery which would lessen the threat of Communist takeovers in Western states as yet beyond the reach of Soviet domination.

In response to Marshall's offer the foreign ministers of France, Britain, and the Soviet Union met to consider the proposal of the United States. Russia soon withdrew from the conference, denouncing the Marshall Plan as an attempt to establish United States dominance in Europe. Shortly thereafter, the Allied commanders in West Germany raised the industrial level of Bizonia by increasing the production quotas of steel and other industrial products. The Soviet Union denounced this action as a renewal of imperialism and responded by organizing the Communist Information Bureau or "Cominform" as a central organization from which, in effect, to pour anti-Western propaganda. Thus, move followed countermove into open hostility.

By 1947, then, the Soviets had come to be viewed in the West as the new enemy of freedom, and the West had come to be viewed by the Russians—as far as can be ascertained—with increasing suspicion and distrust. In the opinion of many Westerners, it was only the atomic bomb, in the possession of the United States, that restrained the Red armies from overrunning Western Europe. To the detriment of mankind, World War II now was followed by the appearance of a Cold War between the Soviets and the West.

The Course of the Cold War (1945-1960)

21

TWO SUPERPOWERS IN OPPOSITION

At the beginning of the modern age the city states of Italy, many of which had been powerful during the height of the Renaissance, began to decline as entities of international importance. They came to be overshadowed by a number of monarchies in Europe, states constructed by something beyond mere princely craft. These burgeoning political complexes were rooted also in a new loyalty of their peoples, who had begun to experience a rising nationalism. In the face of emerging power of this kind Italy, with its checkered political configuration, lay almost helpless—open to invasion by states possessing political leadership and institutions that allowed them to act in force based on large numbers of obedient subjects. Thus Italy became the object of the conflicting interests of non-Italian kings, and the Italian peninsula, its cities sacked and its territories seized, witnessed a rapid fading of the glories of the Renaissance. Political influence passed to the north and west, and the aggressive national states of Europe came to dominate, first, European politics and economics, and then much of the world. In the process, there eventually was established a "balance of power" on the Continent itself, with Great Britain using her influence to keep any one state from becoming dominant. Thus it continued into the twentieth century.

Then, as one of the most important results of World War II, the long-established balance of power among the European states was replaced by a confrontation of superpowers. A move of influence, similar to that which had taken place in the early modern period, away from the smaller political unit to the larger, in which greater numbers of men with more physical resources could act in concert to obtain the ends of the state, once more had come to pass. This

413

might have happened in the case of the United States in 1919, but then Americans returned to their traditional isolationism and Europe was reconstructed in a manner reminiscent of the old system of counterbalancing great powers. Yet, even during this period, there were hints of the potential and growing might of the U.S.S.R. and the United States. After the second worldwide conflict, the potentiality was realized and the two countries emerged as superpowers. Not only were these two states able to command the support of great numbers to carry out the urgings of their national leaders, but each possessed a superior technology that made possible the production of sophisticated military implements in abundance. Their might, accordingly, could be made manifest across the globe.

As early as the 1830's, at least one European observer had seen the shape of such things to come. Alexis de Tocqueville, in his *Democracy in America*, noted that the world of the nineteenth century held "two great peoples" who were "advancing toward the same end," and that some day these two sprawling, as yet underdeveloped territories would hold "the destinies of half the world" in their hands. Since 1945, accordingly, many have looked upon de Tocqueville as a prophet extraordinary. Yet, in light of the immensity of untapped natural resources in both states, evident to some even in the 1830's, the forecast, in the words of one historian, lay in "the realm of the necessary." In his view, indeed, Russia and the United States at some point in history probably would have come to occupy their post-World War II international positions regardless of the coming of Leninist-Marxism to Russia.[1]

From this line of reasoning flows the concept that the behavior of Moscow and Washington during the Cold War was the result of their historic experiences. Russia, for instance, continued the general pattern of national and international behavior under communism that marked its history under the tsars. Throughout the centuries, governmental authority had been highly centralized and typified by authoritarianism. Throughout, also, the approach had been conspiratorial and motivated by a seemingly profound distrust of the outside world. The Bolshevik Revolution of 1917 eventually led to a revived and strengthened authoritarianism in Russia. The Romanov dynasty was overthrown because it was decadent; it was replaced by a new and vigorous Communist Party dynasty which, in many areas, pursued traditional Russian goals.

The position of Russia in the post-1945 world, then, was based on the "age-old response" of the rulers of Russia to what they viewed as the continuing dual spectre of centuries-old backwardness and external aggression. The continuing challenge of Russia's industrial and technological lag underlay the almost frantic drive of the Soviets to industrialize their country along Western lines through successive

[1] Louis J. Halle, *The Cold War as History*, (New York: Harper & Row, 1967), p. 11.

five-year plans. The historic fear of foreign invasions was intensified by the Nazi invasion of 1941.

Though the medieval and early modern incursions generally were from the East, the fact that European Russia opens out into a great plain has made invasion from a technologically advanced Western Europe a tempting and repeated event in more recent times.

It therefore is an oversimplification to hold that the U.S.S.R. has been motivated into "offensive action" against the West because of Communist yearning for power alone. The Russians, having lived through ten centuries of fear of foreign incursions, climaxed by the horrors of the Nazi invasion, felt impelled to create a buffer zone against the West—against even their former allies. The resultant Russian supposedly "defensive" action led to an extension of Moscow's hegemony to a line that ran across Germany, from north to south, 100 miles west of Berlin. But what the Russians regarded as the necessary establishment of a buffer zone, the West, and particularly the United States, regarded as naked aggression rooted in a foreign, nearly incomprehensible ideology.

The twofold goal of the Russians to industrialize and to expand was tied to one policy. The Russian leaders did not rush to industrialize because they were interested essentially in raising living standards and bettering the general welfare of the Russian masses. Rather, they were "interested in economics as a means of enhancing military power, and this goal was usually envisaged . . . as the price of national survival."[2]

The behavior of the United States in the Cold War derives from historical experiences unlike those of the Russians. Americans early developed a feeling of strength and safety. This attitude was based, at least in part, on the geography of North America. For many years the United States could look on the Atlantic Ocean as a barrier, separating her from the "Old World" where, in popular American thinking, political systems were based on outworn and authoritarian concepts.[3] Russia could not escape involvement with Europe, but the United States for a time could and did do so. Keeping this historic development in mind, it was only natural that Americans should return to isolationism after 1919. It was not astonishing that they should seek to hold to the advice of George Washington that the United States must carry on commercial relations with Europe in such a way as to have as "little political connection" with Europeans as possible.[4]

The tendency of early twentieth-century United States policy still

---

[2] Frederick L. Schuman, *The Cold War: Retrospect and Prospect,* (Baton Rouge: Louisiana State University Press, 1967), p. 17.
[3] Probably this notion developed, at least in part, from the circumstances that the United States was founded by refugees from political tyranny and religious persecution in Europe.
[4] Such developments in international relations as the Monroe Doctrine followed logically from the Washingtonian advice.

was to stand fast behind the protection of the Atlantic Ocean in much the same fashion that Britain once had remained separated from Continental squabbles by the English Channel. In this calculation naval power was important, as it long had been to the British on their island fortress. In association with Great Britain, therefore, the United States sought to dominate the Atlantic Ocean and maintain a sea wall against Europe.

As the twentieth century wore on, however, events gradually led to a change in this policy. The United States was pulled into World War I, in part, because Great Britain evidently was unable any longer acting alone to uphold a balance of power on the Continent. Perhaps because there was not yet a clear realization of this factor by United States leadership after the First World War, Americans were destined in 1941 to repeat the 1917–1918 step into the European power-political scene. By 1947, the United States at last turned away from the traditional view that had favored American isolationism based on historical and geographical factors. Now the Atlantic superpower entered Europe's power vacuum and replaced Great Britain as the only logical challenger to Stalin's Russia, which itself had replaced Hitler's Germany as the chief wielder of European continental influence. Thus it was that the two superpowers, motivated by what each considered "defensive" reasons, moved to meet in a struggle of worldwide proportions.

THE EARLY YEARS OF THE COLD WAR

The development of a Cold War situation over Germany already has been described. This, however, was not the only focus of conflict between the two emerging superpowers. In eastern and southeastern Europe the installation of Communist or Communist-friendly regimes proceeded so rapidly that by early 1947 Romania, Poland, Hungary, Albania, Bulgaria, Yugoslavia, and Czechoslovakia had come within the Soviet orbit.

In the case of Czechoslovakia, President Eduard Beneš, in his London wartime exile, was convinced by the experience of the Munich Conference of 1938 that the Western powers would not fight to aid his country in dangerous times. He was equally convinced that the westward military advance of Moscow would leave the Russians free to impose their will on Czechoslovakia at the end of hostilities. Determined therefore to make the best possible bargain with Moscow, he avoided any act of defiance that might provoke the Russians. He and his government-in-exile accordingly approached Stalin and found him apparently friendly. The result, by 1947, was a coalition government headed by a Communist.

In Poland the Russians moved more directly. Here the Red Army had occupied Warsaw at the end of the war. The Russian occupation came, however, only after a Polish resistance army had risen to fight against the Nazis. For some two months, while the city was being destroyed and Poles and Germans were killing one another, the Red Army stood by and waited. When the fighting became only sporadic, the Russians quickly entered and took control of a shattered city. Moscow then imposed its own interpretation of the Yalta promise that Poland would enjoy self-determination through free elections at the war's end. Remnants of the Polish underground decided to fight on against the Russians but soon were suppressed. The Soviets then rapidly established a Polish Government of their own making, a satellite regime completely subservient to Moscow.

Most of the states that came within the Russian orbit went through experiences similar to those of Czechs and the Poles.[5] Several, by the close of 1947, had purged those anti-Communists who earlier had entered the governmental coalitions. Thus, the Hungarian Communists had launched an especially vicious purge of those persons within the coalition government who had striven to resist Hungary's precipitous entrance into the Soviet orbit.

In addition to noting these ominous developments, the Western powers saw with concern the rise of strong indigenous Communist parties beyond the Russian orbit. Not long after the war, for example, the Communists became the strongest party in the French National Assembly and an important factor in Italian national politics. Moreover, it was discovered that French and Italian Reds belonging to the Cominform had attempted to halt economic recovery in their respective nations with strikes and sabotage. The Western powers therefore became aware of a need to halt the spread of Russian influence without resorting to hostilities that might touch off another world war.

Gradually, Western statesmen came to realize the validity of Winston Churchill's remarks at Westminster College in Fulton, Missouri, given on March 5, 1946. On that occasion the British wartime leader had pointed out that an "iron curtain" had "descended across the continent," thus making a new Europe that differed greatly from the one the Allies had "fought to build up." He further had warned, accurately, that "the police governments" of Eastern Europe could not be trusted to work in cooperation with the West to produce a more peaceful Europe.

Maintaining that the Europe born at the end of the Second World War did not contain "the essentials of a permanent peace," Churchill called for a position of strength as the only one that the Russians would respect. That some United States leaders had come to a similar conclusion was shown by the words of George F. Kennan, the director of the State Department's policy-planning staff, who asserted that the West had to apply "counterforce" to the Russian policy of thrusting "at a series of constantly shifting geographical and political

---

[5] For a more detailed discussion of the absorption of the East European states into the Russian orbit see Chapter 23.

points." This was the first American statement of the doctrine that has come to be called "containment," a policy that soon was to be applied with the implementation of the "Truman Doctrine."

TRUMAN DOCTRINE AND MARSHALL PLAN

The Truman Doctrine was first proclaimed in connection with a Greco-Turkish crisis of 1947. It was apparent at this time that Russian influence was reaching out toward the Mediterranean and that Stalin hoped to control the area by penetrating Greece and Turkey through the agency of local communism. Greece had been troubled by political divisiveness since the end of the war, as the Left and Right struggled for control. The British had sought to stabilize the situation by backing the Rightists, who benefited from this support sufficiently to win the first elections after the war, in March 1946. The conservative trend generally was considered to be proof of the revulsion felt by the local citizenry against possible Russian dominance. Indeed, the new government, under Constantine Tsaldaris, held a plebiscite that brought King George II back from London, to which he had fled when the Nazis overran his country.

The return of the monarchy, however, did not end unrest in Greece. The Communists, drawing aid from Greece's neighbors Yugoslavia, Albania, and Bulgaria, who hoped to see a move in Greek politics toward the Left, began guerilla warfare. Soon Greece was caught up in a civil war and the government frantically sought British aid to extricate it from a dangerous situation. The British, however, found it difficult to give the necessary aid because of severe economic difficulties at home. Britain's limited resources were further stretched when it became necessary to help Turkey resist planned Soviet thrusts toward the Dardanelles and Turkish holdings south of the Caucasus.[6]

Then it was that the United States decided to step into the breach, to forestall a power vacuum from which only the U.S.S.R. could benefit. On March 12, 1947, President Truman, declaring that "it must be the policy of the United States to support free peoples who are resisting attempted subjugation by small minorities or by outside pressures," received authority from Congress to assist Greece and Turkey with advisers and funds. What seemed immediately important to those involved in this decision was the establishment of certain programs to help the Greeks and Turks themselves turn back the Communist tide. Looking back on the event with the perspective provided by the intervening years, it seems clear that the decision marked the commitment of the United States to a policy of containment. Later on this policy came to be known as the "Truman Doctrine." And eventu-

---

[6] The seeking of control over Turkish-held territory had been a policy of Tsarist Russia, long before the Bolshevik Revolution.

ally this doctrine became the basis of an attempt to extend a *Pax Americana* far beyond the shores of Europe.

At any rate, with American aid the Greeks and Turks began to emerge from their periods of unrest. The Balkan neighbors were further helped by the fact that Yugoslavia, unwilling to become wholly subservient to the Russians and seeking *rapprochement* with the West, cut off the Greek Communists' major sources of supply. The destructive civil war in Greece thus abated and by 1949 a relative stability had returned to the Athens Government. United States assistance also encouraged the Turks to resist vigorously Russian attempts to annex some territory in the northeast of their country and to ignore Moscow's proposal that the Soviets participate in the defense of the Turkish Straits. Freed, at least temporarily, from internal and external Communist pressures, Greece and Turkey eventually joined the United Nations' forces in Korea and participated as members of the North Atlantic Treaty Organization.

A few months after the beginning of aid to the Turks and Greeks, the Marshall Plan was announced (see Chapter 20) to rehabilitate Europe on a basis of self-help plus United States financial assistance. The Russians looked upon the scheme as "a plan for extortionist speculation" that eventually would enslave Europe economically through the wiles of "American imperialism." The Western European countries viewed the prospect of American help more warmly and responded with the creation of an Organisation for European Economic Cooperation (OEEC) in the spring of 1948 to participate in the European Recovery Program (ERP). Four years of ERP operations saved Western Europe from economic collapse and, perhaps, from Communist control. The Russians meanwhile (1949) countered with a Council for Mutual Economic Assistance, a kind of Marshall Plan for the Communist bloc.

Meanwhile, also, by 1948, a Soviet-devised constitution had been imposed on Romania and the Russians had concluded "mutual aid" pacts with Hungary, Romania, Bulgaria, and Finland. In addition, Czechoslovakia had been absorbed completely within the Russian orbit. On the other hand, the Communists had failed to capture the Italian Parliament in the elections of 1948, as they confidently expected to do. The first significant break in the satellite structure came when Yugoslavia, led by Marshal Tito (Josip Broz), was ordered out of the Communist camp by Stalin. This break came about because Tito, not Stalin, continued to control Yugoslavia's civil and military administrations, and Tito, though a Communist, also was a nationalist. Tito now asked the West for aid and received it, although an angered Stalin imposed a Communist blockade upon the country. The quick establishment of better relations with the West enabled Yugoslavia to survive the Soviet dictator's wrath.

THE GERMAN IMPASSE AND NATO

To examine the next battleground of the Cold War the focus must be sought in Germany once again, for it was in divided Berlin that a situation developed which was fraught with peril for the whole world. As early as December 1947, Secretary Marshall had brought up the matter of Russian intransigence over a German settlement and accused the Soviets of desiring the enslavement of the German people as only a phase of a broad Communist program aimed at "seriously retarding the recovery of Europe."

Eventually, the Russian-Western impasse over Germany led the West to move unilaterally toward a settlement of the German problem. A series of London conferences between the United States and Western European governments followed, despite loud Russian protests against the meetings. Finally, on March 20, 1948, the Soviet delegates walked out of an Allied Control Council meeting and, for all practical purposes, ended the cooperative administration of Germany.

Already in 1947 the United States and Great Britain had joined their zonal economic and financial institutions and established a Bizonia. In 1948 it was decided to merge the French Zone with Bizonia and create an economic Trizonia. It then appeared that the conversion of Trizonia into a German federal government under Western Allied supervision was only a matter of time.

Stalin therefore realized that the attempt to draw all of a demoralized Germany into the Soviet orbit had been frustrated. It also was obvious that a soon to be established federal government in West Germany would receive the same kind of Marshall Plan aid that had helped other European states build higher the walls of prosperity that held back the tide of Communist subversion. The Allies, indeed, in June 1948 introduced into Berlin a new currency, already established in Trizonia, in order to provide financial stability and hamper Soviet efforts to cause inflation by printing excessive amounts of paper money. The Russians responded by introducing a currency of their own design into the Eastern zone and then, on June 23, initiating a total ground blockade of Berlin.

To recapitulate: at the war's end, it was assumed by the Western Powers that the military occupation of Berlin, indeed of all Germany, would be a temporary arrangement. They expected that Berlin eventually would become the capital city of a new Germany, democratically self-governed. But the Soviets, though they had agreed to four-power control of Berlin, later declared that, since the Soviet Zone surrounded the city, the latter rightfully was part of that zone.

Now ground access to Berlin was sealed off and even supplies of electricity and food were halted. First the Russians cited "technical difficulties" as the reason for their action and then they brought up the matter of the "objectionable" currency reform. It soon became clear, however, that the Russians simply wished to take control of

West Berlin and simultaneously prevent the projected economic integration of a new West German state into Western Europe.

The West's counteraction to the blockade was two-pronged: (1) it decided not to resort to military action that might precipitate another war, and instead, to maintain the beleaguered Berliners by air; and (2) it stopped the shipment of goods into the Soviet Zone, so that the economy there, none too healthy at best, would be damaged sufficiently to force the Russians to lift the blockade.

The first course of action followed by the West was called by United States pilots, "Operation Vittles." Though the blockade officially lasted from June 1948 until May 1949, the "airlift" continued until September, with planes from Allied airports in West Germany flying supplies to Berlin at a rate that eventually amounted to about 8000 tons daily. It was the West's proved ability to supply Berlin by air, indefinitely if need be, coupled with the economic measures taken to damage the Soviet Zone, that ultimately led to Russia's raising the blockade.

The Berlin Blockade cost the Russians dearly in international prestige. The airlift, as it went on month after month, proved that the West not only was competent but determined to stop the spread of Russian influence in Europe. The fortitude of the Berliners throughout the blockade demonstrated that the Germans in the Western occupied areas were in solid support of the Western opposition to potential Russian dominance.

It must be remembered, too, that, at this point in the history of the Cold War, Moscow was fully aware that the United States had atomic bombs that could be carried in bombers stationed in Great Britain and West Germany against targets located inside Russia. Although the Russians surrounded the island of Berlin with greatly superior military strength of the conventional kind than that possessed by the Allies, they did not use this force to prevent the Allies from launching West Germany on a Western-oriented course, lest they risk atomic retaliation by the United States. Thus the Berlin episode of 1948–1949 marked a point in the history of the Cold War where it first became apparent that the existence of nuclear weapons and the means of delivering them over great distances presaged a basic alteration in traditional military strategy.

A momentary relaxation of tension following the termination of the Berlin Blockade led to a conference on the German question in May 1949. The Big Four met in Paris, but produced little in the way of positive accomplishments since each side wished to shape the future of Germany to coincide with its own ends, for Germany obviously was the pivot of power on the Continent.

Unable to accomplish anything worthwhile at Paris, the Allies went ahead with their plans to establish a German democratic government in Trizonia. By September 1949 the Federal Republic of Germany was established in West Germany, with the local civilian authorities given basic responsibility for running the domestic affairs of their country.

The Russians' countermove to this Western action was the creation (October 1949) of an East German government in their zone, called the German Democratic Republic.

The Berlin Blockade and the continuing international tension also stimulated a renewed interest in international alliances, chief among them being the North Atlantic Treaty Organization (NATO) established in 1949. Actually, the post-World War II process of alliance making had begun in March 1947, when France and Great Britain concluded a military pact, the Treaty of Dunkirk.[7] This alliance was broadened in 1948, when France, Great Britain, Belgium, the Netherlands, and Luxembourg became signatories to the Treaty of Brussels, which established a fifty-year alliance against armed attack in Europe. With ominous developments in Berlin following soon after, the United States entered into discussions with the West European states, concerning the building of a still more extensive alliance system.

The Europeans welcomed this American interest, knowing that they alone were no match for the Russians. The result of the discussions was the American signing of a North Atlantic Treaty on April 4, 1949, with the members of the Brussels Alliance as well as Canada, Norway, Iceland, Denmark, Portugal, and Italy. These powers were joined in the North Atlantic Treaty Organization by Greece and Turkey in 1951 and by West Germany in 1955. The document stipulated that the signatories would view "an armed attack on one or more of them" as an attack against the whole NATO membership. A NATO military committee was formed, staffed by top-ranking professional experts from member countries, and charged with the task of developing plans for common defense.

In the United States the Senate agreed to ratification of the North Atlantic Treaty by an eighty-two to thirteen vote. Washington warned Moscow, in a politely worded statement, that American interests had been extended beyond traditional boundaries to the division between the two Germanies. The Russians were forced to pay heed to the warning, not because the Atlantic coalition had great strength in terms of conventional forces,[8] but because American nuclear might stood behind NATO.[9]

From the initial stages of the NATO agreement Washington was determined that the alliance should be something more than a paper pact. Hence the United States rushed ahead with the building of a

[7] This alliance initially was aimed at restraining a Germany that might rise again; in response to the developing Cold War, it came to have more significance vis-à-vis the U.S.S.R.

[8] In 1949, NATO forces in Europe numbered only some dozen divisions and a few hundred planes.

[9] A few months after the founding of NATO the Russians exploded an atomic device. However, the entry of the Russians into the select nuclear club did not immediately give them parity in striking power with the United States.

large atomic stockpile. American strategic thinkers, however, decided that atomic might alone was not enough and that NATO must have adequate ground forces, perhaps as many as ninety divisions, to turn back possible Russian aggression in Europe. Others argued at this point that a too rapid buildup of arms might stimulate a Russian attack on Western Europe, a provocation to be avoided because of the immense Communist superiority in number of men under arms.

Courtesy, Foreign Policy Association, *Headline Series.*

In the midst of such discussions NATO headquarters was established in Paris as the Supreme Headquarters Allied Powers Europe (SHAPE). General of the Army Dwight D. Eisenhower was its first Supreme Commander and Field Marshal Viscount Bernard L. Montgomery was his deputy. The establishment of a coordinated command was followed by a buildup of armed forces among the member states. During this process, Communist armed forces on June 25, 1950, attacked, not in Europe, but in the Far Eastern state of Korea. This had a definite impact on NATO since, obviously, the same thing might happen at any moment along the border between East and West Germany. The outbreak of war in Korea made the building of a more effective NATO seem imperative. Now, before the Cold War in Europe can be examined further, it is necessary to turn to events in the Far East.

THE KOREAN WAR

In considering the Cold War in the Far East, it must be noted that misunderstandings and mistakes were evident on both sides. The United States, in filling the power vacuum left by the defeat of Japan, automatically committed herself to the defense of the Japanese mainland. Washington, perhaps insufficiently steeped in the history and culture of the Far East to assume such a role, did not realize, for example, that the Korean Peninsula, because of its geography, for centuries had been a strategically sensitive area, comparable to the Rhineland or the Turkish Straits in the European experience. Korea was important in the past considerations of the Japanese just as it now was important to the defense of Japan, for the Korean Peninsula long offered and still offers a route by which Japan and China can invade each other. Thus, with the coming to power in China, in late 1949, of a government led by the peasant-born Communist Mao Tse-tung (see Chapter 28), and the conclusion of an agreement in February 1950, between the U.S.S.R. and China, newsmen began to refer to a "Moscow-Peking" axis that posed a threat of invasion via Korea to Japan. Once again, as often before in history, the Koreans came to think of their country as "a shrimp among whales."

Meanwhile, in Tokyo in March 1949, General of the Army Douglas MacArthur had told a British journalist that he believed Korea to be beyond the United States defense line in the Pacific. This sentiment was echoed by Secretary of State Dean Acheson in Washington in January 1950. Hence, ironically, the United States Military command and State Department had decided to pull back from Korea on the very eve of a Communist attack on South Korea. It was a North Korean miscalculation not to recognize this direction in American policy.[10]

On June 25, 1950, North Korean forces in Russian-built tanks crossed the 38th parallel, ostensibly to "liberate" the South. The UN Security Council called upon North Korea to withdraw its forces, but the invaders refused to do so. At this point the Council asked member states of the UN to assist the Republic of Korea. Actually, President Truman, having been informed of the situation by Secretary of State Acheson, already had decided to take prompt action. Washington, indeed, sent American forces into the area before the Security Council

---

[10] After the Japanese surrendered on September 2, 1945, Korea was placed under Soviet and United States occupation, pending establishment of a Korean democratic government. Primarily because of Soviet resistance to the democratic establishment through the ballot box of a government for all Korea, a United Nations commission supervised elections for a National Constituent Assembly in Seoul. The North Koreans refused to participate. The elections established the Republic of Korea, which was proclaimed on August 15, 1948. A Korean Peoples' Democratic Republic, claiming authority over the entire country, was inaugurated in Northern Korea. While the United States trained forces in the South, institutions in the North were modeled on those in the Soviet Union.

had urged intervention, and MacArthur had sent in air forces before Washington had approved that step.

Perhaps fortunately for the United States, the UN Security Council quickly adopted a motion to assist South Korea. This could happen because the Russians, since January 1950, had refused to attend the meetings of the Council—in protest over the fact that Nationalist China continued to occupy its seat on that body after it had been ousted from the mainland by the Communist Chinese. Hence, since the Soviet Union had no representative present to veto any action taken against Communist North Korea, the Council was able to place the United Nations' stamp of approval on action that the United States already had launched. General MacArthur now was placed in charge of a United Nations Command, charged with the task of repelling the North Korean aggression.[11]

From a practical standpoint, the United States had little choice but to go quickly to the aid of the Republic of Korea since the latter's forces obviously were no match for the invaders. The weakness of South Korean arms at the beginning of the fighting and the limited initial American aid, caused the war to start badly for the UN forces. The UN army was pushed southward until, by mid-September 1950, it was driven back to a defensive perimeter around the port of Pusan on the southern coast. At that point, however, General MacArthur gambled successfully with an amphibious landing in the north, at Inchon, the port of the Korean Republic's capital, Seoul. The Communist forces thus were cut off from behind, their southern-most units collapsed, and North Korean remnants fled back across the 38th parallel in disorder.

Victory was at hand. The assigned mission had been to turn back the invading armies and that had been accomplished. But success spawned temptation, for the United States and the majority of the UN membership had shared since 1945 the desire of seeing a unified Korea established by an openly elected, representative government. The installation of a Soviet satellite regime north of the 38th parallel had thwarted that aim. Now, with the Communist army shattered, the time seemed opportune to unify the whole country under the Seoul Government.

General MacArthur was anxious to push on; flushed with victory, he wished to drive northward. Properly, the decision to move into North Korea or not should have been made by political leadership, since it was a step with broad political implications. But MacArthur, without awaiting word from Washington, ordered the United States Air Force to bomb North Korean targets.

President Truman apparently hesitated to reprimand MacArthur because the General had become a "gleaming symbol" of heroism for most Americans. MacArthur moreover asserted his confidence that

[11] Eventually fifteen countries in addition to the United States sent military units to aid South Korea.

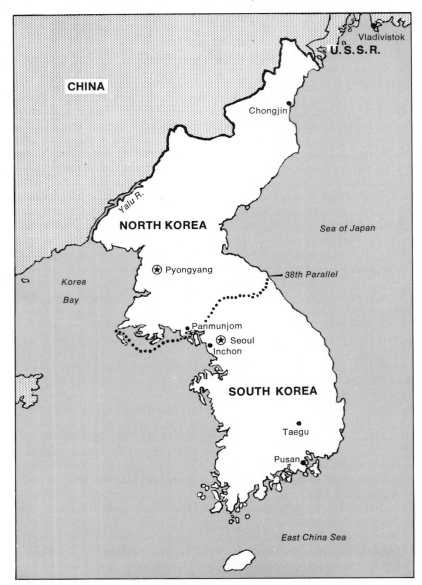

KOREA DURING THE KOREAN WAR

"very little" risk would be involved in pursuing Red forces and that Washington need not be concerned about the possibility of Chinese intervention. Yet, as UN forces drove toward the Yalu River, the border with Communist-Chinese controlled Manchuria, there were repeated warnings from Red China. Chinese "volunteers" began to appear among the defending North Korean forces. At a Wake Island meeting with President Truman in October 1950, General MacArthur repeated his opinion that there was no danger of Chinese intervention in the war and that all formal resistance in North Korea should be finished by Thanksgiving (November 23). Even as these discussions were held, however, the first Chinese units were on their way across the Yalu into Korea.[12]

In November 1950, in keeping with the timetable established at Wake Island, a major drive was launched toward the Yalu. On November 21, United States troops reached the river, and three days later General MacArthur announced a great offensive to end the war. But the offensive hardly was begun when the Chinese counterattacked along the entire front with massive numbers of troops. Within a few weeks the UN forces were driven back across the 38th parallel.

A new determination developed in Washington as the United States Government was urged by other Western powers to reestablish local political control in the south of Korea, since that had been the original objective of the fighting. In keeping with the developing doctrine of containment, it was decided that the war should be a "limited" one. The most important consideration in this decision was the thought that carrying the war into Chinese territory might precipitate a third world war, for China's Red Government had a defensive alliance with the U.S.S.R. General MacArthur became frustrated over the political restrictions placed upon his military action and publicly indicated his objections. The President eventually decided to risk political trouble at home and relieved MacArthur of his command (April 1951). The "liberator of the Philippines" was replaced by General Matthew B. Ridgway as military commander in Korea.

MacArthur, to many the most impressive of the World War II heroes, returned to the United States. He addressed a joint session of Congress and, in a memorable speech, moved many Americans to tears. Truman, on the other hand, seemed humiliated by the triumphal return of the heroic military figure. In Korea the UN forces were trapped in a war which it seemed that they would neither lose nor win, as the conflict stabilized at the 38th parallel. The North Korean and Chinese adversaries of the UN forces had far greater numbers of men in the field; the United States and her allies possessed much greater firepower. The seeming stalemate led, in the summer of 1951, to armistice talks between UN and Chinese representatives at Panmunjom. Two more years of fighting and 575 negotiation meetings occurred before an agreement ending the fighting was signed on July 27, 1953. The boundary between North and South Korea was set slightly

[12] Much of what MacArthur said at the Wake Island meeting probably was based on faulty intelligence.

north of the 38th parallel. At the end of thirty-seven months of fighting, containment apparently had been achieved.

THE COLD WAR THROUGH 1960

If any lesson had been learned by the antagonists at this stage of the Cold War, it was that no major unilateral alteration of the post-World War II situation could be wrought by either side without the risk of a third great war. The result was a period of deadlock in the 1950's, marked chiefly by an arms race, as the United States exerted itself to stay well ahead of the Soviet Union in nuclear technology and the U.S.S.R. in turn struggled to catch up, and by the augmentation of NATO by a series of regional alliances. In these years, however, Tibet was taken over by Chinese Communists, and Southeast Asia experienced the first of a series of Communist disturbances that led to outright war in the next decade.

The years of virtual atomic stalemate and of "competitive coexistence" began about the time that Joseph Stalin died on March 5, 1953. The details of the dictator's death were not made altogether clear. And, as at least one American expert noted, though Stalin at his funeral was eulogized as "our teacher and leader, the greatest genius of mankind," most of the official mourners gave the appearance of having "suddenly been released from bondage."

A few years after the formation of NATO in 1949 a Tripartite Security Treaty (ANZUS), effective in 1952, was concluded among Australia, New Zealand, and the United States, to maintain their mutual security in the Pacific area. In 1954 the Southeast Asia Treaty Organization (SEATO) came into being, with the United States, Great Britain, France, Thailand, Pakistan, the Philippines, New Zealand, and Australia as charter members. In 1955 an association for the military defense of the Middle East, later called the Central Treaty Organization (CENTO), was established by Iran, Iraq (until 1959 only), Pakistan, Turkey and Great Britain. The United States, though not officially a member of CENTO, was pledged to cooperate with it.

These treaties were signed both in imitation of NATO and, in the cases of SEATO and CENTO, in delayed reaction to the invasion of South Korea from the north. Meanwhile, in addition, new leaders had come to power in both of the leading Cold War protagonists. In the United States Dwight D. Eisenhower in 1953 succeeded Harry Truman as President. In Russia, Nikita Sergeyevich Khrushchev gradually emerged as winner of a power struggle among Stalin's former aides and, by 1957, had expelled his rivals from important positions in the party and government. In the late 1950's the former Ukrainian party boss appeared to be leading the Russian system away from the hard line set by Stalin.

The general attitude in the United States towards this seemingly more liberal Soviet line was one of suspicion, mixed with the belief that the moderate trend could be discounted as propaganda. Many Americans held that the U.S.S.R. had merely halted momentarily in its overall plan for world domination in order to concentrate on over-taking the West in nuclear armaments.

Some allies of the United States, on the other hand, began to criticize her foreign policy as being so caught up in neo-nationalism as to drive the U.S.S.R. into renewed Stalinlike position of intransi-gence. The most frequent target of such foreign criticism was Secretary of State John Foster Dulles, who upset some Europeans by advocating a foreign policy conducted, so they said, more in terms of American self-interest than of world responsibility. Dulles further disturbed some European diplomats by referring to the availability of American atomic power for "massive retaliation" in the event of extensive Russian pressure. Some Western governments also objected to Dulles' verbal encouragement of rebellion in states within the Soviet orbit.

Despite these concerns, there emerged some cause for optimism in the mid-1950's. The Big Four foreign ministers, who had discontinued their talks during the troubled years between 1947 and 1953, resumed their conversations at a Berlin Conference in 1954. During this same year nineteen nations, including Communist China, met at Geneva to discuss the tensions in the Far East. The diplomats at Geneva did not reunite Korea, but they brought a temporary peace to troubled Indo-China. The moderate successes of such conferences stimulated hope among some that perhaps the Russians and the West really could move into an era of peaceful coexistence. This optimism was strength-ened when, in May 1955, the Soviet Union declared itself ready to sign an Austrian peace treaty on moderate terms (see Chapter 25).

The search for peaceful coexistence then led to a so-called "summit" meeting in mid-1955. The Big Four leaders agreed to come to-gether for the first time since the Potsdam Conference of 1945. In July 1955, a meeting in Geneva among President Eisenhower, Prime Minister Anthony Eden of Great Britain, Premier Edgar Faure of France, and Premier Nikolai A. Bulganin of Russia proceeded in an atmosphere of cordiality. German reunification, European security, and disarmament were discussed, though there was no real progress to report.

The relatively cordial attitude displayed at Geneva, nonetheless, did seem to improve the general international climate. Thus, in August 1955, scientists from both Western and Communist states met in Geneva to exchange information on the peaceful uses of atomic energy. This was the first international meeting in twenty years of scientists from both sides of the "iron curtain." In 1956 the U.S.S.R. made the generally welcome announcement that the Porkkala Penin-sula, leased from Finland after World War II, would be returned to the Finns. Exchange visits by Russian and Western scholars were encouraged in Moscow as well as the West.

All this somehow made it easier for Westerners to minimize the fact that Russia still wished to break up NATO, and that the Soviet Government priced its recognition of West Germany at the latter's withdrawal from NATO. There also were disquieting reports of arms deals between Soviet bloc nations and certain underdeveloped states (between Czechoslovakia and Egypt, for instance) that seemed aimed at extending Communist influence into new areas.

In 1956, however, the search for peaceful coexistence still seemed to be progressing and the lull in the Cold War continued. The Russians at one point suggested to the United States a twenty-year treaty of friendship and cooperation. Even though this was rejected, on the ground that actual disarmament and the easing of tensions had not proceeded sufficiently to make such a pact meaningful, the very fact of its proposal seemed to presage further cooperation. Then, at the Twentieth Party Congress, Khrushchev denounced Stalin and the old tyrannical ways (see Chapter 24), and there was proclaimed a major cut in Russian armed forces. Then, unfortunately, the vision of a world at peace was dashed by a new series of crises. A Hungarian uprising of 1956 was the major factor in a renewal of the antagonisms of the Cold War.

This crisis and others in 1956 probably were rooted in the fact that the Cold War had been so firmly joined by both sides that it was difficult for either antagonist to disengage quickly without some severe dislocation of its international position. Both the United States and Russia were somewhat overextended in assumed responsibilities and were caught in situations where the delicate balance of power would be upset by a rapid move on either side without a corresponding move on the part of the other. Soviet overextension, indeed, had been predicted as early as 1946 by George F. Kennan, when he had written that the Russian system "will now be subjected by virtue of recent territorial expansions to a series of additional strains which once proved a severe tax on Tsardom."

The new Soviet leaders, perhaps aware of Stalin's overextension of empire, yet hesitated to weaken their iron-handed control lest the satellites join their powerful enemies. It doubtless would have been difficult to control so vast an area even in untroubled times; it certainly was difficult in the 1950's when the dissatisfaction of some satellite peoples took the form of insurrection. For instance, there was an insurrection in Czechoslovakia in June 1953. Hundreds of thousands of East Germans were fleeing to the Federal Republic of Germany. And there was an uprising in East Berlin (June 1953) that brought to the newspapers and cinema screens of the world pathetic scenes of German workers hurling rocks at Soviet tanks. The Russians therefore decided to ease controls gradually in the satellite areas, in the hope thus to allay the seemingly prevalent disaffection.

A major first step, taken between mid-1953 and 1955, was to relax somewhat the economic restrictions, which had been designed essentially, at the end of the war, to benefit the Soviet Union and which had limited the standard of life in the satellites. To reflect this new stance, Khrushchev, at the same Twentieth Party Congress at which he denounced Stalinism, called attention to "the emergence of socialism" from within the boundaries of a single country, and the existence of a number of socialist states. The statement implied a promise of greater freedom of action within the Soviet orbit and, since it was followed by the dissolution of the Cominform in April 1956[13] Khrushchev seemed to have been doing more than mouthing empty words. Throughout the world Communist leaders began to speak of a developing "polycentrism" within global Communism, though it appeared to some observers that polycentrism might be little more than a euphemism for the fragmentation of the Communist world.

As there had been an official reaction against the ghost of Stalin in Moscow, so there now came a reaction against old-line Stalinist leaders elsewhere in the Communist bloc. But when a general ferment threatened to get out of hand, Moscow quickly intervened to limit movements that might sweep away the existing governments. Eventually situations developed that led to the use of Soviet armed forces in Poland and Hungary.

The anti-Stalinist reaction in Poland brought to power Wladyslaw Gomulka, who earlier had been deposed as First Secretary of the Polish Communist Party because he was too "nationalist" minded. Gomulka's emergence, not foreseen by Moscow, created in the Kremlin visions of a Titoist Poland, pursuing a pro-Western course.

In October 1956, the Red Army began to move on Warsaw. Without advance notice, on the morning of the 19th, a delegation from Moscow, headed by Khrushchev himself, arrived in the Polish capital. A meeting was held between Gomulka and the delegation, as Soviet troops continued to advance. The Russians had come to Warsaw apparently believing that Poland was about to move into the Western camp. Some kind of understanding was, however, established between the negotiating leaders. The Russian forces withdrew to the frontiers and Gomulka initiated a series of changes, among them the pardoning of some political prisoners and the release from jail of Stefan Cardinal Wyszyński after three years' detention for "anti-Communist" activities.

As the Polish crisis eased and the Soviets decided that the use of force was not necessary, a more inflammatory situation developed in Hungary. Here Imre Nagy, a Communist with strong nationalist leanings, had become Premier. Nagy was driven by popular pressure to go beyond the position adopted by Gomulka, one that the Russians grudgingly had accepted. On November 1, 1956, Nagy announced that Hungary's ties with Russia had been cut and that, henceforth, Hungary would be a neutral nation like Switzerland. This move

[13] The Kremlin announced that the Cominform was no longer needed because it had "exhausted its function."

united the country behind Nagy, but it also brought the intervention of the Russian army to put down the Hungarian "rebellion."

The Russians evidently believed that their only choice of action was forceful suppression. If they did not move to check the Hungarian political reformation, rebellion might spread to other East European states until, eventually, the Russians would have to withdraw behind their own frontiers—there to erect defenses against potential Western aggression that the Kremlin believed inevitable. Seemingly, they visualized a reunited Germany, allied to the Atlantic nations, and ready under the leadership of the United States to turn against the Soviet Union.

In the dawn hours of November 4, 1956, accordingly, Russian tanks rumbled into Budapest. For ten days the Budapest populace and people of other cities in Hungary held out against the Russians, in some cases fighting the hopeless battle against Soviet mechanized might with bare hands. In the end, the Hungarians were suppressed. Thousands of refugees crossed the border into Austria, seeking escape to the West.[14]

The tragic uprising was followed by police repression. Some 35,000 people were reported imprisoned, and hundreds put to death. When children returned to school they found their teachers intimidated and mouthing the old party line. A new Communist dictatorship was established under János Kádár, and Imre Nagy, as well as those who had worked with him, were sentenced to death by orders from the Kremlin.

The UN General Assembly condemned the Soviets for their Hungarian intervention but took no direct action. Interestingly, a number of "neutralist" nations, which because of their own internal problems generally had tried to stay out of Russian-Western quarrels, now concurred in the UN condemnation of Russia.

Had it not been for the bloody suppression of the Hungarian uprising, the ties that bound the NATO members well might have been weakened in 1956 by a Suez crisis. In the closing days of 1956, Egypt was invaded by troops from Israel, Great Britain, and France. The invaders had various political motives and military objectives, but they shared a single vital interest—the Suez Canal. Let us briefly review the events that precipitated the invasion.

In November 1955, Washington had extended its alliance shield against possible Soviet military expansion by sponsoring the Baghdad Pact (later CENTO) among Turkey, Iran, Iraq, and Pakistan. The United States did not formally adhere to the alliance, because Washington wished to avoid arousing other Middle Eastern hostility toward the West, lest this benefit the Soviet Union. Washington thus established general security interests in the Middle East and was much concerned about any crisis at Suez.

---

[14] Approximately 195,000 Hungarians, some two per cent of the population, were said to have fled.

Meanwhile the Russians had begun supplying various Arabian states with weapons, in attempts to extend Soviet influence. At the same time Great Britain, as she had in other parts of the world, attempted to withdraw entirely from Egypt. As early as 1954, Britain had promised Egypt that her troops would be withdrawn from the Suez Canal area in stages, provided freedom for British commercial traffic through the canal was assured by the Egyptian nationalist leader Gamal Abdel Nasser. As Great Britain then pulled back from another part of her empire, Nasser cast about for material aid against the Baghdad Pact, which he regarded as inimical to Egypt. Refused military assistance by the West, Nasser turned to the Soviet Union. The U.S.S.R. gave such assistance and, indeed, promised extensive aid in building a much needed Aswan Dam on the Upper Nile.

British troops were withdrawn completely from the Suez area in June 1956. Nasser then made himself President of Egypt and promptly asked for American aid, hoping to be served financially by both sides in the Cold War. Washington, however, withdrew earlier offers of economic help, primarily because of the extensive Egyptian dealings with the Soviet bloc.

Denied the aid he had sought from the West and encouraged by the apparent helpfulness of the U.S.S.R., Nasser believed that he no longer needed to worry about the West's concern over Suez. He proclaimed the nationalization of the canal property, although this legally was owned by a foreign company. Never fond of Nasser in the best of times, the British and French governments warned that their interests had been placed in jeopardy by the nationalization of the canal. Washington, however, urged caution and submitted a plan, through the UN, for international control of the waterway. The Russians opposed the American plan and raised the spectre of neo-colonialism to frighten the Egyptians into drawing further away from the West and closer to Moscow.

An atmosphere of international crisis developed in which Israel, long resentful of Egypt because of her support of continued Arabian commando raids into Zionist territory, wished to join France and Great Britain in unseating Nasser and punishing Egypt. Following the delivery of arms from Paris and strategic conferences with the French, Israeli troops, on October 29, 1956, drove across the Egyptian border. Anglo-French air forces bombed the canal area while promising they would localize the Israeli-Egyptian conflict. Washington officialdom reacted by comparing French and British behavior in Suez to that of the Soviet Union in Budapest.

Although preoccupied with trouble in Poland and Hungary, the Russians declared their readiness to send "volunteers" to the Middle East. The threats became more specific as the Israeli armies easily defeated Nasser's forces, Moscow even threatening to send rockets against London and Paris. This hard line on the part of the Soviets helped seal the cracks in the NATO alliance caused by the Suez affair. The United States quickly warned the U.S.S.R. that any attack on NATO states or any member of the Baghdad Pact would bring instant retaliation.

Supported by the United States, the UN General Assembly directed the negotiation of an armistice as rapidly as possible. Israel, France, and England all obeyed within two days.[15] The invaders recalled their forces, and troops from neutral countries—under UN command —took up police duties on the borders of Egypt. The UN also directed the clearing of objects from the canal that angry Egyptians had cast into it during the crisis.

In summary, the NATO alliance, which briefly had threatened to fall apart, once again drew together. The Russian action in Hungary and the bellicose statements issuing from the Kremlin during the Suez crisis helped bring the Atlantic treaty countries into greater harmony. Another healing factor was the replacement in several NATO governments of the leaders involved in the start of the crisis. Great Britain's Prime Minister, Anthony Eden, and French Premier Guy Mollet were replaced by other figures not directly tied to Suez. The outcome of the Suez confrontation, moreover, marked the end of British ascendancy in the Middle East, accompanied by a heightening of American and especially Russian prestige in African and Asian countries.[16] Through the announcement of the Eisenhower Doctrine in 1957, promising aid to any state imperiled by Communist aggression in the Middle East, the United States hoped to contain the spread of Soviet influence there.

During 1957 there were no major crises in the Cold War, perhaps because in that year Russia was preoccupied with domestic developments. In July, Khruschev emerged from a party fight in the Presidium as the supreme voice of Communism. In the area of technological competition between Russia and the United States, the Soviets made great strides by successfully testing an intercontinental ballistic missle (ICBM). The U.S.S.R. followed this triumph by launching (October 4, 1957) a satellite into orbit around the earth (Sputnik I). A second such launching placed a half-ton object in orbit. These Soviet triumphs in space had great significance for international politics since they demonstrated a Russian ability to deliver warheads over the distances between continents. When the United States, in December 1957, failed in her first attempt to launch a satellite, it appeared that the balance of scientific competence was shifting, at least temporarily, to the Russian side. By 1958, Russia claimed a nuclear capacity sufficient to match that of the United States, along with a superior delivery system. Thus the technological superiority of the United States, which was thought by many to have

---

[15] British agreement to an early truce may have been influenced by Commonwealth criticism of the mother country's action.

[16] Russian propaganda continued to maintain for some time after the Suez crisis that it was the threatened use of Soviet missiles that brought an end to the dangerous Middle Eastern situation and enhanced the position of Nasser in Egypt.

been the main deterrent keeping the Russians in check, seemingly had disappeared.

One side effect of the Russian sputnik launching and the proof it gave of Russian possession of a superior delivery system was the Rapacki Plan. In February 1958, the Polish Foreign Minister, Adam Rapacki, proposed the creation of a nuclear-free area in Central Europe (the two Germanies, Poland, and Czechoslovakia). Rapacki urged that no nuclear weapons be produced or stockpiled in this zone. The plan was rejected by the Washington and Bonn governments essentially because it was based on the continuing division of Germany and because it capitalized on Moscow's advantage in delivery systems by depriving the West of forward bases in West Germany, from which nuclear warheads could be fired against Soviet bloc states and the U.S.S.R. itself.

Its technological advances placed Moscow, by the middle of 1958, in a position once again to conduct a dynamic foreign policy. The reaction in the United States to the sputniks was noticeable in the general spread of alarm. There were cries of a "missile gap" and alarmed calls for its closing so that the world balance of power once again might be stabilized. Also frightening some Americans was the fact that so much of the strike capability of the United States was in the form of long-range bombers in North America and medium-range planes based in Great Britain, Turkey, other NATO countries, and the Far East. This more traditional type of conveyance for atomic weapons was vulnerable to destruction on the ground by Russian ICBM's. The United States accordingly stepped up its own production of missiles to counter the threat of the Soviet ICBM's, and hurried the development of the Polaris missile which could be fired from submerged submarines placed within striking distance of Russia. Thus, in 1958, began the period that one American strategic expert called "the delicate balance of terror."

The position of America's European allies, meanwhile, was uncomfortable. United States bombers and missiles, based on their soil, made them prime targets for nuclear attack in the event of a war between the United States and Russia. Consequently, America's allies began to urge that a way be found to stop the arms race through negotiations with the Russians. There was renewed talk of "disengagement" (the Rapacki Plan being the most commonly advanced idea), which would have meant a ban on the further production of nuclear weapons and their removal from the Germanies, Poland, and Czechoslovakia. The establishment of such a nuclear-free zone, it was suggested, might be followed by a reduction of the conventionally armed forces in the area. Russia advanced several similar proposals, but the United States suspected that Moscow's motives were calculated more to weaken NATO than to ease the international situation.

With the start of the "balance of terror," the question of Berlin arose once more. Khrushchev decided to exploit the "missile gap" and tried some "rocket rattling" by announcing, in November 1958, that the time had come for the occupying powers to withdraw from Berlin and to transfer the city to the German Democratic Republic (GDR). He gave the West six months (to May 27, 1959) to get out of Berlin, else Moscow would act alone and turn over the Berlin access routes to East Germany. He further indicated that if the Western Powers attempted to use their accustomed routes without East Germany's consent, Moscow would support its satellite state with force. On Christmas Day of 1958, Soviet Foreign Minister Andrei A. Gromyko warned that any "provocation" by the Allies in Berlin could start "a big war" in which millions would die.

By challenging the Western position in Berlin, Khrushchev reopened the German question. Already, by 1958, the East German authorities had virtually sealed off the long frontier between East and West Germany by building along the border a barricade of barbed wire, watch towers, and machine-gun emplacements patroled by police dogs. The major escape route remaining open for those who wished to flee to the West was the S-Bahn (*Stadtbahn,* an express train) from East to West Berlin and freedom. The frequent use of this route, despite intensive police surveillance, was a constant irritant to Khrushchev and his associates.

In some ways the situation in Berlin in 1958 was more difficult for the West than had been the case a decade earlier. The Western Powers, through NATO, had only 21 divisions facing some 175 Russian divisions in the area of the Germanies. They were not in a good position to fight a ground war because of geographic and strategic considerations. President Eisenhower, when asked if he would use nuclear weapons to free Berlin, replied that one could hardly "free anything with nuclear weapons." On the other hand, he could not wholly dismiss the possibility of nuclear war, for this might have been construed as an open invitation to the Russians to seize Berlin. Therefore he followed his first statement by saying that neither was "nuclear war . . . a complete impossibility." The Western policy clearly was to stand fast in Berlin and resist any transfer to the East German regime of Moscow's Berlin responsibilities. The Big Four had occupied Berlin at the end of the war, and no treaty as yet had been signed to change that situation.

Faced by a firm stand in the West, Khrushchev did an abrupt about-face, demonstrating a Russian strategy dating from the time of the Mongol invasions: retreat until some new occasion to advance presents itself. In March 1959, the Communist leaders virtually endorsed the position of the West by telling a press conference that the Western powers indeed had "lawful rights" in Berlin, emanating from the fact of German surrender "as a result of our joint struggle against Nazi Germany." Meanwhile, early in 1959, Krushchev's associate, First Deputy Premier Anastas I. Mikoyan, made a tour of the United States and urged an early summit meeting to settle major East-West differences. During the summer, plans were announced for an exchange of visits between the United States President and the

Russian Premier, and in September Khrushchev and his family arrived in Washington.

Having told the National Press Club that he had come to the United States to halt the Cold War, he then appeared before the United Nations and created a sensation by calling for an end to all armed forces. He found time also to visit Hollywood and lunch with movie stars. Most importantly, during the last two days of his visit he met President Eisenhower at the latter's Maryland retreat, Camp David. The Camp David talks centered on Berlin and disarmament, but agreement was produced on neither topic. Perhaps the chief gain from this, as with most summit meetings since World War II, was the personal contact between the two most powerful leaders in the world.

In any case, the way was eased for another summit meeting. Prime Minister Harold Macmillan of Great Britain strongly urged another meeting, believing that the United States and Russia were not likely to annihilate one another as long as they were "talking." The next summit conference was agreed upon and scheduled to begin on May 16, 1960, in Paris.

Shortly before this date, a sensational incident cast a pall over the prospect of a successful Paris summit meeting. Apparently the United States since 1956 had been sending high-flying (U-2) reconnaissance planes over the Soviet Union, to gather military intelligence. Moscow had known about these flights, but, because of the altitude and speed of the "spy" planes, the Soviets had been unable to do anything about them. The mission of the planes was vital: they were to collect the same kind of information about Soviet military installations that Russian agents in the United States presumably found it easy to gather in an open society.

On May 5, 1960, eleven days before the scheduled conference in Paris, Khrushchev announced that an American plane had been shot down over Russian territory. The Russian Premier laid a trap for Washington by withholding the full story, for the Soviets not only had recovered the plane's espionage equipment, but had captured the pilot. Washington, acting as nations normally act in such cases, issued a false account of the plane's activities, claiming it to have been a weather plane off course. Then Khrushchev made public his evidence, the intent clearly being to place the United States in a bad light on the eve of the summit conference.

It probably would not have occasioned much international eyebrow-raising had the act been laid at the door of overzealous underlings. Khrushchev, in fact, having obtained propaganda advantage from the event, seemed willing to let Eisenhower escape blame by passing on the responsibility for the spy flights to subordinates. On May 7, 1960, the Soviet leader professed that he was "quite willing to grant" that President Eisenhower "knew nothing about the plane having been sent into the Soviet Union." Eisenhower, however, did not choose this course and, instead, assumed the commander's full responsibility.

As a consequence of the "U-2 incident," Khrushchev, at the opening session of the conference on May 16, attacked the United States and declared that President Eisenhower would not be welcome in the Soviet Union. He also demanded as a precondition for going ahead with the conference that the United States "condemn" the actions of its air force, commit itself to discontinuing permanently such flights, and punish those responsible for the mission of the U-2 spy plane brought down over Russia. Eisenhower replied by indicating only that U-2 flights already had been suspended and would not be resumed.

On the following day Khrushchev repeated his demands and a short time later warned that any more planes sent over the Soviet Union would be shot down and the foreign bases from which they had taken off would suffer "shattering" consequences. To foreign observers it seemed that Khrushchev was under pressure from Soviet "hard-liners" who were using the U-2 incident to force the Premier into a more belligerent pose than he otherwise might have assumed. In any event, when the Russian demands to punish the U-2 "culprits" were rejected, Khrushchev left Paris for East Berlin. But, pulling back once again from ultimate confrontation, Khrushchev disclaimed any desire to precipitate an armed clash and proposed another summit meeting to take place "in six to eight months' time."

The Course of the Cold War (since 1960)

22

THE SINO-SOVIET SCHISM

Before the history of the continuing friction between the Soviet Union and the West is examined, it would be well to consider a feud that appeared in the late 1950's between the Communist leadership in Russia and in China. This confrontation first cracked and then split the seemingly solid front that the Reds previously had presented to the non-Communist world. It was destined to have profound repercussions in the international sphere.

The origins of the split between Russia and China were both immediate and, at the same time, deep seated in the historical positions of both countries. First, it must be pointed out, Mao Tse-tung and his followers in the winter of 1949–1950 had arrived at a stage of optimism similar to that of Lenin and his associates in Russia about 1917–1918. The Red Chinese leadership in 1950 envisioned a world that had developed in terms of an almost Mithraic dualism, a planet divided between the capitalist-imperialists and those whom they exploited. The Communists of China hoped to fulfill the 100-year-old prophecy of the *Communist Manifesto,* though this was written by men whose beliefs were shaped by Western, not Oriental traditions; Mao and his followers would finally destroy capitalism.

It seemed to the Chinese that the United States was the leader of the imperialist camp and thus bound by historical determinism to be the deadly enemy of Communist China. This concept was given additional credence in Chinese governmental circles because of the continued close United States association with the Nationalist Chinese regime on Taiwan. Washington, even had it wanted to, could not disengage itself from Chaing Kai-shek and his government-in-exile on Taiwan because of the force of American public opinion. Hence,

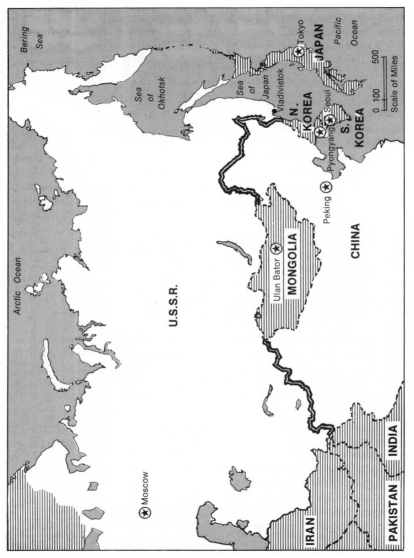

THE CHINESE-SOVIET BORDER 1970

the United States moved into the Formosa Straits with naval strength to prevent the falling of Taiwan into Communist hands. This move hardened an already rigid line that the Red Chinese had adopted in their anti-American propaganda—a line drawn even before American military might arrived off shore because the Maoists needed to create an outside threat so fearful that it would solidify the populace behind the new government. Such a procedure had historical precedence on the part of governments freshly established by revolution or civil war.

With the polarization of the American and Chinese positions, Washington felt impelled to extend the containment doctrine to Asia and to limit Chinese expansion in the same way as the Russian was being contained. This move was to have extensive ramifications including, eventually, United States embroilment in the Vietnam War in the 1960's.

The fixing of Chinese minds upon the United States as the "natural" ideological enemy, underlay a close though historically unusual relationship between Russia and China. Following the proclamation by Mao of a People's Republic of China on September 21, 1949, a thirty-year Treaty of Friendship and Mutual Assistance was signed with Russia on February 14, 1950. The agreement, creating a so-called Moscow-Peking Axis, did not erase the broad differences in culture, language, and general ways of looking at life that existed between Russia and China. From the outset, therefore, the partnership established between Russia and China in 1949–1950 was an uneasy one. Its maintenance was made more difficult by the 4500 miles of boundary shared by Russia and China, a border that was not always clearly defined.

After 1949, China for the first time in modern history appeared on the international scene not merely as an enemy of Russia, but as a potentially powerful enemy. Driven by her accretion of power, and her traditional Asian hostility for the Russians as Europeans, China was ready to challenge Moscow's world Communist leadership. Not surprisingly, the view developed in China during the 1950's that Peking rather than Moscow was the proper model for developing Asian Communist states.

Further stimulus was given to a split between the two Communist giants when, at the Twentieth Party Congress, Khrushchev, in addition to rejecting Stalinism, turned away from Lenin's concept of the inevitability of war. The Soviet Premier's proclamation of the idea of "peaceful coexistence" seemed to the orthodox Leninist-Marxists in China to be nothing short of heresy. The Russian ideological "errors" seemed even more improper when the Russians offered to assist China's capitalist neighbor, India, while at the same time seeking better relations with the North Atlantic powers. The "spirit of Camp David," which hovered over Khrushchev following his visit to the United States in 1959, especially repelled the Chinese Communists, for it led the Soviet leader to urge Mao not to press his claims to the offshore islands in the Straits of Formosa lest there be an impairment of the warmer relations developing between East and West. Then, when, in the winter of 1959–1960, there were border clashes between China and India, the Russians adopted a strictly neutral position. To the Chinese, this seemed little short of treason.

From Peking there now emanated a series of anti-Soviet statements. The Chinese pointed out that the Russians, after all, were Europeans and thus normally demonstrated a special affinity for Europe's decadent civilization. What was even worse, Russia seemed to cower in fear of war with the West. A Russian Government was pictured that was growing more and more like that of the United States in its commitment to the defense of the status quo. In Chinese thinking, the Russians seemed no longer interested in revolution or revolutionary change. These beliefs were accentuated by Moscow's "arrogance" and the attempt of the Russians to maintain a parent-child relationship with the Chinese. The historical divergence of traditional Russian and Chinese interests thus more than counterbalanced the brief sharing of a Leninist-Marxist tradition.

In the midsummer of 1960 there was a public exchange of recriminations between Khrushchev and Mao, and the former recalled Russian technicians who had been sent to help China with industrialization schemes patterned after the Soviet five-year plans. The returning technicians took with them even the blueprints of unfinished projects, and shipments of machinery and equipment were cut back sharply. As far as the Soviets were concerned, this represented little more than the chastising of an unruly subordinate, but it caused a deep schism and initiated a new Cold War for Russia, this time on the Eastern front.

The Kremlin unsuccessfully attempted in 1960 and 1961 to heal the breach with Peking. Khrushchev, seeking to recapture the supreme leadership of world Communism for Russia, again was rebuffed by the Chinese. In 1966 the Soviets once more tried to extend an olive branch to the Chinese, by inviting Mao and his followers to the 23rd Party Congress. But in their refusal the Chinese Communists went far beyond a polite rejection; they accused the Soviet Union of "collusion" with the United States to inhibit the spread of true proletarian revolution.

China's accusation that Russia and the United States were working toward a similar end was based on a fundamental split between Russia and China over the question of war and peace. When Khrushchev made statements, as he had done in 1964, to the effect that something "more to eat" for the people in the Soviet bloc, along with good schools and better housing, were the prime objectives of Soviet policy, the Chinese accused the Soviet Premier of serving "the United States imperialists." The Soviet decision to give a higher priority to domestic prosperity than to the war against the West, opened the way for the Chinese to pose before the underdeveloped world as the new champion of the have-nots, as a dedicated replacement for the newly complacent Soviet Russia.

By early 1967, the schism between China and Russia had become so deep that Chinese newspapers openly insulted the Soviets. On one occasion, the *Peking People's Daily* referred to the Russians as "filthy Soviet revisionist swine." In Moscow, the Chinese *chargé d'affaires* called his hosts "paper tigers" and promised that the day would come when the "Soviet revisionists" would "have to repay their blood debts." A group of Chinese Communist students gathered at Stalin's grave to sing Maoist hymns, and a riot ensued when the Russian police moved in to stop the Asiatic Reds from carrying on "provocative" actions. A few weeks later the Soviet Embassy in Peking was besieged by Red Guards, the teen-age standard bearers of Mao's new "Great Proletarian Cultural Revolution" (see Chapter 28), shouting, "destroy the Soviet swine." Before the year was out, the new Soviet Premier, Aleksei N. Kosygin, publicly urged sympathy for the "people struggling against the dictatorial regime of Mao Tse-tung."

Meanwhile, an event of October 16, 1964, had given the estrangement between the Soviet Union and China, as well as the Chinese hatred of the United States, a new and more ominous meaning. On that date the Chinese exploded their first atomic bomb. In October 1966, the Chinese fired their first intermediate-range missile, and followed that technological triumph in 1967 with a "splendid achievement of the Great Proletarian Cultural Revolution," namely, the detonation of a hydrogen bomb. These triumphs spurred the hard-line Peking Maoists to even greater blustering, and further underscored a seeming fragmentation of the Communist world.

THE THIRD BERLIN CRISIS AND THE CUBAN MISSILE CRISIS

As the split between Russia and China widened, Khrushchev, who sometimes appeared to conduct Soviet affairs in a capricious personal fashion, tried to win concessions from the West that would quiet mounting doubts concerning his leadership among his Kremlin associates. When the administration of President John F. Kennedy succeeded that of Dwight D. Eisenhower, Khrushchev thought he saw the opportunity to bolster his reputation because the new administration did not seem to be as vigorously anti-Communist as had been its predecessors.

Soon after the Kennedy Administration was installed, Khrushchev decided to resume the drive on Berlin. A few days after an unsatisfactory meeting of the United States and Russian chief executives in Vienna, Khrushchev in mid-June again threatened to conclude a peace treaty with East Germany, which presumably would block the Western access routes to Berlin. A solution of the Berlin question along Soviet lines, he said, would have to be found before the end of

1961. In response to these threats and a Russian buildup in armed forces, President Kennedy called for a substantial increase in size of both the United States Army and NATO forces. Kennedy indicated that "we do not want to fight," but that the United States would not be driven out of Berlin.

As the international tension increased over this new confrontation between the Russians and the United States, thousands of East Germans made ready to flee, fearing that if Berlin were absorbed into the GDR it might become impossible to leave. In the first half of 1961, more than 103,000 escaped. Then, in the early morning hours of August 13, 1961, escape to the West was shut off by the Communists in a way that hardly could have been anticipated. East Berlin was sealed off from West Berlin by the erection of a concrete wall, topped by barbed wire. The city was cut into two parts, and passage between the sections was allowed only through a few closely controlled "checkpoints." The Western Allies presumably had the right, under the 1945 occupation agreements, to interfere with the building of the barrier; but they decided not to take the risk.

It is one of the ironies of history that the erection of the wall in Berlin, over which many fugitives came to risk or lose their lives in trying to escape, enabled Moscow to relax its pressures on the West. By stopping the heavy and reputation-damaging drainage of the East German population, the Russians apparently felt able to tolerate the presence of the Western Powers in Berlin. Khrushchev, indeed, removed his deadline and indicated that "if the Western Powers" demonstrated "a readiness to solve the German problem" there need be no time limit set for that solution.

With the crisis in Russian-Western relations unresolved, and in light of a worsening of Russo-Chinese relations, Khrushchev searched for some victory to save his power in the Soviet system and maintain Moscow's influence in the Communist world. This plight spurred him to a well nigh reckless gamble, which brought the world to the brink of war over Cuba.

Cuba took the center of the international stage following a revolution led by Dr. Fidel Castro Ruz, who in January 1959, overthrew the dictatorship of General Fulgencio Batista. Once in power, Castro, lacking a planned program, improvised measures on a day-to-day basis, and soon led Cuba into grave economic difficulty. Much as the Bolsheviks in the early days of their control in Russia had been driven by chaotic conditions to establish a tyranny more thorough than that of the tsarist government preceding them, Castro now installed a dictatorship more rigid than had been Batista's.

The usual approach adopted by revolutionary-autocratic regimes was taken to avert expected disorder. A vicious external enemy was designated—this time in the form of the supposedly "invasion-minded" government of the United States. The resulting intemperate Cuban propaganda campaign led to strained relations between Washington and Havana. Before long, the Cubans found that their political goals had led to action that brought serious economic consequences in its wake. Cuba's economy long had been dependent upon the United States, which had subsidized the island's sugar raisers by buying their produce at a price higher than that of the world market. Now the United States reduced the sugar quota and the Cuban economy suffered a steep decline. There seemed to Castro only one feasible way out of this worsening dilemma: he turned to Moscow for help.

In mid-1960, Cuba in effect proclaimed itself under Russian military protection, declaring that, "in case of necessity, Soviet artillery" could defend Cubans "against aggressive forces in the Pentagon." Thereafter, in his mock struggle against "American imperialism," Castro became increasingly dependent on Russia. Khrushchev's increasing venturesomeness led him to encourage this dependence and thus extended Russia's commitments far afield. One early result of Cuba's new *Fidelismo* was the severance of diplomatic relations by the United States in January 1961.

Meanwhile, throughout 1960, Russian technicians and advisers arrived in Cuba by the thousands. Cuban refugees at the same time were streaming into Florida at such a pace that it became possible to think of creating a Cuban army in exile, bent upon invading the homeland and overthrowing Castro. Such an idea became increasingly popular in Washington, as Russian influence continued to grow in the island dictatorship, only ninety miles off the coast of Florida.

During the last days of the Eisenhower Administration and the first days of the Kennedy Administration (1960–1961), a Cuban refugee invasion actually was organized secretly in Florida. The invaders attempted a landing at the Bay of Pigs (*Bahía de Cochinos*) in Cuba on April 17, 1961. They hoped that the Cubans would rise and support the "liberating" forces against Castro. This failed to happen, the attempted mission ended in disaster for the attackers, and soon the United States was vilified by the international Communist camp as a "proven aggressor." What was, perhaps, a blunder, apparently encouraged Khrushchev to make an even greater error by moving to support Cuba with military aid.

During the summer of 1962, intelligence reports flowed into Washington, indicating that Castro was building up his military strength with the aid of Soviet equipment and technicians. By October, high-flying reconnaissance planes had discovered that the Soviet technicians were installing missile sites and airfields with runways sufficiently long to permit supersonic bombers to take off and land. Further aerial photographs demonstrated that the Russians had installed in Western Cuba missile sites capable of launching nuclear warheads a distance of up to 1400 miles.

On October 22, 1962, President Kennedy informed the nation of this situation in a television speech, in which he said:

This secret, swift, and extraordinary build-up of Communist missiles in an area well known to have a special . . . relationship to the United States . . . is a deliberately provocative and unjustified change in the status quo which cannot be accepted by this country . . . . Our unswerving objective, therefore, must be to prevent the use of these missiles against this or any other country, and to secure their withdrawal or elimination from the Western Hemisphere.

At the same time the President imposed a blockade or "defensive quarantine" on arms shipments to Cuba, to be enforced by the United States Navy and Air Force. On October 24, 1962, when President Kennedy's order went into effect, there were twenty-five Russian ships on course to Cuba. That night twelve of the ships (supposedly those carrying missiles) either stopped or were turned on a homeward course by order from Moscow.

The United States next took to the United Nations a demand that Cuban missile bases be disbanded. Khrushchev promptly was faced both by United States pressure and UN disapproval. He then withdrew further from his original threatening stance by proposing that the U.S.S.R. would remove its missiles from Cuba if the United States were to close its bases in NATO-ally Turkey. Again the United States stood firm and the bargain involving Turkey was rejected. When it appeared that the United States was ready to take military action, perhaps including invasion, to ensure that Soviet weapons were cleared out of Cuba, Khrushchev modified his earlier demands and merely asked that the United States pledge itself not to invade Cuba. When the pledge was given, Khrushchev (October 28, 1962) announced the dismantling and return of missiles and site installations to Russia. In little more than a week, the world had been to the brink of war and back. The disappointed Castro, for a time at least, began to flirt with the Chinese Communists.

A CHANGE IN DIRECTION IN THE COLD WAR

After October, 1962, Russia and the West took stock of the recent frightening events. The shared experience of a great common danger was sobering enough to produce a thaw in the Russo-Western Cold War conflict. From the beginning of the Cold War the Soviets, historically obsessed with the fear of invasion, had taken the initiative. Now the leaders in the U.S.S.R. seemingly became convinced that a world in which there were two (and potentially more) "overkill" arsenals would be least dangerous to the Soviet Union if the status quo were maintained. The final destruction of civilization did not seem a reasonable price to pay for gambles on the international scene. By the end of 1962, too, Moscow recognized that the positions occupied by the West were firmly held and that the Western Powers could not easily be dislodged. The Western states now also could relax, for it appeared unlikely that the Red Army would attempt an early march toward the English Channel.

This all does not mean that the United States and Russia became close friends. The two superpowers still took opposite sides on almost every new global crisis. Nonetheless, in June 1963 a Russo-American agreement was signed establishing a teletype-like "hot line" of direct communication between Moscow and Washington to reduce the possibility of an accidental war.[1] There also developed consideration of a possible joint Russian and United States exploration of the moon's surface. In addition, there were sales of surplus American wheat to the Russians in 1963. Unfortunately, the symptoms of a relaxed attitude on both sides in the Cold War did not reach the foci of international difficulties. President Kennedy, and President Lyndon Baines Johnson after him, made it clear that the West would not budge on Berlin and that there would be no general disarmament unless mutual inspection of arms stockpiles were instituted. The defensive-minded and suspicious Russians, on the other hand, were not interested in elaborate inspection by Western observers of the Soviet defense installations.

The only major breakthrough on disarmament before 1970 was the Nuclear Test Ban Treaty of July 25, 1963, the first significant agreement between Russia and the West in eight years. It was not a really effective pact for, again, the matter of inspection was not agreed upon. Too, the test ban was limited to testing in the atmosphere, outer space, and under water. Consequently, the signatories were not prohibited from carrying on underground blasts. Moreover, a major flaw in the agreement was that not all nuclear powers signed it. By this time both China and France were ready to join the United States, Russia, and Great Britain as nuclear powers. Paris and Peking, indeed, gradually withdrew from their respective blocs into positions of greater independence, and demonstrated this attitude through an increasing tendency to display their nuclear strength before the world, in disregard of the Soviet-United States ban on testing in the atmosphere.

Little more than a year after the Cuban crisis, President Kennedy was assassinated (see Chapter 23). Khrushchev sent his successor, Lyndon B. Johnson, a message in which he called the death of the young American President "a blow" to "Soviet-American" cooperation. But Khrushchev himself was not to remain in office much longer, and, within another year, in 1964, he was removed from power by his associates. Perhaps the most remarkable thing about Khrushchev's removal was the fact that the new Russian leaders defied the tradition of punitive action against former governmental authorities and allowed the ex-Premier to take up a comfortable retirement. The new collective leadership, moreover, seemed more intent on the avoid-

---

[1] The development of the "hot line" seems to have come from the fact that, during the Cuban missile crisis, Kennedy and Khrushchev communicated with each other through diplomatic channels requiring hours for the transmission of a message. This time lag was disquieting when it was realized that a missile could span the distance between continents in minutes.

ance of dangerous "rocket-rattling" than had been the practice of either Stalin or Krushchev. Thus, within two years after the Cuban Missile Crisis, both sides in the Cold War had new leadership, and the strange period of neither war nor peace itself seemed to have altered to a point at which some observers began to use the term "thaw" to explain the transformation that had taken place.

THE WEAKENING OF TIES
WITHIN THE RUSSIAN AND WESTERN BLOCS

By the mid-1960's, the iron curtain had become a somewhat less substantial barrier between Eastern and Western Europe. Ideological tags like "communism" came to mean less in Red bloc countries as they moved slowly into capitalist-like economic and nationalistic political policies. That Russia temporarily should allow greater autonomy in the selection of policies among her satellites was not surprising. Because of the Sino-Soviet conflict, Moscow had to grant concessions to states within the Soviet orbit, for Mao Tse-tung made no secret of his desire to see the Communist states controlled by governments more sympathetic to Peking's "revolutionary" attitude. Accordingly, to maintain satellite loyalty to Moscow and prevent its shift to Peking, the Soviet leadership developed a modified concept of Eastern Europe. The Stalinist line, which envisaged the satellite states virtually as part of a Russian empire, was replaced by a relationship between Russia and the other European Communist states which was more like that of a commonwealth association.

Khrushchev, however, in allowing greater autonomy, unleashed historical forces at work within Eastern Europe. Before World War II, Eastern Europe was a hotbed of national ambitions and antagonisms. The post-1945 Communist regimes hopefully proclaimed an end to the era of nationalism. But among the peoples there remained the yearnings for national autonomy. The exigencies of the Sino-Soviet conflict provided an opportunity for some of the national sentiments to rise again.

There were several instances of national reaction within the Soviet orbit but one example will suffice as illustration. In Czechoslovakia, there had existed before World War II a democratic republic; in 1968, some score of years since the country had been forced into the Soviet Union's East European bloc, a renewed drive toward democratization was manifested. Though long cowed by the grim figure of Joseph Stalin, who was backed by a mighty military machine and an omnipresent secret police force, the Czechs gradually came to regard the growth of polycentrism within the monolithic facade of communism as their signal to seek greater local freedom from Kremlin dictation. This led in 1968 to a crisis within the Communist bloc unequaled since Soviet tanks had moved into Budapest twelve years earlier.

In some ways the Czechoslovak heresy was greater than that of the Hungarians in the previous decade. The Hungarian revolt readily could be interpreted as merely a reaction against "brutal Stalinism." The Czechs, however, were ready actually to challenge Lenin's doctrine at two important points: (1) the view that the Communist Party should hold all political power; and (2) that such power should be exercised in terms of ideological dogmatism. If the Czech Communists could overturn these Leninist dicta, the spectre would be raised of the loss of the party's grip on the U.S.S.R. itself.

The crisis over Czechoslovakia developed when the old-line Stalinist president, Antonín Novotný, was deposed by a group of more liberal colleagues led by Alexander Dubček, who quickly began the bold experiment of tempering Marxist doctrine with democratic reforms.[2] The reforms were widely applauded by the Czech populace and many Czechoslovaks began to believe that they were recapturing a lost heritage. Any rumor that Dubček might buckle under pressure from either the Russians or native Stalinists brought angry cries for liberal leadership to hold firm.

The other satellite bloc states did not react positively to the Czech reforms. On July 14–15, 1968, representatives of the Soviet Union, Hungary, Bulgaria, East Germany, and Poland met in Warsaw to draft a letter to the Czechoslovak Communist Party criticizing the reforms that had been introduced.

There hardly could have been a less auspicious time for a Czech confrontation with traditional Communists. Warsaw Pact maneuvers had just been held in Czechoslovakia, and some 16,000 Soviet troops were still in the country. Instead of going home, the Russian forces lingered on Czech soil in an obvious threat to Dubček's liberal reforms. There were frantic meetings in other Communist capitals, and, at the close of July and the beginning of August 1968, while the Russian forces withdrew just across the border where they continued to threaten the Czechs, there was a summit meeting between Soviet and Czechoslovak leaders. The first meeting was followed by another conference, including delegates from several hard-line satellite states. All conversations, claimed the Communist news agencies, were conducted in an atmosphere of "comradely frankness."

On August 9, 1968, Yugoslav President Tito, the very symbol of deviation from the Moscow line, arrived in Prague and was given a rousing welcome by the people. A few days later East German hard-line leader Walter Ulbricht arrived for talks and was greeted with more reserve by the Czechs. On August 16, the Soviet press resumed attacks it had made earlier on the liberal reform spirit in Czechoslovakia. Despite Dubček's indications that there would be "no break" with the Soviet Union, such attacks continued and became more threatening.

On August 20, invasion forces from Russia and its satellites occu-

[2] Among the reforms promised were freedom of the press and rehabilitation of purge victims.

pied Czechoslovakia. Only sporadic opposition was offered, since the Czech Government realized that resistance against such might could bring on a bloodbath like the one in Hungary in 1956. The Czechoslovak popular reaction was to meet the invaders with spit, wads of paper, and sullen silence. Soon Alexander Dubček was spirited away to Moscow, where talks continued and, although the Czech leader was allowed to return to Prague, it was clear that the Russians did not intend to let the "dangerous" reform movement in Prague continue unchecked. In September 1968, heavy pressure was put on the Czechoslovak Communist Party from Moscow to purge the republic of anti-Russian elements, and, as in the Hungarian case twelve years earlier, thousands tried to make their way out of the country.

Two things, involving Moscow itself, soon became evident. First, regardless of the amount of Soviet authority the Russians might be able to reinstate in Czech affairs, the ruthless intervention in another country's internal life was causing loud reverberations in the international sphere. Secondly, there obviously was a policy conflict within the Soviet leadership. The "tough" Russians believed that the "virus" of Czechoslovak liberalism might spread, perhaps to the Soviet Union itself, unless stern measures were taken to stamp it out. In the world at large, there was an extraordinary chorus of disapproval. The Czechoslovak crisis, moreover, had an immediate and disturbing effect on relations between the United States and the Soviet Union. On August 30, 1968, President Johnson warned that there should be no doubt "where the United States of America stands on a question so fundamental to the peace of the entire World" as the incursions of "would be" aggressors into the political life of another state. Johnson indicated also that if any similar action were taken by the Soviets against other states (such as Romania, where an independent course already had appeared), this would place a still greater strain upon Russo-American relations. The Soviet Union's invasion of Czechoslovakia also tabled any prospect of a summit meeting between Johnson and Soviet Premier Aleksei Kosygin to discuss nuclear disarmament.

In some respects the most profound effects of the Czech invasion seemed likely to transpire within the broader Communist world. The Soviet action sparked resentment among various national Communist parties, and dealt at least a passing blow to the old Soviet dream of Communist international unity. Communist parties generally around the world protested the Kremlin's action. Yet the Russians were aware that, if they hastily backed down, the spectacle of Soviet indecision might well encourage other satellite states to set forth on the path of liberal reform.

In the Western world, the middle sixties similarly experienced a loosening of some ties. There were several serious disputes among NATO states, such as a Greco-Turkish confrontation over Cyprus. Most important, perhaps, France assumed a disruptive pose when President Charles de Gaulle, in an attempt to revive the *grandeur de la patrie,* adopted a policy that, for all practical purposes, pulled France out of the NATO alliance. Eventually he aroused at home sufficient pro-French, anti-British, and anti-American sentiment to force the withdrawal of NATO headquarters from Paris to Brussels.

The Western alliance thus was strong in face of an ominous common threat; when such threat lessened, as in the time of mounting disunity in world communism, splits began to develop within the Allied community. To an extent, de Gaulle seemed to be challenging the influence of the United States in the Western world much as Mao had challenged Russian preponderance in the Communist camp. Hence, another feature of the international politics of the late 1960's was the tightening of the NATO alliance among some of the NATO nations—those which now decided that the Soviet Union had not moderated its stance as much as had been believed, and those which were concerned over the new posture of France as a self-appointed balance wheel between West and East.

OTHER SOVIET-AMERICAN DEVELOPMENTS

The United States regarded it as necessary after the Korean War to maintain the line of containment drawn around Red China along the 17th parallel in Vietnam. Even after it became clear that Peking and Moscow often did not act in unison, Washington believed it necessary further to restrain Communist Chinese expansion. Therefore, the South Vietnamese Government, regardless of its character, assumed it could get United States aid indefinitely in the fight against a Communist Vietnamese liberation movement and the North Vietnamese army. The American motive was simple enough: the Red Chinese had to be contained just as Russian forces had had to be restrained after 1945; and, since the Vietnamese Reds were "tools" of Peking, they must not be allowed to control all Indo-China, unless a majority of the Indo-Chinese in free elections so willed it. This problem was argued extensively in the United States, and the Vietnam War became a major issue in the presidential campaign of 1968 (see Chapter 23).

The United States' Vietnam embroilment placed a renewed strain on Washington's relations with Moscow.[3] For their part, the Russians, if they wished to keep ahead of China in the struggle for world Communist leadership, felt obliged to support the North Vietnamese with propaganda and munitions.

As the Vietnam War continued into 1968 and became more costly to both sides, peace talks were initiated late in the year among the warring parties. Once again there was at least a surface easing of

[3] The renewed turn for the worse in Russo-American relations seemed real enough so that some journalists began to use the term "Neo-Cold War."

tension between the United States and the U.S.S.R. In early July 1968, the two superpowers signed an agreement aimed at freeing the world from the threat of nuclear oblivion, the so-called Nuclear Nonproliferation Treaty. The agreement, designed to limit the nuclear powers to five, was hailed by President Johnson as "the most important international agreement since the beginning of the nuclear age." The high hopes held for the pact were augmented by its signing by other countries, which thus committed themselves not to develop nuclear weapons. Premier Kosygin of Russia, moreover, committed himself to discuss not only the limitation of nuclear armaments, but the broader question of disarmament in general. This developing *détente* was halted abruptly by the Czechoslovak crisis, with the result that consent to ratification of the treaty by the United States Senate was delayed until 1969.

In light of the Czechoslovak invasion, then, Russia's other steps toward seeming moderation appeared minor indeed. The solving of the basic problems that underlay the Cold War, accordingly, could be expected to come only, as one author has put it, "imperceptibly, like the movement of the hour-hand on a watch."[4]

[4] Halle, *Cold War As History,* p. 418.

Events in the
Americas in the
Post-World War II
Period

23

THE UNITED STATES

A. Political and Governmental Activity in the Postwar Years

The United States that was to become a major antagonist in the Cold War continued politics almost as usual during World War II. The general trend in domestic affairs was toward increasing conservatism in both economic and political policies, a drift that was highlighted in the Congressional elections of 1942. In United States politics the party out of power normally gains in the Congressional elections held in nonpresidential years; but in 1942 there was a gain beyond the normal expectancy in both houses. Republican Congressional strength increased significantly, in part because of the military reverses thus far sustained by United States forces.

The off-year success heartened Republicans, who envisaged the possibility of capturing the presidency in 1944. The Republican Convention nominated Governor Thomas E. Dewey of New York, a well-known figure in law enforcement. The Democrats enthusiastically renominated President Roosevelt. During the campaign it became evident that the Republicans, because of the apparent popularity of certain New Deal programs, were ready to abandon some of their traditional positions and, instead, support liberal legislation. But the voters again made Roosevelt their choice. He received 432 votes in the electoral college to Dewey's 99, and lost only 12 states.

The public in general seemed to regard the war as an unfortunate necessity. Unlike the case during World War I, there was relatively little overt hostility toward Americans of German descent. The country's life was mobilized behind the war effort and there was a notable volunteer spirit displayed on all levels of society. In addition to the

453

young men and women who poured into the armed forces, there were millions of citizens, including many women, who entered the defense industries. "Rosie the Riveter" became the propaganda symbol of the wartime woman industrial worker, and it stimulated social acceptance of the idea that women could step into work roles traditionally occupied by men.

Industry, too, was mobilized to bring a quick end to the conflict. In 1941, soon after Pearl Harbor, President Roosevelt had established the Office of Production Management (OPM), which soon transformed the economic system into a war economy. Although the United States' production situation often was confused and sometimes functioned inefficiently, it still turned out, before the end of the war, amounts of combat materials far greater than those produced by any other country. Production mounted until, to those conditioned to the bleak poverty of the depression years, there seemed to have blossomed a miracle of abundance. More and more workers had more and more money. From 1944, they were able to spend some of their new abundance on consumer goods, for the government, satisfied by the success of the production program, gradually relaxed restrictions on the making of civilian goods.

President Roosevelt did not live to see victory in war followed by economic resurgence at home. On April 12, 1945, less than three months after his inauguration for his fourth term, he died at Warm Springs, Georgia. Late that same evening Vice-President Harry S. Truman took the oath of office and became President of the United States. Although on the ticket with Roosevelt in 1944, Truman had been obscured by his famous running mate. Many now asked, "Who is Harry Truman?"

Harry S. Truman was born in 1884 in the little village of Lamar, Missouri, and grew up in his native state. He once had applied for admission to West Point, but had been turned down because of poor eyesight. After graduation from high school in 1901, he spent some time as a blank clerk. From 1906 until 1917 Harry Truman remained on the family farm in Grandview, Missouri. When World War I broke out, Truman went to France and rose to the rank of major. After the war and business reverses, Truman was offered the opportunity of running for the post of county judge by "Mike" Pendergast, brother of "Tom" Pendergast, the Democratic boss of Kansas City.[1] He was elected judge for a term of two years and then was defeated by a coalition that included Ku Klux Klan organizers. By 1927 he was back in politics, again as a county court judge.

In 1934 Truman, with the aid of the Pendergast machine, won nomination to the Senate. With many other Democratic candidates he rode the coattails of Franklin D. Roosevelt to Washington that

[1] Because of this early association with a none-too-scrupulous political machine, Truman was regarded by some with suspicion throughout his public life.

fall. He remained in the Senate for a second term and beyond the beginning of World War II. In 1941 Truman was made chairman of a special Senate committee to study the defense program. He won favorable attention for reportedly saving the Government $15 billion in unnecessary expenditures. Truman's work in this connection gave him sufficient national publicity to make him candidate for vice-president in 1944.

Many thought Truman would be merely a "caretaker president" until 1948, when another could be elected. His unsure manner at the beginning of his term reinforced this idea. But Truman worked hard and mastered the details of governmental operation. In 1946, he urged a full employment bill, which emerged from Congress as the Maximum Employment Act. The Act established a council of economic advisers and required the president to report annually on the state of the nation's economy. Another product of the first Truman Administration was the Atomic Energy Act of 1946, which placed the control of nuclear power, not in the military, but in the hands of a civilian Atomic Energy Commission. Then came the National Security Act of 1947, which brought the sometimes quarreling branches of the armed services under one command in a new Department of Defense. In 1947, also, Truman became deeply involved in Cold War measures such as the Marshall Plan and the Truman Doctrine which were discussed in earlier chapters.

Although he was firm in the Cold War and revived some of the more popular aspects of the New Deal, Truman was disliked by many. This unpopularity derived from perhaps his greatest political weakness, his tendency on occasion to be petty. He was honest, yet, because of his fierce Democratic Party and personal loyalties, he sometimes sheltered corrupt politicians. Damaging to his public image, too, was the lack of dignity he displayed from time to time, as when he vilified a music critic who was not impressed with the vocal talents of the President's daughter. Gradually, political currents, symbolized by the slogan "Had enough?," began to run against the President by the time of the midterm elections in 1946.

By 1948, however, Truman had become more accustomed to the role of the presidency and seemed eager to win the approbation of the electorate. Despite the doubts of the Democratic professionals about his appeal, Truman was the President, and a president in office in the United States has great influence on his party's convention. Thus, the Democratic Convention renominated him on the first ballot. Truman then returned from the convention and called a special session of Congress to reconsider aspects of his liberal legislative program. Unsuccessful in his attempts to sway a conservative legislature, Truman was able to move into the campaign complaining about the "do-nothing" Eightieth Congress.

The campaign trail was littered with obstacles for the President. Because there had been a strong civil-rights plank adopted at the Democratic Convention and incorporated into the party's platform,

Southerners, traditionally an element of Democratic strength, bolted the party and formed a "States' Rights Party." The third-party candidate was Governor J. Strom Thurmond of South Carolina, and it was expected that his candidacy would ruin Truman's chances for election by cutting deeply into the Southern vote.

Another candidacy developed, which seemed to reduce further the potential Democratic vote. Henry A. Wallace ran on a newly formed Progressive Party ticket, holding that the foreign policy of the Truman Administration was so anti-Russian that it was bound to lead the United States into war with the Soviet Union. Wallace was expected to chip away at the extreme left of the Democratic Party, thus further harming Truman's chances for election.

The seeming hopelessness of the Democratic cause made the Republicans more confident of victory than they had been at any time since the beginning of the Great Depression. The Republican nomination again went to Thomas E. Dewey of New York. Dewey's campaign then proceeded with caution, as his forces were certain of victory. During the campaign, Dewey in effect accepted the New Deal reforms, but took the position that his administration could administer them better than could Truman's.

Truman launched an old-style barnstorming campaign during which he continually castigated the Eightieth Congress, charging that it had acted against the people's interests. He also repeated the theme that the Republicans sought a return to the past and intended to sabotage the New Deal's accomplishments for farmers and laborers. During the course of his campaign, Truman traversed some 32,000 miles and made some 350 speeches.

The election results seemed to astound everyone, with the possible exception of Harry Truman himself. Truman was elected by 2,000,000 votes. Senator Robert A. Taft of Ohio expressed well the general Republican opinion of the outcome when he said that Truman's election "defies all common sense." Then more neutral analysts began to point out that Truman had vigorously, and apparently successfully, aroused popular memories of the Great Depression. He had touched the American voter's raw nerves when he indicated that a move toward Republicanism was a step backward toward economic insecurity.

In 1949 Truman launched a domestic program he had christened the "Fair Deal." It was an extension of New Deal programs inaugurated by Roosevelt. Truman emphasized the need for a national health program, aid to education, support for public housing plans, and civil rights. He also asked for the repeal of the Taft-Hartley Act (1947), which unionism tended to regard as an employers' law in that it forbade the closed union shop and union contributions to political campaigns. He also called for a new farm subsidy plan, which laid emphasis on a high income for individual farmers rather than higher prices for farm produce. Though the new Congress had a Democratic majority, it neither repealed the Taft-Hartley Law nor enacted a new farm-subsidy program. Indeed, a coalition of Republicans and conservative Southern Democrats acted to limit the President's whole legislative program. However, Truman did obtain an increase in the minimum wage and a housing act, along with a broadening of Social Security coverage (1950).

The Truman Administration also was troubled with governmental corruption. There were scandals and, although none approached the magnitude of the Teapot Dome affair of the 1920's, each seemed further to damage Truman's effectiveness as a potential vote getter in 1952. Also unfavorable to Truman's chances as a Democratic standard-bearer in the next election was the "Great Fear"[2] of communism, developing in the 1950's as one of the byproducts of the Cold War and, more particularly, the Korean War.

The so-called Great Fear first developed in 1946 and 1947, when American Communists began to regard their citizenship as unimportant when compared to the allegiance they owed the international leader of the Communist world, the Soviet Union. By 1947 the United States Government began to order loyalty checks of government employees. Soon Congressional investigations began, and unearthed Communist spying in government that had taken place as early as the 1930's.

The most sensational espionage case in that era involved Alger Hiss. A former high-ranking State Department official, Hiss was accused of heading a spy ring in the 1930's. His sensational trial and conviction in 1949 aroused widespread public concern over Soviet subversion. Then, in 1950, the Federal Bureau of Investigation revealed that two spies, Julius and Ethel Rosenberg, had transmitted atomic secrets to the Russians when the nuclear bomb was still in its developmental stage during World War II. The Rosenberg couple was tried and executed (1953).

The political implications of the Hiss affair and the Rosenberg case seemed to have been best understood by Senator Joseph McCarthy of Wisconsin. Having noted that Congressman (later president) Richard M. Nixon, a member of the House Un-American Affairs Committee, had become nationally known and more important in his party because of his energetic work on the Hiss case, McCarthy, a month after the conviction of Hiss, gained national prominence through a speech in Wheeling, West Virginia, where he charged that Secretary of State Dean Acheson was "a pompous diplomat in striped pants" who was dangerous to the national security because he tolerated the continued membership in his department of some fifty-seven Communists. A Senate investigating committee later exonerated Acheson and his department, but by that time McCarthy had gone on to other charges, all headline-creating, which gained wide

[2] Although this term previously had been applied only to the French Revolution of 1789, historians writing of the post-1945 United States have come to use it in reference to the "spy-scare" to the end of 1954.

credence for the idea that the United States Government was permeated by people who were "soft" on communism. Interestingly, the instances McCarthy cited always were nameless. Thus, he cited "No. 81" in the Department of State as "one of the big shots" in Communist espionage, or "No. 66," for having once "provided a coffee kitchen for communistically inspired protest groups."

McCarthy's charges continued during the Eisenhower Administration, and it became widely known in Washington that the President harbored deep resentment over the attacks on former Secretary of State George C. Marshall, a respected public figure whom Eisenhower admired greatly. Eventually, in 1954, McCarthy went so far as to imply that perhaps Eisenhower himself had been the victim of Red influence, and charged that Secretary of the Army Robert Stevens was an "awful dupe" of international communism. Suddenly, McCarthy's national popularity shot downward.

Now McCarthy himself was subjected to senatorial investigation. The investigating committee recommended his censure for unmannerly conduct and bringing the honor of the Senate into disrepute. Sixty-seven senators voted his "condemnation" and McCarthy's influence dwindled. By the end of 1954 most Americans apparently believed that the external threat from communism was greater than the internal, and the "Great Fear" faded. Three years later McCarthy died, a discredited figure.

Along with the developing "Great Fear" another factor influenced Truman not to seek reelection in 1952: the negative impact on public opinion of his dismissal of General Douglas MacArthur. As indicated in the previous chapter, Truman had made the decision to dismiss MacArthur because of the General's open criticism of the concept of "limited war." MacArthur had been strongly warned, in December 1950, not to make any further policy statements without Washington's approval. Nonetheless, in March 1951, MacArthur spoke out again, urging publicly that military operations be extended beyond Korea to Manchuria and that attack on "its coastal areas and interior bases, would doom Red China. . . ." Truman's reaction to MacArthur's comments took the form of a cable sent to the General, indicating his shock at the unauthorized statements. Before General MacArthur had time to reply to Truman's message, the Republican Party released another statement given to it by the American commander in Korea, in which the concept of limited war was condemned once more.

Truman now believed the whole issue of civilian control over the military to be at stake. Consequently, he dismissed MacArthur on April 11, 1951. MacArthur returned to the United States a conquering hero, and the Senate undertook a debate on foreign policy with the General as the most important witness. Again MacArthur called for direct strikes against Manchuria and urged the use of the Taiwan Nationalist Chinese troops against the Red armies. However, the Joint Chiefs of Staff, as well as Secretary of Defense George C. Marshall, upheld the national policy and pointed out that the vision of a field commander is limited to his area of conflict as opposed to the view of an Administration that had to concern itself with the total picture of United States security. It also was maintained in Washington that an impetuous attack on Chinese territory could spark World War III by causing a Soviet-Chinese defense pact to become operative.

It was this controversy over the Administration's foreign policy, which raged in the Senate and in the nation's news media, that impressed Harry Truman with his personal unpopularity among the voters. He thus decided to take himself out of the next presidential race early in 1952. The Democratic Convention replaced him with Adlai E. Stevenson, Governor of Illinois, who was well known for his eloquence and, because of his background, unlike the image of the common man that his predecessor had established.

The Republican nominee, emerging from a hard convention fight against Senator Robert A. Taft of Ohio, was General Dwight D. Eisenhower. Eisenhower had great political appeal as a hero of the war, who had risen from common Texas-Kansas origins to world renown. From the outset of the 1952 campaign, Eisenhower was the favorite. Adding to the General's seeming advantage was the fact that Stevenson felt it incumbent upon himself to defend the record of the Truman Administration.

The outcome of the election was a sweeping personal victory for Dwight D. Eisenhower. He won 442 electoral votes to 89 for his opponent, and polled 34,000,000 popular votes to 27,000,000 for Stevenson. The victory seemed to have been more a personal one than a party one, for Eisenhower ran 15 per cent ahead of his party's vote for Congress. Thus, the Republicans held only a slim margin of control in both houses and lost even this in the midterm elections of 1954.

Dwight D. Eisenhower came to symbolize the American national attitude during the 1950's. A moderate Republican, much of his popularity was attributable to the belief that he was a man who had risen above party and faction to serve his nation.

This man, who many Republicans and Democrats believed could heal the nation's wounds and end the Korean war, was born in Denison, Texas, in 1890. He grew up in the old frontier cattle-shipping center of Abilene, Kansas. An average student, he manifested self-confidence despite the fact that he was reared in an atmosphere of frugality. In 1915, he was graduated from West Point and then spent the World War I years as an instructor at Camp Colt in Gettysburg, Pennsylvania. He did not rise rapidly in the military until General Douglas MacArthur asked him to create a military establishment for the Philippine Islands.

Shortly after the outbreak of World War II in Europe, Eisenhower was returned to the United States. In 1941 he became Chief of Staff of the Third Army and commended himself to his superiors by the imaginative and high quality of his staff work and his skill in dealing with men. By mid-1942 he had risen to command the European

Theater of Operations. Thereafter, his name rapidly became a household word in the United States, and he especially endeared himself to the American public through his unpretentious manner. He seemed, indeed, the very antithesis of many swaggering hero-generals of history and was greatly admired because of this.

Once in office, Eisenhower exercized the functions of the presidency quite distinctly from those of Congress. He normally did not comment upon legislation, even as it was discussed extensively in congressional committees or on the floors of the House and Senate. His first Administration also did its best to encourage private business. Government enterprise which competed with private business was discontinued, foreign aid was cut, and government economic controls, a residue of the Korean War, were abolished (February 1952). Eisenhower, however, maintained that economy measures would not be developed to the extent that they placed the national security in jeopardy. In some respects, the Republicans carried on New Deal and Fair Deal policies. Federal authorities, for instance, counteracted the 1954 recession by governmental action to ease the monetary situation, and they expanded the Social Security system.

It also was an Eisenhower Administration policy to attempt the reversal of neo-isolationist tendencies emerging in the Republican Party. One indication of this policy was the President's successful opposition to the Bricker Amendment (1954), which sought to limit the treaty-making powers of the president as it enlarged Congressional control over foreign relations.

In 1956, the immense personal popularity of Eisenhower was reflected by the number of bipartisan supporters who happily wore "I Like Ike" buttons throughout the campaign. The presidential contest was a repetition of the 1952 election since Eisenhower once again opposed Stevenson, who had sought the nomination this time with greater energy than he had displayed four years before. The results of the election were not unexpected. Eisenhower won by a margin of 457 electoral votes to Stevenson's 73. Again it seemed essentially a personal victory, as the Democrats emerged in firm control of the House and Senate.

In his second term, Eisenhower seemed to view his role as the limiter of excessive Democratic spending, and he regularly vetoed government salary increases. Despite the conflict between the President and Congress, important legislation marked the second term. Out of a Senate committee hearing on racketeering in the labor unions came the Labor-Management Reporting and Disclosure Act (1959). This act (1) included a "bill of rights" to protect the union rank-and-file against coercion by labor leaders; (2) required unions to make public a record of their expenditures; (3) forbade unions to exact excessive wages for common labor; and (4) provided for the regular election of union officers.

The Second Eisenhower Administration also produced the Civil Rights Act of 1957, to protect the voting rights of Black Americans, and the National Defense Education Act of 1958. The latter, as its title indicates, emphasized the important connection between the defense of the United States and the improvement of its schools. The law authorized the expenditure of $887,000,000 over four years to encourage instruction and study in science, mathematics, and languages.

Eisenhower could not assure that his tremendous personal popularity would help the Republican cause in 1960. Because of the Twenty-second Amendment to the Constitution (ratified in 1952) he was limited to two terms in office and would have to retire at the end of eight years' service. His Vice-President, Richard M. Nixon, was chosen as the Republican's presidential candidate. Out of the Democratic Convention came the candidacy of John F. Kennedy, Senator from Massachusetts, who had shown strength in the state primaries. His leading opponent for the nomination in the party convention had been Lyndon B. Johnson, Senator from Texas. To prevent a party split, Kennedy asked Johnson to be his running mate.

The campaign was an interesting one, as the candidates appeared jointly on television to debate the issues. These debates turned out to be more advantageous to Kennedy, who previously had enjoyed far less national recognition than Nixon. Kennedy needed all the help he could muster from such appearances, because he was a Roman Catholic. Many Americans still doubted in 1960 whether a Catholic in the Presidency could be more loyal to his own country than to the international church of which he was a member.

The election was one of the closest in American history. Kennedy won 303 electoral votes to Nixon's 219. In the popular vote, however, the new President polled only 113,000 more votes than Nixon, out of a total of 68.8 million votes cast. Despite the closeness of the presidential contest, the Congressional races gave the Democrats heavy majorities in both houses.

John F. Kennedy was born near Boston, in 1917. Both his grandfathers were sons of Irish immigrants who had moved to Massachusetts in 1847 to escape the Irish potato famine. Both of the new President's ancestors had established a family tradition of participation in politics. John F. Kennedy's father, Joseph Kennedy, had carried on the political tradition as United States Ambassador in London in 1937. President Kennedy was educated at Harvard University and then, in World War II, served as a naval officer in the Pacific. After the war, in 1946, he was a successful candidate for the House of Representatives. He remained in the house for three terms and then was elected to the Senate in 1952. It was as Senator from Massachusetts that he mounted his successful campaign for the presidential nomination in 1960.

Throughout the campaign, Kennedy maintained a youthful vigorous image. Now, in the Presidency, he continued that theme by calling his program "The New Frontier." Soon, however, the impetus of the New Frontier encountered a decidedly more conservative Congress. In 1961 and 1962 Congress rejected bills proposed by

Kennedy that would have provided medical care for the aged and federal aid to education. Then the new President proposed the creation of a cabinet post for urban affairs, which was subsequently voted down by Congress. Just as in preceding Democratic administrations, it now was proven that a Democratic majority in Congress did not mean that a Democrat in the White House could enact his programs without difficulty. The House of Representatives actually was dominated by a bipartisan conservative coalition made up of Republicans and Southern Democrats.

Most of Kennedy's political successes were realized in foreign affairs. Even there, however, the record was mixed. The long-range problems of the Cold War, such as divided Berlin and Germany, still were unresolved at the time of his death. Also, Kennedy had sent several thousand advisers and troops to Vietnam to support the South Vietnamese in their anti-Communist fight, and that action was only the beginning of a much deeper American involvement in Asia.

On the positive side, the Alliance for Progress was formed with Latin America early in the Kennedy Administration with the long-range aim of improving conditions "south of the border." The Kennedy regime also provided the drama of the Cuban missile crisis, discussed in the previous chapter, and the resulting thaw in Russo-American relations, which produced the Test Ban Treaty with the Russians (1963) and the establishment of the "hot-line" between the White House and the Kremlin, to prevent the accidental sparking of a nuclear conflagration.

Before the Kennedy Administration had lasted long enough to be fully tested by circumstances, the young President was removed from the historical scene by an assassin's bullet. On November 22, 1963, in Dallas, Texas, a rifle shot terminated the Kennedy Administration. The nation entered mourning, and many young people, who looked upon Kennedy more as one of their own than they had previous older leaders, were horrified and, for a time, despondent.

Within ninety-eight minutes of Kennedy's death, Lyndon B. Johnson was sworn in as President. Lyndon Baines Johnson was a very different type of man from his wealthy, eastern-bred predecessor. He was born in 1908 on his parents' farm located between Stonewall and Johnson City, Texas. The future President grew up in modest circumstances and worked his way through the state teachers' college in San Marcos, Texas. After graduation (1930) he went to Washington as secretary to Texas Congressman Richard M. Kleberg. There he worked hard to absorb knowledge of men and operations on Capitol Hill, and in 1935 and 1936 attended law classes.

During this phase of his career, Johnson was appointed by President Roosevelt as State Administrator for Texas of the National Youth Administration. Early in 1937 he ran successfully on a New Deal platform for a House seat vacated by death. Thereafter, he was reelected to the House at each election until 1946. In 1948 he was elected to the Senate and was returned to the Upper House in 1954. There he rose to become Senate Majority Leader. He was elected to the Senate again in 1960, and was sworn in, only to resign three minutes later to undertake his new tasks as Vice-President.

Now, early in 1964, President Johnson called for "a war against poverty" and, in August of that year, the first step was taken with the enactment of the Economic Opportunity Act. Basic to this new legislation was the concept that most poverty in the United States resulted, not from the dearth of employment opportunities, but from a lack of training and education among the poor. To the total program that hopefully would remedy this situation the President gave the title The Great Society.

Johnson's long experience in the legislative branch soon paid dividends. Programs that had been stalled in the Kennedy Administration, in the fields of education and civil rights, for instance, now were maneuvered through Congress because of Johnson's talents as a political persuader.

Since Johnson seemed to be following the New Deal path blazed first by Roosevelt and then advanced by those Democrats who had succeeded him, some leaders of the Republican Party were convinced that, if it was to defeat the President in the 1964 elections, it would have to find a candidate whose political philosophy was radically different from that of Dewey, Eisenhower, or any of the contemporary GOP moderates. Accordingly, the theme of the Republican campaign in 1964 was "a choice instead of an echo," and the standard-bearer was the representative of the conservative wing of the party, Senator Barry Goldwater of Arizona—scion of a wealthy merchant family.

The contest between Goldwater and Johnson had some unfortunate aspects. Members of various extremist organizations, such as the John Birch Society[3] and the Ku Klux Klan, gave unsolicited support to Goldwater and engaged in "mud-slinging." The Republican candidate, moreover, suffered from the inexperience of his advisers and, on occasion, made rash public utterances. The campaign reflected a larger ideological split than was customary between Republican and Democratic candidates in the United States.

The result of the election was an overwhelming victory for Johnson. The President's margin of votes was the greatest in United States history, exceeding even Franklin Roosevelt's victorious spread in 1936. Johnson carried forty-four states and brought with him a large

---

[3] During the 1950's a group of extreme conservatives appeared on the political right. They hated New Deal and Fair Deal policies and were frustrated by the foreign entanglements of the Cold War. They were ultranationalist in foreign policy, deplored American membership in the United Nations, opposed foreign aid, and regarded attempts to negotiate with the Russians as treasonable. Best known among them was the John Birch Society, named for an American missionary killed by Chinese Communists after World War II. The organization commonly smeared both Republican and Democratic leaders. Even Eisenhower was labeled by some Birchers as a "dedicated, conscious agent of the Communist conspiracy."

Democratic majority into the Congress. An analysis of the election indicated that Senator Goldwater had lost the votes of moderate Republicans, the aged, and ethnic minorities by his repudiation of some of the social gains of the New Deal. Because of Goldwater's position on civil rights (he had voted against the Civil Rights Act of 1964) he lost an estimated 90 to 95 per cent of the Negro vote in urban areas. Conversely, four of the six states he carried were in the Deep South.

The Republicans, however, staged a remarkable resurgence in the 1966 elections. They were able to win forty-seven seats in the House and eight new governorships. It is significant that most of the Republican winners in 1966 had opposed Goldwater's nomination in 1964 or had ignored his ideological theme in their speeches. The results of the 1966 elections seemed to demonstrate that the 1964 Republican abandonment of the middle of the political road had been damaging to the party's national position.

President Johnson for a time continued to secure easy passage of the legislation he wanted. More than a $1,000,000,000 was appropriated to alleviate rural poverty in Appalachia, and $83,300,000,000 for urban aid. The National Defense Education Act of 1964 extended Federal support to college students beyond the sciences to the humanities. Below the college level, $1,000,000,000 was provided by The Elementary and Secondary Education Act of 1965.

Johnson's popularity dropped markedly, however, as he approached the end of his first full term in office. At the core of the public's displeasure were large-scale riots in Northern cities (to be discussed more fully in a later section of this chapter) and the increasing United States involvement in Vietnam.

B.   The Vietnamese War and Johnson's Decision to Step Down

When the French, after much expenditure of funds and numerous military defeats by nationalistic and communistic forces under Ho Chi-Minh, withdrew from their former colonial empire in Indo-China, the country was divided by treaty as earlier had been the case in Korea. The division was established by the Geneva Accords of 1954, which required also that Vietnam be unified within two years on the basis of free elections. In the North, Ho established a Red regime; in the southern half, a strongly anti-Communist government took control.

As the time for elections approached, however, it began to appear that the autocratic policies of President Ngo Dinh Diem, in the south, might lead to his overthrow—by local guerrillas supported by the Vietcong, or Communists from the north.

Hence, despite some of the equivocal characteristics of Diem's regime, Washington decided that it was better to save him than to allow all Vietnam to become Communist. Aid began to flow to the Asian country, but President Eisenhower did not send combat forces to take part in the fighting. During the Kennedy Administration, participation in the Vietnam conflict was increased and military advisors, helicopters, and arms were sent. Still, the fighting remained in the hands of the South Vietnamese. Johnson, in the 1964 campaign, had pledged continuance of this sort of help, while promising that the United States would not become involved in an Asian land war.

Johnson's promise was increasingly difficult to keep as, by early 1965, the southern forces seemed close to military defeat. Such defeat presumably would have meant the installation in the south of a new and unfriendly government. Hence, the President ordered an increase in United States' involvement. By February 1965, the bombing of bases and supply dumps in North Vietnam by American planes had been authorized. Later that year, United States ground forces were involved for the first time. At the end of 1966 the United States was deeply involved in the Vietnamese War. Some 400,000 American troops, their number growing every day, had brought the war to a stalemate, and thus it remained, with minor successes and steady intensification by both sides, into 1968.

Several European allies of the United States now began to fear that the U.S.S.R. or Red China or both might be drawn into the conflict if these powers felt their interests or prestige threatened. The involvement of the Communist world powers, believed some, would then inevitably lead to nuclear war.

In the United States, the policy of gradual but consistent military "escalation" divided the citizenry. Many Americans had voted for Johnson instead of Goldwater in 1964 only, as they now saw it, to find Johnson following the very path that Goldwater earlier had suggested. Others condemned the morality of the Johnson Administration, holding that the South Vietnamese Government was not worthy of United States' support. Corruption and moral decay, they claimed, were more prominent under the South Vietnamese Government than they would be under a more efficient nationalist-Communist regime. Another group criticized the Vietnam involvement on the basis of pragmatism, asserting that the United States had overextended its commitments and overestimated its power by a move onto the mainland of Asia.

Thus, as the presidential campaign of 1968 approached, Vietnam and the disorders in the American cities were major campaign issues. In the spring of 1968, the President attempted to resolve his party's dilemma by announcing his withdrawl from the coming presidential campaign. At the same time he announced a partial bombing halt of North Vietnamese targets as an olive branch extended to the enemy. It seemed to have been Johnson's hope that the divisions racking American society, particularly the war itself, could be terminated more easily if it was known that he would not again seek office. Soon thereafter, peace talks, strikingly reminiscent of the protracted conversations that settled the Korean War, began in Paris between representatives of the United States and the North Vietnamese governments.

The Republicans met in August 1968, and nominated Richard M. Nixon, their unsuccessful standard bearer in 1960. A few weeks later the Democrats met in Chicago and nominated Johnson's Vice-President, Hubert H. Humphrey. As the public-opinion polls seemed to show that both candidates were party professionals' choices rather than the most popular candidates with the electorate, the nominations for the vice-presidency became more important than usual. It was widely thought that each man would choose a glamorous vice-presidential candidate to help the ticket. Nixon surprised many, however, with his choice of a relatively unknown, namely, Spiro T. Agnew, Governor of Maryland. Humphrey picked Senator Edmund S. Muskie of Maine, slightly better known than Agnew nationally, but still not a well-known public figure.

Hubert Humphrey was nominated in Chicago to the accompaniment of nationally televised disorders, as anti-Vietnam War groups and various militant protest formations clashed with police in bloody fighting. To make matters worse for the Democrats, inside the Convention Hall the party split badly over support of President Johnson's Vietnam policy. As in a number of previous election years, therefore, the chances of the Democrats were severely hurt by their own schisms. On the other hand, Nixon's support remained stable, as Republicans refused to bolt his camp.

Another factor in the election was the third-party (American Independent Party) candidacy of the former Governor of Alabama, George C. Wallace. Wallace rode a wave of popular discontent deriving from racial tensions—until he could claim a backing of some 20 per cent in the public-opinion polls. His candidacy clouded the possible outcome of the election because he was expected to draw votes from both Nixon and Humphrey: conservative votes from Nixon in the South and labor votes from Humphrey in the North. The Wallace campaign led some to fear that the election results would give no candidate a majority, thus throwing the presidential decision into the House of Representatives—where each state would have only one vote and the presidency would not be decided until January 1969.

On election night, as the returns began to pour in, Nixon and Humphrey seemed to be running an exceedingly close race in almost every important state. George Wallace, however, failed to make any serious inroads on Democratic and Republican strength outside the Old South, and his third-party candidacy fell far short of gaining the votes outside the South that he had claimed he would win.

It was not until the morning after election night that Richard Nixon's victory was definite. Out of more than 70,000,000 votes cast, just over 310,000 votes separated the Republican and Democratic candidates. George Wallace polled only 13.53 per cent of the votes. The electoral college vote, however, did not reflect the closeness of the popular vote. In the electoral college Nixon received 302 votes to Humphrey's 191, and Wallace's 45. This discrepancy between popular and electoral vote, coupled with earlier fears that the election might be thrown into the House of Representatives, brought forth a popular interest in some revision of the system of presidential election practiced in the United States.

Election analysis indicated that, despite numerous predictions to the contrary, traditional voting patterns were followed, at least outside the Deep South. Northern labor generally did not follow Wallace, but remained in the Democratic camp. Suburbanites stayed with the Republicans, as did small town and rural voters.

C. Black America and the Urban Crisis

Perhaps the gravest issue developing in the United States after the end of World War II grew out of the struggle of black Americans to assume full rights as citizens. After the Second World War, most black veterans returned home to the difficult problem of re-absorption into a society where they were faced with too few jobs and racial discrimination. Many whites also had returned from the war thinking that racial discrimination was wrong, inasmuch as they had just defeated a nation whose armies were imbued with the master-race theory.

The American Negro, sometimes assisted by whites, had formed several organizations to oppose discrimination. Conspicuous among these was the National Association for the Advancement of Colored People (NAACP). During the war there had come into being also the more militant Congress of Racial Equality (CORE). In the late 1940's CORE members picketed segregated swimming pools and attempted to vote in the South, where generally they were not allowed to register.

One of the first and most observable gains nationally for the civil-rights movement was the entry in 1947 of Negro athlete Jackie Roosevelt Robinson into professional sports with the Brooklyn Dodgers baseball team. After Robinson broke the color barrier in major-league baseball, many other black athletes became involved in all professional sports.

At the same time there were attempts by various levels of government to move toward equal rights for black Americans. President Truman established a President's Committee On Civil Rights, headed by Charles E. Wilson, President of the General Electric Company, with Negro members as well as white, to study the whole problem and make recommendations. The Committee reported that the United States still was troubled by lynchings, police brutality, discrimination in housing, discrimination in education, discrimination in employment, and widespread deprivation of voting rights, all aimed largely at the Negro.

On the basis of this report, Truman brought a strong civil-rights program to Congress in early 1948. Although the message of the Administration dramatized the plight of the black American, Congress at the time was far more concerned with limiting the growing power of the Federal Government—a growth which in the minds of conservative congressmen was linked to the New Deal. Thus, no broad civil-rights program emerged from the Eightieth Congress. But, also in 1948, President Truman did issue an order ending segregation in the United States armed forces.

Held back momentarily at the national governmental level, the civil-rights campaign moved forward in the courts and among state governments. In 1946 the Supreme Court declared it unconstitutional to deprive a black man of his seat on a bus to make room for a white passenger. In 1950 came a decision that a Negro could not be denied a place on any train involved in interstate transportation. In 1953 the Supreme Court ruled that anyone acting in a "well-behaved" fashion could not be refused service in any public place in Washington, D.C. Among the states, New York led the way in civil-rights legislation. In 1945 the first fair-employment practices law in the nation's history was passed. By 1963 twenty-two states, including the former "slave state" of Missouri, had passed similar laws.

During the Korean War, full integration of the armed forces was accomplished. Two Negroes were among those who won Congressional Medals of Honor. At the same time American blacks contributed to the peace negotiations, and one of the outstanding diplomats sent to the United Nations by the United States Government was Dr. Ralph Bunche, grandson of a former slave.[4]

On May 17, 1954, the Supreme Court announced a momentous civil-rights decision—one that recalled a prophecy made in 1903 by a black scholar, William E. B. Du Bois, namely, that the major problem of the "twentieth century" in the United States would be the "color-line" dilemma. On that day Chief Justice Earl Warren read the Supreme Court's decision in the case of *Brown versus Topeka School Board*. At the core of the decision was this assertion: "Separate education facilities are inherently unequal." A year later the Court ruled that school districts must become desegregated. Within a year of the school desegregation decision, many school districts in the North and Upper South had complied with the ruling.

In the Deep South, however, there appeared open and highly vocal criticism and even defiance of the Supreme Court decision. In general, the Deep South states admitted Negroes to all-white schools only after they had been compelled to do so by Federal court orders. At times, economic boycotts were threatened by White Citizens' Councils, which battled school integration by threatening loss of

---

[4] Bunche became best known for his efforts in Palestine, where he mediated a tense conflict between Arabs and Jews. In 1950 he received the Nobel Peace Prize.

business to persons who in any way supported compliance with the Court's decision. In March 1956, a group of ninety-nine Southern Congressmen issued a "Southern Manifesto," which denounced the "Brown" decision and called it unconstitutional. The progress of integration of school systems, indeed, slowed somewhat in 1956.

The power of the Federal Government to bring about the integration of schools was first tested in September 1957. Segregated Central High School in Little Rock, Arkansas, was ordered by a federal district court to admit nine qualified Negro students. Governor Orval Faubus of Arkansas objected to the court's directive and warned of bloodshed should black students enter the school. To dramatize his announcement of potential violence, Faubus called the National Guard to the school. Since there was much publicity given to Faubus' statements, a large crowd of segregationists appeared near the school to view the confrontation between black students and the Guardsmen.

The first black student who tried to enter the school, was turned away by a Guardsman. Within a matter of hours, news of the incident at Little Rock and stories of Faubus' defiance of the Federal Government had been flashed around the world. President Dwight D. Eisenhower was reluctant to use Federal force because of his conviction that the states should not be compelled by use of Federal arms to cooperate with court orders. Yet, once the stance of state defiance of the National Government had been adopted by Faubus, the President believed it necessary to take action.

In September 1957, about 1000 members of the 101st Airborne Division were ordered into Little Rock. Paratroopers took up positions in Central High School itself. The nine students in question were escorted to school by the United States Army, and when some of the white students called for a general student strike, only about sixty left classes. Instead of taking part in the strike, others asked the nine black students to eat lunch with them or join student organizations.

This move, however, did not end the Little Rock crisis, for now Faubus closed the city's schools. For more than a year they remained closed, until the local Board of Education reopened them, with Negro students in attendance.

After the Little Rock incidents, national attention for a time remained centered on the racial situation. In 1957, Congress passed a law empowering the Attorney General more effectively to check those who would tamper with the process of school desegregation. The act was shepherded through the Senate by Senator Lyndon B. Johnson of Texas. A second law, in 1960, was guided through the Senate by Johnson with the aid of Senator John F. Kennedy of Massachusetts.

Meanwhile, in December 1955, in Montgomery, Alabama, a black woman had been arrested on a bus for violating a local segregation law when she refused to move from her seat for a white man who had just entered the vehicle. That night a young Negro minister, the Reverend Martin Luther King, Jr., called a meeting at his Baptist Church, where it was decided that all local black citizens would be asked to boycott the Montgomery buses. An estimated 90 per cent of the Montgomery Negroes stayed off the buses for more than a year. The general Montgomery economic situation was damaged and the bus line's business dropped by 65 per cent. Eventually, the city government ordered King and a hundred other black leaders arrested. In November 1956, the Supreme Court ruled that bus segregation violated the Constitution. The Montgomery Bus Company agreed to end segregation and to hire Negro drivers.

On the first day of integrated busing in Montgomery, Dr. King and a white friend were first in line to ride. The driver welcomed them cordially, and a new and important American civil-rights leader came into prominence.

Although the Federal Government had not been very active in the civil-rights crusade until after the "Brown" decision, it now became increasingly involved. President Eisenhower ordered the integration of many veterans' hospitals and speeded the integration of schools in the District of Columbia. The Kennedy Administration had been in office only a few months when it encountered its first civil-rights crisis. James Farmer, CORE director, organized a series of bus rides by CORE members into bus terminals in the Deep South to establish with certainty that such installations were segregated. Violence ensued and Attorney General Robert F. Kennedy sent United States marshals to protect the riders.

Then, on September 30, 1962, James Meredith, the first black man ever to do so, sought to enter the University of Mississippi to complete his studies. He was escorted by 500 marshals. That night there were riots at the university and the marshals fought off a mob of some 2500, who wanted to drive Meredith away from the campus. But both student and government persevered, and in 1963 James Meredith received his diploma with the rest of the graduating class.

In April 1963, Dr. King decided to carry his civil-rights battle to Birmingham, Alabama, regarded by many as the most segregated city in the South. Marches and other nonviolent protests brought wholesale arrests. King was imprisoned, but then released through the efforts of Attorney General Robert F. Kennedy. As the Birmingham demonstrations subsided, after at least partial success, they were replaced by civil-rights demonstrations elsewhere in the country.

The Birmingham situation led President Kennedy to ask Congress for a civil-rights law that would open public facilities to all Americans. In 1964, Congress did pass such a bill, which was signed into law by President Johnson. One of its important terms stipulated that Federal funds would be withheld from any project that was marked by proven discrimination. A 1965 voting-rights act made it possible to obtain Federal voting registrars wherever black men were denied the right to register and vote.

In the mid-1960's the whole question of the future of Black America and the civil-rights struggle became tied to the urban crisis developing in the large cities. Years before the urban crisis became apparent,

Professor Ernest W. Burgess, of the University of Chicago, pointed out that cities in the United States tended to develop in a series of concentric circles. First there developed an inner zone, made up of business and shopping districts. Next came a "zone of transition," characterized by early decay; for this zone, comprising the first residential area of the city, soon lost the people with sufficient funds to move further out and received in their place first-generation immigrants and black people. Beyond this circle one was likely to find a zone of workers' homes and second-generation immigrants. The outermost of the concentric circles then would be characterized by more expensive houses built by more affluent people. Although this analysis of the placing and mobility of social groups has been criticized as an oversimplification, Burgess' zone of transition in numerous cities had become essentially a black ghetto by the 1960's.

World War I stimulated the first large-scale migrations of Negroes out of the South. Thereafter, and especially after World War II, there was a marked population shift in Black America. Dissatisfied southern Negroes imagined the North to be a land of opportunity where relatives had found a way of life freer and financially more rewarding than any they had known in the South. But, unlike many of their relatives who were skilled workers, most of the blacks who migrated northward after 1945 had no labor skills and could not find a place in the job market. Thus they gravitated into the northern ghettos and were caught in grinding poverty. The march toward political rights appeared to mean little to these people as long as their ghetto walls were sustained by economic restrictions.

The mass influx of hopeful blacks, who often became hopeless blacks, accelerated the move of whites into the suburbs. Thus, at the very time when more monies were needed to solve such growing urban problems as air and water pollution, there was an exodus of white people to outlying areas—whites who took with them a goodly portion of the tax resources needed to halt the rot of the inner city.

The hopelessness that came to permeate the black ghettos in the 1960's gave rise to new Negro extremist groups. Among the first of these was the Black Muslims, whose most articulate spokesman, calling himself Malcolm X (previously Malcolm Little), began by asserting the superiority of the black man and calling for an *apartheid* society. Malcolm X, however, had a change of heart after a 1964 trip to Africa, where he became convinced that hatred of the white man was useless and that to attack a Caucasian only because he was a Caucasian gave the latter no option but to reply with force. Before Malcolm could spread his new doctrine, he was assassinated by another black man.

The problem of the black ghetto's existence in a nation of plenty was further dramatized by riots in various large cities. Annually, from 1964, there were fires, fights with police and National Guardsmen, broken glass, and looting in most major northern cities. The rioting generally occurred within the ghetto areas. It resulted in deaths and destruction on a wide scale and brought more bitterness than relief.

Meanwhile the nonviolent campaign for civil rights marched on, with Martin Luther King urging peaceful change for the American nation. King repeatedly said that he was inspired essentially by Henry David Thoreau's essay *On Civil Disobedience* (1849) and by the life and teachings of Mahatma Gandhi. To him the thoughts of these two men merged meaningfully with the Christian instruction to "love your enemies" and "turn the other cheek." He often asserted that nonviolence was not for cowards, since it actually took more courage to remain nonviolent than to allow anger to guide one's actions. But the advocacy of nonviolence became more difficult to uphold as militant "Black Power" advocates of various types argued that the nonviolent way was too slow, that it could not get for the black man socio-economic equality as well as political freedom.

In April 1968, King was in Memphis, Tennessee, to aid local black garbage workers in their campaign for higher wages. He had planned to participate in protest marches and then to speak in the local churches. Before his evening appearance at a meeting, King stepped out on his hotel balcony for a breath of air—and was struck down by an assassin's bullet. Shortly after the death of this most prominent of black civil-rights leaders, there was another outbreak of violence throughout the nation's angry ghetto communities. Then, shortly after this assassination, there was another major shock to the nation's consciousness.

One of the persons who moved into the political spotlight by seeking the Democratic presidential nomination after President Johnson had declared that he would not seek re-election was the brother of assassinated President Kennedy, namely, Senator Robert F. Kennedy of New York. In the important California primary of June 1968, Senator Kennedy ran against rival Democratic presidential aspirant, Senator Eugene McCarthy of Minnesota. After a vigorous campaign, Robert Kennedy won the primary victory. As he left the ballroom of the Ambassador Hotel in Los Angeles after a victory speech, he was shot, dying shortly after. Once again, as it had at the death of President Kennedy and the passing of Dr. King, the nation went into mourning.

Eventually, as weeks turned into months, emotional reactions were tempered by other realizations. Obviously, not all citizens of the United States had killed Martin Luther King and Robert F. Kennedy. Yet, it was obvious also that such violent acts, particularly those directed at prominent persons, had become much too common a phenomenon. President Johnson, indeed, appointed a commission to study the reasons for the conspicuous place of violence in the national life.

Sociologists and social psychologists, meanwhile, began to return to the urban problem and racial prejudice as conditions which, bound together inextricably, produced much of American violence. It was thought by some that ghetto outbursts, portrayed graphically through the mass media, caused chain reactions of similar rioting. It was further theorized that the "wave" of violent acts spurred additional, usually psychotic, individuals to imitate others' misdeeds. Assassination, seemingly, begat assassination and riot spawned riot.

The intensification of violence, the urban crisis, and the civil-rights struggle eventually gave rise to the idea that these phenomena well might be related to a massive population shift in the country. In 1968 approximately 70 per cent of the people in the United States lived on one per cent of the land. It was prophesied by experts that, by the year 2000, more than 80 per cent of a larger population would be crowded into the same area. Social psychologists indicated that psychic development in such situations was likely to be characterized by "depersonalization" of the individual, bewilderment among the unremembered faces in the crowd, and a series of "identity crises." Problems of overcrowding, depersonalization, and lack of opportunity, indeed, did appear to produce a profound despair.

One resolution of all these problems seemed to be relatively simple: rebuild the cities and augment them by new urban centers. However, the cost of such a national rebuilding was estimated at a minimum of $55,000,000,000. It was a moot question whether or not the United States, with all its riches and strength, could continue simultaneously to pursue its power-political course in the world and solve the urban-racial crisis at home.

The urban crisis, the civil-rights struggle, the need to revitalize local and state governments in order to better handle such problems without recourse to Federal aid, and the position of their country in the world—all posed dilemmas of such magnitude for the citizens of the United States in the last third of the twentieth century that the best energies of a vital people would have to be harnessed to resolve them.

THE UNITED STATES AND CANADA

Throughout the twentieth century, Canada gradually pulled away from British control until it enjoyed sovereign status within the Commonwealth. After the end of World War II, Canada became one of the world's major industrial and commercial powers. Particularly important in this development was the exploitation of Canadian iron, oil, and uranium sources. In the development of these resources, one of the most important elements was United States-Canadian collaboration. Perhaps the best example of neighborly cooperation in the economic sphere was the opening of the St. Lawrence Seaway and Power Project in 1959, which substantially helped transportation and industrial activity in both countries.

The United States and Canada also were drawn together militarily by the Cold War. Canada was involved in the United Nations' fight in

Korea, and became, as did her southern neighbor, a contributing member of the NATO alliance. The two powers also joined in establishing a 3000-mile-long line of radar installations (DEW line, for Distant Early Warning) designed to give quick warning in the event of an attack over the North Pole against North America. Moreover, Canada participated with the United States in building a joint defensive air force through the North American Air Defense Command (NORAD).

Some Canadians, however, came to resent what seemed to them an intrusion into Canadian life by United States interests. On occasion, Canadian politics were influenced by such feelings. In the elections of 1957, for instance, the Progressive Conservatives, led by John Diefenbaker, ousted from power the middle-of-the-road Liberal Party, which had been in control of Canadian national affairs for the previous twenty-two years. Diefenbaker's success was due primarily to a manifestation of Canadian nationalism and anti-Americanism.

The Diefenbaker Government remained in office until late 1963, when its refusal to agree to the incorporation of nuclear weapons in the Canadian-United States defense system led to a shift in allegiance of the electorate. The transference of support was not sizable, however, and a new Liberal Government under Lester B. Pearson enjoyed only a narrow margin over the Progressive Conservatives.

As the 1960's went by, more and more Canadians expressed concern lest the growing influence of the United States shape the future of Canada and, indeed, convert their country into a political and economic dependency of the United States. Canada, they pointed out, experienced a substantial yearly deficit in international trade with the United States, and the latter, through its disposal of large grain surpluses on the world market also cut deeply into the Canadian grain trade.

The spectre of "total Americanization of Canadian life" played an important role in 1968 elections in Canada. During the electoral campaign, Pierre Elliot Trudeau, candidate of the Liberal Party and a lively bachelor, became widely popular—apparently at least in part because his style of campaigning reminded young voters of American Senator Robert F. Kennedy. Trudeau won and so, in this fashion, too, the impact of United States political life was felt north of her borders.

In her relations with Great Britain, Canada also generally maintained an independent attitude. Although still a member of the Commonwealth, she followed a course in international affairs that often deviated from the official British line. During the Suez crisis of 1956 (see Chapter 21), for example, UN intervention in Egypt was due largely to Canadian initiative. Though still carrying on extensive trade with her former mother country and receiving preferential tariff treatment fom Great Britain, Canada seemed more and more to be copying the pattern of life displayed across her southern border than that across the Atlantic.

LATIN AMERICA

A. The General Picture

The history of the Latin American states since 1945 has been one of upheaval, based to a considerable extent on overpopulation and widespread poverty. There was a broad similarity in yearning between some Latin Americans and some of the people in Asia and Africa, in that all struggled with only minimal success to gain economic security. They seemed unable to develop the strong economy basic to stable government. Apparently they could not find a way to cooperate harmoniously where joint action was needed to solve common problems. It therefore became the general policy of the United States in Latin America to encourage common hemisphere action through such agencies as the Organization of American States.

In politics, the history of Latin America after World War II reflected a general trend toward the overthrow of military dictators, who, in the past, seemed an integral part of the Latin American scene as they played "musical chairs" with governments through one palace revolution after another. But, beginning in the mid-1950's with the toppling of Argentine dictator Juan Perón, one strong man after another followed his predecessor into obscurity. By 1960, only a few states were still in the hands of the traditional dictatorial regimes.

The usual political form in the early 1960's in Latin America, with the notable exception of Cuba, was a mixture of parliamentarianism and a certain degree of authoritarianism. In most countries a growing middle class gradually took the government into its hands, sometimes in cooperation with moderate leaders of the military and the church. Unlike the situation in most Western democracies, however, government was not yet based on a general society that was literate, economically well off, and informed. Hence, frequently, the rule of the elite coalitions was challenged by representatives of the more radical masses, who commonly were both leftwing and ultranationalist.

Before long, concern regarding the masses' potential threat to order and stability once again led to a return of military dictatorship. Thus, in 1963, military juntas came to power in Guatemala, Ecuador, the Dominican Republic, and Honduras. In the succeeding years the same thing happened in a number of other states, for the stability of the existing order rested on a weak social and economic foundation.

Contributing heavily to the difficulties in Latin America was the unprecedented increase in population after 1945. By 1965 the population was estimated at 200,000,000, and some forecasts predicted double that number within another generation or two. Meanwhile, the average per capita income in Latin America barely reached $200 per year. Ironically, Latin America has vast untapped economic resources, but there has been little efficient economic planning for their development.

In summary, rich resources remained untapped, the masses continued to live in chronic poverty, illiteracy was widespread, and prosperity was enjoyed by a conspicuous few. The circumstances provided a fertile seedbed for the growth of communism.

B.   Communism in Latin America

When Karl Marx and Friedrich Engels first formulated their doctrines, they paid scant attention to Latin America. The major interest of these founders of the Communist movement was in industrialized society, and the Latin America of their time was far from industrialized. Marxist ideas did not filter into Latin America until the end of the nineteenth century, and even then their influence was limited. Even such political groupings as the ephemeral Cuban Socialist Party, founded in 1899, demonstrated only superficial contact with Marxism.

In the twentieth century, as the Latin American order began to undergo political and social transformation, one of the many symptoms of that change was the appearance of native Communist parties. Their development during the 1920's was helped by a large post-World War I migration from Europe of radicals who already had absorbed Marxist doctrines. Moreover, they arrived in a period of beginning industrialization, the start of workers' organizations, and the first wide appearance of strikes.

Communist parties were founded in Latin America soon after the Russian Revolution of 1917. In January 1918, an International Socialist Party which, in 1920, took the name Communist, was founded in Argentina. In 1919 the Mexican Communist Party was organized. Numerous other groupings claiming to be Communist appeared, but their membership grew slowly until World War II and after.

Then, as the Communist parties became more influential, they sought the cloak of legality for their activities and reduced their revolutionary radicalism. They began, also, to aim their propaganda at "United States imperialism" and called for the "neutralization" of Latin America in international politics.

Another factor shaping the growth and influence of Communist parties in Latin America after 1945, was the involvement of Latin American countries as allies of the United States in the Cold War. Several Latin American nations broke diplomatic relations with the Soviet Union and, in 1947 and 1948, the Brazilian and Chilean Communist parties were outlawed. After the death of Stalin, the Soviet Union worked to reverse this tendency by devoting increased attention and intensified propaganda to relations with Latin America. After the Twentieth Party Congress, held in Moscow in 1956, the idea of "nationalistic communism" was promptly incorporated into the program of the Latin American Communist parties.

Despite the external pressures from the United States and the Soviet Union to affect Latin American thinking about communism, the most important factor in indigenous communist growth was the economic one. The relatively favorable economic development of the first years of the postwar period began to fade after 1952. The traditional social and economic divisions seemed to become more pronounced than ever. Many Latin Americans were led to believe that the economic deprivation they suffered was the result of neglect by the United States, which was too involved in the Cold War in Europe to pay attention to the ills developing in her own hemisphere. The Communists capitalized on this anti-American feeling by depicting the great northern neighbor as the "ruthless exploiter" of Latin America.

But then, in the late 1950's and the 1960's, the Communist threat was somewhat lessened by the fragmentation of the Marxist groups into three antagonistic factions—reflecting the splits in Europe and Asia. As a consequence, the local Communist parties were generally not threatening to the regimes in power unless they were strongly stimulated by outside agitators, particularly from Cuba.

The Cuban Revolution discussed in Chapter 22 brought to power in Cuba a group dedicated to Marxist-Leninism (1959). Within a few years, however, there was a drift to the Chinese form of communism, which called for guerilla insurrections against the established governmental order. Exported by Castroite agents into several Latin-American states, this new Cuban line contrasted sharply with that held by Communist Party leaders whose violent revolutionary tendencies had become softened. There thus developed a Communist confrontation with, on the one side, the traditionalists who held that the eventual revolution should not be jeopardized by hasty action before the certain backing of the masses could be assured; on the other side, the groups who regarded such a thesis as defeatist and who maintained that the revolution could be made to happen by the kind of guerilla warfare used so successfully by Castro in Cuba.

The Cuban influence spread so rapidly among the more important Latin American radicals that a reaction was engendered in a number of countries in the form of military coups. On the other hand, the Cuban menace also prompted greater economic aid from the United States, especially after 1961; and, in 1965, it even led to the landing of United States marines in Santo Domingo, lest Castroite Communism spread in the Caribbean area.

As the militant Cubans continued their efforts to win converts among the various Latin American Communists, Castro sent more and more agents to aid local movements that responded to his line. From time to time, Havana played host to international gatherings of self-styled fiery revolutionaries. In July 1967, for instance, the OLAS (Latin American Organization of Solidarity) met there and underscored the position that "the duty of a revolutionary is to make revolution."

The chief Cuban agent who preached the more militant brand of "revolutionary" communism among the Latin states was Ernesto "Che" Guevara, second only to Castro as a hero of the Cuban Revolution, and an acknowledged master tactician of guerrilla warfare. Hence the "hard-line" movement suffered a major setback in October

1967, when Guevara was killed by the Bolivian army during an engagement with some local rebels who were hiding out with the Cuban in a mountain fortress.

The Marxist movement in the Latin American countries thus remained divided. Castro persistently sought to foment violent revolutions, but was not conspicuously successful; many of the older Communist parties continued to reject his leadership. In March 1967, for example, the Venezuelan Communist Party published a harsh answer to criticism hurled against it by Castro for its relatively peaceful ways. The Venezuelan Communists, in their answer, reflected a growing tendency to question openly Castro's role as the model revolutionary. But despite its divisions, communism in Latin America remained an important threat in the Western Hemisphere. The continued stratification of Latin American society and the lack of a reasonably broad prosperity base, were welcome propaganda fuel to the never wearying leftists.

C. The Church-State Conflict in Latin America

Over the centuries, since the time European powers first opened Latin America to Western civilization, the Roman Catholic Church asserted its right to act as the final arbiter of issues that affected the moral and spiritual welfare of people of the Catholic faith. The continuing church insistence on this prerogative frequently led to difficulties in Latin America, all the more as the machinery of secular government developed. Often, matters which churchmen held to be spiritual in nature were considered by secular politicians to lie within their jurisdiction and outside church competence.

In the nineteenth century, as Latin American states became independent of the Spanish crown, church-state relationships, as we have seen, underwent a dramatic transformation. Now the Spanish crown was gone and the church remained. But the crown had protected the churchly position of privilege, and that protection now was removed. To maintain its control over the destinies of the faithful, the church entered more directly into politics, hoping that it thus could protect its established rights and privileges. Heated discussions blossomed into open disputes between church and state and among the officials of each body. Often, as soon as independence from Spain was won through revolution, an argument erupted between church and state over who had the prior right of taxation within the new state. Likewise, as had happened earlier in the European experience, separate church courts with special privileges came under attack by newly installed state officials. Conversely, the clericals generally protested that any lessening of their political role was, in fact, nothing less than an attack upon the Christian religion itself. In the long run, this confrontation tended to end in a reduction of the material and temporal strength of the church.

After 1945, the church came under fire from a continually growing number of critics. In its historic attempts to maintain its temporal power, or acquire more, the church had allied itself with the owners of the large landed estates. The church's continuing political vitality thus was tied to the continued well-being of the landed aristocracy, and the preservation of a semifeudal social structure. Understandably, therefore, the growth of urban centers in the twentieth century tended to lessen the ability of the church to regulate moral behavior through the political structure. As the masses crowded into the industrializing cities, many of their members began to see and to seek opportunities for material advancement and to take advantage of a new social mobility, largely unhampered by rural tradition.

In part as a result of this movement of population, the Church's contact with the masses was lessened. Even among those who remained peasants there developed a loosening of ties with the church and a trend toward radical movements. As a result, the church saw itself forced, in the middle of the twentieth century, to concern itself seriously with the welfare of the masses. Many of its prelates became more "modern" in attitude and began to speak out for social justice for the poor. As perhaps was to be expected, there now developed splits within the church, as some of the clergy wished to cling to the old course favoring the aristocrats, whereas others sought a functional social pluralism with equality of all in personal rights and economic opportunity. How well the church would adapt to the new needs of the many, probably would determine its future survival as an institution. Spurring it to more rapid adjustment were, on the one side, the inroads of communism; and on the other, the vigorous growth of Protestant churches.

Having observed some general developments in recent Latin American history, we now may find it useful to examine two of the more important Latin states in the post-1945 Western Hemisphere.

D. Brazil

In 1942 Brazil had entered World War II as a member of the Allied group. During the war the government led by Getulio Dornelles Vargas, who in 1930 had established his *Estado Nôvo* (New State) by means of a military coup. The rule of dictator-president Vargas eventually aroused opposition among both the upper class Brazilians, who were displeased with his inflexible political and economic policies, and among the poorer elements, whom he had tried to treat benevolently but who resented the wartime price rises and the scarcity of consumer goods. In 1943 a secretly but widely disseminated manifesto, drafted by opposition leaders, called for a return to democratic government. Eventually, in October 1945, a military coup removed Vargas from power and Eurico Gaspar Dutra was elected president (December 2, 1945).

Vargas, however, did not remain in political obscurity. Having succeeded in winning a senatorship, he used his office to organize a strong labor following and again became President through an election held in 1950.

In the early postwar years, Brazil experienced considerable industrial growth. After the overthrow of Vargas in 1945, numerous federal regulatory powers were abolished and social mobility was fostered; but the chief symbol of Brazilian industrial progress, the National Steel Company, remained a government corporation. It was hoped by Dutra that the adoption of a free market system, allowed to operate naturally, would further economic development and prosperity. Yet, the results of the new policies were disappointing and soon outspoken economic nationalists denounced the advocates of free enterprise.

As the economic euphoria of the early postwar years began to lessen, the Dutra Government abandoned its laissez-faire economic policy and returned to a controlled economic system. Centralized economic planning was introduced. One ambitious example of such planning was the short-lived SALTE project, an administration proposal to accelerate the schedule of federal investment in areas regarded as essential to the nation's economic growth, but that were relatively unattractive to the average private investor.[5] With the return of Vargas to office in 1950, the government's role in economic planning continued. Between 1948 and 1953, a period that overlapped portions of both the Dutra and the Vargas administrations, the production of capital goods rose by 77 per cent.

In 1954 the political climate favoring economic nationalism changed abruptly. In that year a scandal, involving an assassination attempt against an opposition newsman, brought a demand for Vargas' resignation. In August 1954, Vargas, discouraged and tired, took his own life. Vice-President João Café Filho assumed power. Under Filho, men of more orthodox political and economic views dominated the administration, although they were not yet ready to reduce greatly the role of government in the national economy. Unable to solve national problems that were "difficult enough to baffle a superman," Filho was ousted by the military in 1955.

In October 1955, Juscelino Kubitschek de Oliveira, grandson of a Czech immigrant, was elected president. Installed in office in January 1956, he soon launched the most ambitious program of economic growth in Brazil's history. Kubitschek called for the vast expansion of investment in the private as well as the public sector of the economy, actively sought to bring foreign capital into Brazil, and tried to break the traditional and economic pattern by moving the national

---

[5] These areas included fisheries, livestock, rails, water transportation, and electric power. SALTE stood for the Portuguese words meaning Health, Food, Transportation, and Energy.

capital to a new city called Brasília, nearly 600 miles northwest of Río de Janeiro.

The material accomplishments of the Kubitscheck regime were impressive, but the illusion of mounting prosperity sometimes was maintained through purposive inflation. As a consequence, there was a threefold rise in the Brazilian cost of living between 1955 and 1960. At the same time, corruption in government increased, perhaps as a result of the lavish expenditures on crash projects, which put temptation in the way of many officials. By 1960, about one fourth of the industrial labor force was unemployed.

In 1960, Dr. Jãnio da Silva Quadros won the presidency, vowing to chart a course that was independent of United States' influence. Although popularly approved, such a policy aroused fears among Brazil's propertied groups and the military. Quickly, a political crisis developed that brought Quadros' abrupt resignation in 1961, and the succession to his office of the Vice-President, João Goulart, a wealthy Leftist. Because Goulart was known to be a Leftist, the parliament, before accepting him, considerably curtailed the presidential power. A national plebiscite in 1963, however, restored the presidential power system.

Following the 1963 plebiscite, it was hoped that Brazil could return to political stability and economic progress. Goulart devised sweeping economic and social reforms to modernize Brazil—but was unable to put them into effect. Prohibited from initiating his program to please the restive masses, Goulart appealed to nationalistic demagoguery to secure popular backing. Eventually, he announced a plan to nationalize the petroleum industries. This decision led to a middle-class revolt that drove Goulart from office in April 1964.

He was succeeded by Marshal Humberto Castello Branco, who strove to purge the regime of Leftists and corrupt officeholders. Castello Branco also adopted stringent measures to deal with the inflationary crisis. Among these acts were the removal of government subsidies from some items, a close control over wages, and a broad tax reform. The net result of the new steps was to bring the economy under more extensive government controls. The program was not well received by the general public, but in 1967, when Castello Branco transferred power to President Artur da Costa e Silva, the economic crisis had become much less acute. In the summer of 1969, Costa e Silva suffered a stroke and died a few weeks later. Following an interim rule by a trio of military men, he was succeeded in late October by Marshal Emilio Garrastazu Medice.

Modern Brazilian society, then, as was the case in other Latin American states, in the postwar years experienced an explosive population growth, unprecedented mobility of the people, and a general restiveness among the populace. In fewer than fifty years, the number of people in Brazil tripled, and the Brazilian rate of increase was expected to remain well above the average for the rest of the world in the foreseeable future. In increasingly large numbers, rural Brazilians crowded into the cities, and this migration coupled with natural growth swelled the ranks of the urban lower classes. In consequence, the sheer pressure of population amid limited resources thwarted the aspirations for a better life among many of the city poor. Meanwhile, however, there was a measure of progress in the areas of health, education, and transportation.

In many of its traits, Brazil at the start of the 1970's still displayed the characteristics of a typical "underdeveloped country." Occupying approximately half of the continent of South America, and accounting by area for one third of the whole region known as Latin America, Brazil's future obviously was of tremendous importance to the Western Hemisphere.

E. Mexico

When Gustavo Díaz Ordaz became President of Mexico in December 1964, he could look at a nation that had taken first place among Latin American states in terms of political stability and economic well-being. Stability had developed when Mexicans had decided to turn away from private armies and the government had become truly national, with the fortunes of one region becoming integrated with those of another.

During World War II, church-state friction, which had been so typical of the Mexican past, dwindled until the Catholic Church and the state managed to live together with a minimum of friction. The church was restricted, after 1941, in that the government officially retained ownership of all churches, and the Catholic Church could maintain no private schools. But, or perhaps because of all the restrictions, the Catholic Church grew stronger as public education was advanced and the priests no longer could be accused of perpetuating illiteracy. By the mid-1960's, indeed, the demand for education had become intense in Mexico, resulting in a literacy rate of 75 per cent.

One of the factors that created an improved and more literate society was the great increase in agricultural and industrial production. In 1965 the net domestic product value was five and a half times greater than it had been in 1939, the major portion of this growth having come in the last decade of that period. Electrical power, upon which so much of the industrial growth depended, far outstripped in progress other areas of the economy.

A substantial and healthy economic growth outran the population increase in Mexico. Between 1940 and 1965 the population doubled, but the total value of goods and services produced, more than quintupled. Thus order and prosperity could be assured, with wages and salaries increasing at a faster rate than population growth. By 1965, virtually any skilled ambitious worker in Mexico, D.F., could support a family of five through his labor.

Prosperity and a higher standard of living were reflected in relatively stable Mexican politics. In 1945 the Mexican Revolutionary Party (PRM) was reorganized to permit wider representation and became the Party of Revolutionary Institutions (PRI). Miguel Alemán, elected President in 1946, and the first civilian candidate to be elected since Francisco I. Madero was killed in 1913, emphasized the need for industrialization and literacy.

He was succeeded in 1952 by Adolfo Ruíz Cortines, among whose first important reforms were a drastic curtailment of graft and the extension of women's suffrage. In 1958, Adolfo López Mateos, another civilian, was elected President, and carried on the tradition of progress. Díaz, elected in 1964, and Luis Echeverria Alvarez, elected in July 1970, became others in the chain of moderately progressive administrators to lead the Mexican state in relative quiet and harmony.

Despite the impressive improvements, however, Mexico at the beginning of the 1970's had not achieved the kind of prosperity and development enjoyed by her northern neighbors, the United States and Canada. Although well-off in comparison with other Latin American nations, Mexico still possessed millions of illiterates, inadequate housing, and an average income that most Americans and Western Europeans looked upon as on the poverty level. Mexico, too, was not well endowed with natural resources. Hence, though the Mexican Government was committed to the betterment of its people's lives, and displayed concern for the common man, advances had not come fast enough to satisfy the young people, especially the graduates of the National University, who often found that society had not yet created sufficient positions for its newly educated. These voiced their discontent with bloody riots just before the opening of the 1968 Olympic Games in Mexico City. The need for the development of further opportunities for the newly educated youth was perhaps the most pressing problem Mexico would face in the 1970's.

THE UNITED STATES AND LATIN AMERICA

During the nineteenth century, as the United States increased its power and world influence, it naturally became concerned about relations with the states of Central and South America. In the period between the two world wars, it was customary to characterize United States-Latin American relations as a "good neighbor policy." After World War II, it became apparent that Latin American considerations were less significant in North American foreign policy than before the war. The exigencies of the Cold War and the United States' consequent global concerns gave rise among Latin American states to some feeling of neglect.

Conversely, it was the international Communist threat that caused the nations of the Western Hemisphere to sign the first regional mutual defense pact aimed at thwarting possible Red expansion overseas. In 1947 most of the American states signed the Inter-American Treaty of Reciprocal Assistance, which provided that an attack against one signatory would be considered an attack against all. It also was indicated that in some cases an attack from within (in other words, an attempted Communist coup) would be considered aggression by the signatories.

In 1948 a permanent body for inter-American consultation, the Organization of American States (OAS), was founded. The Charter of the OAS called for immediate consultation of the member states on all matters of common interest. Once every five years the OAS states were to meet in an Inter-American Conference, conducted at the foreign minister level, to discuss common problems. In the event of an emergency that affected all or a number of the American states, the headquarters of a permanent hemispheric parliament located in Washington was to consider courses of action. Despite the democratic nature of the OAS, the United States, because of her preponderant power and influence, not unexpectedly played in it the dominant role.

This dominant role, as well as criticism from Latin Americans that the United States concentrated far greater attention on Europe, Asia, and even Africa, than on Latin America, caused a mounting wave of anti-North-Americanism in Central and South America. The growth of this sentiment, then, caused a reassessment of Latin American policy in Washington.

In the last years of the Eisenhower Administration, Washington moved to center more attention on Latin American problems. Long-range plans were formulated to help develop Central and South American states. In 1959 the United States contributed 45 per cent of a $1,000,000,000 fund to establish an Inter-American Development Bank. Then, in 1960, the United States Congress voted an additional $500,000,000 toward development funds for Latin America. This action led to another major step in aid for Latin America, the Alliance for Progress.

The Alliance was inaugurated by President John F. Kennedy in 1961. It issued a call for cooperative effort on the part of all American states (except Cuba) to stimulate greater economic prosperity and more social mobility in their midst. President Kennedy insisted that each state develop careful economic planning as a prerequisite for receiving aid from the United States. But such economic expertise was rare in Central and South America; and Brazil, the potential power of the future in the area, was prevented by political instability from taking full advantage of the programs launched by the Alliance. Hence, despite early United States's optimism and faith, Washington's "grand design" by 1970 had run into many roadblocks. Yet this type of international help and guidance from the United States seemed to offer the one best hope for the desired development of the under-developed Latin American republics.

The Soviet Union, the Satellite Bloc, and Their Neighbors

24

THE U.S.S.R. TO THE DEATH OF STALIN

Before World War II, Joseph Stalin had created a one-party, essentially one-man dictatorship in a country of 200,000,000 people. This fact made fighting the war an often difficult task for the Soviets. As the Germans penetrated deeply into the U.S.S.R., many people, whose memories of Stalin's prewar mass executions and slave labor had made them hate Kremlin rule, welcomed the Nazis as liberators. The Nazi forces quickly dispelled the illusion, however, by initiating policies of racial extermination and otherwise brutally treating the conquered peoples.

The Soviets' reaction to the tactics of the Nazis was a practical one. They stimulated nascent Russian nationalism in a variety of ways. For instance, in the Red Army ranks, awards, and privileges for officers were reintroduced. The Russian Orthodox Church was officially recognized again, in 1943, and the people were given to believe that reforms, aimed at improving the style of life in the Soviet Union, would appear after the war.

The widespread destruction wrought by the German armies confronted the rigid, highly controlled Russian system with an overwhelming problem in the postwar era. The ravaged Soviet Union had lost at least 7,000,000 people and some 20,000,000 more were without shelter and sufficient food. Surrounded by a war-produced wasteland, the Soviets, and Stalin particularly, believed that reconstruction could be achieved only by a return to earlier Stalinist methods.

Quickly the Russian Communist Party reemphasized Marxist-Leninist doctrine at the same time that the stress on national patriotism was continued.[1] Propaganda was developed to drive the workers

[1] One of the ways of doing this was by claiming that virtually every techno-

485

on to greater efforts aimed at the rebuilding of the Soviet Union.[2] The West was pictured by *Pravda* and other propaganda organs as a dangerous menace to the welfare of every Russian. It was pointed out repeatedly that the United States had nuclear power, which it might use at any moment against a U.S.S.R. that did not quickly rebuild and, once restored, did not continue technological modernization.

Thus, the Soviet Union began a crash program to combine her own resources with expropriated machinery from occupied countries and aid from agencies like UNRRA. The rebuilding proceeded so rapidly that the Russians soon were able to allot extra resources to scientific research. This research produced remarkable advances, the most important of which was the production, in 1949, of a thermonuclear device.

In 1946, the Fourth Five-Year Plan was launched, and in 1951, the Fifth. In his announcement of the Fourth Plan, Stalin had set as its most important aims, national rehabilitation and expansion of heavy industry.

During the 1930's, people had so crowded into the cities that living conditions had sunk to a level far below Western European standards. The war had made the situation catastrophic by destroying an estimated 40,000,000 square yards of living space. By the early 1950's, the housing aims of the plans had been exceeded in some cities, but fell short in some of the rural areas.

Heavy industry continued to be of utmost importance in Soviet planning because the Kremlin was intent on strengthening the U.S.S.R.'s capacity to make war. Accordingly, by 1951, industrial production in the Soviet Union had risen to second place in the world. But, as had been the pattern throughout the earlier Five Year Plans, consumer goods had to take second place. Even the meager quotas established in the Fourth and Fifth Five-Year Plans were not reached in many instances.

The road back to economic stability could be traversed only if workers labored long hours at little pay. They were urged to do this through a system of incentives like the ones used in the earlier Five-Year Plans (decorative medals, generous publicity for pacesetting, and monetary rewards on a piece-work basis). If the laborers failed to respond to any of these dangled carrots, there was always the stick held threateningly in the other hand by Soviet leaders who warned of imprisonment in a forced labor camp.

The revival of agriculture was particularly important to the development of a balanced economy, but here, as in the 1930's, great

---

logical improvement within the recent memory of men had been the product of a Russian invention.

[2] This rebuilding process was helped by the fact that the Russians already had begun reconstruction before the war ended and, as has been indicated, during the 1930's had moved many of the factories east of the Urals, hopefully out of Nazi reach. This policy of moving factories to the east was continued during the war years.

difficulties were encountered. Many cattle had been killed during the war and not replaced. Moreover, there was a lack of tractors and horses. Therefore, rationing had to be continued into 1946 and 1947 and there were hunger riots in some parts of the Soviet Union. In agricultural affairs, however, the immensely rapid industrialization of the Soviet economy helped a difficult situation. By 1951, machines were handling some 60 per cent of Soviet harvests.

Simultaneously, there was a renewed push toward agricultural collectivization. As before the war, there were two kinds of farms: state farms (*sovkhozy*) and collectives (*kolkhozy*). Between 1950 and the end of 1953, the number of collective farms was cut from some 250,000 to 94,000 by the creation of consolidated collectives with accompanying "argo-towns." These argo-towns brought peasants together in apartment blocks where they lived surrounded by urban social and cultural patterns. In charge of the amalgamation process in the rural districts was Nikita S. Khrushchev, who had instituted increased centralized economic planning in agriculture.

The income of workers on the collectives was determined by yields. Payment to the laborers was made in terms of norms, and there were bonuses of the kind prescribed for industrial workers for those who produced beyond the norms set for them. Each separate household was allowed to maintain a garden plot in which a large portion of the food eaten by the peasant and his family was raised. Should the peasant be able to raise food beyond what was needed at home, he could sell it in free markets in the city at a price determined by supply and demand. Commonly, this established a situation wherein the soil-workers continued to spend as much time as they could on their own land and as little on the collective as possible. Hence, despite the earlier-mentioned mechanization in agriculture, that segment of the economy lagged behind others. At the end of the Stalinist era, grain and livestock were at or below the World War I levels.

Government remained dictatorial and, although the Supreme Soviet remained the highest "legislative" body in the U.S.S.R., the real power, as in the past, rested with the Communist Party. The Party had become larger after the war, since certain military heroes, and others who had performed valuable services to the Soviet Union during the conflict, were included on its lists. This situation meant that the Party was enlarged from some 2,000,000 members before the battle with the Nazis began to more than 6,000,000 in 1947.

Because of its large membership, the Communist Party of the Soviet Union operated through its Central Committee. Within the Committee itself, the most important organ was the *Politburo* (*Presidium* after 1952), usually consisting of about sixteen members. Until his death, the inner core of party machinery was subjected to the arbitrary manipulation of Joseph Stalin.

Since the Soviet state often was governed by dictatorial whim, there was need to maintain a secret police force, a large army, and a vast cadre of bureaucrats, all loyal to the dictator. Through these agencies, movement within Soviet territories by its own citizens was limited severely. Moreover, the repression of dissenting political viewpoints now was enforced as rigidly as it had been before the war, by the use of forced labor camps and summary execution by firing squads.

The party bureaucracy controlled all information media and a strict censorship was enforced. *Pravda,* the official spokesman of the Communist Party, and *Izvestia,* news representative of the Soviet Government, instructed the public in the official and *only* permissible position on matters of importance. Local newspapers mirrored the pronouncements of these giants of the information media. As a result, all news was carefully and unimaginatively edited to produce "correct" stories. Such stories were intermingled with long pronouncements of the *Politburo* and official state utterances. As was the case before the war, this extreme limitation of personal expression was extended to all literary forms. Postwar Soviet intellectuals had to fight a long and difficult battle against the heavy blanket of censorship imposed by Kremlin authorities. Many years passed before any significant amount of creative literature emerged from this land, once so noted for its productive and brilliant literary artists.

In the days of the Stalinist system of repression and limitation, congresses of the Communist Party became rare. During Lenin's lifetime, such congresses were held annually. It was in 1926 that a Party congress was not held for the first time. Thereafter, congresses met only every three to five years. The Eighteenth Congress was held in 1939 and was the last to meet until after the end of World War II. Presumably, Stalin used the Second World War as an excuse to omit such meetings. During this time, a special-interest organ of Stalin and his handpicked bureaucrats, the *apparatchiki,* developed, and the rank-and-file party membership began to demonstrate a moderate degree of unrest as the bureaucracy became increasingly important. It is probable that the Party leadership became aware of this discontent and thus decided to call a Party congress.

The Nineteenth Party Congress met in October 1952. At this meeting, the Party machinery was further centralized and the Secretariat of the Central Committee, ruled by Georgi Maximilianovich Malenkov, assumed the key position in the Party. The Fifth Five-Year Plan (1951–1955) was approved and hydroelectric works were placed at the top of the list of priorities. There was to be produced in Russia a "social system based on waterpower," with mammoth power plants spread across the Soviet Union. Beyond these decisions, there was displayed at the Congress an impressive list of statistics revealing the massive impact of centralized state planning. In many ways, the Nineteenth Party Congress offered a clear documentation of the Soviets' powerful state, which had been shaped by the iron grasp of Stalin, "the Father of the Peoples."

Yet, even the firm hold of Stalin could not last forever. Not long after the Nineteenth Congress, on March 5, 1953, Stalin died. On

March 9, he was buried in the mausoleum on Red Square, next to Lenin. Funeral orations were delivered by Premier and Secretary General of the Party Malenkov, Security Police Chief Lavrenti P. Beria, and Foreign Secretary Vyacheslav M. Molotov. On March 7, the Supreme Soviet had announced the decisions regarding Stalin's successors. Malenkov gave up the secretaryship and emerged as Chairman of the Council of Ministers; his deputies were to be Beria, Molotov, Nikolai A. Bulganin, and Lazar M. Kaganovich.

Little was finally settled, however, by this first emergence of new leadership. Stalin, after all, had held immense power in his hands for thirty years. While Stalin was alive, a myth had been created around him and he became the visible symbol of Soviet hegemony within and outside the Soviet Union. Could this symbol suddenly collapse without the foundations of Communist ideology and the Soviet state shaking severely? In March, 1953, it seemed unlikely that a transfer of power from the dead autocrat to his heirs could transpire without difficulty.

THE STRUGGLE FOR SOVIET LEADERSHIP

Immediately after Stalin's death, there emerged the principle of collective leadership. A *troika* appeared, composed of Beria, Malenkov, and Molotov. Of the three, Secret Police Chief Beria, a Georgian like Stalin, seemed the most important figure. Still, Beria was not sufficiently influential to seize personal authority. Consequently, the troika continued to manage affairs of state, supported by an upper echelon of Soviet officials, among whom were Bulganin and Khrushchev.

Before the end of March 1953, the first convulsion occurred within the collective leadership. Khrushchev took over Malenkov's post as Secretary General of the Party and quickly installed his own supporters in important party offices. As personal alliances had shifted after the death of Lenin, they now began to move with a new fluidity after Stalin's. On July 10, 1953, Moscow information media announced that Beria had been relieved of his offices, expelled from the Communist Party, and arrested. Much of the indictment against Beria appeared contrived. Among the manifold accusations, however, emerged the hard facts that Beria had opposed Khrushchev's agrarian policy and that he had differed with others in the collective leadership over the ways and means of satellite control. After a secret trial, Beria was adjudged guilty and reportedly shot.

Following the death of Beria there were significant shifts in Soviet internal policies. Before the end of 1953, Malenkov announced that production of consumer goods would be increased substantially. This constituted a major alteration in Soviet policy, which, since 1917, had stressed the priority of heavy industry. Malenkov apparently realized that Soviet society had undergone a change in stratification, producing a more sharply delineated social order. The new societal strata were comprised of the party elite at the top, a second order of party bureaucrats, then an emerging middle class of engineers and other technical personnel, and, at the base, the masses of industrial workers and peasants. The higher classes in this more sharply stratified order asked more for their services to party and state than symbolic awards. Another consideration shaping the decision to produce more consumer goods developed from the wartime contact experienced by the fighting forces of the U.S.S.R. with Western living standards. Out of this contact there developed in many a desire for more material things.

Soon after, a cultural "thaw" set in within the U.S.S.R.[3] A process of de-Stalinization was initiatied and a new historical perspective on Stalin was introduced. In consequence, a number of the myths surrounding the former Georgian were dropped. Censorship was lightened and the lessening of controls soon became obvious in the theater, cinema, music, and broadcasting. Soviet scholars also demonstrated the influence of the "thaw" by taking part in international conferences held in the West.

THE EMERGENCE OF KHRUSHCHEV

On February 8, 1955, controversy within the Soviet system accomplished another change in the leadership of the U.S.S.R. The resignation of Malenkov from the premiership was announced and his replacement by Bulganin was indicated. This change reflected a struggle for power behind the scenes that seemed to have benefited Khrushchev. The latter, since his appointment as First Secretary of the Party in 1953, gradually had asserted himself, until Russia's collective leadership was transformed into the two-man team of Malenkov-Khrushchev. In 1955, this duo was replaced by the Khrushchev-Bulganin combination, in which Khrushchev's position was the stronger.

Khrushchev was one of the most prominent examples in the Soviet system, although certainly not the only one, of a man who emerged from proletarian beginnings to rise to the top of his society. Nikita Sergeyevich Khrushchev was born in 1894, not far from the Russian-Ukrainian border in the region of Kursk. He had joined the Communist Party when a worker in the Ukrainian coal region. After the revolution, during the harsh years of the civil war, he fought for the Red cause. From 1929 until 1931, Khrushchev attended a Moscow school of technology. During the same time, the often-jovial Ukrainian advanced rapidly in party circles as an official whose allegiance to

___

[3] The term "thaw" derived from a novel by Ilya Ehrenburg in which he advocated that a less intellectually limiting course be charted by the Government.

Stalin was unquestioned. In 1934, Khrushchev became a member of the Central Committee and, in 1935, advanced to become First Secretary of the Party Organization in Moscow. During 1937 and 1938, Khrushchev carried out purges in the Ukraine ordered by Stalin. As a reward, in 1939, he was promoted to the Politburo. During the Second World War, Khrushchev led the Ukrainian partisan movement. At the end of the fighting, he was placed in charge of the rebuilding of the Ukraine until Stalin called him to Moscow for work at Party headquarters.

Khrushchev seemed mercurial in temperament, stubborn, likely to display childish tantrums, and given to intemperate courses of action. Beneath this misleading exterior, however, there was a shrewd and finely calculating mind. He had the ability to absorb masses of detail without losing perspective. In his ambition to succeed Stalin he was inflexibly committed to a course of action which allowed any means to be employed in gaining the ultimate objective. This objective was achieved in 1957.

Khrushchev took steps, in mid-1957, that caused changes of paramount importance within the Soviet Union. He devised plans to reorganize the Soviet industrial structure by decentralizing the entire economic apparatus. Further, he planned to cultivate virgin lands in Asiatic Russia, thus incidentally arousing hostility among those in the Party who felt such a policy unnecessary. Also, Khrushchev's advance-recede maneuvers in foreign affairs seemed to some Party figures an undue departure from Stalinist orthodoxy. In the minds of others, Khrushchev's was the primary responsibility for the 1956 uprisings in Hungary and Poland. Consequently, Malenkov and Molotov now openly opposed Khrushchev. In this they were supported by Kaganovich and Dimitri T. Shepilov, who recently had replaced Molotov as Foreign Secretary. Khrushchev solved his problem, on June 29, by removing Molotov, Malenkov, and Kaganovich from the Central Committee and the Presidium. Shepilov, too, was forced from his Party post and the foreign secretary's position. The dismissals had to be accompanied by the customary accusations: plotting, resistance against the policy of peaceful coexistence, and sabotage of the new economic plans. In accord with a new softer line developing within Soviet internal politics, the expelled men were transferred to subordinate positions in remote regions of the U.S.S.R. rather than executed. The dismissals were not accomplished with ease, but Khrushchev was able to remove his enemies because he had the support of the Red Army, led by Marshal Gregory K. Zhukov.

After the removal of Khrushchev's antagonists in 1957, Zhukov himself loomed as a possible challenger for the top spot in the Soviet system. In a surprise move in October 1957, he therefore was removed as Minister of Defense and Commander of the Red Army. Khrushchev soon followed this action with the exile of Bulganin, in March 1958, at which time Khrushchev copied Stalin's technique by combining his party leadership with the premiership. Although opposition remained Khrushchev survived party struggles to retain sole leadership until 1964.

THE IMPACT OF DE-STALINIZATION
ON THE SOVIET UNION

The impact of the smashing of the Stalinist cult in the Soviet Union on the Cold War has been examined in earlier chapters. Changes also were wrought within the Soviet Union by de-Stalinization. At the Twentieth Party Congress, Khrushchev called for a new party history, one that would reveal the "true historical facts" about Stalin. He followed with a speech illustrating Stalin's lust for power, despotic procedures, and use of terrorism to control the Russian people.

The first effect of the new de-Stalinization line in Russia was the rehabilitation, by the Central Committee of the Communist Party, of many of the victims of Stalinist terrorism. Since the process of downgrading Stalin had seemed to have come from the government's need to reestablish a relationship of trust between the Kremlin and the people, party propaganda emphasized the new order's ideological connection with Lenin. It also was indicated that the earlier Stalin, who had succeeded Lenin, was a "good" Marxist. It was only the later Stalin who degenerated into a tyrant.

A return to Leninism did not mean democracy. Rather, it meant that one-man rule was to be replaced with the old tradition of one-party rule. Bureaucratic centralism was to be maintained and freedom of expression still was to be limited.

Also coming out of the Twentieth Party Congress was a decision to develop a new party program (more in keeping with the downgrading of Stalin) and a Sixth Five-Year Plan to provide an increase of agricultural and industrial production by raising technical levels of efficiency.

THE SOVIET UNION TO THE FALL OF KHRUSHCHEV

The assumption of leadership by Khrushchev in 1958 put at least a temporary end to collective leadership, but did not mean a return to Stalin's style of governing. In contrast to Stalin's marionette-like manipulation of the Central Committee, Khrushchev had to face in this same body many who supported him only conditionally. Moreover, he did not have at his ready disposal, for use against dissident party members, the former MVD. Indeed, popular fear of the dreaded secret police lessened and the public began to enjoy a somewhat broader freedom.

Since the official Party history of the Soviet Union emphasized the party congresses as important milestones, it may be useful briefly to follow the scheme in examining Khrushchev's career. The

Twenty-first Party Congress, of January-February 1959, dealt with the failures of the Soviet economy, for the Sixth Five-Year Plan had fallen short of its goals. It therefore was decided to launch a Seven-Year Plan to raise industrial output by some 80 per cent.

It soon became apparent, however, that the Soviet economy could not increase heavy industrial production while simultaneously enlarging the output of consumer goods. The government, indeed, found it advisable to redraw the economic blueprint and announce a Twenty-Year Plan, in 1960, before the Seven-Year Plan really had begun to function. After the Twenty-first Party Congress, also, some changes were made in the higher ranks of party leadership, and such "strong men" as Aleksei N. Kosygin and Dimitri S. Polansky came to the fore.

In 1961, between the Twenty-first and Twenty-second Party Congresses, a new program forecast that the Soviet Union's production would exceed that of the United States by 1970. Higher living standards were promised, but there was no mention of greater personal freedom for Soviet citizens. On the contrary, a revised penal code provided harsh punishments for the development of any "bourgeois" symptoms. The first task of the Twenty-second Congress was ratification of this program. Toward the close of the Congress, a clear effort was made to remove older people from the leadership and advance younger men.

During 1962, the rulers continued to wrestle with the problem of a need for heavy industry as contrasted to the public desire for more consumer goods. Agriculture, moreover, once again lagged so badly that Khrushchev openly criticized the backwardness of Soviet farming methods. In an attempt to cope with these recurrent difficulties, the Soviets reorganized the administrative machinery and established two parallel party hierarchies, one concerned with industry and the other with agriculture. In early 1963, a Supreme Economic Council was created and the solution of the economic dilemma became the chief target of Party activity. In this year, too, Leonid I. Brezhnev, an agrarian expert, rose to become the second most important official in the Soviet Union.

By the spring of 1964, when Khrushchev became seventy, there was foreign speculation on a possible heir to his mantle. Aside from the internal difficulties, Khrushchev also was saddled with the responsibility for the steadily worsening Sino-Soviet schism. Antagonistic personal messages were exchanged between Mao and Khrushchev, and when the latter wished to call a World Communist Party meeting to condemn the Chinese position, the satellite governments held back from what they feared would cause a split in World Communism.

At a meeting of the Party Presidium on October 13, 1964, Khrushchev was accused of having erred greatly in office. He was called back from a vacation to defend himself against charges of misconduct, including nepotism, boastfulness, willfulness, and economic ineptitude. On October 14 he was deposed from the premiership and deprived of all party offices. He was replaced by A. N. Kosygin as Premier and by L. I. Brezhnev as First Secretary of the Party.

THE REAPPEARANCE OF COLLECTIVE LEADERSHIP

After the combination of the two highest offices in the Soviet Union was broken and these positions were placed in separate hands, a form of collective leadership again appeared in Russia. The dual leadership of Brezhnev and Kosygin, more impersonal than that of Khrushchev, gave some promise of stability.

Leonid Ilyich Brezhnev was born in the Ukraine, in 1906, into a laboring family. Like many party figures, he was a technician by education, holding a degree in engineering. He was regarded as an expert on land and had held administrative positions in the republics of the Soviet Union. From 1960–1964, he was chairman of the Presidium of the Supreme Soviet and, as such, President of the U.S.S.R.

Aleksei Nikolayevich Kosygin also came from proletarian origins. The son of a laborer, he was born in Leningrad, in 1904, and educated as an engineer. After 1938, he became an industrial administrator, and then, in 1939, Deputy Chairman of the Council of Peoples' Commissars. He eventually held numerous positions in the Ministry of Economics and rose in the party ranks to membership in the Politburo. In 1960, he became a member of the Central Committee's Presidium and the First Deputy Premier of the U.S.S.R. He never had been a hard-line Stalinist.

Late in 1964 and 1965, Brezhnev reorganized the Party, reversing the earlier trend toward decentralization. The administrative separation between agriculture and industry was abolished, larger sums were expended on agriculture, and the burdensome farm quotas were lowered. Higher prices for surpluses and higher wages were promised.

The Twenty-third Party Congress, in 1966, scrapped most of the previous economic schemes and drafted another Five-Year Plan, to run into 1971. The old Politburo was recreated, to take the place of the Presidium, and Brezhnev's title was changed from First Secretary to General Secretary. The Supreme Soviet in 1966 reelected Nikolai Viktorovich Podgorny as President of the U.S.S.R.

The fiftieth anniversary of the Bolshevik Revolution, in November 1967, gave the Soviet Union opportunity to look back and particularly to review the years since the end of World War II. The decades since 1945 had seen major technical and scientific advancements. In addition, some improvement was recorded in the standard of living and in cultural opportunities. The relaxation of control over individual prerogatives, however, had made little progress. Moscow's fear, in 1968, that Czechoslovak liberalism might infect the people of the U.S.S.R., led, as we have seen, to repression abroad and tightening of the governmental reins at home. As the decade of the 1970's opened, freedom of expression still was not a right of the Soviet people.

THE SOVIET UNION AND THE SATELLITE STATES

THE SATELLITE BLOC IN EASTERN EUROPE

The Establishment of the Soviet Sphere of Influence

Soviet influence was established in the satellite states at uneven rates, but a similarity of pattern appears in each case. The first step in establishing Soviet influence in a country involved the obtaining of the active or passive consent of the Western powers. This usually was done in the international conferences held by the anti-Axis leaders near the end of World War II. Next, indigenous Communist parties in the states included within the Soviet orbit generally cooperated, for a time, in some kind of coalition government. The role of native Reds within regimes created after the withdrawal of the Nazis was ensured by the fact that Soviet troops generally were present while the new government was being established. It also was guaranteed by the fact that Communists often had been among the most honored heroes of the wartime anti-Nazi resistance movements, and former members of the underground usually were assured a vote in the forming of a new government. The final phase was entered when the Communists moved into a position of dominance within the government. Of all the states in which the three-step process toward absorption within the Soviet Bloc was attempted, only Finland, traditionally resistant to Soviet maneuvering, effectively stopped short of the third phase.

Once the Communists had moved into power fully, they dubbed their new governments "People's Democracies." These regimes generally were established along the Soviet pattern existing in the U.S.S.R. before the centralization of economic control achieved through the Five-Year Plans. Each People's Democracy was provided with a constitution which, at the same time, gave the Party members power to silence any possible opposition and created a situation wherein the government could take over all means of industrial and agricultural production. Most of these documents established a façade of federalism without sacrificing the reality of centralized power. Private property and initiative in business were allowed to continue within certain limitations. Real authority was reserved for the Communist party hierarchy.

In at least two cases within the satellite bloc the three-step process toward Communist control was not followed. In Albania and Yugoslavia the Communists held unquestioned authority from the beginning. In these two states strong, basically Communist, partisan movements came to power immediately at the end of hostilities, for they were the most vital and highly organized elements there at the time of the Nazis' departure.

Once the Communists had established People's Democracies, Soviet control was exerted in various ways. Most important was the establishing of a link between local Reds and the Kremlin. Long before the end of the war this connection was initiated and maintained. Local party officials were kept in line by the presence of Soviet secret police, who often operated directly from Russian consulates, although these by no means were the only centers of espionage.

Thus, the postwar histories of the satellite states displayed many common characteristics. To a great extent these states were shaped in the image of the Soviet Union. Still they were independent national entitites, each possessing cultural traditions of its own and a separate historic experience, eventually producing a modern nation. It is to these separate patterns of development within the satellite bloc that we now turn.

Poland

The establishment of a postwar government for Poland had been one of the most important items on the agenda at the Yalta Conference. It was decided at Yalta that the Provisional Government already functioning in Poland under Russian supervision should be reorganized "on a broader democratic basis" and retitled the Polish Provisional Government of National Unity. This government was installed in Warsaw with Edward Osóbka-Marawski as Premier. It was pledged to the holding of free elections in Poland. Eventually, this Polish government joined the United Nations.

At the war's end, Poland was devastated. Without natural frontiers, the nation had been left open to destruction as the Soviets and Nazis fought back and forth across its level expanse. During the Nazi occupation, extermination policies had been carried out efficiently. The postwar result of such policies was a population largely deprived of precisely those elements sorely needed in the reconstruction of the country. Also, as described earlier, the establishment of the Oder-Neisse line as the western boundary of Poland had the effect of shifting the prewar Polish nation some 150 miles westward. In consequence, Poland was in a state of extreme flux. It was into such conditions that the Soviets moved and began to reconstruct the nation along Communist lines.

As the Soviets entered Poland, they began to eliminate the opposition. As Polish wartime non-Communist resistance leaders began to reveal themselves, they often were taken to Moscow and tried for treason. The new Polish state police, since it had been created by the Communist-influenced provisional government, began to act in the interests of the Party and terrorized opposition elements. The elections guaranteed at Yalta were not held until January 1947. By that time, potential candidates from the Polish Peasant Party had been placed in jail. Boleslaw Bierut, a Communist, became the President of Poland.

As 1948 began, the Polish United Workers' Party (PZPR) was the sole party of importance. Led by Bierut, its Secretary, the Workers' Party exercised practical control over the government. Following the pattern established within the Soviet Union itself, the Party Politburo became more important than the official organs of state. The Polish economy was then restructured by a Soviet style Three-Year Plan. As the Three-Year Plan was followed by a Six-Year Plan, the Polish economy was tied progressively to the Soviet economic system.

Poland had been primarily a Catholic state and the Church had possessed an elaborate hierarchical system, strongly resistant to secular political pressures. Now it was the Catholic Church that rigidly resisted the onrush of communism. To overcome the Church's resistance, the state confiscated Church lands and removed the clericals from education. By 1953, the government had begun to practice lay investiture and demanded, at the same time, that all priests take an oath of obedience to the government. There was much resistance to the new policies and hundreds of Church officials were placed under arrest, including the Primate of Poland, Stefan Cardinal Wyszyński.

In 1952, a new Polish constitution was adopted, modeled along Soviet lines. It provided for a premier, and that office was occupied by Bierut. Early in 1956, the autocratic Bierut died and there now were those who hoped for a moderation of governmental controls. Moreover, the economic situation was unstable. State planning had brought prosperity to industry, but agriculture had fallen far behind. Grievances were nurtured in sullen silence by large segments of the population.

Then events in Hungary sparked rebellion in Poland. Rioting commenced at Poznan in June 1956, and, to the surprise of many Western observers, the Polish Government compromised with the dissidents. Wladyslaw Gomulka, who in 1947 had been relieved of his posts because of alleged rightist tendencies, now was "rehabilitated" and as Party First Secretary became the dominant figure in Polish affairs.

A period of relative reform began. Cardinal Wyszyński was set free. In 1957, when the elections brought huge majorities to the Communists, it was widely held that the overwhelming electoral tide could be interpreted as approbation of Gomulka's policies by the people. Extreme communization in agriculture was halted and compulsory grain requisitions were abolished. Religious instruction once more was allowed in the schools and, in return, the Church officially requested that Catholics support the government. In the late 1950's, as a result of these more relaxed policies, Poland came to be regarded as a moderate among the states of the Soviet bloc.

As the 1960's began, however, Gomulka, famed as a Communist who could pose as a true socialist and yet observe "national features," began to revert to authoritarianism. His regime became considerably more inflexible than it had been when he first came to power. Cabinet ministers of "liberal" reputation were replaced by orthodox Communists. Perhaps more ominous for the Polish people, the power of the state security police was expanded and arbitrary arrest of political nonconformists reappeared. A harsh censorship was reinstituted and several writers were tried for errors in political and ideological judgment.

In agricultural policy, Gomulka's earlier reforms were retained. Gomulka apparently became convinced that private farmers produced more than was turned out by the same farmers when forced to live and work on a collective. Hence, the bulk of the cultivable land remained in the possession of independent farmers, although the official government pronouncements on the subject constantly maintained that true collectivization would be achieved someday. That the government allowed farmers to retain the land also may have been necessitated by the fact that, after the brief era of good feeling in

1956–1957, relations between church and state had progressively soured as Gomulka moved toward autocracy. The Church traditionally had possessed a strong following among the rural population and Gomulka feared that a dangerous discontent might spread among religiously outraged farmers if the government did not placate them. Thus, concessions were granted to farmers, the faithful of the Church.

But during the decade of the 1960's, Gomulka pursued policies that once again disrupted Catholic-Communist relations. At the beginning of 1967, Stefan Cardinal Wyszyński again was at logger-heads with Gomulka. The Cardinal protested the incursions of state power into all aspects of public and private education. Cardinal Wyszyński indicated that the situation had become so bad that state inspectors often marched into Catholic seminaries to revise the methods of instruction. As Wyszyński put it for the press of the world, "one must obey God rather than men" and "priests should be educated by priests" rather than by bureaucrats appointed by the state.

In foreign affairs, Poland became a hard and fast ally of the Soviet Union. A major factor in the adoption of a Soviet-like "hard-line" in foreign policy was the fear that some day the Germans might press claims for the German territory incorporated into Poland after the war —and now largely de-Germanized. Warsaw traded with various Western powers, but generally remained distrustful of them.

Polish loyalty to Russian aims and Gomulka's opposition to liberal reforms were further indicated by Poland's actions at the time of the 1968 Czechoslovak crisis. In the forefront among those pressuring Prague to retract reforms, and then participating in Czechoslovakia's invasion, was Gomulka's Poland.

Hungary

A Provisional National Government, shaped by the Soviets, was installed in Hungary in April 1945. So-called "People's Courts" soon conducted purges of those who resisted the Sovietization of Hungarian life. Hungary, during the days of Austria-Hungary, had been a land of great estates. What remained of these estates now was fragmented and redistributed to the peasants in individual plots not exceeding 20 acres. As was the case in Poland, the Hungarian economy was closely tied to that of the Soviet Union in an imperialist-colonial kind of relationship.

The first postwar elections, in November 1945, revealed popular discontent with the Communist policies. The election was one of few held in the newly established Russian orbit that was conducted honestly. The result was a victory for the moderate agrarian Small-holders' Party. Following the election, Hungary was declared a republic and a constitution was devised that showed the strong influence of Western democratic traditions. The Smallholders constructed a coalition government composed largely of members of their own party.

However, some important roles in this new coalition government were given to Communists, who worked secretly to pull the Hungarians into the satellite bloc. This first coalition government had been formed by Smallholder Ferenc Nagy. He committed the political error of allowing Matyas Rákosi, Secretary of the Hungarian Communist Party, to become one of his vice-premiers. Even more portentous of troubled times ahead for the new republic was the fact that Nagy in March 1946, took as his Minister of the Interior, Laszlo Rajk, whose new office gave him control of the secret police. Early in 1947, Rajk claimed to have discovered a plot against the government. Using this rumored scheme as an excuse, Rajk launched a series of arrests aimed at the membership of the Smallholders' Party. As top officials of the Smallholders were arrested, they were subjected to interrogation. Out of these interrogations came numerous reports of confessions, which implicated yet other members of the Smallholders' Party.

The wave of arrests of anti-Communists was launched while Premier Ferenc Nagy was in Switzerland. The purge in Budapest transpired so rapidly that Nagy decided it was inadvisable to return to a situation that might prove dangerous to him personally. He resigned his post by telephone and refused to return home. Smallholder Lajos Dinnyés, a straw man in the hands of Vice-Premier Rákosi and Rajk, assumed the premiership.

From this point onward, the Hungarian system was restructured from above. The government, the constitution, and electoral processes, were remolded. Those who voiced opposition to the process were purged.

Inevitably, the church and state came into conflict as the officials of the government removed education from ecclesiastical hands. When the schools were nationalized, Josef Cardinal Mindszenty protested. In response to his protest, the Communists arrested and condemned him, calling the Cardinal an "enemy of human progress."

The death of Stalin and resultant modifications in Soviet methods encouraged some Hungarians to believe that a more moderate rule might be introduced in their country. One result of this moderation was the rise to the premiership of Imre Nagy, a former Minister of Agriculture who was willing to allow some of the peasants to withdraw from the collectives in hope of increasing farm production. Further indicative of the new moderation was a decreed increase in consumer goods and a closing of some of the forced-labor camps.

An intense rivalry soon developed between Rákosi and the more moderate Nagy. Early in 1955, Nagy was forced by the party to halt his easing of communization and was replaced by Rákosi. Land collectivization and emphasis on heavy industry at the expense of consumer goods once again became the national policy. This return to the earlier Communist stance led various Hungarians intellectual groups in 1956 openly to criticize Rákosi. Adding to the discontent was a general atmosphere of unrest created by poor harvests. Feelings of resentment toward the government caused student demonstrations to erupt in

Budapest. Rákosi eventually resigned and Imre Nagy became Premier once again. At the head of a coalition, Nagy began negotiations with the Soviet Government to withdraw its occupying forces.

As October 1956, drew to a close, Budapest was in revolt. But, as described earlier, the Soviets crushed the rebellion and Nagy was put to death. Cardinal Mindszenty, who had been released by hysterical cheering crowds, took refuge in the American Embassy, where he still remained into 1970. János Kádár became the head of a new Hungarian Government, with instructions from the Kremlin to return the country to a Moscow-dictated course.

Beginning in 1959, farm collectivization, which had slipped extensively under Nagy's direction, was intensified. By the mid-1960's, most arable land had been brought under collective cultivation. Typical Communist policies were applied in industry and production was expanded, albeit somewhat less than desired. Hungary's tendency to move out of the Soviet economic bloc, displayed during the Nagy period, now was reversed and the economy was tied more closely to that of the Soviet bloc.

Severe divisions and an undercurrent of anti-government hostility remained in the wake of the events of 1956. Kádár apparently had decided that he could not pursue in Hungary the personally autocratic course chosen by Gomulka in Poland. He thus reintroduced comparatively moderate government in an attempt to rally the nation behind him. Controls on all segments of society were relaxed and tensions between church and state were eased slightly. Greater liberty of foreign travel in Hungary was assured and, in the second half of the 1960's, the Hungarian Government actively sought Western tourists to help the economy. In 1967, the economic expert Jenö Fock became Premier.

As the internal situation bettered, other governments reappraised Kádár's and Fock's Hungary. In the United States, experts on foreign policy noted that Hungary was among the first of the Soviet bloc states to seek greater industrial efficiency by following Western-style business procedures. Representative of the restoration of improved relations with the West, was the United States decision, in 1963, to reopen diplomatic relations with Hungary, broken at the time of the Hungarian uprising in 1956. In 1967, Washington raised Budapest to ambassadorial status.

Czechoslovakia

Czechoslovakia's entry into the Soviet camp had begun in 1943. Still haunted by vivid memories of the Western "betrayal" of Czech interests at Munich, in 1938, and stimulated by the movement of Russian armies into Central Europe, Czechoslovakia's statesmen decided to recognize Russian hegemony in *Mittel Europa.* In 1945, Eduard Beneš visited Moscow and concluded an agreement to form a postwar coalition government including indigenous Communists. Thus the Communists were assured of an important role in the new Czechoslovakia and, in the 1946 parliamentary elections, Reds captured two out of every five seats, to become the largest single party in the country. Klement Gottwald, a pawn of Moscow, became Prime Minister.

This Czechoslovak Socialist Republic, which Gottwald now led, had been subjected to Nazi occupation and the usual persecutions, but, compared with other satellite states, had incurred relatively slight physical damage. As was the case in Poland, most citizens of German descent were driven westward into the newly established occupation zones. Only a relatively few were retained because of their specialized technical skills. The Czechs tried to make certain that there never again would develop in Czechoslovakia another Sudeten situation.

Although Beneš remained as President after the elections of 1946, the Gottwald Cabinet was heavily Communist. Out of twelve members, eight belonged to the Prime Minister's party. The economic policies of the new government indicated its orientation toward Sovietization. A Two-Year Plan was launched and the customary satellite-bloc trade agreement, significantly to the advantage of Moscow, was signed with the Soviet Union.

In 1947 the Soviet Government prevented Czechoslovakia from securing Marshall Plan aid. The lack of sufficient economic help, and a year of poor harvests, paved the way for a political "Second Revolution," as it was termed by the Communists. In February 1948, Gottwald and his followers, backed by the threat of potential Russian military aid, staged a bloodless coup d'etat. The Communist-controlled Ministry of the Interior had, for some time, been preparing for the events of February by dismissing politically unreliable policemen and replacing them with people loyal to the Party. When the non-Communist ministers asked that several dismissed police chiefs be reinstated, the Reds refused and the angry officials resigned in protest. The resignations of the non-Communists played into Gottwald's hands. Without opposition ministers to impede his program, he began to remodel the government along more directly Communist lines. Beneš felt forced to accept the reconstruction, surrounded as he was by the Communist secret police who now ruled Prague with a heavy hand. On March 10, 1948, the body of non-Communist Foreign Minister Jan Masaryk was found under one of the windows of the Foreign Ministry. He was reported to have committed suicide, although the circumstances in which he died were suspicious.

In April 1948, Gottwald presented the Constituent Assembly with a new constitution, designed to institute an authoritarian system. Beneš refused to consent and, rather than affirm Gottwald and his followers' actions, he resigned the presidency. Soon afterwards he died, a broken and tragic figure—and Gottwald was elected unanimously as President by the National Assembly.

Gottwald's Communist Party now began an all out-drive to remake

Czechoslovakia in the image of the U.S.S.R. A series of decrees transferred private property to state ownership and, typically, much emphasis was put on the development of heavy industry. Because Czechoslovakia had possessed such strong Western associations in the past, many Czechs now were suspect. "Action Committees" and "People's Courts" were organized to purge the country of intellectuals and journalists who objected to the government's new course. Commercial ties with the West were weakened and Czech trade was absorbed into the Communist bloc. Since, in Czechoslovakia, the government was able to build on earlier industrial foundations, the republic became one of the satellite system's most important producers of machinery, tools, and electrical equipment.

In accordance with typical Soviet methods, there was a pressing drive to deliver coal, steel, and armaments to Czechoslovakia's allies. Also in the usual Soviet fashion, failure was punished severely. During 1952, following a number of production failures, Rudolf Slánský, Secretary-General of the Communist Party, was selected as scapegoat, brought to trial, and executed. He was blamed for recurrent labor unrest and absenteeism, a shortage of housing and consumer goods, and other unhappy but normal byproducts of the Communists' emphasis on heavy industry to the exclusion of other sectors of the economy.

The Slánský execution, however, did not put an end to popular unrest. When the government, in 1953, instituted a currency reform that inflated the cost of consumer goods, extensive popular disorder resulted. In the industrial town of Plzeň, for example, riots broke out, which could be quelled only by military force.

In agriculture, collectivization was pushed until, by 1960, some 87 per cent of the arable soil was farmed collectively. As in other Communist states, the collective farms' production often fell far short of the amount of foodstuffs needed. Official goals were established, aimed at providing a diet for the average citizen, rich in meat and dairy products; but the aims were not realized, and public officials were reduced to urging city dwellers to work on farms.

In religious affairs, the seemingly unavoidable confrontation between the Communist Government and the Catholic Church came to pass. Outspoken priests who criticized the government were jailed. In the Slovak areas of Czechoslovakia there was a popular devotion to the Catholic Church that resembled the loyalty typical of the devout in Poland. Consequently, it was in Slovakia where trials of the clergy were the most common.

After the trial and hanging of Slánský and nine others implicated with him, Antonín Novotný, who had helped develop the charges against the condemned men, became the most important man in the country after Gottwald himself. Novotný was a "hard-line" Stalinist, who remained the symbol of Soviet dominance over Czechoslovak destinies for some fifteen years. Novotný became secretary-general of the Party following Slánský's downfall and, when Gottwald died, in March 1953, he became the most important figure in state and party. Four years later, he assumed the title of President.

When Poland and Hungary were disrupted by the popular insurrections of 1956, Novotný displayed the mailed fist of the typical Stalinist. The government threatened to strike down any Czechoslovak citizen who tried to emulate the rebellion taking place elsewhere in the satellite bloc. There were no uprisings, and the Stalinist system continued.

By 1962, however, there were signs that perhaps the Stalinist era in Czechoslovakia was nearing its end. Official glorification of Stalin and Gottwald was stopped, and many earlier Communists, like Slánský, were absolved after death of their supposed crimes. Church officials who had resisted the state now were freed. Perhaps this decline of Stalinism developed because of the failures of Communism in the economic sector. In 1964 and 1965, the Prague Government began to decentralize the economic system. Greater independence of action was allowed for plant managers and it was decided that a system of competition between industrial units would be inaugurated. As a corollary, workers were given incentives in the form of higher wages—dependent on how well their plant fared in the competition. Simultaneously, a moderate degree of intellectual freedom was allowed.

The moderating trend culminated in the deposition of Novotný by Alexander Dubček and his liberal colleagues in mid-1968. Unfortunately for those who sought to bring Czechoslovakia to a less Kremlin-directed position, Moscow decided not to tolerate a new, and possibly contagious, liberalization in Czechoslovakia. The Russian invasion of August, 1968, brought the Prague Government back to a degree of repression reminiscent of the pre-1962 Novotný regime. The reality of that repression was more fully indicated in September 1968, when the Czechoslovak legislature, at Russian dictation, passed law after law reinstituting limitations on the press and curbing freedom of expression.

Bulgaria

Although Communism had possessed strength in Bulgaria before 1939, the kingdom during World War II had been one of the Axis satellites. Then, despite the affiliation with Nazi Germany, the Sofia Government had refrained from sending troops against the U.S.S.R. because of a traditional empathy with the Russians. Hence, when Soviet troops in 1944 entered Bulgaria, it was not difficult for native Communists trained in Russia to take charge of the government.

A Soviet-sponsored government and Regency Council were installed in Sofia, and the new order was dominated by a wartime alliance of left-wing parties known as the Fatherland Front. In Bulgaria, too, the Communists entered into a cooperative effort with other parties until they could develop sufficient pressure from within to create a "people's democracy" and pull Bulgaria into the satellite bloc. The most important Bulgarian Communist, Georgi Dimitrov, who as an exile in Berlin had been charged with and acquitted of complicity in the setting of the *Reichstag* fire in 1933, and who ever since had been living in Moscow, returned to his homeland in 1944 and promptly became head of its Communist Party.

In 1946, a plebiscite was held to allow the people to choose between the monarchy and a republic. The voters overwhelmingly picked a republic, and Simeon II, the nine-year-old king, son of the late Boris III, joined his grandfather, Victor Emmanuel III of Italy, in exile. Elections followed, which both London and Washington denounced as coercive and fraudulent, and they resulted in the formation of a Communist-led government and the elevation of Dimitrov to the premiership.

Since Communism now had triumphed, it remained only to eliminate the opposition by means of political trials. The most important spokesman for the non-Communist Bulgarian peasantry was Nikola Petkov, a moderate Leftist. For his opposition to the Communist plans aimed at reshaping radically the lives of the peasantry, he was executed for treason in 1947—not long after the Bulgarian peace treaty had been signed in Paris. Then, in keeping with another familiar pattern in the satellite bloc, the Communist Party purged its Central Committee and all strata of Bulgarian society of suspected anti-Communists. Although the purge was marked by trials, with numerous confessions of treasonous acts, many in the outside world were horrified over the violation of human rights. To demonstrate her displeasure, the United States broke off diplomatic relations with Sofia and did not renew them until 1959.

Once internal affairs were ordered in this manner, Dimitrov involved the government in bridge-building with other satellite states, particularly Yugoslavia.[4] As harmonious relations seemed to be developing among the Communist states, Dimitrov, one of the most zealous Communists in the satellite bloc, proposed early in 1948 that the Red countries of Eastern Europe and the Balkans form a federation in alliance with the Soviet Union. Moscow rejected this idea, holding that a political federation or a "customs union" was not necessary to reinforce the solidarity of idealogically-allied Communist states. In 1949, Dimitrov died while undergoing medical treatment in a Moscow sanitarium.

In the decades of the 1950's and 1960's, Bulgaria moved more and more into the pattern set by the Soviet Union. She joined the Warsaw Pact and the United Nations (1955), collectivized the farms, nationalized industry, and struggled in vain to convert the agricultural coun-

---

[4] This policy was abandoned temporarily, during the period of a Soviet-Yugoslav break from 1948 to 1953.

try into an industrial power. Whenever opposition appeared, trials and purges drove it underground. Indeed, of all the Sovietized regimes in Europe, Bulgaria seemed most prone to resort to purges. In 1962, the Moscow-friendly Todor Zhivkov became Premier and First Secretary of the Communist Party, holding these offices into 1970.

Romania

Before World War II, the form of government in Romania had been authoritarian and rightist. In 1945, under Russian pressure, a new ministry was formed, largely made up of Communists. King Michael, never a strong personality, was ignored during the creation of the new order. As in other similar cases, there were protests from the West. It was pointed out by Western diplomats that the Yalta Conference, in February 1945, had been publicized in Eastern Europe and thus the officials in control in that area could not be ignorant of the Yalta Agreement's provision for free elections in all postwar Europe. The protests were fruitless, for the Soviets were in effective control in Romania and little save military force could have dislodged them.

The Soviets, however, declared themselves willing to enter into a three-power conference to consider the Romanian situation and, on the last day of December 1945, the United States, British, and Soviet foreign ministers met in Moscow. There was obtained at Moscow from Romanian leadership a promise to hold the free and unfettered elections promised at Yalta.

The elections were held, in late 1946, and questionable, probably fraudulent, methods were employed to sweep into office a Communist-controlled coalition. Soon after, King Michael was driven into exile. Into 1948, the usual purges and internal suppression of opposition transpired. In April 1948, Romania officially joined the list of states referring to themselves as "People's Republics." At the same time, Romania became a member of the official military and economic organizations of the Soviet orbit.

Unlike other states in the satellite system, where there were rising stars and plunging comets in the Communist firmament, in Romania, Gheorghe Gheorghiu-Dej became Secretary-General of the Communist Party in 1945 and remained in control of Romanian destinies for twenty years—until his death in 1965. During most of that time, he also filled the post of Prime Minister. Associated with him in the party and as Foreign Minister was Ana Pauker, a former Soviet citizen and fiery revolutionary. As a fervent Stalinist, she was dismissed in 1952, and then slipped into oblivion as de-Stalinization swept through the Soviet bloc.

Romania was largely agricultural in its traditions, and so centralized economic planning, as in other Communist states, dictated a push for heavy industry. By 1953, in keeping with Malenkov's emphasis on consumer goods in the Soviet Union, both the drive for greater industrial production and that for collectivization of farms was moderated.

Gheorghiu-Dej's Government reacted to the 1956 uprisings in Poland and Hungary by cruelly suppressing isolated outbreaks among ethnic minorites, such as those of Hungarian descent who revolted in sympathy with their repressed kinsmen in Budapest. Afterwards, however, Gheorghiu-Dej seemed impressed by the more nationalistic course adopted by Gomulka in Poland. His adaptation of that course to Romanian affairs resulted in policies lightening taxation at the same time that peasants were forced to incorporate their farms into cooperatives.

Between 1950 and 1962, Romanian manufacturing concerns demonstrated one of the greatest industrial growth rates in the world. Bucharest thereupon began to display a somewhat more independent course. She asked aid from hundreds of Western European technicians and engineers. She resisted complete incorporation into the economic system (COMECON) established by the Soviets. Perhaps most importantly, Russian cultural penetration in the schools was resisted and the Bucharest Government even attempted to act as the arbiter in the developing quarrel between Moscow and Peking. Gheorghiu-Dej had found that he was able to maintain a more independent course for his country by playing off the Russians against the Chinese, and by stressing that Romania was an ally of the Russians rather than a satellite.

In 1965, Gheorghiu-Dej died and Nicolae Ceausescu became Party leader, with Ion Gheorghe Maurer as Premier. Ceausescu followed an even more independent policy than had his predecessor by suggesting that Moscow's perennial military headship of the Warsaw Pact was anachronistic and that the command should be rotated among the member states. Ceausescu also joined Tito in suggesting that both NATO and the Warsaw Pact be scrapped and that some type of all-European security system be instituted in their place.

Most of the other satellite countries initially rejected the new Romanian proposals. But it is believed by many that Ceausescu's new and more independent stand did much to encourage Czechoslovakia's 1968 deviationism. It also is noteworthy that when, in 1968, Russia and the other "hard-line" powers of the Soviet Bloc occupied Czechoslovakia, Ceausescu stood with Tito in severely criticizing the action. The Romanian Government further reacted to the 1968 Czechoslovak crisis by proclaiming publically the reorgnization of Romania's defense forces. Ceausescu indicated that, should the Soviet Union and its satellite allies force their way across Romania's borders to reverse independent tendencies, they would be met by armed resistance.

THE HERETICS

A. Albania

A provisional government was established in Albania, in 1944, by Enver Hoxha, a thirty-six-year old Communist resistance leader. Quickly the Communists took over control of the little country (slightly larger than Vermont) through a "Democratic Front" that, in 1946, abolished the kingdom and established a republic. (King Zog died in exile.) Meanwhile, Hoxha had become Premier, head of the armed forces, Foreign Minister, Secretary of the Party, and a fanatic admirer of Joseph Stalin. He copied Stalin in his brutal disposal of opponents and in other ways tried to build Albania along Soviet lines in microcosm. The decanonizing of Stalin by Khrushchev displeased Hoxha, for he saw the new course set by the Kremlin as potentially dangerous to Communism's united world front.

When the Chinese schism with Moscow began, Hoxha entered into the ideological struggle on the side of Red China. Eventually, aid to Albania from Moscow was supplanted by aid from Red China. In 1961 the Soviets evacuated a naval base that they had maintained on Albanian soil and expelled Hoxha from the international party. By 1963 Hoxha had cut the last bonds with the Soviet military alliance and it became common for him to denounce Khrushchev and his successors. Moreover, as several of the people's democracies began to display greater independence in economic matters, Albania increased her trade with them, particularly with Romania.

China tended to regard Albania in the light of a first ideological conquest in Europe. Because of her fortunate geographic position, Albania was able to continue a more nearly independent course in trading with East European states at the same time that she took China's side in doctrinal quarrels. Benefiting from both connections, Albania enjoyed modest material progress and many of her institutions, particularly schools, were modernized.

B. Yugoslavia

Yugoslavia's course after World War II was so generally independent of Moscow that it was only truly a part of the satellite system for a short time after 1945. Yugoslavia became a Communist state at the end of the war. Like so many others, it was, at that point, closely tied to the U.S.S.R. In 1945 Yugoslavia was near economic ruin and was experiencing great political confusion. This condition resulted from the war and from a many-sided partisan conflict, in which Yugoslavs had spent as much time fighting one another as they had the Nazis. Eventually, the prize was won by Josip Broz, a man of Croatian peasant origin, who had become a Communist during World War I and now took control of Yugoslavia as Marshal Tito.

By 1945 Josip Broz Tito both controlled the armed forces of Yugoslavia and served as Secretary-General of the Yugoslav Communist Party. In November 1945, Tito felt it safe to hold elections for a Constituent Assembly. The National Front, a group of left-wing elements among whom the Communists were dominant, won some 90 per cent of the votes. The Constituent Assembly met, abolished the monarchy of exiled King Peter II and launched the Federal People's Republic of Yugoslavia.

In 1946 the Constituent Assembly adopted a constitution modeled after the Soviet constitution of 1936. The document produced a Yugoslavia consisting of six "Socialist Republics"—Serbia, Slovenia, Croatia, Montenegro, Bosnia-Herzegovina, and Macedonia. This new federalism, claimed the government, was the final solution to the ethnic tensions that had rent the fabric of Yugoslav society between World War I and World War II. Tito now, in addition to his Party post, assumed the offices of Premier and Minister of National Defense. In 1953 he became President.

At this point in its history, Yugoslavia still followed the typical pattern displayed by new People's Republics in that wartime resistance leaders who opposed Tito were tried and, in some cases, shot. The Catholic Church, which Tito claimed had been much too passive toward the Nazis during the war, was persecuted. Aloizije Cardinal Stepinac, head of the Catholic hierarchy in Croatia and chief opponent of the antireligious policies, was arrested. He was charged with the failure to protest sufficiently against Nazi occupation and was sentenced to sixteen years' imprisonment. Diplomatic relations with the Vatican were broken, and not fully restored until 1970, ten years after Stepinac's death. The methods used in Tito's purges drew strong verbal but generally ineffective protests from the West.

As was common in other such political configurations, the Yugoslav institutions of autocracy were masked by the outward trappings of constitutionally established democracy. In 1963 a new constitution was drawn up, which, as amended in 1967, assigned even greater power to the Communist Party. Tito was named president for an unlimited term, the Federal Assembly was redesigned to consist of five indirectly elected chambers, and the country's name was changed to Socialist Federal Republic of Yugoslavia.

The first task of postwar Yugoslavia was to repair a shattered economy. It has been estimated that, at the fighting's end, half the farming livestock had disappeared, as had almost every means of mechanized transport that should have been used in agriculture. Immediate aid came from UNRRA, which spent nearly 15 per cent of its budget in Yugoslavia, and many Yugoslavs survived the winter of 1945–1946 only because of the UN agency's energetic efforts. The economic crisis hastened the usual communization. Belgrade quickly began to nationalize industries, collectivize agriculture, and create state corporations to manage the country's foreign trade. In 1947 the First Five-Year Plan was introduced.

At the end of World War II, Yugoslavia's foreign policy was linked with that of the Soviet Union. Hence, the Yugoslav deputation in the United Nations followed Soviet leadership. More generally, Tito's policy was to aid Communist elements wherever he could. The Yugoslavs joined the Cominform, secretly helped Greek Communist guerrillas in their attempt to take control of Greece, and secured close relationships with such satellite neighbors as Bulgaria.

Yet, under the surface of seemingly untroubled Communist relationships, there rumbled tremors of disharmony. Complaints came to Moscow, as early as 1944–1945, regarding the misconduct of the Soviet armies in Yugoslavia. Moreover, in 1945, Soviet diplomacy had failed to secure for Yugoslavia the greatly desired port of Trieste. Therefore, by 1946, Tito was making public pronouncements, which did not have the usual tone of subservience to the Kremlin heard in the satellite bloc. This underlying hostility continued to develop until in March 1948, the Soviet Government complained that its army officers and technicians in Yugoslavia were being mistreated. Charges and counter-charges flew back and forth between Belgrade and Moscow. Tito was willing to compromise on Russo-Yugoslav differences, but Stalin's rule was that Russia must dominate absolutely in the Communist bloc. Tito appealed to other Red countries for moral support, but did not receive it, as those to whom he appealed dared not antagonize Stalin. The other Communist bloc members dutifully agreed that Tito was guilty of improper unfriendliness to the Soviet Union, of Marxist-Leninist deviationism, and of personal ambition and great arrogance. In June 1948, the Cominform expelled Yugoslavia.

After 1948 Yugoslavia charted a new course. She suffered an immediate and total economic blockade from the Soviet Union, but Tito's Government survived. Trade and aid came from the West, and the United States, by 1951, even provided war materials. As part of its new international attitude, Yugoslavia also sought better relations with Greece. In 1954, this *rapprochement* bore fruit in a Yugoslav-Greek alliance.

Despite his new friendliness to the West, Tito made few domestic political or economic concessions. The state continued to be run along Marxist-Leninist lines. The realities of international politics dictated that the West, however much Westerners might be repelled by Tito's political beliefs and practices, had to furnish Yugoslavia with aid. A strong Yugoslavia outside the Soviet bloc might well erode the unity of the Communist world, and the Western powers were well aware of this. Indeed, for several years after 1948, the spectre of "Titoism" did haunt the Kremlin.

During 1955, Bulganin and Khrushchev, in the moderating atmosphere that followed Stalin's death, tried to better relations with Yugoslavia. In 1956, Tito visited the Soviet Union. Yugoslavia remained sufficiently uncommitted, however, to play host to the Conference of Uncommitted Nations in 1961. In 1964, Tito's Government joined COMECON, the economic organization of the satellite bloc. However, this did not mean a complete reabsorption into the Communist sphere dominated by the Kremlin, for Tito continued to criticize *both* NATO and the Warsaw Pact simultaneously. It was characteristic of the uncommitted Yugoslav position that, at the time of the 1968 Czechoslovak crisis, Tito should have denounced in no uncertain terms the brutality of the Soviet Union.

By the 1960's, there had developed in Yugoslavia what Tito called "a socialist market economy." Restrictions were placed on typical Communist planners who urged a complete centralization of the Yugoslav economy. Instead, it was ordered that the rule of supply and demand be allowed to develop much of the price structure and market activity. This meant that individual business enterprises were to be given the opportunity to operate more autonomously than in other Communist states.

By Communist standards, the Yugoslavia of the 1960's and early 1970's was a relatively free country. No criticism of Tito or the government was allowed, but artists and writers could, within these limits, pursue their own objectives. Public discussion of important matters was encouraged, and even the arts demonstrated a marked preference for non-Marxist themes. In 1965, Tito declared that "the practice of political people" deciding what should or should not be built, or what investment policies would or would not be followed, was to be discontinued. In the future, he indicated, such decisions would be left to the operators of the individual factories.

Thus, Yugoslavia remained the triumphant heretic. To indicate that all her policies were decidedly more moderate than those of the other Communist states would be misleading. In the 1960's, for instance, men of letters had greater freedom in Romania. But one thing remained constant. Yugoslavia, given a greater degree of independence than other Communist states by its geographic separation from the Soviet Union, could continue to follow an independent course. She thus could maintain closer relations with the West than would those satellites located on Russia's doorstep.

THE BLOC'S NEIGHBORS

A. Finland

At each end of the long band of Communist states stretching across Central Europe from north to south were nations that were subjected to extreme pressures from the Soviet bloc, but did not succumb. In the far north, Finland, drawn into World War II on the Axis side because of its enmity for the Soviet Union, ceded territory to Russia at the end of the war. The nearly 500,000 Finns living in the lost area moved into a reduced Finland rather than live under Soviet rule. From the date of the peace settlement in early 1947, the need to maintain neutral, yet not subservient, relations with the U.S.S.R. dominated Finnish foreign policy.

Internally, Helsinki strove to reach a high standard of living, in part, to limit the number of dissatisfied unemployed who might be susceptible to the arguments of local Communists. Moreover, the Finnish Government constantly was vigilant so that a coup like the one that swept non-Communists out of the government in Czecho-slovakia, in 1948, might be avoided.

The center of Communist strength in Finland was to be found in the unions. Such elements were counterbalanced by the armed forces, which were antagonistic to communism and steadfastly loyal to the Republic. There was a brief, although not major, participation by Communists in Finnish government at the ministerial level until 1948. In the elections of that year, the moderates made great gains at the expense of the Reds. Communist representatives in the unicameral legislature (*Eduskunta*) numbered 38 out of 200. Thereafter, until 1966, coalition governments regularly were comprised of Social Democrats and Agrarians.

In her diplomatic relations, Finland found it necessary to prove to Russia that she could act as part of the Soviet Union's buffer zone against potential Western invasions without actually becoming a satellite country. Therefore, a treaty was concluded whereby the Finns were to consult with Russia immediately if West Germany, or any other Western state, threatened invasion of the U.S.S.R. There were some occasions following World War II when Kremlin pressure forced Finnish cabinets to resign; however, as late as 1970, complete Soviet domination of Finland in the manner of the states within the satellite bloc had not occurred. Russia had experienced the stubbornness that could be demonstrated by the Finns when pushed too hard by their large neighbor to the east. Moreover, the Soviets were not anxious to alarm Sweden to the point where she would seek an alliance with the Western powers. Periodic difficulties in Soviet-Finn relations normally were resolved by the granting of minor Finnish concessions. Thus, the Finnish authorities allowed the Communist-dominated "World Federation of Democratic Youth" to be held in their country in 1962.

After the 1966 elections, the moderate Social Democrats became the largest party in the country and the Center Party (former Agrarians), the second largest. A new Government was formed, with Social Democratic Party leaders Rafael Paasio and Mauno Koivisto, successively, at its helm. In their cabinets were included variously two or three Communists, as a reflection of what the Finns regarded as a growing *détente* between Russia and the West. The Finns apparently believed that ideological lines were blurring sufficiently in Europe to allow Communists to enter a government without fear of a consequent Communist coup. Koivisto's came to be replaced by Dr. Ahti Karjalainen after the parliamentary elections in 1970.

In economic matters, Finnish ties to the Soviet Union were strong.

About 70 per cent of Finnish land is forested. Thus, Finland's primary exports were timber, pulp, and paper, which were exchanged for Russian fertilizers, cereals, and oil. The bulk of Finnish trade was directed toward the Soviet Union and it remained so, even after the Finns had finished paying their World War II reparations bill to the Soviet Union. It generally was understood among the nations that the Finnish Government, as well as her people, would have preferred greater commercial contact with Western countries and perhaps eventual membership of the Common Market. One of the conditions of continued Finnish independence of Russia, however, was that no extensive commercial intimacy develop between Finland and the West.

B. Greece

At the southern end of the band of Communist nations stretching across Europe lay Greece and Turkey. In Greece, British influence was still extensive during the final years of World War II. Winston Churchill was determined that Greece not be subjected to Soviet domination. When the British forces returned to Athens in the fall of 1944, George Papandreou returned with them, pledged to form a representative government. When the Nazis retired from Greece, however, the Communists in the resistance movement rebelled against the reinstitution of the royal government. British troops intervened and suppressed the rebellious forces. The Greek Government then promised amnesty for political crimes and pledged that civil liberties would be maintained with respect to the Communists.

Many of the Communists wanted no part of a government in Greece that would involve cooperation with royalists. Several Reds escaped into Yugoslavia or hid in the mountains. The Yugoslav, Bulgarian, and Albanian governments began to aid their Communist brethren. By the autumn of 1946, the villages of Greece were torn by civil war. The involvement of Greece's Communist neighbors in this civil conflict was so obvious that a UN commission convicted these states of stimulating guerrilla warfare in the Greek peninsula.

In 1947, the Greek Government asked the United States for aid, for the British had declared themselves incapable of restricting the incursions of communism in the Balkans. The Truman Doctrine, inspired by Greek requests for help, led to the despatch of United States military and economic aid. This help from the United States, coupled with Tito's defection from Moscow, which brought an end to Yugoslav aid to Greek Reds, enabled the Greek Government to break the Communist rebellion. By 1949, the insurrection had died out and prisons were filled with captured rebels. In November 1949, the last British troops returned home.

Three years of vicious civil strife, added to the destruction wreaked by retreating Nazis at the end of the war, had ravaged the country.

Reconstruction, largely with American aid, began at once. The task was not an easy one. Political instability interfered. There were constant reorderings of the cabinet. Intense partisan rivalries prevented national cohesion and stability. In 1946, the prewar royal dynasty had been restored by plebiscite. In 1947, King George II died and was succeeded by his brother Paul. In 1951, the forty-year-old constitution was revised to allow distribution of large estates among the peasantry. The new constitution forbade civil servants from becoming Communists and, in 1952, women were given the vote.

The first really stable postwar government was formed in 1952 by Field Marshal Alexander Papagos, former director of the Greek forces resisting the Italian invasion of 1940. Under Papagos and Constantine G. Karamanlis, another strong man who succeeded him, majority support was commanded for a program that started Greece on an eleven-year period of economic progress. By the mid-1950's, economic conditions had improved markedly and the situation had ameliorated in both agriculture and manufacturing. The Greeks became exceptionally active in shipping and developed an international network of tramp ships that plied the seas to all corners of the world. The Greeks also capitalized on their famous classical heritage and the beauty of the Aegean to build up a substantial tourist trade.

Two elements were particularly important in maintaining the strength of the Greek economy: (1) American foreign aid; and (2) the migration of surplus labor to northern, industrialized Europe. Considerable help from the United States flowed into Greece. From 1945 to 1962, American aid amounted to more than $3,000,000,000, which was canalized into electric power installations, land improvement projects, and factories to produce consumer goods. However, despite beneficial economic development, there still was much unemployment. A long-range program was initiated in 1959 to deal with the overabundance of labor. Fortunately for Greece, at this time, France and West Germany were suffering from labor shortages. Along with workers from Spain and Italy, Greek laborers went west and north and worked in French and German factories. When they returned, they brought with them sizable amounts of money, saved while working in northern Europe, which often was invested in small businesses.

Despite material advances, cabinets commonly were charged with unfair taxing practices and maintaining useless bureaucrats on government payrolls. In 1961, the Karamanlis Government was accused of election fraud and the cabinet assailed as a dictatorship, although Karamanlis placed no restraint on opposition political rallies or public comment. Eventually, in 1963, Karamanlis resigned in protest when the King refused to listen to his advice concerning the impropriety of a state visit to London where he probably would be heckled by Communists.[6] Then a national election followed, which produced no clear majority for one party. It thus was impossible to

[6] Such hostile demonstrations did in fact take place.

form a strong ministry. Another election, in 1964, did give a majority to the Center Union Party of elderly George Papandreou, and ministerial stability was renewed briefly with Papandreou at the head of the cabinet. The line of succession also continued in the monarchy. When King Paul died, in 1964, he was succeeded by his twenty-three-year-old son, Constantine II.

Beginning in 1965, political divisiveness once again appeared. Rumors of a potential Communist coup were common. Eventually, a group of army officers rode the rumors of the Communist threat to power. In April 1967, claiming that the country was in imminent danger of Red insurrection, a junta of army officers took control of the country and muzzled the voices of opposition through the establishment of a tight military dictatorship. Toward the end of the year, King Constantine fled to Italy, after an unsuccessful attempt to oust the military government that came to be headed by Premier George Papadopoulos.

In foreign policy, Greece indicated her affiliation to the Western community by taking up membership in NATO in 1951. Thereafter, the Greeks participated in a small way in the Korean War and provided bases for the Atlantic alliance. In 1962, Greece was granted associate membership in the Common Market. The decade of the 1960's saw continuing dispute with Turkey and Great Britain over the situation in the nearby former British island colony of Cyprus.

C. Turkey

Almost until the end of World War II, Turkey had maintained a strict neutrality. The Turkish stance was a result of an historical experience, indicating that the state controlling the outlet into the Mediterranean constantly would find itself embroiled in European power politics. In consequence, the Turks believed that the best interests of their country would be served if they remained free of European entanglements by pursuing a neutral course.

During the war, Turkey was subjected to pressures from both Germany and Russia. Germany desired Turkish territory as a pathway into the Arab states. Russia sought the same area during the war so that, after the conflict, if the Turkish Straits were not controlled by Russia, at least they would be under the dominance of a Soviet-controlled regime. The Turks, however, managed to resist these influences until 1945.

In early 1945, Turkey at last declared war on Germany, thus qualifying for charter membership in the United Nations. When Hitler's armies were destroyed and the Reich surrendered, the Soviet Union remained an obvious threat to Turkey. When the defeat of Germany had become a certainty, the Soviet Union denounced a Russo-Turkish nonaggression pact dating back twenty years to 1925 and claimed that the time had come when its terms would have to be reconsidered. Then, at the end of the war, Russian total designs on Turkey became clear. The Soviets wanted not only to have a hand in the control of the Straits, but desired a strip of territory in northern Turkey, in the Caucasus. The Turks resisted this pressure and turned to the West for aid. Help from the West subsequently involved them, first under the Truman Doctrine and then in the Western Alliance.

After the death of Mustapha Kemal Atatürk in 1938, General Ismet Inönü had taken over the presidency. But the long tenure of his People's Party had led to criticism of governmental corruption and inefficiency. There also developed, because of the war's impact, an unfortunate economic situation. A tremendous inflation ensued and the government was unable to retard it. This troublous situation gave rise to the development of a strong political opposition. In 1946, the Turkish Democratic Party was founded, and began urging relaxation of the state control over the economy.

In 1950, the Democrats took control of the unicameral Grand National Assembly. Adnan Menderes, a lawyer, became Prime Minister. It was the first time in Turkish history that a government had changed hands because of a truly free election. The step thus was applauded in the West as a move toward final Westernization of Turkish institutions.

In affirmation of the direction being taken by the Turks the United States launched an aid program for Turkey. In the decade after 1947, some $1000,000,000 poured into Turkey from Washington. About three-quarters of this money was appropriated for military use. With this support and foreign loans, the Menderes Government was able to stimulate internal economic growth in both the industrial and agricultural sectors.

The new ministry also chartered a course of religious toleration. The Kemalist period had been typified by a strong anticlericalism (see Chapter 12), but, in the 1950's, the establishment of Moslem schools was allowed. In contrast to Atatürk's order that Turkish dress should be Westernized, the Menderes regime allowed people to wear whatever type of clothes they desired. This meant that, in Turkish rural areas, traditional apparel and ways of life reappeared. This was not unopposed by certain progressives, who desired continued Westernization along the lines set down by Kemal in the between-the-wars period.

Some of the gains of the Democratic regime were paid for by a large indebtedness to the Western European states, which Turkey repaid with United States aid money. This put the Turks in the position of having to ask for more United States help. The Americans declined to expand their aid, and, by the late 1950's, Turkey found it increasingly difficult to obtain foreign credit. This meant that the government had to restrict the import and production of consumer goods to concentrate on essentials. With the initiation of a policy of restriction on consumer goods, popular discontent appeared. The Democrats reacted by using harsh restrictive methods against political opposition. The freedom of the press again was limited, and opposition party members were imprisoned on insubstantial charges. Throughout the Menderes decade that had begun in 1950, popular disaffection increased and culminated, on May 27, 1960, in a bloodless coup d' etat by a group of army officers led by General Cemal Gürsel. Shortly after, a special court convicted Menderes and two other ministers of violating the Turkish constitution. The three men were tried, condemned, and executed in 1961.

As often is the case when one group suddenly is ousted from office and another instituted, the new leaders did not bring well-formulated policies with them. General Gürsel, however, promised to revive parliamentary rule and, in November 1961, a new constitution was adopted, providing for a bicameral legislature and a strong executive. Gürsel became president and the seventy-seven-year old Ismet Inönü was appointed Prime Minister.

Despite the fact that Inönü was a figure around whom most Turks could rally, he tended to introduce a rather rigid bureaucratic system, strictly controlling the economy. Moreover, power actually seemed to reside in the hands of army chiefs. As the economy languished, widespread discontent resulting from a general lack of confidence in the government forced Inönü and his Republican People's Party out of power in 1965.

Following prompt elections, the Justice Party came into office. It included many former Menderes supporters, but they were careful to indicate that they desired no return to the policies of the 1950's. Under Premier Süleyman Demirel, some of the controls now were removed from the economy, which tended then to become more productive. Greater production was a reflection of the fact that Turkey had undergone a major transformation since the revolution of 1922, which had swept Atatürk into power. Turkey now possessed industrial resources and a reservoir of manpower that placed it among the first rank of rapidly developing nations.

In foreign policy, Turkey followed a generally pro-Western course. She extended her international connections to the West by joining NATO, became part of the Balkan Alliance, and joined the Central Treaty Organization (CENTO). Turks fought with UN forces in the Korean War and, despite continual Soviet pressure, Turkey remained closely tied to the West. Nevertheless, in the later 1960's, and into 1970, Turkey began to seek a more flexible and better relationship with the U.S.S.R.—primarily because the Soviets seemed to be moderating their attempts to exert pressure on their non-Communist neighbors.

THE GRECO-TURKISH CONFRONTATION OVER CYPRUS

Both Greece and Turkey were integral parts of the Western alliance system. A NATO headquarters for the Eastern Mediterranean had been established at Izmir, in Turkey, and the military personnel of the two states worked in close cooperation. This working relationship helped both states when, immediately after the war, they had stood alone, threatened by the expansion of communism. This fortunate unity of purpose, however, soon was threatened by disruption. Indeed, the two states came close to an absolute break because of a controversy over Cyprus.

During the late 1950's, Greeks and Turks periodically were inflamed by an emotional dispute over Cyprus, a strategic island that had been under British control since 1878. In World War II, the island played an important role as a British base. Some 80 per cent of the 600,000 people living in Cyprus were Greek, and the others were Turkish. After the war, the possibility of partitioning Cyprus between the two nationalities arose, but they were so intermingled that no division along national lines seemed possible.

When the Turks pressed their claims for Cyprus, they brought up the fact that the island was located only 40 miles from Turkey whereas it was some 660 miles from Greece. The Greeks pointed out in turn that, regardless of its position, the population of the island was mostly Greek. These counterclaims were made more emotional by the fact that the British still remained in control of the island, and thus there were tumultuous anti-British demonstrations in the cities.

In consequence, the British carried on negotiations with both Greece and Turkey. They aimed at the establishment of some kind of independent republic on Cyprus, with meaningful representation for both Greece and Turkey. In 1959, it was arranged that the Cypriot state would have a president who was to be a Greek, and a Turkish vice-president. The cabinet was to be a mixture of the two nationalities. On August 16, 1960, Cyprus did become an independent republic, under President Archbishop Makarios III (Michael C. Mouskos). In 1961, Cyprus joined the British Commonwealth of Nations.

The causes for disagreement remained, however, and it was not long before misunderstandings and hatred led to the renewal of bloody conflict betwen Greek and Turkish Cypriots. In 1963, they fell to fighting once more, the most important cause being the Turks' fear that the Greeks intended to cancel their minority rights. Early in 1964, the UN established a peace-keeping force in Cyprus to maintain order. There followed a variety of proposals to maintain the peace in Cyprus, but, as late as 1970, conflict on the island remained a potentially disruptive force in a Western alliance already weakening because of other problems.

The Two Germanies and Other States of Western Europe

25

WEST GERMANY (FEDERAL REPUBLIC OF GERMANY)

A. The Origins of the West German Republic

At the end of World War II, Germany lay in ruins; bare subsistence was provided for its people by the occupying countries. Since the Western zones now received no food from the breadbasket of prewar Germany in the East, the West Germans were dependent on continued assistance from the Allies, especially the United States. Industrially, as recounted earlier, the developing Cold War situation soon led to a halt in the West in the dismantling of factories and the exaction of reparation. The Allies began to think that West Germany might become a functional part of the Western alliance. Consequently steps were taken to aid the West Germans in creating a self-supporting economy.

Gradually, Allied military officials allowed the Germans to assume many of the tasks of government. Political parties reappeared, most of them based on the politics of Weimar Germany. As in the eastern zone one of the first parties to reappear was the German Communist Party (KPD). In all three western zones the KPD emerged as the fourth largest party. This meant that they were able to gather no more than 5 to 8 per cent of the vote in the elections held at the state government level between 1946 and 1948. When the Federal Republic was created in 1949, the KPD, which had posed as a democratic anti-Nazi organization, struck out in a more clearly Moscow-oriented direction. Then its appeal to the voters lessened markedly. In 1956, the West German Constitutional Court outlawed the KPD as "unconstitutional."

At the same time that the Communists remerged, a new Social Democratic Party (SPD) was formed. Under the leadership of Kurt

Schumacher, who bore the scars of ten years in Nazi concentration camps, the party designed a platform at Wennigsen, in October 1945. The platform rejected a KPD offer to fuse the two political parties and, instead, urged a program of coperation with the democratic parties. The pronouncements of the new party were singularly nationalistic, as Schumacher seemed determined to escape accusations like those hurled against the SPD in the 1920's, namely, that the Socialists were un-German and treasonable.

During 1946, the SPD developed into the second strongest party in the West German states. It therefore was strong enough, when it came time to draft a constitution, to force a compromise with the other parties on such matters as the role of the churches in education and the social duties of the state to its citizens.

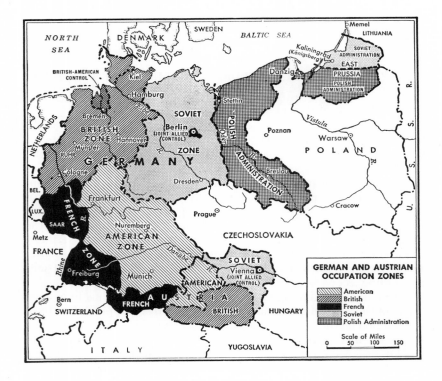

The strongest party developing in Western Germany was the Christian Democratic Union (CDU). Founded at Bad Godesberg in December 1946, the CDU was much less cohesive a unit than the SPD. The only common sentiment that ran throughout its component parts was a conviction that West Germany should have a religiously-oriented middle-class party to stand against the SPD and KPD. Only gradually did the party become more tightly constructed as cohesiveness became necessary to mount election campaigns for national offices in 1949.

The CDU was formed out of many older elements. However, basically, it was a revival of the old Center Party of the Weimar Republic, firmly taking up a stance in the middle of the political road. The Cologne group within the party, particularly Konrad Adenauer, former mayor of the Rhineland metropolis, urged that the narrow Catholic framework of the old Center Party be abandoned and that Protestants should be included to broaden the electoral base of the party. Thus, the CDU was molded along the lines of major political parties in the American two-party system. It embraced people of various religious viewpoints, conservatives, liberals, former Nationalist Party members, and even some Socialists.

The first platform of the CDU was a liberal one in that it demanded the strictest anti-Nazi measures, and adherence to such moderately socialistic concepts then current in the German society as the abolition of monopolistic capitalism. By 1946, its leftist tendencies had lessened somewhat, particularly after Konrad Adenauer emerged as the CDU's most prominent member. Although various of the CDU proposals issued just after the war called for agrarian, currency, and industrial reforms, the schism between the CDU and SPD remained a deep one. It was the CDU that assumed the primary responsibility when the task of planning the reconstruction of West Germany gradually was handed over by the Allies. This made it the strongest political party in West Germany and rapidly gave its program an increasingly conservative cast.

In addition to the major parties there were several smaller political organizations in the West Zone. The most important of these in terms of long-range consequence was the semiconservative middle-class Free Democratic Party (FDP). First organized in 1948, the FDP, by 1949, had become the third largest party. It was composed of many who, before the Nazi years, had belonged to the Weimar Democratic and German People's parties. Standing to the Right of the CDU, its program heavily stressed a program of free enterprise. In 1949, the FDP entered a coalition government with the CDU's Adenauer, as a consequence of which the FDP chairman, Dr. Theodor Heuss, later assumed the presidency of West Germany.

In 1948, the Western powers announced that the U.S.S.R., because of its noncooperativeness, had forced the Allies to go ahead with the establishment of a new state in the West. On July 1, 1948, the military governors of the three Western zones met with the minister-presidents of the eleven West German states. On July 26, the German state governments accepted Allied propositions and called for a Parliamentary Council to convene in Bonn, on September 1, to draft a provisional constitution. For eight months the drafting committee labored. Although the Allies tended to interfere and thus prolong deliberations, the work of the constitutional committee was finished on May 8, 1949. To emphasize its provisional character the document produced was called the "Basic Law" rather than a constitution.[1] On September 21, 1949, the Western Allies formally recognized the Federal Republic of West Germany. Only two weeks later an East German state (the German Democratic Republic) was created by the Russians.

The Basic Law of the Federal Republic demonstrated the influence of the Western Allies and hence Western systems of government. It began with the customary prologue on the rights of citizens. It then provided for a chief executive in the form of a president, who possessed far less authority than his counterpart during the Weimar Republic. The most important tasks of the president were to grant pardons, sign treaties, accredit ambassadors, and appoint the federal chancellor *only* after the *Bundestag* (the lower house) had chosen him. Other than these tasks, the president's duties were largely ceremonial. The first president was Theodor Heuss, who, in addition to being the chairman of the FDP, was one of the chief architects of the Basic Law.

Real executive authority was placed in the chancellor, who had extensive personal prerogatives. The chancellor could be dismissed by a vote of no confidence in the *Bundestag* only if a successor had already been agreed upon.[2] A defeated chancellor, if he wished, could then take his case to the voting public by asking the president to dissolve the *Bundestag* and by ordering national elections.

The national legislative body was bicameral, with most of the authority centered in the lower house, the *Bundestag*, elected every four years. The upper house, the *Bundesrat*, represented the eleven states (reduced to nine, in 1952, by the amalgamation of three states into Baden-Württemberg, and increased to ten in 1957 by the admission of the Saar as a West German state). The *Bundesrat* could veto certain legislation and ratify treaties, but in reality exerted little influence. It was to the *Bundestag* that the chancellor was responsible and all meaningful bills required the sanction of the lower house.

Reflective of fears that Nazism might revive was Article 21, which contained the government's prerogative of declaring anti-democratic parties unconstitutional. After the Basic Law's initiation as a working constitution, Article 21 was used on several occasions to outlaw extremists groups of both the Left and Right.

Article 24 was of great interest in light of the desires of many statesmen in the post-war period to begin working towards the construction of a United States of Europe. It stipulated that the Federal Republic might "transfer sovereign powers" to international institutions.

---

[1] The idea of a provisional document derived from the hope that the constitution might someday become the permanent basis of government for all Germans when the Soviet Zone would be incorporated as part of a reunited Germany.

[2] In this fashion the drafters of the Basic Law hoped to escape the instability that so troubled the Weimar Government.

Once more Germany tried democracy. As was the case after World War I, the new federal state was regarded by many Germans as a creation of the conquerors. It obviously would take time and much testing to satisfy the people with the new form of government. The Federal Republic also found it necessary to combat another dangerous tendency: the desire of many Germans, surrounded by the destruction of much of their material wealth, to shirk civic responsibility as they centered their complete attention on gaining for themselves the material necessities of life.

B.   Politics and Economics in the Young Republic

The Federal Republic early developed many political characteristics that differed from those of the Weimar period. Extremist parties gained little momentum and there was little of the party splintering that so troubled the Weimar Republic. The consolidation of large parties was further reinforced, in 1953, by a regulation granting seats in the legislature only to those organizations obtaining at least 5 per cent of all votes cast in West Germany. By 1961, only three parties were represented in the *Bundestag*.

The outstanding political personality in postwar German life was Konrad Adenauer. At 73, he became Chancellor of the Federal Republic in 1949 and retained that office until his resignation in 1963. A son of the Rhineland, Adenauer had been Mayor of Cologne from 1917 to 1933. In 1933, he was ejected from his office by the Nazis. During the Weimar period, Adenauer had gained many influential friends in Rhineland financial circles. He also enjoyed many contacts with Americans through his second wife, the daughter of a German-American Professor, Ferdinand Zinsser. Although not notably important in the anti-Hitler movement, Adenauer was placed under arrest for a time by the Nazis and his political persecution by the Hitlerites, as it did for many another, proved a valuable political asset in the postwar period. After the war, the British reinstated him as Mayor of Cologne, but he became involved in a dispute with British authorities over where the emphasis should be placed in his city's rebuilding program. In consequence, he was dismissed and he turned to fulltime association with the CDU in which he soon took the most prominent position. He then presided over the convention which framed the Bonn constitution.

The first federal election, in 1949, saw the CDU gain slightly more votes than the SPD, and a coalition ministry was formed with the cooperation of various smaller political groupings. Adenauer was chosen first Chancellor by the margin of one vote (his own), and organized a cabinet. He then proclaimed his objectives: the ending of foreign occupation; the rebuilding of German armed forces; the participation of the Federal Republic in the defense of Europe with Western Allies; the reunification of Germany; the eradication of

Franco-German hostility; the material integration of the West European community; and intimate association with the United States.[3]

Generally, the parties in the Federal Republic grew more conservative as they followed Adenauer's example. The CDU began advocacy of a free-market economy and moved far away from the party's early stress on the need for a degree of socialization by rejecting economic planning (the dismal results of centralized economic planning in East Germany had much to do with this shift). The party also urged reduced taxes on higher incomes to increase incentive. Important in this gravitation toward less restrictive economic policies was the influence of Ludwig Erhard, former Minister of Economics in Bavaria, who brought to the CDU his belief in free enterprise. Erhard continued to proclaim the need for a "Social Market Economy" in Germany, a system combining little restriction on profit-taking with a call for employers' responsibility for the social security of the community.

In 1953, there was an electoral campaign in which the CDU took credit for the economic recovery West Germany had enjoyed to that point. Although the SPD accused the Government of being the tool of large industrial concerns, the CDU's slogan, "The Republic of Prosperity," proved attractive to the voters and Adenauer's party increased its share of the vote from 31 to 45 per cent.

During the 1950's the SPD, like other European Socialist parties, gradually turned its back on doctrinaire Marxism. There were still many major differences with the CDU, particularly did the SPD disagree with Erhard's "Social Market Economy" concept, but the Socialists continued to moderate their system. After the death of Kurt Schumacher, in 1952, Willy Brandt (Karl Herbert Frahm), popular mayor of West Berlin, became the most influential SPD leader. Under Brandt's leadership, the party became much less utopian and far more concerned with immediate social and political gains.

By 1955 West Germany was in the midst of an amazing period of economic growth. Until 1961, when the growth rate slowed somewhat, the economy had expanded at the rate of some 7 per cent annually. Unemployment almost disappeared, and, by 1962, it had become necessary to bring to West Germany more than half a million workers from Italy, Spain, and Greece to fill the available jobs in German factories. The European Common Market greatly stimulated German commerce and industry and a favorable balance of trade was maintained. Economic affluence made it relatively easy for Germany to begin payment on prewar debts. In 1961, to help slow down the gold drain on the United States, Germany repaid debts to Washington at an accelerated rate.

In the 1960's the Bonn Government had recovered from the war

---

[3] Adenauer often voiced the opinion in these early years of the Federal Republic that the generosity of the United States to a vanquished foe had been unequaled at any time in history.

so extensively that it entered into foreign aid programs for various underdeveloped countries. West Germany soon was spending $1,000,000,000 each year on such assistance.

In the presence of such prosperity it was impossible for the SPD to dislodge the CDU from office. Konrad Adenauer continued to direct German affairs, and, during his fourteen years in office, molded the Bonn Government to fit his own concepts of statecraft.

Succeeding elections revealed popular satisfaction with Adenauer's regime. In 1957 the Chancellor's forces took 54 per cent of the *Bundestag's* 270 seats. By 1959, there was a marked trend toward a two-party system in West Germany as the CDU and the SPD continued to grow at the expense of smaller parties.

It was not until 1959 that the CDU suffered its first major crisis. At the end of the 1950's, many began to raise the possibility that Adenauer, at eighty-three, was too old to carry on the functions of government. It often was asserted that Ludwig Erhard, commonly identified with West Germany's prosperity, should succeed the "old one." There were those parliamentarians and bureaucrats, too, who resented the authoritarian manner in which Adenauer conducted the affairs of government.

A search for a suitable successor began, but the CDU found that, outside Erhard, the authoritarian "chancellor's democracy" did not tend to develop talented successors. Too, Adenauer showed little faith in Erhard's ability to direct German foreign affairs. While the search was proceeding, Adenauer, who apparently had decided to move to the largely honorary post of president, which now was open with the retirement of Heuss, astounded Bonn and international political circles by withdrawing his name as a presidential candidate. He indicated that the present Berlin crisis and other pressing foreign problems made it necessary for him to remain in the chancellor's office. Party leaders grumbled, but Adenauer remained chancellor. In July 1959, the presidential election was held and the CDU candidate, Dr Heinrich Luebke, former Minister of Food and Agriculture, became president.

By 1961 disenchantment had developed because the Berlin Wall had been erected and, if for no other reason, simply because Adenauer had been in office so long. The SPD counted on the popularity of Willy Brandt to win the chancellorship for them, and the Socialists did run better. But Adenauer was able once again to form a coalition with the FDP by promising that he would relinquish his post sometime before the 1965 elections.

A political scandal, in October 1962, finally set in motion forces that were to bring the Adenauer era to an end. The West German news magazine, *Der Spiegel*, published an article describing certain defects in the armed forces. The magazine's publisher, Rudolph Augstein, and four of his staff members, were arrested on charges of treason. It was widely held in the press that the arrest was the result of Defense Minister Franz Joseph Strauss' enmity for Augstein. Indeed, it was true that *Der Spiegel* had specialized in attacks on the government. The FDP now threatened to withdraw support from the coalition on the ground that the Free Democratic Minister of Justice, Wolfgang Stammberger, had not been consulted before the arrests were made.

As public cries of "Gestapo" were hurled at the government for infringing the freedom of the press, Adenauer began to search for a way out. The Chancellor persuaded all cabinet members to resign and formed a new cabinet without Strauss. Thus, he was rid of Strauss without having had to dismiss him directly. But the FDP and even some members of the CDU now pressed the Chancellor for the date when he would leave office. Again Adenauer looked for an escape hatch and even discussed the possibility of excluding the FDP from the government and going into coalition with the opposition SPD.

But the FDP's distrust of the Chancellor was too great for them to continue in coalition with him unless the old Rhinelander would name his successor. Despite Adenauer's misgivings concerning Erhard, the leader of the CDU agreed to name the Bavarian as chancellor-designate. In October 1963, the reins of government were passed to Ludwig Erhard. For his cabinet Erhard picked men who already were in office, thus indicating his desire for continuity in state affairs.

Under Erhard the basic style of West German government was altered, and a cabinet-type administration in which individual ministers were given greater responsibility was introduced. Parliament now had a larger role, and there appeared more political brawling in the *Bundestag*, and in German political life generally than had been typical of the Adenauer days. Adenauer became publically critical of the government, and especially objected to Erhard's foreign policy. When the United States would not agree to a reduction of West German debts incurred in arms purchases, and when the upward surge of the economy first leveled off and then dropped slightly, the Free Democrats withdrew their support from the coalition and forced Erhard to resign in November 1966.

Erhard was succeeded by Kurt-Georg Kiesinger, who brought about something of a minor revolution in postwar German politics by engineering a coalition of the CDU and the SPD. His first cabinet demonstrated that pragmatism rather than ideological commitment was now the guiding rule for German politics when he appointed Willy Brandt as Foreign Minister.

The new "grand coalition" brought many changes to German politics. Of importance was the fact that a voter wishing to oppose the policies of the government no longer could give his allegiance to the SPD. The party profiting most from this phenomenon was the new ultra-rightist National Democratic Party (NPD), which preached extreme nationalism and the "moral regeneration" of Germany. The NPD leader was Adolf von Thadden, descendent of a noble Pomeranian family, who received much national and international publicity as his party grew. Some were alarmed at the NPD's radical-romantic talk about German supremacy, because it was so reminiscent of the Hitler period. In 1968, the party demonstrated its burgeoning strength by taking 10 seats in the liberal Baden-Württemberg legislature.

Thus, although it was far from a national danger in 1968, the NPD had frightened many. If, however, the NPD was going to live and thrive it had to avoid a drift into greater right-wing radicalism. Its leaders knew that much of its 1968 showing was based upon the nation's reactions to disorderly Leftist student insurrections in West Berlin. Yet, the NPD was pushed inexorably to the extreme Right by the fact that the CDU and SPD had occupied effectively most of the rest of the political spectrum. Consequently, no matter how vigorously von Thadden protested the charge that he was presiding over a rebirth of nazism, the image of the swastika lingered in the background, a powerful political limitation.

Just how much of a limitation the neo-Nazi charge could be was demonstrated in late 1968. The Soviets, attempting to draw attention from their invasion of Czechoslovakia, threatened West Germany with intervention should the elements of "Nazism" continue to develop. It was widely believed that the Russian threat was not a serious one, but only propaganda. Nevertheless, the voters of Lower Saxony were not willing to take a chance. In an autumn election, the NPD won only 5.2 per cent of the vote and lost strength in both rural and urban areas. It had been only one year earlier that the NPD had begun its rise to prominence. Now the NPD's hopes of making a showing that would bring them representation in the *Bundestag* had been dealt a damaging blow.

The hopes of the NPD leadership that the party ranks would be swollen by those who opposed a governing coalition composed of both major parties were dealt a severe blow at the beginning of the new decade. The strange political bedfellows joined at the end of 1966 in the "grand coalition" were separated at the beginning of the 1970's. The SPD ended the somewhat unnatural combination with the CDU and formed a coalition with the FDP. Kiesinger left the Chancellorship and was replaced in that office by SPD leader, Foreign Minister Willy Brandt. Hence, in 1970, West Germany's affairs were directed by the first Social Democratic government since the Weimar period.

C. Foreign Affairs

The earliest important theme appearing in West German foreign policy was the continued call by Chancellor Adenauer for the Russians to permit German reunification on the basis of "free all-German elections." Adenauer believed that a government so constituted could then conclude a negotiated peace with the Big Four. The Western Allies supported the West German Chancellor in his stand, but the

Russians were adamantine in insisting on separate peaces with the two Germanies (involving *de jure* recognition of the East German regime). The Russians, of course, feared that any Germany established in the manner wished by Adenauer would produce a democratic and pro-Western government.

In 1952, and again in 1953, the Bonn Government, despite the fact that the Occupation Statute required that negotiations on the German question be conducted by the Western powers, expressed the view that there should be an all-German government instituted by free elections. In October 1953, Adenauer indicated that West Germany's foreign policy aims were threefold: (1) the restoration of independence; (2) reunification of Germany; and (3) the political integration of Western Europe, including Germany. In his October speech, the Chancellor declared that the boundary of East Germany, the so-called "Oder-Neisse Line," would never be recognized because it was an artificial boundary created by the Russians. He pointed out that the limits of prewar Germany had been far to the east of the Oder and Neisse rivers.[4]

As has been recounted in Chapters 21 and 22, Russia and the West met several times to attempt a solution to the German problem, but little was accomplished at these meetings. In January 1954, for instance, a Big Four Conference was held in Berlin. In this case, despite much talk, the divergence between the two positions was even more apparent.

Because of the Cold War, an early aim of the West was to bring about the integration of a rearmed Germany into the Western community. In return for Bonn's taking part in the defenses of free Europe, the Federal Republic was to be granted full sovereignty.[5] Along these lines, in March 1951, the Western Allies began revision of the Occupation Statute. The first major alteration allowed the Federal Republic to establish a foreign office and Adenauer himself took the first portfolio of foreign affairs. Shortly thereafter the Western Big Three passed acts ending the state of war with Germany.

In September 1951, Britain, France, and the United States informed Bonn that the Occupation Statute could be replaced with contractual agreements if the Germans would contribute to the European Defense Community (EDC). There was some reluctance to rearm in Germany. Various groups pointed out that Germans had been told repeatedly since the end of the war that German militarism was intrinsically bad and that they had agreed. However, despite strong neutralist opinion prevalent in West Germany in the early 1950's,

---

[4] By 1953, German nationals, for the most part, had been pushed westward from the area lying between the Oder-Neisse Line and the boundaries of 1937.

[5] The Occupation Statute was still in force into the 1950's. Although a West German Government had been established in 1949, it did not have full sovereignty and the Statute reserved to the Allied High Commission control over many areas, including foreign affairs.

Bonn negotiated with the Western Allies and produced an agreement on May 26, 1952. The Occupation Statute was replaced by a "Convention on Relations Between the Three Powers and the Federal Republic of Germany." The effect of the Convention was to grant virtual sovereignty to West Germany at the same time that a defensive alliance among the Western powers was arranged. As one aspect of the agreement, the Allies were allowed to station troops on German soil. The Contractual Agreements, as this pact is usually called, were ratified by Britain and the United States in 1953, and approved by the *Bundestag*.

The EDC did not become a successful project leading to a workable defense alliance,[6] and a new round of negotiations was inititated, aimed at bringing the Federal Republic into the Western defensive system. In a London conference, in October 1954, agreements were worked out allowing a series of Paris treaties to be signed later the same month. The Paris Treaties consisted of four major agreements: (1) The granting of sovereignty to Bonn and reaffirmation of the right of the Allies to station troops on German soil; (2) the bringing of West Germany into the Western European Union (WEU), an extension of the 1948 Brussels Pact; (3) the admission of the Federal Republic to NATO; and (4) the declaring of independence of the Saar, subject to approval of the Saarlanders.[7] Only the Saarlanders, who generally desired to be reincorporated into West Germany, rejected the Paris Agreements. However, as a result of better relations between Bonn and Paris, the Saar was incorporated into West Germany as a state in 1957. Meanwhile, in 1955, West Germany had become a member of NATO as a sovereign state.

In the mid-1950's the Federal Republic developed a firm position with regard to East Germany. The so-called "Hallstein Doctrine" (1955) was intended to warn neutral and nonaligned states not to recognize the German Democratic Republic, since the West German Federal Republic was the only polity possessing the right to speak for Germany as a whole. Foreign Minister Heinrich von Brentano explained the policy in the *Bundestag* on June 28, 1956:

The recognition of the 'GDR' means recognition . . . of the division of Germany into two states. Reunification would then no longer be the elimination of a transitional disturbance in the organism of our all-German state; rather it would be transformed into the infinitely more difficult task of unifying two different German states . . . . The recognition of the 'GDR' by third states would have to be regarded by the Federal Government as agreement to the unlawful splitting off of a part of the territory under

[6] EDC failed primarily because of French intransigence when faced with the possibility of a rearmed Germany. For a discussion of the failure of EDC, see Chapter 27.

[7] In 1946, the French had begun to incorporate the Saar basin into the French economic system, but the Saarlanders began and continued to agitate for a return of the Saar to West Germany.

German sovereignty and as interference with domestic German affairs.
Legally the unity of Germany as a state has not perished . . . .[8]

Thus, the Hallstein Doctrine was designed to notify other governments that recognition of the GDR would adversely affect their relations with Bonn. It had the effect of making relations between the Federal Republic and Communist states very difficult. For instance, in 1957, Tito permitted a legation of the GDR to be established in his country and Bonn then broke diplomatically with Yugoslavia. In 1963, the Federal Republic broke off relations with Castro's Cuba on the same grounds. In the mid-1960's, the Hallstein Doctrine was modified because its maintenance in full force tended to create awkward situations. Bonn could not go on breaking relations with each country allowing a GDR legation on its soil. Consequently, the government began to moderate the doctrine's use and weighed each situation individually.

When Adenauer stepped down, the Bonn Government began to reevaluate its hard-line policies toward Soviet bloc governments. The Federal Republic's higher councils of government began to consider the possibility that the increasingly independent states of Eastern Europe could be won over to a position criticizing the GDR. Thus Bonn's "Eastern Policy" (*Ostpolitik*) took a new turn. On March 24, 1966, the Federal Republic handed to all governments, including those of Eastern Europe, a "peace note," indicating a willingness to consider for the first time a limitation of European armaments along the lines of the Rapacki Plan (see Chapter 21), providing any such agreement "would actively promote the resolution of political problems in Central Europe." The modification of the Hallstein Doctrine did not immediately establish better feelings in mid-Europe, however, because Bonn's peace note could not refrain from reproving the Polish Government for insisting on the recognition of the Oder-Neisse Line.

The most successful relationship opened in Bonn's *Ostpolitik*, in 1966 and after, was with Romania. Trade agreements were signed with that state as it, and then Hungary, Bulgaria, and Poland were placed on a liberalized east-trade (*Osthandel*) list.

With all the eastern countries, however, economic relations could not replace political ones. Consideration of a joint West German industrial project with Poland had to be dropped because of West Germany's continuing talk of recovering the Oder-Neisse territories. The basic problem in Central Europe, by 1969, centered on West German inability to accept the political consequences of a lost war and agree that the area east of the Oder-Neisse Line was simply no longer Germanic. To confound the situation, Germany's eastern neighbors became fearful of a Nazi revival, and tended to arm

[8] Cited by Rudolf Schuster, "Die 'Hallstein Doctrine,'" *Europa Archiv,* September 25, 1963.

themselves against ghosts raised by the rise of the NPD. These troublesome spirits could be laid to rest ultimately by reasonable co-operation between West Germany and her eastern neighbors. This cooperation did not develop rapidly, and was in fact set back measurably by the Russian intrusion into Czechoslovakia in 1968. Intransigence continued to be typical of both sides until Willy Brandt came to the Chancellorship and, in 1970, committed his government to new efforts aimed at creating a rapprochement with West Germany's eastern neighbors.

Brandt's efforts bore first fruit in the signing in Moscow of a Soviet-West German treaty on August 12, 1970. Articles 2 and 3 of the text obligated the two states to be "guided in their mutual relations . . . by the aims and principles which are laid down in the Charter of the United Nations." Moreover, the two powers agreed to "solve their disputes exclusively with peaceful means" and declared "that they have no territorial demands against anyone, nor will they have such in the future." Perhaps most importantly, the treaty proclaimed the inviolability of all European frontiers as they existed on the day of its signing, including "the Oder-Neisse line, which forms the western frontier of the People's Republic of Poland, and the frontier between the Federal Republic of Germany and the German Democratic Republic."

The document was to become effective upon ratification by both parties. Insofar as the Bonn Parliament was concerned, it appeared that ratification would depend on some improvement in the West and East Berlin situation, on a firm understanding that the treaty in no way was intended to weaken West Germany's ties to the Western powers, and on Soviet agreement with Brandt's interpretation that the treaty did not rule out the possible eventual peaceful reunion of the two Germanies. Moscow apparently was pleased at the West Germans' recognition that Russia once more was a part of Europe.

THE GERMAN DEMOCRATIC REPUBLIC

The German Democratic Republic (DDR or GDR) came into being in the autumn of 1949. Since its creation had not been based on free elections, Chancellor Konrad Adenauer immediately declared it illegal. From 1949, the Bonn Government held that the GDR was illegally initiated and therefore refused to recognize its *de jure* existence. It remained common practice, throughout the 1960's, for West German newspapers to refer to East Germany as "the Soviet Zone of Occupation." Yet, the government in the east did exist on a *de facto* basis, and the West Germans, indeed the whole Western world, had to keep that in mind while, officially, the policy of nonrecognition was continued.

The government of East Germany was designed by the Russians. In the state elections of October 1946, the Communist-backed Socialist Unity Party (SED) failed to gain 50 per cent of the vote. Consequently, the Communists decided to suspend all further free elections and instituted a system of people's congresses. An "Anti-Fascist Democratic Bloc," formed out of several political parties,[9] was used to form a "First People's Congress." Although established without regular elections, in December 1947, the Congress issued invitations to West German political parties to attend its meetings. Even though the West German parties declined the invitation, the Congress claimed it spoke for Germany as a whole and demanded that all military occupation end and an immediate peace treaty be signed.

A second congress was convened in March 1948. It appointed a constitutional committee which produced a draft document by October 1948. In March 1949, a People's Council approved a somewhat altered draft and elections were scheduled in May. When election day arrived, the voters were presented with a single list of candidates drawn up by the council. Those who voted were given the opportunity only of voting for the official list and in favor of "German unity and a just peace." The results of the election were less than satisfying to the Communists. Despite the lack of choice on the ballot, only 61.8 per cent of the people voted in favor of the relatively general call for "unity" and "peace," and for the attached list. In East Berlin, barely more than half the voters favored the list.

After the Federal Republic of West Germany was established in October 1949, the Russians, who had held back enactment of the constitution as they waited for political developments in West Germany allowed the East to go ahead with the promulgation of a special law that created a "Provisional People's Chamber" out of the old People's Council. The provisional chamber became permanent in July 1950, when the actions of the government were confirmed by elections.

The new legislature was in theory bicameral, but, in reality, there had been established a unitary state on the Soviet model with the Party elite in control of all facets of government. All state agencies were centralized and the constitution became unimportant in the everyday functions of government. Special government decrees informed the populace of new developments in the agencies controlling financial, police, legal, and even cultural matters.[10]

The reconstruction of war-torn East Germany was to be accomplished by economic planning based on Soviet models. In 1948, a Half-Year Plan was announced, to be followed, in 1949 and 1950, by a Two-Year Plan. The first full-scale Five-Year Plan was launched in 1951. Like their Russian models, the plans concentrated on the build-

---

[9] Most of these parties were artificially established by the Russians to create the illusion of mass support for the regime.

[10] Such decrees were often in violation of the constitution.

ing of heavy industry in an area that had been essentially agricultural in the past. Another feature of economic planning in East Germany was the removal of land and industry from private owners and their placement in semiprivate cooperatives. By 1953, some 85 per cent of the total economy had been sequestered from private ownership. Along with the transition in agriculture and industry, there occurred an intensive effort to permeate cultural and educational life with a materialistic line. As in other Communist states, the aim was to shape the youth in the Red image so that coming generations would not be so troublesome in their resistance to state directives. As had been the case in other states where a similar approach was tried, churches in East Germany resisted the educational programs of the regime. The area that was now the GDR had been the seedbed of the Protestant Reformation and the German Protestant Church was the primary opponent of the materialistic creed proclaimed from East Berlin.

In July 1952, it was decided that progress toward socialization had been too slow and a new program was initiated to accelerate Sovietization. However, the program had to be canceled in June 1953. Too many East Germans had displayed their discontent with the socioeconomic restraints placed upon them by "voting with their feet" and fleeing to West Germany.

Walter Ulbricht, who had been one of the cofounders of the German Communist Party, in 1918, and now was head of state, was forced to adopt a "new course" to try and halt the disastrous refugee drainage to West Germany. In many ways Ulbricht's new direction resembled Lenin's New Economic Policy of the 1920's. A temporary delay in the rapid communization of the GDR was initiated. An increase in consumer's goods and wages was decreed to satisfy the populace.

Extreme dissatisfaction with the state of things in East Germany continued, however. On June 16, 1953, East Berlin workers went on strike to demonstrate against a government demand that they increase their production without an increase in pay. When riots spread to Berlin's suburbs, Russian armor was brought in to put down what had developed into an uprising. Similarly, other risings in various cities in the GDR were put down. Yet, despite the heroic attempts of the workers to budge the Ulbricht regime, the 1953 risings caused little alteration in the basic course of East German development.

After 1955, the economic and foreign policy lines followed in the Democratic Republic were designed more and more to meet the overall needs of the Soviet bloc. Despite economic planning and a traditionally productive population, recovery was slow and the labor force continued to shrink as the skilled departed for West Germany where they could expect a better return on their labors. The First Five-Year Plan fell far short of its goals. It was not until 1957 that industrial production began to grow significantly. The Second Five-Year Plan was helped by the GDR's economic position in the Soviet bloc as trade with the satellite states increased measurably. Nonetheless, the economy suffered as flights to West Germany tended to decrease the population still further.[11]

In 1958, nationalization of small industry and the creation of state farms formed an integral part of a drive for increased productivity. By 1959, the drive had proved at least partially successful. Many aspects of the new programs caused further drains on East Germany's manpower resources. By 1960, all workers were assigned to jobs regardless of their preference, some child labor had been initiated, and industrialization was stressed at the expense of consumer goods. This situation was made worse, in 1961, by new food shortages following the forced collectivization of land in 1960.

In addition to the economic troubles suffered by the GDR, there were other reasons why the government found it necessary to put restrictions on travel to West Germany, lest "tourists" not come back. Walter Ulbricht gradually had converted East Germany into a dictatorship, and established an autocratic rule that he hoped someday to extend to a united Germany.

Much of the opposition to Ulbricht's regime centered in the Lutheran Church, whose Bishop, Otto Dibelius, lived in West Berlin but had a diocese including sizable sections of the GDR. The struggle between the Lutheran Church and Ulbricht's regime continued into the 1960's. As it happened, the Lutheran opposition had been weakened by a split in its ranks, in some ways similar to the one that had existed in the days of Nazi Germany (see Chapter 8). Some of the Lutheran leaders, members of a "Pastor's League," favored close cooperation between the Lutheran Church and any regime in power, even though, in this case, that meant the Communist government. A majority of Lutheran pastors and laymen, however, followed Dibelius and asserted that Ulbricht, no less than Hitler, was a totalitarian, and Christian conscience could not abide cooperation with totalitarian regimes.

Ulbricht alternated between "carrot and stick" policies to weaken the opposition and stem the tide of fleeing East Germans. He fluctuated between pardoning of political prisoners and purging the government and party leaders. Arrests, reprisals, and dismissed scapegoats only seemed to provoke further unrest. In mid-1961, the East Germans began to restrict access between East and West Berlin. An alarm signal thus was sounded for many East Germans, who seemed to sense that the GDR soon would be turned into a huge barbed-wire encampment. In July alone, some 30,000 GDR inhabitants used the last open escape route into West Berlin. Some 22,000 more followed them in August.

Suddenly, on August 13, 1961, the border between East and West Germany was closed. In the ensuing weeks East German *Volkspolizei* and People's Militiamen presided over the building of a permanent

[11] From 1948 to 1960, the population of the GDR dropped from 20,000,000 to 17,000,000.

wall, which eventually grew into a twenty-eight mile long barrier of reinforced concrete, watched over by guard towers. In the wall's first six years, at least sixty-three Germans were shot to death trying to escape over or under it.

The wall, however, had the effect of sealing East Germany from foreign influence and limiting the possibility of escape. Hence, the East Germans had to face the prospect of making the best of what they had. East German industry was rebuilt around a system of eighty great cartels that had borrowed freely from capitalist techniques. Production came to be determined by the rule of supply and demand rather than by unrealistic quotas. By 1968, East Germany was the world's seventh largest industrial power and still growing. Although still far behind West Germany, the GDR had taken first place in production among the Soviet bloc countries.

Dissidents were cleverly manipulated by the Ulbricht regime. Those who cooperated received favors, such as automobiles and cases of liquor. People who were not responsive to state decrees were subjected to an official ostracism. Children of poor workers who demonstrated talent were easily corrupted by surrounding them with lavish facilities and showering them with special attention.

In 1968, East Germany's successes seemed endangered by the tendency toward political liberalization in Czechoslovakia. It was Ulbricht who first warned that the liberal trends in Czechoslovakia might spread to other Communist states when he said, "If things in Prague . . . continue as they are then we are all done for." Ulbricht had still other concerns to worry him, namely, the tendency shown in Czechoslovakia to better relations with the Federal Republic. His major argument in his long struggle to force West Germany to grant his regime *de jure* recognition had been his constant assertion that the GDR had the united support of the various Eastern and Central European nations in the Communist bloc. The new position of the regime in Prague threatened to destroy the validity of that argument.

In addition, Ulbricht faced the possibility that the Czech "contamination" might spread to his own people. The GDR curtailed travel to Czechoslovakia and stopped Czech publications from coming into the country. This rigid censorship, however, was not completely enforced and documents produced by Czechoslovakia's liberalization made their way from Czech intellectuals to East German intellectuals.[12] Students in Leipzig demonstrated against the government and others in Rostow were sentenced to prison for criticizing the regime. It is little wonder then that Ulbricht participated actively in the Russian occupation of Czechoslovakia, in August 1968 (see Chapter 22).

By early 1970, the tendencies toward dissent in East Germany seemed slight when compared with the greater degree of ferment

[12] The most famous of such documents was the democratically-spirited "Manifesto of 2000 Words."

that had been observed in Romania or the reform spirit loosened by Dubček and his associates in Czechoslovakia. Still, in the Soviet bloc, any thought of a possible defection of East Germany must have been considered a disaster of incalculable proportions, for it raised the spectre of a united Western-oriented Germany under the leadership of a Bonn government, that eventually might turn its strength against the Soviet Union. It remained to be seen what influence in this connection might be exerted by the Soviet-West German treaty signed in August 1970.

OTHER STATES OF WESTERN EUROPE

Austria

In April 1945, before Germany's surrender but after the Russians had crossed the Austrian frontier, there came out of retirement in the little town of Gloggnitz a seventy-five-year-old Socialist, who had been chancellor under the Constitutent Assembly of 1919 and a parliamentary leader of the Austrian Republic until 1934. The man was Dr. Karl Renner (1870–1950). The invading Russians agreed to let him go to Vienna on the understanding that he would try to reconvene the non-Fascist rump of the last democratic Austrian Parliament (1933).

When he got to Vienna, Renner found that various underground leaders already had formed nuclei of three revived political parties: the Austrian (Catholic) People's Party, the Social Democratic Party, and the Austrian Communist Party. Negotiations developed among all groups, under Russian observation but without Russian interference. On April 29, 1945, with German surrender still several days off, an Austrian Provisional Government was announced. It comprised a cabinet representing all three parties and was headed by Renner as Chancellor.

Moscow at once recognized this government. The three major Western Allies, however, were suspicious of Renner's cooperation with the Soviets. Before they had even had time to occupy their respective zones, the Western Allies were confronted with a Soviet-sponsored provisional government which sought their recognition as the spokesman for liberated Austria. Such recognition therefore was withheld until October 1945. By that time the Western members of the Allied Council for Austria had required the Renner Government to include more leaders from the rural provinces of Austria, had satisfied themselves that the cabinet really enjoyed widespread popular support, and had deprived the Communist Minister of the Interior of his control over elections and the police. The Renner Government now was empowered to operate "under the guidance and control of the Allied Council." Its chief immediate functions were the encouragement of a free press and preparation for early national elections.

Meanwhile the Renner Government actually had accomplished much. In May 1945, it had restored the democratic constitution of 1920 as amended in 1929. Then it abrogated the whole body of Nazi law as well as the dictatorial measures of the Dollfuss and Schuschnigg regimes; proceeded with denazification and the punishment of war criminals; provided necessary emergency legislation; and established a well-functioning central administration.

Elections for a National Council (*Nationalrat*) were held in November, 1945. No former member of the Nazi Party was permitted to vote. The balloting resulted in the choice of 85 People's Party deputies, 76 Social Democrats, and 4 Communists, for a total of 165. Since it had been agreed in advance that a full coalition government would be formed after the election, the new cabinet (December 1945) contained eight members of the People's Party, six Socialists, and one Communist. Leopold Figl of the People's Party became chancellor. An upper house called the *Bundesrat* or Federal Council was chosen to represent the Austrian provinces. The parliament unanimously elected Renner first President of the Second Austrian Republic, for a term of six years.

The exact occupation zones in Austria were defined by the European Advisory Commission in July 1945. By that time, each of the four occupying powers already had taken over a section of the country and tried to bring order out of the administrative and economic chaos resulting from the war and the collapse of Nazism. The Soviet Zone included Lower Austria and Burgenland. The British Zone embraced Styria, Carinthia, and some of the eastern Tirol. France took over the rest of the Tirol and Voralberg. To the United States was assigned Salzburg and Upper Austria. Vienna, like Berlin, was divided into sectors; each occupying power held one sector, while a fifth was internationalized and ruled in monthly rotation by the occupiers. The Russian zone contained the oil fields, the chief industrial areas, and some of the best agricultural land.

The Allied authority in the country was the Allied Council (AC), composed of the commanding generals of the Big Four in Austria. (In 1950, the three Western powers substituted civilian high commissioners for the military governors.) As in the case of the German counterpart, decisions had to be unanimous. Early in 1946, the AC approved the free exchange of surplus goods among the four zones, but the Russians limited the exercise of this right in their zone. From March 1946, Austria was allowed to exchange diplomatic representatives with all foreign countries save Germany and Japan. An agreement of June 1946, permitted the central government to legislate and administer certain national laws. Any bill not involving constitutional change or international affairs would automatically become law after thirty-one days, unless it had incurred the unanimous disapproval of the AC. Austria now, also, could negotiate bilateral agreements with any of the occupying powers without AC approval. Enjoying this much autonomy, the Austrian Government did a competent administrative job except where it was hampered by Soviet interference.

After early aid from UNRRA and with United States help, Austria made striking economic progress. In mid-1953 the United States Ambassador to Austria reported that the republic's industrial production was well ahead of the prewar peak, the agricultural output was back at the prewar level, the inflation had been checked, and the Austrian schilling was among the most stable of European monetary units.

Only after a peace treaty were signed would Austria be free as well as liberated. The three Western Allies were sympathetic to such a goal and, as has been indicated, strove diligently to convert Moscow to the same view. But the Soviet Union had no desire to quit Austria. Angered to find the Austrian people unsympathetic to communism, the Soviets at least wanted to keep the control they had assumed over Austrian shipping, oil, and industrial assets. Furthermore, it was to their general advantage to leave forces in Austria because then they might legally maintain "communication lines" in Hungary and Romania. Finally, if there were a sufficient accumulation of misery and want in Austria, her people out of sheer desperation might enter the association of Danubian states already within the Soviet orbit.

By way of justifying her refusal to negotiate a treaty, the U.S.S.R. charged Austria with slothfulness in the denazification program and readiness to remain a haven for anti-Soviet displaced persons. In order to prevent the early negotiation of a treaty, the U.S.S.R. continued to demand the cession of Austrian territory to Yugoslavia, and presented a preposterous reparation claim. The Soviets began to appropriate properties Russia had declared to be so-called "German assets." But in the Russians' interpretation almost everything of value that had been seen in German hands at some time or other during World War II was a "German asset."

In order to block Russia's efforts at wrecking the Austrian economy, the Figl Government, in 1946, nationalized the country's big industries. Moscow, however, replied that this action could have no effect on properties already taken over by the Soviets. It therefore disregarded the law and continued to ship eastward all that it wished from Austrian plants, wells, and farms to satisfy Soviet demands for reparation.

The results of the regular parliamentary election of 1949 were gratifying to the West but further increased Russian intransigence. This time the cooperating People's and Social Democratic parties won 77 and 67 seats, respectively, for a total of 144 out of a possible 165. The Communists got 5 seats, and 16 were captured by a new League of Independents, composed largely of former Austrian Nazis who had been reenfranchised since the previous election. Figl remained as Chancellor but during the ensuing years found it increasingly difficult to hold his coalition together.

Elections were held early in 1953, but the result was indecisive. The People's Party got 74 seats, to 73 for the Socialists, 14 for the League of Independents, and 4 for the Communists. After prolonged political jockeying, Figl resigned and was succeeded by his colleague, Dr. Julius Raab, chairman of the People's Party and a foreign-trade expert. Raab's cabinet included members of both major parties.

Regularly during all these years the Western Allies tried to negotiate a peace treaty, and just as regularly Moscow prevented its completion. By the middle of 1953, the Big Four foreign ministers or their deputies had held a total of almost 300 fruitless meetings on an Austrian settlement.

The Soviets continued to object that a revived and independent Austria might rejoin Germany and again raise the threat of Pan-Germanic aggression in Central Europe. Suddenly, in May 1955, the Kremlin changed its seemingly inflexible line on the Austrian situation and expressed a willingness to make a treaty and evacuate the Soviet forces still in Austria. The price for this action was to be reasonable compensation for the "German assets" claimed at the end of the war. The Soviets also demanded that Austria become a neutral state similar to Switzerland.

The abrupt change in Soviet policy aroused much skepticism in the West, but Austrian Chancellor Julius Raab decided that it would be folly for the Austrians to miss an opportunity to win final freedom from the Russians. He led an Austrian mission to Moscow to negotiate an understanding. It was arranged, among other things, for the Second Republic to give the Soviet Union some $150 million as compensation for the "German assets" Russia wanted. It also was agreed that Russia would be supplied with a million tons of oil each year for ten years.

Thus it was that the four occupying powers came to sign a Treaty of Vienna on May 15, 1955. At last Austria was its own master. The last foreign troops had departed by the end of the year.

The Austrian State Treaty was particularly significant in that it was the first time the U.S.S.R. had withdrawn from a Western outpost since the end of World War II. The withdrawal was acceptable to Moscow because an act of the Vienna Parliament designated Austria as neutral territory in perpetuity. Apparently the incorporation of the German Federal Republic into the Western defense system led the Soviets to believe that formal neutralization of countries between the Russian and Western blocs was desirable.

The rejoicing of Austrians in May 1955, was followed by a period of unparalleled prosperity in the small Germanic state. The obligations owed the U.S.S.R. under the treaty proved not to be as burdensome as feared. The Soviets made payment easier by cutting down their claims and allowing other items to be substituted for the oil demanded in the state treaty. Final reparation was paid by 1963.

Austrian exports began to flow into the Common Market to the further benefit of the Republic and the economy flourished. Austrian industry prospered sufficiently for the economy to absorb the refugees who poured in ahead of the Soviet tidal wave, those who fled to Austria after the Hungarian revolt of 1956, and workers from nearby countries who could not find employment at home.

In politics, the domination of the People's Party over the Socialists in the office of chancellor continued into 1970. Raab was succeeded, in 1961, by Alfons Gorbach who, in 1964, was followed by another People's Party Chancellor, Joseph Klaus. On the other hand, the Socialists tended to control the presidency (the president was elected every six years) and they dominated the city elections in Vienna. Early in 1970, the Socialists for the first time won enough seats in a national election so that their leader, Dr. Bruno Kreisky, became Chancellor.

Despite the fact that the Republic was firmly entrenched, the question of a Habsburg restoration arose to haunt the government. In 1962, the Supreme Court of Austria recognized the legality of Archduke Otto's renunciation of any claim to reign and his declaration of loyalty to the republic. This should have paved the way for Otto's return to his homeland, but the possibility stirred up a political crisis. The People's Party tended to go along with the court's ruling, but the Socialists were upset. Heated controversies over the "Habsburg question" threatened to rip apart the ruling coalition cabinet, but a crisis was averted when Otto indicated that he would not enter Austria.

In foreign affairs, after 1955, the Austrians followed a policy supporting the United Nations, which they had joined in December 1955. It was to the United Nations' General assembly that the Austrians brought a dispute with Italy over the South Tirol.

The Tirolian problem developed out of the fact that, at the end of the war, some 250,000 German-Austrians still resided in the Italian district of Alto Adige (the South Tirol). This region had come into Italian hands as a result of the settlement at the end of World War I, and Italy had promised to grant its inhabitants a practical autonomy. But a process of Italianization was begun (see Chapter 6) and sporadic terrorist activities alerted the world to the existence of a minorities problem in the area.

Through the UN, Austria pleaded that real autonomy be granted the South Tirol. The UN, however, recommended that the two nations concerned should settle their problems between themselves. There followed several exchanges of notes and diplomats between Rome and Vienna, which seemed to yield no measurable results. Finally, in 1964, an Italian parliamentary committee recommended a new statute that would increase the degree of autonomy in Alto Adige and strengthen the rights of the German-speaking population. Italy and Austria then appointed a joint committee to prepare an agreement. At last, in 1969, a solution was reached on the safeguarding of local autonomy that was satisfactory to Vienna and Rome, if not to all the South Tiroleans.

In other foreign matters, Austria participated in the Council of

Europe, the European Organization for Economic Cooperation and Development (UECD), the European Free Trade Association (EFTA), and the General Agreement on Tariffs and Trade (GATT). As a result of her involvement in such organizations, Austria undertook a progressive lowering of tariffs. Since the greatest part of Austrian trade was with the Common Market countries, she sought to join the European Economic Community. Although, by 1970, she was not successful in her attempts to join the Common Market, Austria became strong enough to develop a small foreign aid program to help underdeveloped states.

Switzerland

During World War II, Switzerland remained neutral. Hence, the Swiss situation was much less altered during that conflict than was that of most of the other European states. There was, however, during the war, an expansion of federal governmental activity, until, at the end of hostilities, the economy was supervised at a federal rather than a cantonal level.

After the war, many Swiss citizens were disturbed about such controls and it became necessary, in 1947, to hold a national referendum on federal direction of the economy. As a result of the referendum, the constitution was amended and the federal government was given wide powers to control the nation's economic situation. For a brief period the government retained emergency taxing powers, but these were returned to the cantons in 1953.

Much less adversely affected than other European states by the war, it was relatively simple for the Swiss to keep high living standards in a postwar scene that found the rest of Europe in ruins. Since they possessed a stable currency, not touched by wild postwar fluctuations, foreign capital was attracted by the Swiss. In consequence, Switzerland became a leading financial center and supplier of capital to the rest of Europe. Quickly too, as soon as prosperity began to return to other Europeans, peaceful Switzerland, none of her traditional charm damaged by bombs or artillery shells, began to attract a stream of tourists that grew year by year. Low taxes brought affluent foreigners to establish permanent residence in Switzerland.

Postwar elections demonstrated that the Swiss pattern of government would continue to work smoothly, free of the eruptions typical of other continental situations. There was a very slight growth on the political Left. In the 1947 elections, the Communist Party won 7 out of a total 196 seats. However, in the next election, Red representation dropped to five and, eventually, to an average of from three to five. In the parliamentary elections, held every four years, three parties— the Radical Democrats, the Social Democrats, and the (Catholic) Conservatives—demonstrated approximately equal strength.

Although Switzerland developed the usual two-house system (an upper body representing the nineteen full cantons and six half-cantons and a national council chosen by direct election), the national political picture displayed one unusual feature. Referendums, which could nullify a law or create a new one, were commonly held. In 1957 and 1958, for instance, the two Swiss chambers adopted proposals allowing women the right to vote in national elections, to hold federal office, and to accept appointment to the only regular federal court, the Federal Tribunal. Since these proposals involved an amendment to the constitution, they were submitted to a national referendum in 1959. The referendum failed to approve female suffrage.

Democratic forms were zealously preserved in Switzerland. The virtual national literacy well prepared citizens for their roles in national life. Swiss educative processes, particularly at the *gymnasium* or preuniversity level, were widely admired and copied by educators in all parts of the world. The Swiss also pioneered in the field of social welfare. Among the welfare programs developed early by the Swiss Government were the care and education of retarded children, old-age security, and federal insurance plans.

In foreign affairs, the Swiss continued to cling to their traditional neutrality and did not seek membership in the UN, although they worked in several of its specialized agencies. They did not join NATO, nor did they normally seek membership in the several European trade organizations. On the other hand, Geneva remained one of the most cosmopolitan cities in the world. The Red Cross and agencies of the UN retained their headquarters there. Geneva, along with many other Swiss cities, developed international schools and colleges, that attracted numerous students from abroad.

The Low Countries

Although both Belgium and the Netherlands were occupied by the Nazis during World War II, they were faced with somewhat differing situations at its end. Belgium had suffered relatively little physical damage during the years of fighting and was better prepared, in 1945, to initiate national economic recovery. She quickly developed sound monetary policies, and raw materials were permitted to enter the country without a high tariff levy. At the same time, the government announced a policy of slight regulation for local industries. The combined effect of these two policies was to cause the mines and factories of Belgium to move into production quickly and efficiently. Further, thanks to the activities of the Belgian resistance, Antwerp was the only large harbor left intact along the North Sea, and so foreign trade quickly found its way to that port. The amount of foreign trade moving into the Antwerp piers was further augmented by the prompt resumption in the postwar period of Belgian trade with her huge colony in the Congo.

The circumstances of recovery in the Netherlands were somewhat complicated by the injurious Nazi occupation. The destruction of industrial property, to say nothing of private dwellings, was much more extensive. An estimated 200,000 Netherlands soldiers were lost in the war. When Jews had been deported or executed by the Nazis, the local resistance movement had sabotaged the Nazi occupiers' installations. Such actions brought fierce and damaging reprisals against the students, clergymen, and physicians in the population. Further restricting Netherlands recovery was the fact that the country soon became involved in a conflict with her colonies in the East Indies, resulting in a loss of both land and lucrative trade.

Notwithstanding the magnitude of these problems, the Netherlanders set to work with great energy. Areas of the country that had been flooded during the war were drained and the fight to take soil from the sea began again. Old industries were rebuilt and new ones developed. By 1948 industrial production had achieved 1939 levels and thereafter continued to rise.

Perhaps the most significant factor involved in the Netherlands' continued prosperity in the 1950's and 1960's was the intimate economic linkage with West Germany. As West Germany grew more prosperous, Netherlanders were drawn by higher wages to work in West Germany. At the same time, prosperous German tourists made the easy trip to Amsterdam or the Hague to secure retail goods available in some abundance. In consequence, the growth of Netherlands prosperity was nearly simultaneous with the "economic miracle" transpiring in West Germany. Amsterdam again became one of the important international money markets, and Rotterdam rose from the rubble of war to become one of the most attractive and modern ports in the Western world.

In the matter of political reconstruction, Belgium had to struggle with problems after the war that were far more serious than those encountered by the Netherlanders. Many Belgians objected to the restoration of King Leopold III. The objections sprang from the fact that it was King Leopold who had surrendered to the Nazis in 1940 and then spent the war as a "prisoner" in a castle near Brussels. Further, the widowed king had remarried during the war, thus hurting some national sensibilities. There were Belgians who threatened revolutionary violence to prevent the return of Leopold. In 1950, the question was submitted to a national plebiscite and the King was returned by a slim margin. Recognizing the extent of his unpopularity, Leopold abdicated in 1951, and gave the crown to his son, Baudouin.

Another divisive tendency appeared in Belgian life, in the late 1950's, when the constantly-recurrent question of public aid for Catholic schools arose once more. There were fiery demonstrations and counter-demonstrations in the streets of the major cities. Finally, in 1958, a compromise was reached which satisfied the warring factions sufficiently to bring at least a temporary halt to bitter controversy over school support.

One of Belgium's major postwar problems, as in other European states, was the political and economic adjustment necessitated by the loss of empire. In 1957, the first steps toward representative government were taken in the Belgian Congo when partially elected town councils were established. Still, self-government was not established and, when the French began to withdraw from their colonial system, this encouraged some natives residing in Belgian territory to seek independence of European control. Nationalist riots broke out in Leopoldville, in January 1959, and continued to erupt elsewhere in Belgian holdings throughout that year. The Belgian Government, in an effort to meet the demands of the natives, announced a program for the gradual attainment of independence in the Congo. This program was rejected by the nationalist leaders, and prompt independence for the Congo was demanded. It soon was recognized in Brussels that the national independence movement in the Congo had developed too far to be halted. At midnight, on June 30, 1960, by proclamation of King Baudouin, the Belgian Congo became the independent Democratic Republic of the Congo.

To counteract the economic consequences of the loss of the Belgian Congo, the Belgian ministry found it necessary to adopt an austerity program. Taxes were raised and expenditures (including social welfare) were cut substantially. The laboring classes felt the burden of the new austerity efforts most acutely. In the Walloon area of Belgium there were strikes, riots, and attacks on private property. As the economy painfully adjusted to the new circumstances, there were many symptoms of dislocation. There now had to be a great increase in local production to maintain standards of living. When this increase came, it caused a tightening of the labor markets and wages shot skyward, carrying prices with them. In consequence, the government, beginning in 1963, found it necessary to apply price controls, particularly on foodstuffs.

As indicated earlier, the Netherlands, in the long run, did not face such substantial political and economic difficulties as did Belgium. Unlike the situation in Belgium, where such issues as a renewed school crisis in 1968 illuminated the fact that political party lines were sharply drawn between clerical and secular elements, in the Netherlands numerous minor parties existed to soften any ideological clash between Clericals and Laborites. The monarchy continued in the Netherlands, but, in 1948, weary of bearing the responsibilities of the crown, Queen Wilhelmina passed the royal title to her daughter, Juliana.

In foreign affairs, Belgium and the Netherlands abandoned the stances of neutrality to which both had adhered before World War II. Negotiations for trade agreements were carried on by the Benelux countries jointly (thus including Luxembourg). Moreover, the Benelux states entered the Common Market. Economic ties among the Benelux states tended to carry over into the political field, and the three nations jointly participated in NATO and the European Atomic Energy Community (Euratom).

The States of Scandinavia

Since Sweden was neutral during World War II and Denmark and Norway were occupied, the effects of the conflict were varied in the Scandinavian states. Except for some shipping losses, Denmark and Sweden emerged from the war relatively unscathed. On the other hand, Norway suffered widespread physical damage and thus found it necessary to initiate an extensive rebuilding program.

Since productive facilities in Denmark were not greatly damaged, there was little difficulty in achieving a relatively complete reconstruction. Other matters were more troublesome, however. Fleeing in advance of the pursuing Russian armies, over 250,000 Germans entered Denmark, and it was not until 1948 that these exiles were resettled in West Germany. While World War II was being fought, Iceland was established as an independent republic (1944). After 1945, Danish nationalists revived old claims to the German province of Schleswig, in German hands since Otto von Bismarck's wars of national unification. The Danish Government, however, did not take a similar position, and agitation subsided when the West German Government guaranteed the rights of the Danish minority.

Monarchy remained an accepted and popular institution in Denmark and, in 1947, Frederick IX succeeded his father, Christian X, as King of Denmark. A new constitution was approved, in 1953, assigning legislative duties to a unicameral legislature (*Folketing*) and providing for direct representation for the citizens of Greenland and the Faroe Islands.

The economy of Denmark, not greatly disrupted by the war, soon began to depend heavily upon the merchant fleet, which had been reduced only by about one-third. In keeping with the other Scandinavian states, Denmark was active in the field of social legislation. By the 1960's, government-subsidized voluntary sickness insurance programs involved about 80 per cent of the population.

Norway found recovery much more difficult than did her Scandinavian neighbors. Her great merchant marine and hydroelectric works had been severely damaged during the war. Both these sectors of the economy were revived fairly quickly, but other areas lagged sufficiently to require national rationing until 1952.

In 1952, the Oslo Government inaugurated a ten-year economic development plan for northern Norway. The utilization of waterpower in the area was integrated with the cooperative exploitation of rich ore deposits in neighboring Sweden. This development was so successful that, by the 1960's, unemployment was virtually unknown, consumer goods were plentiful, and prosperity had returned.

On the political scene, the Norwegian Government was in exile during the war. It fulfilled an earlier promise at the end of fighting to resign and allow a new government to be formed. A new cabinet, consisting of former officials and resistance leaders, thus was formed smoothly and without a crisis. Election reform, in 1952, ended the earlier overrepresentation of rural districts. King Haakon VII died in 1957, after a reign of fifty-two years. He was succeeded by his son, Olav V. The major political party in the country during this time continued to be the Labor Party which, with only minor interruptions, administered public business until 1965. In September of that year the election results enabled four non-Socialist parties, led by the Conservatives, to form a majority coalition and assume control of the government. This coalition again was victorious in the elections of 1969.

Norway was at the forefront of countries with extensive programs of social legislation. She participated in the common social security programs of the Scandinavian states, established by 1954, agreements that also allowed workers to move from Scandinavian country to country without loss of benefits. In 1956, an obligatory health-insurance program was expanded in Norway to cover all citizens. Old age pensions were made relatively generous.

In Sweden, a type of government and economic structure developed, which has been called a "middle way" between unregulated private enterprise and outright collectivism. Under this system, the population of Sweden (about 7,900,000) was freed from the burdens of insecurity and came to enjoy a remarkably high average living standard. This was accomplished without extensive nationalization of industry (about 90 per cent remained in private hands). The key to the Swedish success story was to be found in the high rate of exports of technologically-advanced products. Automobiles, particularly, were exported to nations across the globe. The state, as is often the case in Europe, took over ownership of all railways and most power sources, and held a monopoly on the sale of products such as wine and tobacco. In addition, there came into being both private and public financial institutions, which competed against one another in the making of loans.

Hence, throughout the Swedish Government and Swedish financial system ran a common thread: cooperation of both management and labor with government to produce a stable and prosperous economic order. Unlike working forces in many other countries, Swedish labor came to realize that Sweden could conduct international trade effectively on a large scale only if the workers negotiated national wage scales without protracted wrangling and disagreement.

A constitutional monarchy also was continued in Sweden. In 1950, Gustav V died at the age of ninety-two and was succeeded by his son, Gustav VI Adolf. Political affairs were conducted in an orderly and productive fashion. All interested groups were consulted and a consensus was reached before any bill was brought before parliament. Because of this constructive groundwork, few pieces of important legislation were held back because of heated bickering. Like the Swiss, the Swedes also made extensive use of the referendum to test public sentiment on important issues. It was through the process of national referendum that the Swedes, in the 1960's, changed their flow of traffic from the left side of the road to the right.

Sweden was one of the postwar international pacesetters in the area of social legislation. On January 1, 1955, a broad universal health-insurance plan was launched in Sweden. Built upon a foundation of older programs, it was financed by a combination of premiums paid by the insured, contributions from employers, and money from the state. In 1957, a national referendum was held, resulting in a compulsory plan that became law in 1959. The 1959 old-age pension law produced a scheme whereby, at age sixty-seven, a pensioner's income equaled 65 per cent of his average salary during those fifteen years of his life when he enjoyed the best average rates of income.

In foreign affairs, the Scandinavian states attempted, in 1949, to establish a defense pact. However, the proposed Scandinavian alliance conflicted with the defense plans of the rest of the Western community and thus collapsed when Norway and Denmark were drawn into the developing Atlantic alliance. Norway was troubled by Russian insistence that she sign a defense pact with the Soviet Union. Eventually, she was forced to seek refuge in the Atlantic pact for demonstrating the "temerity" to refuse the U.S.S.R.'s offer. Denmark and Iceland followed Norway into NATO. When these countries joined the Atlantic alliance, they brought with them strategic elements important to NATO defense plans. Denmark contributed one of Europe's best airfields at Karup, Jutland. Norway allowed the United States a twenty-year lease on valuable air and naval bases in Greenland.

Sweden followed the policy of neutrality established during World War II, as the Cold War took shape around her. Stockholm refused to enter NATO out of fear that Sweden's alignment with the West would produce a Russian occupation of Finland. Neutrality for Sweden did not mean, however, that the Swedes remained openly friendly with the Soviet Union. It was common, during the postwar period, for Swedes to seek out, arrest, and then deport Soviet intelligence agents.

In 1952, Norway, Sweden, Denmark, and Iceland established the Nordic Council to make cooperation easier among themselves. The Council was essentially concerned with the furthering of economic and social collaboration among its members. One of its tasks was to obtain for the citizens of one member country residing in another member state the social and economic privileges formerly enjoyed in his homeland. Further, the Scandinavian states were active in the United Nations operations. Sweden thus furnished peace-keeping forces during crises in the Congo and Cyprus.

Spain

A. *The Dictatorship*

By the end of the Spanish Civil War, General Francisco Franco had established firmly his personal authority over the Spanish nation. Franco combined the top offices of the armed forces, state, and party (*Falange* or Phalanx) in his own person. He had declared his unity of purpose with Mussolini and Hitler, to whose assistance in the civil war he owed much. This linkage was so strong that the economy of Spain was closely tied to the economic systems of the Axis powers during World War II.

For a generation after the ruinous civil war in Spain, Franco and his followers were busy suppressing dissidents, who had fought against the Fascists and many of whom were restive. Loyalists, often wrongly branded as Communists, diligently were sought out by the Franco forces. When captured, they frequently were executed, or herded into concentration camps and put to work as forced labor on public projects. Recollections of the three hard years of desperate civil fighting and the harsh suppression of enemies afterward helped keep Franco, relatively untroubled by meaningful opposition, in power for decade after decade. Not many seemed to hate the Franco dictatorship as much as they did the thought that anarchy and strife might come to Spain again. By the mid-1960's, when a new generation had come along, that had not known the civil disorders of thirty years earlier, the Franco regime had moderated somewhat and the quality of life in Spain had shown improvement. The degree of amelioration was not impressive when compared with other Western states, but was marked when contrasted with the earlier Spanish experience.

There was some opposition to Franco in the postwar era, particularly in the traditionally separatist-minded Basque and Catalan areas. But the Franco Government struck out vigorously at manifestations of separatism. Publication of writings in the Catalan tongue, as well as the singing of the Catalan national anthem, were made punishable under Spanish law. But, as part of the general postwar pattern of moderation in Spain, Franco made some concessions to the Catalans by dismissing officials in Barcelona who were deeply detested by the local inhabitants.

A law of 1947 determined the postwar Spanish succession. In that year, Franco declared Spain to be a monarchy and designed a law, subsequently passed by the Spanish Cortes and ratified in a referendum, which made him chief of state for life. Upon Franco's death, a regency council was to elect a king to be his successor. This king, upon taking the oath of office, would be required to swear fealty to the principles of the Falangist movement. A succession law of 1969 provided that Prince Juan Carlos de Borbón, grandson of Alfonso XIII, was to be declared Chief of State with the title of King, within 8 days after Franco's death or resignation.

With the succession regulated, Franco's Government continued as a Fascist dictatorship. Civil liberties remained curtailed. There eventually developed some popular opposition to this rule, which was independent of the traditional separatism of the Basques and the Catalans. There were periodic student riots, protesting the repressive nature of the government. And the workers began to strike in protest against political oppression and unfavorable economic conditions.

A concordat was concluded with the Vatican in 1953. Roman Catholicism was pronounced the "only" religion of Spaniards, and rules were adopted providing for the nomination of bishops by the state. In return for the privilege of nominating higher clergy, the government appropriated funds for the Catholic Church and allowed it to play a role in Spanish education that appeared anachronistic in Western Europe.

Adherents of minority religions (essentially Protestant and Jewish) formed less than 1 per cent of the population in Spain. Under the law, Protestant and Jewish places of worship were not to be marked. Marriages performed by the clergy of minority religions were not recognized as legal. Attempts to proselytize for religious minorities through publications or schools were forbidden. And laws of this type were enforced with vigor until the mid-1960's, when moderation began to appear also in the area of religious affairs. There was a gradual relaxation of restrictions and Franco, in 1965, stated that he favored freedom of conscience for all Spaniards. This sentiment, however, did not immediately become part of Spanish law.

B. *Spain and the Western World in the Postwar Era*

When a nation declares neutrality, this can become a rigidly held position with scrupulous attention paid to all pronouncements made by the government, so that neither one belligerent nor the other will seem to be favored when international confrontations develop. There is another type of neutral stance, however, wherein a nation which officially declares neutrality will obviously favor one side or another. The latter of these two types of neutrality was the one chosen by Spain in World War II. Franco was diplomatically linked to the Fascist powers and declared technical neutrality chiefly to maintain needed economic relationships with the Allies.

Because of this tendency to lean toward his fellow Fascists and because of the highly dictatorial character of Franco's regime, the first meeting of the United Nations at San Francisco, in 1945, voted to bar Spain from membership. This anti-Franco position was maintained at the Potsdam Conference when a special joint communiqué denouncing Franco was issued. In 1946, the Assembly of the United

Nations urged all member states to withdraw their official representatives to Spain. Franco replied to this international ostracism by blaming Communist influence.

This anti-Franco resentment was a result of the war just finished, a terrible struggle against those same Fascist powers with which Franco had close relationships. As the Cold War developed, and as the fervor of anti-Fascism began to fade in the heat of the new international confrontation, Franco's dictatorship began to be regarded more favorably by the Western powers. The first sign of the easing of hostile feelings against Spain came in 1948, when a bloc of states in the UN, led by South American nations, urged that Spain be admitted to the United Nations. Only Russia and her satellite states continued to maintain a particularly active anti-Franco policy. When the Korean War came, in 1950, and the Atlantic alliance began to seek a stronger European front against possible Communist attack, the strategic potentialities of Spain were realized. The upshot of the softening of attitudes in the West and the recognition of Spain's potential worth to the NATO states was her admittance to the UN, in 1955, as part of the same "package deal" that brought Austria and other states into the international organization.

The growing *rapprochement* between Spain and the Western alliance did not result, however, in Spanish admission to the benefits provided by the Marshall Plan or in an invitation to join the NATO alliance. Instead, in September 1953, the United States negotiated a mutual-aid agreement with Franco which carried with it the stipulation that the United States be allowed use of military installations in Spain. Three years later, in 1956, the Pact of Madrid was signed by Spain and the United States, a ten-year defensive agreement that authorized the joint building in Spain of air and naval installations. Americans were given the right also to erect radar stations and supply depots in Spain. Thus, Spain became a part of the Western defense network, although not an official member of NATO.

In 1963 and again thereafter, most recently in 1970, the original agreement for American leases of the Spanish bases was extended, with much economic benefit to Spain. In fact the mutual defense understanding between Spain and the United States, and the extensive economic aid it carried with it, did much to bolster not only the Spanish economy but the Franco regime, which had been faltering visibly. By the late 1960's, the United States had poured aid into Spain to the extent of $1,800,000.000.

United States cooperation with Spain also did much to break down Spain's isolation elsewhere in international affairs. Thus, in 1958, Spain joined the International Monetary Fund, the Organization for European Economic Cooperation, and the International Bank for Reconstruction. Spain's attempts, albeit unsuccessful, to find a place in NATO and the Common Market also reflected the tendency of Madrid to draw closer to the Western states.

Spain and Portugal also moved closer to one another, primarily because both were dictatorial and found it relatively easy to collaborate. In 1963, an accord was negotiated by Franco with de Gaulle, providing for future cooperation between the fighting services and police forces of their two nations, and in the development of hydroelectric and nuclear power.

C. The Loss of Empire

Spain occupied the free city of Tangier in 1940 and maintained control throughout the war. In 1945, Spanish troops were forced to withdraw and Tangier was taken over by an international commission. Eventually, in 1956, the city, as well as Northern Spanish Morocco, were transferred to the Kingdom of Morocco, after that state had been recognized by France as an independent power.

In that part of her African possessions that remained, Spain was faced with the same restless surge toward independence in her colonies as most European states had come to know so well in their postwar era. An irregular "Liberation Army of the Moroccan Sahara" developed in Spanish Morocco and began to clash with Franco's troops along the West African coast. As a result, in 1958, Southern Spanish Morocco was transferred to the Kingdom of Morocco. In 1968 Madrid granted independence to Equatorial Guinea and, in 1969, ceded Ifni to Morocco. Spain now maintained possession only of the Spanish Sahara, the two ancient enclaves of Ceuta and Melilla, and a few other tiny holdings.

The Spanish overseas empire, global in scope during the early modern history of Europe, now consisted of a few small possessions in Western Africa and some offshore islands. They cost more to administer than they brought in economic return, but Spain held on to them because of sentiment. Moroccan nationalists throughout the 1960's agitated against continuing Spanish control over any North or West African territory and, in 1963, the UN Special Commission on Colonialism urged Madrid to hasten self-government in its African possessions.

D. The Spanish Economy

Due essentially to American aid, the Spanish economy finally recovered from the ravages inflicted upon it during the civil war of the 1930's. Industrial output mounted until, by 1959, it was approximately 75 per cent above the level of 1948. In the 1960's, the production of Spain's factories continued to rise at a satisfactory rate. State-owned irrigation and electric projects were carried out so successfully that, by 1960, available electric power in Spain had tripled in comparison with the immediate postwar level. Utilizing centralized economic planning, a four-year development scheme was invented, which aimed at a 6 per cent annual growth rate. Direction was provided by foreign experts, who worked with scores of Spanish managers, technicians, and representatives of special interest groups within the Spanish society (particularly agriculture and labor).

Despite the anti-Communism of the Franco regime, Spain developed trade with Russia and the countries within her orbit. By the decade of the 1960's, commercial interchange and cultural exchanges with the Soviet Union were quite common. In fact, Spain, starting in the 1950's, became one of the major tourist attractions in Europe for travelers from both sides of the Iron Curtain. Part of the reason for the mass influx of tourists could be found in Spain's distinctive and colorful heritage. Perhaps even more important in attracting visitors, however, was the fact that, compared to foreign standards, life in Spain was inexpensive. Visitors flocked to Spain in such numbers that she was able to amass an impressive gold reserve. Spain thus benefited from several outside stimuli which strengthened the economy greatly, and, at the same time, increased the hold of General Francisco Franco on the country.

Portugal

A.   António de Oliveira Salazar

As intimately as the history of Spain in the postwar era was linked to the name Francisco Franco, so was the experience of Portugal closely tied to the name António Salazar. For thirty-six years, until he became incapacitated in September 1968,[13] Salazar serenely continued to exercise absolute, unchallenged power, whereas statesmen and demagogues in other parts of the world rose up, triumphed, and wielded power, and fell.

Born in 1889, a child of the Portuguese countryside, he grew up to become a financial expert, then a professor of economics. Before he was forty, he had become such an important scholar of law and economics that, in 1926 and again in 1928, he was invited to leave university teaching and become Minister of Finance. He was appointed Prime Minister in 1932, and ruled from that time on with a removed, almost monastic austerity. Indeed, he seemed so impervious to the rapid and cataclysmic changes taking place in the twentieth century that Portugal appeared to be unique in the postwar period. Salazar created about himself a cult of personality, which allowed him to create a political situation more like the benevolent despotism of Europe's past than any modern configuration.

It was indicative of the nature of Salazar's dictatorship that, when

---

[13] Salazar died in 1970 without ever becoming aware that he was no longer Premier.

the seventy-nine-year-old dictator was felled by a massive stroke, there was no hint of a popular rising or coup by the military to bring forth a new dictator. Rather, Portugal displayed no evidence of civil unrest. Instead, the country's new premier was to be chosen by Portugal's most important consultative body, the fifteen-member Council of State. By the end of September 1968, the Council had made its choice, in Marcello José Caetano, a University of Lisbon law professor considered by many to be molded "most closely in the image of Salazar."

B. *Politics and Economics*

In both the political and economic sectors Spain and Portugal resembled one another closely. Salazar permitted the existence of a unicameral legislature, but his National Union Party won all the postwar elections. There developed some opposition to the regime, as proven by occasional arrests of those whose politics deviated from the National Union Party norm. In the 1958 presidential elections, an opposition candidate, who campaigned under great restrictions imposed upon him by the Government, managed to win 20 per cent of the vote. This election so disturbed Salazar that he announced soon after in a national television appearance that there would be no such elections in the future, for it was "inconvenient" for him to tolerate opposition. There followed an amendment to the constitution in 1959, indicating that the president would henceforth be chosen by an electoral college picked by the National Assembly and various state officials. Socialist and Communist parties were banned, and Portugal continued as a paternalistic dictatorship.

The economic situation demonstrated fair improvement in the postwar period. The society, however, remained highly stratified and much of the wealth tended to accumulate in the hands of a small group of affluent families. The great bulk of Portugal's people still lived in poverty.

In the mid-1940's, the Government issued many decrees to stimulate manufacturing. These decrees were succeeded, in 1953, by a Salazar-launched six-year development plan designed to promote electrification and transport, thus providing a strong base for industrialization. The first plan was followed by a second, in 1959, to develop both agriculture and industry. Because so much of the private wealth had been accumulated in the hands of so few, new industries generally were established by the state. Since a poverty-stricken people could not provide the funds through taxation necessary to operate a modern state, much of the earnings of nationalized industry had to be used for that purpose.

Salazar was famed in the Western world for the coldly efficient way in which he operated the machinery of his state. But, for all his economic acumen, Salazar left behind him a large legacy of financial problems. Despite a promising increase of tourism in the late 1950's and 1960's, Portugal's economy continued to suffer from a lack of foreign investment. The gap between the country's wealthy elite and its impoverished masses remained enormous. Adding to the strain on the economy was the fact that Portugal refused to release a colonial empire she no longer could afford and thus was involved in seemingly constant struggles to put down guerrilla revolts in Portuguese Guinea, Mozambique, and Angola.

Many younger Portuguese economists and businessmen urged that their country become more a part of the European community, economically and politically. Traditionalists warned that such a move probably would inflate the Portuguese currency, which would make even more expensive the already costly burden of the colonial struggle. Thus, the severing of the ties of empire and a greater integration into Europe seemed of the highest priority. But Portugal was not as yet able to cut the strong bonds with her seafaring and colonial past.

C. Foreign Affairs

During World War II, Portugal was neutral. Unlike Spain, Portugal leaned toward the Allied side, in keeping with an Anglo-Portuguese alliance, that was several centuries old. Salazar's state formed a sanctuary for wartime refugees and Lisbon became one of the hotbeds of espionage. During the war, the United States and Britain made use of the Portuguese Azores as a midway stop for transatlantic flights. After the war, the Allies continued the use of the Azores and Portugal received American aid.

Irrespective of the authoritarian government of António Salazar, Portugal was "accepted by" the Western states in the postwar era. Portugal was admitted to the UN as part of the "package-deal" of 1955, participated in the Marshall Plan, became a member of the European Free Trade Association (Outer Seven), and belonged to NATO.

As indicated earlier, perhaps the one most important international problem suffered by Portugal was control of her colonies. Salazar was a believer in the "white man's burden" and the "civilizing mission" that the motherland ought to pursue in her overseas colonies. Consequently, Portugal retained a hold on the fragments that remained to her of a once great empire. This hold was tightened by Salazar's conviction that commerce between Portugal and her colonies was essential for maintaining balanced trade and holding already meager living standards in the mother country steady.

It appeared for a time that Portugal might escape the rising tide of native nationalism and anticolonialism, which was sweeping over the world. But such was not to be the case. In 1955, diplomatic relations between Portugal and India were severed as a result of a dispute over a tiny colonial outpost held by the Portuguese on the eastern coast of India. Portugal refused to surrender Goa and Diu Island to the Indian Government, and appealed to the International Court of Justice against India's blockage of Portugal's right of passage from one of her colonies to another across Indian territory. The ruling of the Court, in 1960, was in India's favor. Then, at the end of 1961, the Indian Government used troops to incorporate these territories.

Also burdensome for the strained Portuguese economy were nationalist uprisings, in 1961, triggered by events in the Congo, along Angola's northern border. In 1962, Angolan strife became so intensive and brutal that the UN Assembly adopted a resolution, by a vote of 92 to 2, calling upon Portugal to cease her repressive means against the people of Angola. Portugal denied—and continued to do so—that the UN had any competence to disturb the "internal" affairs of Portuguese colonial territories and she affirmed that the people in these lands already enjoyed the status of "independence" within the Portuguese Empire, a standing equal to that enjoyed by any European citizen.

Despite their "independence," however, Portuguese territories continued to revolt. In 1963, nationalist guerrilla warfare erupted in Portuguese Guinea. Similar, although smaller, uprisings occurred in Mozambique, throughout the 1960's and into the 1970's.

Even after the death of Salazar, the hopes of some Portuguese economists and businessmen, that Portugal would follow the lead of a preponderance of the world's states and withdraw from her colonies, had little promise of fulfillment. The four pillars of the Portuguese governmental establishment—the Catholic Church, the army, the banking community, and the senior civil service—remained determined that Portugal would retain its colonial empire.

Britain, France, and Italy in the Postwar Years

26

THE UNITED KINGDOM

A. Domestic Politics

The British wartime coalition government was made up of elements from both the Conservative and Labor parties. Since it was created only for the purpose of winning World War II, it fell apart at the end of the fighting. In July 1945, the British people went to the polls. Winston Churchill's Conservatives were defeated as 393 Labor members, who advocated fairly radical legislation, were elected to the House of Commons. In consequence, a strong Labor cabinet was established under the leadership of Clement Richard Attlee, former lecturer at the London School of Economics and previous holder of various political offices. The Foreign Secretary was the vigorous Ernest Bevin, a widely known labor organizer and head of The Central Council of the Trades Unions.

With a substantial mandate from the electorate, the Labor cabinet embarked upon an attempt to transform the war-torn British Isles into a "Socialist Commonwealth." Soon a stream of legislation began to alter traditional Britain. The first problem encountered involved rebuilding housing destroyed by bombing during the war. It was estimated that 25,000 dwellings had been ruined during the war and another 300,000 had been made uninhabitable. By the end of 1946, the new government had rehoused some 300,000 families in permanent and temporary dwellings.

A further major area in which there was much activity was education. A new Education Act was passed on April 1, 1945. It provided for reforms in the British public system of education and for regular governmental inspection of all private schools. After April 1947, all children were required to attend school until they were fifteen years old. Facilities for technical training and vocational education for adults were greatly enlarged. Many new schools were constructed and thousands of additional teachers were trained. Eventually, in 1963, an eleven-man committee recommended a considerable expansion of Britain's system of higher education so that larger numbers might enjoy the benefits of university training.

The Labor Government also announced a comprehensive social and economic program. The proclaimed aim of the new program was to provide "against every one of the main attacks which economic ill fortune can launch against individual well-being and peace of mind." By its provisions insurance payments would be made in case of unemployment, maternity, sickness, death of a wage-earner, and in various other circumstances. None of these proposals was presented as an employer's liability, rather they were offered as a social service of the state.

Another Labor social welfare plan eventually developed into the National Health Service. Everyone in the British poulation, regardless of income or occupational status, was to be eligible without charge for care in a hospital, medical service, or special care. This was to be accomplished by combining socialized medicine and private medical practice.

These sweeping social welfare schemes were a novelty in British history. Despite the eventual passing from the political scene of the Labor Government inaugurating these measures, the reforms remained and were accepted. John M. Keynes' motto, "What we can do we can afford," became the rule for postwar British Labor governments.

One of the most important features of the program advanced by the new Labor Government was its nationalization policy. In the election platform of 1945, the Labor Party had pledged itself to the nationalization of the "commanding heights of industry." Nationalization of certain key industries was not a new policy in Britain. The telegraph and telephone system had been operated by the Post Office Department for some time. As early as 1926, the Government had become involved in the public sale of power, and, in 1927, the British Broadcasting Corporation first took over the radio. Hence, the most important aspects of the Laborites' postwar nationalization policy was not its newness, but its wide scope.

The Laborites sought to build what they called a "mixed economy." A mixed economy, in their thinking, was one in which several sectors of private enterprise would be left untouched as certain others were nationalized. As Laborite Herbert Morrison put it, the socialization of each industry "must stand or fall on its own merits." Following this precept, the Labor Government nationalized the overseas wireless services (1946), the Bank of England (1946), the coal mining industry (1947), much of transport (1947), and electrical and gas supply (1948).

In most cases nationalization was achieved by compensating previous owners for their losses, and then government corporations were established. After a number of enterprises had been nationalized, the Labor Government announced that it would take control of the iron and steel industry. In December 1949, a bill was enacted nationalizing the steel industry and, on February 15, 1951, the Iron and Steel Corporation of Great Britain became the owner of the nation's important iron and steel companies. This new government-owned corporation was able to demonstrate a fair net profit by September 1951.

The Conservatives denounced most of the measures inaugurated by the Labor Government. There were those Conservatives who saw the programs initiated by the Laborites as steps sufficiently radical to endanger the very foundations of British liberty. Winston Churchill voiced the typical Conservative concern when he said that the "liberties and free life of Britain" were "in great danger."

In the British political system, the House of Commons is elected for five years. Seldom, however, does one government continue in power that long without an election. The period between 1945 and 1950 was an exception in that Labor held such a comfortable majority that the Parliament lasted until the next regular election in 1950.

As the members of the Government prepared to defend themselves in the election of 1950, they were faced with the fact that their nationalization program had been retarded by an economic crisis. For example, steel could not be spared to improve the British railways, which were badly in need of repair. Thus, the campaign of 1950 roused much heated debate and nationalization was the most important issue. In February 1950, Britain went to the polls. Most of the voters had read the widely-distributed Labor Party campaign literature and many could quote the Laborites' manifesto: "Let us win through together." Laborite campaign posters also indicated all the new areas to be nationalized.

The Conservatives declared, in reply, "This is the road!," pointing a way toward less national control. As a result of the election, the majority held by Labor in the Parliament dropped from some 140 to about half a dozen seats. There would not again pass five years before another election was held.

The popularity of the Labor Party had eroded because many believed that economic and social revolution had been pressed too hastily by the Attlee Government. After a long and crippling war, it was difficult for the British populace to bear the continuing pressures and sporadic crises developing from extensive social and economic experimentation. Labor policies also had brought about a rise in taxes and many yearned for a lowering in the tax rates.

The Labor Party held on with its tiny majority, though the cabinet was immediately faced with severe problems. The British had entered the Korean War on the side of the United Nations, and that policy was not popular in Great Britain. An adverse trade balance developed and created an acute financial situation at the same time that defense needs made the British budget higher than ever. In April 1951, Hugh Gaitskell, the new Chancellor of the Exchequer, presented his budget estimating that the British government would spend £939,000,000 more than in 1950. With much opposition to continued Laborite programs, Prime Minister Attlee felt that another election would have to be fought in late 1951.

In the campaign the Laborites attempted to allay public anxiety. Consequently, there was no mention of new nationalization schemes. The listless Laborite campaign seemed to indicate that Labor temporarily had lost its vitality. The Conservatives appeared to be gaining strength. Churchill and his followers campaigned under the slogan "Britain strong and free" and scored the Laborite Government. In the election of October 1951, the Conservatives and allied groups won a majority of 321 seats to Labor's 295. Winston Churchill once again assumed his familiar role as prime minister.

In February 1952, George VI died, and his daughter was proclaimed Queen, as Elizabeth II.

On the political scene, the Conservative Government launched a series of drastic measures aimed at improving the economy. As a result of these measures, an inflationary spiral was contained by the end of 1953.

Under the Steel Act of 1953 the state corporation controlling the iron and steel industry was dissolved. In its place there was established a private agency, which was entrusted with the task of disposing shares to investors. At the same time, however, the Conservative Government continued developing Labor's house-building activities and social insurance plans.

In April 1955, Sir Winston Churchill, aged eighty years, passed the responsibility of Conservative leadership to Sir Anthony Eden. The internationally respected diplomat led the Conservatives into an election in May 1955. It proved to be an unexciting contest. The Conservatives again won a resounding victory, after which they held 344 seats in the House of Commons to Labor's 277.

During 1956, the Conservative Government was confronted by a series of problems. The British and French armed intervention in Suez led to a brief divergence of United States and British foreign policies and brought extensive criticism of Anthony Eden. At about the same time the level of unemployment rose and inflationary pressures increased. Eden's health was broken by the pressures of office and he was told by doctors that he must resign. The new leader (1957) of the Conservative Party and Prime Minister was Harold Macmillan, former Foreign Secretary and Chancellor of the Exchequer. Macmillan healed the breech that had appeared in Anglo-American relations during the Suez crisis.

The economic policies pursued by Macmillan's government improved financial conditions in Britain during 1957 and 1958. There was a great increase in British exports. Moreover, investments from abroad, especially from the United States, infused Britain's economy with new life. It seemed to Macmillan and his Conservative colleagues that there would be no better time to give the party another victory at the polls. The Conservatives began a campaign in which the Laborites found little in the way of an issue to run on. Conservatives declared to the people of Britain: "You never had it so good."

The Conservative strategy proved to be correct. Hugh Gaitskell and his Laborite followers proposed the construction of new schools, hospitals, and houses. These schemes the Conservatives called "lavish and irresponsible." The general election of October 1959, brought a tremendous victory to the Conservatives, as they won some 100 seats more than Labor. The election victory was so substantial that it caused the Laborites to drop their demands for nationalization as part of a new posture designed to gain the votes of a middle-class that opposed the socialization of British industries.

Under Macmillan's leadership, the Conservative Party continued to control Parliament into the 1960's. Macmillan remained as Prime Minister until illness forced his resignation in 1963. He then was succeeded by his Foreign Minister, the Earl of Home, who resigned his peerage to become a member of the House of Commons,[1] and as Sir Alec Douglas-Home became Prime Minister.

In 1963, too, the Labor Party lost its leader as Hugh Gaitskell died of a virus infection. For seven years, he had shown great ability in leading the party, working long hours to weld together disparate and sometimes antagonistic elements. His most recent efforts had been to win out over the left wing of his party, which continued to attempt the revival of the old Laborite schemes for nationalization. Gaitskell was succeeded by James Harold Wilson, an affable, pipe-smoking intellectual. Wilson insisted that he would follow the moderate policies of Hugh Gaitskell and was emphatic in his support of the Atlantic Alliance. His position placed Wilson at odds with the left wing of his party, which loudly demanded nuclear disarmament.

The British political trend in late 1963 was toward Labor. The Laborites were winning control of local governments where, in earlier elections, the Conservatives had enjoyed comfortable majorities. The reasons behind the Conservative decline were to be found in widespread unemployment, particularly in Scotland, and a morals scandal involving War Minister John Profumo, which filled the headlines of British papers for weeks.

The Conservatives hoped to stop the trend toward Labor by "stealing the opposition's thunder." They promised that, if allowed to remain in power, there would be rapid advances in health, housing, trade, and education, all areas where the Laborites charged the Conservatives with inactivity. On the other side of the political spectrum, Wilson and his Laborites continued to charge that the Conservatives had no plans to stimulate the economy and no answers for the formidable problems developing in industry and trade. In the next

---

[1] Under the provisions of the Peerage Act of July 1963, Lord Home (pronounced Hume) had to renounce his title. Custom also dictated that a prime minister be a member of Commons.

election, held in October 1964, the Labor Party carried the day. However, the winners enjoyed a majority of only four seats.

Despite a "razor-thin" majority that had fallen to three when the House of Commons met in February 1965, Harold Wilson insisted that his mandate from the people was sufficient to press ahead. Wilson indicated that there would be direct government action to deal with problems in housing, and large areas of the cities were to be rebuilt. Complicating Wilson's task were the dark economic clouds hanging over Britain. The ship-building industry, for instance, had been damaged by Swedish and Japanese competition. The Wilson Government resorted to extreme measures—restrictions against corporate mergers, tightening of the laws against monopolies, and the dropping of defense projects when the implements of war could be purchased abroad at lower cost. Yet, the aura of crisis persisted.

Despite difficult times, Wilson's conduct of government apparently satisfied the British. When he called for new elections in March 1966, the electorate was sufficiently impressed with his government's record to give him a majority of about 100 seats.

In the spring of 1966, Britain's economic and military limitations became increasingly evident when the British were forced to slash their overseas forces by a third, openly admitting that they could no longer manage any major military operation without the help of the United States. In 1967 and 1968, Harold Wilson's Government inaugurated an austerity program and the pound was devalued. Trade, however, continued to sag. As the 1970's began, the Commonwealth no longer provided Britain with the major portion of her income. Increasingly, the British traded with European states, and many Britons began to see membership in the Common Market as their only salvation. This entry was continually blocked, however, by de Gaulle's France, on the ground that Britain was not sufficiently independent of the United States to pursue a "European" policy. Thus, despite the energetic efforts of Wilson and his government, Britain's adjustment to the political and economic realities of the late 1960's was less than successful.

In June 1970 Britain prepared to go to the polls in the eighth general election since 1945. The campaign was marred by the issue of race as Conservative candidate for the district of Wolverhampton, Enoch Powell, charged the Labor government with "cruelly" misleading the British public as to the scope of the "problem" caused by immigration into Britain of blacks from Asia and the Caribbean. Powell demanded citizenship legislation to differentiate between those who "belonged" in Britain and those who did not. The furor raised by such charges caused campaigners to pay little heed to the issue of Britain's attempts to enter the Common Market, the most important problem facing the British in 1970.

On election eve the Laborites were definite favorites in the international press. The election itself, however, proved a surprise as the Conservatives emerged from it with a thirty-vote majority in the House of Commons. As a result Britain was led into the 1970's by a new Prime Minister, Conservative leader Edward Heath. It was not known to what extent the racial question shaped election results. But it seemed more probable to observers that voters had supported Conservative candidates in the hope that a Tory government would cut taxes.

B. Economics

After it had come to power at the end of World War II, Clement Attlee's new regime did not remove wartime controls over the economy. Rather, they were extended. Rationing of certain items (food products, for instance) continued until 1954. A coal shortage caused the Government to require domestic consumers to register for each allocation they received. Tight control over the economy was made necessary by an excess of imports over exports. It was essential to bring into Britain basic machinery to replace that which had been lost during the Nazi bombing of industrial facilities.

British industries recovered rapidly. In the reconstruction of industrial centers the United States was particularly helpful. America sent direct aid and Britain also participated in the European Recovery Program. In addition, loans came in from prosperous Commonwealth areas. Britain continued to be bothered by trade deficits, however. In September 1949, with the approval of the International Monetary Fund, the pound was devalued by about 30 per cent. This devaluation was aimed at improving the total balance of overseas payments, and it did bring temporary relief. In the long run, however, the balance of trade remained unfavorable to Britain as the factories were not able to produce a surplus over British domestic needs to sell on the world market.

During Harold Macmillan's tenure in office, Britain became more affluent. Employment was high, and property ownership became more widely distributed throughout the nation. Generally, manufacturing flourished. In 1963, company earnings and stock prices were up and British automobiles sold well in the world market. Despite the fact that the export business was smashing all records, there was a negative side to the new prosperity. Burdened by a growing population, fed by an influx of West Indians, Indians, and Pakistanis from the Commonwealth, the British economy needed a continued increase in imports. Thus, the balance of trade was not restored properly.

When Wilson's Labor Government took office in 1964, the balance of payments deficit had mounted to just over $2,000,000,000. The Government resorted to extreme measures in an attempt to correct the situation. There was placed a temporary charge of 15 per cent on all imports except foodstuffs. The standard rate of personal income tax was raised, as was the gasoline tax.

The new economic measures caused something of an international panic. A run on the pound developed and the Bank of England was able to stabilize affairs only after negotiating $3,000,000,000 in loans. The economic situation continued to worsen, even though British currency had been momentarily stabilized. In 1965, the annual defense outlay was reduced again and, eventually, it became necessary to devalue the pound once more. Many of these severe economic adjustments in the 1960's were tied to Britain's loss of empire and the failure of her leaders to secure full integration into the European Economic Community. To understand this phenomenon more fully, we must turn to an examination of British foreign affairs in the postwar era.

C. Foreign Affairs—World Power or European Partner?

Britain had possessed the greatest of the European colonial empires and thus suffered more than most from the loss of her colonies. After the Second World War, the masses of many lands were filled with a seething nationalism. In many parts of the British Empire, men proclaimed an end to the old order. In India demands for political independence were more vocal than ever. The British decided that their presence in India could be maintained only with difficulty. The granting of independence seemed the easier course. India in 1947 accordingly was divided into two independent British dominions—Pakistan and India.

After the war, the British interests in Palestine could not be maintained without great difficulty and expense. In 1947, therefore, Britain announced her intention of surrendering the mandate of Palestine and withdrawing completely, leaving the awesome burden of difficulties existing there between Arab and Jew to the United Nations. When Britain officially terminated her thirty-one year rule of Palestine on May 15, 1948, the Jews proclaimed at Tel Aviv the independence of the new state of Israel.

These are but two of the many examples which serve to indicate the rapid shrinkage of Britain's empire. In India, Burma, Malaya, Egypt and the Suez Canal, and Cyprus, those who watched over British interests had been forced to leave by 1960.

Some of the territories that broke free from direct British control did not seek complete separation. After 1945, the following new nations joined the Commonwealth: Pakistan, India, Ghana, Ceylon, Cyprus, Nigeria, Sierra Leone, Tanzania, Trinidad and Tobago, Jamaica, Uganda, Kenya, Malaysia, Malawi (Nyasaland), Zambia, and Malta. Some states (Burma and the Sudan, for instance) were members only briefly. Older member nations (Ireland and South Africa) left the Commonwealth completely.

The postwar size of the Commonwealth thus was impressive but illusory. Many of the member states (India, Ghana, and Pakistan, for example) became independent republics and their connection with

Britain was loose indeed. In these cases, the British Government was recognized as "Head of the Commonwealth." The most important bond that held these states together was an economic one. For some time, London's financial houses furnished capital for development areas of the Commonwealth. Gradually, there was a reduction of dependence on former colonies since these states were unwilling to shore up a sagging economic situation in the British Isles by continuing trade that was not to their advantage. At the same time, the majority of nonwhite people within the Commonwealth sought independence. Thus, Britain still appeared to be a world power, although she suffered many hardships that world powers previously had not had to endure.

Because of her former role as the keeper of the European balance of power, Britain's leaders initially believed she would be a world power in the postwar era. Then the emergence of the superpowers diminished the standing of Britain in global affairs. Britain was unable to protect Turkey and Greece against possible Soviet expansion in 1947 and that responsibility was passed to the United States. During the late 1940's and early 1950's, Britain had to admit that she no longer possessed the power to remain isolated from the continent when she wished to do so. She therefore endorsed the idea that the Soviet power could be contained only through collective defense arrangements. Britain became a first-mover in European defense compacts with the Anglo-French alliance (1947), the British, French, and Benelux arrangements of the following year, and the NATO Alliance in 1949. This increasing commitment to the defense of Europe obliged Britain to make considerable outlays for defense.

The rapidly changing economic situation in Britain made her more and more dependent on the United States to meet her defense obligations. Many Britons came to resent this dependence. When Britain became a nuclear power and developed her own H-bomb (1957), she was faced with the necessity of developing a delivery system. The building of a ballistic missile system proved to be too expensive, however, and Britain found it necessary to depend upon the United States for a new type of missile, the Skybolt. In 1962, the United States suddenly announced that Washington had decided to drop production of the Skybolt. When this news reached the British public, a great wave of anti-American criticism developed. Hurt feelings were eased only partially by a Kennedy-Macmillan agreement, in December 1962, which substituted Polaris underwater missiles for the Skybolt system.

After the advent of the Wilson Government in 1964, it became increasingly apparent that Britain was groping for a new stance in foreign affairs. The Labor ministry reaffirmed that the alliance with the United States was basic to British foreign policy. At the same time, however, there were indications that the British Government had realized that Britain was no longer the world power she once had been. As long as the British believed that they could continue to play a leading role in world affairs they were not greatly interested in taking part in European economic or political integration. When it became obvious that the British capability to play such a role had lessened, Britain turned more toward Europe. Prime Minister Macmillan was the first to apply for Britain's admission to the Common Market, only to be blocked by France. Harold Wilson carried on the campaign to secure Britain's entry into the EEC, but he was blocked also. Britain's future lay with continental Europe, and she was impelled to seek closer ties with the Continent in the 1970's.

D. The Irelands

The period between the two world wars was a time of upheaval in Ireland. Out of civil strife came two Irelands. The northern state was constitutionally attached to the United Kingdom and an Irish Free State (Eire after 1937) was established in the south. The six northern counties were called Ulster and were inhabited primarily by people of the Protestant faith, while the south was essentially Roman Catholic. Moreover, the two areas also differed in that Ulster was primarily industrial and Eire was agrarian. The inhabitants of Ulster prized their separation from Eire, whereas the citizens in Eire were often intense Irish nationalists, who believed that establishing a united Ireland was more important than securing any other political objective.

Ulster's Government managed its own local affairs, but foreign relations and national defense were responsibilities left to the British Government. Moreover, Ulster sent representatives to sit in Parliament. Business ties to Britain were close and, consequently, when various indigenous industries suffered a decline in the late 1950's, migration from Ulster to Britain increased.

During World War II, Eire had remained neutral and her ports were closed to certain Allied warships. Despite this fact, many Irish enrolled in the British fighting services and many more took jobs in the British defense plants. After the fighting, the last constitutional ties with Britain were severed, but trade pacts continued to bind the Irish to the British.

Because the southern portion of Ireland was primarily agrarian, politicians in Eire stressed the need for industry. Eventually, because of increased state planning and subsidization, Eire began a noticeable development of diversified industry. Agriculture continued to be somewhat primitive, however. The general trend was for people to hold on to the small farms passed down to them by their ancestors, thus maintaining individual plots so tiny that large-scale machinery could not be used effectively on them. There were some efforts to use land and markets cooperatively, and these were generally successful. In numerous areas the relatively primitive style of life was eased by the Government's insertion of a note of modernity, whereby rural electrification and water supply programs were initiated.

In 1948, the Irish Parliament repealed an earlier External Relations Act and thus broke the remaining legal ties with the United Kingdom. The legislation, effective in 1949, changed the name of Eire to the Republic of Ireland. The London Government recognized that Ireland was no longer to be counted among the dominions, but refused to give it a completely foreign status. Hence, a new British Nationality Act went into effect on January 1, 1949, which created three types of citizens: United Kingdom, Commonwealth, and Irish. Citizens of the Irish Republic, should they happen to live on British territory, were given the right to vote as part of the registered electorate of that area.

In 1959 Éamon de Valéra, six times the Prime Minister, decided to give up his post and run for the presidency. Valéra easily won the election (as he did again in 1966) and from his new post continued to improve relations with Northern Ireland. In 1965, there was a joint conference between the two states, a thing that would have been impossible in earlier days of hostility between the two Irelands. The two Irelands also began, during the 1960's, to encourage tourism together. This era of good feeling was made possible, in large part, by the official announcement in 1962 that the Irish Republican Army, which long had sought to force unity through terrorism, no longer existed.

The religious situation in Eire and Ulster continued to be one of the major bars to the unity nationalists desired so greatly. Strong anti-Catholic sentiments persisted in Ulster, and many of the Protestants there were reluctant even to work beside Catholics or live in the same areas of the cities. This type of discrimination showed up particularly in such matters as the assignment of public housing units and eventually gave rise, from late 1968 into 1970, to mass civil-rights protests and riots. The religious differences also developed strong cultural differences. The stricter Calvinistic Protestants, for instance, believed any kind of activity other than meditation and prayerful repose on Sunday was sinful. At the same time, much of the Catholic population in Ulster indulged in sporting and other similar activities on the Sabbath, which tended to horrify the Protestants. With the example of the Ulsterite Catholics constantly before them, Northern Protestants, despite the hard work of societies to foster interfaith understanding, showed no marked tendency to sympathize with the unity movement. By the late 1960's and early 1970's, old antagonisms between Protestant and Catholic caused continued disruption and violence in Ulster. The establishment of one Ireland seemed to be a matter, if at all, for the distant future.

A. The Establishment of the Fourth Republic

The much-troubled Third French Republic had fallen before the onrushing Nazi armored columns in 1940. During the Second World War, Frenchmen were torn by divided loyalties, sundered between a government in France that cooperated with the Nazis and one in Great Britain, claiming still to be representative of Republican France. As the war continued, those who committed acts of sabotage and rebellion commonly were regarded as patriots and those who were loyal and obedient to the government in power normally were looked upon as either defeatists or collaborators. Hence, there were tremendous divisive strains within the French society. When the Nazis were driven from France, it seemed possible that several disruptions might develop in the newly freed country. But this was not to be the case. Frenchmen gathered around the person of Charles de Gaulle, whose name had become identified with the idea of setting up an independent and well-organized government.

As the Nazis were driven out of France, some resistance groups settled private grudges against those who had collaborated with the Nazis. There were summary executions, stripping and shaving of the heads of female associates of the Nazis, dispossessions, and expulsions. In some areas of France local resistance groups, many of them dominated by the Communists, took control temporarily after the German withdrawal. But wherever the new Gaullist authorities were established, resistance-formed governments at once were terminated. The problem of dealing with collaborators was handed over to the courts.[2]

The French Government-in-Exile, earlier established by de Gaulle in Algiers, came to Paris in 1944. An assembly, formed of members of the Algiers Government and of various resistance groups, was convened. This Provisional Government, with de Gaulle at its head, set about the business of returning France to normal conditions. It remained in power for fourteen months after de Gaulle's entry into Paris on August 26, 1944.

The most important business of the Provisional Government was making a new France. In October 1945, a referendum was held in which 96 per cent of the voters (who for the first time included women) in effect rejected a revival of the Third Republic by electing a Constituent Assembly to draft a new constitution. In the assembly, the Left was heavily represented. The parties of the old Left, the Communists and Socialists, won 25 and 23 per cent of the seats, respectively. Astonishing to observers was the success of a new party, the *Mouvement Républicain Populaire* (MRP), which was

---

[2] A high court was established to try the more notable collaborators. Eventually, Pierre Laval was executed and the aged Marshal Petáin had a death sentence commuted to detention in a fortress for the rest of his life; he died in 1951.

closest to de Gaulle in outlook and drew on the prestige of his name to gather some 24 per cent of the popular vote.

When the Constituent Assembly met, de Gaulle became President of the Provisional Government. It was a role for which he was not prepared by experience, nature, or political views. Although they were the largest party in the assembly, the Communists were excluded from the ministry by de Gaulle. Thus began a series of direct conflicts between the head of the government and the powerful Communist-Socialist coalition. Soon, moreover, relations also became strained between de Gaulle and his MRP Foreign Minister, Georges Bidault.

The basis of confrontation between de Gaulle and many elements within the government and the parties was a difference in view regarding the proper structure of government. De Gaulle wanted a strong executive, who could not be dominated by parliament. His opponents wanted national policy to emerge from party compromises in the legislature, as previously had been the case. In January 1946, de Gaulle, recognizing that his view would not prevail, resigned. A few months later, the electorate rejected a Leftist draft constitution that would have made a figurehead of the president.

A second Constituent Assembly was elected in June 1946. This time the Communists and Socialists lost votes and the MRP became the largest party. Another constitution was produced which, though it still provided for a strong parliament and weak executive, was approved by referendum in October.

The Fourth Republic officially came into being in December 1946. Its first president was the Socialist, Vincent Auriol, chosen in January 1947. Auriol, because of his political prestige and skill, was often to play an influential role behind the scenes; but like his predecessors in the Third Republic, he could not chart a steady course for France. His successor, René Coty, who took office in 1954, was even less effective.

Political instability remained a French habit. From December 1946 to June 1951, there were eight ministries, averaging under seven months each in office. A typical game of political musical chairs was played, with the same faces appearing and reappearing in successive ministries. It was, perhaps, a stroke of good fortune that the foreign ministry, while several times changing leadership during this period, did so only between two MRP members, Georges Bidault and Robert Schuman.

In the early days of the Fourth Republic, in 1947, the MRP, Socialists, and Communists shared power in the government. In May 1947, inflation brought strikes, which the Communist Party was forced by its ideological commitment to support, although the trouble was directed at the very ministry in which Communists played a major role. The Socialist Premier, Paul Ramadier, did not resign in face of the strike crisis, but took the unusual step of dismissing the Communists from the cabinet. This began open political war between the Communists on one side, and the MRP and Socialists on the other. Communist-led strikes in the winter of 1947–1948, failed to regain for the Reds an influential position in the government.

The turning point in the postwar struggle of the Socialists and the MRP against the Communists came with institution of Marshall Plan aid in late 1947. The French Communists lashed out against the idea of aid from the United States and urged that France turn to the U.S.S.R. for economic help. However, even the average Frenchman was aware of France's grave need of economic aid and he also seemed to be at least vaguely aware that such aid could come only from the United States. The result of vitriolic Communist propaganda and open instigation of strikes was a general swing to the right in French politics. As the political center of gravity moved right, MRP and Radical Socialist premiers replaced Socialists in that high office.

As time went on, the three major parties squabbled over almost everything. Fluctuations in the economy caused similar fluctuations in the government. The last eighteen months of the first Assembly of the Fourth Republic witnessed a procession of ineffectual and short-lived ministries. As a new national election approached in mid-1951, the major moderate parties seemed agreed only on the necessity for keeping the Communists out of power on the left and the resurgent Gaullists on the right. In this they succeeded. The parties of a so-called "Third Force" (MRP, Socialists, and Radicals) obtained 62.5 per cent of the seats. The Gaullists managed to obtain 19.6 per cent of the seats and the Communists only 17.8 per cent.

After 1952, the gradual swing to the right continued and the Assembly produced several new premiers. Elements of stability persisted elsewhere in the cabinet, however, as the two earlier-mentioned ministers, Bidault and Schuman, continued to shape foreign policy until 1954. Moreover, the reshaping of the French economy was largely freed from the rapidly shifting influences of French politics by being placed for several years in the capable hands of Jean Monnet.

Ten years after liberation from the Nazis, France seemed to be caught up in political inertia. The structure of the Fourth Republic was even more fragile than that of the Third and its foundations were cracked by the damaging colonial war in Algeria. In November 1955, a cabinet was defeated by a vote of no confidence and the National Assembly dissolved. The ensuing election, however, did nothing to alter the state of inertia that had stricken the Fourth Republic. The parties had just enough vitality to inhibit action by their opponents while, at the same time, lacking energy to initiate positive legislation of their own.

The Fourth Republic could boast of few accomplishments. Territorial disputes with Germany were ended in December 1956, by the return of the Saar to the Bonn Government. In January 1957, the Fourth Republic began negotiations to bring France into a European Common Market. Within France, there was a beginning of economic prosperity, and social reforms had been launched against the worst of the existing social ills.

Yet, all these forward steps did not provide sufficient support for the Fourth Republic to ensure its survival from a colonial crisis. France had cut its ties with certain of its North African possessions (Morocco and Tunisia) in March 1956. In June 1956, a law extended local self-government to other African possessions, thus preparing them for independence in the future. But this action did not resolve the seemingly intractable situation in Algeria.

In November 1954, Algerian Nationalists had initiated a campaign of terrorism. By 1955, the French were forced to maintain some 170,000 troops in Algeria to contain the revolt. In 1956, French reinforcements were poured into Algeria until some 350,000 men were there to suppress the rebels. The latter, despite the fact that their number apparently did not much exceed 15,000, controlled the remote, mountainous areas of the country. From secret mountain bases small groups of terrorists launched continuous raids.

As a consequence of these terrorist activities, governmental functions in Algeria increasingly came into the hands of the military. Whole villages were placed under armed guard and intensive campaigns of indoctrination begun. Despite such efforts on the part of the French, the Algerian nationalists intensified their terrorism. A civil war developed, typified by acts of barbarism perpetrated by both the army and French *colons* (European settlers), on the one side, and the nationalists on the other. As the civil war in Algeria resulted in a mounting toll of young French lives, it became increasingly unpopular in France. Eventually, the outrages perpetrated by Algerian terrorists spread to France itself, greatly augmenting the general feeling of insecurity abroad in the land. This insecurity had its reflection in politics as government instability increased.

In the fall of 1957, France was for five weeks without a government because a majority willing to support any one coalition could not be put together. Again, in April 1958, it took a month before a fallen government could be replaced by a new one. There was a sentiment sweeping throughout France, calling for the French to get out of Algeria no matter what the cost. But to have withdrawn from Algeria would have countered the interests of two powerful groups: the *colons*, who saw Algeria as their homeland and feared the loss of their property should the natives take control; and the army, which sought to continue its colonial control and to maintain the influence such control gave them. All this meant that the army and the *colons* were ripe for rebellion should a premier come to office in France who sought French withdrawal from Algeria. Pierre Pflimlin was such a man. On May 13, 1958, when he was to present his cabinet to the Assembly, French extremists took action.

The Europeans of Algeria were at the edge of hysteria, driven to fear by years of nationalist terrorism. Beating pots and pans and wildly honking automobile horns, they streamed into the streets of their cities screaming "Algérie française." Government offices in Algeria were taken over and a self-elected revolutionary committee proclaimed itself in power. The French Government could only protest the revolt as long as the army took the side of the colonial rebels. There was, at this point, the likelihood that extremists and their sympathizers might extend the revolt into France itself and overthrow the Government.

Charles de Gaulle had been convinced for some time that the Fourth Republic was doomed because it had turned its back on the presidential system he once had proposed. Now he was ready to "save" France and announced, on May 15, 1958, that he was prepared to aid the French nation in its hour of difficulty, should he be called upon to do so. At the same time he pointed out that any move he made would have to be circumspectly legal. In many ways de Gaulle's offer was now the logical choice to solve France's knotty colonial problem, for there were many generals involved in the Algerian revolt who, with a typical political naiveté, believed that de Gaulle, a former military leader, was certain to share their views.

De Gaulle's reaction to the sentiments of any potential supporters was a clever silence. The French President, René Coty, accepted Pflimlin's resignation of the premiership and de Gaulle to succeed him. De Gaulle agreed to accept the office, but only after the acceptance of his condition that he should have decree power for six months. Moreover, he asked that, at the end of the six-month period, a new constitution be submitted to the whole nation for a vote.

De Gaulle made use of his six months to have enacted into law a host of badly needed reforms and to direct the preparation of a new constitution. The new document was submitted to a referendum in September 1958, and accepted by a majority (80 per cent) of the voters. Now effective legislative power was transferred from the Assembly to the premier and the power of nominating a man to the premiership was given to the president. The president was to be chosen by a large electoral college made up of numbers of local government bodies. The general impact of these changes was to place much more power in the hands of the president at the expense of the legislature. Following adoption of the constitution, de Gaulle was chosen President by the electoral college. He took office on January 8, 1959, and thus the Fourth Republic was ended and the Fifth began.

B. Economy and Society during the Fourth Republic

The economic life of the French nation underwent some fundamental changes during the years of the Fourth Republic. To begin, any discussion of the economic changes taking place in postwar France must recognize the fact that the career of Jean Monnet was inextricably intertwined with the financial welfare of France. In

January 1946, de Gaulle signed a decree establishing a *Commissariat du Plan* under the direction of Monnet. The task assigned the Commissariat was nothing less than the reconstruction of the economy of France. Monnet's schemes called for large government investment in railways, mines, and electricity. Other basic industries, particularly steel, concrete products, and farm machinery, also were promoted. By 1951, hydroelectric plants, which in 1929 had produced only 15,000,000,000 kilowatts, had produced 40,000,000,000. By 1954, the productivity of fifteen of the twenty main industries in France had passed that of the greatest boom year of the between-the-wars period (1929).

In addition to the importance of Monnet's planning, the Marshall Plan aid, which flowed into France from the United States until 1955, played an essential part in French recovery. The capital necessary for the restoration and modernization of France was provided by a combination of United States aid and domestic sources. However, some domestic resources were gained through inflationary policies. Consequently, there resulted a temporary mixture of great wealth in some quarters contrasted with grinding poverty in others. As long as this situation persisted, it was possible for the Communists to transform a gulf between rags and riches into a political advantage for the extreme left. Social assistance, first initiated by the Provisional Government, helped to soften the harsh barrier separating the rich and poor, and, by 1952, any possible benefit the Communists might have secured from a poverty-stricken proletariat was greatly lessened.

As in so many other situations where a high degree of centralized economic planning was utilized, industry responded better than agriculture. Some peasants had accumulated savings during the food shortages of the Second World War, but the postwar inflation had wiped out modest reservoirs of paper money. Until French entry into the Common Market, French agriculture, which was rapidly mechanized in postwar years by a massive increase in machinery, produced a surplus the economy could not absorb. In consequence, for some time there were falling prices resulting from overproduction, and farmers commonly protested conditions by dumping their surplus in the marketplaces of the towns.

Because of the situation that prevailed in the countryside between 1949 and 1954, about one-quarter of the rural population left the land and moved into the cities. The population of Paris rose, until it was twice as great as in the beginning of the twentieth century. The portion of the population that remained on the land was continually influenced by changing standards, which first were set in the city and then spread to the countryside. The result was that the great social diversity between country and city in France, which had existed since the medieval age, began to fade and gave promise of eventually disappearing.

In spite of the sometimes damaging inflation, there was remarkable social and economic progress during the Fourth Republic.

Groups in society not sharing in the general progress, however, were the small shopkeepers, minor employers, and peasants who owned only tiny plots. The small shopkeepers found a political rebel to give voice to their despair in 1956. Pierre Poujade organized a revolt against taxes in the Massif Central, attracted much support, and then took his "Poujadists" into national political life. In 1956, the Poujadists won fifty seats in the Assembly. But Poujade's only program was the evasion of taxes, and the lack of variety in his platform soon caused the Poujadists to fade from the scene.

C. Foreign Affairs during the Fourth Republic

After the war ended, a strong sentiment for neutralism ran through France. The influential Parisian newspaper *Le Monde* was an important spokesman for the idea that France remain free of entangling alliances. But the current of postwar events ran against isolationism. By April 1948, there were several calls for European federal institutions, and it was believed by many that some sort of economic union might well form the basis of political union. France moved further from isolationism by entering the Brussels Pact in 1948. And at the first session of a new Council of Europe in 1949, Georges Bidault spoke in favor of German membership in the Council. France also became part of the Western Alliance system and entered NATO at its formation in 1949. It now seemed that *rapprochement* with Germany would give France a greater sense of security and make her more certain about her position in Western Europe. This new direction in French policy was a marked reversal of her traditional position.

For some Frenchmen, however, *rapprochment* with Germany was too great a reversal of traditional policy. Consequently, discussions of a European Defense Community (EDC), which would have included West German troops, foundered in 1954 upon fears that a West German domination of Europe was more threatening to France than any possible benefit she might gain from EDC (see Chapter 27). The National Assembly only grudgingly approved an alternate plan for German rearmament proposed by the British, which carried with it the admission of West Germany to NATO. Only gradually did France move toward an era of good feeling with the old enemies east of the Rhine.

During the Fourth Republic, French world standing recovered notably. The major setbacks were encountered, as has been indicated in the case of Algiers, in colonial areas where the French suffered severe adjustments caused by the loss of colonies. French supporters of the European idea found expression in the Common Market rather than political institutions. With the resurgence of intense nationalism during the Fifth Republic, ideas of a Pan-Europa faded from the scene for a time.

D. The Fifth Republic

Before discussing the history of the Fifth Republic, the life of Charles de Gaulle must be reviewed briefly, for he was most influential in shaping the history of France after World War II. Charles de Gaulle was born into a bourgeois family in Lille in 1890. He became a loyal Catholic and a professional soldier. During the post-World War I era, he pleaded for greater mechanization of the army to prepare it for the mobile warfare of the future, but his conservative superiors decided to rely upon the weapons and techniques of the past. When France fell to the Nazis in 1940, de Gaulle went to London and became the central figure around whom the Free French forces rallied. Throughout the war his person was synonymous with the idea of French patriotism.

De Gaulle's position in French society was unique when the war ended. His personality had captivated the imagination of a broad section of the French population. It was certain that he would not remove himself far from the center of the French consciousness, for he believed himself best suited to restore France to her "proper" position of dominance in Europe. It was this tendency to see himself in an exalted position that brought to de Gaulle the nickname *Le grand Charles.* It also made both Roosevelt and Churchill distrust him by the end of World War II. President Roosevelt, in fact, saw de Gaulle as a potential dictator who ought to be excluded from high office after the fighting was over. De Gaulle's grand design to restore France's lost "grandeur" was delayed by the advent of the Fourth Republic, but the troublesome events of 1958 in Algeria gave him his chance.

No conflict developed between the President and the members of the Assembly in the early days of the Fifth Republic, primarily because the first election under the new constitution (1959) gave a landslide victory to Gaullist candidates. The new Gaullist party, the *Union pour la Nouvelle République* (UNR), obtained some 200 seats. This overwhelming vote of national confidence was reinforced in 1961, when a referendum indicated that approximately 75 per cent of the French people approved of de Gaulle's policies whereas only 24 per cent, mostly Communists, were disposed against him.

The great Gaullist victory brought a pronounced change to France. The Fourth Republic had been directed by men whose political habits had been formed during the Third Republic. The coming of the Fifth Republic brought new men to the government who looked at the business of governing in basically different ways.

The alterations in basic policy were not immediately so sweeping as were the changes in personnel and attitude. The Fourth Republic already had achieved a partial solution of the colonial problem. It had been forced by defeats in war to abandon Indo-China in 1954, but had managed to negotiate independence for Morocco and Tunisia. In 1956, legislation was passed endowing the overseas territories with local assemblies elected by universal suffrage. Hence, the work of the Fifth Republic in the area of the disposition of colonial territories was only to carry to a conclusion policies pursued during the Fourth Republic. Under new constitutional laws enacted by the Fifth Republic, fifteen West and Equatorial African territories, and Madagascar, became self-governing member states of the French community. De Gaulle even offered such territories complete independence from France, but only one country, Guinea, decided to accept.

Many attempts were made by de Gaulle to bring about a cessation of Algerian hostilities. In September 1959, the French President announced a plan to give self-determination to Algeria. It was arranged that no longer than four years after the restoration of peace it would have the choice of integration with France, a special federal relationship to ensure sufficient autonomy, or complete independence. Then negotiations were begun with an exiled Algerian Government. The possibility of an agreement with the nationalists caused the organization of a "Front for French Algeria" among the *colons*, who now made their last stand. The *colons* who had expected de Gaulle to support their call for an *Algérie française* turned against the General in frustrated anger.

A plebiscite was held in January 1961, wherein de Gaulle won the support of both Frenchmen and Algerians for his policies in Algeria. The prospect of a negotiated settlement caused four army generals in Algeria to attempt a coup. They gained the support of dissident officers and some 25,000 paratroopers. Calling themselves the Secret Army Organization (OAS), they seized Algiers and some other North African cities on April 21, 1961. Rumors spread to France like wildfire that the OAS would move on Paris itself. De Gaulle appeared on national television and called for the aid of all Frenchmen against the traitorous actions of the conspiring officers. The appeal caused a widespread demonstration of support for de Gaulle throughout France. Most of the armed forces remained loyal and, in late April, entered Algiers. The danger of a coup which could have overthrown the French Government passed, but the OAS went underground and continued to launch terrorist attacks against Parisian control.

Fighting between French Government forces and Algerian nationalists went on also. Finally, on March 18, 1962, a ceasefire was signed at Evian and eight years of colonial warfare came to an end. On April 8, 1962, 90 per cent of metropolitan France voted to accept the conditions under which the March ceasefire had been signed. Algeria also voted approval. Now the Europeans who had been fleeing Algeria for some time increased in number. Some 900,000 left the former North African colony to come to France during 1962 and 1963. Algeria became independent on July 5, 1962, and the French High Commissioner withdrew. One of France's most pressing postwar problems had been settled.

In October 1962, de Gaulle proposed a constitutional amendment providing that the President should be elected by popular vote. The

"General" was unhappy about the process of nominating a President through the electoral college and criticized the rule whereby national leadership was determined by some "80,000 notables" rather than the people of France. Charges now were hurled at the President that he sought to rule France in the manner of Napoleon, but de Gaulle, albeit by only a modest margin, won the constitutional revision he had sought. It appeared that voters were not particularly enthusiastic concerning the President's proposal, but they seemed to believe that support of de Gaulle was to be preferred to the confusion and irresolution so typical of the Fourth Republic.

During the 1960's, the domestic and foreign affairs of France were directed by de Gaulle and an obedient ministerial team. The Fifth French Republic began with Michel Debré as Premier. Debré was an honest but colorless man, and that was to have been expected since de Gaulle did not veil the fact that he was the real creator of national policies. His subordinates were pushed to the outer edges of the limelight, which illuminated the General's figure alone. There were Frenchmen who protested, calling the de Gaulle regime a thinly disguised "bureaucratic dictatorship." There was substance to this charge since the armed forces and the civil service were staffed with loyal Gaullists in positions of importance.

In the spring of 1962, Debré was replaced by Georges Pompidou, a man without great experience as a legislator. It now appeared to the President's critics that, in selecting a man who had been a teacher and writer without government experience, de Gaulle was drawing more power into his own hands. This impression was reinforced when de Gaulle, in seeking the constitutional amendment to provide popular election for the President, tried to turn the referendum into a vote of confidence in his methods of government. De Gaulle directed Pompidou to bypass the normal consitutional amendment procedures and call for a referendum. Opposition deputies now carried on philippics against the presidential regime and a vote censuring the ministry was passed. Pompidou resigned and de Gaulle dissolved the Assembly. The referendum was held, and, as indicated earlier, the constitutional amendment was passed by a small margin.

In the parliamentary election campaign preceding the selection of a new Assembly, the Gaullist Administration received much criticism for its "dictatorial way" in important French newspapers and magazines. Yet, the elections gave Gaullist deputies some 267 out of 482 seats, gained at the expense of the middle-of-the-road parties. The election results indicated that fears of a Gaullist revival of Bonapartism were outweighed by a widespread political apathy, perhaps produced by material affluence.

During the mid-1960's, the most troublesome opponent of de Gaulle was Gaston Defferre, Socialist deputy and reformist mayor of Marseille. Defferre was a convinced supporter of the Atlantic Alliance and campaigned throughout the country, claiming that de Gaulle was destroying the NATO pact. Defferre also advocated a constitutional revision altering the French politcal structure so that it no longer would be an "elected monarchy." The anti-Gaullist camp, using such arguments, gained enough strength in the Presidential campaign of 1965 to force de Gaulle into a run-off election against Socialist François Mitterand. In this election the General obtained a majority, but only a moderate margin of victory was his (he obtained 55 per cent). Again in March 1967, parliamentary elections indicated a substantial amount of doubt in France concerning the worth of the Gaullist regime, as the General's followers and allies retained only a slim majority in the Assembly.

In certain sectors of the French society discontent continued to grow. Then, in May 1968, anarchy swept across the face of France as several universities were seized by their students and a number of factories were barricaded by their workers. There were ominous rumors of a strike by the Paris police, that could have heralded the final breakdown of order. Late in the first week of insurrections Georges Pompidous appeared before the television cameras to assure the French people that Charles de Gaulle—off on a state visit to Romania—would address the troubled nation "within a few days." France was obviously in the midst of its worst crisis since the Algerian War, those dark days when the armies of France experienced mutiny.

Some of the college youth and industrial workers of France formed an odd ephemeral coalition. A twenty-four-hour general strike and a massive eight-hour march through Paris were arranged. An estimated half-million people joined ranks, marched across the Seine and through the Latin Quarter on the Left Bank. Slogans like "de Gaulle, assassin!" and "Ten years are enough!" demonstrated that the target of students and workers alike was the aging President of the Fifth Republic.

What were the causes of this great upheaval? As far as the students were concerned, spurred on by so-called Revolutionary Committees in the universities, they wanted nothing less than a total change in French society from top to bottom. It was clear from the first that the Government would be unable to accede to such demands. More immediately important was the protest of the workers, who, it was quickly indicated, had relatively few specific new grievances. Indeed, it seemed on the face of things that perhaps there was no real case for the French laboring man. The French economy had suffered a slight recession, but now was recovering nicely. Unemployment only recently had dropped and a rise in the cost of living had been stabilized.

The unrest derived from something more deeply entrenched in modern mass society than the usual surface causes of unemployment and too rapid rises in the cost of living. In all the Western democracies in 1968, a commonly heard criticism, particularly from the students, was that governments had grown increasingly unresponsive to the needs of the citizenry. In France, this alleged unresponsiveness had been greatly exacerbated by de Gaulle's construction of a paternalistic and essentially authoritarian regime.

Moreover, the situation of the workingman in France was not as good as a superficial glance might cause it to appear. There had been a slight upturn in the economy and prices had stabilized. However, for years, the Gaullist bureaucrats had shunned contacts with the working classes. When workers' discontent had been discovered, the Government simply had presented laborers with statistical proof that demonstrated France was more prosperous than ever. But Parisian workers were subject to some of the lowest wage rates and highest prices in Europe. Thus, the workers' demands were for higher wages, shorter hours, and a voice in the setting of their working conditions. De Gaulle's reported response to the demands of students and workers on returning from Romania was to tell his ministers: *"La reforme, oui; la chienlit, non."*[3] De Gaulle's remark was repeated and circulated. Quickly, crude caricatures began to appear on factory and university walls, with the slogan*"Le chienlit, c'est lui."*[4]

De Gaulle then appeared on national television and conceded that the widespread demand for reform—particularly in education and working conditions—made the need for extensive changes immediate. Typically, he asked for sweeping powers to work out France's future. He called for a referendum to give the state a "mandate of renewal" and threatened, as he had many times in the past, that if the people refused him the powers he sought he would not "much longer remain in . . . office."

Students derided de Gaulle's call for yet another national referendum. They pointed out that it would be the fifth such referendum in his ten years in office. Former Premier Pierre Mendès-France voiced the general opinion outside the Gaullist ranks when he claimed that the call for a national referendum was an "appeal for yet another national plebiscite." Even before de Gaulle's speech had ended, street brawling had begun again.

In succeeding weeks de Gaulle made, for him, a large number of television appearances in attempts to quiet the disturbed French nation, as Paris was torn continually by pitched street battles. Meanwhile, the Gaullist regime steadily reasserted its authority. Vital services such as the Paris subway and bus system, shut down by strikes since the early stages of disorder, were reopened. De Gaulle made a defiant announcement that he was dissolving the Assembly and calling for a general election. With the general election only two weeks away, public opinion polls indicated that the weeks of violence and revolutionary extremism had played into the hands of the Gaullists who claimed de Gaulle was the only alternative to a Communist seizure of power. The Gaullists thus drew to their cause what the French journalists labeled the "party of fear," which included the

---

[3] "Reform, yes; . . . in the bed, no."
[4] "De Gaulle himself is the . . . in the bed."

middle class and all other Frenchmen who were frightened that their savings and material comforts might now be swept away by a tide of revolution.

In place of a referendum, came the elections of June 1968. A powerful reaction against France's experiment in rebellion brought the Gaullists 124 of the 487 Assembly seats at stake. The following Sunday a decisive runoff was held and 170 more seats were added, for a total of 294. The Gaullist UDR party thus became an independent majority party (not a frequent phenomenon in coalition political systems). With its allies (essentially the Independent Republicans) the Gaullists controlled a bloc of 357 seats in the new Assembly. The Communist seats dropped from 73 to 34 and the representation of the Federation of the Left, led by François Mitterand, went from 118 to 57 seats.

Not satisfied with the increased power the June 1968 elections had given him and his party, de Gaulle, in April 1969, asked for what actually was his fifth national referendum. He now aimed at weakening France's upper house and obtaining for the President the prerogative of choosing his own successor. Many Frenchmen, with a fickleness typical of politics in France, were swayed by a belief that de Gaulle merely sought to take his revenge on a Senate that had opposed him in the past. Public opinion polls demonstrated that national sentiment was turning against de Gaulle. The President, as he had done many times before, threatened to step down if the nation failed to support him in the referendum. When the referendum was held, more than 53 per cent of the voters rejected him. De Gaulle lived up to his campaign promise and resigned.

Thus, Charles de Gaulle had committed political suicide in a test of strength that hardly anyone except the General himself had deemed necessary. In June 1969, a run-off election for the presidency was held and former Premier Georges Pompidou was elected the second President of the Fifth Republic.

E. Economy and Society in the Fifth Republic

By the mid-1960's, careful economic planning had been part of the scene in France for a long enough period to have produced some definite results. French industrial production had increased by about one-fourth in a four-year period ending in 1962. The Government made large capital investments in new industries, including among them even a space research program. The sectors in which the French economy seemed particularly strong were the merchant marine, steel, chemicals, and automobile production. Especially in the field of automobile production, record-shattering results were achieved, and exports of autos rose steadily.

Employment generally was almost full and, at times, there even developed a shortage of laborers. The shortage of workingmen was solved by imported foreign labor from former French colonial areas and from other Common Market countries. Yet, all this did not benefit the French worker as much as one might think, for inflation was a continuing problem for a wage earner. Between 1959 and 1963, prices rose an average of 4 to 6 per cent each year. Moreover, the wage-price spiral was not balanced and the workers were unable to keep up with the decline in currency values. Thus, there was much unrest among laboring men throughout the 1960's.

The wage-price discomfiture of the workers, in a time of affluence for the middle-classes, established obvious socio-economic gaps between the various levels of French social structure. This, too, became apparent in 1968 as the middle sections of French society gave de Gaulle much support at the same time that the General was the target of vituperative attacks from the working class.

The rapid growth of the French economy brought with it the usual intensive urbanization. Marseille grew extensively and Paris drew within its limits approximately one-fifth of the total French population. This situation produced a crisis in housing. Despite large urban-renewal projects in some areas, the fact that the Government held down rent levels by law caused private investors, who might normally have invested in housing developments, to seek other sectors of the economy where their money could be invested more profitably. The resultant crowding of the French worker into inadequate housing heaped more fuel on the fires of discontent raging among the industrial workers.

French European trade was helped during the 1960's by membership in the Common Market. The tariff reductions agreed to by the member states in the EEC demanded that French industries achieve greater efficiency to meet competition. The increased competition from other European states also had the effect of forcing small French firms to merge with larger companies. Coupled with the heavy tourist trade that France enjoyed, the European Common Market trade gave the French extensive gold reserves and aided greatly in their balance-of-payments situation—although this situation was badly damaged by the disorders of 1968 and there was, for a time, a threat to the stability of the franc.

In French agriculture, too, a continued tendency to amalgamate small holdings was noted in the 1960's. Rural France underwent a transformation and large collectives appeared whereby farm machines were used in common by a number of individual farmers. Unlike those in the Communist world, however, the French agricultural collectives usually were privately organized for greater efficiency and larger profits.

During the 1960's, mass media, particularly television, began to penetrate many cooperatives and villages that only recently had received electricity. The total impact of this technological invasion of the countryside was to blur further the traditional differences in France between urban and rural areas. Like most modern industrialized states, France was becoming a more homogeneous country with startling rapidity.

F. Foreign Policy during the Fifth Republic

After the solution of the Algerian problem, the most important objective pursued by Charles de Gaulle in foreign affairs was the reassertion of French power and influence abroad. Intensely nationalistic, seeing France as the pace setter for Western civilization, de Gaulle made national patriotism a categorical imperative. Also absolutely necessary in de Gaulle's thinking was the idea that France should be strong and independent, a great power again. In the mind of such a man, supranational alignments were bound to arouse suspicion.

As a result of his quest for the lost "grandeur" of France, de Gaulle also tended to turn against international organizations where French leadership was not assured from the beginning. This position made him dubious of the value of the UN, and it made him hostile to NATO. To de Gaulle, the Atlantic Alliance was too much under the direction of an Anglo-Saxon conspiracy, dominated by the United States in cooperation with Britain.[5]

It seemed to some that de Gaulle wished to exclude the United States from Europe completely. It further was believed that he hoped eventually to make a Europe that: (1) stretched to the Urals; (2) was a loose confederation of motherlands; and (3) was led by a France which would provide the moral and political example for other European states.

Since such grandiose schemes called for the increasing of French influence and the development of the apparent trappings of great power standing, de Gaulle became fascinated with the possession and display of atomic weapons. At the core of his development of a nuclear striking force was the doubtful assumption that an unintegrated Western Europe could compete with the United States and the U.S.S.R. in nuclear capabilities and thus form a so-called "Third Force" between the two superpowers.

Since de Gaulle controlled French foreign affairs even more than domestic activity, he was able to transform some of his dreams into action. Yet, despite his feelings about supranational organizations, de Gaulle could not remove his country from a Common Market that

[5] It has been indicated by some scholars that this anti-Anglo-American attitude of de Gaulle's grew out of the Second World War, in which he felt that he was not given a proper share of command responsibilities in the Allied invasion project. During the course of the war, Churchill is reported to have said, concerning de Gaulle and his constant attempt to gain greater stature in the High Command, that the greatest cross that he (Churchill) had to bear was "the Cross of Lorraine" (the standard adopted by de Gaulle).

already had proven to be highly advantageous to France. He could, however, prevent Britain from gaining entrance to the organization, as he did in 1963. De Gaulle seems to have believed British membership in the EEC might have opened the way for yet other European states to join. With a greatly enlarged Common Market it might have proven difficult for France to play the dominant role in European affairs that de Gaulle envisioned for her.

De Gaulle's hostility toward NATO was demonstrated several times in the 1960's. He withdrew the French fleet from the NATO command in July 1963. In late 1964, he reduced the French contingent in NATO's West-German defense line to only two understrength divisions. He refused to take part in the development of a NATO nuclear fleet, and tried to reconstruct NATO agreements. In 1967, de Gaulle was able to stir anti-United States feelings in Europe sufficiently to force the withdrawal of NATO headquarters from France.

De Gaulle did not wish to sever ties with Britain and the United States. He did, however, wish to build better relations with Russia and Eastern European states. It was such a bridge-building expedition to Eastern Europe that had taken de Gaulle from France to Romania at the time of the 1968 insurrection in Paris. Moreover, it was the French policy under *Le Grand Charles* to seek better relations with the whole Communist world. In January 1964, he recognized Red China. Subsequently, he condemned United States policy in Vietnam. By 1967 and 1968, it was common for de Gaulle to point out that French atomic power was aimed not only eastward, but could be directed against *any* power whose intentions might be dangerous to France.

That it was difficult, perhaps impossible, for de Gaulle to continue such policies in hope of raising a "Third Force" between the superpowers became evident at the time of the Czechoslovak crisis of 1968. As the Russians began ensuring that a Moscow-oriented regime would rule in Prague, a somewhat more resolute military posture was detected in the West. All over Western Europe statesmen, who had come to view NATO as a wasting asset in an era when the Cold War seemingly had ended, were shocked by the Soviet recourse to force in Czechoslovakia. Consequently, they were forced to take a new look at the state of the Atlantic Alliance. West German Chancellor Kurt-Georg Kiesinger did not turn to France for help, but sought and received assurance that United States forces would remain in the Federal Republic. In November 1968, de Gaulle himself was forced to admit that, in the face of a potential Soviet threat, he might well have to reevaluate the value of NATO to France.

Early in 1970, when President Pompidou visited the United States shortly after France had seemed to favor the Arabs in the perennial Arab-Jewish conflict, he became the victim of violent demonstrations in Chicago and New York. President Nixon apologized in person, and Pompidou appeared to be satisfied. In April 1970, Paris offered its "active contribution" to any international negotiations arrived at seeking and guaranteeing peace, perhaps through neutralization, in Southeast Asia, the former French Indo-China.

A. The Transitional Governments

The successful march of the Allies north brought the resignation of Mussolini at the dictation of the Fascist Grand Council on July 25, 1943. The new government was headed by Marshal Pietro Badoglio, who signed the armistice terms with the Allies in September 1943. In that same month, Mussolini, who had been held captive by partisans, was freed by German paratroopers. With Nazi protection, he set up a Fascist regime in northern Italy.[6] In the south, the recognized authority was vested in the king and the cabinet. Because the Fascists dominated in the north, it became the main center of partisan activity, for the Italian people, far from rallying to Mussolini, showed a distinct preference for the resistance movement. The partisans, inspired by the widespread sympathy for their cause, believed that, after the war, they could play a major part in Italy's reconstruction and bring about social change.

Badoglio, to demonstrate his good faith to the Allies, brought Italy into the war against Germany in October 1943. However, this failed to placate Italians who thought that the Marshal, despite his present assumption of a fervent pro-Allied stance, had been too close to the higher councils of Fascism in the past. Badoglio was put under great pressure to reform his cabinet. He did so on four occasions and included in it men who had been important in the anti-Fascist movement in the past. The general uneasiness about Badoglio eventually produced a change in government. On June 4, 1944, Rome was liberated by the Allies and the anti-Fascists brought about Badoglio's replacement by pre-Fascist leaders. The control of the Italian Government over Italian affairs was then extended by the Allies until, by January 1946, all northern Italy, except the area immediately surrounding Trieste, was given to the Italian Government.

Immediately after the war, the resistance "Committees of Liberation" attempted to play the role in promoting social and governmental changes that they had planned for themselves during the war. However, the resistance groups quickly lost their political influence and were dissolved by the Allies. It was the more conservative forces who reasserted themselves and it was they who reorganized the cabinet and formed a Consultative Chamber in September 1945. The Chamber consisted of 429 members chosen from lists submitted by

[6] More of Italy was under Fascist control at this time than under the administration of the government sponsored by the Allies and thus the situation remained for several months.

political parties, unions, and certain professional organizations. A cabinet was formed by Alcide de Gasperi, who remained the head of government until 1953. For the time being, the new authority postponed major reforms. Thus, Italy in the immediate postwar period was much as she had been before World War II, a land of singular contrasts. In the Italy of the late 1940's and early 1950's there was a small group of people who possessed great wealth. At the same time an industrial and rural mass of citizens was living in severe circumstances or, in many cases, outright destitution.

Actually, thoughts of a program of sweeping social reforms were difficult to entertain when the most pressing problem of the day was, as it was elsewhere in Europe, that of rebuilding a country shattered by the war. As was the case in Yugoslavia, UNRRA was a major factor in Italian recovery. Before the end of 1946, more than $500,000,000 in supplies had been poured into Italy.

Life for the Italian worker was difficult. Normally, he was hungry and, hence, acutely aware of social injustices within his society. The Communist Party profited from this widespread discontent in the laboring classes and its membership expanded accordingly. Socialist parties proved ineffective in attracting the workingman to a more moderate left-wing stance and disaster threatened the moderate political leadership. At that point, Marshall Plan aid began flowing into Europe and met some of the basic demands of the workers for subsistence.

B.   Postwar Political Developments

After the peace treaties with Italy had been signed and Allied military government had been ended, a new constitution for the Italian Republic was approved by a Constituent Assembly in December 1947.[7] The document, which became law at the end of 1947, generally reflected the views of the dominant middle-of-the-road Christian Democrats, and produced a traditional parliamentary government. The constitution provided for a president, elected by a two-house parliament. Each of the nineteen electoral districts elected members for the upper house of the parliament on the basis of one senator (to serve for six years) for each 200,000 inhabitants. The lower house, the Chamber of Deputies, was to be elected for five years. Each house possessed approximately equal powers, and the ministry was responsible to them. There also was instituted a Constitutional Court similar to the Supreme Court in the United States to decide upon the constitutionality of laws.

---

[7] In June 1946, a referendum on the monarchy had been held and Italians had decided in favor of a republican form of government. Victor Emmanuel III had abdicated shortly before the vote in hope of saving the monarchy for his son, Humbert II. But because the Italians cast their lot with the republic, the new king withdrew to Portugal.

The unsettled conditions in postwar Italy caused the new government to expel the Communists from participation in its deliberations in June 1947. This, of course, made it easier to develop a moderate, middle-of-the-road government. The expulsion of the Italian Reds from the government also caused them to break the bonds of restraint imposed earlier by directives from Moscow. The Communists became increasingly aggressive, and strikes led by them in 1947–1948 were near-insurrections.

The resulting political instablility led to prompt elections in April, 1948. The election was fought as if it alone would determine the future of Italy, and the Communists looked to it as a chance to take control of the government legally.

The left wing in Italy was fragmented, however, and there existed in that part of the political spectrum two separate factions, the Social Democrats and the Communists. In 1947, quarreling between two socialist groups over the possibility of alignment with the Communists developed a severe rift in the ranks of Socialism. A moderate group of Socialists, led by Giuseppe Saragat, favored reform by traditional parliamentary measures. The left Socialists under Pietro Nenni held to the idea that they, as Marxists, should follow the Communists and oppose the pro-Westernism developing in the rest of the political spectrum.

The Italian Communist Party claimed a membership of nearly two million and a half, thus making it the strongest Marxist party west of the satellite bloc. But the Communist following did not derive from a widespread belief in Marxist-Leninist doctrines. Most of the Italians who voted for Communist deputies did so only because they desired sweeping changes to free them from the state of social and economic misery in which they lived. Moreover, the party organization, led by Palmiro Togliatti, had moved quickly after the war to take control of the old Fascist labor organizations, which now formed the basis of much Red strength.

The only party in the center that possessed broad mass appeal was the Christian Democrats (*Democrazia Cristiana*). It was this party which had its roots sunk most firmly in the pre-Fascist days. As its name indicated, it was connected closely to Roman Catholicism. In foreign affairs it was staunchly pro-Western. The Christian Democrat leader, Alcide de Gasperi, desired an environment in which democratic ideas and traditions similar to those of other Western states could be nurtured properly.

During the bitterly fought 1948 election campaign, the Vatican openly supported the Christian Democrats and assumed a fervent anti-Communist position. The United States attempted to help the cause of the anti-Communist forces by giving twenty-nine ships to the government and intimating that the American money flowing into Italy would halt abruptly if the Communists should score an electoral victory. The results of the voting in this crucial election gave the Christian Democrats 48.7 per cent of the vote and nearly half the seats in the Chamber of Deputies. In spite of the forces arrayed against them, the Communists did well. With their left-wing Socialist allies, they captured approximately 31 per cent of the vote. Again it must be indicated that this Red strength probably was not a reflection of the Italian workingman's faith in Marxist-Leninism, but a product of the extreme poverty so common in that sector of the population.

The ascendancy of de Gasperi and his party lasted into 1953. The Christian Democrats possessed a good working majority and Luigi Einaudi, an economist and banker, was elected President. He remained in office until 1955, when he was succeeded by Giovanni Gronchi, another Christian Democrat. Because of a continued threat from the political extremes, de Gasperi managed to get through an electoral reform in the spring of 1953. This was aimed at the Communists and neo-Fascists in that it guaranteed to a party or coalition obtaining 50 per cent of the popular vote a substantial majority of the seats in the Chamber of Deputies.

Political pundits forecast disaster for de Gasperi's party in the national elections of 1953. The Christian Democrats believed, however, that they could, with their new electoral rules, amass enough votes to qualify for additional "bonus" seats. But when the 1953 votes were counted, the Christian Democrats had won only 49.1 per cent of the popular vote. Consequently, the bonus law was not in effect and the Christian Democrats retained only a bare majority of the seats in the Chamber. De Gasperi could not form a government because of factionalism developing in his own party.

From 1953 to 1958, Italy was governed by a number of coalition cabinets. Even after the elections of May 1958, which brought considerable gains to the middle-of-the-road coalition parties, the Christian Democrats still lacked a clear majority. Consequently, the Christian Democrats were beset with all the difficulties normally experienced by a party in a coalition system when it fails to obtain a substantial majority. Such a party has to seek support to the right or left of its own position to put together a cabinet. Such support often is ephemeral, and when it fades away an electoral crisis results. The Christian Democrats, since Pietro Nenni's Socialists had declared a policy of "unity of action" with the Communists, normally looked to the right among Liberals, Monarchists, and even neo-Fascists to find the support necessary to form governments. Thus, until 1962, Italian governments were characteristically right-center. Then, Pietro Nenni apparently realized that his policy of collaborating with the Communists was keeping the Socialists out of government. In February 1962, Nenni renounced his policy of alignment with the Communists.

The new stance of the Socialists caused Premier Amintore Fanfani to attempt the strengthening of the Christian Democratic coalition by including leftists. A revised center-left cabinet was formed in which the Socialists did not actually participate but gave their support.[8] This new arrangement did not work well and, in February 1963, Fanfani dissolved the Parliament.

One political commentator, assessing the significance of the elections that followed Parliament's dissolution in 1963 indicated that: "The ... elections of [1963] can hardly be said to have settled Italy's political problems. The new Parliament is just a little worse than the last two, which were nearly unworkable."[9] Indeed, the election of 1963 hurt the Christian Democrats, whose backing dropped from 42 per cent to 38 per cent of the electorate.

The Communists increased their share of the vote from 22 to 25 per cent. There existed, therefore, no practical alternative for the Christian Democrats except the establishment of a coalition with the Socialists. Negotiations began in which the Socialists, who had not suffered extensive losses in the election as had the Christian Democrats, were in a position to conclude a bargain very favorable to their party. By the end of 1963, there was produced a four-party coalition consisting of Christain Democrats, Socialists, Democratic Socialists, and Republicans. Aldo Moro, a Christian Democrat, became Premier and the Socialist leader, Pietro Nenni, became Vice-Premier. Factionalism soon appeared in this cabinet of strange "political bedfellows." The Moro Government resigned in June 1964, only to be replaced by a new Moro cabinet.

The renewed coalition was not a happy one, bothered as it was by the mutual distrust its members harbored for one another. Attention given to immediate anti-inflationary measures forced the Government to postpone some of its high-priority reforms in agriculture, housing, and education. This postponement caused discontent among the Socialists. When Christian Democratic President Antonio Segni resigned in December 1964, because of illness, conflict developed over who would be his successor. Finally, Giuseppe Saragat, a right-wing Socialist, was selected.

In May 1968, the first general election since 1963 was held in Italy. The Christian Democrats increased their strength in Parliament slightly, but the Communists made their most substantial electoral gains in twenty years. The Socialists' share of the vote dropped about one-quarter, and this loss was attributed to the failure of the Socialists to extract from their coalition partners long overdue social and economic reforms. An ominous portent for the new Moro coalition government was seen by some in the fact that young voters had balloted in record numbers and that many of them had become sufficiently radical to vote for the Communist Party, thus designating it their preferred instrument for reform.

---

[8] "Opening to the Left" became a slogan which obsessed the Christian Democrats. It referred to a Christian Democratic effort to lure the Nenni Socialists from their previous Communist ties, thus building a solid majority while isolating the Communists.
[9] Claire Sterling, "The Italian Elections: Even Worse Than Before," *The Reporter*, May 23, 1963, p. 22.

Moro now was faced with the prospect that the Socialist Party might attempt to regain votes lost to the Communists by demanding reforms with greater vigor than they had demonstrated in their years in the coalition government. These demands seemed likely to create further conflict within the new coalition. There was really no viable alternative to the Social Democratic-Socialist coalition, however. If the coalition failed, the next choice might well be between a popular front including the Communists or a rightist combination. Finally, the unstable Italian situation brought about the fall of Moro. A new coalition was built in which there was a greater participation of Socialists. In December 1968, when the new coalition began with Christian Democrat Mariano Rumor at its head, Pietro Nenni became Foreign Minister. In 1969 and into 1970, Rumor several times fell and rose, to be followed in August 1970 by a fellow-Christian Democrat, the financial expert Emilio Colombo. The latter formed Italy's thirty-second government since the fall of Fascism; it was based on another center-left coalition of four parties. As one observer phrased it, the Italians seemed still to prefer "happy anarchy" to orderly government.

C. Economics

When Mussolini's regime collapsed in 1943, the Italian economy lay in ruins. Parts of the nation had been damaged heavily during the fighting between the liberating Allied armies and the retreating Axis forces. Numberless elements vital to an economy—highways, bridges, and factories—had been destroyed. To make matters worse, the Italian economy had been throughout the twentieth century a "have not" economic structure with few natural resources. War only served to aggravate that situation.

First UNRRA, then aid from the United States, provided funds for emergency rehabilitation. Marshall Plan aid proved to be most important and, from 1946 to 1961, total United States foreign assistance to the Italians amounted to $5,600,000,000.[10] Financial aid from the United States made possible some of Italy's most modern plants and Washington-directed programs of technical assistance brought new methods into Italian industries.

The inauguration of the European Coal and Steel Community in 1952 (see Chapter 27) also influenced Italian industrial growth. When tariffs were lowered in the ECSC, Italian prices for steel were lowered so as to be competitive. This, in turn, benefited various steel-using industries in Italy, since they now were able to afford more steel. In turn, greater numbers of items were produced for sale. Other important industries followed this same general pattern.

[10] Military aid amounted to $2,200,000,000 and other assistance to $3,400,000,000.

An age of selective affluence dawned in a country where poverty was traditional. When new apartment buildings and modern factories began to appear as physical symbols of the new prosperity, the gap between rich and poor in Italy became more obvious than ever. As one labor union official in Rome put it in 1961: "Of course wages have gone up and unemployment has come down. But in the classic —and belated—capitalist boom, I'm afraid the social side has been left behind."[11]

Despite all the advances, Italy remained a country with too many people for its arable land and national resources. Almost 40 per cent of the nation's people lived in Sicily and Sardinia, in conditions of near poverty. In 1953, a parliamentary committee investigated the extent of Italian poverty and found that the housing of nearly 25 per cent of the population was substandard. This contrasted with conditions in the nationalized electric industry where, in 1962, the employees received an almost 20 per cent increase in wages.

The root of the Italian problem was that, in the economic sense, there had developed two Italys. There was the booming north with Milan acting as the dynamic core of the nation's economic revival. Italian postwar production was concentrated in the so-called "iron triangle" of Milan, Turin, and Genoa. In postwar Italy, Milan's 1,500,000 people payed 26 per cent of the taxes. It was in the north that workers were able to own the refrigerators and television sets they produced.

In the south the land was an arid near-wasteland, a place of hunger and hopelessness. In startling contrast to the prosperity of northern Italy, the South did not provide a decent standard of living for its people. Consequently, for many of them, "the iron triangle" replaced the United States, to which immigration now was highly restricted, as the land of their dreams and the target of migration. The Italian Government, between 1950 and 1965, undertook a special fifteen-year development program to lessen the differences between southern and northern Italy. Further, a special five-year plan drawn up in 1964 called for an increased effort to eliminate North-South contrasts by aiding Southern industry and agriculture. Yet, the economic and social contrasts, the consequent sectionalism, and the envy and distrust produced among Italians by this situation remained. There would have to be more progress in the 1970's before the two Italys, north and south, could become one.

D. Foreign Affairs

Generally, after the peace treaty of 1947, Italians favored a pro-Western foreign policy. Through most of the political spectrum ran

[11] *The New York Times,* September 18, 1961.

a sentiment which desired Italy to take its place as a full partner in the Western community. It was hoped by many groups that Italy could by this course recover and perhaps enhance a national prestige that had dwindled under Mussolini. Only the far Left did not whole-heartedly share this view.

With a Christian Democratic-controlled Government in power, it was assured that this general sentiment would be transformed into a policy line. Hence, Italy participated in the Marshall Plan and became a member of NATO in 1949. NATO Command Headquarters in Southern Europe was established in Naples, and Italy provided the first base in continental Europe from which NATO missiles could be fired against an aggressor.

As part of the peace treaty of 1947, Italy was divested of her former colonies. In 1948, a council of Allied powers (the United States, U.S.S.R., France, and Great Britain) was entrusted with the fate of Italy's former colonies. This council failed to reach agreement, however, and the issue was given to the General Assembly of the United Nations. The Assembly passed a resolution in November 1949, providing for the independence of Libya. The United Nations also voted that the territory formerly known as Italian Somaliland eventually should become independent after first having been placed under the trusteeship of Italy for ten years. Later it was decided that Eritrea should be federated with Ethiopia.

A free territory of Trieste was created by the peace treaty of 1947. As early as 1948, however, the Western Allies announced that Trieste would be returned to Italy. This statement brought loud protests from the U.S.S.R. and Yugoslavia. But, eventually, American and British troops were withdrawn and the Trieste Zone was divided between Yugoslavia and Italy whereas the city of Trieste itself retained a free-port status. In the matter of the South Tirol (Alto Adige), Italian politicians presented a solid front against concessions to the German-speaking minority into the 1960's. Not until 1970 did Rome and Vienna reach an agreement that promised greater autonomy and better political conditions to the Tirolese.

Shorn of her empire, Italy felt she could not play a leading role in the Western Alliance. Although she had promised twelve divisions to NATO, the entire army of Italy by 1963, was comprised of only six full strength and supposedly combat-ready divisions.

In other matters, Italy followed a "European" course designed essentially by de Gasperi and his colleagues. This course dictated entry into the Coal and Steel Community and then the Common Market. While it was being considered, Italy also strongly backed the idea of a European Defense Community, until it was wrecked by action of the French Assembly. Later Italy supported Euratom and the admission of Britain to the Common Market. In all this there appeared to be an earnest attempt by the Italian Government to: (1) regain a place of respectability among the nations to which it had lost during World War II; and (2) merge Italian interests with all-European interests in the hope that the Italian effort would count for more on the global scene as part of the power exerted by an integrated Europe.

E. The Vatican

Perhaps nowhere else are governments' relations with the Catholic Church so important as they are in the country that provides a home for the papacy. Generally, after World War II, these relations were cordial and the Pope gave outright support to the Christian Democratic Party.[12] Most members of the Italian government also supported papal actions against satellite bloc governments where the privileges of Roman Catholics had been restricted. In 1949, for instance, the Papacy, because of their anti-Catholic measures, excommunicated all persons who were Communists or aided Communists in certain satellite states. In this the Pope had Italian government support. Eventually, however, Vatican relations with parts of the Communist world improved sufficiently to allow papal appointments once more in the hierarchies of churches where, previously, Communist governments had restricted such appointments.

When Pope Pius XII died in October 1958, a great innovator came to the papal throne in the person of Angelo Giuseppe Cardinal Roncalli of Venice, who took the name, John XXIII. Quickly, Pope John broke with tradition by increasing the number of cardinals (who by 1970 numbered some 130). In doing so he continued a tendency that had appeared during the pontificate of Pius XII who, for the first time since the fourteenth century, made appointments producing a College of Cardinals in which non-Italians formed a majority. John XXIII further tipped the scales in favor of non-Italians by appointing new Cardinals in Africa and the East.

John XXIII used his short pontificate (just over four years and a half) to call repeatedly and eloquently for peace and disarmament in the world. Most importantly, he announced, in January 1959, that he hoped to convoke the first Ecumenical Council of the Church to be called together since 1870. From October to December 1962, John XIII presided over an all-Church Council, with more than 2500 important church figures in attendance. Out of the Council came the first major change in the mass since the seventh century.

In June 1963, John XXIII died, loved and admired by many non-Catholics as well as Catholics. He was succeeded by Giovanni Battista Cardinal Montini of Milan, who ascended the papal throne as Paul VI. Characteristic of Paul VI's pontificate was a trip to Jerusalem

---

[12] Alcide de Gasperi, while he led the Christian Democratic Party, kept close watch on tendencies towards clericalism in his party and seemed to believe that such tendencies could be neutralized by coalitions with other moderate parties.

in January 1964. Paul VI was the first pontiff to leave Italy since 1814, and he left it repeatedly to visit the United States, Latin America, and other areas of the world.

Among Paul VI's most progressive measures were the following: attempts to bring the Roman Church and the Greek Orthodox Church closer together again; statements urging toleration of Jews; affirmation of the principle of religions liberty for all; and several steps which tended to democratize the church. One position maintained by the Pope, in the late 1960's, caused a certain degree of upheaval within the church's membership and criticism from without. After consideration of the matter, the Pope reaffirmed the church position against artificial birth control. In the United States, where planned families were part of the middle-class national social pattern, and in Latin America, where an ever-burgeoning population threatened disaster, the decision caused much criticism. Some commented that a modernizing papacy would have to modernize even more rapidly its position on birth control if it wished to make the church relevant to the problems of the 1960's and 1970's.

Attempts to Integrate Europe | 27

THE IDEA OF EUROPEAN UNITY
AND SOME EARLY ORGANIZATIONS

A. The Organization for European Economic Cooperation

World War II, and the Cold War developing shortly afterward, strengthened both the political and economic arguments for greater unity among European nations. For a brief period of illusion it was hoped that unity could be established in Europe, and it was immediately after the war that the major effort to build a supranational state was expended.

Concepts of European integration several times were voiced during the Second World War. Many of the political refugees who fled to the United States and Britain helped to keep interest in the subject alive. At the suggestion of Jean Monnet, who was in London in 1940, Winston Churchill proposed that eventually there should be a Franco-British Union. In 1943, Churchill voiced an appeal for a postwar "Council of Europe." Even more common during the war was the notion of an economic federation, a union to which even Great Britain eventually might adhere. All this created early postwar hopes that European union might not be far away.

The postwar cleavage between East and West described in Chapters 21 and 22 caused attempts to initiate political integration to be restricted to Western Europe. Economic aspirations had to be scaled down as well. Out of the unhappy Moscow Conference of March and April 1947, came the firm indication that East-West trade might take place, but that it would be far too restricted to permit an open flow of goods between Eastern and Western Europe.

Marshall Plan aid provided an opportunity for Europeans to attempt unified action in the economic sphere after 1945. Indeed, it was the desire of the United States that the Europeans replace their old institutions and former trade relations with a system of cooperation. The Europeans responded by establishing a Committee of European Economic Cooperation, which met in Paris, prepared a report on Europe's needs, and then drafted a program for what became the sixteen-nation Organization for European Economic Cooperation on April 16, 1948.

The member states of the OEEC imposed a number of restrictions on themselves. Yet, the OEEC proved a remarkable economic success in spite of such limitations. Quota limits on trade and attempts to bring the economic policies of member states in line with one another assisted recovery over a broad area. The habit of consultation and cooperation continually was urged by the OEEC. The work of the Organization proved that the very presence of an international body at a time when there are disputes among nations can ease the solution of such difficulties immediately. Time after time the OEEC helped achieve informal agreement, thus avoiding substantial difficulties. It might have worked even better had its founding states given it greater latitude of operation, but much of its activity was confined to the removal of quota restrictions. It could do little to regulate international trade in other areas. In consequence, the greatest successes of the OEEC were realized in the area of short-term problems. Long-term quandaries, such as the problem of full employment throughout Europe, could be met only by an organization given fuller powers to deal with the whole European economic situation.

OEEC was given limited scope because European governments were not anxious to initiate a customs union "with no internal trade barriers," as the United States recommended. Indeed, it was only at American urging that the Committee of European Economic Cooperation actually sat down to discuss the possibility of a European *Zollverein*. These discussions were aided by the fact that a smaller-scale union already was being established. Belgium, the Netherlands, and Luxembourg had been at work on steps to lower trade barriers since September 1944. Great Britain, however, was, at this time, still possessed by the memories of imperial glories. The British particularly, therefore, caused the work of the Committee to be transformed from a start on a concrete customs union into final diluted statements to the effect that there should be general "economic cooperation" among European states.

Precisely because the OEEC was so limited at the beginning by its members, any one of its member states could impede progress toward greater integration of Western Europe. In 1948, at one of its meetings, France put forth the idea that the OEEC was too powerless and that it should have a strong executive board empowered to make major policy decisions on its own. Again, Britain was cool toward this kind of idea, because of a reluctance to give up her right of independent action in the economic sphere, especially in Commonwealth relations. This dispute was typical of the continued debates over how much authority should be given OEEC's governing board.

B. The Council of Europe

The debates that took place in the councils of the OEEC had counterparts in a second Western European organization. The Council of Europe was established on May 5, 1949, the outcome of strong sentiment for European unity. The Council was made up of members of the Brussels Treaty Organization and five other states. Three months after its formation, a first meeting was held in Strasbourg and Paul-Henri Spaak of Belgium was elected its first president. Many plans were discussed that would, their proponents claimed, have given Europe "a political authority ... with limited functions but real powers." A European Economic Union was proposed as was a European Bank. There even were some so ambitious as to demand a political authority of a supranational character. Spaak was optimistic enough to leave the meeting believing that a "United States of Europe" was possible. In 1949, there was an electric excitement in the air and many shared Spaak's belief that European union was imminent.

In the long run, the accomplishments of the Council fell far short of European integration. The Council normally performed unspectacular but useful tasks such as cultural and legal coordination among the member states. But generally the spirit of Strasbourg had been illusory. By 1951, Paul-Henri Spaak was so distressed by the Council's failure to move Europe toward unity that he resigned the Presidency of the Consultative Assembly.

The basic problem again was to be found in the restrictions placed upon an all-West European organization by member states fearful of giving up their sovereign political rights. In the early days of the Council's Consultative Assembly, it was not allowed even to decide what matters were to be on the agenda for meetings. The Consultative Assembly could only submit resolutions to the Council's Committee of Ministers, but even that body could not make decisions committing member governments to courses of action. The committee members merely could recommend to their governments that certain steps be taken, but, often, such recommendations were disregarded if they seemed likely to clash with national interests.

Many who desired a greater degree of European integration sought to restructure the Council of Europe to allow it greater freedom of action. Such attempts failed uniformly. In 1957, the Consultative Assembly sadly issued a statement to the effect that the member states obviously had "no common political will" on the important questions pertaining to the problem of European integration. Others were not so polite. It even was charged that the Council was a two-body organization, one standing "for" Europe and the other aligned with the forces "against" it.

Thus the OEEC and the Council of Europe accomplished a slight movement toward economic integration, but they did not move Europe noticeably toward political unity. By early 1950, many were convinced that it was time for new initiatives toward European integration. Most important among those who shared this view were Jean Monnet, director of French economic recovery, and French Foreign Minister Robert Schuman.

C. The European Coal and Steel Community

On May 9, 1950, journalists representing the world's major newspapers were called to the French Foreign Office, for a press briefing. Robert Schuman, French Foreign Minister, appeared before them to make the startling announcement that: "The French government proposes to place the whole . . . Franco-German coal and steel output under a common High Authority, in an organization open to the participation of the other countries of Europe." The Schuman Plan established as its long-range goal the achievement of European unity in hope that a united Europe would stabilize world relations and bring international peace. Before that could be achieved, however, it was decided that the "age-old opposition" between France and Germany had to be ended. This was especially meaningful in 1950 as the Federal Republic of West Germany only recently had come into existence. Thus, as the French saw it, the most rational policy was to cement a resurgent West Germany firmly to the Western powers. The Schuman Plan was aimed at accomplishing just that.

The whole atmosphere of attitudes and opinions surrounding the Schuman Plan was more realistic than the false optimism of those desiring European unity immediately after the war's end. The Plan's basic premise was that a united Europe "will not be made at once," but rather through first creating *"de facto"* solidarity. It seemed to Schuman and his colleagues that the best way to establish such solidarity was through common economic institutions. Coal and steel were the ideal items with which to begin an economic community because, for many years, it had been precisely the related mineral deposits that had provided one of the major causes of dispute between France and Germany. Europe's coal and iron ore, and consequently its steel production, were to be found in a relatively small area—Lorraine, the Ruhr, a part of northern France, the Saar, Luxembourg, parts of Belgium, and the Netherlands. Since the beginning of industrialization, this zone of concentrated resources had been of the highest importance. The boundaries of several nations criss-crossed the area and thus created jealousies among various states over the amount of valuable resources each could draw from the zone. Consequently, for several years, economic and political experts had pleaded for the integration of this set of resources.

There had been some attempts to integrate the European coal and steel resources earlier in the twentieth century. In 1926, an international cartel (Belgium, France, Luxembourg, and the Saarland) had been formed among steel producers. This arrangement aroused suspicion among many who saw the area in question as the basis of European armament production. There was a fear that private individuals would wield too much power through possession of important resources. Later, in 1947, France had proposed a system of international control that would have involved Allied ownership of German resources in the area. This proposal was not accepted in its original form by Britain and the United States, but it did lead to a 1949 agreement that established the International Authority of the Ruhr. The Authority, in which Germany possessed only a minor voice, proved to be too weak and unsatisfactory. The Schuman Plan was a more workable successor in that it established international control of the zone where resources were located. Moreover, it satisfied the Germans because it meant that Germany would not lose the benefits of the area through heavy-handed French control as they had in 1923. At the same time, it assured the French that the resources of the coal and iron mines in the Ruhr would not be used, without international agreement, to build a West German army that might threaten France in the future. The Plan aimed at weakening traditional forces of nationalism by establishing "common bases" for economic development in Europe.

The Schuman Plan[1] also helped lessen antagonism between France and Germany over the Saar. The Saar, unlike the Ruhr, had been attached to France since 1947. Negotiation of the Franco-Saarland Conventions during 1949 confirmed that the Saar was politically autonomous, but economically French. This arrangement created tensions between Paris and the new West German Government at Bonn. But the Schuman Plan provided a resolution of the problem by pooling the Saar's resources with others in the area, thus paving the way for West Germany to retrieve the Saar in 1956. The French no longer were greatly worried about the loss of the Saar at that point, because they recently had been assured by the functioning of the Coal and Steel Community that they would be able to tap the rich resources of the Saarland on a continuing basis in the future.

When the Schuman Plan first was proposed, the usual strong reservations concerning supranational authority appeared. However, some of the leaders of those countries debating the proposal were particularly sympathetic to it. Since the 1920's, Konrad Adenauer had held that lasting peace between France and Germany could be

---

[1] Despite the fact that the 1950 plan presented by Robert Schuman bears his name, it is widely recognized that the initiative behind the plan was that of Jean Monnet.

attained best through the establishment of common economic interests and he now repeated that opinion. Alcide de Gasperi also was favorably disposed toward the idea, although Italian territories did not play the major role in considerations that did land in France and West Germany.

Those influential men who were sympathetic to the Plan helped along negotiations which, in 1951, produced a treaty creating the European Coal and Steel Community among Belgium, France, Italy, Luxembourg, the Netherlands, and West Germany. The ECSC was provided with a Council of Ministers and a Common Assembly. There was some debate in July 1952, over the location of the ECSC headquarters. It finally was decided that Strasbourg would be the seat of the Common Assembly and that the High Authority, as well as a special Court of Justice created for the organization, would reside in Luxembourg. Jean Monnet was the Community's first President and the rest of the seats on the High Authority were occupied by representatives of the various member states.

There were three distinct aspects of the work to be accomplished by the ECSC. These were: (1) the "fusion" of markets by removing barriers in the coal and steel trade; (2) the expansion of the European economy to improve living standards in the member states; and (3) steps toward eventual economic and political unity in Europe. Work on the first task, the removal of customs barriers, began rapidly. A common market for coal and iron ore came first, then steel, and finally "special steels" in August 1954. In the next four years intra-Community trade increased spectacularly.

Those who had forecast doom when the "fusion" of markets took place now were happily surprised. Economic adjustment came with relative ease during a period of healthy financial growth. Careful steps were taken to ensure that workers within the member states of the ECSC were not subjected to deprivation through technological unemployment. Sizable funds were provided for the resettlement of those unfortunates who lost their jobs during the transitional stages of the Schuman Plan.

Obviously, then, the second aspect of the work to be accomplished by the ECSC, the expansion of the European economy and the general betterment of the style of life enjoyed by its people, was realized with considerable success. The Schuman Plan that had seemed to many to be nothing more than a utopian fantasy had turned out to be a prosperous undertaking. Moreover, its success story pointed the way to the establishment of the Common Market and Euratom.

The third task set for the Community had not, by 1970, been completed. There were some halting steps taken in the direction of European political unity in the formation of ECSC's institutional structure. The Community's Council of Ministers, whose members were national representatives, was subject in many cases to majority international vote. Thus was provided, some hopeful experts claimed, a precedent for a supranational assembly in which matters could be decided by majority vote. The Common Assembly as formed was not a parliamentary body, but it did have some substantial powers, such as that to oust members of the High Authority if need be. The High Authority, particularly, was a supranational organ in that it was constituted of members forbidden to receive instructions from their own national governments. The High Authority was to decide matters by simple majority vote. The rule of the majority obligated the minority to accept the collective responsibility for actions taken, much as a national cabinet, regardless of internal squabbles, presents a united front to the world. Moreover, the High Authority levied its own taxes on coal and steel production, and the proceeds were used to facilitiate the functions of the ECSC.

These institutions clearly were designed to point the way toward a united Europe. Monnet was so enthusiastic about the Community's possibilities that he called the ECSC, "the first expression of the Europe that is being born." This kind of enthusiasm, coupled with the first successes of the Community, led to further plans for integration. The most important of these were the European Defense Community and the European Atomic Energy Community.

D. The Failure of the European Defense Community

There is no doubt that French leadership was a constructive influence in early steps toward West European unity. It is equally true that France dealt a damaging blow to hopes that there would be a common West European army. On August 30, 1954, the French National Assembly rejected a treaty that would have inaugurated a European Defense Community (EDC). Britain also had made it clear that she would not take part in any common European fighting force, although British troops were pledged to help maintain the defenses of the continent for the foreseeable future. Britain's reason for failing to support the EDC was to be found in the fact that the British believed their special relationship to the United States could not be maintained if they submerged themselves in all-European organizations.

Despite indications of doubt from Britain, the six countries working together in the ECSC, guided by the same French diplomats who had been so active in the building of European economic integration, constructed a treaty for a European Defense Community. The treaty was to be a giant step toward European unity. It was to run for fifty years, and, more importantly, be directed by a supranational authority. The EDC draft treaty obligated its signatories to integrate their military resources and form an international peacetime army. It was assumed that West Germany would contribute forces that would be part of an integrated army with common uniforms, common equipment, and a common paymaster. Hence, the

EDC was to mean an end to purely national armies in Europe and the various European states would be forced to pass on sovereignty in matters of defense to a supranational body. The overall scheme for European unity then went something like this: nations were to give up their sovereignty first in economic affairs (in the ECSC and its successors), then in defense matters, and finally a federal European union would be formed. There was to be a permanent assembly to operate the supranational organizations, which might well be the cornerstone of a future federal structure.

It was the intention of the EDC planners to produce a force that could serve eventually as an all European unit under the NATO command with other units contributed by the United States and Great Britain. The legislatures of West Germany and the Benelux states ratified the EDC treaty, indicating that they were in substantial agreement with the idea that sovereignty should be surrendered in the securing of greater unity and strength on the continent. Italy, however, straddled the fence, waiting to learn what France would do. Italy's hesitation was caused by a debate raging in the French press and the Assembly. Intensively applied pressure came from the United States Secretary of State John Foster Dulles. The position of the United States was interpreted in France as meaning that French ratification was the price of additional United States assistance to France. The French reacted negatively to American pressure and the cause of the EDC was damaged.

The political center in France supported the EDC and the extremes opposed it. From the left came Communist opposition, excited in large part by Soviet apprehension concerning a West European army. The Gaullists saw in the EDC the destroyer of French national pride, an army that would wreck the French army at the same time that it "rebuilds the German." The old spectre of Franco-German hostility was raised from a very shallow grave and was nourished by apprehension over the possible revival of West Germany as a military power. Old wounds also were opened by delays in settling the fate of the Saar and worry over the fact that Britain would not enter the EDC to balance the possible might of a resurgent Germany.

Thus, French support for the treaty was eroded, and the proposal was defeated in the National Assembly in 1954. The defeat of the EDC was of decisive importance. Those who believed in a practical Western European federation based on EDC's framework were forced to devise other plans. Ironically, it was not long until the Atlantic Alliance admitted a rebuilt German army from the Federal Republic, which was a national force and therefore not directly subject to limitations that might be imposed upon it by other European states. When the EDC failed, the European political community failed with it. Discouraged, Jean Monnet announced that he would not seek reelection as president of the ECSC High Authority. It now was widely believed that the postwar movement towards unity had lost its vitality.

E. Euratom

The movement towards European unity was not dead, however. In December 1954, the ECSC's Common Assembly called for the establishment of a working group to study possible extensions of the Coal and Steel Community's functions. In May 1955, the group that had been constituted in the previous December urged that a conference be called to discuss further steps toward European integration. In June, a conference of European foreign ministers met at Messina, Italy, to discuss additional moves toward integration. Out of the Messina Conference came a Committee of National Representatives, under the presidency of Paul-Henri Spaak, which met periodically until it was ready to present its conclusions to the foreign ministers in April 1956. When the ministers met, they, in effect, transformed the Spaak Committee into a treaty-making conference which, within a year, produced treaties establishing a European Atomic Energy Community (EURATOM) and a European Economic Community (EEC or the Common Market).

At their beginnings, Jean Monnet was more concerned with Euratom than the Common Market. He, as did many others, believed that the next logical step in the march to unity was the pooling of atomic resources. Spaak agreed, saying that "the atom and automation are the future."

Actually, Euratom had been preceded by several intra-European organizations whose concern was primarily atomic energy. In 1952, the European Nuclear Research Council was founded, and the European Atomic Energy Society was initiated in 1953. Europeans then took part in an International Atomic Agency in 1954. This tendency developed because the prospect of diverting atomic research into peaceful avenues had caught the enthusiasm of Europeans. It was this widespread enthusiasm that caused discussions of an atomic pool among European states in the spring of 1955.

In January 1956, a committee was appointed to report on "the quantities of atomic energy that can be produced" by the six Coal and Steel Community States. The central conclusion of the committee's report was that the six nations faced a long-term shortage of nuclear energy when compared with the resources possessed by Britain, the Soviet Union, and the United States. The impact of this report was to hasten the ratification of the Euratom Treaty in 1957. But the building of atomic reactors proceeded somewhat slowly after Euratom's organization. By June 1961, only about 1,500,000,000 kilowatts of capacity had been authorized. By 1964, atomic capacity had risen to more than 2,000,000 kilowatts and it rose more rapidly thereafter in the later 1960's and early 1970's.

In addition to the building of reactors, the Euratom program included the establishment of four joint research centers—in Belgium, Italy, West Germany, and the Netherlands. There also was extensive cooperation with several international organizations. Further, in the industrial field, Euratom guided and stimulated investment by providing technical and financial aid to private nuclear projects.

F. The Common Market

By far the most important step taken toward an eventual European political union was the institution of the Common Market. In 1955, there were few who believed that there would be a Common Market at any time in the foreseeable future, but by January 1959 it was a reality. Jean Monnet again played a central role, as did Paul–Henri Spaak. Washington also gave firm support to the building of the Common Market because of the commonly held view in United States' State Department circles that the EEC's institution would speed final European political integration. The United States believed that a unified Europe would prove a stronger ally for Washington in the Cold War.

The Common Market was based on the idea of a customs union, within which the individual tariffs of the member states would be averaged into a common tariff. This common tariff would then be imposed upon all trade entering the EEC from the world outside its borders. Obstacles to trade within the EEC were to be eliminated through a phasing out process, extending over a maximum time span of seventeen years.

The scope of the customs union could not be confined to tariff regulation alone. The problem of quantitative restrictions had to be considered and a common trade policy produced. Some railways, for instance, charged so-called "terminal charges" for merely crossing a frontier, and these fees had to be eliminated. Certain state railways also imposed charges for loading and unloading at frontiers, even when trains did not stop and no loading operations actually took place. A Common Market also had to act in private areas to restrict monopolistic practices, which might cause trade to flow for the benefit of one country at the expense of another.

It also was planned that the EEC could allow the free flow of capital, the establishment of a joint investment bank, joint agricultural policy, and even common taxation and social welfare legislation. It was believed, too, that the problem of labor shortages in some states and abundances in others might be solved by removing restrictions on the free movement of workmen and citizens from one state within the EEC to another.

Therefore, in all the planned aspects of the EEC there was a common element: the intention to dismantle national economic barriers. The Coal and Steel Community had provided valuable lessons in this area. The first lesson was that it would take time to adjust to the new situation. In consequence, it was decided that the pact establishing the Common Market would provide for a transitional period during which the barriers would come down gradually and national policies with the other states of the world would be aligned. The second lesson learned from the ECSC was that the period of adjustment could not be unlimited, else traditional economic nationalism might well hold back the lowering of barriers indefinitely. Therefore, barriers had to come down according to a strict timetable.

THE MEMBER STATES OF THE COMMON MARKET
(**Unshaded areas**)

The earlier successes of the Schuman Plan fortified the logic of the promoters of EEC. Negotiations among the six partners in the ECSC began in mid-1955 with the earlier-mentioned conference in Messina, Italy. In June 1956, it was agreed that European economic integration was absolutely necessary for the future. These discussions then led to the Treaty of Rome on March 25, 1957.

The Treaty of Rome, containing the various arrangements detailed above, was a compromise document. For instance, low-tariff states had to raise import duties whereas those at the higher levels lowered theirs until the two met. The longe-range objectives of the Treaty were declared to be the bringing of European peoples closer together, at the same time that a general raising of living standards could be realized throughout Europe.

The Treaty of Rome was not, as is sometimes implied, a document automatically establishing free trade within the member states of the EEC. In agriculture, for instance, it was decided that immediate disbanding of trade barriers would lead to chaos and resultant hardship for farmers. Consequently, it was decided that, in the area of agriculture, a managed market would be introduced gradually. In interstate transport it once again was decided that a program of free competition could not be immediately initiated.

The working machinery of the Common Market was carried over from the Schuman Plan. There was instituted an assembly with a consultative role. It was composed of deputies sent by the national parliaments of the member states. A Council of Ministers representing the cabinets of the member states was to make decisions, generally by majority vote. A court of justice, similar to that of the ECSC, was to settle disputes that arose among member states. Beyond these basic organs, several bodies, staffed by civil servants, were established to operate the functioning machinery of the Common Market.

Finally, in July 1968, eighteen months ahead of schedule, all trade barriers were dismantled in accordance with the agreements reached in the Treaty of Rome. A full-fledged customs union encompassing 183,000,000 people was inaugurated. All remaining tariffs within the Common Market were eliminated and uniform duties on imports received from nonmember states were fully established. Meanwhile, associate membership in the EEC, involving the establishment of a number of agreed-upon reciprocal economic rights and obligations, had been extended to several other European and non-European countries.

The appearance of this customs union was hailed by some as a milestone in the march to a new European order; this evaluation was less than realistic. When the EEC was formed, international opinion concerning its portents and potentialities was varied. In West Germany, opponents of the EEC claimed that it would be but one more complication making it impossible to reunify the German people. The Kremlin denounced the Common Market as a plot intended to make the capitalistic order healthier, thus retarding the eventual and unavoidable uprising of the proletariat against its capitalistic masters. Behind the propaganda smokescreen, the Russians seemed to see that EEC might build a stabler Europe, potentially militarily stronger, and thus less susceptible to Communist subversion. Lastly, there were those optimists who saw the Common Market as a natural step toward European political consolidation much as the nineteenth-century *Zollverein* had been a move toward the unification of Germany. By 1970, these optimistic men had not realized their dreams as the EEC—owing mainly to strong French hostility toward the expansion of the organization to include other European states—had not yet moved Europeans significantly closer to a United States of Europe.

G.   The Common Institutions of the European Communities

French hostility toward the expansion of common European economic communities to include states other than those among the original "Inner Six" was demonstrated again in an event transpiring in the last half of the 1960's, an event which otherwise might well have been the prelude to political integration. In a treaty signed by Belgium, France, West Germany, Italy, Luxembourg, and the Netherlands in 1965 (effective in 1967) the "Common Institutions of the European Communities" were established. The treaty fused EURATOM, the ECSC, and the EEC and established for them a single Council, Commission, Parliament, and Court of Justice. The newly-merged commission was headed by President Jean Rey of Belgium, former Vice-President for External Relations of the EEC. It was hoped by some of the member states that the new body would bring closer the establishment of a unified Europe. However, through early 1969, those on the commission who advocated unity in Western Europe were opposed by France. With de Gaulle's resignation as Head of State, new enthusiasm for unification was aroused among members of the commission. But French President Pompidou took no decisive steps toward political integration, as consideration of the first of such steps, British entry into the Communities, was postponed by France's chief executive while he pondered internal problems.

EUROPEAN INTEGRATION IN HISTORICAL PERSPECTIVE

The history of postwar Europe reveals that the traditional centers of influence and importance—the nation states of Western Europe—no longer were large enough or strong enough individually to play a major role in world affairs. The attempts to set up supranational organizations indicated that there were a number of Europeans who well understood this fact. The relative diminution of power resulted from the dissolution of colonial systems and from the developments in science and technology that resulted in an increase in the quantitative requirements for world-power status. The new superpowers in effect established new qualifications for membership in the elite international grouping of first-rate powers, qualifications that only a politically integrated European society with a population beyond 200,000,000 people and a gross national product in excess of $300,000,000,000 could have met. Without integration, West European states had to seek the protection of a superpower in times of stress. The nervous appeals for greater United States presence in Western Europe after the 1968 Russian incursion into Czechoslovakia provided an example of the postwar dependence of the medium-sized European states upon a protector superpower.

As nuclear striking forces grew after World War II, the prospect that a serious clash could occur in the sensitive Western European area and unleash the forces of worldwide destruction became an omnipresent factor in international calculations. Yet, the states of Western Europe were reluctant to put aside their traditional and destructive national rivalries. Evidently, "the persistence of archaic political arrangements in Europe" was at the heart of the continent's difficulties.

During the days of Europe's colonial empires, relatively small, but technologically advanced European states could exercise extensive control over large populations. When the period of empire passed, it greatly weakened the European states' capacities to play the role of world power. Confused as to their place in a postwar world dominated by emergent superpowers, Europeans withdrew from their share in global responsibility. Moreover, the populations of the various European states echoed the stance of neo-isolationism adopted by their leaders. This greater isolationism manifested in European states gave a distorted emphasis to the United States' role in international affairs, forcing on several occasions the overextension of American resources to fill the vacuum created by Europe's abandonment of world wide responsibility.

Even a Europe in which there was a Common Market could not compete economically with a superpower. Since the common European economic institutions that existed did not allow for the easy merging of corporations and facile pooling of ideas, a "technological gap" between the United States and Europe appeared and persisted. This gap could not be closed by a new technological aid plan from the United States, but only by the removal of the old political barriers of Europe's traditional nationalism.

Thus, European industry had not organized properly by the late 1960's to serve the Common Market area as well as it might have. In consequence, companies based in United States cities such as New York and Detroit became the enterprises acting as all-European corporations, since they were not limited by the same political strictures retarding European industrial amalgamation. Many Europeans began to argue in the late 1960's that the only way in which

Europe could resist American industrial absorption was by a modern political and economic consolidation.[2]

United States enterprises by the end of the decade of the 1960's had accomplished an efficient adjustment to a world economy. This meant that United States concerns had managed better the difficult tasks of selling, obtaining raw materials, financing investment, and production, than had the large European corporations. The activities of great world companies based in the United States raised for the first time the possibility of standardizing the degree of industrial efficiency across the globe. The accomplishments of these world companies aroused concern in Europeans such as Charles de Gaulle. Some resented the "American invasion" that seemed to be sweeping over Europe's economic system.

An important result of the "technological gap" was the failure of European nations to export capital in amounts consistent with national reserve holdings, and a consequent balance-of-payments deficit in the United States. This balance-of-payments deficit came into being partly because United States business concerns were able to corner much of the European market in crucial areas at the same time that European business enterprises, too small and too inefficient, were unable to move into the United States market with equal force.

What seemed to many observers to be needed at the beginning of the 1970's, then, was a sweeping reorganization of European political and economic institutions to meet "the American challenge." For economic integration among the Common Market countries had proceeded to the point where it apparently could not go much further without the achievement of greater political unity. Consequently, a hope persisted among those who supported European unity that eventual frustration over the political limits set upon economic expansion might make it possible to remove those strictures. If such a phenomenon occurred, it would not be the first time that pressure in the economic sphere had forged a change in the European political order.

---

[2] A book by Jacques Servan-Schreiber entitled *The American Challenge,* which maintained this point of view, became a best-seller in Europe in the late 1960's.

The Emergence of   28
a New Asia

A. The Communist Seizure of Power

Perhaps even more than the success of Communism in Russia, the advent of a Marxist-Leninist state in China probably would have astounded Karl Marx and Friedrich Engels, for these two ideologists lived in cities and saw the coming of the new Communist order as an urban phenomenon. What happened in essentially rural China was that adjustments were made in Marxist doctrine similar to those that Lenin had made in Russia during 1917. Mao Tse-tung, the leading figure in Chinese Communism, went even further than Lenin in transforming communism. He restructured the Marxist-Leninist doctrine until communism emerged as an entity to serve his Chinese goals. Instead of being an urban-oriented ideology, it was based on the peasant masses whose task it became to overthrow "the authority of the landlord class."

To understand the development of communism in China it must be realized that the Bolshevik Revolution in Russia took place at a time when Chinese intellectuals were examining Western ideas closely. A number of Chinese political thinkers knew China was a living anachronism in 1917, and that she must be divested of her old ways and given new ones if she wished to live in the modern world. At Chinese universities Adam Smith, John Locke, and other famous Western political and economic thinkers were studied with the intention of using this knowledge to modernize China. Then came news of Lenin's successful revolution in Russia and Chinese attention turned to the writings of Marx and Lenin. Moreover, in 1918 and 1919, the Russian Bolsheviks still believed that the export of their revolution to other states throughout the world would be easy. Consequently, they tried to better relations with potentially communist elements in other states. Agents were sent from Russia to China in 1920 to help in the founding of the Chinese Communist Party.

The Chinese Communist Party was established in 1921. The founders were intellectuals organized by the Russian agents. Foremost among them were Chen Tu-hsiu and Li Ta-chao, professors at Peking University, and Mao Tse-tung, a young library clerk at the university. For the first ten years of its existence the Communist Chinese Party followed the Soviet Union's "line" in almost all matters.

When Chiang Kai-shek took over the armies of the Kuomintang (see Chapter 13), he conquered much of the Chinese territory previously held by the regional warlords (1926–1928). Chiang also sought victory over the Communists. In 1927, he ordered his forces to destroy the Reds, ignoring an earlier agreement providing for cooperation between the Kuomintang and the Marxist-Leninists. Chiang's war of annihilation against the Communists almost succeeded. At Stalin's direction, the Reds were concentrated in the cities, and thus were easy to find and destroy. But, as the decade of the 1930's began, Mao Tse-tung avoided destruction of the movement he now led by gathering a small band of followers and retreating to the mountains. There, gradually, he began to build up the movement again, seeking mass support among the peasantry.

Mao Tse-tung was born, in 1894, of peasant parents about forty miles from Changsha. In 1912, he entered the Hunan Normal School where he remained for six years, graduating in 1918. After World War I, Mao enrolled at Peking University, where he was remembered by associates as an eager student. In 1919, as new intellectual movements from Europe were shaping the minds of China's intelligentsia, revolutionary groups were formed and Mao joined one of them. In December 1919, China's first Society for the Study of Socialism was established in Peking and one of its members was Mao Tse-tung. From this group he moved into the Communist Party when it was established in 1921.

As the 1930's began, Mao already had developed a master plan, which he followed until he came to power nearly twenty years later. At the heart of his scheme was the idea of building strongholds of Communism in the countryside, thus establishing self-contained political-military units. Important in this type of organization were the techniques of guerrilla warfare. The tactics used by Mao against the larger forces of Chiang's Kuomintang have, in written form, become classics in the literature of guerrilla war. Mao's formula for proper guerrilla activity was as follows:

> The enemy advances: we retreat.
> The enemy halts: we harass.
> The enemy tires: we attack.
> The enemy retreats: we pursue.

Mao's armies were weak at first. He therefore devised a two-part program to build his forces even while suffering losses in the field: (1) his armies were taught to obtain supplies by capturing them from the enemy; and (2) they were instructed to replenish their combat-depleted ranks by convincing soldiers captured in battle to serve the Communist cause.

Despite the ingenious nature of his plans, Mao Tse-tung suffered many setbacks before he won control of China. In the early 1930's, Chiang tried time after time to destroy the Communist forces north of Canton. Mao's armies survived only by following his basic plan closely. When Chiang halted, they harassed, until the Kuomintang forces were sufficiently tired for the Reds to attack.

In 1933, the Nationalist Government decided to overcome Mao's tactics by preparing more carefully and by placing a larger force in the field. Some 700,000 troops, supported by artillery and airplanes, were sent against the Reds by Chiang. A year of hard fighting followed, and finally Mao found his forces encircled. Mao decided to retreat and began a forced march across China. This "Long March," as the incident has come to be known, lasted a year and ended 6000 miles from its point of origin. The Long March began with 100,000 men and ended at the other end of China (Shensi Province) with less than one-third of the original force remaining. Mao now had to begin again, with one of the most poverty-stricken areas of China as a base.

To have climbed back from this deep pit of misfortune might have been impossible had it not been for certain conditions at work elsewhere in China. From 1937 to 1945, the Japanese invaders drained the strength of the Nationalists. The series of Japanese military victories early in the war forced an unnatural bond of alliance between the Nationalists and the Communists. Indeed, Moscow urged the strange union and backed its urging with arms.

The agreement to cooperate between Mao and Chiang was characterized by mutual cynicism. Even while the war against the Japanese continued, Mao and Chiang sought positions which would help them in the postwar resumption of the Nationalist-Communist struggle. Mao fared better than Chiang in this endeavor. During World War II, he greatly extended the area of the countryside under his control.

When the war ended in 1945, Mao immediately received aid from the Soviets. The U.S.S.R. had seized Manchuria from the Japanese during the last days of the war. Now it helped Mao's followers to build major bases of operation in the Manchurian area. From this newly controlled territory the Communists launched an attack on Chiang's forces.

When the Japanese surrendered to the Allies, the Communists controlled most of the northern Chinese countryside. The Nationalists were still strong in the towns, but the Communists had begun to erode their strength even in these former Kuomintang bastions.

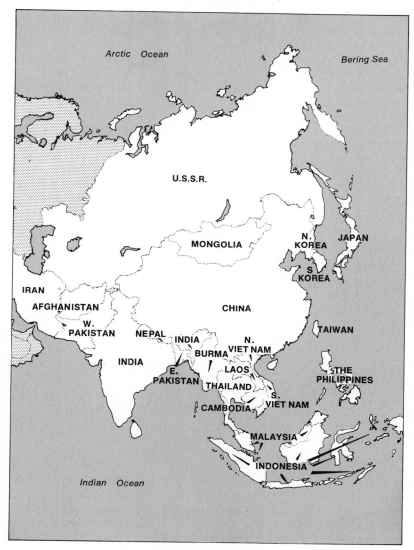

ASIA IN 1970

The United States now entered the struggle with extensive aid to the Nationalists. American transport planes were used to deploy a total of between 400,000 and 500,000 Nationalists troops in different locations. While the Nationalists troops were riding "in style" in American aircraft to northern China, thousands of Communist troops were arranging themselves for battle on foot.

At first the Nationalist advances seemed to presage Chiang's eventual success. The Communists allowed the Nationalists to extend themselves by letting Chiang's forces take town after town. Impelled by a false optimism, the Nationalists drove on deeply into Manchuria and even fanned out to take positions on the Yalu River, the border with Korea. But then the Communists began to appear, almost from nowhere it seemed, behind the Nationalist "front."

During the winter of 1946, the Communist strength continued to grow in the Manchurian countryside. The Nationalists now were so over-extended that their lines of communication and supply were fragile. They believed that the Manchurian winter was too cold to allow the Communists to continue the fight. They therefore decided to protect their gains until spring by building elaborate pillbox and barbed-wire systems around the various Nationalist-held towns.

Then, across the frozen plains of Manchuria, the Communists launched a number of unexpected attacks. By May 1947, the Communist People's Liberation Army (PLA) was advancing rapidly southward in Manchuria through the thinly held countryside. By summer, the Nationalists had been forced to withdraw from most of southeastern Manchuria. As the second year of the war began, northeast China had become a gigantic strategic trap for the Nationalists, and Mao was beginning to close that trap.

From September 1948, disaster followed disaster for the forces of the Government in Manchuria, in Shantung, and in Central China. The Communists methodically cut communications lines around battlefield areas and divided the defending forces into segments that could be attacked and destroyed individually. The direction the war was reflected in the Chinese Nationalist economy as a supposedly "stable" new currency plummeted in value.

In January 1949, the Nationalist Government requested the governments of Great Britain, the United States, France, and the Soviet Union to intervene and assure a "peaceful settlement with the Chinese Communist Party." An American observer earlier had written that he was "convinced that the military situation had deteriorated to the point where only the active participation of United States troops could effect a remedy," and that the Nationalist's military setbacks could be attributed to "the world's worst leadership."

On January 21, 1949, Chiang Kai-shek transferred authority to his Vice-President, General Li Tsung-jen, although he maintained his influence over the Government. In April, a Nationalist delegation headed by Chang Chih-chung, close associate of Chiang Kai-shek's, began negotiations with the victorious Communists. The Communists set an early deadline for conclusion of the negotiations and when that deadline was reached without an agreement, the PLA continued its advances on all fronts. The new Central Peoples' Government of the Chinese People's Republic already had most of China under its jurisdiction when it was installed formally at Peiping[1] on October 1, 1949. The Nationalists withdrew their

[1] The Communists promptly renamed the city Peking.

government to Taiwan (Formosa) in December 1949. The Communist era in China had begun.

B. The People's Republic of China (1949-1957)

After many years of Western presence in China, an awakened nationalism now dictated that the influence of the West be expunged. Western businesses were confiscated on a wide scale and government officials and private businessmen from the United States were forced to leave the country. Quickly the Communists began an "all-out" assault on the minds of the people by organizing small "study groups" in factories, shops, schools, and offices. In these study groups the average Chinese was indoctrinated with the ideology and politics of the new regime. Such meetings were held regularly under leaders whose task it was to report the thinking of each group member to higher authorities.

Conforming the thoughts of the Chinese masses to the way of the new order was accomplished by other means as well. All public media were controlled and saturated with propaganda. Loudspeakers were set up in the streets to convey the message of the mass party to the people. Ideological heretics were to be reported at the first sign of deviation. Opposition meant certain death as the Communists took control of all military and police organs within the state. In short, by the early 1950's, the Communists were well along the road toward the establishment of a totalitarian state.

Extensive reorganization of land use was achieved between 1950 and 1952. Into each Chinese village went a "Land Reform Squad" to organize complaint meetings, where dissident peasants vented their anger against village landlords. Great emotion was stimulated at these meetings until the peasants finally would be roused sufficiently to demand the execution of their landlords; executions normally followed such demands. Some estimates of the number of landlords killed in this manner approach 2,000,000. This purge had the effect of eliminating the larger landowners as a class.

Having finished with the landlords, the Government turned to businessmen as early as 1952. Meetings were held for businessmen, who were expected to accuse one another of crimes and "confess' their own.[2] Frightened into submission by this campaign, Chinese businessmen were not likely to resist the sharing of control over their businesses with the Government. Later in the decade of the 1950's, the Government suggested that businessmen transfer their jointly-held concerns to the State. Ceremonies were held wherein businessmen "celebrated" in public demonstrations their "joy" at being allowed to leave the capitalist class at last.

[2] These "crimes" were: bribery, fraud, and theft of Government property and "economic secrets."

The China that the Communists had taken from the Nationalists possessed a singularly underdeveloped economy. It thus became the dream of Chinese Communists to build the country's economy and make China a modern nation. Mao's basic resource in this endeavor was the seemingly limitless manpower of China, and he promptly put the teeming masses to work. Particularly in agriculture was there intensive activity, and great drives were launched to kill the hordes of insects that damaged crops, to irrigate dry areas, and to cultivate land cooperatively. Agricultural production was increased sufficiently by this program to make it possible by the mid-1950's to use profits from agriculture to finance industrialization.[3] Experts came from the Soviet Union to teach Chinese factory workers new skills. Arrangements also were worked out whereby Chinese technicians could study in the Soviet Union.

Despite some progress, Mao felt it necessary to achieve more from the agricultural sector and, at the same time, eliminate certain relatively well-off peasants who had benefited from the redistribution of other landlords' former holdings. In the mid-1950's Mao decided to deal with peasant landlords, who resisted taxation, by an intensive campaign to collectivize agriculture. Within a year, 91.6 per cent of all farmers were included within collectives. Thus, peasants, who originally had come to the Communist Party because of hopes for land reform, were deprived of their recently gained holdings.

At the end of 1956, Mao and his associates began to worry about potential unrest among the people. The example of the Hungarian uprising of 1956 indicated that insurrection against a Communist regime was a distinct possibility. For a brief period in the spring of 1957, the Communists relaxed control over those who wished to criticize the regime, perhaps hoping that such a liberalization would strengthen loyalties to party and state. However, criticisms began to pour in and many demanded that the Communist Party relinquish power.

Suddenly, the time of free expression was ended. The Government launched a campaign to purge the dissidents and those who had protested were severely punished. Uniformity of opinion was reintroduced.[4] Mao and his colleagues had learned something from the so-called "hundred flowers" incident.[5] The basic discontent of the masses ran just beneath the surface of Chinese life. Mao and his associates came to believe that the basic factor tending to general

---

[3] There was some financial aid from Russia during this period, but it did not nearly meet the needs of China.

[4] It is not known whether this time of free expression was a trap set by Mao and his colleagues for nonconformists, or, whether it was a case of miscalculation on the part of the leadership and the extent of popular discontent was unexpected.

[5] The term derives from a speech given by Mao in which he called for conflicting opinions. He said: "Let a hundred flowers bloom, let a hundred schools contend."

discontent was the lack of the necessities of life (food, housing, and so on). It therefore was decided to push China forward rapidly into a time of plenty when she also would wield world power. The scheme that was to provide this miracle was called the "Great Leap Forward."

C. The People's Republic of China (1957-1965)

The "Great Leap Forward" was designed to end China's backwardness within a few years. It seemed to begin well and, in early 1959, the Chinese Communists boasted that this supreme effort to raise industrial and agricultural levels of production quickly was beginning to succeed.

To help industrialization, the Chinese decided to go ahead with the development of large and expensive plants. These installations, first begun in 1950, were constructed under Soviet tutelage and with Russian equipment. At the same time, the government decided to utilize the massive available labor force by opening small mines, primitive factories, and other similarly crude industrial establishments all over China. It became the patriotic duty of many Chinese to have a small furnace in their backyard where they were to make metal for the national industrialization effort.

In agriculture an effort was made to abolish, finally, private property and disrupt family life by moving people into "dormitories." It was thought that in communal life would be found the key to greater agricultural production. The aim of these systems was expressed by Mao-Tse-tung when he said that the "whole nation" was to "be organized as militia" to accomplish the establishment of the new China.

The "Great Leap Forward" failed to realize the achievements Mao had expected of it. In agriculture, flood and drought hampered the program. In 1960 and 1961, famine swept the land. Factories stood idle as many were sent from the cities to the farms in an attempt to increase food production. The backyard furnaces now had to be replaced by gardens.

The government blamed the national disasters on the Soviet Union, which had withdrawn many of its technicians from China in 1960 as the great schism between the two Communist monoliths developed. But it was the planning that went into the Great Leap Forward which was at fault. The metal produced by amateur backyard efforts was of such poor quality as to be nearly useless, and much labor was wasted in furnace tending. The collective farm effort ran into the same difficulties that other Communist countries had experienced when collectivization was initiated too rapidly. Peasants refused to work hard on land owned by the state and demonstrated a strong preference for working on their own plots, where they could work for profit. Mao and his associates perhaps had not been cognizant of the fact that Chinese agriculture had fed vast numbers in the past, primarily because peasants worked their own plots with methods learned over the centuries, thus drawing from the soil the highest possible yields.

In 1960, the government leaped backward by dissolving many of the people's communes. The peasant was given back his plot and production increased. By now, however, it was difficult for food supplies to keep pace with the expansion of population. The Communist Government, aware of statistics indicating that the population had increased by perhaps 150,000,000 people during the 1950's, launched a vigorous campaign to cut the national birthrate.

Simultaneously, the Communists introduced new methods of sanitation and improved health as well. This produced a situation in the early 1960's, in which the death rate fell sharply whereas the birth rate remained high. In consequence, the Chinese population in 1960 reached perhaps 700,000,000. Moreover, statisticians estimated that, if the birth rate continued, it would give China a population of 1,600,000,000 by the year 2000. The government attempted to limit the populace through a campaign of population retardation. Those males who were voluntarily sterilized were praised loudly and it was suggested that others follow their example. The propaganda campaign assumed the proportions of an antisex movement.

In such difficult times the Communists found it necessary to control the people by intensive propaganda. They attempted to develop support by appealing to patriotism and by indicating that it was Mao Tse-tung who would eventually restore the ancient lost glories of China. In this context, the Sino-Soviet split discussed in Chapter 22 was a logical outgrowth, at least in part, of Mao's need to prove that he was a China-first man, and not a mere plaything of Moscow.

China in the Communist era followed the typical propagandist pattern that had been established by totalitarian states troubled by potential internal difficulties, namely, by portraying a dangerous outside enemy, in hope of uniting the nation against an external threat. This created enemy was the United States. Loudspeakers and wall posters depicted the evil country that "stole" Taiwan from Communist China and sought to "enslave" the Chinese people.

China's explosions of atomic weapons (the first one detonated in October 1964) were singularly important to Mao. These were not only the greatest Chinese technological accomplishments in centuries, but they were the ultimate weapons developed by "Protector Mao" to defend China from the outside threat posed by a menacing United States and, after the Sino-Soviet schism had deepened, the hardly less fearsome danger of the U.S.S.R. That the Chinese might possess adequate delivery systems for these weapons was demonstrated by the launching of their first earth-orbiting satellite in April 1970.

D.   The People's Republic of China since 1965

During the second half of the 1960's, Mao seemingly became disturbed that Red China might lapse into the "sinful, bourgeois" ways of Soviet Russia. A Communist Party bureaucracy had developed which desired the easing of Mao's pressure to remake society at once. These men were believed by observers in the outside world to be "pragmatists." Mao's answer to the pragmatists was to organize millions of teenage paramilitary "Red Guards," whom he sent on a rampage in 1966, hailing them as the true embodiment of Maoism.

Apparently at the direction of Mao and his close associates, observers from foreign nations in the late summer of 1966, saw the teenage Red Guards rioting in the streets of China's major cities. Buddhist shrines, always highly respected by even those Chinese living under communism, now were defaced. Crudely lettered marching orders for the Red Guard appeared on the walls, indicating "reactionaries" within the party who would have to be punished.

The persistent defamations and disruptions of the Red Guards turned the Chinese workers against them. In January 1967, crowds of workers poured into Nanking, where they fought in the streets with the Red Guards. Soon the Red Guard-workers struggle spread to other cities as the Red Guards further established their scorn for all "reactionary" elements within Chinese society by marching to Shantung to wreck the birthplace of Confucius. In February, even soldiers joined the anti-Red Guard forces.

The actions of the Red Guard were called the "Great Proletarian Cultural Revolution," a term invented by Mao to describe the struggle to purge the Chinese society of all "revisionist" elements. By late February 1967, it seemed possible that the Great Proletarian Cultural Revolution would so disrupt Chinese society that the annual harvest would be below minimal levels. Consequently, after seven months of "cultural" disorder, it became necessary to send some Red Guards back to school and work, for famine threatened.

The activities of the Guard continued, however. By May, Mao felt ready to "consolidate" the gains of his "Cultural Revolution." The Chinese dictator created provincial "revolutionary committees" in which loyal government workers, Red Guards, and militant leaders were combined to replace the old party-government apparatus, that had proven to be filled with anti-Maoists. This action did little to quell disorder, however, and, two weeks later, in southwestern China, some thousands were killed in fighting between Maoists and anti-Maoists.

On June 16, 1967, Vice-Premier Lin Piao was given the task of controlling disorders. By this time the nature of the struggle taking place in China had become clearer. A new form of traditional Chinese particularism had developed. Mao's thinking postulated a monolithic state with all theoretical and practical power reposing in the apex of the political-administrative pyramid. The bureaucrats who controlled the provinces took a contrary view. Although they did not care to oppose Mao, they wanted practical control of their own provinces. Around this jockeying for power between local and national elements a continued surge of riots and streetfighting swirled throughout 1967.

By 1968, the Great Proletarian Cultural Revolution had produced a badly damaged economy, an all but defunct educational system, and factional strife that frequently verged on outright civil war. In August 1968, the Peking Government broadcast that the disbanding of the Red Guards was under way. During the Great Revolution young people had flocked to the cities until they became over-crowded. In late 1968, and into 1969, the government reversed the process and ordered youth back to the countryside to help a failing agricultural situation. In April 1969, the Ninth Congress of the Chinese Communist Party formally closed the period of Cultural Revolution and designated Marshal Lin Piao as eventual "successor" to Mao Tse-Tung.

E.   The Republic of China (Taiwan)

The Government of Nationalist China, after it left the mainland in 1949, remained on the island of Taiwan (Formosa). Thereafter, it was recognized as the legitimate government of China by the United States, many other nations, and the United Nations. In 1968 the total population of the island was about 13,470,000. Thus, Taiwan could not form a major threat to Mao's mainland China. Yet, Mao's Government continually was disturbed by Taiwan because it offered the mainland Chinese a possible alternative pattern of life. The Communists also believed that Chiang Kai-shek's regime, aided by the United Sates, might seek to attack mainland China.

The Communists were disturbed further by the fact that, after its departure from the mainland, the Chinese Nationalist Govern-ment maintained steadily that it someday would return to China. A very large army for such a small state was maintained on Taiwan and, periodically, spies, saboteurs, propaganda planes, and reconais-sance aircraft were dispatched to the mainland. Moreover, Commu-nist jealousy was aroused by the Taiwan Government's successful attempt to make the island a splendid showcase of prosperity in contrast with the grinding poverty of the mainland.

The progress achieved on the island redounded to the benefit of most inhabitants. The government sponsored a program of land re-form that made most of the farmers the owners of their own land. Industry was encouraged with extensive help from the United States. Health, education, and welfare, were improved. Eventually, Taiwan came to enjoy one of the best living standards in Asia. One social result was the appearance of a middle class that was relatively much larger than those normally found in Asian countries.

In the political realm, Taiwan remained a one-party dictatorship. The Kuomintang, dominated by President Chiang, sought out and arrested both Communists and Taiwanese members of dissident political groups.

At the end of the 1960's, the United States continued to use Taiwan as a military and intelligence base, forming the keystone of the entire American position in the western Pacific. The ominous possibility remained that, if the mainland Chinese organized an invasion of Taiwan, this might draw the United States into a conflict with Communist China, the most heavily populated nation in the world. In 1969 Chiang Kai-shek's son, Chiang Ching-kuo, became Vice-Premier; he generally was regarded as likely to succeed his father in the republic's leadership.

JAPAN IN THE POSTWAR ERA

A. Occupation

The occupation of defeated Japan was officially an Allied project. Actually, it was almost solely a venture of the United States. Allied interests in Japan were represented by a policymaking body which met in Washington, known as the Far Eastern Commission, and a four-nation body, the Allied Council for Japan, which normally met in Tokyo. The Allied Council (the United States, the Soviet Union, China, and Great Britain) was never of consequence, and real authority rested with the Supreme Commander for the Allied Powers (SCAP), an office first directed by General Douglas MacArthur.

The occupying victors decided not to depose the emperor of Japan nor to erase the basic structure of Japanese government. Rather, SCAP worked through the Japanese to carry out a direct military administration of Japanese affairs. The basic documents of the occupation listed the first tasks of this United States-controlled Japanese administration as follows: political parties were to be developed; undemoractic laws left over from the past were to be abolished; secret societies were to be outlawed; political prisoners released; and war criminals tried.

In the first year of SCAP's existence, several hundred directives flowed through administrative channels to the Japanese Government. Soon Japan was bustling with activity as tons of weapons were tossed into the sea, war criminals were placed on trial,[6] and Japanese troops and civilians were brought home from overseas. Aside from the official demilitarization activities, the Japanese were a people al-

---

[6] Emperor Hirohito, who had ascended the throne in 1926, was exonerated of crimes against peace.

ready beaten and so much impressed with the nuclear bombing of their cities that there had developed in them a deeprooted pacifism. Therefore, much more important among the tasks given to SCAP than demilitarizing an already demilitarized Japan, was the work of clearing away debris to build new structures and the assignment to initiate new political forms for the Japanese.

It was not easy for a military organization like SCAP, possessing the autocratic tendencies normally displayed in military hierarchies, to strengthen basic democratic tendencies in Japan. The first step toward building a parliamentary democracy was the presentation of an American-drafted constitution to the Japanese. When the constitution went into effect, in May 1947, the emperor became only a symbolic head of state, deriving his position from the sovereign will of his people. Japan was to be governed by a bicameral legislature, elected by universal adult suffrage. The legislature was to control budgetary affairs at the same time that it was responsible for selecting the prime minister and his cabinet. The rest of the constitution contained guarantees of basic civil rights and, in the well-publicized Article 9, there was set forth the promise of the Japanese people never again to engage in war, maintain armed forces, or threaten force against another state.[7]

Japan had held her first postwar elections in April 1946, before the new constitution was in effect. The old prewar Minseito and Seiyukai political parties now appeared with new platforms and new titles as the "Progressives" and the "Liberals." On the left of the political spectrum, Social Democrats and Communists sought the approval of the electorate.[8] Shigeru Yoshida, leader of the Liberals, emerged victorious from the election campaign and eventually became the foremost Japanese politician to appear during the occupation period.

Before Japan could build truly democratic institutions, however, her people had to be fed, for starving people have little time or energy to expend in the calm and thoughtful deliberations necessary for democracy. Consequently, SCAP, which at first was reluctant to do so, began to revise the economic structure of Japan. SCAP broke up large holding companies by forcing members of exceptionally wealthy families to resign from the boards of corporations and by selling the properties of this elite to workers, trade unions, and private purchasers outside the traditional controlling group.[9] Trade unions were encouraged, but when the unions became active enough

---

[7] This article was inserted by SCAP, partially because of the widely held belief among United States authorities that Japan would never be able to defend herself again with her own forces. Following the outbreak of war in Korea in 1950, Japan, with United States approval, enlarged both its police and "self-defense" forces.

[8] The Japanese electorate now contained women for the first time.

[9] To reinforce this action the Japanese Diet passed the Anti-Monopoly Law of 1947 and the Trade Association Law of 1948.

to threaten a general strike in 1947, General MacArthur forbade it as possibly damaging to Japan's recovery. Lastly, an ambitious program of land reform was carried out. Absentee landlordism was abolished and land redistributed so that three out of four former tenants could experience the pride of ownership.

The Cold War's appearance, in 1948, forced the United States to make a decision with regard to Japan similar to the one forced in Europe by Russo-Western antagonism over Germany. It was decided to give more generous assistance to the Japanese lest they succumb to the influence of communism. The merchant marine and new industries were built up. By 1950, the 1930–1934 level of production had been achieved and wages were on their way up while prices had been stabilized.

The social impact of these political and economic reforms was extensive. Education was reformed and made more widely available to people regardless of social origin, and nationalism and militarism were eliminated from instruction. Land reform in the countryside caused a social leveling there, and religion and state were separated. Most Japanese regarded the social changes which transpired as no more than extensions of tendencies toward modernization begun in Japan during the 1930's. In consequence, the occupation accomplished an impressive degree of modernization and westernization in a relatively short time.

B. The Peace Settlement and the Return to Independence

As 1950 began, Japan seemed to have been transformed into a nation which was well along the road toward modernization and prosperity. Then came a substantial shock with the beginning of the Korean War. The war called attention to the fact that Japan lay helpless, dependent on the protection of the United States. Once again the possibility that Korea might form the invasion route between China and Japan became an important consideration. The Japanese, as a people, apparently had been satisfied with a constitution that enforced pacifism upon them. They now reconsidered their position. With the approval of SCAP, Japan began to increase enlistments in its national police force and coastal defense services. General MacArthur pointed out to the Japanese that to turn one's back on war as an instrument of national policy is not necessarily to give up the right of self-defense against unprovoked attack. Japan reacted to the threat posed by the Korean War by placing all her military strength at the disposal of the United Nations. This step further convinced the United States that Japan was ready to resume sovereign power status.

Actually, President Truman and General MacArthur, as early as 1947, had agreed upon the desirability of a peace treaty with Japan. This sentiment grew out of an apprehension caused by the developing Cold War. It was believed that a freed and strengthened Japan would become a strong ally of the United States. Yet, the United States could not alone settle a treaty with Japan. Because of a 1942 United Nations' declaration to the effect that none of the participating states would sign a "separate peace," the United States could not act unilaterally to sign a peace treaty with Japan.[10]

Finally, Truman decided to risk charges that he had violated the 1942 United Nations' declaration. The President of the United States called for peace with Japan and, on September 8, 1950, appointed John Foster Dulles to the post of special ambassador to make peace with Japan. For nearly a year Dulles was involved in negotiations conducted in ten world capitals. After a series of drafts of a treaty were scrapped, the British and Americans finally agreed. In August 1951, copies of the proposed treaty were cirulated among the nations invited to a conference in San Francisco.[11]

The peace treaty was constructed along lines demanded earlier by the United States. It was, therefore, essentially nonpunitive with relatively easy terms, as Washington looked to a future in which Japan would be a staunch ally. In the preamble was included a statement declaring Japan's intention to join the United Nations and, in her future actions, to conform to the UN Charter. Most important for the Japanese, the end of the state of war existing between the Allies and Japan was declared along with the full sovereignty of the Japanese people.

This regained sovereignty was limited by the terms of the treaty to the four main islands and the minor isles of the Japanese homeland. Japan renounced title to Formosa, the Pescadores, the Kurile Islands, Korea, and Southern Sakhalin, along with its former mandates.

As indicated earlier, Japan was bound to the peaceful principles expressed in the United Nations Charter, but it was recognized that Japan did have the right of self-defense and the privilege of entering into collective defense arrangements. Japan was not to be subjected to any permanent trade discriminations and her economy was to be benefited by the right to free trade.

Reparation was considered and it was at least implied that those nations suffering material damage at the hands of the Japanese were entitled to payment in compensation. However, Japan could not afford to pay the usual kind of reparation. Consequently, the Japanese were obligated to make people available for production, salvaging, and other work the Allies desired done.

The menace posed by the Korean War to Japan's security brought

[10] Russia and Nationalist China were in no hurry to see an end to the *status quo* in Japan until they were sure that the Japanese would not again threaten expansion in Asia.

[11] The conference was not called to initiate the negotiation of a proposed treaty. Nations were invited to sign or reject a treaty already composed.

about the signing of a bilateral security pact between Japan and the United States on the same day that the peace treaty was signed. The provisions of the security pact allowed the United States to deploy its forces in and around Japan. It was guaranteed that such forces not only would be used to protect American interests in the Far East, but to provide greater security for Japan against armed attack.

Fifty-two nations were represented in San Francisco and, surprisingly, considering the fact that the treaty was designed primarily by the United States and Great Britain, the Soviet bloc decided to attend. The reason the Russians had come to the conference soon became evident when the Soviet representatives objected vigorously to the treaty and then proposed a number of amendments. The major Russian objection was that Japan shared collective guilt with the other Axis powers and should therefore be treated no better than had been Nazi Germany. Despite the objections the treaty was signed, although the Soviet bloc nations refused to become signatories. Japanese Premier Yoshida addressed the gathering and generally praised the treaty. He promised that Japan's unfortunate imperial ambitions of the past now had truly disappeared and that she was ready to live at peace with her neighbors.

In Japan itself there was a generally favorable feeling about the end of occupation. Many Japanese were upset, not by the treaty, but by the accompanying Japanese-United States security pact. The nuclear-induced pacifism, which had swept Japan in the postwar period, now caused many to indicate that they did not wish to take sides in an international confrontation that might lead to atomic warfare. This sentiment was defeated by the practicality of the majority, however. It generally was realized that alignment with the United States was the only possible alternative to rebuilding a national defense force. The former president of Keio University, Koizumi Shinzo, voiced the prevailing Japanese opinion when he said that defense by foreign troops might not be "honorable" but could be tolerated if it maintained peace.

Both houses of the Japanese Diet overwhelmingly approved the treaty of peace and the Emperor signed it on November 9, 1951. The treaty entered into force on April 28, 1952, the same day on which Japan made peace with Nationalist China. On June 9, 1952, Japan made peace with India, and, on November 5, 1954, a similar agreement was reached between Japan and Burma.

C. Government and Politics

Japan, within seven years of her surrender to the Allies, had once again become a sovereign state. The architect of the new sovereignty had been Premier Shigeru Yoshida, who held that high office through the decisive years 1948–1954. It was Yoshida who was the foremost exponent and defender of democratic procedures, and the constitution of 1947 supported his efforts to provide greater democratization.

The constitution established a 250-member upper house (House of Councilors) and a 467-member (later 486) lower house (House of Representatives). The lower house, elected every four years, was the more important of the two parliamentary bodies in that it made most of the laws and controlled finances. It also had the power to name prime ministers. The constitution ensured that the democratic procedures inaugurated during the occupation would be continued.

Japanese political parties, nearly driven out of existence by the militarists before World War II, reappeared. A coalition known as the Liberal Democratic Party (LDP) normally operated the Japanese Government. The LDP was made up of three political parties, the Liberals, Democrats, and Progressives, which basically were conservative despite their names. Businessmen, farmers and bureaucrats filled the ranks of the LDP. Its platform approved of the general spirit of pacifism abroad in the nation, and called for peace in keeping with the principles set forth in the United Nations Charter. The platform was against war, but advocated a partial arming for the sake of defense. The LDP was dedicated to a free enterprise system and was thus a natural ideological foe of the Left and, especially, of the Communist Party.

The most important party in the political opposition was the Japanese Socialist Party (JSP). The term Socialist in Japan did not necessarily indicate an adherence to Marxism, but rather indicated belief in a program designed to help the numerous underprivileged spawned by any modern industrialized society. The strength of the JSP was centered in the large cities, organized labor, and intellectuals. The JSP normally suffered from a lack of funds and was troubled by factionalism.

The factionalism within the JSP eventually produced a party cleavage in 1959. A group of party rightists defected and re-formed as the Democratic Socialist Party (DSP). The splintering of the Socialists was caused by a 1949 statement from the Red Chinese Government to the effect that American imperialists acted as "the common enemy" of China and Japan; the left wing of the JSP agreed and the right dissented.

The Communists were less politically influential than the Socialists, because they were associated in the minds of most Japanese with the disliked Russians. Their sole means of securing a following among the electorate was their often vitriolic anti-Americanism. Another limitation on their appeal was the fact that the police kept them under strict surveillance. If one was to become an active Communist it meant that he was immediately suspect as far as the authorities were concerned. Relatively few Japanese seemed willing to pay this price for a party allegiance. The lack of appeal of the Communists was indicated by the fact that, in 1949, they were able to capture only 10 per cent of the vote. By 1963, they could manage only 4 per cent. In 1969, they elected fourteen representatives.

Between 1952 and 1969, eight general elections were held in Japan, all which revealed the political spectrum to be relatively fixed. The vote usually was slightly less than two-thirds LDP and one-third Socialist, with the rest gong to the Communists and other minor parties. The normal political picture in postwar Japan was one of stability and, despite periodic student riots on such occasions as the docking of a United Sates nuclear submarine in a Japanese port, Japan's politics continued on a democratic course.[12]

D. Foreign Affairs

In the 1950's and the 1960's, Japan took on a special symbolic importance in foreign affairs. She occupied a strategic location between the mostly Communist-controlled Asian mainland and the United States-dominated Pacific. Although not a pawn of the United States, Japan remained more closely tied to Washington than to any capital on mainland Asia. Moreover, she continued to be a symbol of prosperity and stability under democracy for the whole Asian area. It thus was believed by some that this prosperous Japan had more power to build the future by example than the combined military potential of the other Asian non-Communist states.

The basic aim of foreign policy in Japan was to use international relations and international trade to raise the level of living standards in the mother country. The United States' primary concern in Asia was the containment and eventual elimination of Asian Communism. United States policies worked to the advantage of the Japanese as Japan profited from vast sums spent there by the American Government and private individuals during the Korean War and after, as the United States continued its containment effort.[13] Of the first billion dollars of postwar investment money flowing into Japan, approximately 80 per cent came from the United States. One-third of Japan's foreign trade was conducted with the United States and, in the 1960's, more than a billion dollars in goods flowed annually from one country to the other.

In late 1969 Premier Sato and President Nixon agreed on a continuance of the Japan-United States Mutual Security Treaty, and the return of administrative control over Okinawa to Japan in 1972 (with retention of military-base facilities by the United States). Japanese

[12] In July 1968, an upper-house election, and in December 1969, a lower-house election were won easily by the pro-American LPD. Forces of Premier Eisaku Sato and the LDP captured 47.63 per cent of the vote in December 1969.

[13] Bases from which troop deployment to Asia was carried out were maintained on Japanese soil, and much money passed into the economy through the hands of the servicemen.

parliamentary elections held in December 1969 provided a strong endorsement of Sato's action (see footnote 12).

Some Japanese were highly critical of Japan's relationship to the United States, but even these critics admitted that close ties with such a powerful ally often served the nation well in dealing with Communist neighbors. Consequently, the only attempts made by Russia to help Communism in Japan or to move the Japanese closer to the Soviet's point of view, both before and after Stalin's death, were peaceful. Japanese soldiers, taken prisoner by the Russians during the war, were repatriated with relative ease. Trade was expanded between the Soviet Union and Japan until, in 1963, Japan signed a pact providing for the exchange of $700,000,000 in goods over a three-year period. When the Soviets attempted to instruct the Japanese concerning international relations, as they did in 1961, when Deputy Premier Anastas I. Mikoyan visited the country and advised the Japanese not to renew the security treaty with the United States, they were rebuked politely but coolly by the Government of Japan.

Japan's relationship with Communist China was a cordial but cautious one. The Japanese Government did not care for Maoism, but it refused to let ideology interfere with business. Consequently, trade grew steadily between the two countries until 1958. At that point, trade stopped for four years because the Japanese refused to grant diplomatic status to the Red Chinese trade mission in Tokyo. In November 1962, however, a new trade agreement was signed between the two oriental powers.

Such friendly relations with Peking posed a potential problem for the Japanese. Considering the pronounced anti-Communist-Chinese stance of the United States, there was the possibility that Tokyo might offend Washington. The Japanese avoided this pitfall by maintaining official silence concerning Communist China at the same time that trade continued to move between China and Japan. The Japanese had judged correctly that the attitude in Washington was much more antagonistic toward official recognition than unofficial trade, whatever its volume.

A major problem area for the Japanese in immediate postwar Asia was the task of regaining the confidence of the Southeast Asian nations they had damaged during the war. These nations feared the rapid recovery and rearmament of Japan in the same way that many Europeans reacted to the possibility of a rearmed and resurgent Germany. Japan eased such fears by paying over a billion dollars in reparation in the form of goods and services to Southeast Asian states. By 1954, Japan was participating in international programs of assistance to underdeveloped countries, including many in Southeast Asia. Thus, Japanese financial help began to close the wounds opened by war.

E. Economics

Japan's economic recovery from the war was remarkable. Yet, the Japanese could not forget their basic problem: there were too many people living on too little land. Moreover, population increased at a rate of approximately one million people per year. Hence, rapidly increasing prosperity was imperative to raise the average living standard and even a momentary recession might spark an economic crisis of gigantic proportions. The political result of this kind of population pressure was that even conservatives sponsored a certain degree of welfare-statism.

Japan developed a large number of modern and fully automated factories in the postwar period, comparable to similar establishments in the United States and Europe. The output of the nation's industries accounted for more than one-half of the national income, and Japan was able to move into the first rank of the world's industrial nations in the manufacture of textiles, precision instruments, toys, and a variety of other products. The quality of these products, despite popular jokes to the contrary, was high enough to compete successfully with American and European products in the world market.

For a small nation with so many people, extensive foreign trade was an absolute necessity. The government was forced to tax United States and European products out of competition, and allow reasonable entry only to needed essentials such as petroleum, coal, and iron. Trade, to bring in needed items and assure the selling of Japanese-produced items abroad, was assured by a series of bilaterial agreements. Such agreements regulated the kind of exchange which would take place with each country (machinery to Burma in return for rice, for instance). The Japanese also offered extremely favorable terms to various states so that the products of these countries (Arabian oil, for example) could be transferred from one location to another in the bottoms of the expanding Japanese merchant fleet.

All these economic measures, necessary to the survival of Japan, were not accomplished easily. Not all states would sign bilateral agreements on a permanent basis. Moreover, the expansion of the Japanese merchant fleet brought serious and potentially limiting complaints from various international competititors in Britain and the United States. Japan's arguments for obtaining more trade usually quieted such criticisms, however. First, the Japanese pointed out that they always bought more than they sold in the international market. Secondly, they indicated that Japan had to export or face extinction. Further, they warned that if the West could not provide what the Japanese needed, they would be forced to trade with the East. Since Washington and London were aware that a prosperous, democratic Japan was symbolically and practically important in the struggle to hold back Asian Communism, such arguments from the Japanese usually were effective.

A. The Federation of Malaysia

The British administration of Malaya traditionally had been a benevolent despotism directed by the British Parliament. Under the watchful guidance of Great Britain the Malayans enjoyed a degree of prosperity, modernization, and extension of public welfare services. Moreover, British direction seemed to have been appreciated by the three major ethnic communities that had taken up residence in an area about the size of Florida. The Chinese, Indian, and Malay inhabitants generally were satisfied because the alternative to the British might well have been chaos, as Malaya was organized into eleven separate governments. It seemed on the surface, in 1939, that Malaya was moving steadily along a path that would permit little change in the years to come and, in truth, slight alteration was desired.

The war changed this apparently tranquil scene in Malaya. For six months after the Japanese had surrendered, the British directed government affairs with a military administration. Then the British established a protectorate, which was to be called the Malayan Union. But the establishment of the Union stirred up a storm of protest, and the British quickly transformed the Malayan Union into a new Federation of Malaya (begun February 1, 1948), which commenced to operate with British "advice." The British then turned their attention to economic affairs and London-based firms eagerly reestablished the profitable rubber and tin trade, which had been so important to the Commonwealth before the war.

Life in Malaya did not return to its relatively tranquil prewar pattern, however. After 1948, Malayan Communists, who had been busy promoting strikes and riots in Singapore, turned their attention to the whole peninsula. As was the case with most Southeast-Asian Communists, the Malayan variety mixed traditional Marxist-Leninist anticapitalism with a strong nationalism. This meant native hatred of foreigners and a fervent desire for their expulsion. Their fanaticism spurred the Communists to acts of sabotage, ambushes, destruction of rubber trees, and wrecking of trains. A hard core of some 6000 Red guerrillas retreated into the jungle and raided from there with such intensity that Malaya came to spend one-fourth of her national income yearly for pacification programs.

There also was a rising demand for national independence in Malaya, originating with a Western-educated elite. The British, faced with a choice between communism and nationalism, decided to aid national aspirations, hoping that nationalism would provide the best deterrent to the Communist threat. Under pressure from the Red menace, Malayans put aside old differences existing between various ethnic communities and political districts and installed a cabinet system. In 1955, the first national elections were held and the

Malayan-Chinese-Indian Alliance Party (MCI) won fifty-one of fifty-two contested seats, while gathering 84 per cent of the vote. The British now conceded that Great Britain had no future in Malaya and began to work out a plan for transition to self-rule.

In August 1957, the British signed an agreement ending their jurisdiction in Malaya. Singapore was launched as a separate state and given the right to choose its own style of government in 1959. The first election held in Singapore on May 30, 1959, resulted in a sweeping victory for the People's Action Party. The new government was to control its internal affairs, but was bound by treaty to confer with the British on foreign affairs.[14]

By 1960, Malaya had become peaceful. Its economic development proceeded well and, despite an official policy of nonalignment, its sympathies were with Great Britain and the United States in the Cold War. In Singapore, although the government functioned smoothly enough, the tiny state suffered economic difficulties since it was not easy to keep commerce and industry at a sufficiently high level to compensate for the annual increase in population. In 1961, the governments of Singapore and Malaya worked out a plan to solve the problems of the city-state. A new Federation of Malaysia was proposed, joining Malaya and Singapore to the crown colonies of North Borneo, Sabah, and Sarawak. This consolidation of territories was to establish a single state extending over 1600 miles from Thailand to the Philippines.

On September 16, 1963, the Federation of Malaysia was born. European ties to Asian territory virtually came to an end with the creation of this new territory. The major remaining exceptions were Portuguese Macao, off the southern coast of China, and the British-controlled port of Hong Kong. The MCI controlled the Malaysian Government until 1969 with a substantial majority. In 1969, however, elections cut the majority of the multiracial party sharply. An unfortunate racial polarization between Malay and Chinese was evident in the election, and riots which followed further demonstrated that a Malay-Chinese schism might fragment what had seemed to be one of the world's most promising multiracial states. Meanwhile, in 1965, Singapore had been ousted from the Federation and became an independent republic within the British Commonwealth. The ouster was based on the Malay's fear that the Chinese of Singapore would come to dominate the Federation. Malaysia continued, after 1965, as a constitutional monarchy within the British Commonwealth of Nations.

[14] This limitation on Singapore's freedom of action derived from the British concern about the strategic location of Singapore and the importance of Britain's naval base there.

B.   Burma

The dependency of Burma prospered under British control in the prewar era, although there were some Burmese who believed that they had received less than their fair share of the prosperity. During World War II, this discontent gave rise to the formation of "Peasant Unions." In 1942, the Japanese moved into Burma, occupying Rangoon and the fertile rice-producing Irrawaddy valley. The Japanese then established a puppet government called the Independent Republic of Burma.

Next to the Philippine Islands, Burma was more extensively damaged by the war than any other country in Southeast Asia. When the British first retreated, they implemented a scorched-earth policy. To add to the destruction this caused, Burma was the base from which Japan's abortive attack against India was launched. Consequently, its cities and transport systems were constant targets for Allied air attack. In addition, there was nearly constant fighting between the Burmese resistance groups and the Japanese.

Thus, when Chinese-United States forces swept across northern Burma and British-Indian armies drove into Lower Burma, they began liberating a country that bore extensive physical and psychological scars. At the end of April 1945, the Japanese left Rangoon and retreated to the hills, where "mopping-up" campaigns continued for months. The puppet government was dissolved and the British again took control. Quickly, it became apparent that the British had returned with new ideas about how Burma should be governed. These were summed up in a British White Paper of May 1945.

The White Paper indicated the British intention to reestablish normal governmental operations, hold elections, and commence drafting a constitution which would, eventually, help Burma begin self-government within the Commonwealth.[15] The establishment of order and security for the Burmese was not to be so easy. One of the wartime resistance leaders, U Aung San, insisted on a voice in Burma's future and immediate independence for his country. In July 1947, Aung San was assassinated and political responsibility passed into the hands of U Nu, who provided the leadership necessary for the drafting of a constitution in 1947. The document proclaimed the Union of Burma. U Nu then journeyed to London where he signed with Prime Minister Attlee, who by now was convinced that the dissension-torn Burmese state could not remain tied to Britain, a treaty granting Burma independence in January, 1948.

When British economic power and the British army were removed from Burma, stability went with them. Extreme factionalism became typical of all sectors of society. Even the Burmese Communists

---

[15] Britain reestablished the prewar financial arrangement in Burma and thus continued the mutually profitable business that British firms had enjoyed there in the past.

divided themselves into Stalinist and Trotskyite factions and carried on an intra-party civil war. Various factions took up arms against the government and travel in the countryside became unsafe.

In this time of trial for his government, Premier U Nu decided to use force to "pacify" the countryside. He was helped by the fact that the enemies of the government were as bitterly turned against each other as they were against the authority of Rangoon. U Nu also proclaimed programs promising a redistribution of the land and, despite the fact that his promises were mostly empty talk, they quieted people who now hopefully waited for reform. By 1951, U Nu felt that Burmese conditions had improved sufficiently to risk a general election. After emerging from the election a winner, U Nu continued the campaign to make the country a safer place in which to live. This was difficult, especially after 1954, when the bottom fell out of the rice market. It was during such calamities that the Communists used economic disruption to increase their following.

Burma, from the time her independence was gained, maintained an international position of "neutralism." She was the first nation outside the Soviet orbit to extend recognition to Communist China. At the same time, Burmese relations with the United States and Britain normally were cordial. Although Peking referred to U Nu as an "imperialist tool," the Burmese Prime Minister usually stayed apart from the Free World–Communist Bloc conflict and emphasized "coexistence," maintaining that the real war in Asia should be fought against poverty instead of ideology.

U Nu continued as Prime Minister until 1958. Despite his long term in office, he was unable to solve the problem of bloody clashes between rival factions, which had made Burma one of the unsafest places to live in all Asia. Consequently, U Nu frequently was criticized because he did not deal harshly enough with guerrillas and bandits. Finally, in 1958, U Nu turned the government over to a military junta, hoping that a militaristic rule might bring order. The military junta then concentrated vigorously on pacifying the countryside. When that task had been finished the leaders of the junta retreated to the background.

U Nu was returned to the office of prime minister by an election in 1960. But, without the martial control of the junta, the republic was troubled by renewed disorder. In 1962, a military strong man, General Ne Win, seized power and jailed U Nu. The constitution was abolished and parliament disbanded. Ne Win announced the establishment of a single party, the "Burmese Socialist Program Party," and began nationalizing major industries. But banditry and terror were just as typical of Burma in the 1960's and into the 1970's as they had been in the previous decade, and the foreign policy of the Ne Win Government was essentially the same as it had been under U Nu. The latter, released from prison, founded a revolutionary movement in Thailand toward the close of 1969.

C. Indonesia

During World War II, Indonesia was subjected to Japanese occupation. While still under Japanese rule, the Netherlands East Indies declared their independence of Holland and officially took the name Indonesia, in August 1945. This declaration was meaningless, however, without the consent of the Hague. In March 1946, an agreement was concluded between the Hague and certain Javanese leaders whereby Indonesia and the outer islands were joined to form the United States of Indonesia—a part of the Netherlands Union. This arrangement broke down almost immediately. Finally, the Netherlands, troubled by rebellion and a near civil war between native Nationalists and Communists, transferred sovereignty over all the old "Netherlands East Indies," except West Irian. (West New Guinea), to the Republic of Indonesia in December 1949. In June 1950, the new state was admitted to the United Nations. (The Netherlands gave West Irian to the UN in 1962, and the UN turned it over to Indonesia in 1963).

A constitution was proclaimed in 1950, providing for a president, a cabinet, and a legislature. President Achmed Sukarno, who first organized the *Partai Nasional Indonesia* (PNI) in 1927, maintained a delicate political balance while party organizations multiplied. The multiplicity of political parties, as well as religious and ethnic differences, resulted in an instability from which the Communists in particular profited.

Indonesia's political problems were compounded by a sustained economic crisis. President Sukarno maintained, as he would for the nearly two decades of his presidency, that "the life of a nation depends on its national consciousness—not on industry or airplanes or asphalt roads." This view plunged the nation into an economic disaster with few parallels in modern times. Retail prices rose 650 per cent between 1945 and 1965. The national debt soared and the country's whole economic infrastructure—its roads, factories, canals, and ports—moved toward a state of collapse. More than four-fifths of Indonesia's 113,000,000 people sank back into a barter economy.

With all these problems at home Sukarno characterized his foreign policy as basically anticolonialist and generally tolerant towards communism. He showed scant interest in foreign capitalistic enterprises. Consequently, his deprived state received little of the help from outside that it needed to vitalize industries.

Because of the internal disorder, Sukarno in 1957 denounced "chatterbox democracy" and announced a new concept of government called "guided democracy." Guided democracy meant the proclamation of martial law and the placing of government under a national advisory council made up of Moslems, Nationalists, and Communists. The new machinery of government did not end the chaotic conditions in Indonesia, however, and the Communist Party continued to grow, numbering perhaps 2,000,000 members by

1962.[16] In view of this strong internal position of communism, Sukarno was circumspect in his attitude towards Red China.

In 1965, Sukarno decided further to consolidate his power with the help of the Communist Party. In late September, the Communists tried to take control of the state, backed by the President himself. The army moved rapidly to prevent the power seizure and the Communists' attempted coup was smashed. The army's leader, Major General Suharto, became the acting head of state, and the battered Communists went underground. Sukarno was kept on as a closely watched figurehead president for a time and then, in the spring of 1968, Suharto, having been Acting President for a year, became President.

Immense problems now confronted Suharto. It seemed likely that the Communist movement, weakened though it might be, could not be kept underground forever unless there were basic improvements in the Indonesian style of life. To make matters worse for the Indonesian Government, the United States and other Western nations adopted a "wait and see" attitude concerning Indonesia before giving extensive foreign aid. In 1970, the Indonesian Government still was struggling painfully to provide a better life for its people, but the problems were so difficult that they obviously would not permit an early solution.

D. The Indo-Chinese Peninsula

At the end of World War II, the French slowly moved back into their protectorates in Indo-China. This was not particularly difficult in the case of Laos and Cambodia, but in Vietnam the desire for independence was pronounced. Those willing to carry on the revolutionary fight against France gathered around Nguyen Ai Quoc, later famous as Ho Chi Minh. Soon Ho had set up a government in North Vietnam within which he could carry out his anti-French, nationalistic, and Marxist-oriented ideas. In March 1946, Ho obtained an agreement from the French in which they recognized Vietnam as a free (although not independent) state within the French Union. Shortly after, war broke out between the Vietnamese and the French. As charge and countercharge were exchanged between the French and Ho, Paris decided to continue the war to keep Vietnam out of the grasp of the Communists. Thus, an eight-year-long struggle, and one that was to be disastrous for France, was joined.

From 1950 to 1954, the character of the civil war in Indo-China altered markedly, as Ho formulated new military tactics. His scheme of battle was a three-step process: (1) win over the people; (2) cut off the enemy supply lines and isolate strong points; and

[16] This membership figure made it the largest Communist party outside China and the Soviet Union.

(3) then attack the strong points. Soon the North Vietnamese Communists (the Viet Minh) began emptying the ranks of French officers faster than the military establishment of France could supply them.

The dire situation in North Vietnam soon allowed the other Indo-Chinese states to wring concessions from France. Cambodia took advantage of France's embarrassment in Vietnam, in 1953, to gain full sovereignty in military, judicial, and economic matters—a situation only slightly short of full independence. In 1953, France also signed a treaty with Laos declaring it to be fully independent within the French Union.

After a particularly disastrous loss at Dien Bien Phu, the French were willing to quit their Pacific empire, and, by a series of accords signed at Geneva, in 1954, hostilities were terminated. Vietnam was partitioned as had been Korea, and the question of unity was left up to elections scheduled for 1956. The Geneva Agreement marked the end of imperial rule in Vietnam. During 1954–1955, two Vietnams (Communist Democratic Republic of Vietnam in the North and Nationalist Republic of Vietnam in the South), Cambodia, and Laos became independent governments bearing the responsibility for growth and development within their own territories.

Of the four political entities emerging from the former French empire, Cambodia seemed the most prosperous. Ruled by Prince Norodom Sihanouk, Cambodia maintained a neutralist stand. Her "neutralism" allowed Cambodia to draw foreign aid from all available sources willing to help in the building up of the country's economy. When the United States took France's place in attempting to stem the tide of Indo-Chinese communism, Sihanouk decided Washington could not win the struggle. He, therefore, began to shift toward Red China, the power he saw as the eventual victor in the Southeast Asian conflict. He erected an anti-United States monument built from captured American equipment and accepted greater amounts of aid from his Communist neighbors.

During the period of Red Guard enthusiasm in China which threatened to spread to neighboring areas, Sihanouk decided to change policy directions. Faced with a mounting Communist insurgency, he, who once had scorned heavy-handed American methods in Vietnam, himself became more ruthless with indigenous Reds. But in 1970, when he once again flirted with the Reds, he was deposed in a coup and exiled while away on a foreign visit. North Vietnamese Reds then infiltrated the country, thus posing another dilemma for Washington in the matter of possible intervention for the sake of "containment." In April 1970, President Nixon decided on limited American intervention alongside South Vietnamese forces. The joint operations into Cambodia from South Vietnam were continued for some weeks until the United States withdrew according to a predetermined time table and the South Vietnamese remained to continue with the Cambodians the fight against Red invaders.

Laos was the smallest in population of the countries made independent by the Geneva agreements in 1954, and perhaps the most primitive. It possessed a limited elite made up of the king and his household, great landlords, and the Buddhist priesthood. In Laos the government was engaged in a constant struggle to prevent the local Communists, the Pathet Lao, from taking over the state. The Laotian situation developed strong international complications as a continuing conflict in the tiny state kept the great powers alerted. The Laotian anti-Communists were consistently backed by the United States, and the Laotian Communists by the North Vietnamese, the Russians, and the Chinese. Neither side appeared to place much confidence in Premier Prince Souvanna Phouma, but he was accepted as a compromise candidate in the hope of peace.

As already indicated in Chapters 21 and 22, there existed a chronic civil war in Vietnam from the time of the signing of the Geneva accords. Ho Chi Minh in Hanoi emerged from the Geneva talks with the feeling that it was his destiny someday to control all Vietnam. In consequence, he announced a Fatherland Front for all the people and asked the Republic of South Vietnam to participate in the 1956 all-Vietnamese elections (according to rules established by Ho). These elections would then determine the future shape of the government controlling all Vietnam. However, the South Vietnamese regime at Saigon refused to take part in any election governed by rules set down in the north. Ngo Dinh Diem rose to power in the south and both he and Ho continued to indicate that they were the rightful rulers of all Vietnam.

A constitution of 1956 gave Diem unusually strong powers in the south. Further, it guaranteed the rights of citizenship only in the absence of a crisis. Diem was assisted by the United States and, with this material aid, set out to win the loyalty of the common people from "Uncle Ho." This was no easy task, for the civil war had greatly intensified after 1956. Over the years the United States became more deeply enmeshed until, by 1963, thousands of American "advisors" were involved in trying to help the South Vietnamese Government, which seemed likely to lose the war to its native Communist insurgents, the National Liberation Front (NLF).

In November 1963, President Diem was killed during a coup d'état and one military junta after another succeeded him. The junta promised to continue the war against the NLF with renewed vigor. But, as the struggle continued, the United States and North Vietnam were both increasingly involved and the end of fighting was not in sight. Eventually, the military junta was replaced by a regime led by President Nguyen Van Thieu. Regardless, however, of changes in control the South Vietnamese were not able alone to hold back the combination of North Vietnamese and native Red insurgents.

During 1968, the war stalemated, due to the presence of a sizable United States expeditionary force. On November 1, 1968, President Lyndon B. Johnson ordered a bombing halt to speed up the Paris peace talks on the Vietnam War, which had begun the previous spring. However, a war of attrition continued in Vietnam during 1969 and into 1970, while the Paris peace talks fruitlessly went on and on. The only major change was to be found in the United States' policy of Vietnamization, which aimed at eventual withdrawal of American troops.

E.   The Republic of the Philippines

President Sergio Osmeña had been chief executive in exile after the Japanese had conquered the Philippines. When the United States forces came ashore, Osmeña came with them. By February 1945, he had returned his government to Manila. Real authority, however, still rested in the hands of the United States. Gradually, the United States worked toward Philppine rehabilitation, reconstruction, and independence. The United States Congress helped reconstruction by passing measures such as the 1946 Philippine Rehabilitation Act (or Tydings Act), which made available $620,000,000.

Elections were held in the Philippines in April 1946, and the Liberal Party candidate, Manuel Roxas, supported by the United States and the more prosperous segments of Philippine society, won the presidency. On July 4, 1946, the United States flag was lowered and the banner of the Republic of the Philippines was raised. Despite extensive aid from Washington, the Philippine islands suffered some of the same problems known elsewhere in Asia after the end of the war. An unfavorable balance of trade developed with the United States, and dollars were siphoned off to America. Production lagged and the amount of available tax resources lowered dangerously.

By 1948, the greatest problem faced by President Roxas was agrarian unrest, as the former anti-Japanese peasant movement had fallen into Communist hands. The Communist-led *Hukbalahap* or People's Liberation Army, commonly known as the Huks, opposed the Roxas administration, branding it a puppet of United States imperialists. When the Huks were placed outside the law by the government, they began brutal forays (kidnappings and attacks on busses, trucks, and trains) against the established order. Roxas countered by initiating a program of land reform to offset the ideological appeal of the Communists. Yet, the economy continued to deteriorate and, by the beginning of the Korean War, in 1950, the Government was at the edge of bankruptcy.

In 1950, when both the Philippine and United States governments had become aware of the economic crisis building in the Philippine islands, it was decided that the two would cooperate in an improvement program.[17] The cooperative project soon helped the Philip-

---

[17] The United States pledged $250,000,000 in loans over a ten-year period.

pine economic situation. At about the same time, national leadership was invigorated by the addition of the dynamic Ramón Magsaysay to the cabinet as Secretary of Defense. Magsaysay initiated a successful campaign against the Huks which brought him national popularity. The renown thus gained helped Magsaysay become President of the Philippines in 1953. Under him, the Philippines clung to a United States-style democracy and announced a firm anti-Communist position. Further, Magsaysay bettered the lot of the common man by beginning community development and welfare programs. His work remained unfinished, however, for he was killed in 1957, when his plane crashed into a mountainside on the island of Cebu.

The next president of the Philippines was Carlos P. Garcia, a representative of the Nacionalista Party. Garcia hoped to raise Philippine living standards above the subsistence level by employing a scheme to increase agricultural production and industrialization. However, this plan was restricted by the national economic policy, which was one of "Filipino First," a slogan indicating a preference for economic nationalism. This policy discouraged private capital from the United States and restricted a proper flow of raw materials from abroad. Consequently, hundreds of new factories were built in Manila, but these packaged goods rather than manufacturing them. Thus, trade dwindled and so did the government's reserves.

In 1961, Liberal Party candidate Diosdado Macapagal became president. Macapagal was a sincere advocate of Western-style democracy, and he deemphasized the "Filipino First" idea in hope of attracting foreign private investment. Moreover, he sought to assure honesty in government and encouraged agrarian reform.

In foreign affairs, the Philippines stood for "open cooperation with the United States" into the 1960's. Philippine-American ties became particularly strong after the Communist victory in China. In 1954, the Philippines became one of the founders of the Southeast Asia Treaty Organization (SEATO).

In 1965, Nationalist Ferdinand E. Marcos swept into the presidency with a call to "make the country great again" and an idealistic platform promising social revolution. During his first two years in office, Marcos built 8400 schools and, in three years, 1500 miles of road. With the help of the Ford and Rockefeller foundations, a new rice strain was produced that grew quickly enough to allow two crops a year. This variety of rice had just begun to increase substantially the Philippine harvest as Marcos came into office. Consequently, under his leadership, the Philippines became an exporter of rice rather than an importer.

Still, as in most Asian states at the beginning of the 1970's, there had been no fundamental social revolution in the Philippines. An oligarchy of aristocratic families, that had ruled the country for generations, still controlled business and continued to block land reforms. Moreover, Marcos' regime was no different from that of his predecessors in that political corruption seemed to be endemic. All this led to a revival of the Huks, whom Magsaysay seemed to have destroyed in the 1950's.

In foreign affairs the Marcos regime moved awkwardly at times. He involved his government in a fruitless dispute with Malaysia over the Malaysian state of Sabah, located on the island of Borneo. At another time, Marcos claimed that the Philippines was the American "strong right arm in Asia," and backed the title with deeds when he sent 2000 Philippine soldiers to aid the United States forces in South Vietnam. Marcos' maintenance of the traditional American-Philippine relationship was unpopular with some, for the Asian nationalistic and anti-American sentiment sweeping over Southeast Asia in the 1960's had made an impact on the Philippines as well. Nonetheless, he was reelected in November 1969. Before the end of the year, he reestablished diplomatic relations with Malaysia and recalled the Filipino troops from Vietnam. In 1970, he concentrated on attempts at economic improvement.

F. Thailand

Thailand (Siam) took sides with the loser in World War II and had to "do penance" after the war was over. In alliance with the Japanese, the Thais annexed Burmese and Malayan territory in the early days of the war. At its end, several short-lived governments came and went including that of guerilla leader Pridi Phanomyong, who was one of the main negotiators of peace. The Thai negotiating team denounced the country's Japanese affiliation during the war and volunteered to return territory taken from Burma and Malaya. Recognizing the altered nature of the Thai regime, the United States urged a generous peace; consequently, the peace agreements treated Thailand less harshly than other losers. Shortly after the war, in 1947, Thailand (or Siam as it was known briefly) became a member of the United Nations.

The postwar political scene in Thailand was dominated by a struggle for power among intriguing elites. In theory, the country was a democracy with a cabinet government that was responsible to a unicameral legislature. In fact, power was in the possession of a few thousand people who controlled the bureaucracy, the army, and the police. The cabinets succeeded one another, not as a reflection of the will of the people, but mainly as a result of intrigues. In 1948, Plaek Phibunsongkhram, a former collaborator with the Japanese, came to control the state and changed the name of the country back to Thailand. While he led the government (1948–1957), there were frequent attempts on his life, and the atmosphere of suspicion and intrigue continued.

Despite sometimes comic and sometimes tragic happenings at the cabinet level, the Kingdom of Thailand displayed socio-economic stability. Food generally was abundant and land was available for those who desired to own it. Unlike the situation in other Asian states, the ordinary Thai farmer was customarily unexcited by calls for land reform. He seemed willing to put up with a political elite as long as the country prospered.

At the outbreak of the Korean War, Thailand sent a small contingent of troops to fight for the United Nations. Moreover, Thailand adopted an anti-Communist stance which gained her the gratitude of the United States and considerable assistance from Washington. Thailand, also an original SEATO member, had regional commitments equally as important as those assumed in the broader pact, but the Thais seemed most disposed to concentrate on internal matters.

The Thais' contentment with their lot reinforced authoritarian government. Plaek Phibunsongkhram was prime minister for ten years and then, in 1957, Field Marshal Sarit Thanarat took control of the government in a bloodless coup. This change at the top brought little alteration in the life of the average Thai, however. Generally, the people were unaware until sometime after the coup that anything had happened. Until his death in 1963, Sarit exercised supreme power, having abolished all political parties except his own. He pursued a policy of friendliness toward representatives of the United States—particularly military men. A cautious attitude was maintained toward geographically neighboring China. Sarit, however, made it clear that he would not tolerate Communists in Thailand and this policy was pursued after his death by Prime Minister Thanom Kittikachorn. During the Vietnam War, the Thais moved further in the direction of the United States by providing important air bases for American attacks on Communist forces.

SOUTH ASIA

A.   The Partition of India and Pakistan

As soon as the British Labor Government entered office in 1945, it commenced a series of steps aimed at the independence of the Indian subcontinent. In the granting of independence, however, some decision had to be made concerning the respective satisfaction of territorial demands by the Moslems and the Hindus. The Moslems professed an often fanatic belief in the teachings of their religion and were tied together by a strong sense of community. Consequently, they desired a religious state, which would pursue an active course designed to convert nonbelievers to Islam. On the other hand, the Hindus did not seek the same degree of uniformity or intensity of belief in the followers of their religion. Thus, the Hindus wanted a secular government. The coming of the British to India did not diminish these traditional differences between Moslems and Hindus, whose political leaders before World War I had formed the Moslem League and the Indian National Congress Party. The religious split made more difficult the structuring of an independent India.

When Indians gathered around British and United States installations, tore down flags, and otherwise violently demonstrated their anti-imperialist, anti-Western mood, the British in 1946 sent a mission to India to assist in the framing of a constitution. The mission attempted to reconcile the opposing points of view maintained by the Moslem League and the National Congress, but encountered great difficulty. Increasingly, as discussions proceeded, it seemed that the logical solution was partition. The British, however, were reluctant to divide India, fearing that the threat to peace might well be magnified if two, mutually suspicious, antagonistic nations took the place of a united India. As it turned out, however, no plan which would preserve the political unity of India was feasible because the country was torn by constant and bitter strife between Moslems and Hindus. Eventually, in June, 1947, Great Britain announced a partition scheme under which areas with a majority of Moslem population would be allowed to form a dominion separate from that of India.

By the provisions of the Indian Independence Act of 1947, India and Pakistan were to become dominions within the British Commonwealth, and the various princely states were free to join whichever dominion they might choose. The drawing of boundaries produced much bloodshed as religious majority made war on religious minority in each dominion. Seemingly endless lines of Moslem refugees began to flee westward as Hindus trekked eastward.[18]

With these chaotic conditions as a background, a Constitutional Assembly in New Delhi declared, in August 1947, that India was a Dominion within the British Commonwealth and, in Karachi, the Pakistanis followed suit. Both new governments proclaimed their independence days as the harbingers of new eras.

B.   The Union of India

Even after a steady stream of Moslems had poured out of the new Union of India, about 11 per cent of the population was still composed of the followers of Allah. Another related problem troubling the new government was the crowding of Hindu refugees, who had fled from the newly created Pakistan, into special camps where they suffered great hardships. There was little hope for these refugees in the immediate future, since the Indian economy was unable to absorb them. The situation was further complicated by the death

[18] It has been estimated that as many as 10,000,000 people fled their homes in the upheaval of populations caused by partition and that more than 600,000 died.

of the Hindus' most prominent leader and their champion for decades, Mohandas K. Gandhi, who was killed at a prayer meeting by a Hindu extremist in January 1948.

Without Gandhi's leadership, the construction of a new Indian state was made more difficult. India, at the time of independence, had some 340,000,000 people within her boundaries. These millions lived in 600 states, which quickly were consolidated into 30 states and territories. This number varied from time to time, but autocratic rule in the former Indian Native States did come to an end.

In this process of streamlining the administrative machinery of the new Union, the problem of Kashmir was particularly troublesome. Beautiful Kashmir in the Western Himalayas was of great significance to the Pakistanis, who believed its possession was necessary to strengthen their national economy. India desired the territory because of its wealth and prestige value. Further, the religious problem, which troubled the whole subcontinent, was particularly intense in Kashmir where seventy per cent of the population was Moslem. Deep-seated resentment had grown among the Moslems, who suffered repression and discriminatory practices at the hands of an autocratic Hindu elite. Antagonisms were further heightened when thousands of religious refugees from Pakistan came into Kashmir. In 1947, Moslem tribesmen from the northern areas of the state burned and looted their way toward Srinagar, the capital. These fierce tribesmen came to control most of northern Kashmir and set up their own government in the area. The Maharajah of Kashmir thereupon appealed to India for help, which he received in return for the promise of accession of his state to India.

The Kashmir dispute eventually was placed before the United Nations. The UN proposed that the Pakistani-supported tribesmen be withdrawn from Kashmir into Pakistan and that Indian troops should be withdrawn. With the area thus neutralized, it was planned that a plebiscite could be arranged to settle the future of Kashmir. However, little progress was made in troop withdrawals, agreement on the nature of the plebiscite, or on the composition of a new government of Kashmir that was acceptable to both India and Pakistan. The Kashmir situation remained rancorous even after 1952, when the Kashmiri Government signed a treaty establishing a special relationship with the Union of India, short of full incorporation.

Despite turmoil, India adopted a constitution effective in January 1950. It made India a secular state and prohibited the discrimination against "untouchables" commonly practiced in public places. Moreover, the need for decent working conditions, equality of pay scales regardless of sex or caste, and a free education for children were stressed. The government's structure was basically federal except that, unlike the case in the United States, all powers not mentioned in the constitution resided with the national government and not the states. In other things, too, the new government directly reflected the Anglo-Saxon model in that India was a parliamentary democracy with an independent judiciary, a primarily figurehead president, an influential prime minister, a two-house legislature, and a group of states presided over by governors who were to be appointed by the president.

Now that India possessed a governmental structure she was faced with the problem of making it work. The most influential statesman in the new India was Prime Minister Pandit Jawaharlal Nehru, who concurrently was President of the Congress Party. Soon Nehru and his Congress Party were forced to meet the challenge of rising political parties on the left and right. The parties that developed on the right were based on various factions within the Indian religious community, such as the Hindu Mahasabha, or Hindu People's Association. A much more serious challenge to the Congress Party was mounted on the left by the Federation of All-India Scheduled Castes, agitating for more rapid improvement in the status of untouchables. There were also a Socialist Party and a proletarian party, the KMP (Peasants, Workers, and People's Party). These leftist parties basically were anti-Communist, sharing the general view in India that the Communists were the tools of a foreign state. Moreover, this was a time when no foreign country was welcomed in India, but each was regarded as a potential "interferer" in India's affairs. For a time, the Communists resorted to violence, hoping to cause the masses to become more radical. Failing to achieve their goal, the Indian Communists began, after 1952, to behave as did other political parties in India.

The Congress Party took few steps to improve the lot of the impoverished rural masses in the postwar period until the left parties seemed to be attracting support through their calls for agrarian reform. The Congress Party then restricted the rights of the landlords over the peasantry and secured the passage of laws in some Indian states, which allowed the peasants to purchase land at low prices fixed by the state government.

The Congress-controlled Government also promoted the industrialization of India. The new state possessed reasonably large amounts of raw materials, but few factories. The Government monopolized the manufacture of armaments and of any industry vital to the nation's defense in time of national emergency, but other enterprises were left to private initiative.

All these steps were just the beginning of an attack on India's basic problems. India suffered from linguistic chaos since language differences tended to heighten old provincial loyalties. Most of India's people lived in poor housing, both in the sun-baked villages and in the growing cancer of city slums. There were 500,000 villages which had no schooling facilities whatsoever. Before the new Government had a chance to catch up with the problems existing at any given moment, those problems were made worse by an expanding population. In 1951–1952, the Congress Party submitted its programs to an electorate, which was 85 per cent illiterate. The Congress slate captured 45 per cent of the votes and a variety of parties took the remaining votes. The Socialists and Communists made a relatively strong showing. This caused many to assert that the Congress Party had suffered because its reform program was too conservative, and, hence, too slow to aid the impoverished masses. Still, primarily because of the prestige of Jawaharlal Nehru, the Congress Party was able to maintain control and put its programs into effect.

Nehru's first two tasks, as he saw them, were to assure India's territorial sovereignty and ensure the perpetuation of democratic government. To obtain these goals he secured the abandonment by the French of their two tiny outposts in India, in 1954, and forced the retirement of the Portuguese from Goa in 1961. He saw to it that sixteen Indian states were established along linguistic lines and made these the basic functioning units of government in the subcontinent. Nehru encouraged voting by all and, in the 1962 election, nearly two-thirds of the eligible voters went to the polls. In the, election, the Congress Party polled enough votes to give it more than two-thirds of the seats in the lower house.

The Congress Party's increased popularity seems to have derived from Nehru's active interest in fighting poverty and his government's efforts to secure economic improvement. In 1951, India launched its First Five-Year Plan for economic development, which placed much emphasis upon agriculture, dams, and flood control. It was only natural that the Government should place a high priority on agriculture, for starvation in India was endemic. Age-old ways of farming were set aside and new ones initiated under government supervision. Transportation systems were modernized and irrigation projects were begun all over the Union. The result of all this was an increase of 18 per cent in national income. Since the population was growing even more rapidly, however, this increase produced an expansion of only about 9 per cent in per capita income, which had been $300 a year.

Of greatest importance for the future was the fact that the First Five-Year Plan laid a base upon which greater industrial growth could be built. India's objective was a mixed industrial economy, and toward that end the Government worked by placing steel, machine industries, chemicals, petroleum, aircraft, locomotives, and shipbuilding in the public sector, and placing textiles, cement, and automobiles, only to mention a few, in the private sector. The Second Five-Year Plan (1956–1961) more heavily emphasized industrialization than the first plan, and thus many improvements were made. These gains were realized, however, only by borrowing from abroad and subjecting the people to an austerity program.

The Third Five-Year Plan began in 1961. In the next period, although it might have seemed on the surface that great advances had been made, very little net gain transpired in the attempt to raise general living standards, because of a further massive population increase. Thus, as the 1960's ended, most of India was still illiterate (more than 70 per cent), the population burgeoned, and India remained socially backward. The advances that had been made were sufficient to make life better for many, but any "great leap forward" was no more possible in India than it had been in China. In both countries, because of the number of people involved, Government-sponsored crash programs to improve the lot of the common man generally were ineffectual.

After 1962, it became clear that India was developing a party structure which was neither one-party nor, as was the case in many Western states, a number of parties directly competing with one another. Rather, the political scene was dominated by a party of consensus although there still were several minor parties. The Congress kept itself in power by keeping factionalism within its ranks to a minimum while at the same time "stealing the thunder" of other parties by copying the best features of their proposed programs.

This inner-party solidity was severely tested in 1964 when Nehru died after seventeen years in the prime minister's office. There was a momentary furor over the choice of a successor, which raised hopes in the opposition that the Congress might fragment without its great leader. This, however, did not happen. Moderate Lal Bahadur Shastri, "a Nehru-trained crown prince," was chosen shortly afterwards. When Shastri died in January 1966, the cohesiveness of the Congress was tested once more. But the storm was weathered when it was agreed that the new prime minister should be the daughter of Jawaharlal Nehru, Mrs. Indira Gandhi. Mrs. Gandhi was a respected political leader in her own right. Under her leadership, India displayed a continued willingness to abide by the results of elections.

In foreign affairs, India continued to place great value on its membership in the Commonwealth of Nations. Much economic benefit in the form of trade came from close association with her former British master. India also came to be known as the leading neutralist power in the world, playing the role of peacemaker in dispute after dispute. In maintaining this neutralist stance, India achieved a prominent position in world affairs which she would not have occupied had she been close to either the Communist or anti-Communist bloc. Nehru personified the neutralist spirit, which argued passionately that no nation was inherently or permanently bad or good. Therefore, he held that each nation should be judged on an assessment of its actions in a particular circumstance. Just as passionately, he argued for disarmament.

The motivating impulse behind Nehru's foreign policy was anti-imperialism. This tendency was apparent in Nehru's disapproval when the United States gave aid or support to a state involved in what he considered imperialist activity. When, however, the United States refused to cooperate with the British and French in the Suez crisis of 1956, Nehru applauded the position taken by Washington.

When peaceful coexistence between the United States and the Soviet Union appeared to develop, the Indian Prime Minister obviously was heartened.

Generally, as the United States began to understand the Indian policy of nonalignment, better relations between the two countries came about. Washington increasingly was inclined to accept India as the most important country in South Asia. Because of India's size, Washington desired to help it maintain its parliamentary democracy as a positive example that other Asian states might copy. Consequently, in 1962, when the Chinese infringed upon certain border areas of India, there was a prompt response from the United States to Nehru's appeal for material assistance. Moreover, the Indian attempt to continue good relations with the United States was matched by bridge building between Moscow and New Delhi.

Apart from her difficulties with Pakistan, India's greatest problem in foreign affairs was her breach with Red China. Beginning in 1954, India and China reached agreement on their relations in Tibet, although the matter of the exact boundary between India and her Communist neighbor was not defined. The Indians believed the border to have been firmly settled by the British-Chinese negotiations of 1914. This was the situation in 1959 when some Tibetans, after revolting against harsh features of the Chinese military administration in Tibet, fled with their spiritual leader, the Dalai Lama, to India. Peking immediately became hostile, protesting New Delhi's granting of hospitality to political refugees. Border incidents became numerous soon after.

In the northwestern area of India, where Kashmir and Tibet face one another, 20,000-feet-high peaks had made it difficult to fix a boundary. After 1958, boundary disputes recurred over this region as the Chinese began building a military supply road into the territory. Finally, in April 1960, India and China began diplomatic negotiations aimed at fixing a definite boundary line. At the same time, a thousand miles to the east, along the MacMahon Line (the generally recognized border between Tibet and India), similar troubles developed in the relatively unexplored and inaccessible hill country.

The Chinese built new roads across the MacMahon Line and set up outposts in Indian territory. In October 1962, the Chinese began military operations at both ends of the 1000 mile border with Tibet. The Chinese pushed some eighty miles into Indian territory with little opposition from the Indians. Then the Reds stopped, pulled back, and announced a cease-fire. Nehru appealed to the West for help, indicating, at the same time, that he would be willing to turn over the dispute to the Permanent Court of Justice.

The Chinese insisted that they merely desired to define their national boundaries. The occupying of this territory was, indicated Peking, merely the beginning of an understanding with India, similar to those Peking had with all other states on China's borders. Although China continued to regard the border dispute with India as of minor importance, India did not. New Delhi's attitude toward China from this point on, although it did not mean an abandonment of an overall neutralist stance in international affairs, was watchful. The Indians prepared for a permanent condition of tension with China and built up the frontier defenses against attack.

While relations with China were unsettled, the difficulties with Pakistan continued. Even after January 1957, when the Indian Government declared Kashmir fully integrated with India, the Pakistanis refused to accept the Kashmiri status quo. Although the protests of Pakistan were continuous, the Government of India paid little heed. The incorporation of Kashmir into India had become a point of honor and India could not relinquish her hold on the province without losing face. Until India could be certain that a plebiscite in Kashmir to decide the fate of the territory would be in her favor, New Delhi would ignore Pakistani demands that the Kashmiri be allowed to decide their own territorial allegiance. Consequently, the Kashmiri issued remained a deeply emotional one for both India and Pakistan.

In 1963, Pakistani hopes were raised when the Communist Chinese agreed upon a border with Pakistan that tacitly recognized the latter's claims to Kashmiri territory. Tension over Kashmir built up until, in August 1965, India attacked along the sixteen-year-old cease-fire line. Ostensibly, the attacks were in retaliation for incursions by Pakistani armed forces into Kashmir. The fighting then spread into the Lahore area, where the Indians feared that Pakistan might attempt an invasion of Punjab. Finally, the heads of the governments of the two states agreed to a cease-fire (Declaration of Tashkent) in early 1966. Yet, the hard feelings created by the Kashmiri situation continued into the 1970's. Red China helped keep the situation unstable, working to arouse the hostility of Moslems and Hindus against each other in the subcontinent.

C. Pakistan

At the time of partition, Pakistan did not exist as a nation. The name of this new state, which began as the seventh largest in the world, was derived from the Urdu words for "Land of the Pure." Newly created Pakistan was composed of two sections (East Pakistan and West Pakistan) separated by the breadth of India. It was governed initially under a makeshift structure which had some of the characteristics of democracy, but, from the first, the executive branch assumed authority.

From the outset, Pakistan was troubled by the question of religion in politics because many Moslems wanted a government based on the teachings of the Prophet. Yet, there were 11,000,000 non-Moslems in the state of Bengal alone. Here was sufficient voting strength to block any measure tending to deprive non-Moslems of participation in public affairs.

Pakistani leaders had not planned so carefully for independent status as had the leaders in India. The first explicit demand for a Pakistani state had come only seven years before its actual formation. Hence, most of the activity of the leaders had been aimed at creating Pakistan, not in devising a governmental and political structure that would serve the state, once it was established. Except for the Moslem League, political parties were not broadly based. Moreover, India inherited most of the British administrative machinery.

Soon the Moslem League, which seemed likely at the outset to be the dominating force in Pakistani politics, was in trouble at the polls. It was supported largely by a traditional landlord group rather than the rising middle class. In 1954, the League was defeated by a coalition of opposing factions in the provincial elections in East Pakistan and, in 1956, suffered another defeat in West Pakistan.

The decline of the Moslem League was attributable largely to internal factionalism, which brought Pakistan in the first eleven years of independent governmental operation, a rapid succession of cabinets, both in the states and in the central government. This instability led in 1958 to a suspension of parliamentary government.

President Iskander Mirza abrogated the constitution and appointed Mohammad Ayub Khan, to control the government. A few weeks later, Ayub Khan became President and dictator as political parties were abolished.

Under Ayub Khan's military dictatorship, order was restored, corruption in government was lessened, and there was marked progress in agriculture and industry. Gradually, a program of "Basic Democracy" was initiated, and the people were allowed to vote for government personnel at the local level. The local governing bodies, then, chose members for district councils, who, in turn, selected the membership of regional councils. So it went on up through the regional, provincial, and national levels until a National Council was produced. All councils chosen above the local level were to be constituted of members appointed by the administration. Moreover, it was these appointed members who tended to dominate the affairs of government. Thus, it was not surprising that these "representatives of the people" made Ayub Khan president for five years and asked him to promulgate a new constitution rather than having it drafted by a constitutional convention. A new constitution went into effect in 1962. It retained the important aspects of "basic democracy" and provided for an electoral college of 80,000, chosen by universal suffrage, to elect the president and various assemblies.

It had been Ayub Khan's intention to govern without political parties. As time passed, however, public objections to the government's restrictions on political activity became too extensive to ignore. In consequence, in 1962, political parties again were allowed to form, but only an offshoot of the old Moslem League, that backed

Ayub Khan, achieved any degree of importance. In 1964, when elections were held on the local level for Basic Democrats, the opposition parties managed to secure more than one-third of the electoral seats. Despite these opposition gains, Ayub Khan's followers maintained a firm hold on the presidency and, in 1965, he was reelected for a five-year term.

After his reelection, the most important problem encountered by Ayub Khan grew out of nationalistic resentment over his relatively moderate position on Kashmir. When the Tashkent agreement was signed ending the India-Pakistan conflict of 1965–1966, Zulfikar Ali Bhutto, pro-Chinese and former foreign minister, broke with Ayub Khan and formed his own Pakistani People's Party in 1967. Bhutto then began speaking tours in West Pakistan where he vehemently denounced government corruption and called for the "liberation of Kashmir." Then violent student riots plunged West Pakistan into turmoil.

Ayub Khan traveled to Peshawar, the center of such activity, in November 1968. He attempted to make a calming speech, only to have a student attempt his assassination. The abortive murder attempt enabled the government to suppress its critics. Among those arrested was Zulfikar Ali Bhutto. With presidential elections scheduled for 1969, Ayub Khan faced the possibility of a political reaction. During early 1969, there were continued disorders in Pakistan. Finally, Ayub Khan stepped down and was succeeded by a military regime that reestablished order by proclaiming martial law. General Agha Mohammad Yahya Khan proclaimed himself President and promised to hold elections for constitutional assembly in late 1970.

In the matter of economic growth Pakistan, like India, was faced with the constant problem posed by extremely low living standards. Thus, Pakistan followed India's example and launched a series of Five-Year Plans, beginning in 1955. The plans were aimed at producing a truly diversified economy and a free exchange of goods and services. It was hoped that the nation could be raised above the stage of development where most people were tied directly to the land and lived at a minimum level of subsistence. Consequently, Pakistan, like India, placed emphasis on industrial growth.[19]

Since three-fourths of the Pakistani population lived in rural surroundings, the Government designed programs to bring the people into the cities. It was believed that once people were persuaded to sell their land, the many scattered and tiny plots could be incorporated into larger units where more modern farming methods could be implemented. Ayub Khan therefore initiated a program of land reform with two goals: (1) the consolidation of existing small holdings, in order to produce land units which could be farmed effici-

[19] In Pakistan, particularly, Ayub Khan placed considerable emphasis on the fact that industrialization was necessary for the maintenance of strong armed forces.

ently, and (2) the breaking up of a few large landlord holdings so that the units thus farmed would be approximately the same size as those created by consolidation.

The First and Second Five-Year Plans promoted the rapid growth of industry in Pakistan. As in India, many outside sources—British, United States, Western European, and even Soviet bloc aid after 1955—helped the Pakistanis to develop a stronger economy. Yet, like India, economic steps forward did not bring a rapid improvement in the lot of the average Pakistani, since the population growth rate continued to increase at a high level. Consequently, most of the increase in industrial and agricultural output was used to keep people alive. The continued failure to halt the population growth rate dismayed those whose responsibility it was to plan for Pakistan's future.

In foreign affairs, whereas India sought nonalignment, Pakistan chose a policy of cooperation with Britain and the United States in the Central Treaty Organization, developing out of the Baghdad Pact. Pakistan also joined the Southeast Asia Treaty Organization. In all international alignments and negotiations the Pakistani motivation was essentially the same: seek friends to help her should there be a confrontation with India. Hence, early in the postwar period, Pakistan joined the United States-British sponsored alliances. When the Chinese encroached upon Indian-claimed territory, Pakistan immediately became friendlier with Peking. Then, when Britain and the United States pledged support to India, the Pakistanis reacted by turning to the Communist Chinese for diplomatic support. Thus, no one nation's friendship seemed as important to Pakistan as her continued anti-Indian posture.

The Rise of New Nations in Africa and the Middle East

29

THE EUROPEAN INFLUENCE IN AFRICA

It is common to refer to the upsurge of new nations in postwar Africa as the end product of the rise of nationalism. In reality this new nationalism was more anticolonialism than nationalism in the usual sense. At the end of the war, nearly all the continent was divided among European powers. For three-quarters of a century Africans had been ruled by Europeans, who often were despised by the natives as aliens. After the end of World War II, there was a revolt against this European control in Africa.

It was unfortunate for Afro-European relations in the postwar era that the early contacts historically between Europeans and Africans had been through the slave trade. In the twentieth century, the emotional inheritance of this traffic left a residue of subservience to Europeans among some Africans. At the same time, it inspired an aggressive, sometimes vicious, repudiation of European overlordship among others.

During the last twenty years of the nineteenth century, the Europeans moved from a partial control of the continent to its nearly total partition. The tendency was to decide African affairs in Europe's diplomatic chambers. By the 1930's, this tendency had become tradition. Many developing African nationalists were inflamed by the memory of it in the middle of the twentieth century.

Deep seated hostilities also grew from the fact that, during the early stages of African colonization, the imperial governments placed little or no social and economic responsibility in the hands of Africans. The usual attitude toward the natives, if not openly cruel and harsh, was paternalistic. Africans were regarded as simple, ignorant, or "unspoiled" children, whose society had to be maintained at the tribal level to give them the security they needed.[1] The ultimate effect of this policy was the development of people who would be set free in the twentieth century basically unprepared for participation in modern life. On the one hand, imperialism had brought to Africa an advanced technology, which promised the natives an easier way of life; on the other hand, it built walls of distrust between European and African.

Out of the two World Wars came the principle of self-determination. It first was enunciated by Wilson and later repeated in such documents as the Atlantic Charter. Moreover, imperialism had, to some extent, derived its justification from the principle that "might is right," and that view was discredited by the events of the two World Wars.[2] Yet, in 1945—with the exception of South Africa, Egypt, Liberia, and Ethiopia—Africa still was controlled by the same European states that had dominated the life of the continent for more than seventy years. But an explosion of African nationalism was building. When it came, it removed in fifteen years the direct influence of European imperialism from nearly the whole continent.

WEST AFRICA

The removal of foreign control from West Africa began at the end of World War II. Since the 1930's, signs of political militancy had been appearing among some West Africans. As they studied in the metropolitan centers of the Western world, they formed small groups of political activists. In these discussion groups they talked —in cities like London and Paris—about political independence in Africa. Because they normally were educated in those European states that controlled the territory from which they had come, these nascent nationalists usually reflected the political milieu of the host country.

The impact of World War II was felt more directly in French than in British West Africa. After the fall of France, in 1940, until the invasion of North Africa, in 1942, most of French West Africa was under Vichy rule. This meant increased authoritarianism, compulsory labor, and forced cultivation of land. The harsh treatment of Africans by the French during the war aroused many of those same people who had joined political clubs in Paris during the 1930's.

---

[1] It has been pointed out that many Europeans who went to Africa "felt a subconscious nostalgia" for the village life of feudal Europe, which was rapidly being erased through industrialization. These men thus placed much emphasis on the image of the simple respectful peasant "on whose subservience they could no longer feed their egos at home." See: John Hatch, *A History of Postwar Africa* (London: André Deutsch, 1965), pp. 21–22.

[2] Many pointed out, during and after World War II, that the Nazis and the Fascists were imperialists.

Thus, in 1944, de Gaulle and his associates were led to understand that, after the war, there could be no return to the prewar situation in French West Africa.

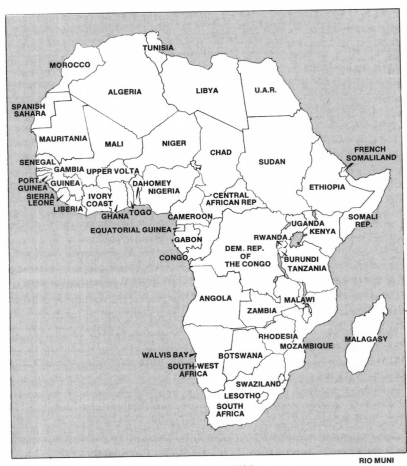

AFRICA IN 1970

By 1946, the African leaders in French West Africa were demanding equal French citizenship, the abolition of forced labor, and the raising of living standards for the native masses. As has been noted in the discussion of European international organizations, French leaders generally were in a progressive mood in the postwar era. The parliament thus devised a constitution which would have created a federal relationship between Paris and the French African territories. This constitution was rejected by the electorate, however. Then business lobbies, fearful that lucrative colonial interests might be damaged, began pushing for a minimizing of concessions granted to the colonies. The result of this pressure was a reaffirmation of traditional colonial policies. The constitution finally devised allowed French West Africa only 13 of 622 seats in the French National Assembly, thus belying earlier assertions that the African colonies would be granted a role in French life equal to that enjoyed by Metropolitan France. African leaders understandably were critical of this imbalance.

In this same 1945–1946 period, British West Africa, too, had its economic and social tensions. In the colonies of Nigeria, the Gold Coast, and Sierra Leone, the British traditionally had followed a policy of recognizing chiefs as "black squires." These chiefs were regarded by Britons as socially superior to urban residents generally, or the small rising middle class of lawyers, journalists, and teachers. At the same time, the British encouraged education and local elections. Thus a situation was established wherein the British expanded and built up an urban middle class that resented the elite class that was created by Britain's favoring of the tribal chiefs. Consequently, social and political revolt developed in West Africa, not only against the British, but against the social system maintained by some of the chiefs.

In 1945, a Manchester Pan-African Conference was convened in Great Britain. It was organized by African nationalist Kwame Nkrumah from the Gold Coast, and by George Padmore, the latter of whom had considerable experience in the international Communist movement.[3] Reflecting the social and political tensions in West Africa, the declaration that emerged from this conference asserted that Africa needed to transform its society, and warned that this could be accomplished only in nations freed from foreign control.

In Nigeria and the Gold Coast the call for breaking the "shackles" of imperialism found a response among a new intelligentsia. For two generations, West Africans had been educated abroad, and thousands of African soldiers had served in the war and had observed conditions in modernized countries. Imperial power and traditional authority were widely denounced among this growing group of dissidents.

In late 1944 and early 1945, new constitutions were promulgated in the Gold Coast and Nigeria. These documents angered the intellectuals in both countries because they reflected the outlook and perpetuated the power of traditional African rulers. The British apparently believed that traditional chiefs represented the popular mood of the people and that loud nationalistic politicians were mere agitators. But the opposition to colonial and traditional rule gave rise, in 1947, to the United Gold Coast Convention, a meeting of

[3] Also prominent in this conference was Jomo Kenyatta, later the chief executive of Kenya.

middle-class groups and radicals who advocated bringing control of national affairs into the "hands of the people."

In Nigeria, Benjamin Nnamdi Azikiwe in 1946 helped found an association of protest organizations called the National Council for Nigeria and the Cameroons (NCNC). The first aim of the National Council was to secure universal suffrage in Nigeria. Azikiwe and his followers selected the colonial government as their major target for attack.

When Azikiwe organized an NCNC delegation to protest to the Colonial Secretary concerning Nigerian conditions, he became a national hero. His council became a political party which was, at that time, probably most accurately representative of the aspirations of those Nigerians who wished to modernize their state.

While revolution was not yet abroad in the land, many areas were ripe for revolt. The greatest common denominator among the various West African peoples was the decline of respect for Europeans. There long had been a superstitious belief that the technologically advanced Europeans were something more than mere men. These beliefs gradually were dissipated by education and increasing familiarity with the ways of the modern world.[4]

The general spirit of restiveness produced new constitutions in 1951 in Sierra Leone and Gambia, that oddly shaped territory some 20 miles wide along 200 miles of river. In Nigeria and the Gold Coast, however, events occurred that were to determine the course of revolution in West Africa.

The revolutionary period in West African postwar history began in December 1947, when Kwame Nkrumah came home from Britain to serve as secretary of the United Gold Coast Convention. Educated in Great Britain and the United States, Nkrumah possessed an experience in political strategy shared by few Africans. Soon after his return, he organized a drive to recruit membership for the United Gold Coast Convention Party (UGCC). He then arranged boycotts and demonstrations against colonial rule that finally led to the Accra riots of 1948. The Governor, Sir Gerald Creasy, blamed the UGCC for the disorders in which nearly 30 had lost their lives and some 300 suffered injuries. Many of the leaders of the UGCC, including Nkrumah himself, were banished from the Gold Coast, although they did not remain in exile long.

A British Commission of Enquiry was appointed to study the causes of the disorders, and it quickly found that part of the problem was rooted in an "outmoded" constitution. London thereupon appointed an all-African body under an African judge, Henley Coussey, to propose a revision of the governmental structure.

[4] Education was spreading extensively. The number of educated people in French West Africa in 1948, for example, was about double the figure in 1938.

Nkrumah was ignored in the composition of the committee, but several more conservative members of the UGCC were included.

In October 1949, the Coussey Committee reported and recommended that a new Legislative Assembly be constituted. Only a few of the members were to be elected directly. Nkrumah immediately attacked the Coussey proposals, and his new party, the Convention People's Party (CPP) held a mass meeting at which the condemnation was repeated.[5] In place of the Coussey proposals, immediate self-government, dominion status in the Commonwealth, and a new constitution were demanded. The demands were rejected by the new British Governor, Sir Charles Arden-Clarke.

At the beginning of 1950, Nkrumah and his party adopted the Gandhian method of passive resistance to secure their ends. A general strike was planned for January 8, 1950. The Governor reacted by declaring a state of emergency and imprisoning Nkrumah and a number of his associates. Nkrumah's party remained loyal to him and, when the state of emergency was ended, in March 1950, Nkrumah's lieutenants directed renewed agitation.

The first general election under the Coussey constitution was held in February 1951. The CPP fought the election campaign as a disciplined party and won thirty-four of the thirty-eight seats that were directly or electorally chosen.[6] Despite the fears of many, the supposedly undemocratic constitution had provided a basis for party government, and the dominant party was nationalist, antitraditionalist, and anticolonial. Nkrumah, elected while in jail, was released and in 1952 became Prime Minister.

The Gold Coast now exerted an important influence throughout the African continent since Kwame Nkrumah and his colleagues had set an example that caused even assimilationist-minded French Africans to change their views and strive for independence. Moreover, the Gold Coast, with an estimated population of about 5,000,000, possessed a convenient size and sufficient affluence to act as a model for other experiments in national self-determination. In addition, the development of a nationalist role in government was helped in the Gold Coast by the British governor, who was more liberal and imaginative than most other similar officials on the African continent. Sir Charles Arden-Clarke worked closely with Nkrumah to produce a relationship between imperial governor and leading African nationalists, which finally brought imperial rule to an end.

After the election of 1951, there was a two-year period in which the semi-autonomous government consolidated its position. Then the frontal attack on colonial rule began. In 1953, Nkrumah introduced a motion demanding responsible self-government based on direct

---

[5] The support given by some members of the UGCC to the Coussey Committee caused a split in the party and the formation of the CPP.
[6] The other thirty-seven seats were elected by Chiefs' Councils or outlying territories.

elections and universal adult suffrage. The motion further requested that the British declare independence as soon as the new constitution came into force. When a new and more representative draft constitution, providing for more autonomy, emerged from the deliberations of an appointed commission, the British Government in 1954 accepted it almost without amendment. Yet independence did not come immediately, since there were traditionalist-minded elements in the country itself opposing it.

In 1954 and 1956, new legislatures were elected in which the CPP obtained a substantial majority. Finally, the Colonial Secretary promised that, if a "reasonable majority" in the new legislature passed a motion calling for independence, he would set a date on which the Gold Coast might be proclaimed a sovereign state. The independence motion was introduced and passed. The Colonial Secretary then designated March 6, 1957, as independence day for Ghana, formed through union of the Gold Coast and the British Trust Territory of Western Togoland. Three years later, in 1960, Ghana became a republic. The impact on colonial Africa was immense. Ethiopia and Liberia were not regarded by most Africans as being in the same category as Ghana. To those who still lived under colonial rule Ghana was the first state to break free of European control. Nkrumah's call for the emancipation of Africa from white imperialism now echoed in other parts of the continent.

Actually, the transformation of the Gold Coast into Ghana had more immediate impact on further-removed African regions than it had on much of West Africa itself. Gambia, for instance, was still dominated by traditionalists who worked closely with tribal chiefs to control the society. Still, constitutional progress was made and a ministerial system was introduced in 1954. Soon after, progressives in Gambia began to fight for universal suffrage, which was achieved in 1960. In 1962, internal self-government was attained and in February 1965, Gambia became an independent member of the British Commonwealth. The events in Ghana influenced Sierra Leone, also, to move slowly toward a greater degree of constitutional government. Liberians were inspired to institute female suffrage, and increase the pace of socio-economic progress.

Much larger in area and population than Ghana in West Africa was Nigeria. It, too, underwent constitutional evolution in the 1950's, although progress was less smooth than in Ghana. In Nigeria, the power of traditionalism and sectionalism was much stronger.

The influence of Nigerian sectionalism was evident in a 1951 constitution. This document reflected the fact that the British themselves wanted to lead the Nigerians to unified national statehood, by giving stronger powers to the central rather than the regional governments. At the same time, it limited the powers given to the central government by preserving much of the regional authority over elections. In consequence, the political energies of Nigerians often were diverted from support of national to regional efforts. In the north of Nigeria, conservatism was deeply-rooted, whereas there was a strong independence movement in the South.[7] Hence, there was a strong hostility between North and South, which undermined the constitution. In 1953, the southerners tried to secure passage, through the Federal House, of a motion demanding that Nigeria be granted self-government by 1956. Discussions ensued and, in October 1954, a new federal constitution was written, which allowed the majority political parties a strong influence over affairs in their own regions. Thereafter, each major regional party won the elections in its own region, but could not influence the outcome in others. Consequently, a united Nigerian nation seemed increasingly further from realization, as each region went its separate way. As a result, the first move toward independence in the area was in the direction of regional self-government—achieved by East and West Nigeria in 1957.

The North seemed anxious to maintain British administration a few years longer. Despite this tendency, and to the surprise of other Nigerians, the northerners, in March 1957, participated in a motion passed in the Federal House demanding national independence in 1959. By the passage of this motion, it became clear that Nigeria would not divide along regional lines, but that one nation would be formed. The British, however, believed that the Nigerians were not yet ready for independence, and London required that they wait somewhat longer. Independence then did come on October 1, 1960. Thus, the largest country in Africa, with a population well over 50,000,000, became a sovereign state. In 1963, Nigeria became a federal republic. It comprised North, West, and East Nigeria and the Federal Territory of Lagos (the capital).

Even after the British grant of independence Nigeria continued to be troubled by Black Africa's most troublesome difficulty—recurrent tribalism. In the relatively primitive north, the Moslem Hausa-Fulani group dominated. In the west, the politically aggressive Yoruba were ascendant. In the east, the Ibo, ambitious and activist, controlled political life. In January 1966, the Ibo led a military coup, murdering the northern-born Prime Minister Sir Abubakar Tafawa Belewa. The northerners then struck back, killing the leading Ibo officers. In the summer of 1966, Lieutenant Colonel (later Major General) Yakubu Gowon, a northern-born graduate of Britain's Sandhurst, took control of Nigeria as Chief of State.

Many Northerners believed, in the autumn of 1966, that they had not evened the score properly with the Ibo for their attempt to take over the government. In September a wave of mass murder broke out in the northern cities, and thousands of Ibo, who had migrated

[7] The dominant people in the northern region were the Hausa; in the southern area, the western part was dominated by the Yoruba and the eastern part by the Ibo.

there to find employment were slaughtered.[8] Uncounted thousands of Ibo fled back to their homeland in the southeast corner of Nigeria. In the spring of 1967, the military governor of the Eastern region, Colonel (later General) Chukwuemeka Odlumegwu Ojukwu, declared that his territory had seceded from Nigeria, and become the Republic of Biafra.

A civil war followed between the majority Nigerians and minority Biafrans, which continued into 1969. Humanitarians throughout the world were aroused by the nature of the war. The protests did not stem from the regular casualties of battle, for these were relatively slight; but untold tens of thousands of victims were civilians who died of starvation.

The landlocked Ibo homeland was so infertile that the Biafrans were faced with the necessity of winning the war rapidly or suffering starvation. Accordingly, they launched a drive at the beginning of the war, in 1967, that carried them to within 136 miles of Lagos, the federal capital. Then Nigeria's great superiority in men and machines began to take effect. The tide turned and the Ibo were blockaded within their barren homeland.

By mid-1969, when Biafran resistance virtually collapsed, the Nigerian Civil War had caused the Lagos government to develop the most effective army in Black Africa. Moreover, at least for the time being, the civil conflict had forced the Nigerians to consolidate the previously particularistic state. Chief of State Gowon, who broke the power of the secessionists during the war, also reorganized Nigeria. The previous four regions were divided into twelve more easily controlled states. Foreign capital flowed back into the country for restoration and development and, by 1970, the government was collecting substantial royalties and taxes on (Biafran) oil.

It is less difficult to follow the course of events in French than in British Africa, because French colonial policy was more uniform. The French colonies stepped forward virtually in unison to obtain nearly identical institutions. In the first half of the 1950's, French West and Equatorial Africa were relatively calm. The electorate increased and schools, industry, and agriculture all demonstrated a marked growth.

Despite the comparative quiet however, African pressure was mounting for a revision of the constitution governing the French colonial territories. In addition, France was beset by military and political failure in North Africa and Southeast Asia. In June 1956, a new constitutional act (the *loi cadre* or "skeleton law") was passed by the French Assembly. It was an enabling act, giving power to the Paris government which would allow it to fill in the details later. The *loi cadre* marked a dramatic departure from the traditional colonial

[8] It has been estimated that 30,000 men, women, and children were killed in this outburst of violence.

policy of assimilation. Paris now recognized that the destiny of African states was independence.

The new act essentially dismantled French West Africa and French Equatorial Africa, allowing each territory a semiresponsible government. The decrees putting the *loi cadre* into force, in territory after territory, were promulgated in 1957. One of the immediate effects was to stimulate greater political activity in the West African territories as the natives made ready for new elections. While new party alignments were being constructed, reconstructed, and then constructed again, the Fourth Republic toppled in France and de Gaulle came to power. The French West Africans decided that this was a propitious time to present to Paris a united front. They called for a federal republic of autonomous states, leaving the nature of the relationships among them to be decided later.

De Gaulle wished to maintain strong links to Africa. He seemed to believe that the African colonies might be useful in restoring France's lost influence. Consequently, plans were offered to the French Community, in 1958, proposing a situation wherein the African territories would no longer be represented in the French parliament, but would participate in the election of the president. This compromise took a position midway between imperial government from Paris and full federalism. It was calculated to forestall a "flood" of African deputies in the French Chamber, and, as one observer put it, would keep France from becoming "a colony of her colonies." Most of the African territories, except in Niger, where a sizable majority voted against it, approved the plan through a referendum.

The newly-arranged government of the French Community soon proved unworkable. Calls for independence were heard again from all over French West Africa. In April 1959, Senegal and the French Sudan joined to form the Federation of Mali.[9] Representatives of the new union asked France for independence as a new federal state within the Community. De Gaulle was, at this point, embroiled in Algeria. He thus raised little objection, and independence within the Community was granted to French Mali in 1960. But the federation broke up after a few months, the French Sudan keeping the name of Mali and the other state reverting to the name Senegal.

Elsewhere in French West Africa, representatives of United Nations Trust Territories Togoland and the Cameroons went to Paris to negotiate independence. Since the two states were Trusteeships, the United Nations debated the question and expressed doubt only over whether the Cameroons should have elections before independence. By 1960, both states were independent as, respectively, the Republic of Togo and the Federal Republic of Cameroon.

[9] Mali was the name of a medieval African Kingdom in the Upper Niger Valley.

Now the other Community states followed the examples set by the Mali Federation, Togoland, and the Cameroons. In June 1960, the Ivory Coast, Niger, Upper Volta, and Dahomey requested France to accord them independence outside the Community. With this, the Community—as its unrealistic construction had foretold—virtually collapsed. In 1960, eight new French West African states took their seats in the UN.

The creation of nations went on in all West Africa. States sometimes separated, as in the case of the Mali Federation. On other occasions they were joined, as in the case of the Spanish colonies of Río Muni and some offshore islands including Fernando Póo in 1968. The United Nations' "Special Committee of 24," which was charged with the responsibility of arranging self-determination for new states, proposed that Spain join Fernando Póo with Río Muni; thus was formed Equatorial Guinea (the world's 133rd nation-state). Some of these newly-created territories were too small to secure economic well being for their people, and some were tempting targets for larger African states with imperialistic tendencies of their own. These situations promised a tempestuous future for most of West Africa.

SOUTHERN AFRICA

The transformation of the spirit of black nationalism into the reality of national independence in West Africa was not matched by similar developments in the southern part of the continent. There the white rulers looked with mixed scorn and fear on the anti-colonial upheavals in the north. They took measures that they hoped would inhibit native independence movements in the south. This resistance to black nationalism probably was "white nationalism" only among the Afrikaner of South Africa. Elsewhere—in the Portuguese possessions of Angola and Mozambique, for instance—what some have called white nationalism basically was an attempt to maintain European colonial empire, after such empires had become anachronistic in Africa.

Perhaps because of the special history and rugged spirit of its inhabitants, the heart of resistance to change was the Afrikaner community, an amalgam of German, French, and Netherlands heritages. The Afrikaner nation grew out of a colony first settled by the Dutch East India Company in the eighteenth century. The descendants of the first Netherlands colonists fled from contact with the English settlers in the nineteenth century to form the Orange Free State and the Transvaal. The first frontier colonies were developed along strictly caste lines, and thus it remained. After the Boer War, the Afrikaners accepted the opportunity offered by the British and formed a Union of South Africa with the Cape Colony and Natal in 1908.[10] The caste idea was based on the belief that the Afrikaners were God's special people. It was thus assumed, even in the twentieth century, that Afrikaners were superior to other and lesser beings, and South African social and political structures reflected this outlook.

The industrial revolution followed a normal course in South Africa, with the usual flow of people from rural to urban areas and a growth of industrial classes according to diversification of skills. Urban slums developed, with the attendant appearance of disease and social discontent. Because a caste system had existed prior to the industrial revolution, the socio-economic order continued along similar lines. Unskilled workers almost entirely were black, semiskilled workers were both black and white,[11] and skilled workers and management were white.

During World War II, the economy expanded to meet war needs and thus a demand was created for new skilled workers. Yet, the color bar hindered the drawing of such workers from among the unskilled or semiskilled blacks. At the same time, economic expansion had drawn an increasing number of people from the countryside to the cities to fill new unskilled jobs. As this process continued, the economic reality made the traditional social order anachronistic. Not unnaturally, then, a number of prominent African nationalists became critical of South Africa during the war. The political structure came under particularly intense fire, for the whites were governed according to parliamentary rules, whereas the rest of the population was subjected to autocratic rule. At the end of the war, some 8,000,000 Africans were represented by 3 of the 153 members of the Assembly and 4 of the 44 senators. Moreover, all members of both houses were white.

The major differences between South Africa and colonialism in other parts of Africa was that, in South Africa, the Government represented the white population of the country itself instead of a removed electorate in Paris or London. Consequently, the Government followed procedures which reinforced the development of two separate camps in the nation—white and non-white. As the racial schism widened, the Afrikaners developed a deep-seated fear of the millions of black Africans in their country.

The people in the English-speaking areas of Northern Rhodesia, Southern Rhodesia,[12] and South Africa seemed less interested in

---

[10] A draft constitution produced by a constitutional convention went into effect in 1910 when it was approved by the British Parliament as the South Africa Act.

[11] There was a tendency at this level of skill, however, to train whites so that they could move into the skilled classes and out of proximity to blacks.

[12] In 1911–1912 the Northeastern and Northwestern provinces of Rhodesia united to form Northern Rhodesia. In 1923 Southern Rhodesia was formally annexed to the British crown.

politics than the Afrikaners and more interested in making money. They lived in Africa rather than Britain because they there could enjoy a more comfortable existence. Yet, the British South Africans could not escape the growing social tensions, and the white inhabitants of major cities tended to remain aloof from the black population; firearms became a necessity of life.

Thus, the postwar period saw a hardening of segregation in attitude and practice. In its first year, the United Nations called upon government leaders from the Union of South Africa to account for their pursuance of illiberal racist policies. South-West Africa, which had been mandated to the Union after World War I, was subjected to the same policies. Yet, when questioned by the UN membership about South West Africa, the Union leadership claimed that a referendum taken there had demonstrated that the majority of blacks supported incorporation into the Union on the Union's terms. The referendum was not regarded seriously by the UN membership, and no action was taken by the international body beyond extracting the promise that the Union would report to the Trusteeship Council on the administration of the territory.

By 1948, three distinct views could be identified, all claiming best knowledge of how the social order should be arranged in South Africa. First, there were those who advocated the absolute division of territory between European and native to produce an "apartheid" society. A second view favored a social order without discrimination. Between these two polarized positions, some held that European and native communities should continue to exist side by side, with certain differences between them recognized by law. Out of these differing views came a spate of legislation, during 1949 and 1950, which, among other things, prohibited sexual relations between blacks and whites, and officially classified by race the peoples living within the Union.

In the 1950's and 1960's, the Union defied the UN by virtually incorporating South West Africa. The newly enlarged territory rapidly became the core of white nationalism throughout the southern half of the continent. Britishers generally in Kenya, as well as in Northern and Southern Rhodesia, approved of the Union's policies with regard to blacks. In the Portuguese colonies of Mozambique and Angola, however, apartheid was rejected. In these territories a small African elite was allowed to enter white society and, because of the scarcity of white women, miscegenation was permitted. Yet, despite this separation of the Union and the Portuguese colonies in matters of racial policy, a common authoritarian outlook served as a bond between the two areas. Thus, throughout South Africa, there developed a reversal of the social and economic evolution transpiring elsewhere in Africa.

Throughout the 1950's and 1960's, while black Africanism was creating independent states in Central and Northern Africa, the white oligarchies in the South restricted any upsurge of black nationalism which might be stimulated by the northern example. The Afrikaners weighted the constitution in favor of the white man, and worked out a racial strategy that removed the threat of African political power without destroying a much-needed black labor force.

The white nationalists, through a merger of the National and Afrikaner parties under the name of the National Party, gained control of the Union Parliament in 1951 and still held control in 1970. Successive apartheid laws were passed, some of which impinged on the personal freedom even of white citizens. With this control the whites forced the non-European community into a subservient pattern of life. From 1951, the so-called Bantu Authorities Acts restored tribal communities even in towns where black African residents and workers had lost their tribal identities. There also was a deepening in the division of employment between Europeans and Africans. The Industrial Conciliation Act of 1956 allowed the Ministry of Labor to reserve some categories of employment to whites only. The same act segregated white and black workers into separate unions and made it a criminal offense for black Africans to strike.

The blacks nonviolently protested such treatment and strove to improve their lot through such black associations as the African National Congress (ANC). Some of the 3,500,000 ruling whites, however, demonstrated a deep-seated fear of the Africans. In 1960, at Sharpeville in the Transvaal, for example, police shot more than sixty Africans in a crowd peacefully demonstrating against apartheid legislation. World public opinion was turned against the white nationalists by the "Sharpeville Massacre" and South Africa eventually felt impelled, by British disapproval of apartheid, to leave the Commonwealth. She became an independent republic in May 1961. Soon after, a state of emergency was declared and thousands of Africans and their few white supporters were imprisoned without trial.

Such policies caused a black nationalist reaction. As early as 1959, a more radical wing of the African National Congress had broken away to form a Pan-Africanist Congress (PAC), under the leadership of a former university lecturer, Robert M. Sobukwe. The PAC departed from the nonviolent policy established by the ANC, and Sobukwe soon was imprisoned; from 1969, he was restricted in his movements to Kimberley. Meanwhile, in 1966, the United Nations had ended South Africa's mandate over South West Africa, but the republic simply refused to acknowledge any trusteeship authority. In 1968, the UN adopted the name Namibia for South West Africa, and, into the 1970's, still and vainly asked the Union to extend independence to the region and its 600,000 inhabitants.

In the Portuguese possessions of Angola and Mozambique, policy was shaped more along traditional colonialist lines than along the South African pattern. But, unlike other European powers, Portugal declared that her place in Africa was a permament one. When the tide of black African nationalism surged into Portuguese territories, it was met with ruthless suppression. In Angola there were purges of the opponents of the regime. Repression was so severe in Mozambique that it was denounced by the Catholic Church.

In 1961, despite some political reform and economic development, there was an uprising in Angola. The rebels were subjugated by Portuguese reinforcements, but in 1962 a group of Angolan refugees in the Republic of the Congo organized to overthrow Lisbon's authority. The uprisings received considerable attention in Western capitals, lest failure to criticize the perpetuation of Portuguese empire antagonize the new African nations.

Rhodesia followed the example of maintaining the dominance of whites over blacks at all costs.[13] In November 1965, the Rhodesian Government reacted to British pressure to democratize black-white relationships by unilaterally declaring its independence, though still recognizing the Queen as sovereign. For the next three years a Government dedicated to preserving the rule of 232,000 whites over 4,000,000 blacks withstood all the economic pressures that Britain and the United Nations could bring to bear. British Prime Minister Harold Wilson negotiated with Rhodesian leader Ian Douglas Smith through 1968, in an effort to win majority rule for Rhodesia's blacks. It was hoped in London that blockade by Britain and other nations eventually would force the Rhodesians to make concessions to their black population. But in 1969, Rhodesia severed all ties with London and became a republic.[14]

CENTRAL AFRICA

The Second World War profoundly affected the peoples of Central Africa when, in 1940, Belgium and France were overrun by the Nazis. By November 1940, the whole of Central Africa was engaged in support of the war against the Nazis. Many Africans from the central belt served overseas, and brought back with them to their homelands Western concepts of the freedom of the individual and the dignity of man. In addition to arousing an increased political and social awareness, the war had an impact on the Central African economy, for it stimulated an increased production of gold, rubber, cotton, and other supplies. The increase in production brought the

[13] Northern and Southern Rhodesia in 1953 became part of the Federation of Rhodesia and Nyasaland. In 1963, the Federation was dissolved, and in 1964 Northern Rhodesia became the independent Republic of Zambia. Nyasaland in 1963 became the Dominion and, in 1966, the Republic of Malawi. Southern Rhodesia reverted to dominion status in 1963, with a white-supremacy policy.
[14] Rhodesia generally is included in histories as part of Central Africa. It is included here in the section on South Africa because the attitudes and policies which developed there in the postwar period were closer to those common among whites in the Union of South Africa than those typical of the Congo or French Equatorial Africa.

usual consequent growth of cities,[15] the formation of new workers' associations, and a further development of social and political awareness.[16]

The colonial aims of the British, French, and Belgians differed in the area. The French hoped eventually to make of their subjects "black Frenchmen." The Belgians paternalistically worked at the schooling of Africans in Roman Catholicism and taught them manual skills. The British balanced economic interests against the traditional British policy of "settler self-government."

The practical administration of the colonies, however, was similar. They were dominated by large European companies, which often took over the role of government. In Congolese Katanga, for instance, the companies began to provide welfare and housing services, which were unavailable from other agencies.

The years immediately after the war saw boom conditions continuing in the central-belt territories. Europe was war-torn and many Europeans fled from the rubble of their cities to an apparently privileged and comfortable life in Africa. In many Central African urban areas this situation established tensions, because the Europeans normally were favored over the natives when housing space was made available.

Belgian policy in the Congo was "paternal;" it assumed that Africans had arrived at only an early stage of social and political evolution. Both before and after the war the Belgians thus attempted to rear their charges by teaching them the middle-class Belgian virtues of thrift, industry, and Christianity. By 1945, however, the policy was slow-moving when compared to the pace of African advances elsewhere on the continent. But the Belgians believed that it was necessary to achieve material progress first, with political development later following naturally.

The traditional Belgium policies did not satisfy the (small) politically conscious section of the African community in the Congo, which emerged in the postwar period. From 1948, this emerging African intellectual elite began pressing for salaries and working conditions similar to those enjoyed by Europeans. There were some minor moves made to appease these political activists. For instance, in 1948, a certificate of "civic merit" was given to those members of the restive elite who were able to prove that they had behaved with civic virtue. The certificates were almost valueless, however, as they carried with them few privileges beyond commendation. More significantly, in 1948, European schools were opened to Africans and, in 1950, all discrimination was abandoned in the schools.

The impact of the war on French Equatorial Africa was some-

---

[15] Léopoldville, for instance, increased its population from 40,000 in 1939 to 100,000 in 1945.
[16] One form of this increased awareness in the Congo was indicated by the appearance of strikes and rioting in 1941 and 1944.

what different. The French territories had remained loyal to de Gaulle during the war and thus were regarded favorably in Paris at the war's end. Consequently, it was decided that they would be given parliamentary representation in the French Union, which was to succeed the Empire. Hence, as with French West Africa, the Central African colonies sent delegates to help draft a constitution with the Constituent Assembly meeting in Paris in November 1945. But when the constitution was approved, in 1946, Central Africa was given only 6 seats out of the 622 in the National Assembly. Still, this new participation in government brought radical changes to African life in French Central or Equatorial Africa, particularly in the formation of local assemblies (one in each territory) and a Grand Council for the Federation.

Despite this first step, political development was slower in French Equatorial Africa than in French West Africa. Economic and social conditions were miserable. Hence, the time still had not come when important considerations of how best to survive, begin to shape a political awareness within people. Many, indeed, still believed that Europeans should continue in power at the territorial level, and they regarded the traditional chiefs as the natural wielders of local political power. Only over a period of time did the new representative institutions broaden political activity. The basic significance of the new assemblies was that they presented the machinery necessary for participation in the African political revolution.

Thus, the immediate postwar period was the scene of profound alteration in the attitude of Paris toward its Central African subjects, although tribalism remained more important to the natives than a sense of Africanism. In 1951, the electorate was expanded in French Equatorial Africa, but the effect of this was slow in coming, perhaps because urbanization had proceeded more slowly in Central Africa than in West Africa. In the working class that did exist, there was very little unionism. Politics, in consequence, remained attached to local feeling, and nowhere did a really strong radical group, urging independence, emerge.

French Central Africa, because of its retarded political development, eventually became independent through external pressures rather than by its own intent. When the *loi cadre* was passed in 1956, the Europeans voluntarily left the political field and confined themselves to technical and economic matters. They thus created a vacuum in politics. For the next four years the four states that made up French Equatorial Africa (Chad, Gabon, French-Congo, and Ubangi-Shari) moved haltingly forward, establishing among themselves agreements on common services, customs, and defense. Then, in 1960, the four states were swept by the great move toward nation-making, sparked by West Africa, into a sovereignty perhaps not strongly desired (as the Republics of Chad, Gabon, Congo, and Central Africa). They still remained, however, within the French

Community and heavily dependent upon France for economic support.

In contrast to French Equatorial Africa, where political life was stimulated with difficulty, the Belgian Congo experienced intense activity in politics. Until the mid-1950's, the Belgians governed from Brussels, seldom consulting the Congo natives. In the midst of a rising tide of African nationalism on the continent, they pursued a policy of improving the Congolese people's lot although barring them from political life. Part of the program of improvement involved an attack on illiteracy. By the mid-1950's, some 42 per cent of the Congolese could read. Thus, there was the possibility of stimulating political awareness among the Belgian Congo's African population through the written word that did not exist elsewhere in Africa. As the Congolese earned more money, gained more skills, and learned to read, it was inevitable that they should begin to think of running their own country. Hence, it was Belgian policy itself that stimulated the beginnings of African nationalism in the Congo.

Since 1953, a group of Congolese intellectuals had been publishing a journal called *Conscience Africaine.* In the middle of 1956, these men published a special issue of their journal in the form of a manifesto calling for the ultimate independence of the Congo. The authors of the manifesto probably thought that the process of gaining independence would take decades, but the Belgian Administration was thrown into a panic.

Although those involved in the issuance of *Conscience Africaine* did not become activists, the journal did inspire others to do so. One of these was Joseph Kasavubu, a leader in an African nationalist association known as Bakongo Tribe Association or ABAKO. In 1957, the Belgians attempted to adjust to the mounting political pressures by permitting elections to be held in the municipalities. The ABAKO and its followers demonstrated strength by gaining nearly half of the seats in the Léopoldville Assembly. In 1958, a rival political party, inspired by Bakongo successes, organized as the *Mouvement National Congolais* (MNC). Foremost among its leaders was Patrice E. Lumumba, who realized that if the Congo ever were to become independent, it would be necessary to move away from traditional tribalism. The MNC, therefore, established a national organization in order to get the rank-and-file support that could sweep the Congo to independence.

Then the long-dammed-up political flood broke loose in the Congo. At the end of 1958, Patrice Lumumba attended an All-African Conference in Accra and heard emotional accounts describing the continent's surge towards independence. He returned to Léopoldville, and, in early 1959, announced that his goal now was immediate independence from Belgian rule. The declaration was made in near revolutionary circumstances, for a recession had caused widespread unemployment.

Meanwhile, events transpiring since 1956 had convinced the Belgians that they should grant concessions leading toward independence in the Congo. In January 1960, a roundtable conference was called to sit in Brussels, and soon it was announced that independence would be granted.

A centralized system of government, of which Kasavubu disapproved, came out of the roundtable conference. The machinery to create independence thus was established. In the last days before independent status was realized, however, the shadow of tragic days to come was cast across Congolese affairs. Kasavubu's ABAKO demanded that an autonomous government be created in Bas-Congo. Moise K. Tshombe, who recently had formed a new federalist-orientated party, cabled the Belgian Government and demanded that the constitution be revised. Soon Congolese particularism developed along tribal lines and attempts were made to proclaim secession.

On June 30, 1960, the Belgians abruptly turned the Congo over to Head of State Kasavubu and Premier Lumumba, and the path to chaos was opened.[17] The newly emerging politicians had whipped up emotions to support the cause of independence, between 1956 and 1960, and now were unable to control these passions. Violence swept through the towns and cities as the army mutinied against its officers and Kasavubu and Lumumba fell to quarreling. Districts broke loose from the Federal Government, particularly in the south, where mineral-rich Katanga led the way with Tschombe as president.

When the Government's authority shrank to a small area around the capital, Léopoldville, barbarism and anarchy reigned. The UN decided to intervene in order to restore order. It recruited an emergency army from thirty-four countries. The UN army, numbering some 20,000, was flown into the Congo. A radical faction of Congolese politicians, led by Prime Minister Patrice Lumumba, seemed on the verge of opening full-scale war. Lumumba, however, was deposed in 1961, thrown in jail, and subsequently murdered. In the UN General Assembly, the Soviets now demanded the withdrawal of United Nations forces.[18] Despite Soviet pressure, UN Secretary General Dag Hammarskjöld ordered the UN armies to push ahead. Even after his death in a plane crash in September 1961, in Northern Rhodesia, the UN forces continued to fight rebellion and to pressure Tshombe into surrendering and reuniting Katanga with the Congo. In 1964, Tshombe was called home from voluntary exile to organize a ministry that ran across most party and tribal lines.

[17] Alongside the new Democratic Republic of the Congo was the populous Belgian trust territory of Ruanda-Urandi which, in 1962, became the two separate nations of Rwanda and Burundi. Almost immediately tribal divisions brought turmoil to both countries.
[18] There was some evidence that Soviet agents were at work in the Congo crisis, encouraging the radical Lumumba faction. His death was a setback for the U.S.S.R.

In July 1964, the last UN forces were withdrawn from the Congo.[19] When the UN troops left, rebellions broke out in at least three areas and Tshombe's poorly trained army could not suppress the uprisings. Communist-led insurgents seized whites in the interior of the Congo and massacred them. Once again the issue of the Congolese situation was brought before the UN. The specter of "white colonialism" was raised by several African delegations, who indicated that the murders of whites in the Congo had been caused by colonials who would not let go the imperial privileges of the past. Testimony of hostages saved by a Belgian-American rescue mission refuted this charge. Eventually, the turbulence in the Congo subsided, after Lieutenant General Joseph D. Mobutu assumed the presidency in 1965. In the ensuing years, however, he, too, resorted to forceful methods to curb tribalism and personal political rivalries.

EAST AFRICA

Most of East Africa before 1945 was governed by the British, except for Tanganyika, which was German East Africa until the end of World War I, and Ethiopia, which, except for a period of Italian occupation between 1936 and 1941, was controlled by its own native rulers. Despite the general prevalence of British control, the area had a more cosmopolitan population than any other bloc of African territories. Europeans of all types, Indians, and other Asians were settled in the region as the result of early exploration and of colonization. The voyages of Arabs down the East African coastline, and their establishment of trading posts, dated from the era before the explorations of Vasco da Gama.

The racial mixture in East Africa created unfortunate antagonisms. The Europeans generally disliked the Indian-Asian community because of the economic competition it provided. Both Africans and Europeans developed an animosity toward the Asiatics because they believed that the Asians retarded African progress through their monopolization of small business and their clannish living pattern. The antagonism against the Indians and other Asians maintained by the Africans revealed the fact that the Africans had developed a European-oriented cultural outlook. The Africans' educative and cultural institutions had been modeled along European lines. The natives therefore resented an Oriental society in their midst which excluded their participation. This tension between Africans and Asians was most apparent in Kenya, Uganda, and Tanganyika.

Immediately after the Second World War, there did not seem to be the same threat to European control developing among East

---

[19] At one time some 93,000 men had been involved in UN operations in the Congo.

Africans as was the case elsewhere in Africa. Despite this surface appearance, however, the roots of conflict were there and were growing, particularly in Kenya. In Kenya, during the war, the number of factory workers had risen to nearly 10,000. These were concentrated mainly in Nairobi. Consequently, there developed the usual politically-oriented byproducts of industrialization within a context of urbanization. In 1943, trade unions were legalized and strikes broke out. By this time, about 70,000 Africans were living in Nairobi, forced into a barracks-like existence. These Africans were required to live apart from their wives because it was assumed by the Europeans that the natives would maintain the old family plots at the same time that they sought employment in the cities. Thus a system was established that prevented the development of a stable urban family population.

As political consciousness became evident in the after-the-war period, the British Government generally adopted a policy in its territories of slow evolution in the direction of representative institutions. To many Africans, this seemed nothing more than a series of token advances aimed at maintaining Europeans in control.

After 1945, the British began the appointment of a few Africans to governmental councils. This policy was adopted at least partially in response to pressure from the United Nations Trusteeship Council to grant greater African representation in Trustee territories like Tanganyika. As a phase of this slow constitutional progress there appeared in Uganda, the *Bataka*, the first genuine political party in that territory. The Bataka now began to work for more rapid economic and social reform.

One constant influence upon those Africans who began to assert themselves politically in East Africa was the status of Ethiopia. It was true that Ethiopia was a primitive, underdeveloped land with semifeudal institutions and a dictatorial emperor. Yet, Ethiopians had, except for the Italian occupation in World War II, always lived under their own rulers. Hence, Ethiopia might be so backward as to have few recognizable roads outside the capital, Addis Ababa, and still other East Africans could draw inspiration from the fact that the empire was self-governed.

There were signs of desires for self-government in Tanganyika and Uganda, but the prinicipal locale of political development was in the East African territory of Kenya. In Kenya, there lived some 20,000 Europeans, who occupied the most important positions in government and business, 120,000 Asians (mostly Indians), and aproximately 5,000,000 Africans. The Africans lived in traditional tribal groupings, functioned as workers on European farms, or existed in urban surroundings.

Before the Europeans had come to Kenya, life was primitive and highly organized along tribal lines. When the Europeans came, they brought with them missionaries who criticized what seemed to them cruel practices (female circumcision, for instance). Yet, the missionaries were not trained anthropologists and thus condemned these practices with a fervor based on moral concepts that the Kenyans did not comprehend. Consequently, those same Christian missionaries who brought the positive benefits of education, health, and general welfare, profoundly disrupted the African society. Hence, over the long run, the breaking down of traditional societal patterns by well-intentioned Europeans caused a massive erosion of good feeling between the races in Kenya.

From the African point of view, their tribal customs were being destroyed without anything more attractive being offered in their place. This feeling was particularly intense among the Kikuyu, who lived near Nairobi. As early as 1922, the Kikuyu organized as the Kikuyu Central Association (KCA) to fight the tendency toward erosion of their institutions. After the war, the KCA, which was proscribed during the conflict, was reborn and its leadership was assumed by Jomo (Burning Spear) Kenyatta, an imposing man instantly recognized everywhere he went by his black beard, huge red ring, and elephant-head stick.

When Kenyatta returned to Kenya from England in 1946, conditions were bad. Unemployment, overcrowding, and homelessness were epidemic in Nairobi. The Kikuyu area was overpopulated. Kenyatta built up a political party, the Kenya African Union (KAU), hoping to use it in securing amelioration of the Kikuyu's plight. At the core of the KAU was the "Forty Group," formed by a number of Kikuyu who had been initiated into the old KCA in 1940. Many of these men had served in the war and, afterwards, were still disposed to violence. From 1950, tension mounted rapidly and secret societies were formed by the Kikuyu. The most important of these was the Mau Mau movement, which perpetrated terrible atrocities against white settlers.

There was a section of the KAU which strongly opposed violence and made efforts to disassociate the KAU from the Mau Mau. Kenyatta himself declared the Mau Mau to be a bad thing at a public meeting in February 1951. But Mau Mau depredations continued and even grew in number. Europeans began to demand emergency powers to deal with the violence.

In October 1952, there were many attacks made on the European farms in Kenya. At about the same time that this was occurring one of the most prominent Kikuyuans was assassinated. On October 20, Great Britain declared a state of emergency. The following day Kenyatta, along with ninety-eight of his followers, was arrested. British troops were flown in and Kenya was caught up in the turmoil of civil war. By 1960, many had been killed, mostly among the Mau Mau.[20] Moreover, there were massive roundups of the Kikuyu, who were forcibly returned to already overcrowded areas.

---

[20] The Mau Mau lost 7800 people in the fighting, to 470 Africans, 2 Asians, and 38 Europeans killed among the security forces.

The civil war in Kenya caused the British to consider bringing to a close the era of their political power. In 1961, Jomo Kenyatta was released from prison, and began strenuous efforts to bring dissident African political factions together. Constitutional conferences, attended by Kenyatta, were held in London. It was hoped that a government could be devised which would be sufficiently powerful to form and maintain a new Kenyan state after independence was obtained. Elections arranged by these constitutional conferences were held and, in 1963, Jomo Kenyatta became Kenya's first prime minister; in 1964, he became President.

Immediately after the launching of an independent Kenya, Kenyatta entered into earnest discussions with the governments of Tanganyika and Uganda, hoping to establish an East African Federation. But national sovereignty seemed as difficult to surrender in the African situation as it was in postwar Europe. The hope of federation faded away.

The march to independence in Kenya was matched by parallel developments elsewhere in East Africa. During the decade of the 1950's, a constitutional revolution transformed Tanganyika from a country almost completely under British control to near independence. This process was instigated and directed by Julius Nyerere, president of the Tanganyika African Association and founder of the Tanganyika African National Union (TANU) in 1954. With the backing of TANU, Nyerere engineered smooth progress in the direction of independence, and, while still under British control, the Tanganyikans achieved a genuinely representative structure. In December 1961, Tanganyika became a sovereign state within the Commonwealth possessing a constitution that spelled out individual rights and the qualifications for citizenship. In 1964, the offshore former British territories of Zanzibar and Pemba merged with Tanganyika to form the new state of Tanzania, under President Nyerere.

In Uganda there did not develop the strong nationalist movement present in so many other African countries. Actually, traditionalist African leaders tended to hold back the movement toward independence more than did colonial administrators. It was the British who accorded greater influence to Africans in government. In spite of obstruction from traditionalist-minded African elements, the British administration pressed on with constitutional reforms. It was interference from traditionalists, anxious to preserve their own influence within the imperial system, that stiffened the determination of more nationalistic-minded politicians to lead the country to independence.

In 1960, pro-independence parties coalesced under the leadership of Milton Obote to form the Uganda People's Congress, which negotiated with the British. It was agreed that independence would be granted in July 1961. Although the Obote group worked vigorously with the British, independence could not be achieved at such an early date. Finally, on October 9, 1962, with Milton Obote as

Prime Minister, Uganda became an independent state within the Commonwealth. In 1966, Obote was chosen President.

Elsewhere in East Africa, out of the Italian Trust area of Somaliland and the protectorate of British Somaliland, there was developed a unified Somali state. In the Italian case, the United Nations set 1960 as the deadline for independence and ordered Italy to prepare the inhabitants of its trust for independent status. Italy, particularly since it was still regarded suspiciously in the postwar period because of its wartime activities in East Africa, worked hard in the 1950's to train sufficient administrators among the natives and create the machinery of government in Somaliland. In contrast, in British Somaliland, virtually nothing was done before 1958 to prepare the Protectorate for self-government. In 1960, the two territorial assemblies merged and the two states united. Aden Abdullah Osman, who had been Prime Minister of Italian Somaliland, became President of the new Somali Republic. He was succeeded in 1967 by Dr Abdirashid Ali Shermarke. An irredentist movement developed to absorb the 350,000 Somalis living in neighboring French Somaliland, Kenya, and Ethiopia.

During the same time span, little was changed in Ethiopia. The Government was particularly patriarchal and a basically feudalist structure was maintained. Since the Ethiopians already were independent, the drive for modernization could not link itself with the surge for independence as it had in so many other African countries. The Emperor retained the power given to him by the majority of his people who regarded him with a mystical reverence. However, a constitution of 1955 did move in the direction of political modernization.

The only important opposition to Emperor Haile Selassie appeared in December 1960, when the Imperial Guard revolted and placed the Crown Prince on the throne. The Emperor was, at this time, away in Brazil on a state visit. He returned immediately and led a loyal army and air force to dislodge the rebellious guard.

Once the revolt was over, the Emperor realized that his regime was so little open to change that many had become dissatisfied. He thus decided to bend with the winds of change and began appointing younger and more progressive ministers. He also took an initative in African politics, and Pan-African conferences were held in Addis Ababa with regularity. As 1970 arrived, however, he was still a virtually absolute ruler.

NORTH AFRICA AND THE MIDDLE EAST

A. Egypt

At the end of World War II, Egypt was moving steadily toward revolution. Britain had maintained a presence in Egypt primarily because of the Suez Canal. Since London's interest in Egypt had seemed to Egyptians essentially exploitive, many young Egyptian nationalists, including the young army officers who were to become so important after the end of the war, hoped that the Germans would be successful in driving the British from Cairo and, eventually, from all of Egypt. Consequently, when the war ended, many Egyptians felt a disappointment akin to that experienced by nationalists among the defeated powers.

Immediately after the war, attempts were made to secure revision of the Anglo-Egyptian Treaty of 1936, which would be more satisfactory to the Egyptians. The bitter nationalist temper of the public was revealed, however, when every effort made by the government to secure a compromise with the British was criticized violently. This criticism developed in spite of the fact that such compromises were aimed at lessening the British hold on Egyptian affairs. Apparently, nothing short of the exodus of all foreign forces would satisfy the average Egyptian.

By the end of 1948, Egypt was in turmoil. King Farouk I, who controlled both the Senate and the Chamber of Deputies in the exercise of his normal executive powers, decided to hold new elections. The Wafd-controlled Government had been dismissed in 1944, but the Wafd Party, which had been the spearhead of mass revolt against the British since the 1920's, won the election. Then, in a desperate attempt to gain the backing of a majority of the people, the Wafd turned guerrilla forces against British troops in the Suez zone and in 1951 denounced the agreement of 1936. Nationalist revolts now flared up throughout Egypt and merged with protests against an anachronistic social system. The king dismissed the Wafd Government, but he could no longer control the emotions of the masses. The mob turned against the upper strata of Egyptian society at the same time that it lashed out at foreign control.

The Egyptian revolution, as it developed, had two formidable obstacles to overcome. First, the winds of change, when they blew in Egypt, normally were stirred by a foreign occupying power. Therefore, Egyptians were not accustomed to looking to their own to bring about the alteration of the existing order. Secondly, the Moslem elements in the country were essentially conservative and intent on resisting change. Thus, there was in Egypt an identification of liberal democracy with the foreigner and conservatism with the Egyptian tradition. Consequently, there did not develop the dynamic, revolutionary-oriented bourgeoisie of the European experience. The only element capable of effecting radical change in the social order was the army.

In the Egyptian army there had developed a body of young officers, who were better educated than most other segments of Egyptian society. They now assumed a role normally played by bourgeois revolutionaries in the European past. Moreover, these officers held a strategic position in the Egyptian monarchial structure since the king depended upon their support to maintain himself in power.

After Cairo riots in January 1952, the Farouk regime appeared to be disintegrating rapidly. Urged to action by the prospect of a tottering government, Lieutenant Colonel Gamel Abdel Nasser (1918–1970), organized a Free Officers' Committee. In the early hours of July 23, 1952, the Committee acted as the Farouk regime seemed to be disintegrating. Tanks were moved to strategic locations in Cairo and the centers of civil administration were taken over. There was virtually no opposition to the army's seizure of power. Farouk was forced into exile, after abdicating in favor of his son. One of the most respected senior officers of the army, General Mohammed Naguib, was brought in to become Chairman of the Revolutionary Command Council, and Nasser served as Deputy Chairman. By September, Naguib had become Prime Minister and in June 1953, the monarchy was abolished. Egypt now became a republic in which Naguib was both President and Prime Minister. Nasser occupied both the offices of Deputy Prime Minister and Minister of the Interior.

The new regime revolutionized Egypt politically and socially. First, the estates of large landowners were divided among the landless. "Arab Socialism" was introduced, which meant, in part, that measures were initiated to increase industrialization and reduce the dependency of the economy on cotton. The major hope for the years to come was based on the building of the Aswan High Dam. It was envisaged that, when this project was completed, it would irrigate a million new acres of land. This concentration on one project as the primary salvation for the future, coupled with Anglo-American displeasure over events at the Suez Canal, allowed the Soviet Union to extend its influence in Egypt. After 1958, the U.S.S.R. lent the first two fifths of the capital needed for the dam and a great number of Soviet technicians to aid in the project.

Despite the high hopes of some, Egypt's revolution did not produce a genuine social democracy in the 1950's. National cohesiveness had to be cemented so that there could be economic reconstruction. To accomplish this it was necessary to maintain a high degree of state control, based on military power. Unions, universities, and other institutions which normally follow an independent course in more democratic states, were rigidly controlled in Egypt.

By 1954, Nasser had taken control from Naguib and destroyed the influence of the only other forces which might have challenged his power. The Communist Party was proscribed. The Moslem Brotherhood had hoped to control the country once the British left. Then Nasser obtained, subject to certain rights of reentry, British evacuation of the Canal Zone. After securing British withdrawal, however, Nasser indicated that he had no intention of establishing a Moslem-influenced government. Rather he was set upon a course designed to produce a secular state. When the Islamic organization objected to Nasser's new course, it was suppressed. In October 1954, members of the Brotherhood attempted to assassinate Nasser. The Government reacted by ruthlessly crushing the movement, hanging a number of its leaders.

In 1956, Nasser was elected President of Egypt, with virtually dictatorial power. In the same year, because London and Washington refused to supply funds for the Aswan Dam, he suddenly nationalized the Suez Canal. A joint British-French-Israeli invasion was halted when Washington and Moscow persuaded the UN to arrange a ceasefire and send an international army to supervise the withdrawal of the invaders.

The Suez affair made Nasser the anticolonialist hero of the African continent. Nasser's influence, however, was much greater in the Middle East than in Black Africa. From 1958 to 1961, he used that influence to secure the temporary formation of a United Arab Republic (UAR) with Syria. But in 1961, Syria, disillusioned with Nasser's attempts to establish greater Egyptian control over the UAR, withdrew and reasserted its independence; Egypt continued to be called the UAR. Later he tried to form another union with Syria and Iraq.

By the early 1960's, Nasser had accomplished many major changes only through the use of authoritarian methods, but the people still seemed to be in support of his regime. Much of the fervor observed in the public's support of Nasser's policies was created by a constant stirring through propaganda of the population's hatred for Israel. To maintain a threatening stance toward Israel, it became necessary to drain off valuable resources for military purposes. Nasser and his associates did nothing to halt this drain even as 1970 dawned. This was the price Nasser paid for continuing acceptance as the leader of the Arab world.

Then, in June 1967, Nasser led the Arab states into war with Israel and suffered a humiliating defeat. A festering stalemate followed and Nasser's prestige declined throughout the whole Arab world, including Egypt. At the beginning of December 1968, Egyptian students demonstrated violently against a lack of democracy— which had never bothered them as long as Nasser seemed successful. Hence, at the end of 1968, Nasser faced restless students and a young officers corps, which was clamoring for another strike against Israel. It was then observed by one diplomat that, "whenever Nasser feels threatened at home, he strikes out at the enemy." The recurrent necessity for such a political tactic in Egypt made life among Arabs and Israelis indeed uncertain. And by the spring of 1970, Nasser had become dependent on Moscow for technicians to set up missile bases and flyers to provide air cover against Israeli reprisal raid (See page 687.)

B.   The Arab States of the Middle East

To define the Middle East is not easy. For more than a century before World War I, it meant Persia, Afghanistan, India, and Burma. After 1920, Middle East sometimes was applied to those lands where the Arab tongue was in common use. On other occasions, the term was used more broadly to refer to all those areas where populations followed the Moslem faith. The Middle East, as discussed here, comprises the states of Saudi Arabia, Iraq, Iran, Syria, Lebanon, Jordan, and Israel.

Saudi Arabia, richly endowed with oil, had embarked on an independent political career on the morrow of World War I. After World War II, Saudi Arabia represented one of the last patriarchal societies to be found anywhere. All power was concentrated in one king who claimed to rule by the authority of God. In 1953, the second king of modern Saudi Arabia, Saud Ibn Abdul Aziz al Saud, promulgated a royal decree which represented the first serious attempt to give the country an organized form of government. Although the decree produced a system which clearly prescribed certain principles of legislative action, the king still possessed final authority in all executive and legislative matters.

After 1945, with the fullest exploitation of Saudi Arabia's oil resources, the country experienced material progress. Hospitals, schools, and farms were built, and in basic services, such as electricity, fresh-water supply, and sanitation, expansion was noted. Still, the social order in Saudia Arabia remained highly stratified. There existed only two social classes, the very rich and the very poor. Even though the country drew in tremendous profits from the vast reservoirs of oil that lay beneath her arid sands, this money usually ended in relatively few hands. There was only gradual modification in this pattern during the postwar era.

In foreign policy Saudi Arabia maintained "but a remote concern" for the solution of the Palestine question of 1947, and was in favor of "some form of partition." Under the new king, from 1953, the country made a serious bid for leadership in the Arab world and took a greater interest in Israeli affairs. Finally, however, the Saudi Arabian monarchy came to realize that leadership in the Arab world could not be wielded by so weak a country. After 1964, when Faisal Ibn Abdul Aziz al Saud became king, he held that Saudi Arabia's best interests could be served by maintaining a policy of neutralism, which would guarantee its independence and ensure peaceful enjoyment of the wealth derived from oil sales to Western states.

A major factor in the development of modern Iraq was the British Government's installation in 1921 of the Hashemite kings in Baghdad. After 1945, the Hashemite regime remained authoritarian. There was little regard for the desires of a new nationalist generation and basic disregard of public opinion. Consequently, in the decade of revolutionary nationalism that swept over the Arab world after its defeat in Palestine, in 1948, the ruling order in Iraq lost contact with the people. This kind of rule was ended by an army coup d'état on July 14, 1958, led by Abd al-Karim Qasim. Shortly after, the Republic of Iraq was proclaimed, with strong backing from the Soviet Union and the Communist bloc. By 1961, the system of government had solidified into a military hegemony based on centralized power and personal leadership. Qasim, however, soon alienated the nationalists by accepting help from the Soviet Union and the Communist bloc in both military and economic affairs. In 1963, he was overthrown and executed following an army-air force revolt. His successors during the next five years co-operated with the nationalists but the structure of government was much the same.

In foreign affairs, Iraq generally followed Cairo's lead until 1968. In July 1968, Iraqi soldiers displaced President Abd al-Rahman Muhammad Arif with Ahmed Hassan Bakr, who made no secret of his deep dislike for Egypt's President Nasser. It was generally believed that the coup represented a delayed reaction to Nasser's disastrous defeat at the hands of Israel in the Six-Days' War of June 1967. The Iraqi coup produced an even more autocratic dictatorship, which aroused Arab nationalism and kept it at feverish pitch. This was accomplished by publicly hanging spies, who were allegedly in the pay of Israel.

One of the most vexing problems facing each Iraqi government was the continuing strife and intermittent warfare with the Kurds, who lived in the north and demanded autonomy. A compromise agreement at last was reached in 1970, whereby some autonomy was extended.

In Iran, World War II brought an ordeal of foreign occupation, economic upset, and political disorder. Until 1946, when the evacuation of all foreign troops was finally effected, the Allied Command represented the real center of power in the country, and the Shah was virtually powerless. The most effective political force to appear in the postwar period was the National Front, which was not really a party in the usual sense, but a loose coalition of various political groups typified by extreme nationalism. Its leader was Dr. Mohammed Mossadegh, a landowning politician well known for his nationalistic tendencies.

For a time in the early 1950's, Mossadegh used the premier's office to demand and receive dictatorial powers. These he used to upset Western statesmen by tampering with foreign oil rights in Iran. Finaly, a severe economic crisis and the Western powers' continual demand for oil rights caused the Shah, Mohammed Reza Pahlavi, to dismiss Mossadegh. The forces of the status quo then gathered around the Shah and his army. From that time forward, the Shah himself was the most important figure in the Iranian Government.

The reformist-minded Shah introduced new agrarian schemes, submitted social programs to popular referendum, introduced compulsory education, established profit-sharing in industry, and gave the voting right to women in national elections. Much of this was repugnant to right-wing elements, who on at least one occasion tried to assassinate the Shah; but he persisted on his reform course.

In foreign policy, Iran was subjected to much Soviet pressure, and it was only through the influence of the UN that the U.S.S.R. evacuated its troops from Iran after the end of World War II. Soviet Iranian policy after that consisted of blandishments and threats rather than direct aggression. This caused Iran to break away from her historical tradition of nonalignment and commit herself to a pro-Western policy. Agreements were concluded with the United States in the early postwar period. Iran then entered the Baghdad Pact in 1955, and signed a bilateral mutual defense treaty with the United States in 1959. Through the 1960's and into the 1970's, Mohammed Riza continued a pro-Western policy but did try to improve relations with Moscow.

In Syria and Lebanon, the defeat of Vichy French forces by the British sounded the death knell of the French mandate in those states. For two more years the Free French under de Gaulle attempted to maintain French hegemony in the two countries. In 1943, however, elections were allowed to take place and nationalist victories transpired. In 1944, the French reluctantly transferred most of the governmental power to the new national regimes. In 1946, France evacuated Syria and Lebanon, thus ending twenty-five years of mandate government. Even then, it required some UN prodding to persuade the French to leave.

In 1949, partly in reaction to Arab defeat by the Israelis in 1948, an army coup d'état overthrew the old nationalists in Syria and began an era of army involvement in politics. The army leaders displayed a general incapacity to rule. There was also the problem of continuing intrusion into Syrian affairs by Moscow and Cairo, as happened throughout the Middle East after World War II. In Lebanon, too, the army remained overly enmeshed in political affairs, although it was not allowed direct political control.

On February 1, 1958, Egypt negotiated a shortlived union with Syria, which proved not to be particularly advantageous for the Syrians. On September 28, 1961, that arrangement was dissolved. At this point, Egypt tentatively formed a United Arab Republic (UAR) in collaboration with both Syria and Iraq. The proposed UAR was was to be the nucleus of a universal Arab community, but, typically, intense bickering broke out among Arab leaders over the character of the common institutions of government to be instituted. Despite the fact that the new Cairo plan came to naught, there was a mutual defense pact betwen Cairo and Damascus signed in 1966. Syria also became a base for Palestinian Arab guerrillas, who were bent on destroying Israel. This situation helped bring on the oft-mentioned Six-Days' War of 1967, described later in this chapter. Be it noted here, however, that the Israeli victory and the Syrian loss of territory frayed the already thin ties betwen Egypt and Syria and added to the already unstable political life of Syria.

From 1921 until 1948, Trans-Jordan was a small patriarchy stretching along the eastern bank of the Jordan river from the border of Syria to the Gulf of Aqaba. A few weeks before the termination of the British mandate in Palestine on March 15, 1948, a treaty was signed between Trans-Jordan and Great Britain. This document limited the British forces there to only two bases. Three weeks after an armistice agreement between Trans-Jordan and Israel was signed on April 26, 1949, King Abdullah of Trans-Jordan annexed Arab Palestine to Trans-Jordan and proclaimed the union as the new Hashemite Kingdom of Jordan.

This action was resented by the other Arabs, and, in 1951, Abdullah was shot by a Palestinian refugee, and his eldest son Talal became king. Talal, however, was very ill when he came to the throne and hence resigned in favor of his seventeen-year-old son Hussein Ibn Talal in 1953. In Jordan, as in almost all the Arab states, the regime depended upon the army for support and thus to some extent was dominated by it. King Hussein, after the rise of Nasser to Arab leadership, enjoyed the full support of the army and his subjects as long as he maintained support of Egypt. When Hussein moved out of the Egyptian camp in 1957, he was thus forced to appeal to the West for protection. This protection was promptly extended by the United States, and, by 1961, American aid to Jordan amounted to 40,000,000 dollars annually.

In 1967, pressured by Arab nationalist elements within Jordan, Hussein reversed his policy of separation from Egypt and flew to Cairo on May 30 to sign a military pact with Nasser. It was this pact that involved Jordan in the disastrous six-day war with Israel. Among the vanquished Arabs after the war, Hussein's perhaps was the most realistic voice, for he sought a settlement with Israel. During 1968, however, Hussein was unable to remain an effective voice for moderation in his own country. Some thousands of guerrillas trained in his domain and made periodic raids into Israel. Those incursions drew Israeli reprisals. Palestinian commandos training in Jordan constantly vowed to fight until Israel no longer existed. These commandos were so popular among the people that Hussein could not prohibit their existence and was forced by the guerrillas' popularity into the maintenance of a more belligerent stance against Israel than he otherwise might have assumed. (See page 687.)

C.   Israel

Following World War I, Britain was given the Mandate of Palestine, for centuries under Turkish control. The British had promised Zionists that in Palestine would be established a homeland for the scattered Jewry of the world. At the same time, the Arab population living there was assured that its rights would be protected. After a number of international meetings and conferences to discuss the question of Palestine, the independent Republic of Israel came into existence in 1948. This, unfortunately, could not take place without a mass displacement of Arabs, and thus was born a feeling of deep-seated hostility between Arab and Jew, which worsened over the years.

Between the wars, the Jewry of the world combined its impressive energy, brains, and talent to convert Palestine into a country that culturally and technically moved far ahead of the other states in the Middle East. After 1945, the British were forced to use military might to subdue chronic clashes between Arabs and Jews. Hence, in 1947, it was decided in London that Great Britain should be rid of the troublesome task of managing its Palestinian mandate, and the problem was given to the General Assembly of the UN. The Assembly shortly brought forth a recommendation that Palestine should be partitioned. The United States strongly supported the notion than an independent state of Israel should be created.[21]

The discussion and disagreements over a partition plan were so prolonged that London eventually declared her intent to lay down the mandate in mid-May 1948. This spurred a group of Israeli leaders in Tel Aviv to declare the independence of a new state of Israel at midnight on May 14–15, 1948, with no mention of specific boundaries.

Dr. Chaim Weizmann, the British scientist-Zionist who had persuaded London in 1917 to promise a Jewish homeland, became Provisional President, while David Ben Gurion, a Palestinian labor leader of Polish origin, was made Premier. Arabs from several states quickly took up arms to prevent the foundation of Israel, but the Israeli forces repelled the disunited Arabs and forced a truce.

In this manner was born the only country in the world which is characterized by "a race, a language and a religion, none of which nationally characterizes any other state."[22] Apparently one of the most heterogeneous states in the Middle East, it became one of the most united. Its Jewish population of 650,000 was increased during the decade following 1948 by over one million immigrants, which streamed into a new state smaller than Vermont.

In the immediate after-the-war period Israel had been a magnet for the hardy Jews of Europe who had been strong enough to live through the terrors of the Nazi death camps. As Israel became more prosperous, it increasingly attracted Jews from Asia and North Africa, and enjoyed a high birth rate. By 1970, the population of Israel exceeded 2,600,000, including more than 2,000,000 Jews or approximately one-sixth of world Jewry. The remainder were Moslem

[21] The strong support from Washington for the fledgling state of Israel created the lasting view in the Arab States that Israel could not have been born without the help of the United States.
[22] Charles Malik, "The Near East: The Search for Truth," *Foreign Affairs* (January, 1952), p. 244.

or Christian Arabs and Druses. The constitutional structure of the new state of Israel was based on the so-called Transition Law, which declared that:

the Constitution will be constructed chapter by chapter in such a way that every one of them will constitute a law by itself. The chapters will be brought before the Knesset as and when the [constitutional] Committee completes its work and will together be confirmed into the Constitution of the state.[23]

According to the Transition Law, Israel was established as a republic. She was given a weak president with a strong executive cabinet and parliament. A judiciary was instituted with nine judges appointed for life, and was separated from the legislative and executive branches. The fact that national elections were carried out regularly in accordance with provisions set down in the constitution brought into existence political parties. That Israel developed a dozen or more of such parties was due to the country's cultural heterogeneity, as well as a residue of factionalism from the old Zionist movement.

Thus, Israel began her life as a state, owning a government obviously based on Western democratic principles and, at first, clearly supported by the major Western countries. This new polity became much more politically stable than did its Arab neighbors. Because of Israel's early and obvious Western orientation, the Soviet Union quickly became antagonistic to the Republic. The U.S.S.R. tended to regard Israel as a potential outpost for the Western powers, threatening the Black and Caspian seas through the possible expansion of anti-Soviet influences in the Middle East.[24] Consequently, when Nasser or other Arab leaders sought arms or propaganda backing to use against Israel, they usually found a ready response in Moscow.

Despite a tendency toward political fragmentation caused by her strong cultural and linguistic differences, Israel was held together by firm government control and a workable parliamentary democracy. Much stability resulted from the fact that a vigorous leadership was provided from 1948 until 1963 by David Ben Gurion, who retained the premiership (with one brief interruption) until his retirement.

Stability in government, hard work, imagination and ingenuity, and an amazing national spirit and pride helped economic and cultural activity. The Israelis expended much labor in converting desert lands into productive farmlands. Through use of a combination of private and communal farming techniques, the limited economic potentialities of the area were exploited to the fullest. To add to this agricultural prosperity, much money poured into Israel from the West German Government, in payment for the depreda-

[23] *The Israel Yearbook, 1960,* (Jerusalem, 1960), p. 33.
[24] The Soviets also held a traditional ideological dislike of Zionism.

tions committed by the Nazi regime against European Jewry. There was also extensive investment by wealthy Zionists in other parts of the world, particularly the United States and Great Britain. All this helped produce an Israel much more affluent than its neighbors. Thus, to the traditional hatred held for the Republic of Israel by the Arabs, was added the element of envy.

D.   The Arab-Israeli Confrontation

There is a common tradition shared by Arabs and Jews that the two peoples sprang from Ishmael and Isaac, both sons of Abraham. According to the tradition, Ishmael, despised because his mother was an Egyptian slave, was forced to leave the land of his birth and take up exile in the wilderness. Ishmael was believed to be the founder of twelve tribes, from whom the present-day Arab nations supposedly have descended. Isaac, who remained at home, became the ancestor of the twelve tribes of the Jews, of which two eventually were lost. Hence, the rivalry of Jew and Arab is by tradition the intense rivalry of brothers both claiming the same territory as their home. Thus, when the British Mandate over Palestine ended on May 15, 1948, tradition added to the actual agony caused by the displacement of peoples. Fighting between Jew and Arab grew more intense after the creation of Israel in May 1948, and still was going on in 1970.

It was not until November 1948, that an armistice resolution offered by the United Nations was accepted by the warring parties, and there was another ten days of fighting in the Negev desert against Egypt in 1949. By 1950, the Israelis had defeated decisively all Arab attempts to expel them from Palestine. However, the armistice lines drawn were not conducive to the maintenance of security.[25]

To conpound the problem of the Arab-Israeli relations there was the plight of some 800,000 Arabs who had fled from Israel to adjoining states. In Jordan alone they came to form more than one-third of the population. These refugees lived a miserable existence, subsisting on aid supplied by the United Nations. As year after year went by with little relief in sight, several states offered schemes of resettlement. It was often pointed out that many Arab states were only thinly settled and that there was much room for the refugees in these underpopulated areas. Spokesmen for the displaced Palestinian Arabs, however, continued to demand that all refugees should be allowed to return to their ancestral home in what was now Israel.

With the Palestinian refugee problem augmenting the traditional Arab-Jewish antagonism, the Arab countries refused, in 1948, and

[25] At this point, the various nations of the world began, one after another, to recognize the state of Israel.

persisted thereafter, to recognize the state of Israel. Simultaneously, the Arab countries continued to assert that they were in a permanent state of war with the nation they refused to recognize.

In the early 1950's, when Nasser came to power in Egypt, a campaign of sabotage was initiated to drive the British out of the Canal Zone before 1968, when the Suez Canal was scheduled to revert to the government of Egypt. During the same period, Israel was harassed by constant commando raids from Egypt, Syria, and Jordan. When the British and French struck out at Egypt following Nasser's seizure of the Canal in 1956, the Israelis, primarily because of their weariness of Arab raids, were drawn into a series of collusive plans (particularly with France). They participated with the British in an attack upon Port Said and struck against Egyptian positions in the Sinai desert. A *blitzkrieg* attack brought them to within fifty miles of the Suez Canal and allowed them to reopen the Gulf of Aqaba, which had been closed to them. Through this campaign the Israelis achieved temporary security along their southern border, but eventually they withdrew from territories held in the Sinai as a result of UN negotiations.

After the Suez crisis had faded, the problem of terrorist raids across Israeli borders became even more troublesome. In Jordan and Syria particularly, *fedayeen* military units were formed and swift strikes into Israel were carried out. Between 1957 and 1962, Israel complained to the United Nations of some 422 raids and breaches of the 1956 truce by the Syrians alone. The raids caused the Israelis to mount major reprisal attacks into Jordan and Syria.

In October and November 1966, there was an intensification of Arab terrorist activities against Israel by the commando organization called al-Fatah. On November 4, 1966, Syria and Egypt concluded a defense agreement. Retaliatory strikes by Israel in reaction to Arab commando raids continually embarrased President Nasser. The Egyptian President already had been humiliated by the continued presence of a United Nations Emergency Force in Egypt, which had first come there as part of the settlement of the Suez crisis of 1956. Other Arab nations were asking with some scorn why there was so little commando activity against Israel from Egypt. Because of the UN presence, Nasser could not participate in anti-Israel activities to the extent that the Jordanians and Syrians did. Hence, Nasser's position of leadership in the Arab world was weakened and he needed a confrontation with Israel to revive his flagging prestige.

On May 15, 1967, large bodies of Egyptain troops were seen moving through Cairo on their way to the Suez Canal. Under pressure from Nasser's forces, which had advanced in the UN-occupied area, and fearful of a disruption of international peace, UN Secretary-General U Thant announced that the United Nations' troops were being withdrawn from the Canal area. On May 22, Nasser declared that the Straits of Tiran and the Gulf of Aqaba (Israel's out-

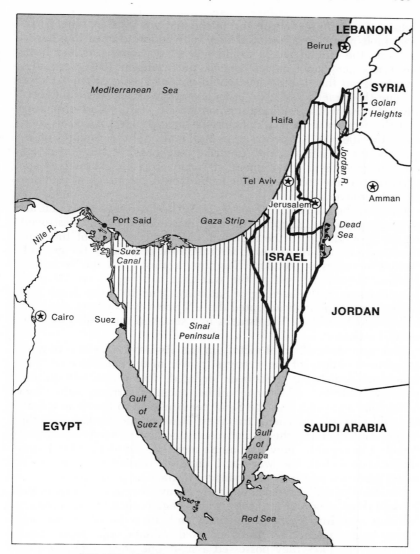

ISRAEL AFTER THE SIX-DAYS WAR OF 1967

let to the Red Sea) were closed to Israeli shipping. On the following day the Government of Israel replied that interference with Israeli shipping in the Straits of Tiran would be regarded as an act of war. Gradually, an international crisis took shape as the U.S.S.R. moved to support Nasser and the United States, along with Great Britain, favored Israel.

Through diplomatic channels, the Israeli Government became

certain of two things by the end of the first weekend in June. First, the Israelis were certain that, if they took action to open the Straits of Tiran, the United States would not act negatively, as had been the case when Israel moved against the Arabs in 1956. Secondly, they believed that the Soviets would not intervene. Another factor causing the Israelis to decide upon a surprise attack was the generally held and well-publicized opinion among Middle East observers that the Israelis were in a difficult strategic position, faced as they were by 100,000 Egyptians and 800 tanks in the Sinai. Consequently, the Israelis decided to strike quickly while the climate of opinion gave them the element of surprise, as the Arabs had apparently become convinced that Israel would not attack in the face of such unfavorable odds.

Early in the morning of June 5, 1967, the first wave of Israeli air strikes began. The Egyptian air force was almost totally destroyed on the ground. Up to the nightfall of the second day of the war, the Israelis destroyed 416 Arab aircraft, most of them on the ground. Similar successes marked Israeli fighting against Lebanon, Syria, and Jordan. The official end to the war that had begun on Monday, June 5, came on the evening of Saturday, June 10, when Israel and its last Arab opponents accepted the UN Security Council's repeated call to end hostilities. The Israelis had smashed the Arab forces on every battlefield.

The immediate effect of victory in the Six-Days' War was to raise Israel to the status of the strongest power in the Middle East. The power of Arab unity had been deflated. Israel was left on the morrow of battle holding much of her enemies' territory—the Gaza Strip, Shar el-Sheikh and the Sinai peninsula up to the Suez Canal; the Old City of Jerusalem; the West Bank of the Jordan; and the Syrian or Golan Heights which commanded the northern part of Israel. The republic now had much more readily defensible boundaries than before the war—and rapidly installed modern roads, water facilities, and even new villages in the occupied zone.

The Six-Days' War seemed basically to have solved very little in the Middle East. Soon after, the Arabs began anew their military buildup with Russian help. Guerrilla raids from Jordan, Syria, and Egypt began again. The Arabs amassed military implements until, in November 1968, they possessed a six-to-one advantage in supersonic jet planes over the Israelis. Such an advantage was far superior than the four-to-one superiority of Arab over Israeli aircraft that had existed at the time of the June 1967, war. The fact that another international crisis might easily boil up out of the Middle-Eastern cauldron at any time was indicated by the attitude of the thousands of Jordanian terrorists, training for attacks on Israel. They vowed to imbue their sons with a burning hatred of Israel, expecting eventually to carry on the fight until Palestine was "freed."

Perhaps nowhere else in the world were the paradoxical situations, which so troubled contemporary affairs, as evident as they were in the Middle East in 1970. In Israel, irrigation and modernized agriculture had broken the bondage of centuries. Nearby in Jordan the harvest was reaped by sickles—as it had been 2000 years earlier—and was thrashed by donkeys walking around a tether. And into the arid countryside of Jordan and its neighboring Arab states marched ten-year-old boys to be taught the hatred of Israel and the art of killing in the fashion of commandos.

And then, in the spring of 1970, at the time of the third anniversary of the Six-Days' War, Palestinian guerrillas based mainly in Jordan launched new attacks against Israel with the avowed object of taking from her the Arab lands she had annexed in 1967. This time the terrorists were led by Yasir Arafat and they again got support from Egypt, Syria, and Lebanon. The Israeli reaction was swift and effective, and once again war threatened. The situation was further complicated by the forceful but unsuccessful attempt of the guerrillas to involve the Jordanian King Hussein and his army in the fight.

Whereas Moscow backed the Arab cause and Washington was favorable to Israel, neither great power wanted a Middle East conflagration that might ignite a third world war. Accordingly, and with UN assistance, a ceasefire was arranged in August 1970. During the period of uneasy truce, Nasser died of a heart attack. This sudden demise at 52 of the influential Arab leader caused national hysteria in Egypt and shock throughout the world.

Amid charges and countercharges of truce violations by both Israelis and Arabs, the Egyptians elevated Vice President Anwar Sadat to the Presidency. He indicated a determination to carry on Nasser's policies at home and abroad. And the UN, 25 years old, debated the Arab-Israeli issue, with its New York headquarters under heavy guard.

Thus, in the early 1970's, in the Middle East as in nearly every part of the globe, humanity could still cry with Jeremiah, "Peace, peace; when there is no peace."

Bibliography

In view of the existence of numerous bibliographies, general and specific, on national and international events since the First World War, there seems little need to present here another extensive list. Hence this section will merely indicate some of the bibliographies, a few general reference works, and selected books relating to the individual chapters. Titles followed by an asterisk are available in paperback editions.

GENERAL AND SPECIAL BIBLIOGRAPHIES

Almond, N., and Lutz, R. H. *An Introduction to the Bibliography of the Paris Peace Conference,* 1935.

Aufricht, H. *Guide to League of Nations Publications. A Bibliographical Survey of the Work of the League, 1920–1927,* 1951.

Besterman, T. *A World Bibliography of Bibliographies,* 3 ed., 4 vols., 1955–1956.

Borton, H., Elisseeff, S., and Reischauer, E. O. *A Selected List of Books and Articles on Japan in English, French, and German,* 1941.

Chih–Yi, M. Chang. *A Bibliography of Books and Articles on Mongolia,* 1950.

Childs, J. B. *Government Document Bibliography in the United States and Elsewhere,* 3rd ed., 1942.

Conover, H. F. *Introduction to Europe: A Selective Guide to Background Reading,* 1950 Supplement for 1950–1955, 1955.

Embree, J. F., and Lasker, B. *A Selected Bibliography on Southeast Asia,* 1952.

Franz, G. ed. *Bücherkunde zur Weltgeschichte,* 1956.

Gooch, G. P. *Bibliography of European History, 1918–1939,* 1940.

Grierson, C. L. *Books on Soviet Russia, 1917–1942,* 1943.

Howe, G. F. and others, eds. *Guide to Historical Literature,* 1961.

Humphreys, R. A. *Latin America: A Selective Guide to Publications in English,* 1949.

Langer, W. L., and Armstrong, H. F. *Foreign Affairs Bibliography; A*

Selected and Annotated List of Books on International Relations, 1919–1932, 1933. See also Roberts and Woolbert below.

Langsam, W. C. *The World Since 1914,* 6 ed., 1948. This edition contains a list of *c.* 3000 titles on the period 1914–1947.

Launay, J. de. *The Two World Wars: A Selected Bibliography,* 1965.

McCune, S. *Bibliography of Western Language Materials on Korea,* 1950.

Morley, C. *Guide to Research in Russian History,* 1951.

Neumann, I. S. *A Bibliography of the European War Crimes Trials,* 1951.

Paklons, L. L. *European Bibliography,* 1964.

Ragatz, L. J. *A Bibliography for the Study of European History 1815 to 1939,* 1942. Also *Supplement,* 1943 and 1945.

Roberts, H. L. *Foreign Affairs Bibliography. A Selected and Annotated List of Books on International Relations 1942–1952,* 1955.

———. *Foreign Affairs Bibliography. A Selected and Annotated List of Books on International Relations 1952–1962,* 1965.

Savord, R., and Wasson, D. *World Affairs. A Foreign Service Reading List,* 1954.

Scott, F. D. *The Twentieth Century World: A Reading Guide,* 1954.

Strakhosky, L. I. *A Handbook of Slavic Studies,* 1949.

Sztachova, J. *Mid–Europe. A Selective Bibliography,* 1953.

The Europa Year Book, 1926 ———. 11 ed., 2 v., 1970.

Thomas, S. B., and Biggerstaff, K. *Recent Books on China: 1945–1951,* 1951.

United Nations. *Latin America 1935–1949, A Selected Bibliography,* 1952.

United States, Library of Congress. *French Colonies in Africa. A List of References,* 1942 (comp. by H. F. Conover).

United States, Library of Congress. *Introduction to Africa. A Selective Guide to Background Reading,* 1952 (comp. by H. F. Conover).

United States, Library of Congress. *Official Publications of Present-Day Germany,* 1942 (comp. by D. Neuburger).

United States, National Historical Publications Commission. *List of World War II Historical Studies Made by Civilian Agencies of the Federal Government,* 1951.

Walsh, W. B. *Russia under Tsars and Commissars. A Readers Guide,* 1946

Woolbert, R. G. *Foreign Affairs Bibliography. A Selected and Annotated List of Books on International Relations 1932–1945,* 1945.

REFERENCE WORKS, GENERAL AND DOCUMENTARY READINGS

Annual Register of World Events.

Aron, R. *The Century of Total War,* 1954.*

Banks, A. S., and Textor, R. B. *A Cross-Political Survey,* 1963.

Barraclough, G. *An Introduction to Contemporary History.* 1964.

Carr, E. H. *International Relations Between the Two Wars,* 1948.

Council on Foreign Relations. *Political Handbook of the World,* 1927 ———. Since 1970, called *Political Handbook and Atlas of the World.* Indispensable.

Craig, G. A., and Gilbert, F. eds. *The Diplomats, 1919–1939,* 1955.*

Duroselle, J. B. *Historie diplomatique de 1919 à nos jours,* 1962.

Einaudi, M., Domenach, J.-M., and Garcosi, A. *Communism in Western Europe,* 1951.

Fischer–Galati, S. *Twentieth Century Europe,* 1967. Documents.*

Fourastie, J. *La grande metamorphose du XX siècle,* 1961.

Freymond, J. *Western Europe Since the War; A Short Political History,* 1964.

Funk, A. L. *Europe in the Twentieth Century,* 1968. Documents.*

Gatzke, H. W. *The Present in Perspective–A Look At the World Since 1945,* 1965.*

Ginsburg, N. *Atlas of Economic Development,* 1961.

Hayter, W. *The Diplomacy of the Great Powers,* 1961.

Helmrich, E. C. *History at a Glance: Chronological Chart of European Civilization,* 1965.

Hudson, M. O. *International Legislation; a Collection of the Texts of Multipartite International Instruments of General Interest Beginning with the Covenant of the League of Nations,* 1931–

Kirk, D. *Europe's Population in the Interwar Years,* 1946.

Kulischer, E. M. *The Displacement of Population in Europe,* 1943.

Kull, I. S. and N. M. *A Short Chronology of American History,* 1952.

Langer, W. L. *An Encyclopedia of World History,* rev. ed., 1952.

Langsam, W. C. *Documents and Readings in the History of Europe since 1918,* rev. ed., 1951. Krauss Reprint, 1969.

———. *Historic Documents of World War II,* 1958.*

Martin, M. R., and Lovett, G. H. *Encyclopedia of Latin American History,* rev. ed., 1968.

Morris, R. B. *Encylopedia of American History,* 1953.

Peaslee, A. J. *Constitutions of Nations,* 3 v., 1950.

Rowse, A. L. *Appeasement: A Study in Political Decline, 1933–1939,* 1961.

Russett, B. M., and others, eds. *World Handbook of Political and Social Indicators,* 1964.

Seton–Watson, H. *From Lenin to Malenkov. The History of World Communism,* 1953.

Taylor, A. J. P. *From Sarajevo to Potsdam,* 1965.*

Thomson, D. *World History 1941–1961,* 1963.

Vogt, W. *Road to Survival,* 1948. Relation of man to his environment.

White, T. H. *Fire in the Ashes, Europe in Mid–Century,* 1953.*

Woytinsky, W. S. and E. S. *World Commerce and Governments,* 1955.

CHAPTER 1. THE PEACE OF PARIS, 1919–1920

Albrecht–Carrié, R. *Italy at the Paris Peace Conference,* 1938.

Almond, N., and Lutz, R. H. *The Treaty of St. Germain,* 1935. Documents.

Bailey, T. A. *The Great Betrayal,* 1945.*

———. *Woodrow Wilson and the Lost Peace,* 1944.*

Birdsall, P. *Versailles Twenty Years After,* 1941. Supports Wilson.

Bonsal, S. *Unfinished Business,* 1944.

Burnett, P. M. *Reparation at the Paris Peace Conference from the Standpoint of the American Delegation,* 2 v., 1940. Documents.

Grebler, L., and Winkler, W. *The Cost of the World War to Germany and to Austria–Hungary,* 1940.

Jessop, T. E. *The Treaty of Versailles—Was it Just?,* 1942.

Keynes, J. M. *The Economic Consequences of the Peace,* 1920. Prophetic.

Langsam, W. C. "Maladjustments of the Peace Settlement," in *The Annals of the American Academy of Political and Social Science*, September 1934.

Lederer, I. J. *Yugoslavia at the Paris Peace Conference*, 1963. Excellent.

Luckau, A. *The German Delegation at the Paris Peace Conference*, 1941.

Macartney, C. *Hungary and Her Successors*, 1947.

Mantoux, E. *The Carthaginian Peace or the Economic Consequences of Mr. Keynes*, 1952. The rejoinder to Keynes.

Miller, D. H. *My Diary at the Conference of Paris, with Documents*, 21 v., 1928. By U.S. legal adviser. Forty sets distributed to large libraries.

Nicolson, H. *Peacemaking, 1919*, 1933.*

Pink, G. P. *The Conference of Ambassadors (Paris 1920–1931)*, 1942.

Shotwell, J. T. *What Germany Forgot*, 1940. Holds that the war, not Versailles, was to blame for many German troubles.

Tillman, S. P. *Anglo–American Relations at the Paris Peace Conference*, 1961.

United States, Department of State. *Foreign Relations of the United States: Paris Peace Conference 1919*, 13 v., 1942–1947.

CHAPTER 2. THE LEAGUE OF NATIONS

Bentwich, N. *The Mandate System*, 1930. Emphasizes Class A Mandates.

Berdahl, C. A. *The Policy of the United States with Respect to a League of Nations*, 1932.

Cecil, Viscount (Lord Robert Cecil). *A Great Experiment: An Autobiography*, 1941.

Davis, K. W. *The Soviets at Geneva; the U.S.S.R. and the League of Nations, 1919–1933*, 1934.

Hudson, M. O. *The Permanent Court of International Justice*, 1934.

———. *The World Court 1921–1938*, 1938. Documents.

Knudson, J. I. *A History of the League of Nations*, 1938.

League of Nations. *Report on the Work of the League*, 1942.

Miller, D. H. *The Drafting of the Covenant*, 2v., 1928. By one of the draftsmen.

Russell, F. M. *The Saar, Battleground and Pawn*, 1951.

Walters, F. O. *A History of the League of Nations*, 2 v., 1952. The standard work.

Wambaugh, S. *Plebiscites since the World War*, 2 v., 1933. Documents.

———. *The Saar Plebiscite*, 1940. Authoritative.

Wilson, F. G. *Labor in the League System; A Study of the International Labor Organization in Relation to International Administration*, 1934.

Wright, Q. *Mandates under the League of Nations*, 1930. Exhaustive.

Zimmern, A. *The League of Nations and the Rule of Law, 1918–1935*, rev. ed., 1939.

CHAPTER 3. THE POSTWAR SEARCH FOR INTERNATIONAL EQUILIBRIUM

Alpert, P. *Twentieth Century Economic History of Europe*, 1951.

Angell, J. W. *The Program for the World Economic Conference; The Experts' Agenda and Other Documents*, 1933.

Carr, E. H. *International Relations Between the Two World Wars*, 1947.

Condliffe, J. B. *The Commerce of Nations*, 1950.

Crane, J. O. *The Little Entente*, 1931.
Dawes, C. G. *A Journal of Reparations*, 1939.
Galbraith, J. K. *The Great Crash, 1929*, 1955.
Hodson, H. V. *Slump and Recovery, 1929–1937*, 1938.
Langsam, W. C. "United States and British Press Opinion of the Proposed Austro–German Customs Union of 1931," in *Journal of Central European Affairs*, January 1943.
League of Nations. *World Production and Prices, 1925–1933*, 1934.
Miller, D. H. *The Peace Pact of Paris; A Study of the Briand–Kellogg Treaty*, 1928. Documents.
Moulton, H. G., and Pasvolsky, L. *War Debts and World Prosperity*, 1932. The standard work.
Rappard, W. E. The Quest for Peace since the World War, 1940.
Robbins, L. *The Great Depression*, 1934.
Shotwell, J. T. *War as an Instrument of National Policy and Its Renunciation in the Pact of Paris*, 1929. Complete.
Soule, G. *Prosperity Decade: From War to Depression: 1917–1929*, 1949.
Wheeler–Bennett, J. W. *The Pipe Dream of Peace; The Story of the Collapse of Disarmament*, 1935. Covers 1932–1935..
Wiskemann, E. *The Rome–Berlin Axis*, 1949.
Wolfers, A. *Britain and France between Two Wars: Conflicting Strategies of Peace since Versailles*, 1940.
Youngson, A. J. *The British Economy: 1920–1957*, 1960.

CHAPTER 4. GREAT BRITAIN AND IRELAND

Beaslai, P. *Michael Collins, Soldier and Statesman*, 1938.
Brand, C. F. *British Labour's Rise to Power*, 1941. Essays.
Bullock, A. *The Life and Times of Ernest Bevin*, v. 1, 1960.
Carr, E. H. *Great Britain: A Study of Foreign Policy from the Versailles Treaty to the Outbreak of the War*, 1939.
Eden, A. *Facing the Dictators*, 1962.
Gooch, R. K. *The Government of England*, 1937.
Graves, R., and Hodge, A. *The Long Weekend: A Social History of Great Britain 1918–1939* ,1940.*
Hamilton, M. A. J. *Ramsey MacDonald*, rev. ed., 1929.
Jones, T. A. *A Diary with Letters: 1931–1950*, 1954. Appeasement examined.
Laski, H. J. *Reflections on the Constitution: The House of Commons, The Cabinet, The Civil Service*, 1951, Three lectures.
Macmillan, H. *Winds of Change: 1914–1939*, 1966.
McDunphy, M. *The President of Ireland*, 1945.
Medlicott, W. N. *British Foreign Policy since Versailles*, 1940.
Mowat, C. L. *Britain Between the Wars, 1918–1940*, 1955. Valuable.
Nicolson, H. *Diary and Letters: 1930–1939*, 1966.
Rowse, A. L. *Appeasement: A Study in Political Decline: 1933–1939*, 1961.
Royal Institute of International Affairs. *Political and Strategic Interests of the United Kingdom*, 1939.
Ryan, D. *Uniqe Dictator: A Study of Eamon de Valera*, 1936.
Somervell, D. C. *British Politics Since 1900*, 1950.
Taylor, A. J. P. *English History: 1914–1945*, 1966.

Tucker, W. R. *The Attitude of the British Labour Party Towards European and Collective Security Problems, 1920–1939,* 1950.
Wilcox, W. B. *Star of Empire. A Study of Britain as a World Power, 1485–1945,* 1952.
Young, G. *Stanley Baldwin,* 1952.

CHAPTER 5. FRANCE.

Bainville, J. *The French Republic, 1870–1935,* 1936. Royalist view.
Brogan. D. W. *France under the Republic: The Development of Modern France, 1870–1939,* 1940.
Challener, R. D. *The French Theory of the Nation in Arms: 1866–1939,* 1955.
Clough, S. B. *France: A History of National Economics, 1789–1939,* 1939.
Colton, J. *Léon Blum: Humanist in Politics,* 1966.
Earle, E. M. ed. *The French Labour Movement,* 1954.
Franck, L. *French Price Control,* 1942. Blum to Pétain.
Gagnon, P. A. *France Since 1789,* 1964.
Howard, J. E. *Parliament and Foreign Policy in France,* 1948. Covers 1919–1939.
Joll, J. ed. *The Decline of the Third Republic,* 1959.
Knapton, E. J. *France since Versailles,* 1952.
Larmour, P. J. *The French Radical Party in the 1930's,* 1964.
Lorwin, W. R. *The French Labor Movement,* 1955.
Marcus, J. T. *French Socialism in the Crisis Years: 1933–1936,* 1958.
Michaud, C. A. *The French Right and Nazi Germany, 1933–1939; A Study of Public Opinion,* 1943.
Paul–Boncour, J. *Recollections of the Third Republic,* 1958.
Reynaud, P. *In the Thick of the Fight,* 1955. Memoirs.
Stokes, R. L. *Léon Blum: Poet and Premier,* 1937.
Thompson, D. *Democracy in France since 1870,* 1964.*
Weber, E. *Action Française: Royalism and Reaction in Twentieth Century France,* 1962.
Werth, A. *Which Way France?* 1937.
Wright, G. *France in Modern Times,* 1960.

CHAPTER 6. FASCIST ITALY

Albrecht–Carrié, R. *Italy from Napoleon to Mussolini,* 1950.*
Binchy, D. A. *Church and State in Fascist Italy,* 1941.
Chabod, F. *A History of Italian Fascism,* 1963.
Ciano's Hidden Diary, 1937–1938, 1953.
Ebenstein, W. *Fascist Italy,* 1939.
Fermi, L. *Mussolini,* 1961.*
Finer, H. *Mussolini's Italy,* 1935. Full treatment; hostile.
Germino, D. L. *The Italian Fascist Party in Power: A Study in Totalitarian Rule,* 1959.
Grahan, R. A., Jr. *Vatican Diplomacy,* 1959.
Halperin, S. W. *Mussolini and Italian Fascism,* 1964.
Jemolo, A. C. *Church and State in Italy 1850–1950,* 1960.
Kirkpatrick, I. *Mussolini: A Study in Power,* 1964. Valuable.
Macartney, M. H. H., and Cremona, P. *Italy's Foreign and Colonial Policy, 1914–1937,* 1938. Good.

Martelli, G. *Italy Against the World*, 1937. Good on Italo–Ethiopian conflict.
Meenan, J. *The Italian Corporative System*, 1945.
Monelli, P. *Mussolini: An Intimate Life*, 1953.
Royal Inst. of Int. Aff. *The Italian Colonial Empire*, 1940.
Salvemini, G. *Under the Axe of Fascism*, 1936. Anti–Fascist.
Schmidt, C. T. *The Corporate State in Action*, 1939.
Smith, D. M. *Italy*, 1959.
Sprigge, C. J. S. *The Development of Modern Italy*, 1943.
Swire, J. *King Zog's Albania*, 1937.
Villari, L. *Italian Foreign Policy Under Mussolini*, 1956.

CHAPTER 7. SPAIN

Alvarez del Vayo, J. *Freedom's Battle*, 1940. Loyalist foreign minister.
Blanshard, P. *Freedom and Catholic Power in Spain and Portugal*, 1962.
Bowers, C. G. *My Mission to Spain: Watching the Rehearsal for World War II*, 1954. Memoirs.
Brenan, G. *The Spanish Labyrinth*, 2 ed., 1950. Excellent.
Cattel, D. T. *Communism and the Spanish Civil War*, 1955.
———. *Soviet Diplomacy and the Spanish Civil War*, 1957.
Descola, J. *A History of Spain*, 1963.
Jackson, G. *The Spanish Republic and the Civil War: 1931–1939*, 1965.*
Kleine–Ahlbrandt, W. L. *The Policy of Simmering: A Study of British Policy During the Spanish Civil War, 1936–1939*, 1962.
Livermore, H. V. *A History of Portugal*, 1948.
———. *A History of Spain*, 1958.
Madariaga, S. de. *Spain: A Modern History*, 1958.
Mendizabel, A. *The Martyrdom of Spain*, 1938. Objective; 1923 to 1936.
Padelford, N. J. *International Law and Diplomacy in the Spanish Civil War*, 1939.
Spanish White Book. *The Italian Invasion of Spain. Official Documents and Papers Seized from Italian Units in Action at Guadalajara*, 1937.
Thomas, H. *The Spanish Civil War*, 1961. Excellent military and political history.*

CHAPTER 8. GERMANY

Allen, W. S. *The Nazi Seizure of Power: The Experience of A Single German Town, 1920–1935*, 1965. Excellent.*
Angress, W. T. *Stillborn Revolution: The Communist Bid for Power in Germany, 1921–1923*, 1963.
Baumont, M., Fried, J. H. E., and Vermeil, E. eds. *The Third Reich*, 1955. Essays.
Baynes, N. H. *The Speeches of Adolph Hitler, April, 1922 – August, 1939*, 2 v., 1943.
Brecht, A. *Federalism and Regionalism in Germany. The Division of Prussia*, 1945.
Bretton, H. L. *Stresemann and the Revision of the Versailles Treaty*, 1955.
Bruck, W. F. *Social and Economic History of Germany from William II to Hitler, 1888–1938: A Comparative Study*, 1938.

Bullock, A *Hitler. A Study in Tyranny, rev. ed. 1964. The best biography.*

Carsten, F. L. *The Reichswehr and Politics 1918–1933,* 1966.

Childs, H. R., tr. *The Nazi Primer. Official Handbook for Schooling the Youth,* 1938.

Clark, R. T. *The Fall of the German Republic: A Political Study,* 1935.

Comfort, R. A. *Revolutionary Hamburg: Labor Politics in the Early Weimar Republic,* 1966.

Craig, G. A. *The Politics of the Prussian Army: 1640–1945,* 1954.* Excellent.

Dodd, W. E., Jr., and M. *Ambassador Dodd's Diary, 1933–1938,* 1941.

Dorpalen, A. *Hindenburg and the Weimar Republic,* 1964.

Duncan-Jones, A. S. *The Struggle for Religious Freedom in Germany,* 1938.

Ebenstein, W. *The Nazi State,* 1943.

Epstein, K. *Matthias Erzberger and the Dilemma of German Democracy,* 1959.

Eyck, E. *History of the Weimar Republic,* 2 vols., 1963–1964.

Feder, G. *Hitler's Official Programme and Its Fundamental Ideas.* 1934. By author of Nazis' "25 Points."

Fraser, L. *Germany between Two Wars: A Study of Propaganda and War Guilt,* 1944.

Frey, A. *Cross and Swastika,* 1938. On Lutheran struggle.

Gatzke, H. *Stresemann and the Rearmament of Germany,* 1954.

Gay, P. *Weimar Culture: The Outsider As Insider,* 1968.

Goerlitz, W. *History of the German General Staff,* 1953.*

Gordon, H. J. *The Reichswehr and the German Republic, 1919–1926,* 1957.

Hale, O. J. *The Captive Press in the Third Reich,* 1964.

Halperin, S. W. *Germany Tried Democracy: A Political History of the Reich from 1918 to 1933,* 1946.*

Hartshorne, E. Y. *German Universities and National Socialism,* 1937.

Heiden, K. *A History of National Socialism,* 1934. Still valuable.

———. *Der Führer,* 1944. Excellent.

Helmreich, E. C. *Religious Education in German Schools,* 1959.

Heneman, H. J. *The Growth of Executive Power in Germany: A Study of the German Presidency,* 1934.

Hertzman, L. *DNVP: Right Wing Opposition in the Weimar Republic 1918–1923,* 1963.

Hilberg, R. *The Destruction of the European Jews,* 1961.

Hitler, A. *Mein Kampf,* in various English translations, 1939 and after.*

Holt, J. B. *German Agricultural Policy, 1918–1934,* 1936.

Hoover, C. B. *Germany Enters the Third Reich,* 1933. Economic background.

Hunt, R. N. *German Social Democracy, 1918–1933,* 1964.

Jetzinger, F. *Hitler's Youth,* 1958.

Kaufmann, W. *Monarchism in the Weimar Republic,* 1953.

Kessler, H. *Walter Rathenau, His Life and Work,* 1930.

Klein, B. H. *Germany's Economic Preparation for War,* 1959.

Kubizek, A. *The Young Hitler I Knew,* 1955.

Lerner, D. *The Nazi Elite,* 1951.

Lutz, R. H. *The German Revolution, 1918–1919,* 1922.

Marx, F. M. *Government in the Third Reich,* 2 ed., 1937.

Meinecke, F. *The German Catastrophe: Reflections and Recollections,* 1950.

Mendelssohn–Bartholdy, A. *The War and German Society. The Testament of a Liberal,* 1937.

Miller, D. *You Can't Do Business with Hitler,* 1941.

Mitchell, A. *Revolution in Bavaria, 1918–1919,* 1965. Excellent study.

Morrow, I. F. D. *The Peace Settlement in the German Polish Borderlands,* 1936.

Neumann, F. L. *Behemoth: The Structure and Practice of National Socialism,* 1942.*

Nicholls, A. J. *Weimar and the Rise of Hitler,* 1968.*

Pounds, N. J. G. *The Ruhr. A Study in Historical and Economic Geography,* 1952.

Rauschning, H. *The Revolution of Nihilism, Warning to the West,* 1939. Aims and methods of Nazism by former Nazi leader in Danzig.

Reich, N. *Labour Relations in Republican Germany: An Experiment in Industrial Democracy, 1918–1933,* 1938.

Rothfels, H. *The German Opposition to Hitler,* 1948.

Ryder, A. J. *The German Revolution of 1918,* 1967.

Schacht, H. *My First Seventy-six Years,* 1955.

Scheidemann, P. *The Making of a New Germany; The Memoirs of Philipp Scheidemann,* 2 v., 1929. Early years of the republic.

Schoenbaum, D. *Hitler's Social Revolution,* 1967. Valuable.*

Shirer, W. L. *Berlin Diary. The Journal of a Foreign Correspondent 1934–1941,* 1941.*

Speer, Albert. *Inside the Third Reich,* 1970. By important Nazi official.

Stammler, E. *Churchless Protestants,* 1964.

Stern, F. *The Politics of Cultural Despair. A Study in the Rise of German Ideology,* 1961.*

Stolper, G. *German Economy, 1870–1940,* 1940.

Strasser, O. *Hitler and I,* 1940.

Stresemann, G. *Essays and Speeches on Various Subjects,* 1930.

Taylor, T. *Sword and Swastika: Generals and Nazis in the Third Reich,* 1952.

Thyssen, F. *I Paid Hitler,* 1941. By German industrialist.

Turner, H. A. *Stresemann and the Politics of the Weimar Republic,* 1963.*

Waite, R. G. L. *Vanguard of Nazism: The Free Corps Movement in Postwar Germany: 1918–1923,* 1952. Excellent.*

Wheeler-Bennett, J. W. *The Nemesis of Power: The German Army in Politics: 1918–1945,* 1953. Excellent.*

————. *Wooden Titan, Hindenburg in Twenty Years of German History, 1914–1934,* 1936.

Zeman, Z. A. B. *Nazi Propaganda,* 1964.

CHAPTER 9. CENTRAL EUROPE

Almond, N., and Lutz, R. H. *The Treaty of St. Germain,* 1935. Documents.

Ball, M. M. *Post War German–Austrian Relations. The Anschluss Movement, 1918–1936,* 1937. Excellent.

Beneš, E. *My War Memoirs,* 1928.

Bethlen, S. *The Treaty of Trianon and European Peace; Four Lectures Delivered in London, November 1933,* 1934.

Bloss, E. *Labor Legislation in Czechoslovakia,* 1938. Scholarly.

Buell, R. L. *Poland: Key to Europe*, 1939. Excellent.

Bullock, M. *Austria, 1918–1938: A Study in Failure*, 1941.

Buschbeck, E. H. *Austria*, 1949.

Buttinger, J. *In the Twilight of Socialism. A History of the Revolutionary Socialists of Austria*, 1953.

Crankshaw, E. *The Fall of the House of Habsburg*, 1963.*

Diamant, A. *Austrian Catholics and the First Republic: Democracy, Capitalism, and the Social Order, 1918–1934*, 1960.

Feierabend, L. *Agricultural Cooperatives in Czecholovakia*, 1952.

Felinski, M. *The Ukrainians in Poland*, 1931. Polish view.

Fuchs, M. *Showdown in Vienna: The Death of Austria*, 1939. Good.

Gehl, J. *Austria, Germany, and the Anschluss, 1931–1938*, 1963.

Glaise–Horstenau, E. von. *The Collapse of the Austro–Hungarian Empire*, 1930. By director of Austrian War Archives.

Gulick, C. A. *Austria from Habsburg to Hitler*, 2 v., 1948. Favors socialists.

Hindus, M. G. *We Shall Live Again*, 1939. Fall of Czechoslovakia.

Hiscocks, C. R. *The Rebirth of Austria*, 1953.

Horthy, N. *Memoirs*, 1956.

Jászi, O. *The Dissolution of the Habsburg Monarchy*, 1929.

Kertesz, S. D. *Diplomacy in a Whirlpool: Hungary between Nazi Germany and Soviet Russia*, 1953.

Leonhardt, H. L. *The Nazi Conquest of Danzig*, 1942. Covers 1928–1938.

Macartney, C. A. *Hungary and Her Successors: The Treaty of Trianon and its Consequences*, 1937.

———. *Hungary: A Short History*, 1962.

———. *October Fifteenth: A Short History of Hungary 1929–1940*, 1961.

———. *The Social Revolution in Austria*, 1926.

Macdonald, M. *The Republic of Austria 1918–1934*, 1946.

Masaryk, T. G. *The Making of a State*, 1927.

Perman, D. *The Shaping of the Czechoslovak State: Diplomatic History of the Boundaries of Czechoslovakia, 1914–20*, 1962.

Rothschild, K. W. *Austria's Economic Development Between the Two World Wars*, 1947.

Schuschnigg, K. *My Austria*, 1938. Tragic Story.

Seton–Watson, H. *Eastern Europe Between the Wars*, 1962.

Seton–Watson, R. W. *Slovakia, Then and Now; A Political Survey*, 1931.

———. *Treaty Revision and the Hungarian Frontiers*, 1934.

Sharp, S. L. *Poland: White Eagle on a Red Field*, 1953.

Shepherd, G. *The Anschluss*, 1963.

Shotwell, J. T., and Laserson, M. M. *Poland and Russia 1919–1945*, 1945.

Sinos, D. *History of Hungary*, 1959.

Strong, D. F. *Austria, October 1918–March 1919: Transition from Empire to Republic*, 1939.

Taylor, J. *The Economic Development of Poland: 1919–1950*, 1952.

Wheeler–Bennet, J. W. *Munich: Prologue to Tragedy*, 1948.*

Wiskemann, E. *Czechs and Germans: A Study of the Struggle in the Historic Provinces of Bohemia and Moravia*, 1938. Excellent.

Zweig, F. *Poland between Two Wars*, 1944.

CHAPTER 10. THE SOVIET UNION

Armstrong, J. A. *The Politics of Totalitarianism: The Communist Party of the Soviet Union from 1934 to the Present*, 1961.

Barghoorn, F. C. *Soviet Russian Nationalism,* 1956.

Baykov, A. *The Development of the Soviet Economic System,* 1946.

Beloff, M. *The Foreign Policy of Soviet Russia, 1929–1941,* 2 v., 1947–1949.

Carr, E. H. *The Bolshevik Revolution, 1917–1923,* 3 v., 1950–1953.

———. *The Interregnum, 1923–24,* 1954.

Cattell, D. T. *Soviet Diplomacy and the Spanish Civil War,* 1957.

Chamberlin, W. H. *The Russian Revolution, 1917–1921,* 2 v., 1935.

Curtiss, J. S. *The Russian Church and the Soviet State,* 1953.

Dallin, D. J. *The Real Soviet Russia,* 1947.

Daniels, R. V. *The Conscience of the Revolution: Communist Opposition in Russia,* 1960.

Degras, J. *Soviet Documents on Foreign Policy, 1917–1941,* 3 v., 1951–1953.

———. *The Communist International, 1919–1943: Documents,* 2 v., 1956–1960.

Deutscher, I. *Stalin,* 1949.*

———. *The Prophet Armed. Trotsky, 1879–1921,* 1954.*

———. *The Prophet Outcast: Trotsky, 1929–1940,* 1963.*

———. *The Prophet Unarmed: Trotsky, 1921–1929,* 1959.*

Fainsod, M. *Smolensk Under Soviet Rule,* 1958. Excellent.*

Fischer, L. *Men and Politics,* 1941.

———. *The Fundamentals of Marxism–Leninism,* rev. ed., 1962.

———. *The Life of Lenin,* 1964.*

———. *The Soviets in World Affairs,* 2 v., 1930. Soviet sources.

———. *The Soviets in World Affairs: A History of the Relations Between the Soviet Union and the Rest of the World,* 2 v., 1951.

Florinsky, M. T. *Russia. A History and an Interpretation,* 2 v., 1953. Scholarly and thorough; to 1917.

———. *World Revolution and the U.S.S.R.,* 1933.

Gilksman, J. *Tell the West,* 1948. Soviet labor camps.

Harcave, S. *Russia. A History,* 4th ed., 1959.

Hilger, G., and Meyer, A. G. *The Incompatible Allies. A Memoir–History of German–Soviet Relations 1918–1941,* 1953.

Hodgman, D. R. *Soviet Industrial Production 1928–1951,* 1954.

Howe, I. ed. *The Basic Writings of Trotsky,* 1963.

Kennan, G. F. *Soviet Foreign Policy, 1917–1941,* 1960.

Kohn, H. *Nationalism in the Soviet Union,* 1933.

Kolarz, W. *Russia and Her Colonies,* 1952. Non-Russians in the U.S.S.R.

Leites, N. *A Study of Bolshevism,* 1953.

Lenin, V. I. *Selected Works,* 12 v., 1935–1936.

Liberman, S. *Building Lenin's Russia,* 1944.

Lorimer, F. *Population of the Soviet Union: History and Prospects,* 1946.

Marcuse, H. *Soviet Marxism: A Critical Analysis,* 1958.

Maynard, J. *Russia in Flux,* 1948.*

Meyer, A. G. *Leninism,* 1957.

Moore, B., Jr. *Soviet Politics: The Dilemma of Power,* 1950.

———. *Terror and Progress in the U.S.S.R.: Some Sources of Change and Stability in the Soviet Dictatorship,* 1954.*

Possony, S. T. *Lenin: The Compulsive Revolutionary,* 1964

Robinson, G. T. *Rural Russia under the Old Regime,* rev. ed., 1949. Excellent.

Schapiro, L. B. *The Communist Party of the Soviet Union,* 1960.*

———. *The Origin of Communist Autocracy: Political Opposition in the Soviet State, First Phase, 1917–1922,* 1965.

Schwarz, S. M. *Labor in the Soviet Union,* 1952.

Scott, J. *Behind the Urals,* 1940.

Seton–Watson, H. *From Lenin to Malenkov: The History of World Communism,* 1953.

Shub, D. *Lenin: A Biography,* 1948.*

Sorokin, P. A. *Leaves from a Russian Diary,* 1950.

Stalin, J. *Leninism,* 2 v., 1933.

Timasheff, N. S. *The Great Retreat: The Growth and Decline of Communism In Russia,* 1946.

Towster, J. *Political Life in the U.S.S.R., 1917–1947,* 1948.

Trotsky, L. *My Life,* 1930.*

———. *The History of the Russian Revolution,* 3 v., 1932.

Von Laue, T. H. *Why Lenin? Why Stalin? A Reappraisal of the Russian Revolution, 1900–1934,* 1964. Excellent.*

Wheeler–Bennett, J. W. *Forgotten Peace: Brest–Litovsk, March 1918,* 1938. The standard work on the subject.

CHAPTER 11. SOUTHEASTERN EUROPE

Abbott, G. F. *Greece and the Allies, 1914–1922,* 1922. Critical of Venizelos.

Alastos, D. *Venizelos: Patriot, Statesman, Revolutionary,* 1942.

Baker, E. *Macedonia. Its Place in Balkan Power Politics,* 1950.

Beard, C. A., and Radin, G. *The Balkan Pivot: Yugoslavia,* 1929. Politics.

Black, C. E. *The Establishment of Constitutional Government in Bulgaria,* 1944.

Clark, C. U. *Bessarabia; Russia and Roumania on the Black Sea,* 1927.

Evans, S. G. *A Short History of Bulgaria,* 1960.

Forster, E. S. *A Short History of Modern Greece, 1821–1940,* 1941.

Geshkoff, T. I. *Balkan Union,* 1940.

Gibbons, H. A. *Venizelos,* 1923.

Graham, S. *Alexander of Yugoslavia, Strong Man of the Balkans,* 1938.

Hoptner, J. B. *Yugoslavia in Crisis, 1934–1941,* 1962.

Kerner, R. J., and Howard, H. N. *The Balkan Conferences and the Balkan Entente, 1930–1935,* 1936. Documents, bibliography.

Kerner, R. J. ed. *Yugoslavia,* 1949.

Logio, G. C. *Bulgaria Past and Present,* 1936. Well balanced.

Macartney, C. A. *Refugees; the Work of the League,* 1931. Greco–Bulgarian.

Machray, R. *The Struggle for the Danube, and the Little Entente, 1929–1938,* 1938.

Mitrany, D. *The Land and the Peasant in Roumania; the War and Reform, 1917–1921,* 1930. Analytical.

Mittleman, E. N. *Nationality Problem in Yugoslavia: A Survey of Developments, 1921–1953,* 1954.

Moodie, A. S. *The Italo-Yugoslav Boundary,* 1945.

Pasvolsky, L. *Bulgaria's Economic Position,* 1930.

———. *Economic Nationalism of the Danubian States,* 1928.

Pavel, P. *Why Rumania Failed,* 1944. Covers 1921–1940.

Roberts, H. L. *Rumania: Political Problems of an Agrarian State,* 1951.

Roucek, J. S. *Contemporary Roumania and Her Problems,* 1932.

Royal Institute of Int. Aff. *The Balkan States I: Economic,* 1936.
Seton–Watson, R. W. *A History of Rumania from Trajan to Trianon,* 1934.
Stavrianos, L. S. *Balkan Federation: A History of the Movement toward Balkan Unity,* 1942.
Trouton, R. L. *Peasant Renaissance in Yugoslavia, 1900–1950,* 1950.
Wolff, R. L. *The Balkans in Our Time,* 1956. Very good.

CHAPTER 12. TURKEY FOR THE TURKS

Allen, H. E. *The Turkish Transformation,* 1935. Sociological.
Berkes, N. *The Development of Secularism in Turkey,* 1964.
Edib, H. *Conflict of East and West in Turkey,* 1935.
———. *Turkey Faces West,* 1930. By Turkish feminist.
Ekrem, S. *Turkey Old and New,* 1947.
Froembgen, H. *Kemal Atatürk,* 1937.
Heyd, U. *The Foundation of Turkish Nationalism,* 1950.
Howard, H. N. *The Partition of Turkey: A Diplomatic History, 1913–1923,* 1931.
Kinross, B. *Ataturk: A Biography of Mustafa Kemal,* 1964.
Mikusch, D. von. *Mustapha Kemal; Between Europe and Asia,* 1931.
Price, M. P. *A History of Turkey,* 1956.
Robinson, R. D. *The First Turkish Republic,* 1963.
Shotwell, J. T., and Deák, F. *Turkey at the Straits,* 1940.
Ward, B. *Turkey,* 1942. Good; brief.
Webster, D. E. *The Turkey of Atatürk,* 1939. Factual.

CHAPTER 13. THE AROUSING OF ASIA AND AFRICA

Abbas, M. *The Sudan Question: The Dispute Over the Anglo–Egyptian Condominium, 1884–1951,* 1952.
Allen, G. C. *Japanese Industry: Its Recent Development and Present Condition,* 1940.
Andrews, C. F., and Mookerje, G. *The Rise and Growth of the Congress in India,* 1939.
Bandurant, J. V. *Conquest of Violence: The Gandhian Philosophy of Conflict,* rev. ed., 1965.*
Beasley, W. G. *The Modern History of Japan,* 1963.
Bentwich, N. *Fulfilment in the Promised Land, 1917–1937,* 1938.
Berkov, R. *Strong Man of China: The Story of Chiang Kai–shek,* 1938.
Borton, H. *Japan's Modern Century,* 1955. Excellent.
Brandt, C. *Stalin's Failure in China, 1924–1927,* 1958.*
Buss, C. A. *Asia in the Modern World,* 1964.
Castle, W. T. F. *Syrian Pagent,* 1948.
Chen, S., and Payne, R. *Sun Yat–sen, a Portrait,* 1946.
Christian, J. L. *Modern Burma,* 1942.
Cleland, W. *The Population Problem in Egypt,* 1936.
Clubb, O. E. *Twentieth Century China,* 1964.*
Crouchley, A. E. *The Economic Development of Modern Egypt,* 1938.
Dean, V. M. *The Nature of the Non-Western World,* 1957.
Du Bois, W. E. B. *Black Folk—Then and Now,* 1939. By black educator.
Dulles, F. R. *Forty Years of American–Japanese Relations,* 1937.
Easton, S. C. *The Twilight of European Colonialism: A Political Analysis,* 1960. Africa.

Edwardes, M. *Asia in the European Age, 1498–1955,* 1961.

Ennis, T. *Eastern Asia,* 1948.

Fabunmi, L. A. *The Sudan in Anglo–Egyptian Relations, 1800–1956,* 1960.

Fage, J. D. *An Introduction to the History of West Africa,* 1962.

Fischer, L. *The Life of Mohatma Gandhi,* 1951.

Fortes, M., and Evans–Pritchard, E. E. *African Political Systems,* 1940. Native institutions.

Friedman, I. S. *British Relations with China, 1931–1939,* 1940.

Gandhi, M. K. *The Story of My Experiments with Truth,* 2 v., 1927–1929.

————. *Untouchability,* 1944.

————. *Women and Social Injustice,* 1945.

Grant, C. P. *The Syrian Desert,* 1937.

Griffiths, P. *Modern India,* 1957.

Griswold, A. W. *The Far Eastern Policy of the United States,* 1938.

Haas, W. S. *Iran,* 1946.

Haddad, G. M. *Fifty Years of Modern Syria and Lebanon,* 1950.

Hailey, Lord. *An African Survey. A Study of Problems Arising in Africa South of the Sahara,* 1938. Encyclopedic.

Hallberg, C. W. *The Suez Canal,* 1931.

Hitti, P. K. *History of Syria,* 1951.

————. *History of the Arabs,* 1937.

Issawi, C. *Egypt: An Economic and Social Analysis,* 1947.

Jansen, M. B. *The Japanese and Sun Yat-sen,* 1954.

Kirk, G. E. *A Short History of the Middle East,* 1948. Readable.

Kohn, H. *A History of Nationalism in the East,* 1929.

————. *Nationalism and Imperialism in the Hither East,* 1932.

Latourette, K. S. *A Short History of the Far East,* 1946.

————. *The Chinese, Their History and Culture,* 2 v., 4th ed., 1964.

————. *The History of Japan,* rev. ed., 1957.

Levy R., Lacam G., Roth A. *French Interests and Policies in the Far East,* 1941.

Liu, C. *A Military History of Modern China, 1924–1949,* 1956.

Lockwood, W. W. *The Economic Development of Japan: Growth and Structural Change, 1868–1938,* 1954.

Longrigg, S. H. *Syria and Lebanon under French Mandate,* 1958.

MacNair, H. F. *The Real Conflict between China and Japan: An Analysis of Opposing Ideologies,* 1938.

Maxon, Y. C. *Control of Japanese Foreign Policy: A Study of Civil–Military Rivalry, 1930–1945,* 1957.

Mehrotra, S. R. *India and the Commonwealth, 1885–1929,* 1964.

Nehru, J. *Toward Freedom: An Autobiography,* 1941.

Ogata, S. N. *Defiance in Manchuria: The Making of Japanese Foreign Policy, 1931–1932,* 1964.

Oliver, R., and Fage, J. D. *A Short History of Africa,* 1962.*

Pollard, R. *China's Foreign Relations, 1917–1931,* 1933.

Quigley, H. S. *Far Eastern War 1937–1941,* 1942. Excellent.

Rawlinson, H. G. *India: A Short Cultural History,* 1938.

Reischauer, E. O., and Fairbank, J. K. *A History of East Asian Civilization,* 2 v., 1962–1965.

Romein, J. *The Asian Century: A History of Modern Nationalism in Asia,* 1962.

Rotberg, R. T. *A Political History of Tropical Africa,* 1965.

Rowe, D. N. *Modern China: A Brief History*, 1959.
Royal Institute of Int. Aff. *Great Britain and Egypt, 1914–1951*, 1952.
———. *Great Britain and Palestine, 1915–1945*, 1946.
Schumpeter, E. B., and others. *The Industrialization of Japan and Manchoukuo, 1930–1940*, 1940.
Sitaramagya, P. *History of the Indian National Congress*, 2 v., 1946–1947.
Smith, T. C. *The Agrarian Origins of Modern Japan*, 1966.*
Starry, R. *The Double Patriots: A Study of Japanese Nationalism*, 1957.
———. *A History of Modern Japan*, 1960.
Stimson, H. L. *The Far Eastern Crisis*, 1936. By U.S. Sec. of State.
Sun Yat–sen. *San Min Chu I; The Three Principles of the People*, 1927.
Tang, S. *Russian and Soviet Policy in Manchuria and Outer Mongolia 1911–1931*, 1959.
Townsend, M. E. *European Colonial Expansion since 1871*, 1941.
Vinacke, H. M. *A History of the Far East in Modern Times*, 6th ed., 1959.
Ward, W. E. F. *A History of the Gold Coast*, 1949.
Weizmann, C. *Trial and Error*, 1944. Memoirs of a Zionist leader.
Willoughby, W. W. *The Sino–Japanese Controversy and the League of Nations*, 1935.
Wills, A. J. *An Introduction to the History of Central Africa*, 1964.
Wiser, W., and Wiser, C. *Behind Mud Walls, 1930–1960*, 1963. On India.*
Yamasaki, K., and Ogawa, G. *The Effect of the World War Upon the Commerce and Industry of Japan*, 1929.
Young, A. N. *China and the Helping Hand, 1937–1945*, 1963.

CHAPTER 14. LATIN AMERICA

Braderman, E. M. *A Study of Political Parties and Politics in Mexico since 1890*, 1938.
Calogeras, J. P. *A History of Brazil*, 1939. Old but still authoritative.
Carnegie End. for Int. Peace. *The International Conferences of American States, 1933–1940*, 1941.
Cline, H. F. *The United States and Mexico*, rev. ed., 1963.
Davis, H. E. *History of Latin America*, 1968.
Dulles, F. R. *America's Rise to World Power, 1898–1945*, 1955.
Fenwick, C. G. *The Inter–American Regional System*, 1949.
Galdames, L. *A History of Chile*, 1942.
Herring, H. *Good Neighbors*, 1941.
Ireland, G. *Boundaries, Possessions, and Conflicts in South America*, 1938.
James, P. E. *Latin America*, 1942.
Levene, R. *A History of Argentina*, 1937.
Lieuwen, E. *Generals vs. Presidents: Neo–Militarism in Latin America*, 1964.
Loewenstein, K. *Brazil uder Vargas*, 1942. Sympathetic.
Mecham, J. L. *Church and State in Latin America; A History of Politico-Ecclesiastical Relations*, 1934.
Perkins, D. *Hands Off! A History of the Monroe Doctrine*, 1941.
Tannenbaum, F. *Peace by Revolution: Mexico After 1910*, 1968.*
———. *Ten Keys to Latin America*, 1960.
———, *Whither Latin America?*, 1934. Economic and social problems.
White, J. W. *Argentina: The Life Story of a Nation*, 1942.

CHAPTER 15. THE UNITED STATES

Adamic, L. *Dynamite; The Story of Class Violence in America,* rev. ed., 1934.
———. *From Many Lands,* 1940. Immigration.
Adams, S. H. *Incredible Era: The Life and Times of Warren Gamaliel Harding,* 1939.*
Bailey, T. A. *A Diplomatic History of the American People,* 4th ed., 1950.
Beard, C. A. and M. *America in Mid-Passage,* 1939. The Depression Years.
Chambers, C. A. *Seedtime of Reform: American Social Service and Social Action, 1918–1933,* 1963.
Cochran, T. C., and Miller W. *The Age of Enterprise,* 1942. Industry.
Dulles, F. R. *America in the Pacific; A Century of Expansion,* 1932.
Freidel, F. *Franklin D. Roosevelt: The Apprenticeship,* 1952.
———. *Franklin D. Roosevelt: The Ordeal,* 1952.
———. *Franklin D. Roosevelt: The Triumph,* 1956.
Griswold, A. W. *The Far Eastern Policy of the United States,* 1939.
Handlin, O. *Al Smith and his America,* 1958.*
Hawley, E. W. *The New Deal and the Problem of Monopoly, 1933–1939,* 1966.
Hicks, J. D. *The Republican Ascendancy, 1921–1933,* 1960.*
———. *Agrarian Discontent in the Middle West, 1900–1931,* 1951.
Hoover, H. *Memoirs,* 3 v., 1951–1952.
Hull, C. *Memoirs,* 2 v., 1948.
Ickes, H. L. *The Secret Diary of Harold L. Ickes. The First 1000 Days, 1933–1936,* 1953.
Leopold, R. W. *The Growth of American Foreign Policy,* 1962.
Leuchtenberg, W. E. *The Perils of Prosperity, 1914–1932,* 1958.*
Madison, C. A. *American Labor Leaders,* 1950.
Noggle, B. *Teapot Dome: Oil and Politics in the 1920's,* 1962.
Pratt, J. *Cordell Hull, 1933–1944,* 1964.
Pringle, H. F. *Alfred E. Smith,* 1927.
Rauch, B. *The History of the New Deal,* 1944.*
Rice, A. S. *The Ku Klux Klan in American Politics,* 1962.
Romasco, A. U. *The Poverty of Abundance: Hoover, the Nation, the Depression,* 1965.
Roosevelt, F. D. *Public Papers and Addresses,* 9 v., 1938–1950.
Schlesinger, A. M. Jr. *The Age of Roosevelt: The Crisis of the Old Order, 1919–1933,* 1957.
———. *The Coming of the New Deal,* 1958.
———. *The Politics of Upheaval,* 1960. Covers 1934–36.
Schuman, F. L. *American Policy Toward Russia Since 1917,* 1928.
Sherwood, R. E. *Roosevelt and Hopkins,* 1948.
Sinclair, A. *The Available Man: The Life Behind the Masks of Warren Gamaliel Harding,* 1965.
Soule, G. *Prosperity Decade: From War to Depression, 1917–1929,* 1947.
Tugwell, R. G. *The Democratic Roosevelt,* 1957.
Warren, H. G. *Herbert Hoover and the Great Depression,* 1959.*
Wecter, D. *The Age of the Great Depression, 1924–1941,* 1948.
Witte, E. F. *Development of the Social Security Act,* 1962.

CHAPTERS 16–19. THE SECOND WORLD WAR, 1939–1945.

Anders, W. *An Army in Exile: The Story of the Second Polish Corps,* 1949.
————, *Hitler's Defeat in Russia,* 1953.
Aron, R. *The Vichy Regime,* 1958.
Badoglio, P. *Italy in the Second World War,* 1948.
Bailey, T. A. *America Faces Russia: Russian–American Relations from Early Times to Our Day,* 1950.
Beloff, M. *The Foreign Policy of Soviet Russia,* 2 v., 1947–1949.
Butow, R. J. C. *Japan's Decision to Surrender,* 1954.
Carr, E. H. *German–Soviet Relations Between the Two World Wars, 1919–1939,* 1951.
Cave, F. A. *et al. The Origins and Consequences of World War II,* 1948.
Churchill, W. S. *The Second World War,* 6 v., 1948–1953. Fascinating.
————. *While England Slept: A Survey of World Affairs, 1932–1938,* 1938. Speeches.
————. *Blood, Sweat, and Tears,* 1941. Wartime speeches.
Conquest, R. *The Soviet Deportation of Nationalities,* 1960.
Dallin, A. *German Rule in Russia,* 1957.
Dallin, D. J. *Soviet Russia's Foreign Policy, 1939–1942,* 1942.
Debicki, R. *Foreign Policy of Poland, 1919–1939,* 1962.
Drummond, D. F. *The Passing of American Neutrality,* 1956.
Dulles, A. W. *Germany's Underground,* 1947. Authoritative.
Eisenhower, D. D. *Crusade in Europe,* 1948.*
Falls, C. B. *The Second World War,* 1950.
Feis, H. *The Road to Pearl Harbor,* 1962.*
Fleming, P. *Invasion: 1940,* 1957.
Fuller, J. F. C. *The Second World War,* 1949. By a British general.
Gantenbein, J. W. ed. *Documentary Background of World War II, 1931–1941,* 1949.
Goerlitz, W. *Paulus and Stalingrad,* 1963.
Gouré, L. *Siege of Leningrad,* 1962.
Greece. *The Greek White Book,* 1942.
Greenfield, K. R. *American Strategy in World War II: A Reconsideration,* 1963.
Guderian, H. *Panzer Leader,* 1952.
Hinsley, F. H. *Hitler's Strategy,* 1951.
Ismay, H. L. *Memoirs,* 1960. Memoirs of Churchill's chief of staff.
Jacobson, M. *The Diplomacy of the Winter War,* 1961. Russo-Finnish War.
Keith, A. B. *The Causes of the War,* 1940.
Kingston–McCoughry, E. J. *Defense: Policy and Strategy,* 1960.
Langer, W. L. *Our Vichy Gamble,* 1947. Documented.*
Langer, W. L., and Gleason, S. E. *The Challenge of Isolation, 1937–1940,* 1952.
————. *The Undeclared War, 1940–1941,* 1953.
Langsam, W. C. *In Quest of Empire: The Problem of Colonies,* 1939.
Lee, A. *The German Air Force,* 1946.
Lee, D. E. *Ten Years: The World on the Way to War, 1930–1940,* 1942.
Liddell Hart, B. H. *The Rommel Papers,* 1953.
————. *Strategy: The Indirect Approach,* 1954.
Lundin, C. L. *Finland in the Second World War,* 1957.

Manstein, E. von. *Lost Victories,* 1958. Memoirs of a German Field Marshal.

Matloff, M., and Enell, E. M. *Strategic Planning for Coalition Warfare,* 2 v., 1953–1959.

Montgomery, B. L. *El Alamein to the River Sangro,* 1949. By a British field marshal.

———. *Memoirs,* 1958.

———. *Normandy to the Baltic,* 1948.

Moorhead, A. *Montgomery: A Biography,* 1946.

Morrison, S. E. *The Two Ocean Wars,* 1963.

Motter, T. H. Vail. *The Persian Corridor and Aid to Russia,* 1952.

Namier, L. B. *Diplomatic Prelude, 1938–1939,* 1948.

———. *Europe in Decay: A Study in Disintegration,* 1950.

O'Neill, H. C. *A Short History of the Second World War,* 1950.

Possony, S. T. *Strategic Air Power,* 1949.

Pratt, F. *Fleet Against Japan,* 1946.

Robertson, E. M. *Hitler's Pre-War Policy and Military Plans,* 1963.

Rossi, A. *The Russo–German Alliance, August 1939 to June 1941,* 1950.

Ryan, C. *The Longest Day: June 6, 1944,* 1959. A popular history of the Normandy landing.

Salvemini, G. *Prelude to World War II,* 1954.

Schroeder, P. W. *The Axis Alliance and Japanese–American Relations,* 1958.

Schröter, H. *Stalingrad,* 1958.

Smith, J. E. *The Defense of Berlin,* 1963.

Snell, J. L. *Illusion and Necessity: The Diplomacy of Global War, 1939–1945,* 1963.

Snyder, L. L. *The War: A Concise History, 1939–1945,* 1960.

Soloviev, M. *My Nine Lives in the Red Army,* 1956.

Speidel, H. *Invasion 1944,* 1949. By a German general.

Taylor, R. L. *Winston Churchill,* 1952.

Taylor, T. *Sword and Swastika: Generals and Nazis in the Third Reich,* 1952.

———. *The March of Conquest,* 1958. To the collapse of France.

The Ciano Diaries 1939–1943, 1946.

The Goebbels Diaries 1942–1943, 1948.

The War Reports of General of the Army George C. Marshall, General of the Army H. H. Arnold, and Fleet Admiral Ernest J. King, 1947.

Trevor–Roper, H. R. *The Last Days of Hitler,* 1947.*

United States, Department of State. *Foreign Relations of the United States. Japan 1931–1941,* 2 v., 1943.

United States, Department of State. *Foreign Relations of the United States. The Soviet Union, 1933–1939,* 1952.

United States, Department of State. *Nazi–Soviet Relations, 1939–1941,* 1948.

United States, Department of State. *Peace and War, United States Foreign Policy, 1931–1941,* 1943.

Vaughan–Thomas, W. *Anzio,* 1961.

Warmbrunn, W. *The Dutch under German Occupation,* 1963.

Werth, A. *Russia at War,* 1964.*

———. *The Twilight of France,* 1942.

Wiskemann, E. *Prologue to War,* 1940. Informative on Nazi "infiltration."

———. *The Rome-Berlin Axis,* 1949.
Young, D. *Rommel,* 1951.

CHAPTER 20. "WHEN THERE IS NO PEACE"

Alperovitz, G. *Atomic Diplomacy: Hiroshima and Potsdam,* 1965.
Bailey, S. *The United Nations,* 1963.
Boyd, A. *The United Nations: Piety, "Myth" and Truth,* rev. ed., 1964.*
Byrnes, J. F. *Speaking Frankly,* 1947. U.S. Sec. of State, 1945–1947.
Cohen, B. V. *The United Nations and How it Works,* 1962.
Dallin, A. *The Soviet Union at the UN,* 1962.
Feis, H. *Between War and Peace: The Potsdam Conference,* 1960.*
Glueck, S. *The Nuremberg Trial and Aggressive War,* 1946.
Jäksch, W. *Europe's Road to Potsdam,* 1963.
Kennan, G. F. *American Diplomacy 1900–1950,* 1951. Emphasis on
    Soviet relations.*
Leiss, A. C., and Dennett, R. eds. *European Peace Treaties after World
    War II,* 1954.
Nazi Conspiracy and Aggression, 8 vols., 1946. Nuremburg Trial record.
Neumann, W. L. *Making the Peace 1941–1945. The Diplomacy of the
    Wartime Conferences,* 1950.
Nicholas, H. G. *The United Nations as a Political Institution,* 1959.
Royal Institute of Int. Aff. *Documents on International Affairs 1947–1967,*
    1952–1970.
Snell, J. L. ed. *The Meaning of Yalta,* 1956.*
Stettinius, E. R. Jr. *Roosevelt and the Russians, The Yalta Conference,*
    1949.
United States, Department of State. *Making the Peace Treaties, 1941–
    1947,* 1947.
———. *Participation of the United States in International Conferences,
    July 1, 1945—June 30, 1946,* 1947.
Van Alstyne, R. W. *American Crisis Diplomacy. The Quest for Collective
    Security 1918–1952,* 1952.
Woetzel, R. K. *The Nuremberg Trials in International Law,* 1962.

CHAPTERS 21–22. THE COLD WAR, 1945–1970

Armstrong, J. P. *Southeast Asia and American Policy,* 1959.
Bailey, T. A. *America Faces Russia: Russian–American Relations from
    Early Times to Our Day,* 1950.
Barghoorn, F. C. *Soviet Foreign Propaganda,* 1964.
Beloff, M. *Soviet Policy in the Far East, 1944–1951,* 1953.
Blackett, P. M. S. *Atomic Weapons and East–West Relations,* 1956.
Boorman, H. L., and others. *The Moscow–Peking Axis,* 1957.
Boyd, R. G. *Communist China's Foreign Policy,* 1962. Background of
    Sino–Soviet split.
Brandt, W. *The Ordeal of Coexistence,* 1963.
Buchan, A. *NATO in the 1960's,* 1963.
Burnham, J. *The Struggle for the World,* 1947.
Chatham House Study Group. *Atlantic Alliance: NATO's Role in the
    Free World,* 1952.

Cole, S. D. H. *World in Transition: A Guide to the Shifting Political and Economic Forces of Our Time,* 1949.

Cottrell, A. J., and Dougherty, J. E. *The Politics of the Atlantic Alliance,* 1964. An objective study.

Davison, W. P. *The Berlin Blockade: A Study in Cold War Politics,* 1958.

Dean, V. M. *The United States and Russia,* 1947.

Deutscher, I. *The Great Contest: Russia and the West,* 1960.

Dubois, J. *Fidel Castro,* 1959. Journalistic but useful.

Dulles, A. W. *The Craft of Intelligence,* 1962. Soviet and U.S. intelligence methods.

Dulles, J. F. *War or Peace,* 1950. By U.S. Secretary of State.

Eichelberger, C. M. *U.N.: the First Fifteen Years,* 1960.

Fischer, L. *Russia, America, and the World,* 1961.

Fleming, D. F. *The Cold War and its Origins: 1917–1960,* 1961.

Gaitskell, H. T. *The Challenge of Coexistence,* 1957.

Gardner, B. *The Wasted Hour: The Tragedy of 1945,* 1963.

Halle, L. J. *The Cold War As History,* 1967. Excellent.

Henkin, L. *Arms Control,* 1961.

Herz, M. F. *Beginnings of the Cold War,* 1966.

Hsieh, A. L. *Communist China's Strategy in the Nuclear Age,* 1962.

Hudson, G. F. ed. *The Sino–Soviet Dispute,* 1961.

Ingram, K. *History of the Cold War,* 1955.

Ismay, H. L. *NATO, the First Five Years,* 1954. By first Secretary-General of NATO.

Jackson, W. A. D. *The Russo–Chinese Borderlands,* 1962.

Kennan, G. F. *On Dealing with the Communist World,* 1964.

——. *Russia and the West under Lenin and Stalin,* 1961.

——. *Russia, the Atom and the West,* 1958.

Luard, E. *The Cold War: A Re-appraisal,* 1964.*

Lukacs, J. *A History of the Cold War,* 1961.*

Mander, J. *Berlin, Hostage for the West,* 1962. Excellent.

Marcus, J. T. *Neutralism and Nationalism in France,* 1958.

Morray, J. P. *From Yalta to Disarmament: Cold War Debate,* 1961.

Patcher, H. M. *Collision Course,* 1963. The Cuban Missile Crisis.

Pinder, J. *Europe Against De Gaulle,* 1963.

Price, H. B. *The Marshall Plan and Its Meaning,* 1955. Valuable.

Rees, D. *Korea; the Limited War,* 1964.

Roberts, H. L. *Russia and America: Dangers and Prospects,* 1956.

Robertson, T. *Crisis: the Inside Story of the Suez Conspiracy,* 1965.

Salvadori, M. *NATO,* 1957.

Schuman, F. L. *The Cold War: Retrospect and Prospect,* 1967.

Seton-Watson, H. *Neither War Nor Peace,* 1960.

Shulman, M. D. *Stalin's Foreign Policy Reappraised,* 1963.

Smith, J. E. *The Defense of Berlin,* 1963. Covers 1945 into 1962.

Smith, H. K. *The State of Europe,* 1949.

Tompkins, P. *American–Russian Relations in the Far East,* 1949.

Vatcher, W. H. *Panmunjom; The Story of the Korean Military Armistice Negotiations,* 1958.

Williams, W. A. *American–Russian Relations, 1781–1947,* 1952.

——. *The Tragedy of American Diplomacy,* 1959.

Wright, M. *Disarm and Verify,* 1964.

Zagoria, D. S. *The Sino–Soviet Conflict, 1956–1961,* 1962*

CHAPTER 23. EVENTS IN THE AMERICAS IN THE POST–WORLD WAR II PERIOD

Alba, V. *Politics and the Labor Movement in Latin America,* 1968.
Aguilar, L. E. ed. *Marxism in Latin America,* 1968.
Albertson, D. *Eisenhower as President,* 1963.
Alexander, R. J. *Today's Latin America,* 1962.
Bennett, L. *Before the Mayflower: A History of the Negro in America, 1619–1964,* rev. ed., 1966.*
Berle, A. A. *Latin America—Diplomacy and Reality,* 1962.
Berman, R. *America in the Sixties: An Intellectual History,* 1968.
Christman, H. M. *The Public Papers of Chief Justice Earl Warren,* 1966.
Cumberland, C. C. *Mexico, The Struggle for Modernity,* 1968.*
Daniels, J. *The Man of Independence,* 1951 on H. S. Truman.
Dickey, J. S. ed. *The United States and Canada,* 1964.
Dreier, J. C. *The Organization of American States and the Hemisphere Crisis,* 1962.
Eisenhower, D. D. *The White House Years: Mandate for Change,* 1963.
———. *The White House Years: Waging Peace, 1956–1961,* 1965.
Fall, B. B. *The Two Viet-Nams,* 1965.
Franklin, J. H. *From Slavery to Freedom: A History of American Negroes,* 1956.
Freeman, R. E. ed. *Postwar Economic Trends in the United States,* 1960.
Goldman, E. F. *The Crucial Decade and After, 1945–1960,* 1961.
———. *The Tragedy of Lyndon Johnson,* 1969.
Goodman, J. F. *While You Were Gone: A Report on Wartime Life in the United States,* 1946.
Rippy, J. F. *Latin America, A Modern History,* rev. ed., 1968.
Schlesinger, A. M. Jr. *A Thousand Days,* 1965. The Kennedy administration.
Sorenson, T. C. *Kennedy,* 1965. By Kennedy aide.
Tannenbaum, F. *Ten Keys to Latin America,* 1960.*
Truman, H. S. *Memoirs,* 2 v., 1955–1956.
Wagley, C. *An Introduction to Brazil,* 1963.*
White, T. *The Making of the President,* 1960, 1961.
———. *The Making of the President,* 1964, 1965.
———. *The Making of the President,* 1968, 1969.

CHAPTER 24. THE SOVIET UNION, THE SATELLITE BLOC, AND THEIR NEIGHBORS

Armstrong, H. F. *Tito and Goliath,* 1951. The rift with Moscow.
Barghoorn, F. C. *Soviet Russian Nationalism,* 1956.
Bass, R. H., and Marbury, E. eds. *The Soviet–Yugoslav Controversy,* 1959. Documents.
Belov, F. *The History of a Soviet Collective Farm,* 1955.
Berliner, J. S. *Factory and Management in the U.S.S.R.,* 1957.
Betts, R. R. ed. *Central and Southeast Europe,* 1951.
Blodniek, A. *The Undefeated Nation,* 1960. Latvia under Soviet rule.
Brown, J. F. *The New Eastern Europe The Khrushchev Era and After,* 1966.
Brzezinski, Z. K. *The Soviet Bloc,* 1961. Valuable.
Conquest, R. *Power and Policy in the U.S.S.R.,* 1961.*

Counts, G. S., and Lodge, N. P. *The Challenge of Soviet Education,* 1957.

Craciunas, S. *The Lost Footsteps,* 1961. On Romania.

Crankshaw, E. *Khrushchev: A Career,* 1966.*

————. *Khrushchev's Russia,* 1959.

Cressey, G. B. *How Strong is Russia?,* 1954.

Deutscher, I. *Stalin,* 1949.*

Djilas, M. *Conversations With Stalin,* 1962.

————. *The New Class,* 1957. Communist Bureaucracy.

Dziewanowski, M. K. *The Communist Party of Poland,* 1959.

Fainsod, M. *How Russia is Ruled,* 1953.

Fischer–Galati, S. A. ed. *Eastern Europe in the Sixties,* 1963.

————. *Romania,* 1957.

Fisher, R. T. *Pattern for Soviet Youth,* 1959.

Freidin, S. *The Forgotten People,* 1962. On the satellite states.

Gibney, F. *The Frozen Revolution,* 1959. On Poland.

Hazard, J. N. *Law and Social Change in the U.S.S.R.,* 1953.

Hiscocks, R. *Poland,* 1963.

Hoffman, G. W., and Neal, F. W. *Yugoslavia and the New Communism,* 1962.

Hoptner, J. B. *Yugoslavia in Crisis,* 1962.

Jasny, N. *The Socialized Agriculture of the U.S.S.R.,* 1949.

Karpat, K. H. *Turkey's Politics,* 1959.

Kellen, K. *Khrushchev,* 1961.

Kertesz, S. D. ed. *East Central Europe and the World,* 1962. After Stalin's death.

Kolkowicz, R. *The Soviet Military and the Communist Party,* 1967.

Kostiuk, H. *Stalinist Rule in the Ukraine,* 1960.

Lane, A. B. *I Saw Poland Betrayed,* 1948.

Lasky, M. J. ed. *The Hungarian Revolution,* 1957.

Leonhard, W. *The Kremlin Since Stalin,* 1962.

Lewis, B. *The Emergence of Modern Turkey,* 1961.

Maclean, F. *The Heretic,* 1957. A biography of Tito.

Mazour, A. G. *Finland between East and West,* 1956.

Michal, J. M. *Central Planning in Czechoslovakia,* 1960.

Mikolajczyk, S. *The Rape of Poland,* 1948.

Modelski, G. A. *The Communist International System,* 1961.

Montias, J. M. *Central Planning in Poland,* 1962.

Mosely, P. *The Soviet Union Since Khrushchev,* 1966.

Munkman, C. A. *American Aid to Greece,* 1958.

Nagy, I. *On Communism,* 1957.

Neal, F. W. *Titoism in Action,* 1958.

Noel–Baker, F. E. *Land and People of Greece,* 1960.

Nove, A. *The Soviet Economy,* 1962.

Palmer, A. W. *Yugoslavia,* 1964.

Pietromarchi, L. *The Soviet World,* 1965.

Reshetar, J. S. *A Concise History of the Communist Party of the Soviet Union,* 1960.

Ripka, H. *Eastern Europe in the Post–War World,* 1961.

Rostow, W. A. et. al. *The Dynamics of Soviet Society,* 1954.

Salisbury, H. E. *To Moscow—And Beyond,* 1960.

Schapiro, L. B. *The Communist Party of the Soviet Union,* 1960.

Schmidt, D. A. *Anatomy of a Satellite,* 1952. Czechoslovakia.

Schwartz, H. *The Red Phoenix*, 1961.
Seton–Watson, H. *From Lenin to Khrushchev*, rev. ed., 1960.
———. *The East European Revolution*, 1950.*
Shaffer, H. G. ed. *The Soviet Economy*, 1963.*
Simmons, E. J. ed. *Continuity and Change in Russian and Soviet Thought*, 1955.
Skendi, S. ed. *Albania*, 1957.
Slonim, M. *Soviet Russian Literature: Writers and Problems*, 1964.*
Spulber, N. *The Economics of Eastern Europe*, 1957.
Starr, R. F. *Poland, 1944–1962*, 1963.
Stroyen, W. B. *Communist Russia and the Russian Orthodox Church, 1943–1962*, 1967.
Sweet–Escott, B. *Greece, 1939–1953*, 1954.
Syrop, K. *Spring in October*, 1958. 1956 uprising in Poland.
Taborsky, E. *Communism in Czechoslovakia 1948–1960*, 1961.
Tucker, R. C. *The Soviet Political Mind: Studies in Stalinism and Post–Stalin Change*, 1963.*
Ulam, A. B. *After Stalin*, 1963.
———. *Tito and the Cominform*, 1952.
———. *The Unfinished Revolution*, 1960.
Váli, F. A. *Rift and Revolt in Hungary*, 1961.
Zinner, P. E. *Revolution in Hungary*, 1962.

CHAPTER 25. THE TWO GERMANIES AND OTHER STATES OF WESTERN EUROPE

Andersson, I. A. *History of Sweden*, 1955.
Arango, E. R. *Leopold III and the Belgian Royal Question*, 1963.
Bader, W. B. *Austria Between East and West, 1945–1955*, 1966.
Balfour, M., and Mair, J. *Four Power Control in Germany and Austria*, 1956.
Bölling, K. *The Republic in Suspense*, 1963. West German political history.
Bonjour, E., and others. *A Short History of Switzerland*, 1952.
Bourneuf, A. *Norway: The Planned Revival*, 1958.
Brandt, W. *My Road to Berlin*, 1960.
Brenan, G. *The Face of Spain*, 1950.
Clay, L. D. *Decision in Germany*, 1950. By U.S. Commander in Germany.
Coles, S. F. A. *Franco of Spain*, 1955.
Davidson, E. *The Death and Life of Germany*, 1959. Excellement treatment of U.S. occupation.
Edinger, L. J. *Kurt Schumacher: A Study in Personality and Political Behaviour*, 1965.
Erhard, L. *Germany's Comeback in the World Market*, 1954.
Figueiredo, A. de *Portugal and its Empire: The Truth*, 1961.
Franks, H. G. *Holland as an Industrial Country*, 1957.
Freund, G. *Germany Between Two Worlds*, 1961.
Friedrich, C. J. *The Soviet Zone of Germany*, 1956.
Friis, H. K. ed. *Scandinavia Between East and West*, 1950.
Garnier, C. *Salazar*, 1954.
Gillen, J. F. J. *State and Local Governments in West Germany, 1945–1953*, 1953.
Gimbel, J. A. *German Community Under American Occupation*, 1961.

Golay, J. F. *The Founding of the Federal Republic of Germany*, 1958.
Gottlieb, M. *The German Peace Settlement and the Berlin Crisis*, 1960.
Grosser, A. *The Colossus Again*, 1955. On West Germany.
Gruber, K. *Between Liberation and Liberty: Austria in the Post–War World*, 1955.
Heidenheimer, A. J. *Adenauer and the CDU*, 1960.
Hills, G. *Franco: The Man and his Nation*, 1967.
Hiscocks, R. *Democracy in Western Germany*, 1957.
———. *The Adenauer Era*, 1967. Excellent.*
Huber, H. *How Switzerland is Governed*, 1947.
Hughes, C. *The Federal Constitution of Switzerland: Transition and Commentary*, 1954.
Kohn, H. *Nationalism and Liberty: The Swiss Example*, 1956.
Lauring, P. A. *A History of Denmark*, 1960.
Lindgren, R. E. *Norway–Sweden: Union, Disunion, and Scandinavian Integration*, 1959.
Mander, J. *Berlin: Hostage for the West*, 1962.
McInnis, E. *The Shaping of Postwar Germany*, 1960.
McVittie, W. W. *Economic and Commercial Conditions in Portugal*, 1955.
Merkl, P. H. *Germany: Yesterday and Tomorrow*, 1965.
———. *The Origin of the West German Republic*, 1963.*
Michener, J. A. *Iberia, Spanish Travels and Reflections*, 1968.
Nettle, J. P. *The Eastern Zone and Soviet Policy on Germany, 1945–50*, 1951.
Outze, B. ed. *Denmark During the German Occupation*, 1946.
Plischke, E. *Contemporary Government of Germany*, 1961.*
———. *History of the Allied High Commission for Germany: Its Establishment, Structure and Procedures*, 1953.
———. *The West German Federal Government*, 1952.
Pollock, J. K. *German Democracy and Work*, 1955.
Pritchett, V. S. *The Spanish Temper*, 1954.
Prittie, T. *Germany Divided*, 1960.
Rothschild, K. W. *Austrian Economy Since 1945*, 1951.
Ruhm von Oppen, B. *Documents on Germany under Occupation, 1945–1954*, 1955.
Schuman, A. *Codetermination: Labor's Middle Way in Germany*, 1957.
Siegfried, A. *Switzerland*, 1950.
Slusser, R. M. *Soviet Economic Policy in Postwar Germany*, 1953.
Stahl, W. ed. *The Politics of Post–War Germany*, 1963.
Stanislawski, D. *The Individuality of Portugal*, 1959.
———. ed. *The Memoirs of General Delgado*, 1964. By Portuguese political exile.
Statistisches Jahrbuch für die Bundesrepublik Deutschland, 1952 ff.
Stearman, W. L. *The Soviet Union and the Occupation of Austria: An Analysis of Soviet Policy in Austria, 1945–1955*, 1961.
Stolper, G. *German Realities*, 1948.
Stolper, W. F. *The Structure of the East German Economy*, 1960.
U.S. Department of State. *East Germany Under Soviet Control*, 1952.
Wallich, H. C. *Mainsprings of the German Revival*, 1955.
———. *The Financial System of Portugal*, 1951.
Weymar, P. *Adenauer: His Authorized Biography*, 1957.
Whitaker, A. P. *Spain and the Defense of the West*, 1962.

Willis, F. R. *France, Germany and the New Europe, 1945–1963*, 1965.*
————. *The French in Germany*, 1962.
Zink, H. *The U.S. in Germany*, 1957.

CHAPTER 26. BRITAIN, FRANCE, AND ITALY IN THE POSTWAR YEARS

Ambler, J. S. *The French Army in Politics, 1945–1962*, 1966.
Attlee, C. R. *As it happened*, 1954.
Aron, R. *France Reborn*, 1964. Much on de Gaulle.
————. *France: Steadfast and Changing*, 1960.
Baum, W. C. *The French Economy and the State*, 1958.
Birch, A. H. B. *Representative and Responsible Government*, 1964. British government.
Boyd, F. *British Politics in Transition, 1945–63*. 1964.
Butler, D. E. *The British General Election of 1951*, 1952.
————. *The British General Election of 1955*, 1956.
————. *The Electoral System in Britain, 1918–1951*, 1953.
Butler, D. E., and King, A. *The British General Election of 1964*. 1965.
Carlyle, M. *The Awakening of Southern Italy*, 1962.
Caute, D. *Communism and the French Intellectuals*, 1964.
Clark, S. F. *The Man Who Is France*, 1963. On de Gaulle.
Douglas–Home, A. *Peaceful Change*, 1964. Speeches.
Einaudi, M., and Goguel, F. *Christian Democracy in Italy and France*, 1952.
Foot, M. *Aneurin Bevin*, 1962. Left–wing Labour view.
Gallagher, F. *The Invisible Island*, 1957. The Irish Question.
Grinrod, M. *The Rebuilding of Italy*, 1955. Useful.
Hackett, J., and Hackett, A. *Economic Planning in France*, 1963.
Hoffman, S. ed. *In Search of France*, 1963. Essays.
Hopkins, H. *The New Look*, 1963. British social history.
Hughes, H. S. *The United States and Italy*, 1965. A concise history of postwar Italy.
Kogan, N. *The Politics of Italian Foreign Policy*, 1963.
Laponce, J. A. *The Government of the Fifth Republic*, 1961.
Lüthy, H. *France Against Herself*, 1955. The Fourth Republic.
Lutz, V. C. *Italy, A Study in Economic Development*, 1962.
Mander, J. *Great Britain or Little England?*, 1963.
Mathiot, A. *The British Political System*, 1958.
McKenzie, R. T. *British Political Parties*, 1955.
Micaud, C. A. *Communism and the French Left*, 1963.
Neufeld, M. F. *Italy: School for Awakening Countries*, 1961.
Pickles, D. M. *The Fifth French Republic*, 1963.
Rieber, A. J. *Stalin and the French Communist Party 1941–1947*, 1962.
Robson, W. A. *Nationalized Industry and Public Ownership*, 1960.
Taylor, D. *The Years of Challenge*, 1960. General history of Britain.
Thomson, D. *Democracy in France*, rev. ed., 1958. Excellent.
Webster, R. A. *The Cross and the Fasces: Christian Democracy and Fascism in Italy*, 1960.
Werth, A., *France, 1940–1955*, 1956.
Williams, P. M., and Harrison, M. *De Gaulle's Republic*, 1961.
Wright, G. *Rural Revolution in France*, 1964.
Youngson, A. J. *The British Economy, 1920–1957*, 1960.

CHAPTER 27. ATTEMPTS TO INTEGRATE EUROPE

Ball, M. M. *NATO and the European Union Movement,* 1959.
Beever, R. C. *European Unity and the Trade Union Movements,* 1961.
Deutsch, K. W. *Political Community and the North Atlantic Area,* 1957.
Florinsky, M. T. *Integrated Europe?,* 1955.
Gilpin, R. *France in the Age of the Scientific State,* 1968.
Hartog, F. *European Trade Cycle Policy,* 1959.
Haviland, H. F. Jr. ed. *The United States and the Western Community,* 1957.
Hays, D. *Europe: The Emergence of an Idea,* 1957.
Kraft, J. *The Grand Design: From Common Market to Atlantic Partnership,* 1962.
Lerner, D., and Aron, R. eds. *France Defeats E.D.C.,* 1957.
Linsay, K. *European Assemblies,* 1960.
Lippman, W. *Western Unity and the Common Market,* 1962.
Mayne, R. *The Community of Europe,* 1962.
Servan–Schreiber, J. J. *The American Challenge,* 1968.
Stadler, K. R. *Adult Education and European Co-operation,* 1960.
Zurcher, A. J. *The Struggle to Unite Europe,* 1940–1958, 1958.

CHAPTER 28. THE EMERGENCE OF A NEW ASIA

Alastair, B. *China and the Peace of Asia,* 1965.
Albright, J., Cash, J. A., and Sandstrum, A. W. *Seven Firefights in Vietnam,* 1970.
Allen, G. C. *Japan's Economic Recovery,* 1958.
Allen, R. H. S. *A Short Introduction to the History and Politics of Southeast Asia,* 1970.
Barnett, A. D. *China on the Eve of Communist Takeover,* 1963.
———. *Communist China in Perspective,* 1962.
———. *Communist China: The Early Years, 1949–1955,* 1964.
Bastin, J. ed. *The Emergence of Modern Southeast Asia,* 1967.
Beasly, W. G. *The Modern History of Japan,* 1963.*
Bone, R. C. *Contemporary Southeast Asia,* 1962.*
Boyd, R. G. *Communist China's Foreign Policy,* 1962.
Brecher, M. *Nehru: A Political Biography,* 1959.
Burling, R. *Hill Farms and Padi Fields: Life in Mainland Southeast Asia,* 1965.*
Buttinger, J. *Vietnam: A Political History,* 1968.
Butwell, R. *Southeast Asia Today and Tomorrow,* 1961.
Campbell, R. D. *Pakistan: Emerging Democracy,* 1963.
Chen, T. H. E. ed. *The Chinese Communist Regime,* 1967.*
Clubb, O. E. *Twentieth Century China,* 1964.*
Cohen, A. A. *The Communism of Mao Tse-Tung,* 1964.*
Corpuz, O. D. *The Philippines,* 1965.
Dore, R. *City Life in Japan,* 1965.*
Emerson, R. *From Empire to Nation—The Rise to Self–Assertion of Asian and African Peoples,* 1962.
Fairbank, J. K. *The United States and China,* 1963.
Fels. H. *The China Triangle: The American Effort in China from Pearl Harbor to the Marshall Mission,* 1965.*

Feuerwerker, A. ed. *Modern China*, 1964.

Fu–sheng, M. *The Wilting of the Hundred Flowers*, 1963, Chinese intelligentsia under Communism.

Higgins, B., and Higgins, J. *Indonesia: The Crisis of the Millstones*, 1963.

Hinton, H. C. *Communist China in World Politics*, 1966.

Jacobs, D. N., and Baerwald, H. H. eds. *Chinese Communism—Selected Documents*, 1963.

Lamb, B. P. *India: A World in Transition*, rev. ed., 1968.*

Legge, J. D. *Indonesia*, 1964.

Lewis, J. P. *Quiet Crisis in India—Economic Development and American Policy*, 1964.

London, K. ed. *New Nations in a Divided World—The International Relations of the Afro–Asian States*, 1963.

MacFarquhar, R. K. ed. *China Under Mao: Politics Takes Command*, 1966.*

Maki, J. M. *Government and Politics in Japan*, 1962.

Mancall, M. ed. *Formosa Today*, 1963.

McNelly, T. *Contemporary Government of Japan*, 1963.*

Melby, J. F. *The Mandate of Heaven*, 1969. The Chinese Civil War.

Milne, R. S. *Government and Politics in Malaysia*, 1967.*

Morris–Jones, W. H. *The Government and Politics of India*, 1964.*

Moussa, P. *The Underprivileged Nations*, 1963.

Olson, L. *Japan in Postwar Asia*, 1970. Covers 1952–1969.

Palmer, N. D. *The Indian Political System*, 1961.*

Patterson, G. *Peking vs. Delhi*, 1964.

Pye, L. W. *Southeast Asia's Political Systems*, 1967.*

Rowe, D. N. *Modern China*, 1959.

Sayeed, K. B. *The Political System of Pakistan*, 1967.*

Scalapino, R. A., and Masumi, J. *Parties and Politics in Contemporary Japan*, 1964.

Schram, S. R. *The Political Thought of Mao Tse–Tung*, rev. ed., 1968.

Scigliano, R. *South Vietnam; Nation Under Stress*, 1963.*

Stucki, L. *Behind the Great Wall*, 1965. Mao's China.

Tinker, H. *India and Pakistan*, rev. ed., 1968.

Tsou, T. *America's Failure in China: 1941–50*, 1963.*

Ward, B. *India and the West*, 1961.

———. *The Rich Nations and the Poor Nations*, 1962.*

Wint, G. *Communist China's Crusade*, 1965.

Wolpert, S. *India*, 1956.*

Woodman, D. *The Republic of Indonesia*, 1955.

Wu, Y. *The Economy of Communist China*, 1965.

Zinkin, M. *Development for Free Asia*, 1963.

CHAPTER 29. THE RISE OF NEW NATIONS IN AFRICA AND THE MIDDLE EAST

Abraham, W. E. *The Mind of Africa*, 1962.

Apter, D. E. *Ghana in Transition*, 1963.

Atiyah, E. S. *The Arabs*, 1955.

Ben–Gurion, D. *Israel: Years of Challenge*, 1964. By long-time Premier.

Berger, M. *The Arab World Today*, 1964.*

Burke, F. G. *Africa's Quest for Order*, 1964.

Carter, G. M., and Brown, W. O. eds. *Transition in Africa*, 1958.

Chilcote, R. H. *Portuguese Africa*, 1967.

Collins, R. O., and Tignor, R. L. *Egypt and the Sudan*, 1967.

Cowan, L. G., and O'Connel, J. eds. *Education and Nation–Building in Africa*, 1965.

Cremeans, C. D. *The Arabs and the World—Nasser's Arab Nationalist Policy*, 1963.

Davidson, B. *The African Awakening*, 1955.

Duffey, J. E. *Portuguese Africa*, 1959.

Duncan, P. *South Africa's Rule of Violence*, 1964.

Elston, D. R. *Israel: The Making of a Nation*, 1963.

Fisher, S. N. *The Middle East*, 1959.

Fisher, S. N. ed. *Social Forces in the Middle East*, 1955. Excellent.

Flint, J. E. *Nigeria and Ghana*, 1966.

Hance, W. A. *African Economic Development*, 1967.

Hargreaves, J. D. *West Africa: The Former French States*, 1967.

Hatch, J. A. *History of Postwar Africa*, 1965. Excellent.

Hempstone, S. *Africa, Angry Young Giant*, 1961.

Hoskyns, C. *The Congo Since Independence*, 1965.

Hughes, J. *The New Face of Africa South of the Sahara*, 1961.

Hunter, G. *The New Societies of Tropical Africa*, 1964.

Hurewitz, J. C. *Middle East Politics: The Military Dimension*, 1968.

Issawi, C. P., and others. *The Economics of Middle Eastern Oil*, 1963.

Italiaander, R. *The New Leaders of Africa*, 1961. Sketches.

Kamarck, A. M. *The Economics of African Development*, 1967.

Karpat, K. H. *Political and Social Thought in the Contemporary Middle East*, 1968.

Kimble, G. T. H. *Tropical Africa*, 2 v., 1960.

Kraines, O. *Government and Politics in Israel*, 1961.

Laqueur, W. Z. *Communism and Nationalism in the Middle East*, 1956.

Leaky, L. S. B. *Defeating Mau Mau*, 1954.

Legum, C. *Congo Disaster*, 1961. Concise.

———. *Pan–Africanism*, 1965.

Luthuli, J. *Let My People Go*, 1962. Anti-apartheid.

McEwan, P. J. M. ed. *Twentieth–Century Africa*, 1968.

McKay, V. *African Diplomacy: Studies in the Determinants of Foreign Policy*, 1966.

———. *Africa in World Politics*, 1963. Excellent.

Nkrumah, K. *I Speak of Freedom*, 1961. Autobiography of Ghanaian president.

Nuseibeh, N. Z. *The Ideas of Arab Nationalism*, 1956.

O'Brien, C. C. *To Katanga and Back*, 1966.

Padelford, N. J., and Emmerson, R. eds. *Africa and World Order*, 1963.

Partner, P. *A Short Political Guide to the Arab World*, 1960.

Quaison–Sackey, A. *Africa Unbound*, 1963.

Rivkin, A. *Africa and the West*, 1962.

Wallbank, T. W. *Contemporary Africa*, 1956.

Warriner, D. *Land Reform and Development in the Middle East*, 1962.

Wynn, W. *Nasser of Egypt*, 1959.

Zartman, I. W. *Government and Politics in Northern Africa*, 1963.

Index

Names preceded by "de" or "von" are listed under the names themselves, e.g., under Valera and Hindenburg. The first names of persons may generally be found on the first page reference to those persons. The dates given for persons are those of birth and death, except for rulers and popes, whose dates are those of incumbency. Battles are listed under the cities or places after which they are named. All treaties, pacts, agreements, protocols, conventions, and concordats are listed under Treaties.